Letters to Véra

VLADIMIR NABOKOV

Letters to Véra

Translated and edited
by Olga Voronina and Brian Boyd

PENGUIN CLASSICS

PENGUIN CLASSICS

Published by the Penguin Group
Penguin Books Ltd, 80 Strand, London WC2R ORL, England
Penguin Group (USA) Inc., 375 Hudson Street, New York, New York 10014, USA
Penguin Group (Canada), 90 Eglinton Avenue East, Suite 700, Toronto, Ontario, Canada M4P 2Y3
(a division of Pearson Penguin Canada Inc.)
Penguin Ireland, 25 St Stephen's Green, Dublin 2, Ireland (a division of Penguin Books Ltd)
Penguin Group (Australia), 707 Collins Street, Melbourne, Victoria 3008, Australia
(a division of Pearson Australia Group Pty Ltd)
Penguin Books India Pvt Ltd, 11 Community Centre, Panchsheel Park, New Delhi – 110 017, India
Penguin Group (NZ), 67 Apollo Drive, Rosedale, Auckland 0632, New Zealand
(a division of Pearson New Zealand Ltd)
Penguin Books (South Africa) (Pty) Ltd, Block D, Rosebank Office Park,
181 Jan Smuts Avenue, Parktown North, Gauteng 2193, South Africa

Penguin Books Ltd, Registered Offices: 80 Strand, London WC2R ORL, England

www.penguin.com

First published in Penguin Classics 2014
001

Set in Joanna Mt Pro 11.5/16pt
Typeset by Claire Mason
Printed in Great Britain by Clays Ltd, St Ives plc

A CIP catalogue record for this book is available from the British Library

ISBN: 978–0–141–19223–9

www.greenpenguin.co.uk

Contents

List of Plates vii
List of Abbreviations ix
Chronology xiii

Envelopes for the *Letters to Véra* xxi
Brian Boyd
'My beloved and precious darling':
Translating *Letters to Véra* liii
Olga Voronina

LETTERS TO VÉRA 1

Appendix One: Riddles 525
with Gennady Barabtarlo
Appendix Two: Afterlife 539
Brian Boyd

Notes 543
Bibliography 731
Acknowledgements 737
Index 739

List of Plates

All illustrations from the Estate of Vladimir Nabokov, unless otherwise noted.

Nabokov family at Vyra, their summer estate, 1907
The five Nabokov children, Yalta, 1919
VN and VéN, Berlin, c. 1924
VN and pupil Aleksandr Sack, Constance, 1925
VN, Berlin 1926
VéN, Berlin, 1927
Yuly Aykhenvald
Ilya Fondaminsky
Savely and Irina Kyandzhuntsev, Nicolas and Nathalie Nabokov and VN, Paris, 1932
Ivan Bunin (*Foto Centropress Prague, Leeds Russian Archive*)
Vladislav Khodasevich (*Nina Berberova collection*)
VN, VéN and DN, Berlin, 1935
Elena Nabokov, Prague, 1931
Irina Guadanini (*Private collection*)
VN with editorial board of *Mesures*, near Paris, 1937 (*Gisèle Freund*)
VN, VéN and DN, Cannes, 1937
VN and VéN, Cambridge, Massachusetts, 1942
VN and VéN, Ithaca, New York, 1954

VN and VéN, dictation, Montreux, c. 1968 (*Time & Life Pictures/Getty Images*)

VN and VéN, lepping (butterfly hunting), near Montreux, c. 1971 (*Horst Tappe*)

VN and VéN, Montreux, 1968 (*Philippe Halsman*)

List of Abbreviations

Books are by Vladimir Nabokov unless otherwise noted. For full bibliographical details, see Bibliography. This list includes abbreviations used in the letterheads.

AL	autograph letter, unsigned
ALS	autograph letter, signed
AN	autograph note
ANS	autograph note, signed
APC	autograph postcard, unsigned
APCS	autograph postcard, signed
BB	Brian Boyd
DBDV	*Dear Bunny, Dear Volodya: The Nabokov–Wilson Letters, 1940–1971*
DN	Dmitri Nabokov
EN	Elena Nabokov (mother)
EO	Alexander Pushkin, *Eugene Onegin*, trans. with commentary by Vladimir Nabokov
Gift	*The Gift*
KQK	*King, Queen, Knave*
LL	*Lectures on Literature*
LRL	*Lectures on Russian Literature*
MCZ	Museum of Comparative Zoology, Harvard University

MUSSR	*The Man from the USSR and Other Plays*
NG	*Nikolay Gogol*
N'sBs	*Nabokov's Butterflies*
PP	*Poems and Problems*
RB	*Russian Beauty and Other Stories*
Schiff	Stacy Schiff, *Véra (Mrs. Vladimir Nabokov)*
SL	*Selected Letters 1940–1971*
SM	*Speak, Memory*
SO	*Strong Opinions*
Sog	*Soglyadatay*, 1938
SoVN	*Stories of Vladimir Nabokov*
SP	*Selected Poems*
Stikhi	*Stikhi*, 1979
TD	*Tyrants Destroyed*
TGM	*Tragediya gospodina Morna*
TMM	*The Tragedy of Mister Morn*
V&V	*Verses and Versions*
VC	*Vozvrashchenie Chorba*
VDN	Vladimir Dmitrievich Nabokov (father)
VéN	Véra Nabokov
VÉNAF	Véra Nabokov audiofile (for 1932 letters, from BB tape recording)
VF	*Vesna v Fial'te*
VN	Vladimir Nabokov

VNA	Vladimir Nabokov Archive, Henry W. and Albert A. Berg Collection, New York Public Library
VNAY	Brian Boyd, *Vladimir Nabokov: The American Years*
VNRY	Brian Boyd, *Vladimir Nabokov: The Russian Years*

Chronology

In order to situate the letters to Véra quickly in time, the following Chronology offers only: (1) key dates in the lives of Nabokov and his immediate family; (2) the dates of his novels and autobiography (and the titles of their translations, where important in the letters); and, with most precision, (3) the dates when VN and Véra Slonim/VéN were separated long enough for VN to send VéN more than a single letter.

Bold italics indicate a departure of either from the other's location (or departure and return in a single short trip); **bold roman** indicates a return. A line break precedes each departure or follows each return.

1870	Vladimir Dmitrievich Nabokov (VDN) born.
1876	Elena Ivanovna Rukavishnikov born.
1897	VDN and Elena Rukavishnikov (EN) marry.
1899, 23 April	VLADIMIR VLADIMIROVICH NABOKOV (VN) BORN IN ST PETERSBURG.
1900	Sergey Vladimirovich Nabokov born.
1902, 5 January	VÉRA EVSEEVNA SLONIM (LATER VéN) BORN IN ST PETERSBURG.
1903	Olga Vladimirovna Nabokov born (later married name Shakhovskoy, then Petkevich).
1906	Elena Vladimirovna Nabokov born (later married name Skulyari, then Sikorski).
1911	Kirill Vladimirovich Nabokov born.

1917	February and October Russian Revolutions; Nabokovs flee at end of year to Crimea.
1919, April	Nabokovs flee to Greece and then (May) London.
1919, October	VN goes up to Cambridge (Trinity College), Sergey to Oxford.
1920	VDN takes wife and younger children to Berlin, then the centre of the Russian emigration, and founds and edits Russian liberal daily, *Rul'*.
1921	VN, who has published since 1916 under his own name, now begins to publish as V(ladimir) Sirin.
1922, 28 March	VDN assassinated by Russian right-wingers.
1922, June	VN completes Cambridge BA and joins family in Berlin.
1923, January	Svetlana Siewert's family force end of her engagement to VN.
1923, 8 May	VN meets Véra Slonim at émigré charity ball in Berlin.
1923, May	***VN heads to Solliès-Pont (Var), in the south of France, to work as farm labourer.***
1923, c.18 August	**VN returns to Berlin and meets Véra in September on her return from vacation.**
1923, c.29 December	***VN travels with family to help them settle into Prague.***
1924, 27 January	**VN returns to Berlin.**
1924, 12–28 August	***VN joins mother in Prague and Dobřichovice, Czechoslovakia.***
1925, 15 April	VN AND VÉRA SLONIM MARRY IN BERLIN.

1925, c. 16 August	*VN accompanies his pupil Aleksandr (Shura) Sack to the Pomeranian beach resort of Zoppot, then on a walking tour through southern Germany (Freiburg and Schwarzwald).*
1925, 4 September	VéN joins VN and Shura Sack in Konstanz.
1926, 1 June–c. 21 July	*VéN sent to sanatoria in Germany's Schwarzwald for her health (depression, anxiety, weight loss).*
1926	Novel *Mashen'ka* (*Mary*) published
1926, 22–26 December	*VN visits his family in Prague.*
1928	Novel *Korol', dama, valet* (*King, Queen, Knave*) published.
1929	Novel *Zashchita Luzhina* (*The Defence*; *La Course du fou*) begins serial publication.
1930, 12–25 May	*VN travels to Prague to visit his family and give public reading.*
1930	Novella *Soglyadatay* (*The Eye*) published serially.
1931	Novel *Podvig* (*Glory*) published serially.
1932, c. 3–20 April	*VN visits his family in Prague*
1932, May	Novel *Kamera obskura* (*Camera Obscura*, *Laughter in the Dark*) begins serial publication.

1932, October	*VN and VéN join cousin Nicolas Nabokov and his wife Nathalie for two weeks in Kolbsheim, near Strasbourg; VéN returns to Berlin on 13 October; VN heads on 18 October to Paris, by now the centre of the Russian emigration, for Russian and French literary readings, contacts and contracts, and returns via Belgium.*
1932, c. 28 November	VN returns to Berlin.
1934	Novel *Otchayanie* (*Despair*; *La Méprise*) published serially.
1934, 10 May	DMITRI VLADIMIROVICH NABOKOV (DN) BORN IN BERLIN.
1935	Novel *Priglashenie na kazn'* (*Invitation to a Beheading*) begins serial publication.
1936, 21 January–29 February	*VN travels to Brussels and (on 29 January) to Paris for literary readings and contacts.*
1936, c. 9–c. 22 June	*VéN and DN spend holiday with Anna Feigin, on Anna's visit to her cousins in Leipzig.*
1937, 18 January	*After Sergey Taboritsky, one of the assassins of VDN, is appointed as Hitler's deputy director of Russian émigré affairs, VéN insists that VN leaves Germany; he heads first for Brussels, then (22 January) to Paris, for readings and to set up the family's move to France.*
1937, February	VN begins affair in Paris with Russian émigrée Irina Guadanini.
1937, c. 17 February	VN travels to London for readings, contacts and contracts and job prospects.

1937, 1 March	*VN returns to Paris.*
1937, April	Novel *Dar* (*The Gift*) begins serial publication.
1937, 6 May	*VéN and DN escape Germany and join EN in Prague.*
1937, 22 May	**VN rejoins VéN, DN and his mother in Prague; from there VN, VéN and DN travel to Franzensbad (now Františkovy Lázně), Czechoslovakia.**
1937, 17 June	*VN travels to Prague for reading and to arrange trip from Czechoslovakia to France.*
1937, 23 June	**VN and VéN reunite in Marienbad (now Mariánské Lázně) and travel to Paris on 30 June.**
1937, July	Nabokovs settle in Cannes, France; VN admits to affair, VéN forces him to decide, and he chooses her.
1937, c. 9 September	Irina Guadanini visits Cannes, against VN's wishes; VN asks her to leave; the affair definitively ends.
1937, October	Nabokovs move to Menton, France.
1938, July	Nabokovs move to Moulinet, above Menton, VN captures butterfly he will name *Lysandra cormion*.
1938, August	Nabokovs move to Cap d'Antibes, France.
1938, October	Nabokovs move to Paris.
1939, 2–23 April	*VN travels to London for English and Russian readings, contacts, contracts, and in hope of position as Russian lecturer.*

1939, 2 May	Mother (EN) dies in Prague.
1939, 31 May–14 June	***VN travels to London for publishing and lecturing prospects.***
1940, 28 May	After months of trying to escape France, VN, VéN and Dmitri arrive in New York, where they settle.
1941, 15 March–2 April	***VN leaves for two weeks of guest lectures at Wellesley College, Massachusetts.***
1941, September	VN begins one-year resident lectureship in comparative literature at Wellesley (where family now lives) and begins volunteer work at Harvard Museum of Comparative Zoology.
1941	Novel *The Real Life of Sebastian Knight* published.
1942, September	Nabokovs move to Cambridge, Massachusetts. VN on annual Russian-language teaching contract at Wellesley and annual lepidopterological research fellow contract at Harvard's MCZ.
1942, 30 September–12 December	***VN leaves on whistle-stop lecturing tour: in October in South, in November in Midwest, in December to Farmville, Virginia.***
1944, 1–15 June	***VéN takes DN to New York for appendicitis operation.***

1945, c.8–11 February	***VN travels to Baltimore to give lecture.***
1947	Novel *Bend Sinister* published.
1948, January	VN begins serial publication of his autobiography, mostly in *New Yorker*.
1948	VN appointed professor of Russian literature at Cornell.
1951	Autobiography *Conclusive Evidence* (US) / *Speak, Memory* (UK) published.
1952	Novel *Dar* (*The Gift*) published.
1954, c.16–22 April	***VN travels to Lawrence, Kansas, to give lectures.***
1955	Novel *Lolita* published in Paris.
1957	Novel *Pnin* published.
1958	*Lolita* published in US and elsewhere.
1959	In the wake of *Lolita*'s success, VN resigns from Cornell and travels with VéN to Europe.
1961	VN and VéN move into Montreux Palace Hotel, Montreux, Switzerland.
1962	Novel *Pale Fire* published.
1969	Novel *Ada* published.
1970, 4 April	***VN travels on vacation to Taormina, Sicily, ahead of VéN.***
1970, c.13 April	**VéN joins him there.**

1972	Novel *Transparent Things* published.
1974	Novel *Look at the Harlequins!* published.
1977, 2 July	VN DIES IN HOSPITAL IN LAUSANNE, SWITZERLAND, AFTER TWO YEARS OF ILLNESS.
1991, 7 April	VÉN DIES IN VEVEY HOSPITAL.
2012, 22 February	DN DIES.

Envelopes for the Letters to Véra

Brian Boyd

I dreamt of you last night—as if
I was playing the piano and you
were turning the pages for me.
VN to VéN, 12 January 1924

I

No marriage of a major twentieth-century writer lasted longer than Vladimir Nabokov's, and few images anywhere encapsulate lasting married love better than the 1968 Philippe Halsman photograph of Véra nestled under her husband's right arm and looking up towards his eyes with steady devotion.

Nabokov first wrote a poem for Véra in 1923, after having spent only hours in her company*, and in 1976, after over half a century of marriage, dedicated 'To Véra' the last of his books published in his lifetime. He first dedicated a book to her in 1951—his autobiography—whose last chapter turns directly to an unidentified 'you': 'The years are passing, my dear,

* See Chronology for key details of the lives of the Nabokovs. Literary and historical figures mentioned here will be briefly identified in the Notes on their first introduction in the Letters. See Index to find their first occurrence there.

and presently nobody will know what you and I know.' He had anticipated the sentiment in a letter to Véra, barely a year into their relationship: 'you and I are so special; the miracles we know, no one knows, and no one loves the way we love'.

Nabokov would later call his marriage 'cloudless'. He had done so even in a letter to Irina Guadanini, with whom he fell into an intense affair in 1937. That year was the darkest and most painful in the Nabokovs' marriage, and an exception, as the letters attest. But although the sun of young love shines or shimmers in many of the early letters, other troubles becloud much of the correspondence: Véra's health and his mother's, their constant shortage of money, their distaste for Germany, and his exhausting search for refuge for his family in France, England or America as Hitler's rise threatened the very existence of the Russian émigré community where he had shot to not-quite-starving stardom.

Véra Slonim first encountered Vladimir Nabokov as 'Vladimir Sirin', the pen-name he had adopted in January 1921 to distinguish his own byline from that of his father, also Vladimir Nabokov. Nabokov senior was an editor and founder of *Rul'*, the Russian-language daily in Berlin, the city that in 1920 had become the centre and magnet for the post-1917 Russian emigration. Nabokov junior had been publishing books and contributing to journals in Petrograd since 1916, when he still had two years of high school to complete, and by 1920, in the second year of his family's emigration, his verse was already being admired by older writers like Teffi and Sasha Chorny.

Much of the time *Letters to Véra* features unfamiliar profiles of Vladimir and Véra. The familiar images begin when Nabokov added the first dedication 'To Véra' in 1950, exactly halfway through the story of their love. And when *Lolita* was published in America in 1958, and in the years that followed, a flood of translations of his old Russian *oeuvre*, as well as his new English work–fiction, verse, screenplay, scholarship and interviews–would appear with more dedications to Véra. The writer and his wife were photographed together in the many interviews his fame precipitated, and the story of her editing, typing, driving, teaching, corresponding and negotiating for him became part of the Nabokov legend. Yet the second half of their life together, from 1950 to 1977, occupies only 5 per cent of the letters that follow, and the remaining 95 per cent reflects years much more strained than this final spell of worldwide fame.

The Slonim family (father Evsey, mother Slava, and daughters Elena, Véra and Sofia) escaped Petrograd via many adventures in Eastern Europe before settling in Berlin early in 1921. There, Véra told me, she was 'very well aware' of Nabokov's talent before she met him, 'despite having lived in non-literary circles, especially among former officers'. (A strange choice of company, perhaps, for a young Russian-Jewish woman, given the anti-Semitism common in the White army. But Véra's own courage as she and her sisters were fleeing Russia had turned a hostile White soldier from aggressor to protector, and she insisted to me there were many decent former White officers in Berlin.) The earliest samples of his verse she had clipped from newspapers and journals date from November and December 1921, when she was still nineteen and he twenty-two. A year later the young Sirin, already richly represented in émigré periodicals and miscellanies, as a poet, short-story writer, essayist, reviewer and translator, scooped the productivity stakes in Berlin's émigré book world: *Nikolka Persik*, a translation of Romain Rolland's 1919 novel *Colas Breugnon*, in November 1922; a sixty-page collection of recent verse, *Grozd'* (*The Cluster*), in December 1922; a 180-page collection of verse over several years, *Gorniy put'* (*The Empyrean Path*), in January 1923; and a translation of *Alice's Adventures in Wonderland*, *Anya v strane chudes* (*Anya in the Land of Wonders*, March 1923).

Of much more interest for one attractive and strong-willed young woman with a passion for literature was the evidence of a romantic rift in Sirin's recent verse. In the wake of the assassination of his father on 28 March 1922, Nabokov had been allowed by the parents of the vivacious beauty Svetlana

Siewert to become engaged to her, despite her being much younger than him, seventeen to his twenty-three. Poems he wrote for Svetlana within the first year of his knowing her filled the volume of his most recent verse, *Grozd'*. But on 9 January 1923, he was told that the engagement was over: she was too young and he, as a poet, much too uncertain a prospect.

If meeting Svetlana had released a torrent of verse, so did parting from her. Over the next few months, a number of poems reflecting the poet's loss in love began to appear in the émigré press: 'Zhemchug' ('The Pearl') in March ('like a pearl-diver sent to know the depths of passionate torments, I have reached the bottom–and before I can bring the pearl back to the surface, I hear your boat above, sailing away from me'); 'V kakom rayu' ('In what heaven'), also in March ('you have captured my soul in era after era, and have just done so once again, but once again you have flashed on by, and I am left only with the age-long torment of your elusive beauty'); the most explicit, 'Berezhno nyos' ('I carefully carried'), on 6 May ('I carefully carried this heart for you but someone's elbow knocked it down and now it lies shattered').

Another poem, 'Ya Indiey nevidimoy vladeyu' ('The Ruler': 'An India invisible I rule'), written the same day as 'I carefully carried', and published on 8 April, signals a readiness for a new beginning: the poet is an emperor of the imagination, and swears he can conjure up untold wonders for a new princess–though she, whoever she will prove to be, remains still unseen. The princess, though, may well have seen the poem, as well as the glimpse of the end of romance in the other poem that Nabokov wrote the same day. For on 8 May 1923, two days after the poem 'I carefully carried' appeared in *Rul'*, Véra Slonim appeared before Vladimir Sirin, wearing, and refusing to lower, a black Harlequin demi-mask. Nabokov would later recall meeting Véra at an émigré charity ball. *Rul'*, the exhaustive record of émigré Berlin, notes only one charity ball around that date, on 9 May 1923, although it is 8 May that the Nabokovs would continue to celebrate as the day of their first meeting. When I cited to Véra her husband's account of their meeting, and the evidence in his diaries for 8 May as the day they commemorated, and the evidence from *Rul'* of a 9 May charity ball, she responded: 'Do you think we do not know the date we met?'

But Véra was an expert at blanket denial. Whatever we do not know of 'what you and I know', at an émigré charity ball Véra singled out Vladimir Sirin, while keeping a mask up to her face. Nabokov's favourite sibling, Elena Sikorski, thought Véra wore that mask so that her striking but not unmatchable looks would not distract him from her unique assets: her uncanny responsiveness to Sirin's verse (she could commit poems to memory on a couple of readings) and her sensibility uncannily in tune with the one behind the poems. They stepped outside together into the night, they walked the Berlin streets, marvelling together at the play of light and leaf and dark. A day or two later, Nabokov set off for a planned summer as a farm labourer on an estate in the south of France managed by one of his father's colleagues in the Crimean Provisional Government of 1918–19, in the hope that the change would help dull his grief at his father's death and his severance from Svetlana.

On 25 May, from the farm of Domaine-Beaulieu, near Solliès-Pont, not far from Toulon, Nabokov wrote Svetlana one last forbidden farewell letter, full of passionate regret, 'as if licensed by the distance that separated them'. A week later he wrote a poem to the new possibility in his life:

THE ENCOUNTER

enchained by this strange proximity

Longing, and mystery, and delight . . .
as if from the swaying blackness
of some slow-motion masquerade
onto the dim bridge you came.

And night flowed, and silent there floated
into its satin streams
that black mask's wolf-like profile
and those tender lips of yours.

And under the chestnuts, along the canal
you passed, luring me askance.
What did my heart discern in you,
how did you move me so?

In your momentary tenderness,
or in the changing contour of your shoulders,
did I experience a dim sketch
of other– irrevocable– encounters?

Perhaps romantic pity
led you to understand
what had set trembling that arrow
now piercing through my verse?

I know nothing. Strangely
the verse vibrates, and in it, an arrow …
Perhaps you, still nameless, were
the genuine, the awaited one?

But sorrow not yet quite cried out
perturbed our starry hour.
Into the night returned the double fissure
of your eyes, eyes not yet illumed.

For long? For ever? Far off
I wander, and strain to hear
the movement of the stars above our encounter
and what if you are to be my fate . . .

Longing, and mystery, and delight,
and like a distant supplication ...
My heart must travel on.
But if you are to be my fate ...

The young poet knew that the young woman who had accosted him so strangely followed his verse assiduously. He sent this new poem to *Rul'*, where it featured on 24 June. Here, in a sense, Vladimir's letters to Véra begin, in a private appeal, inside a public text, to the one reader who could know about the past the poem recorded and the future it invited.

Just as Nabokov had responded in verse to Véra's bold response to the heartache of Sirin's recent verse, so Véra appears to have responded boldly to this new verse invitation. She wrote to him in the south of France at least three times during the summer. The letters do not survive – the highly private Véra later destroyed every letter of hers to Vladimir that she could find – so that we cannot be sure that her first letter followed the appearance of 'The Encounter' in *Rul'*, but the logic of their passion strongly implies such a sequence. She had made her masked appeal to him in person on 8 May, and could not know whether she had roused more than a passing interest. Reading *Rul'* on 24 June, she could know that he wanted *her* to know the effect she had had and the hopes she had stirred.

If Véra wrote to Vladimir almost immediately after reading the poem, Vladimir may have responded to her first letter with another poem, 'Znoy' ('Swelter'), that he wrote on 7 July. Here he hinted at his desire stirring in the heat of a southern summer. He did not send it to her yet, but after at least two more letters from her, he wrote another poem, on 26 July ('Zovyosh'–a v derevtse granatovom sovyonok': 'You call–and in a little pomegranate tree an owlet'). He then wrote his first letter to her, just a few days before his planned departure from the farm, enclosing both 'poems for you'. He begins this first letter with memorable abruptness and no salutation (' I won't hide it: I'm so unused to being–well, understood, perhaps,–so unused to it, that in the very first minutes of our meeting I thought: this is a joke, a masquerade trick ... But then ... And there are things that are hard to talk about–you'll rub off their marvellous pollen at the touch of a word ... They write me from home about mysterious flowers. You are lovely ... And all your letters, too, are lovely, like the white nights'), continues with the same sureness ('Yes, I need you, my fairy-tale. Because you are the only person I can talk with about the shade of a cloud, about the song of a thought') and ends, before offering her the poems, with 'So I will be in Berlin on the 10th or 11th ... And if you're not there I will come to you, and find you'.

From here, Vladimir's first letter to Véra, we need to follow the trail chronologically, to orient the letters in their life, their love and their world, before considering what makes the correspondence so special and what light it throws on Nabokov as man and writer.

At the end of summer 1923 he found Véra in Berlin with her mask and guard down. Like other young lovers with no space of their own, they would meet day after day to stroll together on the evening streets. A single letter of this time, dated November 1923, from Vladimir in one part of Russian west Berlin to Véra in another, reflects their passionate early understandings and misunderstandings.

At the end of December 1923, Vladimir travelled with his mother and his youngest siblings, Olga, Elena and Kirill, to Prague, where his mother, as the widow of a Russian scholar and statesman, was entitled to a pension. In their first stretch of weeks apart, Vladimir wrote to Véra of his intense focus on his first long work, the five-act verse play *Tragediya gospodina Morna* (*The Tragedy of Mister Morn*), of his impressions of Prague (looking out at the frozen Moldau: 'along that whiteness, little black silhouettes of people cross from one shore to the other, like musical notes ... some boy is dragging behind him a D-sharp: a sledge'), and of the shock of being without her for almost a month.

Back together in Berlin by the end of January 1924, they soon considered themselves engaged. When in August Vladimir travelled for two weeks to join his mother at the riverside town of Dobřichovice, near Prague, his first letter back to Véra began: 'My delightful, my love, my life, I don't understand anything: how can you not be with me? I'm so infinitely used to you that I now feel myself lost and empty: without you, my soul. You turn my life into something light, amazing, rainbowed–you put a glint of happiness on everything.' A few short notes in Berlin, in a similar vein, reflect the foreglow of their marriage there on 15 April 1925 (sample letter, complete: 'I love you. Infinitely and inexpressibly. I've woken up in the middle of the night and here I am writing this. My love, my happiness').

Both Vladimir and Véra earned their main incomes by tutoring in English, and in late August 1925 Vladimir was paid to accompany his principal tutee, Aleksandr Sack, first to a Pomeranian beach resort, then on a high-spirited walking tour through the Schwarzwald, which he recorded in short postcard-prose snapshots, before Véra joined them in Konstanz.

A year later, the summer of 1926 introduced more complex moods. Véra was sent with her mother to sanatoria in the Schwarzwald to gain weight she had lost to anxiety and depression, while Vladimir remained in Berlin with his regular tutees. Véra had made her husband promise to send her a daily report–what he ate, what he wore, what he did–and Vladimir loyally obliged.

Never again do we have such a sustained day-by-day record of his response to his world. In the gap between his first novel, *Mashen'ka* (*Mary*), written in 1925, and his second, *Korol', Dama, Valet* (*King, Queen, Knave*), written in late 1927 and early 1928, his life seemed relaxed and summery: tutoring (which often seemed little more than long bouts of sunbathing, swimming and cavorting in the Grunewald), tennis, reading and patches of writing; a critique of recent Soviet fiction for his friends in the Tatarinov literary circle; a poem he wrote for Russian Culture Day; a mock-trial of Pozdnyshev, the murderer in Tolstoy's story 'The Kreutzer Sonata', with Nabokov playing Pozdnyshev and triumphantly reinterpreting the role; a short story swiftly conceived and swiftly executed; for the Tatarinov circle again, a list of what made him suffer, 'starting with the touch of satin and ending with the impossibility of assimilating, swallowing, all the beauty in the world'. In order to buoy up Véra and to keep her at a sanatorium until she had gained the weight that he and her father both thought she needed, Vladimir, always playful by nature, laboured – and here the effect is sometimes laboured indeed – to entertain and amuse her, upping the ante as the separation continued. He started each letter with a new salutation, at first apparently in honour of the names of the small animal toys they collected, and becoming more and more bizarre (Lumpikin, Tufty, Little Old Man, Mosquittle); he added puzzles for her, crosswords, codes, labyrinths, riddles, word-combination games; and finally he invented a German editor of his puzzle section, a Mr Darling, who supposedly interfered with what *he* wanted to write.

Berlin had been the hub of the first Russian émigrés to flee the Bolshevik coup of October 1917. Between 1920 and 1923 the city housed over 400,000 Russians, many of them artists and intellectuals. But when the German Mark was restabilized after the end of the hyperinflation of 1923, life in Germany rapidly became dearer. By the end of 1924 most émigrés had moved to Paris, where they largely remained until the Second World War convulsed the continent.

To ensure he would not dilute his Russian by living in a city where he knew the local language, Nabokov stayed in Berlin. By 1926 he was already the recognized literary star of the emigration there, as can be seen in the rapturous reception he provoked at Russian Culture Day celebrations, which he describes in a slow prose striptease to Véra. Nabokov continued to grow rapidly as a writer – although *Rul'*, where he still published most of his work, was little read in Paris – and he and Véra lived relatively carefree in Berlin thanks to their extremely modest lifestyle and a spare but adequate income from his tutoring, from the German translations of his first two novels, and from Véra's part-time secretarial work.

By 1929, when Sirin began to publish *The Defence* in the Paris journal *Sovremennye zapiski*, the best-paying and most prestigious émigré literary outlet, the novelist Nina Berberova could respond to the first instalment: 'A tremendous, mature, sophisticated modern writer was before me, a great Russian writer, like a Phoenix, was born from the fire and ashes of revolution and exile. Our existence from now on acquired a meaning. All my generation were justified. We were saved.' Novelist and poet Ivan Bunin, the doyen of émigré writers and soon to become the first Russian Nobel laureate in literature, commented on *The Defence* in his own mode: 'This kid has snatched a gun and done away with the whole older generation, myself included.'

Prague was the third most important of European émigré centres, with a lively group of scholars attracted by grants from the Czech government. When Nabokov travelled there in May 1930 to see his family, he was a literary star there too, though he was more concerned with his mother's straitened circumstances (including bedbugs and cockroaches), his sisters' marriages, his younger brother's literary longings, and Box, the dachshund too old now to recognize him.

His next trip away from Véra, in April 1932, was again to Prague and his family. He was fascinated by his new nephew, Olga's son Rostislav, and appalled at the boy's neglect by his parents. Only rereading Flaubert, rediscovering with wry detachment his own early verse, and being introduced to the butterflies in the National Museum redeemed his displeasure with the dark city without and the bedbugs within.

Perhaps the gloom also owes something to the absence of the glow of endearments throughout the 1932 letters, which we have been able to access only through the recordings Véra Nabokov made into my tape-recorder in December 1984 and January 1985. Researching my Nabokov biography, I had persisted for years in asking Véra for the letters. Rather than allow me to read them myself, she at last agreed to read out as much as she could bear into my cassette-recorder. Somehow since then (apparently in the late 1990s) the entire batch of 1932 originals has vanished. Since much of the passion and play evident in the other manuscript letters was selected out by Véra as she read, 1932 suffers, and the April 1932 trip in particular.

The letters of October and November 1932 also depend on what Véra chose to record, but lose less of their force because so much of this trip reports a triumphal progress that she was only too happy to help commemorate. In October, Vladimir and Véra travelled to Kolbsheim, near Strasbourg, to stay with Nabokov's cousin Nicolas, the composer, and his wife Nathalie. When Véra returned to Berlin, Nabokov remained a few days in Kolbsheim then travelled on to Paris, where he stayed a month. Here Sirin's fame made him the toast of émigré writers (Bunin, Vladislav Khodasevich, Mark Aldanov, Boris Zaytsev, Berberova, Nikolay Evreinov, André Levinson, Aleksandr Kuprin and many more) and editors (above all Ilya Fondaminsky and Vladimir Zenzinov of *Sovremennye zapiski*), most of whom he had not or had barely known in person before. Many of them made him the focus of a campaign to earn him as much money as possible through public readings and through contacts with French publishers (Grasset, Fayard, Gallimard), writers (Jules Supervielle, Gabriel Marcel, Jean Paulhan) and translators (Denis Roche, Doussia Ergaz). Nabokov's letters of autumn 1932 abound with incisive pen-portraits of Russian and

French literary figures, and his surprised delight at their generosity to him, especially that of the 'very sweet and saintly' Fondaminsky, an editor and the chief funder of *Sovremennye zapiski*.

In 1932, still in Berlin, the Nabokovs moved into the quiet–and for them cheap–apartment of Véra's close cousin Anna Feigin. Their son Dmitri was born in May 1934. With Hitler consolidating power, Véra no longer able to earn an income, and Dmitri to feed, they had good reason to seek extra money in the short term and a more secure future elsewhere in the long term. In pursuit of the longer term, Nabokov translated *Despair* into English himself and wrote his first French story, the half-memoir 'Mademoiselle O', before travelling in January 1936 to Brussels, Antwerp and then Paris to give a series of literary readings to both Russian and French audiences and to forge still stronger ties with the French literary world. He swiftly became friends with Franz Hellens, Belgium's best writer. In Paris, staying with Fondaminsky and Zenzinov, he found himself inducted into the highly sociable émigré literary set, often more deeply than he wanted–his description of being dragged off to dinner by Bunin is a classic of social discomfort–and he had a major success in a joint public reading with Khodasevich. Again, his impressions of other writers and his energy and persistence as a rather desperate networker dominate the letters.

Late in 1936 Sergey Taboritsky, one of the right-wing assassins of Nabokov's father in 1922, was appointed Hitler's second-in-charge of émigré affairs. Véra insisted to her husband that he had to flee Germany and find a way for the family to set up a life in France or England. Late in January 1937 he left Germany for the last time, stopping again to give a reading in Brussels before heading to Paris to stay again with Fondaminsky. He had written an essay in French for the centenary of Pushkin's death and had begun to translate his stories into French. His readings to Russian and French audiences in public spaces and grand private homes were highly successful, but he could not obtain a *carte d'identité*, let alone a work permit. At the end of January he began a passionate affair with Irina Guadanini, a part-time poet, supporting herself as a dog-groomer, whom he had met the previous year. The stress of deceiving Véra exacerbated Vladimir's chronic psoriasis to nightmarish levels. Meanwhile, he was trying to bring Véra to France, but with her anxiety about finances and her sense that he was too blithely optimistic about prospects, she refused to move from Berlin. In late February he crossed to London for readings and to establish contacts in the literary and publishing worlds there, especially in the hope of finding not only publishers for a short autobiography he had written in English and an English collection of his stories but possibly even an academic post. Despite his excellent contacts and strenuous efforts, he earned little and could establish no beachhead.

He returned to Paris at the beginning of March and resumed the affair. The correspondence with Véra became more and more fraught as he tried to persuade her to quit Germany and join him in the south of France, where Russian friends of friends had offered places to stay. He wanted Véra to bypass Paris, but she had got wind of the affair and wanted to join him anywhere but France: Belgium, Italy or especially Czechoslovakia, where they could show Elena Nabokov her grandson. When Véra reported the rumour of the affair, Nabokov denied it. The persistent tension between them expressed itself not in further explicit accusations and denials but through moves and counter-moves in the plans for their reunion–'a painfully atonal duet', in Stacy Schiff's apt phrase. Complicating their lives and their letters were the nightmare difficulties of arranging visas for Véra and Dmitri to leave Germany, and for Vladimir to leave Paris, for Prague, where Véra's firm resistance to his French plans meant they were eventually reunited–Vladimir travelling via Switzerland and Austria to avoid Germany–on 22 May.

After six weeks there they travelled back to France, again skirting Germany, and settled in Cannes. When Nabokov confessed to the affair, marital storms ensued before subsiding into a spurious calm, after he swore it was all over–though he continued to write to Guadanini. Fearing the end of their relationship, Guadanini travelled down to Cannes, despite his telling her not to, on 8 September. He saw her, sent her back to Paris, and the affair was over, although it would take longer for Vladimir and Véra to return to their old emotional footing. After over a year in Cannes, Menton and Cap d'Antibes, they travelled north to Paris. Nabokov now had an American agent, who managed to place *Laughter in the Dark*, his rewriting of a translation of his *Kamera obskura*, with Bobbs-Merrill. But despite the critical acclaim from Russian-speaking readers in France, England and the United States for his other, more complex fictions, his work proved too original to find other publishers outside the emigration. Unable to obtain a work permit, Nabokov found it increasingly difficult to support his family by his writing. Poverty began to bite, and he looked more and more gaunt.

Hoping to find a refuge beyond France, Nabokov wrote his first novel in English, *The Real Life of Sebastian Knight*, early in 1939. In April he travelled to London where he had learned of a vacancy in the Russian department at Leeds University, which might open a space in London or Sheffield, if the Leeds appointment went to one of the candidates applying from universities there. His letters back to Véra in Paris record that the exhausting pace of his networking in his 1936 and 1937 trips had intensified still further, but despite high-level support from Russian and English academics and literati, he came away with friendships but little else except hopes that were soon dashed. A return trip at the beginning of June, occasioning another spate of letters, advanced his prospects no further.

Only chance allowed him to extricate himself and his family from Europe. Novelist Mark Aldanov, who had been offered a teaching position in creative writing at Stanford University for the summer of 1941, felt his English too poor to accept and passed the invitation along to Nabokov.

This at last allowed Nabokov to obtain an exit permit from France, and although visas and funding across the Atlantic took a long time to secure, the Nabokovs sailed into New York on 28 May 1940, only two weeks before the fall of Paris. In New York Nabokov found tutoring jobs and reviewed for New York newspapers, and, through his meeting with Edmund Wilson, for the *New Republic*. Through his cousin Nicolas he secured an invitation to two weeks of lectures at Wellesley College in March 1941, prompting his next batch of letters to Véra. At the time of the Hitler–Stalin Pact, Nabokov's anti-Sovietism amplified the appeal of his lectures – he could not quite believe the compliments – and led to a full-year appointment at Wellesley in 1941 – 2. But after that academic year, and despite having published *The Real Life of Sebastian Knight* at the end of 1941 and appearing regularly in the *Atlantic* and even in the *New Yorker*, Nabokov found himself financially compelled to undertake lecture tours through the American South in October 1942, the Midwest in November, and to Virginia in December. Even more than during his Wellesley tour in 1941, he had the time to pass on to Véra his observations and adventures in encountering America, his most Pninian day producing the longest letter of all – three thousand words.

With impermanent but annually renewed positions teaching Russian at Wellesley and researching Lepidoptera at Harvard's Museum of Comparative Zoology from 1943 until 1948, then the security of a professorial appointment at Cornell from 1948 to 1959, Nabokov had few occasions now to be separated from Véra for long. In June 1944, while Véra took Dmitri to New York for an exploratory operation that turned into an appendectomy, Vladimir remained at work in Cambridge. On 6 June, D-Day, he succumbed to a spectacular bout of food poisoning, which he relished describing in hilarious detail, along with the ordeal of hospitalization – from which he fled in his pyjamas. Only a distinguished lecture invitation to the University of Kansas in 1954 produced another thin sheaf of letters to Véra during the years he was writing his autobiography, *Lolita*, *Pnin* and his translation of and commentary to Pushkin's *Eugene Onegin*.

In 1958, Hurricane *Lolita* swept North America and much of Europe. By 1959 Nabokov could take early retirement from Cornell and travel with Véra to Europe, partly to visit his sister Elena, now in Geneva, and partly to watch over Dmitri, now training as an opera bass in Milan. Although not planning to remain there, the Nabokovs soon found Europe a welcome refuge from the pressures of fame in America. In these European years there was little to keep them apart. Only one sustained volley of letters fills this spell, when Vladimir, eager to catch the first butterflies, travelled on ahead to a holiday in Taormina, Sicily, in early April 1970. After that, the 'correspondence' dwindled to scraps, like the shortest of all, a three-word note, 'forty-five springs!' accompanying a wedding anniversary bouquet. Three words, but they manage to pun on the Russian words for 'year' and 'summer': when the plural is needed for the usual Russian word for 'year,' *god*, the plural of 'summers,' *let*, usually fills the gap; Nabokov's further substitution suggests that all their years together had been springs.

II

As the change of pace in describing these last years and decades indicates, circumstances had changed enormously for the Nabokovs. That is part of the fascination of the letters: the continuity of the writer's voice and vision, but expressed so differently through all the marked changes in his life and love, through all the shifting contexts and demands on him as character and correspondent: farmhand and incognito poet in 1923; son, brother and budding playwright in early 1924; tutor and paid travelling companion in 1925; relaxed stay-at-home support in 1926; returning son and brother in 1930 and 1932; touring writer and literary networker in 1932, and later, compounding these roles, also frazzled job-seeker and exasperated visa-seeker in 1936, 1937 and 1939, as well as marital deceiver and near-suicidal psoriatic in 1937; prospective teacher on a charm campaign in 1941; impoverished travelling lecturer in 1942, hospital patient in 1944, distinguished travelling lecturer in 1954; relaxed vacationer in 1970. In some ways the changes reflect normal life-stage progressions, in others emphatically singular experiences: a carefree young and early married life as a part-time professional; an acclaimed but uncommercial author for a disappearing émigré audience; a hit visiting lecturer, an itinerant jobbing lecturer, a secure professor; and a rich and famous writer. And in some ways the changes reflect the normal progression of lasting love, as well as the singularity of Vladimir's and Véra's characters from that first masked moment: passionate early declarations and the difficulties of adjustment; coping with other anxieties and demands, including a boisterous child, an affair, an ailing mother and an encroaching tyranny; recalibrations to a new and in some ways still-precarious life in a new country; final attunements so serene they needed only the quietest of reaffirmations.

Oddly, this correspondence of a long-lasting marriage remains doubly single-sided. Véra appears to have destroyed every letter of hers to Vladimir that she could find, and even her contribution to joint postcards to Nabokov's mother, where she wanted to preserve his part, she rendered illegible by thickly crossing out every word.

I had remembered all her letters to Vladimir as destroyed, until just before writing this introduction I rediscovered the transcripts I had made of three short functional letters from her. Two were found in a small briefcase that had been brought to me, perhaps in 1981, by one of Véra's secretaries, who knew I was cataloguing the archive and had discovered the briefcase in an unlikely corner where it had escaped Véra's vigilance. To dispel misplaced anticipation, let me quote one of these in full, from the time of the trip to New York for the exploratory operation on ten-year-old Dmitri, from about 1 June 1944:

> The trip went well. The heat was intense. Today we were at D.'s, they're doing extra tests etc., but the operation has been definitely scheduled for Wednesday. I'll write in more detail on Monday when I see D. again. There'll be more X-rays in the morning. We're waiting for a letter. All send their regards.
>
> Véra

No letters from Véra to Vladimir survive, or at least none has yet been catalogued, in the Vladimir Nabokov Archive at the Berg Collection of the New York Public Library. But after I thought I had completed this introduction, including the paragraph above, I discovered to my surprise in my own files my partial transcript of a letter Véra had written to biographer Andrew Field on 9 May 1971, in which she cites a letter 'just come to light' that she had written to her husband. What Véra quoted to Field reports a little more of the strange fate of the 'Life of Chernyshevsky', chapter 4 of *The Gift*. *Sovremennye zapiski* was proud to publish 'Sirin' and particularly proud to feature all the rest of his greatest Russian novel, *The Gift*, but nevertheless firmly refused to publish chapter 4 because of its irreverent critique of the nineteenth-century radical writer Nikolay Chernyshevsky. When he arrived in the USA, Nabokov was still anxious to publish this chapter and, if he could, *The Gift* intact, without this hundred-page hole. When Vladimir Mansvetov and other Russian writers now based in America invited him to contribute to an anthology, he offered them the 'Life of Chernyshevsky'. On 17 March 1941 Véra wrote from New York to Vladimir, in the midst of his guest lectures at Wellesley College:

> Mme Kodryansky was here today. 'Chernyshevsky is an icon for socialists, and if we print this, we'll destroy the anthology, since the Workers' Party won't buy it up.' She's in despair, but an utter chicken. Repeats Mansvetov's words. I asked for all this in writing to send to you. I told her your opinion of censorship of any kind. Again: 'This thing is impossible to print in America, since he'll destroy his reputation.' To this I told her straight: 'Tell them he doesn't give a damn, he can look after his reputation himself.' ... They're having a meeting about this today.

Véra quoted this to Field because of her pride in her husband's principles and his triumphs in the face of tribulation, and *despite* its showing something of her character, her steeliness in his defence. But in general she destroyed her letters because she thought they were not worth keeping and because they were no one else's business. (She told me she thought her sister-in-law Elena Sikorski vainglorious to publish *Perepiska s sestroy* (*Correspondence with his Sister*) and incorporate her own letters as well as her brother's.) In later years the woman who kept her mask up before the man she wanted to enchant now wanted to keep her mask up before the whole world, even when she had done all she could to help him become the world-famous writer she always thought he deserved to be.

I wrote that the correspondence was 'doubly single-sided'. Even odder than Véra's destroying her letters is that she wrote so few in the first place. After she followed up the night of the mask, and Sirin's poem about that night, by writing several letters to him in the south of France before she received a single letter back, their correspondence became overwhelmingly one-sided the other way, Véra often writing, it seems, only about one letter to every five of Vladimir's. He was an assiduous and even an uxorious letter-writer, and although often exasperated by her silence, remarkably tolerant of what many in his position might have seen as a failure of the reciprocity expected in a loving relationship. The imbalance persists through every sustained spell apart, from Prague in 1924 ('"You are voiceless, like all that's beautiful . . ." I'm already used to the thought that I won't get a single letter more from you, my bad love, you'; 'Don't you find our correspondence somewhat . . . one-sided? I'm so cross with you that I've begun this letter without a salutation'), through Véra's sanatorium stay in 1926 ('Tufty, I think you write too often to me! A whole two letters over this time. Isn't that too much? Believe it or not, I write every day'; 'Will I get a letterlet tomorrow? Is it sitting now in a railroad car, in the heat, between a letter from Mrs Müller to her cook and a letter from Mr Schwarz to his debtor?'), to Prague in 1930 ('I am sad that you write so little, my endless happiness'), all the way to Taormina in 1970 ('Won't I really get news from you?').

Despite his recurrent disappointment, Vladimir could also be extravagant in his delight at some of the letters he *did* receive: 'I received today – finally – your wonderful (stellar!) letter'; 'My sweetheart, my love, my love, my love – do you know what – all the happiness of the world, the riches, power and adventures, all the promises of religions, all the enchantment of nature and even human fame are not worth your two letters'; 'My love, I keep walking around in the letter you wrote on, on every side, I wander over it like a fly, with my head down, my love!'; 'I read parts of your little card (about the move – terrible! I can imagine . . .) out loud to Ilyusha and Zinzin and they said they understood now who writes my books for me. Flattered?'

Those who know how much Véra did for Vladimir, as administrator, agent, archivist, chauffeur, editor, research and teaching assistant and secretary and typist in four languages, often presume she was somehow subservient. She was not: she dedicated herself to serve Nabokov, but on her own terms. She was resolute and bold from the moment, just turned twenty-one, when she approached Sirin in a mask, and when she followed her invitation and his response with a whole series of letters before he had written a word to her. She carried a gun in Europe and America, and she was proud of the fact that Dmitri, a successful racing-car driver and the owner of multiple Ferraris and speedboats, was proud to say she drove like a man.

There was something fierce in Véra, something steely as well as, in the early days, something frail. From the first she showed she would set her own terms. In his first letter to her, from that farm in the south of France, Vladimir wrote: 'And all your letters, too, are lovely, like the white nights–even the one where you so resolutely underlined several words.' In his next, in the phase of their evening rendezvous and strolls through glistening Berlin streets: 'I can't imagine life without you–in spite of your thinking that it is "fun" for me not to see you for two days … Listen, my happiness–you won't say again that I'm torturing you?'

She shared Nabokov's delight at the enchantment of life's trifles and literature's treasures, and he rated her as having the best and quickest sense of humour of any woman he had met. But where he was buoyant by nature, she was inclined to sink towards gloom. He wrote as he was about to return from his American lecture tour: 'I love you, my darling. Try to be cheery when I come back (but I love you when you're low, too).' As she admitted, she was critical by nature. She never stinted on reproaches, even to the man she loved so unwaveringly. From his first exhausting trip to Paris to establish literary contacts, Nabokov wrote with exasperation: 'but why should I tell you all this if you think I'm doing nothing?' From London, on his first trip there for the same purpose: 'My darling, it *is* unfair (as I have already written to you) to talk of my thoughtlessness … I beg you, my love, do not direct at me any more of these childish reproaches, *je fais ce que je peux*.' From London, two years later: 'I'm ready to come back to Paris, having left the Leeds castle hanging in the lilac dusk an inch above the horizon, but if this happens, believe it, it won't be my fault–I'm doing all in my powers and possibilities,' and the next day, 'Do not write to me about "*don't relax*" and "*avenir*"–this only makes me nervous. I adore you, though.'

That toughness could be turned on others, of course. If T. H. Huxley was Darwin's bulldog, Véra was Vladimir's, albeit in the shape of a greyhound. But that Nabokov built his life around Véra's steely support reveals an aspect of his character not often recognized.

His work was acclaimed with increasing force throughout the 1920s and 1930s, as the letters record, often with embarrassment as well as justified pride, but he never sought meek acclamation. He liked his companions independent rather than deferential: acid-tongued Khodasevich, pugnacious Edmund Wilson, ebullient Ellendea Proffer, irrepressible Alfred Appel. Notoriously undeferential to others, even at moments to Shakespeare, Pushkin and Joyce, let alone to Stendhal, Dostoevsky, Mann, Eliot or Faulkner, Nabokov shows in his letters to Véra his hatred of any kind of fawning before class, power, wealth or reputation. He rarely reported on news, but this 1926 column provoked an outburst: 'The Finnish president came to visit the Latvian one, and on this occasion, the "Slovo" editorial repeats eight times within forty-six lines the words "distinguished guests", "our distinguished guests". The toadies!' His distaste for self-importance produces a damning and hilarious vignette of critic André Levinson and his adulatory family, or quick thrusts at the incidental Aleksandr Halpern, 'who's not very pleasant and moves carefully, to avoid spilling himself, of whom he is full', or Kisa Kuprin, with her '"let's-talk-about-me" smile', or Véra's sister Sofia, whose arch coiling of herself in her sense of her own momentousness he records with fascinated distaste. He remains friends with novelist Mark Aldanov, but laments that 'it's as if he drinks in praise'. Nabokov could be youthfully ebullient about appreciation, even cartwheeling with pleasure as he leaves a gathering of his friends in Berlin on a night when everything he does earns their admiration, but while he spins his body he does not let his head get turned: 'praise and more praise ... I am beginning to get sick of it: it even went as far as them saying I was "subtler" than Tolstoy. Terrible nonsense, really'; 'To avoid later embarrassments (as happened with my letters from Paris—when I re-read them) I now and henceforth absolutely refuse to quote all the direct and indirect compliments I receive'; Gabriel Marcel 'wants me to repeat the *conférence* (which he overpraises)'. He could be critical about earlier and even recent work ('Don't know how my '*Mlle*' will go down today—I'm afraid it's long and boring'; 'I don't give a damn about these French excrements of mine!'). Those who confuse Nabokov with his vain heroes—Hermann, Humbert, Kinbote and Van Veen—should think again. Vanity is his target, not his mode.

Although of course capable of being irked or stingingly dismissive, Nabokov comes across in the letters as naturally generous and appreciative in his opinions of others: 'And he, with his protruding eyes which seem to pop out from the sockets because his (morbidly sunken) cheeks are pressing on them, is very sweet'; 'I am surrounded by hundreds of very nice people'; 'He turned out to be a large springy darling'. In the Paris Métro, 'I once asked a conductor what was in the composition of the stone steps that sparkled so nicely—the sparks were like the play of quartz in granite, and at this he, with unusual eagerness—giving me *les honneurs du Métro*, so to speak,—started explaining to me and showed me where to stand and how to look to enjoy the glitter at its best: if I described this, people would say I made it up.'

Like any lepidopterist of his day, Nabokov pinned his butterfly catches after killing and spreading them, leading many a later headline writer to label him Vlad the Impaler. But writing to Véra, a lover of animals (they donated to the Anti-Vivisection Society), his own tenderness to animals, and his sense of their enchantment, emerges again and again:

> I save mice, there are lots in the kitchen. The servant catches them, and the first time she wanted to kill one, but I took it and carried it out into the garden and set it free there. Since then, all the mice have been brought to me with a snort: '*Das habe ich nicht gesehen*.' I've already set free three of them this way, or maybe it was always the same one. It'll hardly have stayed in the garden.

> what a cat they have! Something perfectly stupendous. Siamese, in colour dark beige, or *taupe*, with chocolate paws . . . and wonderful, clear-blue eyes, turning transparently green towards evening, and the pensive tenderness of its walk, a sort of heavenly circumspection of movement. An amazing, sacred animal, and so quiet–it's unclear what he is looking at with those eyes filled to the brim with sapphire water.

> How light and obedient their little puppy seems,–yesterday he dived head-down in my side pocket where he got stuck, having burped a little blue milk.

He showed the same tenderness towards children. He himself provides a natural transition: 'There's a cat sitting on each central heating stand, and a twenty-day-old wolf puppy whining in the kitchen. And how is our puppy [i.e. Dmitri], I wonder? It was strange to wake up today without the little voice walking past my door in your arms.' Two days later, still from the home of the Malevsky-Maleviches in Brussels:

> The servant here, Boronkin, has a melancholy face but he's very nice, fusses over the puppy and cooks wonderfully. I keep looking at babies–all the carriages here are on thick tyres. I woke up yesterday *en sursaut* utterly certain that my little boy had got into my suitcase and I had to open it up at once or he'd suffocate. Write me as soon as you can, my love.

> Boings, boings, boings against the highchair footstep in the kitchen each morning. I feel new words hatching there without me.

'I feel agonizingly empty without you (and without the little warm portable boy).' And two days later, again:

> And he, my little one? I just physically miss certain sensations, the wool of the breeches' straps, when I unbutton and button them up, the little ligaments, the silk of the crown at my lips when I hold him over the potty, carrying him up the stairs, the circuits of a current of happiness when he throws his arm across my shoulder.

He was taken by children's beauty, their vitality, their vulnerability. The son of his cousin Sergey: 'How charming little Niki is! I couldn't tear myself away from him. He was lying, a red little thing, dishevelled, with bronchitis, surrounded with automobiles of all makes and sizes.' Or his sister Olga's 'extremely attractive' boy: 'I gave my mite towards buying Rostislav something to wear. The only word he can say is "yes", with lots of feeling and many times in a row: "yes, yes, yes, yes, yes", affirming his existence.'

Or the family of his friend Gleb Struve:

> Three of the children take after their father, very unpretty with thick freckled noses (the eldest girl is very *attractive*, though), but the fourth child, a boy of about ten years, also takes after his father, but a different one: he is absolutely charming, a very sweet appearance, with a haze, Botticellian,–quite lovely! Yulen'ka is chatty and dirty as in the old days, is carried away with Scouts, wears a brown jacket and a wide-brimmed hat with elastic. There was no tea when there should have been, while their 'dinner' consisted of Easter cake and a paskha (both dreadful)–that's all the children got, and not because of poverty, but because of lack of discipline.

Nabokov's concern for children lies behind David's role in *Bend Sinister*, Lolita's, or Lucette's in *Ada*. Nothing could be further from Humbert's leering at schoolgirls than Nabokov's eye for the littlest and frailest girl in a gym class he could see from his boarding house: 'The teacher was clapping her hands, and the schoolgirls–really tiny–were running around and jumping in time. One girl, the littlest one, was always left behind, getting muddled and coughing thinly.'

III

On the jacket of Nabokov's *Selected Letters, 1940–1977*, John Updike would write: 'Dip in anywhere, and delight follows. What a writer! And, really, what a basically reasonable and decent man.' Although there is much more these letters to Véra disclose about the man, what do they allow us to discover about the writer? That depends on the reader, of course, but here are some things that strike me. The volatility, the quick changes in subject and tone and point of view, as if impersonating Véra's reaction for a moment, or an interlocutor's peculiar speech, or a reviewer, or a heroic Sirin:

> Now I'm floundering in the muddy water of scene six. I get so tired that my head feels like a bowling alley–and I can't fall asleep earlier than five or six in the morning. In the early scenes there are a thousand reworkings, deletions and additions. And ultimately I'll be rewarded with the routine sarcasm: '. . . not without poetic talent, but we must admit . . .' and so on. And on top of that you–staying silent . . .
>
> No–not on your life! I'll show myself so that the gods will flinch, covering themselves with their elbows ... Either my head will burst

open or the world will – one or the other. Yesterday I ate goose. The weather is frosty: straight pink smoke puffs and the air tastes of sugar-glazed cranberries.

His playfulness infected not only endearments but even reproaches ('I'll go out to buy stamps it's bad that you write to me so seldom and a Gillette razor') and the evasion of Hitler's vigilance. In 1936–7, reporting to his Jewish wife, still in Berlin, on the money that he was earning from his readings and publications abroad and either sending to his mother in Prague or storing with an intermediary for Véra, he invented nonce or recurrent proxies for himself – Grigory Abramovich, Victor, Calmbrood – and would encode the currency that the proxy earned in terms that could change each time: books, journals, pages, columns, butterflies, or even 'Semyonlyudvigoviches' (since Véra knew Semyon Lyudvigovich Frank, and Vladimir was writing from Brussels, she could decode that this registered an amount in Belgian francs).

His imagery could turn the duty of reporting mundane details day by day in 1926 into delight ('The weather this morning was so-so: dullish, but warm, a boiled-milk sky, with skin – but if you pushed it aside with a teaspoon, the sun was really nice, so I wore my white trousers'), or amplify romance ('You came into my life – not as one comes to visit (you know, "not taking one's hat off") but as one comes to a kingdom where all the rivers have been waiting for your reflection, all the roads for your steps'), or immortalize a vista or a person ('How he, Bunin, looks like a wasted old tortoise, stretching its old sinewy grey neck with a fold of skin instead of an Adam's apple and chewing something and waving its dull-eyed ancient head!'), or alleviate the irritation of border bureaucracy ('my German visa – that lichen on the dilapidating wall of my passport').

He observed everything with fascination, animals, plants, faces, character, speech, skyscapes, landscapes, cityscapes ('In the métro it stinks like between the toes and it's just as cramped. But I like the slamming of the iron turnstiles, the flourishes ("*merde*") on the wall, the dyed brunettes, the men smelling of wine, the lifelessly sonorous names of the stations'). Oliver Sacks, musicophile and psychologist extraordinaire, rightly singles Nabokov out as a case of amusia ("'Music, I regret to say," he confesses in his autobiography, "affects me merely as an arbitrary succession of more or less irritating sounds"'), yet the letters disclose him enjoying music in the right circumstances: 'I read for an hour–while the "loudspeaker" in the yard played wonderful dancing music. The violin-like languor of the saxophone, reedy pirouettes, the even beat of strings'; 'I went to the gypsies, to a very pleasant Russian establishment, *Au Papillon bleu*. There we drank white wine and listened to the truly beautiful singing. Real gypsies plus Polyakova.'

Nabokov's haphazard reading would be hard to anticipate: not just the expected *re*-reading of Flaubert, Proust and Joyce, but also surprises like the Soviet fiction he forces himself to read, or Henri Béraud, Ralph Hodgson or Arnold Bennett, all of whom he reads with enthusiasm. But even more valuably his letters to Véra reveal his writing. They document his creative energies, letting us see the plethora of projects–poems, plays, stories, novels, memoirs, screenplays, translations–that suggest themselves and go nowhere, like will-o'-the wisps around the forest of finished works. While most of the letters are too early to throw light on the great English works, or even on the great late Russian works–he was simply too busy pursuing contacts and prospects in his Paris and London trips of the 1930s to have much time to write–the letters of the 1920s show the creative intensities of the composition of his first long work, *The Tragedy of Mister Morn*, and the genesis and composition of two poems, including one of his best. A strange idea for a story about a room modulates into (and now helps explain) the poem 'Komnata' ('The Room'). Most illuminating of all is the making of the poem 'Tikhiy shum' ('Soft Sound'), which we can follow all the way from frustration to triumph. Nabokov had been a star of Berlin's first Russian Culture Day in 1925, and the next year wanted to top this with something new. With only a few days left, he first felt anxiety at having nothing ready, then the rhythmic perturbance that precedes a poem, then disgust at the first snatches of nostalgic cliché washing back from the temporarily blocked drain of his imagination. Then recent impressions, including a memorable downpour in the letters a few days before he began to brood on a poem, and older memories, and current impressions, like a toilet's persistent flush, coalesce in scraps that will become late stanzas in what gradually forces itself on him more insistently, as he falls to sleep, when he wakes, as he walks to the home of his pupil, until he finally sets it down on paper while visiting Véra's cousin's apartment, learns it by heart and then earns a rapturous reception, encore after encore, at Russian Culture Day.

Nabokov wrote his letters for Véra, not for future readers, as we can see most clearly in the 1926 letters where he keeps his promise to report on each day's meals, clothes and activities. In this, the letters to Véra contrast with those to Edmund Wilson, where, although Nabokov was spurred to write so intensely by the match-and-mismatch of their literary passions, he could also not help being conscious that the letters would see print one day. But by the late 1960s he had become probably the most famous writer alive. When Andrew Field, author of the first widely noticed critical book on Nabokov, heard from the Nabokovs in 1968 that they had received from Prague Nabokov's letters to his parents, he asked if he could undertake a biography. They approved, and when he arrived in Montreux at the end of 1970 they had photocopied the letters to Nabokov's parents, with some personal passages blocked out, and a few of the letters to Véra, especially those from 1932 that showed Nabokov's reception in both Russian and French literary Paris. They kept passages of these letters too off limits, but Nabokov also wrote in for Field identifications of some of the individuals mentioned. Perhaps it was before Field arrived that Véra destroyed her own letters to Vladimir.

Nabokov wrote *almost* all his letters to Véra with little thought of posterity looking over his shoulder. But in Taormina in April 1970, knowing that Field would be undertaking his biography, and would be shown some of the letters he had written to Véra, Nabokov on his last multi-day separation from his wife–apart from the succession of enforced sojourns in nearby hospitals that would mark the 1970s–could not help, in his first letter back to Montreux, writing with a wider ultimate audience in mind. The letter splendidly combines his late public style–its parody, poetry, speed and verbal play–and his intimacy with Véra. Unlike so many of the earlier letters that testify to the tension of their uncertain lives, it bespeaks the serenity he had earned through fame, wealth, leisure and a near half-century with Véra. His subsequent letters in this final batch appear to become less conscious of posterity, as he settles back into daily dispatches to Véra. They end, as Véra is about to join him, with what seems a premonition that this may be the last occasion he will ever have to enjoy writing just for her day after day:

> Now I'm waiting for you. I'm a little sorry, in one sense, that this correspondence is coming to an end, hugs and adoration.
>
> Will note down the laundry, and then, around nine, go collecting.
>
> V

'My beloved and precious darling': Translating Letters to Véra

Olga Voronina

Matrimonial correspondence can be awkward to showcase. When even famous writers address their spouses, minutiae may smother amusement. Joyce's letters to Nora Joyce are remembered mainly for their obscenities, rather than their lyricism. Among Virginia Woolf's letters to her husband, only her last—the 'suicide note', in which she thanks him for 'all the happiness in [her] life'—tends to be etched in the reader's memory. Remarkably, Nabokov's letters to his wife are memorable in their entirety. Almost always playful, romantic and pithy, they cannot be reduced to a few unforgettable lines.

In *Speak, Memory*, Nabokov weaves patterns of the past into a 'magic carpet' that the reader can fold and unfold while traversing through the text. In *The Gift*, in *Lolita*, in *Pnin*, in *Ada*, he creates multi-dimensional artistic universes, in which every textual detail is intricately connected, bringing together each novel's time and space and linking quasi-divine predestination and human consciousness. In spite of their spontaneity, the letters to Véra exhibit a similar integrity of vision. Two of them, for example—one from the beginning of the correspondence, the other from the end—form a narrative arc that spans forty-six years of meticulous observation and virtuoso storytelling.

Visiting his family in Prague in 1924, Nabokov goes to see the Church of Saints Peter and Paul in Vyšehrad. Generally displeased with the city, he nonetheless admires the heads of court jesters carved above the door of the cathedral's Basilica Minor, writing in his report to Véra: 'I like to think that the carver, insulted by the ungenerous reward, by the stinginess of the sullen monks he was ordered to depict on the walls, turned their faces, without altering the likenesses, into those of jesters.' In 1970, he again notices a face of a friar – now in good spirits. It reappears on the wall of the Taormina hotel where Nabokov took rooms for a vacation with his wife: 'The door right opposite yours is a funny *trompe l'oeil*: it's fake, painted on, and from behind it a rather cheerful monk is sticking out his white-bearded head.'

Thematic designs created by recurrent images exemplify the continuity of Nabokov's personality and illuminate the consistency of his epistolary style. We deferred to both when translating the letters. We also paid tribute to the master's own creed that a good writer is also an enchanter whose deceptions readers should at least acknowledge and, ideally, see through. An ardent chess problem composer, dedicated maze-maker, and inveterate punster, Nabokov turned quite a few of his letters into a game of codes and brief forays into fiction. In the letters from 1937 in particular, his whimsical aliases acquired personalities, itineraries, even biographies. Giving readings and selling his novels to publishers in Brussels, Paris and London, he avoided reporting his income to Véra directly – a comment not only on his reluctance to deal with the German Finanzamt, but also on his disgust over the vigilance of a putative perlustrator. Instead, he invented two characters to convey by post how much he had earned. The *Doppelgängers* parody their creator while featuring certain qualities bizarrely unlike those of Nabokov. Grigory Abramovich, who makes his appearance on 13 February 1936, is 'sharp, businesslike, good-looking' (19 February 1936), has a family and wishes to settle down in Paris (17 February 1936), and cannot travel to London as Nabokov plans to do because he is unable to procure a visa (4 February 1937). Victor, the other double, emerges on 22 January 1937, has a less comprehensive life-story, and temporarily vanishes two weeks later (5 February 1937). He is somewhat closer to his maker: Nabokov, who was almost christened Victor owing to a mistake of a half-deaf priest, gave the name to the narrator and hero of 'Music', then allotted it to Victor Wind, the young artist of genius in *Pnin*. In the letters, Victor possesses greater vitality than Grigory, reappearing right after getting kicked out, making more money, and begetting, in a confounding stunt of identity alteration, a flesh-and-blood father in the person of Vadim Victorovich Rudnev, the editor of the Russian émigré journal, *Sovremennye zapiski* ('Vadim Victorovich was offering his father a few hundred as an honorarium. Father will take it.'). Four years after composing the letter about Rudnev, Nabokov would praise Gogol's knack for creating 'peripheral personages' who 'are engendered by the subordinate clauses of… various metaphors, comparisons, and lyrical outbursts'. No doubt he knew exactly how Gogolian his own epistolary prose was.

Like Gogol, Nabokov did not miss a chance to turn a morsel of life–or a crumb of language–into a feast of fiction. Even his fiscal reports surround factual detail with fictional curlicues. The transformation of the Belgian franc into Semyon Lyudvigovich Frank, the philosopher and a personal acquaintance, allows Nabokov to write about the currency as if it were hundreds of men replicating themselves in quick succession. His earnings in Britain and France become 'butterflies' (in a letter of 5 February 1937, he talks about amassing 'a collection of three thousand butterflies–so far'), which 'Victor', now turned a butterfly expert, accumulates at the British Museum, a place Nabokov dreams of as a scholarly paradise free of financial worry and other earthly considerations. Eventually the butterfly code too loses its lustre. In the spring of 1937, he starts writing about collecting, storing and sending his mother 'books'–the money transfers she desperately needed. 'Journals' or 'books' add to his fiscal ciphers, with 'pages'–in an array of languages–representing amounts earned in a succession of currencies.

Nabokov's preoccupation with encoding his earnings can make this game seem mundane and even drab in comparison to the sheer exuberance of Gogol's literary imagination. But most of his fictional inventions in the letters spring from pranksterism, not pragmatism. In 1926, when Véra was recuperating at a sanatorium in Southern Germany, he invented a zoo of minuscule creatures, some of which may be spin-offs from the unheard-of names he painstakingly coined for her, a fresh appellation in every letter. Many of these 'beasties' are indeed little animals, feline and canine in origin–for instance, Pooch, a relative of Poochums, one of Nabokov's pet-names for his wife in 1925 and 1926. Others are strikingly human, such as Mrs Tufty, a snappy dresser, or Mr Darling, the lisping, sensitive German-born 'editor' of the letters' 'puzzle department', who is in love with Véra and takes an easy offence at her reluctance to respond to 'his' numerous crosswords and verbal games. Mr Darling's crying in a wastebasket, or his brave attempt to steal Nabokov's pen to add a few words to the letter to his beloved, are chefs-d'oeuvre of the art which, just as Darling himself, has a name but avoids classification. It is literary tightrope-walking, an exercise in 'life-generating' fiction.

Nabokovian verbal jauntiness has overwhelmed many a translator, but his quirky Russian endearments are a new challenge: never before have they been converted to English in such profusion. The letters of 1926 abound in sweet talk with a 'sch' or 'shch' attached to some words. Thus the Russian 'мышь' (*mysh'*, mouse) becomes 'мысч' (*mysch*) and even 'мыс-ш-с-ч-щ-с-ш' (*mys-sh-s-ch-shch-s-sh*), with several other variations of such spelling to follow ('ознобысч,' 'обезьянысч,' 'тушканысч,' 'ужинысч,' etc.). It is unclear whether the wordplay originated in an attempt to recreate the scurrying rodent by means of alliterative animation and then went rampant, drawing in other creatures and objects, or whether Nabokov borrowed part of the German diminutive '-chen' suffix (as in 'Greta–Gretchen' or 'Brot–Brötchen'), truncating it for a half-soothing, half-grating effect. In translation, we relied on our stylistic intuition to choose between adding 'sch' to English roots ('Mousch,' 'Feverisch') or replacing Nabokov's ending made of Russian hushings with an English diminutive suffix, '-kin(s)' (as in 'monkeykins').

Even when Nabokov chooses to address Véra in a less eccentric fashion, his choices may not have English equivalents. Most often, he prefers to call his wife *dushen'ka*, literally a diminutive of the Russian word *dusha* ('soul', 'psyche'). It would have been possible to translate this word as 'darling' (our choice), 'sweetheart' or 'dearest' (options from a discard pile), had the writer not bedecked it with other tender adjectives: *dorogaya* ('dear'), *lyubimaya* ('beloved'), *milaya* ('lovely', 'sweet'), and *bestsennaya* ('priceless'). We used 'dear darling' a few times in spite of its sounding too alliterative, resorted to 'beloved darling' rarely, tried 'sweet darling' once or twice, and once (15 April 1939) had to go along with 'My beloved and precious darling'. Unfortunately, even that baroque phrase does not fully convey the fretful and persistent affection of the Russian 'dushen'ka moya lyubimaya i dragotsennaya', with its one and half times as many syllables and with the adjectives coming cajolingly after the noun.

In some cases, readers simply have to accept it as a given that Nabokov did not use his tenderness sparingly. The closest they can get, in English, to the understanding of his epistolary passion, is by comparing the sentence from the letter of 3 July 1926 ('I love you, my Pussms, my life, my flight, my flow, darling pooch . . .') to the beginning of his most famous novel: 'Lolita, light of my life, fire of my loins. My sin, my soul. Lo-lee-ta.'

Nabokov's endearments reflect his fascination with verbal games in his native tongue. His move to the United States and the transition to English opened even greater prospects for exploring new lexical possibilities. The letters are full of enthralling details of the writer's linguistic adjustment to his post-European American existence. Unlike his Russian translation of *Lolita*, jammed with carefully chosen equivalents of English expressions, they boldly slip transliterated English into Russian grammatical slots. This is especially noticeable in Nabokov's reports of his adventures in the American South in 1941–2, which he peppers with such words as *khintiki* ('little hints'), *prufsy* ('proofs'), *glimpsnul* ('I've glimpsed'), *brekfastayu* ('I am having breakfast') and *tribulatsii* ('tribulations'). We have italicized English (as well as French and German) words Nabokov used in the letters, but these Cyrillic steals have remained unmarked.

From his first letter to his last note, Nabokov used the pre-revolutionary orthography to write to Véra. Echoing his father, who called the spelling reform of 1917–18 a 'disgrace', he could never disconnect his awareness of the cultural loss from the perception that there was something vaguely criminal about the outlawing of the old spelling. No matter where the Nabokovs lived, the endearment 'Vérochka' would always be written with a *yat'*, while all hard consonants at the end of words would invariably be followed with a *yer*, letters expelled, along with three others, from the Russian language. A deviation from this rule could mean only a joke or a scornful remark on Nabokov's part, as in the riddle in the letter of 11 July 1926. He asks Véra why 'M. M. Sukotin'–a fabricated 'peripheral character'–writes his name without the hard sign at the end. The answer: because M. M. Sukotin is an anagram of 'communist' and therefore a barbarian mutilator of language.

Following modern practice, inside and outside Russia, *Letters to Véra* retains Nabokov's politically and culturally pointed use of the old orthography only in commentaries or in the snippets of manuscript reproduced as illustrations. Neither this English edition, nor other translations, will be able to pay full tribute to his nostalgia for the lost spelling. Yet it would be hard to appreciate the letters without understanding Nabokov's yearning to cross boundaries of time as well as space by eloping through language. In the story 'The Visit to the Museum', written in 1938, he clinches the protagonist's nightmarish journey from France to Soviet Russia with an image of a lonely street sign, '. . . OE REPAIR', where the Russian genitive plural for 'shoes' ('. . . САПОГ') is spelled without a *yer*. To his horror, the character realizes that 'it was not the snow that had obliterated the "hard sign" at the end'. But if in the story the abolition of the 'ъ' signifies the definitive and irrevocable loss of one's native land, its reappearance in Nabokov's letter of 19 March 1941 intimates hope. Having playfully composed a quotation from a future Russian book about himself, Nabokov deliberately, and perhaps even triumphantly, has the yet unborn reviewer use the old-fashioned spelling: "Living at Wellesley College, among the oaks and sunsets of peaceful New England, he dreamed of changing his American fountain-pen for his own incomparable Russian feather-pen." (From "Vladimir Sirin and His Time", 2074, Moscow)'.

Not only idiosyncrasies of the old orthography disappear in translation – some stylistic deviations become invisible as well. For example, in this edition we had to leave unmarked Nabokov's spelling of certain Russian words which now would seem charmingly antiquated ('галстухъ', 'шофферъ', 'притти'). Aware of the dearth of suffixes denoting smallness or more or less tender familiarity in English, by contrast with their abundance and naturalness in Russian, we also reduced the number of diminutive noun forms, rampant in Nabokov's early letters, especially in descriptions of food, clothes and other trivia (the phrase 'cold-cuts and macaroni' in the letter of 3 July 1926 would otherwise have to be rendered something like 'teeny cold-cuts and macaronikins'). When translating the intimate-sounding word 'mama' Nabokov used to refer to Elena Ivanovna Nabokov, we chose the more reserved 'Mother' and thus avoided contemporary 'mom' or 'mum' as words that would not have belonged to the Nabokov family in that era.

We have transliterated Russian proper names, as well as the names of periodicals, according to a simplified version of the Library of Congress system, introducing a number of deviations from the norm in favour of the spelling accepted in Nabokov studies and Anglophone academia. Fixed English spellings remain intact ('Rachmaninov' instead of 'Rakhmaninov'). We used *y* for the spelling of й and *jot*-based vowel sequences, such as ая and ую, as well as for rendering ы ('Sergey' but 'Sovremennye'; 'novyi' but 'goluboy'). Adjectival masculine name endings ий or ый are transliterated as *y* ('Fondaminsky' instead of 'Fondaminskiy'). We have omitted the Russian soft sign whenever reasonable ('Gogol' instead of 'Gogol''), transliterating it as *ie* in some names (Vasilievna) and as ' before a consonant and in word-end positions ('Izobretenie Val'sa'; '*Rul*'') or before a vowel (p'esy). The vowel ë is transliterated as *yo* (Fyodor, Seryozha, Zyoka).

Like all other correspondents of his era and upbringing, Nabokov customarily used name and patronymic ('Vadim Victorovich'), calling only some family members and intimate friends by their first names (Kirill, Ilya, Sonya). We have retained all the patronymics as well as affectionate names (Ilyusha, Fondik), providing the latter with explanations in endnotes.

When rendering Russian feminine surnames in English, we have adhered to the system which Nabokov preferred, dropping the final 'a' in 'Anna Karenin', unless it was a well-established literary or artistic name (Berberova, Akhmatova). In several cases, it proved impossible for us to figure out whether the woman in question was married or not. Thus, in the letters of 3 and 11 November 1932, Nabokov mentions either a daughter or wife of Sergey Rachmaninov. We had to preface the name with 'Mme [Mlle?]' to avoid suggesting with certainty that it was the composer's wife. In another case, it was easier to surmise that Mlle Novotvortsev, Nabokov's former girlfriend who kept accosting him at readings in Paris in 1932 and 1936, remained single and thus was able to profess her feelings freely.

When writing to Véra about his diet in 1926, family matters in 1924 and 1932, his income or the women who commented on the colour of his eyes in 1937, Nabokov's diction is the same as when he describes his hospital stay in 1944 or butterfly collecting in 1942 and 1970. From the first letter to the last, his writing remains buoyant and whimsical, lyrical and lucid, rich and nimble. This stylistic consistency is one of the noteworthy features of the letters, especially in view of the fact that at the end of his life he became painfully self-conscious about his Russian. Reaching out to readers to whom Nabokov is, first and foremost, a master of English prose, this translation aims at preserving the lushness, flow and tang of Nabokov's more intimate style.

Dmitri Nabokov, who endorsed this publication of his father's letters to his mother, looked forward to editing our translation. It is sad indeed to recall that his health declined so that he could see only the earliest preparation for this edition and would never see the final product. We missed his insights, his touch and tone, his irreplaceable knowledge of the details that constituted Vladimir and Véra Nabokovs' biography and, to a large degree, his own.

LETTERS TO VÉRA

*1923**

[ALS, 2 PP.]
[c. 26 July 1923]

[TO: Berlin]

[Domaine de Beaulieu, Solliès-Pont, Var, France]

I won't hide it: I'm so unused to being – well, understood, perhaps, – so unused to it, that in the very first minutes of our meeting I thought: this is a joke, a masquerade trick ... But then ... And there are things that are hard to talk about – you'll rub off their marvellous pollen at the touch of a word ... They write me from home about mysterious flowers. You are lovely ...

And all your letters, too, are lovely, like the white nights – even the one where you so resolutely underlined several words. I found it and the

* Notes to the letters begin on p. 550. People referred to in letters only by first name, first name and patronymic (in full, abbreviated, or by initials only), or nickname, will be identified in the notes the first time for each variant form but not always thereafter, especially if identities are obvious from the continuous context. But each short name will be noted in the Index, with a cross-reference. *Fond*, *Fondik*, *I. I.*, *Il. Is.*, *Ilya*, *Ilya Isidorovich*, and *Ilyusha*, for instance, all refer to Ilya Isidorovich Fondaminsky, and in the Index will each be cross-referred to 'Fondaminsky, Ilya Isidorovich'. Words and phrases, other than proper names, written in Roman rather than Cyrillic characters are indicated in italics. Underlined emphases remain in underline. Occasionally VN spells out an English or French word in Cyrillic characters. We indicate this by spacing out the word, as in 'b r e a k f a s t'.

previous one when I got back from Marseilles, where I was working in the port. It was the day before yesterday, and I decided not to reply to you till you wrote me more. A little joke ...

Yes, I need you, my fairy-tale. Because you are the only person I can talk with about the shade of a cloud, about the song of a thought – and about how, when I went out to work today and looked a tall sunflower in the face, it smiled at me with all of its seeds. There is a tiny Russian restaurant in the dirtiest part of Marseilles. I ate my grub there with Russian sailors – and no one knew who I was and where I was from, and I was surprised myself that I used to wear a tie and thin socks. Flies circled over spots of borsch and wine, a sourish chill and the hum of portside nights wafted in from the street. And listening, and watching – I thought that I remember Ronsard by heart and know the names of skull bones, bacteria, plant juices. It was strange.

I am very drawn to Africa and Asia: I was offered a place as a stoker on a boat going to Indochina. But two things are forcing me to return to Berlin for a while: the first is that Mother must be so very lonely – the second ... a mystery – or rather a mystery I desperately want to resolve ... I leave on the 6th, but will spend some time in Nice and in Paris – at the home of a man I studied with in Cambridge. You probably know him. So I will be in Berlin on the 10th or 11th ... And if you're not there I will come to you, and find you ... See you soon, my strange joy, my tender night. Here are poems for you:

EVENING

You call – and in a little pomegranate tree
an owlet barks like a puppy.
In the evening height the moon's curved blade
is so lonely and ringing.

вернуться во время въ Берлинъ: первая — то, что мамѣ уже очень одиноко приходится, — вторая… тайна — или вѣрнѣе, тайна, которую мнѣ мучительно хочется разрѣшить…] Выѣзжаю я 6го, — но нѣкоторое время пробуду въ Ниццѣ и въ Парижѣ — [у человѣка съ которымъ я учился вмѣстѣ въ Cambridge'ѣ. Ты вѣроятно знаешь его.] Такимъ образомъ въ Берлинѣ я буду 10го или 11го… [И если тебя не будетъ тамъ я пріѣду къ тебѣ, — найду… До скораго, моя странная радость, моя нѣжная ночь. Вотъ тебѣ стихи:

Вечеръ

Зовешь, — а въ деревцѣ гранатовомъ совенокъ
    полаиваетъ, какъ щенокъ.
Въ вечерней вышинѣ такъ одинокъ и звонокъ
    луны изогнутый клинокъ.

Зовешь, — и плещетъ ключъ вечернею лазурью:
    какъ голосъ твой, вода свѣжа, —
и въ глиняный кувшинъ, лоснящійся глазурью,
    луна вонзается, дрожа.

Зной

Я стеръ со лба укусы капель жгучихъ
и навзничь легъ на скользкій теплый скатъ,
гдѣ голосами сплюснутыхъ цикадъ
гремѣло солнце въ сосенкахъ пахучихъ.
И я поплылъ въ пылающую тьму
дня южнаго, — подъ пьяный плескъ тимпана,
подъ лепетъ флейтъ — и ротъ пурпурный Пана
прижался жадно къ сердцу моему.]

Здѣсь очень много написалъ. Между прочимъ — двѣ драмы „Дѣдушка" и „Полюсъ". Первая будетъ въ альманахѣ „Гамаюнъ" — вторая въ слѣд. номерѣ „Русской мысли".

В.

You call – and a spring splashes with the turquoise of evening:
the water is fresh, like your voice,
and the moon, quivering, pierces a clay jug,
gleaming with its glaze.

SWELTER

I wiped the prickles of burning drops off my forehead
and lay supine on the slippery warm slope,
where the sun thundered among fragrant pines
with the voices of flattened cicadas.

And I floated into the scorching darkness
of the southern day, to the drunken swash of a timbrel,
to the babbling of flutes, and Pan's purple mouth
pressed greedily to my heart.

I have written an awful lot here. Among other things, two plays, 'The Granddad' and 'The Pole'. The first will be in the collection 'Gamayun' – the second, in the next issue of 'Russkaya Mysl''.

V.

[ALS, 4 PP.]

[8 November 1923]

TO: 41, Landhausstrasse, Berlin W.

[Berlin]

8–XI–23

How can I explain to you, my happiness, my golden, wonderful happiness, how much I am all yours–with all my memories, poems, outbursts, inner whirlwinds? Or explain that I cannot write a word without hearing how you will pronounce it–and can't recall a single trifle I've lived through without regret–so sharp!–that we haven't lived through it together–whether it's the most, the most personal, intransmissible–or only some sunset or other at the bend of a road–you see what I mean, my happiness?

And I know: I can't tell you anything in words–and when I do on the phone then it comes out completely wrong. Because with you one needs to talk wonderfully, the way we talk with people long gone, do you know what I mean, in terms of purity and lightness and spiritual precision–but I–*je patauge* terribly. Yet you can be bruised by an ugly diminutive–because you are so absolutely resonant–like seawater, my lovely.

I swear–and the inkblot has nothing to do with it–I swear by all that's dear to me, all I believe in–I swear that I have never loved before as I love you,–with such tenderness–to the point of tears–and with such a sense of radiance. On this page, my love, I once (Your face betw) began to write a poem for you and this very inconvenient little tail got left–I've lost my footing. But there's no other paper. And most of all I want you to be happy and it seems to me that I could give you that happiness–a sunny, simple happiness–and not an altogether common one.

And you should forgive me for my pettiness–that I am thinking with aversion about how–*practically*–I will mail this letter tomorrow–and yet I am ready to give you all of my blood, if I had to–it's hard to explain–sounds flat–but that's how it is. Here, I'll tell you–with my love I could have filled ten centuries of fire, songs, and valour–ten whole centuries, enormous and winged,–full of knights riding up blazing hills–and legends about giants–and fierce Troys–and orange sails–and pirates–and poets. And this is not literature since if you reread carefully you will see that the knights have turned out to be fat.

No – I simply want to tell you that somehow I can't imagine life without you – in spite of your thinking that it is 'fun' for me not to see you for two days. And you know, it turns out that it wasn't Edison at all who thought up the telephone but some other American, a quiet little man whose name no one remembers. It serves him right.

Listen, my happiness – you won't say again that I'm torturing you? How I'd like to take you off somewhere with me – you know how those highwaymen of old did: a wide-brimmed hat, a black mask, and a bell-shaped musket. I love you, I want you, I need you unbearably . . . Your eyes – which shine so wonder-struck when, with your head thrown back, you tell something funny – your eyes, your voice, lips, your shoulders – so light, sunny . . .

You came into my life – not as one comes to visit (you know, 'not taking one's hat off') but as one comes to a kingdom where all the rivers have been waiting for your reflection, all the roads, for your steps. Fate wanted to correct its mistake – as if it has asked my forgiveness for all of its previous deceptions. So how can I leave you, my fairy-tale, my sun? You see, if I'd loved you less, then I would have had to go. But this way – it makes no sense. And I don't want to die, either. There are two kinds of 'come what may'. Involuntary and deliberate. Forgive me – but I live by the second one. And you can't take away my faith in what I am afraid to think about – it would have been such happiness . . . And here's another little tail.

> Yes: an old-fashioned slowness of speech,
> steely simplicity . . . Thus the heart's more ardent:
> steel, incandesced by flight . . .

This is a fragment of my long poem – but didn't go in it. Wrote it down once, so not to forget, and here it is now – a splinter.

У меня прощенье за всѣ свои прежнiя
обманы. Какъ-же мнѣ уѣхать отъ тебя,
моя сказка, мое солнце? Понимаешь:
если-бъ я меньше любилъ-бы тебя, то
я *долженъ* былъ-бы уѣхать. А такъ —
— просто смысла нѣтъ. И умирать мнѣ
не хочется. Есть два рода „будь что будетъ"
безвольное и волевое. Прости мнѣ — но я
живу вторымъ. И ты не можешь отнять
у меня вѣры въ то о чемъ я думать
боюсь: такое это было-бы счастье...
Вотъ опять — хвостики. Это кусочекъ
моей поэмы — не вошедшiй въ нее.
Записалъ какъ-то чтобы не забыть
и вотъ теперь — даю.

Вотъ: старинная медлительность рѣчи
сталистая простота... живыхъ сердецъ грозы
сталь накаленная полетомъ...

Все это я пишу лежа въ постели,
опирая листокъ объ огромную
книжку. Когда я долго ночью
работаю то у одного изъ портретовъ
на стѣнѣ — (какая-то прабабушка
нашего хозяина) дѣлаются
пристальные пренеприятные глаза.
Очень хорошо что я дошелъ до конца
этого хвостика; очень мѣшаютъ
Любовь моя, спокойной ночи...
Не знаю разберешь ли ты это безграмотное
письмо... но все равно... Я люблю тебя.
Буду ждать тебя завтра въ 11 ч. вечера — а не то
позвони мнѣ послѣ 9 час. В.

All of this I'm writing lying in bed, resting the page on a huge book. When I work long into the night, the eyes of one of the portraits on the wall (some great-grandmother of our landlord) become intent and very unpleasant. So good to have reached the end of this little tail, such a nuisance.

My love, good night ...

Don't know whether you'll be able to make sense of this illiterate letter ... But never mind ... I love you. Will wait for you tomorrow at 11 p.m. – otherwise call me after 9.

V.

[ALS, 1 P.]
[30 December 1923]

[TO: Berlin]

[Prague]
30–XII–23
Praha Třida Svornosti 37
Smichov

My dear happiness,

How charming, lovely, light you were at that bustling station ... didn't have time to say anything to you, my happiness. But I could see you through the window of the carriage, and, for some reason, while looking at you standing there pressing the fur coat to your sides with your elbows, hands deep in your sleeves – looking at you, at the yellow glass in the station window behind you, and at your grey little booties – one in profile, another *en trois quarts* – for some reason it was precisely then that I realized how I loved you – and then you had such a fine smile when the train began to glide off. But you know – our trip was absolutely, exceptionally awful. Our things were scattered all over the train, and we had to hang about standing upright, in the draught, till the border. I wanted so much to show you how amusingly the frozen snow, like kernels of silver corn, attached itself to the inner side of those, you know, leather aprons that connect the carriages. You'd have enjoyed it.

Imagine three little rooms: furniture, a deal table, a dozen chairs hiding splinters, seven beds – entirely wooden, without mattresses, with crosspieces instead of bottoms – and one couch, bought by chance. That's it. A thin mattress is stretched along the crosspieces – but you can feel these wooden ribs through it, so in the morning you're all aches . . . and bed-bugs inhabit the couch. They'd almost vanished after a turpentine attack, but here today they've reappeared, on the ceiling, from where they will, at night, like larks, fall onto those asleep – onto Kirill and me. I told him that twelve (it is more correct to spell it with an 'e') bed-bugs would be enough to kill a man, but having remembered how charmingly you say: 'But he's so small!' I took, as they say, my words back. Add to this the furious cold in the rooms and the two tiled stoves' unwillingness to give off warmth (which, of course, would be unpleasant for them), and you get the picture of our life here. No money at all, no forks either – so we have to subsist on sandwiches. At the first opportunity I'll bring Mother back to Berlin, where I'll arrive myself on April 5th – minus eighty-five days (have you worked this out?). I have not seen Prague yet – and generally we're on bad terms with each other.

Listen: as soon as I have a chance, I will call you on the only telephone to be found in this city: in Kramář's house. I will try it on the twenty-third (old style), at seven o'clock.

I love you very much. Love you in a bad way (don't be angry, my happiness). Love you in a good way. Love your teeth. I have been working, Morn sat down here with me. He asks me to send you his 'cordial greetings'. My love, you know, I'm simply very bored without you. I have a feeling you're still standing at the station as I saw you at that last moment – just as you, probably, still think I'm standing at the carriage window, in my bowler. Till the court scene, your Spanish novel is enchanting; after that, it's bad. I will give them the package tomorrow.

How I wish you were saying, right now, with feeling: 'But you promised me!?. . .' I love you, my sun, my life, I love your eyes – closed – all the little tails of your thoughts, your stretchy vowels, your whole soul from head to heels. I'm tired, off to bed. I love you.

V.

[ALS, 2 PP.]

[postmarked 2 January 1924]

TO: 41 Landhausstr., Berlin W. 15

[Prague]

3[1] – XII – 23

Trida Svornosty, 37

Smichov Praha.

Not a word from you yet, my love – probably, tomorrow. But if not? You know, I didn't think I'd miss you so much ('Ah, you didn't think! . . .'). No – it's just a turn of phrase – to tell you, my lovely, my happiness, how I long for you (how I need you). Meanwhile, I'll get out of here only on the 17th – I want to finish my Morn – If there were yet another move, he'd fall apart. He's a man who absolutely cannot bear the feeling of relocation. Yesterday I wrote only two lines all day, and even those I crossed out today. Now it's been going unexpectedly well, so tomorrow I'll finish the first scene of the third act. For some reason I am very *touchy* about this thing. And yet, what a pleasure it's been to read it to two people – to you and, the other day, to Mother. The third person who understood every comma and appreciated the trifles dear to me was my father. Mother always recalls this when I read her something – and it hurts.

I have just written to Tatarinov, asking him to place an announcement on the 6th or the 7th, in *Rul'*, that I (name given) am looking for a room with board in a Russian family. Otherwise it would work out too expensive. Unfortunately I left your package on the train. I am 'in total despair'! In fact, two days ago I took it to the address – which you wrote in a barely audible whisper ... You know what I'd like to do now? To watch you slightly curtsy when stepping up from the street to the sidewalk ('Stop it! ...'). I love you so much today that I seem to be writing nonsense.

And here's what I have noticed so far in Prague: a huge number of cart-horses, and in the shops, signs like when a Frenchman, wanting to show off, puts Russian words in his novel – and shows off illiterately. There's also a wide river here – under the ice. Here and there areas have been cleared for skating. On each of these ice squares a single boy skates, falling down every minute. Idle passers-by look down at him from the huge ancient bridge, along which horses drag their carts, one after the other. A fat man in a uniform stands at one end of the bridge, and every passer-by must pay him a copper coin for the right to cross to the other side. The custom is old, feudal. The trams are small, russet-flanked, and inside the latest magazines hanging on hooks – for general consumption. Great city?

Yesterday, one professor told me that when his daughter was just a few months old, she often pretended to faint. Later, when she'd grown up a little, he'd scare her like this: he'd sit down, reading; she'd play on the floor. Suddenly he would lower his book, make terrible eyes, wipe his forehead and say slowly: 'You know, Mashen'ka, I seem to be turning into an eagle ...' She – in tears: 'Why do things always happen to you when there's no one in the apartment? ...'

Tomorrow at seven I will try to 'call' you. It will probably be painful, but I want to hear if only a little edge of your voice. And how will it be in Berlin, my love? Will you come to America with me? Oh, if you only knew how disgusted I am with this poor fit of a life, the fuss about money, the repulsive translations I have to sweat over – and the pennies, the pennies ... But I'm *bourgeois* in everyday things. Kramář's automobiles, his marble bath, his servants drive me mad ... Buffon put on lace cuffs when he sat down to work. I need comforts, you understand, not for the sake of comforts, but so I need not think about them – and can just write, write – and unfurl myself, and explode ... But after all, who knows, maybe because I am writing 'Mr Morn' sitting in a fur coat, on a prison bed, by the light of a candle-end (this is getting almost poetic), it will turn out still better. I can't wait to read you the fifth scene.

Do you know that you are my happiness? You are made entirely of tiny arrow-like movements – I love every one of them. Have you ever thought how strangely, how easily our lives have come together? Probably God, bored in Heaven, had his hand in Patience come out, which doesn't happen often. I love this marvellous quickness in you, as if in your soul there's a place prepared in advance for my every thought. When Monte Cristo came to the palace he had bought, he noticed, among other things, a small casket on his desk. He said to his majordomo, who'd arrived earlier to arrange everything: 'There should be gloves in here.' The man beamed, opened this unremarkable casket and, indeed, there were gloves. I've got a bit lost in the image – but somehow this all relates to you and me. You know, I have never trusted anyone as I trust you. In everything enchanted there's an element of trust.

I am afraid that this has turned out to be a rather stumbling letter. And not completely literate. I have been speaking in iambic pentameter so much lately it's hard to write prose. Listen: can you call my former apartment some time at midnight or even later? I have also asked the

Tatarinovs and the Struves to do this. I want to make the tenants happy.

I kiss you, my happiness – and you cannot stop me ...

V.

1924

[ALS, 2 PP.]
[8 January 1924]

TO: 41, Landhausstr., Berlin W.

[Prague]
8–1–24

Hullo! (slightly short of breath). Gre-etings (quietly and softly,—it's such a cushion-word).

No, I didn't manage to call you, my love ... But then I received today—finally—your wonderful (stellar!) letter. You know, we are terribly alike ... For example, in letters: we both like 1) to slip in foreign words unnoticed, 2) to quote from favourite books, 3) to translate impressions from one sense (for example, vision) to another (for example, taste), 4) to apologize at the end for imaginary nonsense; and much more. You wrote so well about yourself, my lovely: I saw you. And I wanted to tousle you even more. As for the mask, indeed, don't you dare wear it. You're my mask ... Would you like to know the view I have out of my window, since you love snow? So here you are: the broad whiteness of the Moldau, and along that whiteness, little black silhouettes of people cross from one shore to the other, like musical notes. For example, the figure of some boy is dragging behind him a D-sharp: a sledge. Across the river there are snowy roofs in a distant, lightweight sky, and to the right, that feudal bridge I've already written you about.

Morn is growing like fire on a windy night! I have only two scenes to write; and, I already have the very end of the last – eighth – scene. I am writing to Lukash that it's all a brilliant trifle – but I don't believe that ... However ...

Lord, how I wish to see you ... My dear eyes ... I don't know what I'll do with you when we meet. Can't write more today – have to go to a party. They are taking me out into society! Of all my acquaintances, there's only the eternally youthful Sergey Makovsky here. I love you. Without end.

V.

I'm just come back from the party at Kramář's. I have to quote the dialogue which 'took place' (a Gallicism) there.

A lady (elderly)

And how do you like Prague? (Several lines follow about the beauty of Prague. I'll skip them. Then:)

You're at the local gymnasium?

I

???

The Lady

Ah, sorry – you have such a young face ... Then you will be going to lectures. What field?

I (with a melancholy smile)

I finished university two years ago. Two majors, Natural History and Literature.

The Lady (confounded)

Er ... so you work?

I

For the Muse.

The Lady (livening up a bit)

Ah, you are a poet. And have you been writing long? Tell me, have you read Aldanov – amusing, isn't he? Overall, books are a great help in our difficult times. You pick up, say, Voloshin or Sirin – and at once your heart lifts. But nowadays, you know, books are so expensive …

I

Yes, extremely expensive. (And disappear modestly, incognito.)

Isn't it an amusing little conversation? I have quoted it to you word for word.

My happiness, you know, tomorrow will be exactly one year since I broke up with my fiancée. Do I regret it? No. It had to happen this way, so I could meet you. After Mr Morn I will write the second – final – act of 'The Wanderers'. I suddenly feel like it. And now I am putting the candle out and going to bed. No, I will read for a bit longer. I love you, my lovely. Do write to me more often otherwise I won't cope. And meet me at the station on the seventeenth.

V.

[ALS, 2 PP.]
[10 January 1924]

TO: 41, Landhausstr., Berlin W.

10–I–24
Smichov, Třida Svornosty, 37
Prague

My love, today I was sure my sister would fly in to me with a shout: 'A letter from Madame Bertran!,' – but no. I became so sad … 'And what are letters? White patches on partings' tattered black' (paraphrasing Mr Lermontov's famous line).

Yesterday evening was straight out of a Flemish painting, motionless in a languorous mist. Over the snows, in the mist, the sunset shone through tenderly, dimly, like the undeveloped colours of decalcomania (you know what I mean?). After crossing the river on ice, I climbed a hill – white, with black bushes of naked elder. On one side the hill is suddenly cut off by a fortress wall; on its top stands a dark two-towered cathedral, girded here and there with scarlet fretwork – like a Slavic sheen falling on Gothic geometry. There, too, behind a cast-iron railing, is a Catholic cemetery: straight little graves, golden crucifixes. Above the cathedral door, a vaulted bas-relief, ending on both sides of the door with two heads – the moulded, protuberant faces of two ... jesters. One of them has large, sly features, the other's face is twisted in a crooked grin of contempt. Both are in those paddle-shaped leather hats or hoods (recalling simultaneously bat wings and a rooster's comb) that medieval jesters used to wear. I found a few such faces on other doors too, and each has a different expression: one, for example, has a beautiful, austere profile from under the folds of his rough head-gear: an angel jester. I like to think that the carver, insulted by the ungenerous reward, by the stinginess of the sullen monks he was ordered to depict on the walls, turned their faces, without altering the likenesses, into those of jesters. Or perhaps this is a nice symbol for me, that only through laughter can mortals enter Heaven ... You agree?

I walked around the cathedral along a slippery path between snow-drifts. The snow was light, dry: grab a handful, throw it up, and it disperses in the air like dust, as if flying back up. The sky darkened. In it appeared a thin golden moon: half of a broken halo. I walked along the edge of the fortress wall. Old Prague lay below in the thickening mist. The snowy roofs clustered together, cumbrous and dim. The houses seemed to have been piled anyhow, in a moment of terrible and fantastic carelessness. In this frozen storm of outlines, in this snowy semi-darkness, the streetlamps and windows were burning with a warm and sweet lustre, like well-licked punch lollipops. In just one place you could also see a little scarlet light, a drop of pomegranate juice. And in the fog of crooked walls and smoky corners I divined an ancient ghetto, mystical ruins, the alley of Alchemists ... On the way back I composed a short monologue, which Dandilio will say in the penultimate scene:

... ... Matter must decay
for matter to be resurrected – and from that,
if we guess the ancient symbol right,
it comes out thus – follow me, Tremens:
space is God, and matter is Christ, and time
is the Holy Ghost. Hence my conclusion:
the world is divine, and therefore all is happiness,
and so we must all sing
as we work (for our *existence*
means to work for the master
in three forms: space, matter,
and time), but the work ends,
and we depart to the eternal feast,
having given our memory to time, our image
to space, and our love to matter . . .

To which Tremens answers: 'Opposites meet, I agree with you, – but the point is, I rebel against a sovereign-existence: I don't want to work for it, but rather, to go and party right away.'

My literary labours notwithstanding, I love you very much, my happiness – and I am very angry that you're not writing to me. All these days I've been in a tense and exalted mood, because I have been composing, 'literally', non-stop.

They told me that there was a note in *Rul'* by Mme Landau about our *Ahasuerus* reading. Have you read it?

So long, my lovely. You've not 'fallen out of love' with me, have you?

V.

[ALS, 2 PP.]
[12 January 1924]

TO: 41, Landhausstr., Berlin W.

[Prague]
12–I–24
12 midnight

'You are voiceless, like all that's beautiful ...' I'm already used to the thought that I won't get a single letter more from you, my bad love, you. I am sending you my countenance, which I happened to find among Mother's things (she has another like it). I had it taken two years ago, in Cambridge *of sweet memories*, on the eve of an exam – so that in case I 'failed', I could find a sign of doom, a fatal little feature in my image. But, as you can see, I'm proud and care-free.

Yesterday our furniture *u. s. w.* finally arrived. It seems to have gone a roundabout route (Hamburg–America–Singapore–Constantinople) – which explains the delay. Now our apartment has cheered up a bit, i.e. first there was only one chair in each (tiny!) room, now there's a whole regiment of them, so it recalls the look of a room where children are having a magic lantern show. (Damp linen and very long explanations with each picture: I hated it as a child.) Do you know that on the cover of the first issue of 'Grani' our surnames are side by side? A symbol?

Kadashev-Amfiteatrov has just been visiting me and talking about famous typos. One provincial newspaper printed 'veterinary' instead of

'Virgin Mary'. The authorities would certainly not have noticed, but the newspaper apologized next day for its mistake – and was immediately shut down. And Nemirovich-Danchenko had a fight with 'Spolokhi' because in one of his stories, in the most dramatic episode, instead of 'Beppo, saddle the horse!' was cosily and modestly printed: 'Beppo, paddle the horse!' Such things happen ...

The lamps have arrived too, so that now the paper and my writing hand are bathed in a cone of light.

Today we had an unlucky accident: I went to visit a sick professor with Mother and Kirill. Kirill was dragging his sledge behind. When I caught sight of a high steep snow slope, I decided to show how to really slide down. I lay face down on the sledge, sat him on my back, and pushed myself off. (Meanwhile, a crowd of gawkers had gathered.) Halfway down something cracked – and I was already flying down without the sledge and without Kirill, in a whirlwind of snow. It turned out that one of the runners had given out, snapped (I've put on a lot of weight since being here). Weeping and reproaches went on for several hours. And here's what Morn says, farewelling Midia:

> ... You will leave; we'll forget one another;
> but now and then the name of a street,
> or a street organ weeping in the twilight,
> will remind us in a more vivid and more
> truthful way than thought could resurrect
> or words convey, of that main thing which
> was between us, the main thing which
> we do not know ...
> And in that hour when the soul
> will sense the charm of past trifles –
> *the soul will understand* that in eternity all is eternal:

the genius's thought and the neighbour's joke,
the bewitched suffering of Tristan
and the most fleeting love.

. . . not unlike yours (are you angry?). My darling, today I love you so sweetly, so joyfully – you don't know how . . .

I dreamt of you last night – as if I was playing the piano and you were turning the pages for me . . .

V.

[ALS, 1 P.]
[postmarked 14 January 1924]

TO: 41, Landhausstr., Berlin W.

[Prague]

Date – not interesting.
Address: the same, 'svoronosty'.

Don't you find our correspondence somewhat . . . one-sided? I'm so cross with you that I've begun this letter without a salutation. At first I decided to send you just a blank sheet of paper with a little question mark in the middle, but then I didn't feel like wasting the stamp. Honestly, why aren't you writing to me? This is my fifth letter, but I've had only one from you. Or perhaps you're ill? Or are there 'sharp corners' again? Or, finally, you're acting like this on purpose, so I'll forget you? I am a surprisingly bad writer today.

I have to postpone my return to Berlin indefinitely, in view of the infinite slowness with which I'm working. Sometimes, after a whole day of creative pangs I manage to write only two or three lines. I've cut out from scene two Kliyan's story and everything connected with it. Now I'm floundering in the muddy water of scene six. I get so tired that my head feels like a bowling alley – and I can't fall asleep earlier than five or six in the morning. In the early scenes there are a thousand reworkings, deletions and additions. And ultimately I'll be rewarded with the routine sarcasm: '. . . not without poetic talent, but we must admit . . .' and so on. And on top of that you – staying silent . . .

No – not on your life! I'll show myself so that the gods will flinch, covering themselves with their elbows . . . Either my head will burst open or the world will – one or the other. Yesterday I ate goose. The weather is frosty: straight pink smoke puffs and the air tastes of sugar-glazed cranberries.

The seventeenth is approaching, but on which street in Berlin I'll land that day, where I'll live – I know not. Tatarinov doesn't write, my *boss* doesn't write, Drozdov doesn't write, you don't write . . . I'm the only one writing – and not well at that.

Let me repeat that this is very poor on your part. But if you do not love me, tell me frankly. Sincerity above all! All the same: you are my happiness.

V.

[ALS, 2 PP.]
[16 January 1924]

TO: 41, Landhausstr., Berlin W.

[Prague]
16–I–24

Thank you, my love, for your two amazing letters. Here's a silly aphorism I've thought up: the mind writes with a pen, the heart, with a pencil.

My happiness, I won't be able to come on the 17th, either. Besides the tragedy, there's another, secondary reason – which, unfortunately, is more important than the first one. The fact is, to be blunt, I'm waiting for money from Berlin (for those translations). They promised to send it to me on the 7th – ten days have gone by and I'm still waiting. As soon as I get it, I'll leave that day – and this could even be tomorrow. I had a little with me, but yesterday I had to squander it all on household needs; meanwhile it's dangerous to just chance it, coming to Berlin with five marks. As for the tragedy, it will reach a point any day now where I can finish it where I like. I'm so vexed by all this I can hardly write to you.

Had I met that shaggy troglodyte who first thought of approaching the neighbour in the next cave to offer him a deerskin for a handful of precious stones, I'd have gladly torn his head off. My sweet love, my joy, what a turn-up! I didn't come back for one silly reason, and now another, even sillier, has come up, almost like a pretext. And now I'm concerned only about you; I no longer need any of those Morns. Well, this new year has got off to a rather bumpy start.

I'm sorry I wrote nonsense to you. My brains are dishevelled – their hairpins have fallen out: just as there are bare-headed people, I'm somehow bare-brained ... Do you understand?

I'll wait two or three days more and set off for Berlin on foot. When the sun comes out, you are downy. I still don't know what I'll do with you when I come back. But you won't change my mind about those elders! I've read Nilus and Krasnov – *c'est tout dire*. Do you know, for example, that it was the masons who arranged the earthquake in Japan? I love you, truly, more than the sun.

V.

A VISION

In the snows of a midnight wilderness
I dreamt of the mother of all birches,
and someone – some shifting hoar-frost –

quietly walked to it carrying something:
carried on his shoulder, in high anguish,
my Russia – a child's coffin,
and under the lonely birch,
in a pale-dusting snowdrift,

he bent, in a white quivering,
bent, like smoke under wind.
The little coffin with its light body
was committed to the purest and silent snow.

And the whole snowy wasteland,
praying, looked on high,
where clouds drifted, brushing
the moon with slender wings.

In a gap of moonlit ice,
the naked birch now swayed,
now bent like a bow,
and there were shadows on the snow:

There on this snowy grave
now pressed together, now straightened out, now
wrung in hopeless despair,
like the shadows of God's hands.

He rose up; and along the plain,
he withdrew forever into the night –
the face of the Divine, the vision, the hoarfrost,
leaving no trace.

Vl. Sirin

[ALS, 2 PP.]
[17 January 1924]

TO: 41, Landhausstr., Berlin, W.

[Prague]
17–I–24

My love, I'm returning on Wednesday the 23rd. This is final. My announcement has already appeared in *Rul'*. My name is printed in such bold type that I thought for a moment it was a death announcement. If you happen to come across a room with board, costing no more than a dollar a day (but preferably 3 marks), then inform this Mr N. himself. You know I am now so used to my pen-name that it's strange to see my real name.

Frost and sunshine today, and because of that the snow on the roofs looks like a layer of purplish gouache; every little bit of smoke stands out in the air. I have a scene and a half left till the end of my cursed tragedy; I will try to publish it in Berlin. Do you know, two days ago our poor Yakobson threw himself in the Spree, wanting, like Sadko, to give a little concert to the mermaids. Fortunately, a 'greenie's' valiant dive interrupted his underwater tour; he pulled the composer out, the score under his arm. Lukash writes me that the poor fellow has a terrible cold, but has generally perked up greatly. There you go.

I never thought I'd dream about Berlin as a heaven on ... earth (the heaven in the sky is, most likely, quite boring – and there is so much fluff there – seraphims' – that, they say, smoking is forbidden. Sometimes, though, angels themselves smoke – in their sleeves. But when the archangel goes by, they throw their cigarettes away: this is what falling stars are). You will come to my place once a month to tea. When my income dries up, I will Amerigo, with you. Just now, both of my sisters went off for an exam. I composed a 'song about failure' for them, after which they both burst into tears. I love you.

I have re-read, over this time, all of Flaubert. Read – or re-read – 'Madame Bovary'. It's the most brilliant novel in world literature – in the sense of the perfect harmony between content and form – and the only book which, in three places, makes me feel hot under my eyeballs: *lacrimae arsi* (this is not in Latin).

Somehow it seems to me today that you and I will soon be very happy. 'The scarlet ribbon of dawn I will entwine like silk around your waist' (or something like that) – though it's not very fashionable, my love.

I'll sit down to Morn again now. My God, how I want to read it to you … I love you furiously and endlessly: your handwriting, like your gait, your voice, the colour of a cautious dawn. Kisses, on your eyes – and further, along the black tape. Love you.

V.

[ALS, 3 PP.]
[24 January 1924]

TO: 41, Landhausstr., Berlin W.

[Prague]
24–I–24

My dear love,

I arrive in Berlin at five p.m., on Sunday the 27th, at the Anhalter station. The reason for my delay was money. On top of that Mother got sick, and I caught a bad cold too, crossing the Moldau over melting ice. My cold is lifting, and Mother too is better, so nothing now can prevent me from arriving on Sunday. It seems to me, my happiness, that you're angry with me for my slowness? But if you only knew how many trifles crowd around me, how many stupid thorns at every step … My family has to move from this apartment to another one – and once again, frustrations flock on my shoulders – and gloomy conversations. Only one thing makes me happy: the day after tomorrow, Morn will shoot himself: I have some fifty or sixty lines left, in the last – eighth – scene. I will certainly have to keep sanding and polishing the whole thing, but the essential will be done.

As for our pantomime, a certain Asta Nielsen has taken a liking to it – but she's asking for some changes in the first act. Our other pantomime, 'The Living Water', will be on in a few days at 'Sinyaya ptitsa'.

I am incredibly worn out by my work. At night, my dreams rhyme, and all day I have an aftertaste of insomnia. My thick notebook with drafts will go to you – with a dedication in verse. Indirectly, in some meandering kind of way – like the story of the Medes – you inspired me with this. Without you I wouldn't have moved this way, to speak the language of flowers.

But I am tired. When I was seventeen, I used to write on average two poems a day, each of them taking me about twenty minutes. Their quality was doubtful, but I didn't even try to write better then, thinking that I was performing little miracles and that over miracles I didn't need to think. Now I know that, indeed, reason is a negative part of creativity and inspiration a positive one, but only through their secret conjunction is the white spark born, the electrical flicker of perfect creation. Nowadays, working seventeen hours on end, I can write no more than thirty lines a day (that I won't cross out later), and that by itself is already a step forward. I remember myself, hazy and excited – in our mushroom birch-grove – gathering chance words to express a chance thought. I had favourite words then, such as 'gleams', 'transparent', and a strange propensity for rhyming 'rays' and 'flowers' although I was very punctilious about my feminine rhymes. Later – and even now – I had real philological passions, when for a whole month and even longer I would overindulge one particular word I'd lovingly selected. For instance, I have recently had a little episode with the word 'hurricane'—maybe you noticed . . .

I can talk about all this only to you. I am becoming more and more firmly convinced that art is *the only thing that matters* in life. I am ready to endure Chinese torture to find a single epithet—and in science, in religion what excites and engages me is only the colour, only the man in side-whiskers and a top-hat, lowering—on a rope—the smoke-pipe of the first funny locomotive passing under the bridge and dragging behind it the little cars full of ladies' exclamations, the movements of tiny coloured parasols, the rustle and squeaking of crinolines. Or, in the domain of religion, the shadows and red highlights sliding across the knitted brow, the sinewy shaking hands of Peter, warming himself by the fire in the cold dawn, when the second cocks are crowing now closer, now further off—and a light wind passes by, and the cypresses bow with restraint . . .

Today, I looked over a huge calico plan of my estate (fortunately it had stayed with my other papers), and walked along its paths in my imagination, and now I have a feeling as if indeed I really have just been home. There must be snowdrifts there now, branches in white mittens, and ultra-crisp sounds from beyond the river—someone is chopping wood . . . And in the papers today is the news that Lenin is dead.

My love, what happiness it'll be to see you again, to hear the singing of your vowels, my love. Come to the railroad station—because here's what has happened (only don't be angry!)—I can't remember (for God's sake, don't be angry!)—I can't remember (promise, you won't be angry?)—I can't remember your telephone number!!! I recall, there was a seven in it, but beyond that?. . . And this is why, when I get to Berlin, I'll have to write to you—but where will I get stamps for the letter?—since I'm scared of the post office!!!

We'll have a wonderful time in Berlin. I led a very modest life here.

Visited only the Kramářs – and that rarely – but today I am going, for a change of air, to Marina Tsvetaeva's. She is absolutely charming (Ah ... indeed?).

See you soon, my love, don't be angry with me. I know that I am a very boring and unpleasant man, drowned in literature ... But I love you.

V.

[ALS, 2 PP.]
[13 August 1924]

[TO: Berlin]

[Prague?]
13–VII[I]–24

My delightful, my love, my life, I don't understand anything: how can you not be with me? I'm so infinitely used to you that I now feel myself lost and empty: without you, my soul. You turn my life into something light, amazing, rainbowed – you put a glint of happiness on everything – always different: sometimes you can be smoky-pink, downy, sometimes dark, winged – and I don't know when I love your eyes more – when they are open or shut. It's eleven p.m. now: I'm trying with all the force of my soul to see you through space; my thoughts plead for a heavenly visa to Berlin *via* air ... My sweet excitement ...

Today I can't write about anything except my longing for you. I'm gloomy and fearful: silly thoughts are swarming – that you'll stumble as you jump out of a carriage in the underground, or that someone will bump into you in the street ... I don't know how I'll survive the week.

My tenderness, my happiness, what words can I write for you? How strange that although my life's work is moving a pen over paper, I don't know how to tell you how I love, how I desire you. Such agitation – and such divine peace: melting clouds immersed in sunshine – mounds of happiness. And I am floating with you, in you, aflame and melting – and a whole life with you is like the movement of clouds, their airy, quiet falls, their lightness and smoothness, and the heavenly variety of outline and tint – my inexplicable love. I cannot express these cirrus-cumulus sensations.

When you and I were at the cemetery last time, I felt it so piercingly and clearly: you know it all, you know what will happen after death – you know it absolutely simply and calmly – as a bird knows that, fluttering from a branch, it will fly and not fall down ... And that's why I am so happy with you, my lovely, my little one. And here's more: you and I are so special; the miracles we know, no one knows, and no one loves the way we love.

What are you doing now? For some reason I think you're in the study: you've got up, walked to the door, you are pulling the door wings together and pausing for a moment – waiting to see if they'll move apart again. I'm tired, I'm terribly tired, good night, my joy. Tomorrow I'll write you about all kinds of everyday things. My love.

V.

[ALS, 2 PP.]
[17 August 1924]

[TO: Berlin]

[Dobřichovice]
17–VII[I]–24

I'm more than thinking about you – I'm living about you, my love, my happiness ... I'm already expecting a letter from you – although I know that it'll be late, since they'll have to forward it to me from Prague. Mother and I are in a beautiful hotel, where it's all so expensive that we have to stay in one room – huge, it's true. The view from the window is wide and open: rows of poplars along the river, farmed fields beyond – green, turquoise, greyish brown squares – and further on, wooded hills through which it's lovely to roam: it smells of mushrooms and there are damp, wild raspberries. Not many people: all elderly couples from Prague, like slow quiet pedestals. No Russians – too expensive for them – but the Chirikovs and Tsvetaeva live nearby, where the roofs of the little village glow red in the valley.

My dear love, my priceless joy, you haven't forgotten me, have you? The whole way I ate your sandwiches and plums and peaches: very tasty, my love. I arrived in Prague around nine and had quite a long bumpy ride home in a big black coach. My family has a small apartment, but excellent – only the cost's going up and they have no funds. Besides, from five o'clock in the morning a thundering procession of drays, wagons and trucks starts up, so that while you're half-awake you feel as if the whole house is slowly rolling somewhere, rumbling and rattling.

It turns out that it makes no sense for Olga to go to Leipzig. If she leaves, she loses her grant; and her singing is all arranged here: she has an extraordinary voice and will soon start performing. Please thank your cousin in my name and Mother's – thank her warmly.

I'll return to Berlin next Monday or Tuesday. I want to pile up more lessons – please help if you can, my darling. But in general things are bad, there's nothing to live on, Mother's very sad and nervous, dreams about going to Berlin, to Tegel. I'd be ready to break rocks if only I could help her in any way. The ten dollars I brought with me will be enough to live on for a week – very comfortably and quietly. Only it's raining drops like beads today, and I have to crack balls at billiards.

My sunshine, my tremor of joy, had you been here with me I would have been completely happy. Here there's quiet, solitude and greenery.

Terrible clay storks and dwarves here and there in the garden—obviously of German origin. Terraces, fountains. We have lunch and dinner outdoors.

A little task: copy please (retype) the poems 'Prayer' (the Easter one) and 'Rivers'. Send the first to *Rul'* and the second to *Rul'* too. No typos, my joy. Can you do this? Also, write to me whether anything's appeared in 'Segodnya'.

I must go to lunch, my joy. I love you. I can hear your little toothy sigh. And the rustle of your lashes against my cheek. You're my happiness. If you want—call Mme Tatarinov and tell her I'm arriving in a week. And please give my best regards to your father.

Kisses, my love, deep ones, to the point of fainting, I am waiting for your letter, I love you, I move carefully so as not to break you, as you ring out inside me—so crystal-like, so entrancingly ...

V.

[ALS, 2 PP.]
[18 August 1924]

[TO: Berlin]

18–VIII–24
Dobřichovice

I still haven't received anything from you, my love. But I am full of hope (with a small 'h'). You delicately bite your lower lip, then say: 'I don't like it when you joke like that . . .' Forgive me, my joy.

I love you today with a special kind of wide, sunny love, saturated with a pine smell—because all day long I have been wandering in the hills, seeking out amazing footpaths, bowing with tenderness, to familiar butterflies ...

The down of flowers was fluttering above the glades like soft sparse snow, grasshoppers stridulated and golden cobwebs – wheels of sunlight – stretched across the trail, clinging to my face … And a lush soughing ran through the trees, and the shadows of clouds glided along distant slopes … It felt very free, and light, and like my love for you. Meanwhile, in Mokropsy (there is such a hamlet), Chirikov, tiny, in a Russian shirt, was standing there on his terrace. A little old man completely devoid of talent.

I go to bed at nine o'clock and I get up at nine. I drink raw milk by the bucketful (another of my weaknesses). Mother and I are separated by a white wardrobe placed in the middle of the room. We argue in the morning who'll take the *tub* first.

There's only one unpleasant thing: a little pooch, shaggy, female, with a timid expression on her face and with a tail curved like a French horn. Just as soon as we go to bed, this pooch begins to yap under our windows. It stops and starts. At first Mother was touched, then she began to count the seconds between the bouts of yapping, then we had to close the window. We met the pooch in the garden today. She looked at us intelligently and affectionately. But I dread to think what will happen tonight. It's worse than the dray-carts in Prague.

How are you, my wonderful happiness? Have you learned lots of new English words? Are you playing chess? I'm sick with longing to see you walk in this room now, flutter your eyelashes and become soft all of a sudden, like a little piece of cloth … My sweet legs …

Oh, my joy, when will we really live together – in a charming spot, with a view of the mountains, with a pooch yapping under our window? I need so little: a bottle of ink, a speck of sun on the floor – and you; but the latter is not all that little, and fate, God, the seraphs know this perfectly well – and withhold and withhold …

I'm deliberately not writing anything now, I suppress metric lines that jump out from God knows where, I respectfully but firmly evade the muse's temptations. I only translate – with quiet rage – such phrases of Korostovets's as this: 'Contemporary Europe after, on the one hand, heavy scrapes in the area of political achievements *par excellence*, but nevertheless, doomed, as such, to perish or in the best case, to be forgotten, and, on the other hand ... ' And so on. Such hogwash.

Well, my love, time for bed – almost nine ... What are you doing now? Lowering the shutters, maybe ... I've come to love their tense clatter. Good night, my happiness. Have to get to bed. The pooch has already started.

V.

[ALS, 2 PP.]
[24 August 1924]

TO: 41, Landhausstr., Berlin

24–VIII–24
Prague

My love, your letters – four letters so far – are simply wonderful, – they're almost touches, and that is the greatest thing you can say about a letter. I adore you.

Yesterday Mother and I returned to Prague from the country, where the whole time it was damp and sunny, where alongside the paths coloured stripes are daubed on beech and oak trunks, and sometimes simply on the rocks, like little flags to show the way to this or that hamlet. I noticed too that peasants put red ear-flaps on their percherons and are cruel with their geese, of whom they have plenty: they pluck off their breast feathers when the geese are still alive, so that the poor bird walks around as if in a décolleté. I have seen a lot of the Chirikov family (he has two charming daughters and a son, who's chasing after my youngest sister), and the old man and I thought up scenarios and tried to guess what our 'pictures' will look like in the Riga newspaper. And on the eve of my departure the Directorate of Western and Eastern Skies treated us to a monstrously beautiful sunset. Above, the sky was deep blue, and an enormous cloud stood, only in the west, in the shape of a mauve wing spreading wide its orange ribs. The river was pink, as if someone had dribbled port into the water – and beside it the express train from Prague to Paris flew past. And right at the horizon under that violet cloud, trimmed with orange down, a strip of sky shone like light-green turquoise – and little fiery islands were melting in it. It all reminded me of Vrubel, the Bible, the bird Alkonost.

Have you found a room, my sweet love? Can you simply set up in my boarding house – they have an extra room, don't they? Arrange it so it'll be easy for us to meet. I'll have to see you forty-eight hours a day, after this week of faithlessness (is this witty?). I am leaving on Thursday, at 9 a.m. – can't do it earlier because of various family combinations. Don't be angry with me, my love, for this delay – don't say 'I knew it'd be like this . . .' And if I don't arrive even on Thursday, you can consider me an indecent man and a talentless writer. It's cold today, drizzling, at seven a.m. the orchestra of the butchers' guild played right under our windows – the Sunday custom.

And last night I read my father's notes and diaries, and his letters to Mother from Kresty, where he spent three months after the Vyborg Appeal. I remember his return so vividly, how in all the villages from the station to our estate arches of pine and flowers were set up – and crowds of peasants with bread-and-salt surrounded his carriage – and how I ran out onto the road to meet him – I was running and crying with excitement. And Mother was wearing a large light-coloured hat, and a week later she and father left for Italy.

I will see you soon, my happiness. I don't think there'll be more separations like this. This whole year has passed by like a sail swollen by the sun – and now nothing can interfere with this smoothness, with my heavenly gliding through the air of happiness ... You understand my every thought, – and my every hour is full of your presence – and I am all a song about you ... See, I am talking to you like King Solomon.

But let's leave Berlin, my love. It's a city of misfortunes and mishaps. That I met you precisely there is an incredible blunder on the part of a fate so badly disposed towards me. And I think with dread that once again we'll have to hide from the people I know – and the thought irritates me that the unavoidable will happen – and my dear friends will raise a predatory chatter about the most marvellous, divine, inexpressible thing I have in life. You understand, my love?

My love, oh, my love, there's nothing to dread when you're with me – so I am writing this in vain, am I not? Everything will be all right, won't it, my life?

V.

1925

[AL, I P.]
[19 January 1925]

TO: Luitpoltdstr 13, bei Rilcke, Berlin W.

[Berlin?]

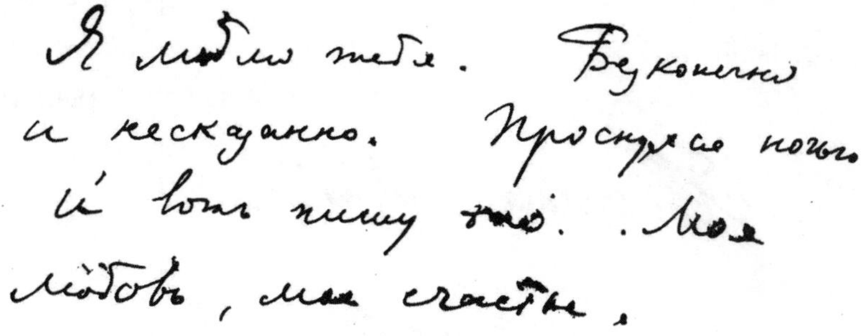
Я люблю тебя. Безконечно и несказанно. Проснулся ночью и вотъ пишу это. Моя любовь, мое счастье.

I love you. Infinitely and inexpressibly. I've woken up in the middle of the night and here I am writing this. My love, my happiness.

[ALS, I P.]
[c. March–April 1925?]

TO: 13, Luitpoldstr., Berlin W.

[Berlin]

My sweet, sweet love, my joy, my sunny rainbow,

I seem to have eaten the entire little triangle of cheese, but I really was so very hungry . . . But now I'm full. I'm walking out now into the soft light, the cooling hum of evening, and I will love you tonight, and tomorrow, and the day after tomorrow, and still many more, so very many more tomorrows.

That's all, my tender one, my inexpressible delight.

Oh yes: I forgot to say that I love you.

V.

P.S. Love you.

[AL, 1 P.]

[14 June 1925]

[TO: Berlin?]

[Berlin?]

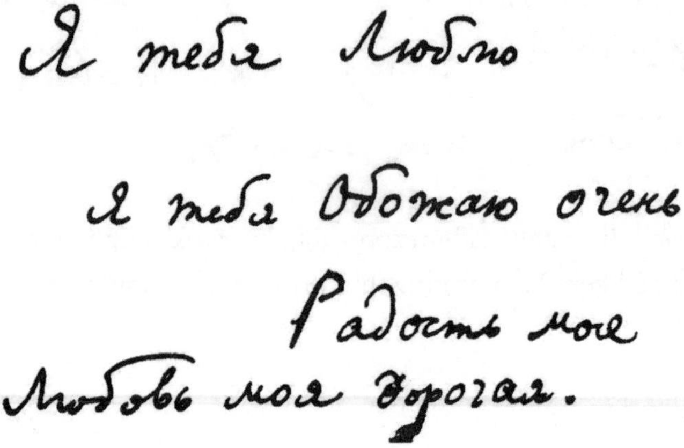
Я тебя люблю
Я тебя обожаю очень
Радость моя
Любовь моя дорогая.

I Love you

I Adore you very much

My Joy

My dear love.

[ALS, 4 PP.]
[postmarked 19 August 1925]

TO: 29, Neue Winterfeldtstr., Berlin–Schöneberg

[Zoppot]

My sweetheart, my love, my love, my love–do you know what–all the happiness of the world, the riches, power and adventures, all the promises of religions, all the enchantment of nature and even human fame are not worth your two letters. It was a night of horror, terrible anguish, when I imagined that your undelivered letter, stuck at some unknown post office, was being destroyed like a sick little stray dog … But today it arrived–and now it seems to me that in the mailbox where it was lying, in the sack where it was shaking, all the other letters absorbed, just by touching it, your unique charm and that that day all Germans received strange wonderful letters–letters that had gone mad because they had touched your handwriting. The thought that you exist is so divinely blissful in itself that it is ridiculous to talk about the everyday sadness of separation–a week's, ten days'–what does it matter? since my whole life belongs to you. I wake at night and know that you are together with me,–I sense your sweet long legs, your neck through your hair, your trembling eyelashes–and then such happiness, such simmering bliss follows me in my dreams that I simply suffocate … I love you, I love you, I can't stand it any longer, imagination won't replace you–come … I am perfectly healthy, feel <u>magnificently</u> well, come and we will swim–the waves here are like at home. We are planning to return on Sunday–but these last days I must spend with you, do you hear? And you know what: I think we had exactly the same illness. Even on the day before I left I'd been hurting all over inside–somehow sharp-edged–it hurt even to laugh–and then here the fever started. Now I feel wonderful. I am afraid that here at the hotel they thought that I had simply gone on a drinking binge. The weather is cool, but no rain. Shura doesn't swim much, today I will write to S. A. Really I don't know what to do next. Go to Bavaria, perhaps?

Will you come, my love? Why don't you take off the day after tomorrow (21st) – we'll spend two or three days here. The trip costs 12 marks, the room 1½ marks (you can move in with me), lunches and dinners – barely anything.

My little kitten, my joy, how happily I love you today … I kiss you – but won't say where, there are no words for that.

V.

[APC]

[27 August 1925]

TO: Postlagernd, Konstanz i. / Baden

[Hotel Römischer Kaiser]

Freiburg

27–VIII–25

Hello, my kitty, my dear love,

We had an excellent journey, climbed the nearest hill today, tonight went to the cinema. Tomorrow at 9 we're leaving for Döggingen, will arrive there at noon, have lunch and set out on foot to Bol[l], where we'll spend the night. I'll send you a card from there. It's lots of fun. F. is a wonderful town, somehow like Cambridge. In the centre is the old cathedral, the colour of raw strawberries, stained glass inside – all sorts of ornaments, wheels of paradise, as well as a black jackboot on a golden background, very sweet, in the vicinity of saints' little faces. I love you, my poochums. Our hotel is good. I love you, my K.

[APC]
[28 August 1925]

TO: Postlagernd, Konstanz i / Baden

[Freiburg]
28–VIII–25

Hello, my darling, we walked about 20 versts today (from 1 p.m. till 8), walked through Bad-Bol[l], and are now waiting at the Reiselfingen station for a train to Titisee, where we will spend the day tomorrow. A murky evening, a flock of crows is flying over black firs, their wings rustling. We've had a wonderful stroll, romantic spots. Rather dark for writing here, on a bench at a local train stop. The flock of crows is cawing, I can hear the silky rainy murmur as they fly low and spread out among the firs. It's very beautiful. But the walking was muddy in places, so I was happy I'd put on the black boots. Have just changed into the other pair. The moon is shining yellow; the crows have settled, gone silent. I love you, my happiness; our train's coming.

[APC]
[29 August 1925]

TO: Postlagernd, Konstanz

[Titisee]
29–VIII–25

Hello, poochums,

I am writing to you from the shore of the Titisee, where we are now sucking on chocolate ice. We'll spend the night here and tomorrow climb up Feldberg. We had a wonderful time today swimming and lying in the heat.

I love you. Very much.

We passed through here.

[APC]

TO: Postlagernd, Konstanz

[postmarked 30 August 1925]
[Feldberg]

On the way here, to the summit of Feldberg, I composed and kept repeating to myself this little ditty: 'I love noittything except one kittything'. The weather is dampish, beads of rain on the wires and between them the lacy wheels of cobwebs. The view is covered in fog. I love you.

We'll spend the night here, and tomorrow move to St Blasien.

[APCS]
[31 August 1925]

TO: Postlagernd, Konstanz am Bodensee in Baden

[St Blasien]
31–VIII–25

Shura suggests calling this poem: what I thought upon walking through the Schwarzwald and meeting a familiar plant.

Hello, my sun,

We have walked from Feldberg to the very lovely St-Blasien. Tomorrow we walk to Wehr and probably on Friday will be in Konstanz. Retype this poem exactly and send it to 'Rul'' with a request ('my husband . . .') to publish it. The weather is wonderfully hot. I love you. V.

THE SUMMIT

I like that mountain in its black pelisse
of fir forests – because
in the gloom of a strange mountain country
I am closer to home.

How should I not know those dense needles
and how should I not lose my mind
at the mere sight of that peatbog berry
showing blue along my way?

The higher the dark and damp
trails twist upward, the clearer
grow the tokens, treasured since childhood,
of my northern plain.

Shall we not climb thus
the slopes of paradise, at the hour of death,
meeting all the loved things
that in life elevated us?

V. Sirin

Schwarzwald

[APCS]
[31 August 1925]

TO: 14, Neuhausenstr., Pension Zeiss, Konstanz

31–VIII–25
St Blasien

Hello, my lovely,

I have just mailed you (*poste restante*) a postcard with a poem, but, stopping at the post office, I found the little card from you, my happiness. I had to get the black half-boots repaired here – the rubber sole had come unstuck; I seldom walk in the grey ones and they're still intact. All in all, the trip has turned out wonderfully well, we walk through entrancing spots. The musical stream of cowbells on the slopes is melodious and delightful. Up to tonight, we've spent exactly 100 marks (500 left). I adore you.

V.

[APCS]
[1 September 1925]

TO: 14, Neuhausenstr., Pension Zeiss, Konstanz

[Todtmoos]

Tomorrow we walk through Wehr to Säckingen on the Rhine. I love, love, love you.

1–IX–25

Hello, my life,

You can follow the route we covered today. It's now 4 o'clock. We are sitting in a café in Todtmoos. The day is cloudless, I walked without a shirt on, and rolled about on heather slopes. Todtmoos is a charming little place, they give you a good shave here. Two Russian girls at the hotel (!). V.

[APC]

[2 September 1925]

TO: 14, Neuhausenstr., Pension Zeiss, Konstanz a/ Bodensee

2–IX–25

Wehr

Hello, my dear life, we arrive on Friday, take two rooms for us at your boarding-house.

Here in Wehr I have found a delightful letter from Véra. I'll send you a telegram about the train we arrive on (on Friday). We won't stay in your namesake (we'll just drink some milk) and will walk on to Säckingen (about 30 versts in all from Todtmoos). I love you.

[APC]

[2 September 1925]

TO: 14, Neuhausenstr, Pension Zeiss, Konstanz

[Säckingen]

2–IX–25

Hello, my song,

We are in Säckingen, on the shore of the Rhine, and on the other side is Switzerland. Tomorrow we walk to Waldshut and the morning after we'll come to Konstanz. The weather is delightful. Enjoy the charming postcard.

[ALS, 1 PP.]
[1925? No date]

[TO: Berlin]

[Berlin, probably in early marriage]

I called there, and, fortunately, it turns out that the room is already taken, so we have to find something else. I went to look for it. If you're not too late getting back, go and have a wander around yourself.

V.

1926

[HOLOGRAPH MANUSCRIPT, 1 P.]
[26 April 1926]

Ivan Vernykh

I.

Electric lights lit up, at oblique angles, the dark-blue night snow, the huge snowdrifts coming up to the house. All was strange and somehow, not artificially, bright in those dips in the glimmering lustre, and black shadows from the lamps, breaking over the snowdrifts, cut the sheer, fine patterns across the snow, the shadows of bare lindens. Ivan Vernykh, after stamping a little in his soft felt boots around the inner porch and pulling on his leather mittens, pushed the glass door, which did not yield at once – from the frost – and then suddenly, tightly shot out into the snowy gloom of the garden. The Chernyshevs' dog, shaggy and senile, like old man Chernyshev himself, quickly tumbled out after, but you've just gone out and I won't write any more, my joy. Now you've moved a chair in the bedroom, and now you've walked back in, clinked a little plate, given a dog-like yawn, and a little whimper, asked me do I want some milk. Pupuss, my kittykin.

26–IV–26

[ALS, 4 PP.]
[2 June 1926]

TO: b/ Frau Doktor Slonim,
Sankt Blasien, Sanatorium Pr. Backmeister, Schwarzwald

[Berlin]
2/VI–26

Puss, my p-pus-ss,

There, I've lived through my first you-less day. It's now a quarter to nine. I have just had supper. I'll always write at this time. Every time, there will be a different salutation – only I don't know whether there will be enough little critters. Maybe I'll have to create a few more. Little epistolaries. Oh, my darling, I don't even know where you are now – in St Blasien or Todtmoos or Gotter-knows-where ... They took you away by car. I came here (the hall-boy did not give me a stamp, since he'd disappeared somewhere, after abandoning the little trunk in the middle of the room), read 'Zveno' for a while, but soon gave up because the lamp cord would not reach the couch (but today I've already asked the landlady to fix it for me. She promised – tomorrow). I crawled into bed around ten, had a smoke, extinguished it. Someone was flailing away on the piano but soon stopped. I'll get up now to mix myself a drink – water with some sugar. I found it. I thought it was in a little bag. I rattled things about in the cabinet for quite some time, squatting. Had a drink, put everything back in place. Now the maid's come in, she's making the bed. She's left. I had a very good sleep. In the morning, about eight, I could hear the schoolgirls thundering up the stairs. At nine I got an egg (I have to write very small, or my whole day won't fit on the page), hot chocolate, and three rolls; I got up, had a cold shower and as I got dressed, looked out into the yard where a gym class was going on. The teacher was clapping her hands, and the schoolgirls – really tiny – were running around and jumping in time. One girl, the littlest one, was always left behind, getting muddled and coughing thinly. After that (still obeying the claps), they sang a song: my dress is blue, blue, and everything I have is blue as well. They repeated this several times, replacing 'blue' with 'red' then 'green' and so on. They also played cat-and-mouse, then another game, which I did not understand, with refrains – and then collected their little bags piled in the corner and left. The shadows of leaves were moving about so nicely on the wall of the yard. I read (*Albertine*, then a rather vulgar Soviet short story) and without waiting till the tailor's man came I went (no, now I can see I'll definitely need to take another sheet) to Kaplan's, but it turned out that Maman Kaplan had gone to the dentist. In a dark-blue suit, a cream shirt and a bow tie with white polka dots, I sailed off to Regensburger Str., where, however, no one was at home. But I did meet Sofa on the stairs, and she gave me your address. From there (it was windy, dullish-sunny; beneath the trees nets of shadow were sliding over the passers-by, but couldn't hold them, they slipped without catching, turning coats into moving spotted skins) I went to the butterfly shop, received my wonderful *Arctia hebe* and argued with the owner about this and that (he thought *Daphnis nerii* doesn't occur in Sicily, and I told him that not only does *nerii* occur there, but so do *livornica* and *celerio* and even *niceae*. He showed me such wonderful *Aporia crataegi-augusta!*). I came back home and asked to have lunch in my room. Broth with vermicelli, meat stew, lots of vegetables, and a wobbly thing in sweet juice (I didn't eat it). While I was having lunch my little grey trousers arrived: excellently done. I changed twice – first the grey pair, then the white one – and went – for three – to Shura's. I met the landlady in the hallway (no, it was earlier, before lunch, when I was re-pinning my butterflies to free space for the *hebe* and then went out to the hallway, after hearing the landlady's voice and deciding to ask her for a longer lamp cord), and she told me that she thought of me like a son – and 'if you have any burden on your heart, come and we'll talk it over'. (Right there, before lunch, the maid brought the register with tenants' names in it – and I wrote – *Nabokoff-Sirin*). I had a cup of tea at Shura's and talked to Sofia Ad. about B. G. She thinks things are going really badly. Tuberculosis. Fortunately, B. G.'s sister arrives on the fifteenth. After tea, Shura and I played tennis. On the way there, we saw where a fire had been: a barn had burned down that had served as a warehouse for some sort of theatrical accoutrements. It was very beautiful to see, among the charred rubbish, chunks of carpets and mattresses showing red and blue. We played for a while, I walked Sh. home and rode to my own club, where I hit around again (windy, clouds of dust, bells ringing on the kirk) till half-past seven. I came back (oh, forgot again: when I was leaving for Shura's, I met not the landlady (I remembered I'd met someone!), but the man with the other trousers – from cleaning. I paid one mark fifteen), read a little more of the Soviet rubbish as well as 'Rul'', where there's a note about my reading on the eighth. I'll keep it. On the table, I found the little sheet that arrived by mail from the Finanzamt. (I'm forwarding it to you. Answer them that in fact, I'm not a Catholic but a Russian Orthodox and that they should stop bothering me.) Around half past eight they brought me dinner (same as yesterday except macaroni and cheese instead of the egg). I ate and sat down to write to you. And there's my whole day, my puss. I'm off to bed now – it's already a quarter past ten. I've been writing to you a long time! Oh, my sweet, oh, my darling, don't worry and don't mope ... You know, it's so strange not to hear trams and cars when I lie in bed. Good-bye, my puss, my pusschen. You'll never guess the little critter at the start of my letter tomorrow.

V.

[ALS, 2 PP.]
[3 June 1926]
TO: b/ Frau D[tr] Slonim, Sanatorium, Sankt-Blasien, Schwarzwald
[Berlin]
3/VI–26

Little old man,

This morning I got the notice from the police that our passports are ready,–please report and pay, they say, twenty state marks. I don't have that. What now, little old man?

Today the day turned out greyish, inclined to rain, so I didn't go swimming with Shura as we'd planned. We met at the Charlottenburg station (I in my new, very wide, ash trousers) and went to the zoo. Oh, what a white peacock they have! He was standing there, his tail spread out like a fan, and his tail was like shimmering hoarfrost on star-shaped branches–or like a snowflake magnified a million times–and this wonderful tail, sticking out like a puffed-out fan (puffed out from behind, like a hoop skirt inflated by the wind)–crackled from time to time all of its frosty spokes. And later in the ape house we saw two enormous russet orangutans. The husband with a red beard moved slowly, with a certain patriarchal sedateness: he solemnly scratched himself, solemnly pulled snot from his nose (he had a cold), and sonorously sucked on his finger. And there was such a kindly bitch with hanging nipples, who had been nursing two plump little lion-cubs, sitting on their rumps, motionlessly watching with their yellow eyes the warden painting the fence in front of their cage. And other amazing animal stares: the mother of those cubs trying, through the bars of her cage, to look around the corner–at the cage where her children were with their canine nanny–and the father, thoughtfully contemplating the croup of a percheron harnessed to a cart from which a labourer was offloading some planks.

I took Sh. as far as the corner of Wilmersdorfer Strasse, and, after buying the *Observer* on the way, returned home and read till lunch. They served me (in my room – as I asked) some broth with a rice-filled pastry, a lamb chop, and apple mousse. After that I rang the Tatarinovs (I'll visit them on Saturday). Then I changed and went to the club. I played – not badly at all – till six, and on the way back I called in at Anyuta's. I saw everyone there, we sat around in the dusk, and I returned home for dinner (fried eggs, fried potatoes with bits of meat, radishes, cheese, sausage). After having dinner, I sat down to write to you (it's exactly nine now). So there you are, little old man, my enchantment, my dear life. I am such a grass widow … But I feel very good here, very cosy. Good night, my little old man. I'll compose a poem now, then go to bed at 10.30.

V.

[ALS, 4 PP.]
[4 June 1926]

TO: Sankt Blasien, Sanatorium, Schwarzwald

[Berlin]
4/VI–26

Mousch, mouse-sh-s-ch-sch-sh …

In the morning, I had a postcard from Stein: 'I need to talk to you about translating "Mary" into German. Would you kindly phone, or, still better, call in on me at "Slovo".' I could do neither, since I was hurrying to Shura's. (Oh yes, there was another letter – from my mother. They almost turned her back at the border, owing to the absence of a German visa! She is very happy with her Czech village.) Shura and I went to the swimming establishment on Krumme Strasse. There was a man without an arm (cut off right at the shoulder, so he was like the statue of Venus. I kept thinking his arm was hidden somewhere. Looking at him, I felt a kind of physical unease: just a smooth place with a fringe of armpit hair), while another man had the most detailed tattoos all over his body (by his left nipple he had two little green leaves that transformed the nipple into a disgusting pink floweret). We swam, drank a bottle of Seltzer water at the villa, and I took off (for one o'clock) to my Kaplan lesson (with Madame). At two I returned home (white trousers, white sweater, mackintosh), and having locked myself in a telephone booth, called Stein. Awfully tongue-tied, with an agonizing abundance of 'obli-obli', he informed me that 'in German literary circles they are interested in Oblimary and the short stories as well, and so they want to translateobli both Mary and the oblistories; and that, ifobli I agree, they ask me not to undertake any steps on the side (this is in connection with Gräger) before June 20th. And please, obli, deliver all your stories to me and wait for further news, and this is an oblisolutely sure thing.' I am somehow worried that they will obliswindle me. I've decided to ask six hundred marks and no Spaniards for 'Mary', and five hundred for the book of short stories. I will talk to Evsey Lazarevich about this tomorrow (he is leaving for Amsterdam tomorrow evening, but today went to Wannsee for a whole day off). In any event, I'm very pleased. And, considering how excited Stein was, and how he oblioblied, it really is a sure thing. My Mousch, I love you. For lunch, they gave me a couple of meatballs with carrots and asparagus, a plain brothy soup, and a little plate of perfectly sweet cherries. I have been getting my litre of milk from day one. After lunch, I went straight to the Kaplans' again, and then played tennis till seven. The weather was rather cloudy all day, but very warm. By some miracle I received 'Rul'' in the evening. After getting back I read it for a bit, and began tortuously composing a poem about Russia, about 'culture' and about 'exile'. And nothing came of it. Only separate silly images swim up: 'and the alley / of cypresses went to the sea . . .' or 'in Bohemia in a beech-wood / there is a reading-room . . .' and make me feel nauseous, set my teeth on edge and put my head in a fog. Only old phrases used long, long ago, surface ... I have to grab hold of some kind of vision, immerse myself in it–but now only fake visions are rushing past; they irritate me terribly. At dinner (a couple of meatballs–cold cuts, sausage, radishes), I suddenly grasped the future music, the tone, but not yet the metre–a scrap of musical mist–undoubted proof that I will write this poem. I love you, Mousch. They have extended the cord, it's now very comfortable (ah, what a downpour just now ... at first an indistinct rustle, then the drumming of drops on some tin,–a windowsill, maybe–and a mounting noise, and somewhere in the yard a window banged shut with a crack. Now it's booming at full bore ... this is a broad, sheer noise, a tinny pounding, a sodden weight . . .). I forgot to write that all the same I didn't go right at once to my three o'clock lesson (the noise of the rain has become remoter, softer, more even), but had fifteen minutes to lie down and heard–from some balcony–two girls memorizing French sentences out loud: 'il est evidang ... evidang . . .' (the noise rose for a moment, now it's quieter again ... magnificent rain ...). The roses on my table haven't withered yet, but I finished off the candy today (one drop fell completely separately, with a separate clear sound. Now it's not a noise but a rustle ... And subsiding). It is exactly nine now, at ten I'll go to bed. I want to write to Mother too. My Mousch, where are you? I dare say there'll be a little letter tomorrow morning. Do you know what the look of the envelope will remind me of? Not at all the trip to Prague (my sisters, screaming: from Mme Bertran!!), but that postman who summoned me in a peasant woman's voice from the white road I was working near–under the huge two-ton Provençal sun –: '*Ouna lettra por vous, mossieu* . . .' So, Mousch. Today's already the third you-less day. The rain's gone almost entirely silent, it's cooler, the dishes are clinking delicately in the kitchen. Good night, my

Mousch, my mousikins. My dear one. My sweet one ... Here again, a scrap of little music. Maybe I'll still compose it today. My Mousch ...

V.

[ALS, 2 PP.]
[5 June 1926]

TO: Sanatorium, Sankt-Blasien, Schwarzwald

[Berlin]
5/VI–26

Goosikins,

I've now returned home (7 o'clock) and found your little letter on the marble of the wash-stand. Goosikins, what is this? Leave S. B. immediately (not Slava Borisovna, but Sankt-Blasien) and go somewhere warm. Talk to your doctor. Find out how things are in Todtmoos or Titisee. My poor little one ... Do you have your fur coat with you? Shall I send you something else warmish? You know, when I was in S-B last August, it was so sultry there. This is all very unpleasant. Please, don't stay there, my sweet one. I won't tell your folks anything meanwhile, I'll wait for your next little letter (which will come tomorrow). My Feverisch ... And why did your idiot-doctor send you to the mountains of all places? This is all wrong. But it'll all turn out right, my goosikins, you'll move tomorrow, won't you? Today it rained all day, it's only just cleared. This morning I went to find out about the watch – it turns out that only next week will it become clear how much it'll cost. Then under a warm drizzle, I sailed off to Ladyzhnikov's for Soviet fiction. I signed up – it cost me seven marks (five as a bond) – per month – I couldn't do it any other way. They told me there that more than a hundred copies of 'Mary' had been sold. I took the idiotic stories of Zoshchenko and read them through by lunch. Not much of a lunch today: a soup with some kind of groats, beige thick-skinned sausage, and a rice cake. After lunch, I went to Sergey K.'s lesson and got caught in a downpour–such heavy rain that my little grey (old) trousers got soaked through under the hem of my mackintosh and immediately lost their fresh crease. At five, after the lesson, I called in at Ladyzhnikov's again and exchanged the idiot Zoshchenko for two other little books. Then I visited the denizens of Regensburg. I had a conversation with E. L. (who is leaving only on Monday), asked him for advice about those translations. I returned by seven, found your letter. A really small day today. Now they'll bring me dinner and then I'll go to the Tatarinovs (there, Mlle Ioffe–pleasant name–is giving a talk about Freud–pleasant topic). Kosten'ka, my warmest regards, thanks, and all that–I won't write about this in my letters to you. I didn't compose that little poem last night,–and the Day of Culture is nigh. I have five marks left. They give me milk in a large sealed bottle–very appetizing. Last night mice were scuttling about a lot. My joy, my happiness, my goosikins, I feel so unhappy that you are cold and uncomfortable ... But everything should work out, there are other places around ... Well, here comes my dinner. Till tomorrow, my sweet love.

V.

[ALS, 2 PP.]
[6 June 1926]

TO: Sanatorium, St-Blasien, Schwarzwald

[Berlin]
6 / VI

My poochums, pooch-chums,

Last night, at the Tartars, there was a lecture and discussions about that quack Freud (in a dispute 'about modern woman', Karsavin was trying to prove that men shave themselves and wear wide trousers thanks to the influence of women. Deep?). Aykhenvald received an anonymous letter after his article about Purishkevich. 'How could you spit so upon the grave of your friend?' A journalist called Grif informed me he'd sent a big article about me to a Dutch literary magazine; too bad I don't understand Dutch. Generally speaking, it was rather dull, it was mostly Kadish who spoke. We left around one – so I got up late today, around eleven. I went for a walk – in a loop, past Gedächtniskirche, down to the embankment, where I watched the windy-cubist reflections of the chestnut shuttlecocks in water. And at Schillstrasse, in an antique shop, I saw an ancient little book, opened on the first page – a journey of some Spaniard to Brazil in 1553. The drawing is charming: the author in knight's armour – chain-mail, cuirass, helmet – all fit and proper – he is riding a llama, and behind him there are natives, palm-trees, a snake around a tree-trunk. I can imagine how hot he was ... I am wearing my new dove-grey trousers today and the Norfolk jacket. Before lunch I read Leonov's 'Badgers'. A little better than all the other rubbish – but still not genuine literature. For lunch they served broth with dumplings, meat roast with fresh asparagus, and coffee with cake. And then I lay down on the couch and spent the whole day in books: finished Leonov, read through Seyfullina's 'Vireneya'. A nasty hag. The dinner was the same as yesterday: fried eggs and cold cuts. See, what a quiet little Sunday I've had. Today I heard so much peasant talk – from the books – that when someone in the yard suddenly shouted something in German – I was startled: where did the German come from? Now half past eight; in a little while I'll go for a stroll, post the letter, and then it will be lights-out right away. My dear joy, where are you? Are you shivering still? My poochums ... Time to turn the lamp on. There. I thought there would be a little letter this morning ... But tomorrow, for sure. Don't go to Todtmoos – there, apparently, it's even higher. I can't wait for you to be all sorted out. My poochums, my love ... My sweet little legs. Seems tomorrow the weather may be fine—such a delicate sky.

V.

[ALS, 3 PP.]
[7 June 1926]

TO: Sanatorium, St-Blasien, Schwarzwald

[Berlin]
7–VI–26

My monkeykins,

Last night around nine, I went out for a stroll, feeling through my whole body that thunderstormy tension that's the harbinger of a poem. Back home by ten, I clambered inside myself, as it were, rummaged about, tormented myself for a little, and wriggled out with nothing. I turned the light off—and suddenly an image flashed by—a little room in a poorish Toulon hotel, the velvet-black depth of the window opened into the night, and somewhere far beyond the darkness the hissing of the sea, as if someone is slowly drawing in and letting out air through his teeth. Simultaneously, I was remembering the rain which rustled so nicely in the yard one recent evening while I was writing to you. I felt there'd be a poem about the soft sound—but here my head clouded over with fatigue and to fall asleep I began to think about tennis, imagining I was playing. After a while I turned on the light on and schlepped along to the toilet. The water there squelches and tweets for ages after you pull the string. And now back in bed with this soft sound in the pipe, accompanied by my recollection-sensation of the black window in Toulon and the recent rain, I composed two stanzas of the enclosed poem: the second and the third. The first of these scrambled out almost at once, whole – but I fiddled longer with the second, setting it aside a few times to trim the corners or to think a little about the remaining stanzas, still unknown, but palpable. After composing this second and third, I calmed down and fell asleep – and in the morning, when I woke up, felt happy with them – and immediately began to compose more. When at half past twelve, I set off for my lesson with Kaplan (Madame), the fourth, the sixth, and part of the seventh were ready – and at this point I experienced that miraculous, inexplicable feeling that may be the most pleasant of all at the time of composition, namely, the precise extent of the poem, how many lines it will have in all; I knew by now – although perhaps a moment before that I hadn't known – that there would be eight stanzas and that in the last there'd be a different rhyme pattern. I composed in the street and then over lunch (I had liver with mashed potatoes and a plum compote) and after lunch, before leaving for Sack's (at three). It was raining, I was glad I'd put on the navy suit, black shoes, and mackintosh, and on the tram I composed the poem right to the end, in this order: eighth, fifth, first. I finished the first at the moment I opened the garden gate. I played ball with Shura, then we read Wells to terrible peals of thunder: a wonderful thunderstorm had broken – as if in accord with my liberation – since later, on the way home, looking at the gleaming puddles, buying 'Zveno' and the '*Observer*' at Charlottenburg Station, I felt a luxurious lightness. In 'Zveno', there happened to be an announcement of 'Volya Rossii' (I am sending it to you; I'll get the issue tomorrow). On the way home I stopped in at Anyuta's. I saw E. L., he had just received a letter from S. B. Around seven, they set off for some shop, I went home and, as agreed with Anyuta, raked out your little fur coat from underneath newspapers and naphthalene (it has such a sweet little monkey on its collar . . .). Anyuta will pack it up tomorrow, and I'll send it to you. I read newspapers before dinner (a letter from Mother: they live cramped but not badly), then ate potatoes with bits of meat and a lot of Swiss cheese. I sat down to write to you around nine, i.e. I reached out for a writing pad and suddenly noticed the little letter that had arrived in my absence and that I somehow hadn't noticed. My sweet. It is such a monkeykins little letter ... It seems it's not so much the air as 'family matters' that are driving you out of S. B.? Anyuta says – and I think she's right – that mountain air often acts that way at first – but later, in two or three days, you get used to it – and then it becomes very pleasant. No, monkeykins, don't come back – you will be shoved into the oldest, vilest little suitcase and sent off again. I will mail your reprimand to the Catholics tomorrow – thank you, monkeykins. I'll leave the back of this sheet blank – I am sleepy. The little man brought the cigarettes when I was out. I borrowed 30 marks from Anyuta and will receive exactly that from the Kaplans tomorrow. I love you, monkeykins.

V.

SOFT SOUND

When in some coastal townlet, on a night
of low clouds and ennui, you open
the window – from afar
whispering sounds spill over.

Now listen closely and discern
the sound of seawaves breathing upon land,
protecting in the night
the soul that harkens unto them.

Daylong the murmur of the sea is muted,
but the unbidden day now passes
(tinkling as does an empty
tumbler on a glass shelf);

and once again amidst the sleepless hush
open your window, wider, wider,
and with the sea you are alone
in the enormous and calm world.

Not the sea's sound ... In the still night
I hear a different reverberation:
the soft sound of my native land,
her respiration and pulsation.

Therein blend all the shades of voices
so dear, so quickly interrupted
and melodies of Pushkin's verse
and sighs of a remembered pine wood.

Repose and happiness are there,
a blessing upon exile;
yet the soft sound cannot be heard by day
drowned by the scurrying and rattling.

But in the compensating night,
in sleepless silence, one keeps listening
to one's own country, to her murmuring,
her deathless sleep.

V. Sirin

[ALS, 4 PP.]
[8–9 June 1926]

TO: Sanatorium, St-Blasien, Schwarzwald

[Berlin]
8/VI–26

My joy,

Before describing today's extraordinary, deafening success (about which there will probably be a hint in the newspapers), I must tell you, as promised, about my day. In the morning I rolled along to Sack's, played ball with him in the rain. On the way home I went into 'Moskva', but it turned out they didn't have the last issue of 'Volya Rossii'. I came home in the rain. They served white, tasteless fish and cherries for lunch (No, you can't even imagine such success!). Then – still in the rain – I took your fur-coat to Anyuta (after carefully wrapping the thing – not Anyuta, but the coat). I found Lena's lovely soap at Anyuta's, for which I am very, very thankful. I dashed to the Kaplans' (you know, it's the first time I've had such a success. I felt passionately sorry that you weren't there, my joy) and was back at home at five – with two new little books, checked out from 'Ladyzhnikov' on my way. I read for a while, recited my poem out loud a few times, changed into a dinner-jacket, had dinner (cold-cuts, a bit of Weisskäse), and, after a wee shot of cognac, set out to 3 Bellevuestr., where the festivities were taking place, for eight. There were already lots of people there, I chatted with Aykhenvald, with Sergey Gorny, with the unexpected Kardakov. Kardakov told me astonishing stories about the peasants' attitude towards him, an entomologist, working in the Ussuri region. Their attitude was nasty (almost to the point of murder) for two reasons. First: he asked boys to deliver him beetles and paid 2 kopecks per bug. The peasants began to say that the 'doctor', you know, buys a beetle for next to nothing and then sells it for a thousand rubles. Once he advised the lads to look for a rare Siberian beetle for him among stacked firewood. The lads found the beetle, but they also thoroughly scattered the logs, and the peasants decided to finish Kardakov off. Secondly: they all thought (I've now understood what 'thunder of applause' means. It was a real ovation) that Kardakov was a doctor, and those who were ill, and pregnant women too, thronged to him. He tried to explain to them that he didn't know how to treat them, but they were certain he said this on purpose, out of malice or pride. Finally he couldn't stand it any longer and moved to other places. Then Lyaskovsky jumped up at me – not a man, really, but a hook (I must also tell you that this morning he wrote to me, asking me to be there precisely at eight and adding that, you know, you don't need a ticket – 'you have a place in the presidium') and carelessly, without looking at me, he remarked: 'You know what, Vl. Vl., it'd be better if you took a place in the first row – here's a ticket. Please, take it.' The bell rang, we all sat down. When the presidium were seated (Yasinsky, Zaytsev, prof., Aykhenvald, Tatarinov, and so on), it turned out that one place was left empty, but, in spite of the imploring whisper of Yasinsky and Aykhenvald, I refused to take it. Lyaskovsky, meanwhile, was sitting at the edge of the table and avoided making eye contact with me. Surprising character. It started. Ilyin gave a rather good speech after Yasinsky's introductory word, and then some young folk acted out Chekhov's 'The Jubilee'. A small intermission followed, finally a bell, and Lyaskovsky, flying past, throws out: 'You, Vl. Vl., tell them to have someone announce you, since the Ofrosimov Group will probably be on now.' Here I got angry with him at last and said to him, literally: 'No, my dear man, you're arranging it all. And I will sit here in the green room.' He flashed his pince-nez and obediently ran off. From behind the curtain, I heard how, in total silence, Yasinsky named me. And immediately the applause exploded. I pushed the curtain aside and went out to the front of the stage. After I finished reading (I recited without stumbling and, apparently, loudly enough), the entire huge hall, jam-packed, began to clap so hard and make so much noise it even began to feel gratifying. I came on three times. The roar still didn't stop. Lyaskovsky scampered backstage, muttering drily: 'Why such a din? Is this really for you?' A few people pushed me back on stage again – and the hall didn't want to quiet down; they shouted 'encore' and 'bravo' and 'Sirin'. Then I repeated my poem again and recited it even better – and again a boom of applause. When I went down into the audience, all sorts of people threw themselves on me, began to shake my hand, Hessen kissed me smack on the forehead, tore out my page, to print the poem in *Rul'*. And then, after one act from 'It's Not Always Shrovetide for the Cat', they all congratulated me again, and I feel very sorry, my joy, that you were not there. Somewhere far away, pale little Shura was sitting with his father, the Kaplans were there too, and all kinds of girls, and that deaf lady who helped you translate the dictionary. I got home at two, sat down to write to you – but did not finish and am continuing today. The weather's better, but windy. I've got letters from Mother and from – Panchenko. Now I will go to Maman Kaplan's lesson. Oh, my joy, my sweet love, how are you, what are you doing, do you remember me? I love you very much today. And last night, when I was walking down Potsdamer Str. – I suddenly felt so warm that you exist – and what a joy you are. Just think, if I get a good amount for the translation of 'Mary', we could still take off for the Pyrenees. I paid the landlady yesterday (when I returned from K.). It came out at 55 m. 20 pf. (52+ milk). My sweet, my happiness, sweet, sweet ... Don't you worry, I will write to you tonight, too. Here, my darling (such a darling . . .), I must go – and the second page has finished at just the right spot.

V.

[ALS, 2 PP.]
[9 June 1926]

TO: Sanatorium, St-Blasien, Schwarzwald

[Berlin]
9–VI–26

Tufty,

After writing to you – and to Mother as well – I popped the letters in a blue box on the street of winter fields and at the post office drafted a card to Kaminka, who yesterday was asking me to give him Mother's address. Then I sailed around to Mme Kaplan and explained to her, for the hundredth time, that 'Joan' is not some Mr 'Ivan', but a young girl Joanna. Then I came home and ate: chicken with rice and rhubarb compote. Then I read Gladkov's 'Cement', from which I must quote the following sentences for you: 'She wouldn't turn off her smirk, and the smirk reflected off the wall back to her face, and the face fire-glowed with dim heat between the black spots in her eye-sockets. Then Gleb filled his fists with blood and gnashed his teeth. Recovered and crushed his heart. Smirked himself and swallowed his Adam's apple with saliva. But a burning tremor tore the muscles from his heart with a convulsion. Gleb, tamed, bony, dashing, with jaws clenched to his sucked-in cheeks, gnashed his teeth from the splinter in his brain.' How do you like this pearl, Tufty? I read and took notes until supper. 'Rul'' came, I am sending you a clipping not without interest. Dinner consisted of fried eggs and cold-cuts. It's now half past eight. I would like to go for a stroll before sleep.

Tufty, I think you write too often to me! A whole two letters over this time. Isn't that too much? Believe it or not, I write every day. Today there was a somehow quiet but penetrating row behind our wall – unfortunately in German dialect. 'In amazement, Zhuk bulged out his eyes, and his face said "ah" and burst into smithereens. The paralysed engineer Kleist stood, pressing his back straight to the parapet, and his head kicked up the hat with rare jerky movements.' I think that engineer Kleist ... could have been a good forward.

Yes, Tuftikins, this is not good ... I, for example, very much counted on getting a little letter today. The littlies are wasting away (by the way, Lalodya isn't in the list on the first page of 'Mary'. He is very offended), I don't even know what to do. Today, the letter went under the sign of Tufty – but tomorrow? I'm in new trousers today.

V.

[ALS, 2 PP.]
[10 June 1926]

TO: Hôtel Pension Schwarzwaldhaus, Schwarzwald

[Berlin]
10/VI–26

Dipod,

This morning, they brought me your third little letter, along with my fastbreak. Oh, dipod ...

The weather this morning was so-so: dullish, but warm, a boiled-milk sky, with skin – but if you pushed it aside with a teaspoon, the sun was really nice, so I wore my white trousers. I went to Sack's for eleven, played ball with him. Then the skin thickened up – and it began to drizzle. When I got home it was pouring hard and continued all day. A large puddle formed in my courtyard, – and concentric circles were spreading through it – some smaller, others bigger – quick-quick – so there was a rippling effect in my eyes – and then in place of the circles thin, countless, wavelike lines began to flow and flow – and I had to somehow cut off my vision to see the circles under the raindrops again. So I didn't go out the whole day. Lunch wasn't bad – a lamb chop and gooseberry compote. After lunch I read Fedin, then decided to sort out my manuscripts: after all, I need to prepare all my stories for Stein – he's been asking for a while, – but it turns out that I don't have 'The Fight' here. Besides, I need to copy it all on a typewriter (so far, only 'Beneficence' and 'The Seaport' are in decent shape) – so I do not know how this'll be done. I read again after that, then opened up my chessboard, started to compose a problem, but soon gave up. They brought me 'Rul'' and dinner (I don't know why there is such a hubbub in the kitchen area today. Our good landlady's probably out of sorts). The 'Rul'' review of the soirée is abominably written ('V. Sirin recited his last poem about his homeland (as if I won't be writing again!), 'Soft Sound', published in 'Rul'' yesterday, talented and especially intimate in its rendering of specific settings as a pretext [?!] for fundamental, deep, experiences'). Dinner consisted of an egg and the usual cold cuts. 'Rul'' I will save for you, but I ate the dinner. The lecture will be on Saturday, and I think it will turn out all right. (Where did I put the matches? Things seem to have some sort of survival instinct. If you throw a ball in a huge room without any furniture, except for one armchair – nothing at all except that – the ball will roll under it without fail. I've found the matches, though. They were in the ashtray.) You know, I haven't played tennis for a week now, owing to the rain ... Tuftikins, I've decided to kiss you at the end of my letter. Wait, don't move ... No, wait. My little Tuftikins ... Oh, my love, my sweet, my dear one. We walked to Todtmoos from St Blasien on foot. It was burning hot, and I took my shirt off. Tuftikins ... My fabulous dipodikins ... I'll read a bit and go to bed.

V.

[ALS, 2 PP.]
[11–12 June 1926]

TO: Hôtel Pension Schwarzwaldhaus, Schwarzwald

[Berlin]
11/VI–26

Lumpikin,

This morning, taking my time, I set out for Ladyzhnikov's. Returned the books, got my deposit back, and sailed off to 'Moskva', where I wasted two marks on 'Volya Rossii'. Mme Melnikov-Papoushek (whose papa ushered no good news in) writes that 'Mary' is not a novel, that I imitate Proust, that some of my descriptions are 'miniature', that there are longueurs, which, apparently, Proust does not have, that the overall conception is not bad, but the performance is weak – and that she, Madame Melnikov-Papoushek, does not understand those critics who have seen in 'Mary' a symbol of Russia. The review, overall, is ladyish and ill-disposed. After getting home I sat down to write the talk and wrote it non-stop all day (the Kaplans had cancelled their lesson), till half past one in the morning. Interspersed with the lecture, I was writing a little short story in today's 'Soviet' style. If I have enough gall, I'll read it tonight at the Tatarinovs, passing it off as a Russian production. The lecture, though, took up twenty-eight large pages (not these – but the other sheets that you bequeathed me, Lumpikin) and seems to have turned out not badly. I mock and I tear to pieces. Will send it to you as soon as I am done with the reading.

Lumpikin, don't be surprised that I write 'today at the Tatarinovs'. The thing is, I was too tired to write to you on the night of the 11th – and although the letter sounds as if I'm writing on the evening of the 11th, in fact this is now the morning of June 12th, I'm just up and have sat down in my untidy little room to write to you. Lunch yesterday consisted of a veal chop and a banana in the company of cherries. For dinner, they treated me to fried eggs and cold-cuts. It rained yesterday, today's sunny although chilly, and the wind is fluffing out the bright crooked acacia by the wall of the yard. My lecture is entitled: 'A Few Words on the Wretchedness of Soviet Literature, and An Attempt to Establish the Cause Thereof'. I will send it tomorrow for you to read.

There is a whole island of ashes under my writing desk. The maid is knocking, she wants to clean up. I'll go out to buy stamps it's bad that you write to me so seldom and a Gillette razor. I also have for you two programmes illustrated by Golubev-Bagryanorodny, in connection with the day of my triumph. I haven't sent the books to Bunin and Uncle Kostya yet, Panchenko and the Polizeipräsidium are still waiting, and I still have not managed to inform 'Rul'' of my address, although, by an incomprehensible miracle, I receive the newspaper every evening. Stein, too, is waiting for my stories. I haven't found time to call B. G. All this is very bad. My Lumpikin, how are you keeping? How are your little furs? There is something birdy or parroty in my acacia. Till this evening, Lumpikin – I will definitely write you tonight. The lecture will be at nine, at the Tatarinovs. My joy . . .

V.

[ALS, 2 PP.]
[12 June 1926]

TO: Hotel-Pension Schwarzwaldhaus,
Todtmoos Bad, Schwarzwald

[Berlin]
12/VI–26

Katyusha,

After finishing the letter to you, I went out to post it, stopped in at the clock shop (turns out that they still can't tell me how much the repairs will cost!), then bought a razor, then acquired a stamp collection for two marks–ten tens and five twenties–and on top of that, from a stand, two English books for fifty [pfennigs]: Squire, *Steps to Parnassus* (literary parodies) and the renowned Henry James, *The Outcry* (a novel). I returned home (the weather, meanwhile, has turned warmer, and I'm wearing the new trousers) and had lunch (meat stew and apple spittle). After lunch I began to read through my lecture–and here, Sofa called, to say E. I. had arrived. On the way to the Kaplans' I stopped by at Regensburg, saw there E. I. and E. L., who got back yesterday. I haven't learned especially much about you from E. I. She is unusually unforthcoming. I learned in any case that you've moved to Todtmoos–which I very much welcome. Your fur-coat is being sent to you all the same. Then I was at K.'s for his lesson, quietly came home, thinking I'd find a little letter from you and of course was mistaken. I think I'll also stop writing to you. Before dinner I read the books I'd bought, had dinner (macaroni and cold-cuts) and, around nine, sailed off to the Tatarinovs. Gradually, a great multitude of people gathered there (of course, Aykhenvald, Volkovysky, Kadish, Ofrosimov, and so on), and I began. I spoke (I did not read, only peeked in from time to time–when quoting) for more than an hour. They found the lecture brilliant but very vicious and somewhat 'fascistic'.

Volkovysky especially attacked me. It all finished about one. I saw Mme Falkovsky to the corner of Augsburg[er] Strasse and quietly returned to my solitary little room. It's now a quarter to two, tomorrow is Sunday, I'll sleep in. I'm sending you the lecture – of course I changed and added an awful lot when I was speaking – this is only a summary. There you are. Beddy-time, Katyusha. I more than adore you. You are my happiness and life. When I think about you, I get so happy and light, and since I think about you always, I'm always happy and light. And tonight, someone will be writing a little short story – or rather composing it till sleep comes. My joy, Katyushen'ka, my little music, my love. Todtmoos is cosy, isn't it? We stayed at the Adler inn there. Good night, Katyushen'ka.

V.

[ALS, 2 PP.]
[13 June 1926]

TO: Hotel-Pension Schwarzwaldhaus,
Todtmoos, Schwarzwald

[Berlin]
13/VI–26

Nice-and-warm,

Rain, rain, since morning ... Such a pretty June, I must say ... It drips onto the windowsill, it crackles as if endlessly opening thousands of tiny cabinets, chests, caskets – senselessly and purposefully, in the dark, in the yard, where my crooked acacia receives the rain in its own way, with an obedient steady rustling. I went out in the morning to post letters and after that didn't stir. I mulled. Here's the little story I want to write. It'll be called 'Rooms'. Or even 'A Room for Rent'. About rooms, about this long enfilade of rooms through which one has to travel, about each room's having its own voices (locks, windows, doors, mice, the wardrobe's moan and the bed's squeak) unlike the voices of another room, about the mirror's staring at a person like a quiet invalid who has lost his mind, his ability to perceive and retain what he sees – with a clear insane look – and about how we unfairly insult things with our inattentiveness, about how touching are the moulded ceiling ornaments, which we never look at, which we never notice. And do you remember, Nice-and-warm, a couple of little cobwebs hanging over my bed on Trautenaustr.? I was thinking this over for a while, then read Henry James, drank some milk. From time to time, the sounds of the pension would reach me. From the thickets of the hallway, snatches of an argument between the landlady and her son:

'And at four –'
'I don't understand, mama, why you never listen to my opinion –'
'At four we will go to the Zoo, come back at five, at six –'

But generally the pension is very quiet, very pleasant. The maid and her sister are obliging to the point of submissiveness. I'm very happy I settled here. We had a Sunday lunch today: soup with dumplings, meat served well, a tart with strawberries and whipped cream. Dinner, however, was as always – egg, cold-cuts.

Nice-and-warm, there wasn't anything from you today, either. Maybe the rain got in your way.

It's now a quarter to ten, I'll write to Mother now, then go to bed. This is terrible – I'll probably not be able to send her anything on the fifteenth: the Sacks owe me 120 mar[ks], 30 will go to Anyuta, 60 – for the apartment and little things, 25 – to Tegel, 5 in reserve. And the passports?

Nice-and-warm, we love you very much, we greatly respect you. The roses have dried out completely, but they're still standing on the table.

My writing hand and the orange tulip of the lamp are reflected in the black, mirrory gloss of the window. Nice-and-warm …

V.

[ALS, 2 PP.]
[14 June 1926]

TO: Hotel-Pension St Blasien, Sanatorium,
b Frau Dr Slonim, Schwarzwald

[Berlin]
14/VI–26

Love,

I'm just back from the cinema and found your sad little letter. Love, move to another place on Wednesday – try Titisee, where there's a wonderful lake and where I didn't find the mountains oppressive. Or try the place the doctor recommended – in any case, look for something – since the whole problem is that you are unhappy living in a funnel, in a valley – but you can find other places – on a slope, on a summit, on a plateau. You need not get so down, my love. I realize you're sick of the bad weather – but bad weather is everywhere these days – I'm complaining of the rain, too. Can't you really find a nook for yourself in the Schwarzwald (I've spilled a drop of milk here)? Collect a few sanatorium addresses – and go. Understand this, my love, none of us wants to see you till you're completely well and rested. I beg you, my love, for my sake shrug off all that gloom and move to another place, to a second, a third – only find some refuge at last. Think what I must feel knowing things are bad for you– and try to arrange something better for yourself. My love, my little one, my sweet happiness …

Around one I went to read about the Maid with Madame K, and on the way there I met the Walrus and the little saintly Nuki. I bent down to touch him, but he ran past paying absolutely no attention. I had lunch (ragout, salad, cherries), then went to Sack's. We walked through the thickets of the Grunewald: the weather is windy today, and it was wonderful. Then I stopped by at Regensburg, where they were discussing your letter, and where they gave me a delicious dinner (vegetables in sour cream, wild strawberries). Veryovkin dropped in–he's severely dizzy, and he's very scared. About nine, I went to the cinema with Sergey K. and saw the new version of the film 'Ways to Strength and Beauty', hardly different from the first. Now I am drinking milk, eating the cold-cuts left for me and looking at your letter. My darling, you needn't cry ... You'll see–I'm sure that if you find a place where you don't feel the mountains–everything will go well. And here's more about objects: I keep the stamps I put on my letters to Todtmoos in the folding aluminium tumbler I drank from at the creek on the way to Todtmoos ... A sweet coincidence. My love, what can I do so things will be better for you?

V.

[ALS, 4 PP.]
[15 June 1926]

TO: Hotel-Pension Schwarzwaldhaus,
Todtmoos, Schwarzwald

[Berlin]
15/VI–26

Sparrowling,

It's poured down all day without a moment's break–ghastly–and it's still pouring. I wanted to go to Sack's by motorcycle, but the driver refused to go–too slippery because of the rain. A whole row of motorcycles, but no drivers in sight. A passer-by pointed out a tavern to me. They were all sitting there and drinking coffee with milk, in big mugs. I had to ride by tram – and when I arrived at Sack's the front of my mackintosh was a sodden chocolate hue. We did gymnastics, we read. I got home and found a letter from Mother, who'd forwarded me a letter from Bobby de Calry (very sweet, he's planning, I think, to invite us) and a letter to her from Sergey. I can't stop myself copying it out: '.... I did not reply to your letter right away. I could not write because of the awful storm in my soul. Today I want to explain the situation to you. You must understand the utter importance of the decision I've come to, which I couldn't *not* come to. You know my whole life for the last ten years has been a terrible one, not only a sinful life, but even a crime against myself. I never resorted to that power that helps and directs us to other ways. You know that we were not brought up in the Orthodox spirit. For me, Orthodoxy has never been and could never be any help. But, as always happens in life, a moment came when I received a jolt from without. I was facing a fatal and frightening dead-end. On the other hand, the man I've linked my life with, the man I love more than anything else in the world – had gone back to the church, i.e. he had received the same jolt from without. Those were terrible days. I am becoming a Catholic in full awareness of the inescapability of this step and with absolute belief in its necessity. Yes, of course, there's been an influence on me: but not a momentary influence, not a passing one. More like help. An unconscious influence coming from God. The Catholic Church is stricter, more demanding than the Orthodox. I need the power directing and restraining me. Faith has come, God has come to me in earnest. The ceremony is taking place this week, and I ask you to think and pray about me. I know this is not superficial, but rather right, true, genuine. I will take communion every day to kill the sin in me, so God can give me strength, energy, and will. I will live alone. We aren't separating in the full sense of this word. I am with him as before. But our life together in one room is incompatible with joining any kind of church. This is not easy for me, it's very hard: I cannot cut off a huge part of my self with one blow. This part must change, and make way for something new and not sinful. If I could take communion more often than four times a year in the Orthodox Church, I would not have left it. Do understand how important all this is and don't reproach me: it's hard for me, too, but I am waiting for divine grace.'

I had lunch (veal cutlet, cherry compote), then sailed off (in the chocolate mackintosh) to Kaplan for the lesson. Once I was home, I sat down to write letters – to Bobby, to Mother (I am sending her twenty-five marks), to Panchenko (also 25) and to Lena. And then … Puss, what a little story! I was licking my lips as I began. It is called 'Odd (A Fairy-Tale)' and it's about how the devil (in the form of a large elderly woman) has offered a little civil servant to set up a harem for him. You will say, frivolous Hebe, that the topic is strange, you may even wince, my Sparrowling. But you will see. *Je ne dis que cela* …

The dinner was as usual. It's now half past nine, and I'm in my old grey trousers.

Sparrowling, how're your spirits? I hope you'll no longer be in Todtmoos when you get this letter. I'm afraid that if you open it on the second page you'll think I've gone mad. In fact I've added all those quotation marks just in case. I think, overall, this is good for Sergey. It is true – Catholicism is a feminine, arrow-arched faith – the sweetness of painted glass, the suffering tenderness of young Sebastians … I personally prefer the most worthless, baldish little Russian parish priest to the rustling abbot with a pseudo-inspired, waxy countenance. And when I thought of the wonderful, happy, religion I have, my very own … But never mind. Probably, Sergey's carried away by this, but in a deep, good way, that will help him a lot. And you, my Sparrowling, don't be too angry at the rain. You realize it has to fall, it can't help itself – it's not its fault, after all, it can't fall up. My happiness, because of it I haven't played tennis for almost two weeks (I'm not comparing things, of course). But I simply – love you.

V.

[ALS, 2 PP.]
[16 June 1926]

TO: Hotel-Pension Schwarzwaldhaus,
Todtmoos, Schwarzwald

[Berlin]
16/VI

My sweet,

I dreamt that I was walking along the Palace Embankment with someone, the water in the Neva is lead-coloured, flowing thickly, and there are masts, masts without end, large boats and small ones, colourful stripes on black pipes – and I say to my companion: 'The Bolsheviks have such a big fleet!' And he replies: 'Yes, that's why they had to remove the bridges.' After that we walked around the Winter Palace, and for some reason it was purple all over – and I thought that I must note this down for a short story. We stepped out onto the Palace Square – it was squeezed from all sides by buildings, some kind of fantastic lights were playing. And my entire dream was lit up by some threatening light – the kind you find in battle paintings.

I went out around twelve (wearing the new trousers, thanks to the sun), changed books at the *Librairie*, paid eight and a half [marks] there and headed off for a little garden on Wittenbergplatz. There I read for half an hour on a bench between an old man and a nanny, enjoying the intermittent but hot sun. Near one I went to explain to Madame K. that Joan is a woman, a historic persona, and, having explained this (till Saturday), returned home, had lunch (meatballs, wild strawberries with cream). Then sat down to write 'Odd'. Around six I stopped by at Regensburger, but saw only Sofa, came back, gave the laundry to the maid (and wrote it down) and sat down to my little story again. Already seven (large) pages written, but I think it'll be around twenty.

Meanwhile, it began to rain – and the rain may stop me from going for a walk before bed. And for dinner, besides cold-cuts, they served three little sweet pies – macaroni-like, fried on top and sprinkled with sugar (and very unpalatable). About the milk: this milk is different, more expensive, in hermetically sealed bottles, marvellous – it doesn't go off. Here, my sweet, is what the sixteenth day of my grass widowhood was like. Neither sight nor sound of you. Why do you write so seldom, my sweet? I regret terribly not arranging for you the same kind of note-pad you arranged for me – with dates. It is five minutes to nine now. Two plumpish coffee-coloured dachshunds are frolicking below in the yard – from above, it looks like two pawless sausages rolling about. My sweet, I don't know where you are now (where you'll be reading this letter). I love you. My sweet, I love you. Do you hear?

V.

[ALS, 2 PP.]
[17 June 1926]

TO: Hotel-Pension Schwarzwaldhaus,
Todtmoos, Schwarzwald

[Berlin]
17/6–26

Mosquittle,

I received your little letter this morning. What's really going on? Mosquittle, cheer up . . .

As soon as I got up I sat down to write (no, I went to post the letter to you and exchange the French book) and finished the story by seven. Dismal fish and cherries for lunch (I stopped writing about the soups a while ago: I can't tell them apart). Generally speaking, they feed me a lot and constantly ask whether I am full. I am absolutely full. A few days ago, I complained that the cocoa was weak – and since then they have been giving me fine stuff – dark and sweet. And the little story turned out not bad (ah, yes, why am I so forgetful today ... In the morning, the postman brought me twelve marks – for your wee little lessons – and I have paid ten of them to the cigarette man who arrived five minutes later. Very lucky), it's rather long – about twenty pages, as I thought. I'll rewrite it tomorrow. I stopped by at Regensburg at seven, saw everyone, had dinner there (the Bolsheviks are making concessions. They don't have *full-size*, but they have other sizes. They're knocking off between 20 and 25%. I heard this with half an ear. Everyone's well. L. got the tickets for E. I., E. L. and Anyuta will probably see her off to Stettin. Anyuta was wearing a blue dress which had ripped open between her shoulder blade and armpit. I secretly threw the dead trunk of my cigarette under the couch – nobody noticed, it seems.) Near nine I went to the Tatarinovs – no crowd there, we had a very nice chat. A few days ago, Aykhenvald was visiting with them, and they managed to convince him that the little old lady Sofia S. rode a bike. On Saturday, they will have an evening of ... aphorisms. Everyone must think of an aphorism on the subject of suffering and pleasure. No squeaking, Mosquittle. I got home around half past eleven and now I'm writing to you. The weather today was bearable (only one downpour – between five and six). My tender Mosquittle, I love you. I love you, my superlative Mosquittle. Maybe you'll settle near Heidelberg – they say it's wonderful there – won't you? I can't wait, generally speaking, for you to settle down very soon. My sweet creature ... I don't know 'pleasure' and 'suffering', I only know 'happiness' and 'happiness', i.e. 'the thought of you' and 'you yourself'. They are very nervous here about some princes and some millions. I don't know what the matter is exactly. I love you. I am going to bed, Mosquittle. I so much want you to be happy. Good night, my darling, my tenderness, my happiness.

V.

[ALS, 3 PP.]
[18 June 1926]

TO: Hotel-Pension Schwarzwaldhaus,
Todtmoos, Schwarzwald

[Berlin]
18/VI–26

Pussykins,

You write disgustingly rarely to me. In the morning, under the invariable rain (which is beginning to drive me mad), I floated to Sack's, composing a poem along the way which I began yesterday before sleep and today, just now, I've finished. It's enclosed. I did gymnastics with Sack and dictated to him. I returned home (composing all the while), had lunch – for which they served very tough meat – the landlady later ran in to apologize (and to make up, she sent me an excellent dinner: a large dish of fried eggs and ham). After lunch, I went to give Kaplan his lesson – we translated Rousseau – then came back, composed till six, and set off for Regensburger Str. Only Sofa was there. I sat at the table and wrote down several stanzas. A few minutes later E. I. arrived. We said good-bye very warmly – and I dragged myself home, half-stunned by the labour of my muse. I had dinner – and here the labours delivered, and I composed the whole poem. I think I'll send it to 'Zveno'. My sweet, you see what a little day I had today. I'm unshaven and when I rub my palm over the stubble on my cheek, it sounds like a car braking. I forgot to write to you that when I was at Regensb. yesterday I asked them for nail scissors and a file, and neatly clipped my nails, which I had thoroughly neglected. Tomorrow I plan to perform the same operation on my feet too (but at home). On Wednesday, the landlady leaves for Terijoki for a month with her son and daughter.

Pussykins, how are you? Will you recognize me when you see me? Little Show has grown up a lot and we'll soon have to buy him toys. Tuftikins wanted to have a Bubikopf, but they misunderstood and shaved her little head smooth (she now looks absolutely like a pawn). The rest of the little ones are all well.

My sweet, my dear one, have you found a refuge? When will you finally write to me that you are well, comfortable, in good spirits? As for me, don't worry about anything, my joy, Pussykins: I live very well, eat my fill, read and write a lot. I'm very curious to know if you'll like my little poem.

It's now ten minutes past nine, I'll go to bed soon. The rain has stopped, but – to judge by the puddle in the courtyard – I won't be able to play tennis tomorrow, either. This is extremely boring. My Pussykins, today I've decided to kiss you again. The stock-market has been amazingly peaceful recently. Isn't there any demand in the Schwarzwald for some kind of crockery? Write, Pussykins. I didn't think you'd write to me so rarely. Good night, Puss.

V.

A trifle – a mast's denomination, plans – trailed
by a seagull, soars my life;
and, on the deck, a man, lap-robed,
inhales the radiance – it is I.

I see, upon a glossy postcard,
a bay's depravity of blue
and, white-toothed, a townlet with a retinue
of countless palms, and the abode in which I dwell.

At that same instant, with a cry, I'll show you
myself, myself–but in a different town:
like a parrot snapping with its beak,
I scrabble at the scrapbook with its cards.

That one–that's me, with phantom suitcase;
and that's me on a chilly street
walking at you, as if from a screen,
and blurring into blindness.

Oh . . . I sense inside my legs, grown heavy,
the trains that leave without me
and what a wealth of countries have not warmed me,
where I shan't live, and never shall be warmed!

And, in his armchair, the voyager from Eden
describes, his hands behind his head,
sucking the pipe smoke with a whistle,
his love of loves–a tropic bay.

V. Sirin
18–VI 26

[ALS, 2 PP.]
[19 June 1926]

TO: Hotel-Pension Schwarzwaldhaus,
Todtmoos, Schwarzwald

[Berlin]
19/VI–26

Kidlet,

This morning I began to rewrite 'Odd', then I gave S. K. his lesson. Back home I had lunch (veal cutlet, compote) and carried on rewriting. I finished around seven and then – for the Tartars' soirée – listed all that makes me suffer – starting with the touch of satin and ending with the impossibility of assimilating, swallowing, all the beauty in the world. It turned out about two pages in small handwriting – and, forgive me, my Kidlet – I've mislaid this sheet somewhere, or I'd have sent it to you. I had dinner in the company of cold-cuts and two sausages and by nine, with the story, the poem, and the list of sufferings sailed off to Mlle Ioffe's. There I found the Tatarinovs, Mme Falkovsky, Danechka, Rusina, Kadish with his wife, Trotsky with his wife, Grif, the repulsive Zvezdich, Aykhenvald. I read them the story. An absolutely deafening success. I promptly read them the poem. They made me read it three times. They discussed it for about an hour. Zvezdich and Aykhenvald almost had a fight. Then Mme Tatarinov gathered all the written aphorisms about 'suffering and pleasure' (Aykhenvald, Mme Tatarinov, Mlle Ioffe, Mme Falkovsky, and Grif had all had a go) and read them. One was not bad: 'A man cannot achieve pleasure single-handed.' Finally, she read my little list too – and again, there was a burst of inexplicable excitement. All in all, the whole soirée turned into a celebration of the present writer – and he, in order to put, so to speak, the proper full-stop, to crown the soirée – when we got out on the street (Passauer Strasse), when everyone was saying good-bye to one other, turned a somersault right there, on the pavement.

And when I got home, I landed like a rooster in soup, at a *grand gala* in the landlady's dining-room. Everybody there was completely drunk: some German actors (friends of the son), employees of the American consulate (friends of the daughter), and a professor Poletika (the Korostovets couple should have been there, too, but they did not come). I drank some vodka, a cup of hock, ate a sandwich, danced one fox-trot with the landlady's daughter (a very unattractive lady) and retired unnoticed. It's now almost two, and here I am writing to you, Kidlet. My Kidlet, I'm so sorry that you weren't the first to hear my story and all in all that the whole soirée went on without you ... I'll give the story to 'Rul" on Monday, they'll type it up there, and I'll send you the little manuscript straight away. 'They say that misfortune is a good school. Yes, true. But happiness is the best university.' Isn't this great? That's Pushkin. And here is an émigré-political aphorism: 'The zeros realized that in order to become something they had to stand on the right.' And do you know the German translation of this line from the Chekhov story: 'I walk on a carpet, you walk on false talk'? '*Teppich, tepst du.*' My Kidlet, my happiness, where are you? I love you so much now, my sweet ... I am going to bed, I'm rather tired. I put everything away neatly in the wardrobe, there's nothing lying about the room. Love you infinitely.

V.

[ALS, 2 PP.]

[20 June 1926]

TO: Hotel-Pension Schwarzwaldhaus,
Todtmoos, Schwarzwald

[Berlin]

20/VI–26

My life,

It's been raining all day. This morning I wrote a letter to Mother and sent the poem to 'Zveno'. I thanked them for placing the translation and added: 'My brother writes me from Paris that the author of the review of my "Mary" thinks that I have "taken offence". Be so kind as to tell him that this is not so. I was only surprised by the factual inaccuracies in the review, which convey a wrong impression about the book's very plot and style.' Short and caustic. By the way: Aykhenvald told me yesterday that Elkin (who'd gone to Paris) wrote to him that Mochulsky was 'remorseful'. This whole story is rather stupid. I had lunch (good meat, strawberries with whipped cream), read after lunch, and then slept for two hours. I looked out of the window and felt sorry that I had not added to my letter to 'Zveno': 'Blaming a critic is like blaming the rain.' I had a good yawn, my thoughts were dawdling, I didn't want either to read or write. They brought me dinner (an egg and cold-cuts), I ate it, lit the lamp, and here I am writing to you, my life. You know, I'll have nothing to tell you when you come back – you'll know everything, down to the details, from my letters! But you'll have such a heap ... My sweet life, I love you. I love your little dachshund paws and the little pink lines around your eyes. I got another epistle from the Catholic Church. Let it sit for a while. I didn't understand a thing. It's now a quarter to nine, the maid's making my bed. I'll finish the letter and step out for a stroll, in the light drizzle. I have to buy some cigarettes – I've run out. The little man will come tomorrow. Today I sat at home the whole day – I only nipped out before lunch to post the letters. In the mornings, if I'm not going to Sack's, I do gymnastics – I've got a grand headstand! – and then bathe in my *tub*. (I don't bathe in the bathroom – there's a bleeding red rug there – and everything would turn a bright raspberry colour: my heels, the edges of my bath towel, the heels of my socks.) How are you, my life? How does the morning sleepyhead stretch? How is my happiness, my long, warm happiness? I'm wearing the blue suit today – and, of course, the speckled, which I've got to like more than all the other jumpers and sweaters I've ever had. There's a strange friendship between my neighbour (a young Dutch artist) and my wrinkled landlady … But, let me repeat, I'm very happy with the boarding-house – and they feed us really well. I've got used to the sausage and sometimes eat it without disgust. But you, my love, take care that you eat well, too … We love you so. We adore you. Please forgive us for writing so seldom. I've put in a new nib today. My life …

V.

[ALS, 2 PP.]
[21 June 1926]

TO: Sanatorium, St Blasien, Schwarzwald

[Berlin]
21/VI–26

Skunky,

This morning about half past ten I went to 'Rul'' and handed Hessen my story (I still don't know whether I'll call it simply 'A Fairy-Tale' or 'Odd'. It's rather large – eighteen pages; in fact, it's unclear all in all whether it will suit. If it does, then by Wednesday they'll type it out and I'll check it. If it doesn't suit, then I'll send it to 'Slovo' on this condition: 30 marks by the 1st. Not a pfennig less and not a day later. Good?). I returned to my neighbourhood and when I saw I had a whole hour till my lesson with Mme Kaplan, I first called at Berta Gavr.'s (according to Shura, she's doing much better), but no one opened up for me, and since I had nothing to do, I sat for a while in an open café on the corner of Bavarian square and drank a glass of dark beer. Then I gave my lesson (it's very warm here today, but raining from time to time. I'm wearing the new grey pair). I had lunch (excellent cutlet and strawberries) and after a lie-down on the little couch (my joy, I am in the same room – I think I wrote to you that I had refused to move to the other), went, by four, Sackwards. I played ball with him. On the way back (I bought the 'Observer'), I stopped by at Regensburg. I saw them all, stayed half an hour, picked up clean laundry and returned home for dinner (excellent fried eggs and cold-cuts). Today in 'Rul'' there's an article by Konoplin about Taboritsky and Shabelsky-Borg. It's strange to read. They have eight years hard labour left. I found your dear little skunky letter. I'm happy that you're better. Stay, Skunky, in Saint Blasia. You can't describe butterflies that way. What does 'yellow' mean? There are a million shades of yellow. That little one, with black speckles, must be not simply yellow, but orangey-russet, rather like yellow wax for boots. If that's the case, then it belongs to the genus *Brenthis* or *Melithea* (butterflies with a motley, often nacreous underside). The other one, you write, is white with a yellow piping? I don't know. Describe it in more detail – and in general note a few others too. Yesterday I went out for a stroll in the evening – and watched with a crowd (on Nollendorfplatz) a wonderful illuminated advertisement – a ribbon of words passing by like a well-lit train: the news on voting and simply the news – a whole newspaper of lights. Amazingly beautiful. And now it's a quarter past nine. I won't go out again tonight. What can I write you about the Regensburgers? They are all well, comfortable, I sat down in the dusk with E. L., telling him about the soirée at Ioffe's, then I read him my poem – he liked it. As he spoke he'd get up, thrust his hands in trouser pockets, bend his head a little to the side; he'd slowly walk across the room, turn around on a heel, walk again, just lowering his head. I love all of this and I feel very good around him.

Well, Skunky, good night. You will never guess (I am kissing you) what exactly I am kissing.

V.

[ALS, 5 PP.]
[22 June 1926]

TO: Sanatorium, St Blasien, Schwarzwald

[Berlin]
22/VI–26

Mymousch,

(The critter I've chosen today isn't handsome – but very furry) this morning I met (my handwriting is so small because I've just rewritten the poem in small script, and my hand hasn't yet got out of the habit. Well, here I'm getting bigger) with Sack and – since the weather was wanly sunny and very hot – we set out (now at last it has evened out – not Sack, my handwriting) to the Grunewald, where we had a splendid time swimming. We were lying on the sand, when the rain suddenly burst, thunder broke out a huge purple chunk of sky and little silver arrows began to dance on the lake. A thick oak shielded us from the rain. I came back via Roseneck (I'm in the old grey suit today) and had a rather dense lunch (good meat, cherry compote). Simultaneously, I continued composing a poem that arose overnight. I went to the Kaplans (not on foot, by car – since it was raining deafeningly). On the way home (by five o'clock the weather had become heavenly) I continued to compose, bought a razor blade, exchanged a book, bought new garters (the old pair is torn) as well as … a nice grey neck-tie (a long one), and having completely gone on a spree, I ruined myself further with a *Nestlé* chocolate bar with nuts. Getting home, I found, Mymousch, your little letter, nice and warm, like you yourself, and was quite overjoyed that you seem in better spirits. But, my happiness, don't come back on the first! You must get still better – remember. Come back no earlier than the 20th, Mymousch ... Later, lying on the divan (oh yes, I paid 52 marks on the bill today and 5 to the cigarette man) I composed, meanwhile a terrible thunderstorm broke out, and I finished the poem to claps of thunder. I enclose it for you. I am also forwarding Mother's letter to you. There were cold-cuts for dinner (veal and ham). It's now ten o'clock. The roses, now completely faded, are still standing on my table. I am curious whether you'll like my little poem ... And the tie is the colour of one little dress which I cannot think of without a sob (it greeted me with its little wool-wisps!), darker barely noticeable rhombi, silk. The house was noisy today: our landlady leaves tomorrow morning. The servants are exulting. Mymousch, hello!. ... love you. Good that you're taking lots of pictures. I would also like to take a lot off ... My joy, floridithy, owlthy, lovethy, my love ... The other day, as I was falling asleep, tiny word nightmares tormented me. Here's one: 'Popes pounced on poplars, the port where Rappoport rapped out a report.' I could not get rid of it. It sounds somehow ... ritual. Well, my happiness, time for bed. For some reason, I'm tired tonight. This poem will go to 'Rul''. I love you, my life.

V.

THE ROOM

Here's the room. Still half-alive,
but it will recover by tomorrow.
The mirrored wardrobe looks at me
without recognition, like lucid madness.

For the nth time I unpack my things,
get used once more to the keys' caprices,

and slowly the whole room quivers,
and slowly it becomes mine.

Done. All has been summoned
into my existence – every sound:
the squeak of the drawer that takes layers of linen
from my hands in its kindly maw;

and the badly locking window frame's
bang in the night – revenge for a draught;
the bustle of mice, their dwarfish din;
and someone's approaching step:

he'll never get entirely close –
like circle after circle on water, he moves
and falls away – and again I hear
how he sighed and moved on.

I turn on the light. All's quiet. On the quilt
falls a scarlet mound of light.
All's well. And soon I'll abandon
this room too, this house too.

I've known many such submissive rooms,
but if I look closer, I feel sad:
no one here will fall in love with, or remember,
the painstaking patterns on the wall.

This dry watercolour and this lamp,
in its old, see-through summer frock,

I too'll forget when I leave
this room too, this house too.

I will enter another: again the monotony
of wallpaper, the same armchair by the window ...
But I'm sad ... The less the difference seems,
perhaps the more divine it is.

And perhaps when we grow cold
and cross from life into a bare heaven,
we'll regret our earthly forgetfulness,
not knowing how to furnish our new home.

V. Sirin 22–VI–26

18–VI–26

Dear Véra,

How annoying that you have had such bad luck with the weather! It's just terrible! How can one get better this way. I am awfully sad, it's such a pity, I was really counting on this rest time for you. It's very hard on you. Our weather is also vile, we are bathing in mud everywhere. But I feel well in such damp weather; my asthma is completely gone. My daughters are starting their exams now, and Olga is very nervous. Her stomach is better, and she has recovered. Kirill's finishing his classes soon. At the start of July Ev. K. is going to France for 3 months. I am very happy for her, although it will be very hard to be separated from her for so long. But overall our life is hard, we still can't pay out our debts. We are all terribly worn out. E. K. and the girls send many thanks for the stockings, and K. for the trousers. They fit him perfectly and are very elegant. Our life here is monotonous, especially in such weather. All three of us sleep together, which is, of course, rather cramping for me. We haven't yet let out the rooms in Prague, but I am not losing hope. How is Slava Borisovna's health? How long will you be away? I was happy with Volodya's successes, but even more with his beautiful poems. It's a pity I was not there. If you can write, let me know how you're feeling.

I am kissing you lots.

With love, E. N.

Tender regards from E. K. and the girls.

[ALS, 2 PP.]

[23 June 1926]

TO: Sanatorium, St Blasien, Schwarzwald

[Berlin]

23/VI–26

Long bird of paradise with the precious tail,

In the morning I rode to the Grunewald and had a splendid swim there. I lay on the sand for an hour. (The sun is milky, but hot.) From there, for one, I went to the lesson with Mme K. She is trying very hard to convince you and me to go to Biarritz (they are going there on July 1st for five weeks). She says – rather sensibly – that, first of all, those 15 marks a month that I'd get there for the lessons with her and Sergey would be almost enough (given the franc's low conduct) for one person's keep – and that, secondly, along with expensive hotels they have very, very cheap boarding-houses there. Moreover I dare say I can convince Sack (whose school vacation begins on July 20th) to come along. All in all the only expensive thing is the trip (around one hundred twenty marks for two). So, if we have 150 (the trip) + 150 (your board) + 50 (miscellaneous expenses) + 150 (return trip) = 500 marks, then we could head off boldly, let's say, on the 20th (I could pick you up from St Blasien) and stay till the day when our money dries up. Of course as soon as the Kaplans arrive in Biarritz, they'll try to find a cheap little shelter for us. A journey like this could finish off your recovery wonderfully. The question is, how can we get 500 marks? Of course we could borrow them. In any event, my long bird of paradise, please ask Lena (if she gets back soon to Paris) if she could go to a little trouble for a visa for us (I don't know – maybe she can?); from my side, I will procure the passports, talk to F. and – even if we have to get in touch with Paris – we can manage this by the 20th. You know, the Tatarinovs have around 500 marks a month, 200 of which they give to the mother-in-law – and, all the same, they're borrowing money and travelling (to Italy). Why can't we as well? Meatballs and rhubarb for lunch. The landlady has left. I read after lunch, then went to play tennis – hit around for two hours. Came back and read some more. There were cold-cuts for dinner. It's now half past eight. My heavenly, please think about Biarritz. It seems possible to me. If I get the money for the translation of 'Mary', or if Sack agrees to go, too – then, of course, everything will work out. Write to Anyuta and E. L. for advice. Try not to look at this as if it were myth. My swimming trunks are drying on the windowsill. I forgot to find out from 'Rul'' today whether they are buying 'Odd'. Tomorrow I will call them before leaving for Sack's. The sky is ashy-blue, the gramophone is scorching out a foxtrot from the next window. Yes, it'd be nice in Biarritz ... Such a sea! And a Basque selling waffles on the beach. Huge waffles, like corsets. My love, I could finally feel the sun today. Off to bed soon. Will write to Mother too. I have fifty pfennigs left. I love you very much. Goodbye, my heavenly, my long one, with the dazzling tail and the little dachshund paws.

V.

[ALS, 2 PP.]
[24 June 1926]

TO: Sanatorium, St Blasien, Schwarzwald

[Berlin]
24/VI

Bushms,

This morning I met Sack at the Charlottenburg station. We wanted to go to the Dog Show – but it turned out it had closed. We strolled about in the thickets of Westend. I came back and called 'Rul''. The story will appear in the Sunday issue (the day after tomorrow). On Saturday morning I'll go to the 'Editorial Office' to correct the proofs. Hessen is delighted. The weather is cloudy, but dry (morning and afternoon). After lunch (liver and gooseberry jelly – a sort of frog caviar), I lay down and re-read 'Mary' (I liked it), and near four went to play tennis. I forgot to tell you yesterday that five strings broke as a result of a powerful serve. Fixed today. I played well. A charming borzoi with ash-blue (like yesterday's evening sky) specks on her forehead was walking near the pavilion. She was playing with a russet dachshund, and these two long tender snouts, prodding each other, were wonderful. At six, it began to rain (and it's still raining). On the way home, I changed a book at the library: I am reading two French novels at once, both in several volumes – according to Proust's system – but how petty and dull compared to his perfect artistry, depth, divine tongue-tiedness ... I get home – open the door – go in – look at the table – see – a little letter. What is it – where from – from whom? – I take it – open it up – and suddenly – something falls out! O, my sweet! Such a wonderful, wonderful picture ... I keep looking at it, and chuckling, and keep repeating: 'What a sweet beastie ... What a funny beastie . . .' And how nicely your legs are standing there. And some little bushes in the background. And for dinner, my Bushms, I had: fried eggs with potatoes and spinach, two pieces of ham, Swiss cheese and so on.

Before dinner, I read Martin du Gard. It's now half past eight. The rain is sprinkling at full force. My Bushms between bushes stands propped up by the cigarette carton in which two weeks ago I brought from the entomological shop a Berlin Hebe and a couple of Lapland *Brenthis borealis* (a variety of *pales* or *aphirape*–I do not know exactly). Bushms, it is too early to discharge you ... Wait a little, Bushms ... And a terrible thing you should think about Biarritz anyway has happened do think about it to the skiing pictures: they have warped from dampness (after all, they were on the dressing table by the open window), and won't stand up ... I have moved them it would be so marvellous on the beach there to the little yellow briefcase where your letters pile up. The Finnish president came to visit the Latvian one, and on this occasion, the 'Slovo' editorial repeats eight times within forty-six lines the words 'distinguished guests', 'our distinguished guests'. The toadies! It's a quarter to nine now–time for bed soon. Now it's ten to. Now five to. Nine. Good night, my Bushms. The little skirt is very nice–which one is that? *I love you, my own darling, my sweetheart, my life* ...

V.

[ALS, 2 PP.]
[25 June 1926]

TO: Sanatorium, St Blasien, Schwarzwald

[Berlin]
25/VI–26

My tenderness,

This morning Shura and I went to the Grunewald–since the weather is sunny; we swam there, ran around the lake just in bathing trunks, blissed out on the sand. A little old Russian lady came by and asked: 'Excuse me, this is not a male beach, is it?' (beach!). I came back for lunch (incomprehensible meat and a tart with wild strawberries) and hauled myself off to the Kaplans. They were still having lunch. Kaplan will advise Sack tonight to send his son with me to Biarritz. There was no lesson today because Sergey was having a tooth taken out. I went to tennis, played till half past six. On the way back, I exchanged a book and stopped by at Regensburger. They have your letters; Anyuta says: 'I am pleased with the letter. That's all I can say: I am pleased with the letter.' I consulted with E. L. about the trip to Biarritz: he's against it: the sea is not good for your health. I think, my tenderness, he's right. And he's right when he says you must stay in St Blasien till the first of August. I know how hard it is. But you need to get better ... He advised me to go to B. anyway – but I don't know, really. Without you, I don't want to. On the other hand, here, too, I'm not with you. What do you think about all this, my tenderness? Cold-cuts for supper as always – and macaroni too – and, too – one little letter. My softness, what a delicious sunset! I read your description, and – straight away – began to drool. As for the money ... I borrowed 5 more marks from Anyuta today, and borrowed more money so I can extend S. B.'s subscription tomorrow, when I'm at 'Rul''. They brought back my laundry yesterday (no, what am I saying: today), and it cost 3.85. I gave them another batch. I left my white sweater with Anyuta – to have the elbow darned. It's now half past nine. The sky is clear. Thank God. Oh, my tenderness, I keep looking at the photographie ... Did I write you that Bushms had sent me a photographie? It looks very like her. I will show you, when you come back. In today's 'Rul'' they say that Uncle Kostya has received an honorary degree from Cambridge Univ. I don't know whether he has received anything else, 'Mary', for example. In any case, his copy and Bunin's are lying very cosily next to each other in my bedside table.

Sweet, no? I'm all tanned from the bathing. Only the places covered with trunks – i.e. the upper legs and the loins – are pale. Not pretty, but it's original. And has my softness also got a tan? What a suntansch met me – in a terrible checkered coat – at the railroad station in Konstanz once! . . And here I am kissing you, my tenderness. I am kissing everything that could be called you, yours . . . Don't miss me, my tenderness. Do you want me to write twice a day?

V.

[ALS, 2 PP.]
[26 June 1926]

TO: Sanatorium, St-Blasien, Schwarzwald

[Berlin]
26/VI–26

Pupuss (a little cross between a puppy and a kitten),

I went to 'Rul'' this morning, corrected proofs. Hessen invited me to dinner. (The first half came out today; the second will come out on Monday, and then I'll send you both issues, my Pupuss. I have renewed the subscription for S. B. Maybe they will hold the delivery for these three days. But I have arranged for them to send every issue from the day (probably the 23rd) when 'Rul'' stopped reaching you. All the same, just in case, I'll send you the issues with 'A Fairy-Tale'.) While at 'Rul'', I have also agreed with Ludwiga that on Monday (when I come to proofread the second part (by the way, there are quite a lot of typos in the first one, since I made corrections in a very pale pencil)) I'll drop off the books for Bunin and Uncle K, to be sent to each of them. I returned home with a little book of poems by Shakhovskoy (he'd sent it to me via 'Rul''), read it: not bad at all – lucid darkness, coolness, excitement. I wrote exactly this to him and mailed the letter at once (to 'Blagonamerenny'). Then I replaced the inscription (I had to tear a page off) on the book intended for Uncle K, and instead of the idiotic inscription that had been there, wrote congratulations on the receipt of the honorary degree. Pupuss, I love you. Then I had lunch (rather good meat, plum compote), and sailed to Kaplan's lesson by three. Got back by five (rather chilly today; I am wearing the new grey trousers, the Norfolk, and the new tie) and, after a shave, took the underground to Hessen. Dinner there was absolutely delicious. Hessen flashed his bald spot, the golden rims of his pince-nez, and talked a lot, palpating the air with one hand. From their place, at nine, I took off to the Tatarinovs, where there was a rather boring lecture on Pirandello. Then I recited 'The Room', and ... well, the usual consequences. Next time, Volkovyssky will talk on émigré literature. We broke up late, I accompanied Aykhenvald, we talked about Russia. Pupuss, Pupuss, when will we return? It is quarter past two now, I'm a little tired. I forgot to tell you that I received a very puppypuppish letter. Puss, I beg you to stay longer in St Blasien ... You must understand, your health is more important than anything else. Pupuss, my sweet, my lightness, you really must ... Your father insists on it – and he's absolutely right. Pupuss, my joy, since you are there, make the most of it ... You must gain some weight too – to become at least like Anyuta. At least. If you love me – you will understand all of this. And I have decided not to go anywhere: I am closer to you here, after all. And I don't feel like travelling without you. Will you stay, Pupuss? And I have set up a dictatorship: Showen'ka and all the rest of the little ones have no right to vote ... Pupuss, the 'list of sufferings' has disappeared. And this, you know, is letter number twenty-five. I love you, my little one, my happiness. Good night. The day seems to be breaking. The sky is green.

V.

[ALS, 2 PP.]
[27 June 1926]

TO: Sanatorium, St Blasien, Schwarzwald

[Berlin]
27/VI–26

Mothling,

I got up late, took my time dressing, did lots of gymnastics. Veal and wild strawberries with cream for lunch. Then had a stroll. I looked over old lithographs and books in antique shops on Schillstrasse. Here's what I thought: what enchantment there will be in antique photographs! In 2126, let's say. A photograph two hundred years old–a photograph of a street with people in jackets and with automobiles ('jacket' will sound like 'jerkin' for us, and 'automobile', like, for instance, 'pyroscaphe'). There'll be terribly expensive photographs. There'll be collections of photographs costing millions. 'Will you come over to look at my collections of photographs from the beginning of the twentieth century?' 'With great pleasure.' 'Here, look: a street, automobiles, motorcycles.' 'Yes, but Mr X has an even older photograph: you can see a horse in it!' Composing such little conversations, I walked, my Mothling, past the splendid fountain near the Lukashes' old place, and admired the wet, glossy backs of the stone Tritons smiling through the gleam and quiver of the water trickling down. On the Hercules bridge I felt sorry for the poor lion, the restored part of whose tail was pale, naked, like a poodle's. I roamed on, deep into an alley in the Tiergarten, where now and again shadows lost consciousness whenever the sun vanished. After sitting on a bench for a while, I walked back along the same way, and on Schillstrasse a stout old woman all in black stopped me and asked me to help her across the street. I put my arm in hers, and with slow steps we crossed to the other side. I felt like a painting: '*The Boy-Scout or One Good Deed Every Day*'. When I got home, I read for an hour–while the 'loudspeaker' in the yard played wonderful dancing music. The violin-like languor of the saxophone, reedy pirouettes, the even beat of strings ... And then I dozed off—when I woke up it was already half past seven. The sky is pale-blue now, in melting little clouds—like on a ceiling with an allegorical apotheosis. And the jazz-band on the radio keeps playing—an idolized doggy-whining. Dinner: cold-cuts. And now I'm writing to you, my Mothling ... How are your wings and antennae, and all their little spots and their silky fluff? I'll go out again today to post the letterlet. My Mothling, my happiness, love ... How do you like this definition: a dream that one person has is a dream, a dream that two people have is semi-reality, the dream which dreams all this is reality. By the way, I have a wonderful title for a newspaper or magazine: 'Real'. You like? Mothling, what's it like settling on the flowers of St Blasien? My love ...

V.

[ALS, 2 PP.]
[28 June 1926]

TO: Sanatorium, St Blasien, Schwarzwald

[Berlin]
28/VI

My Rollikins,

In the morning, I washed, shaved, put on the new grey trousers and the dark-blue jacket and went to 'Rul'' to correct the second part of the little story. How do you like it? Not bad, to me. By the way, it turns out that there really is a Hoffmann street (Shura, of course, was the one who told me), only not 'past Kaiserdamm' but in Treptow. The books have been sent (a huge relief). From 'Rul'' I went to my lesson at the Kaplans, then came home, had lunch: a roulade and plum compote (not good . . .). Before three

I went off to Dernburgstr., played ball with Sh., ate wild strawberries and gooseberries in the garden, then–around six–we went to Zoo together, where I bought the '*Observer*'. There, your little sister fluttered up to me. What she was doing there I don't know. I left Sack, came home on foot, my Rollikins, read the newspapers. I am sending you a clipping from 'Slovo': an absolutely charming poem, the form and the substance are absolutely exceptional. I also bought 'Zveno', but they don't have my poems in it. On the other hand, Adamovich has given Mrs Papoushek a thorough scolding. Dinner: fried eggs and ham. Now it is five past nine. Rollikins, Rollikins, my heavenly creature, what's new with you? Will you be sensible and stay in St Blasien for twenty or thirty more letters? You know, sometimes it seems to me that only now do I understand <u>how</u> I love you and <u>how</u> happy we are together... My Rollikinsie. Save Perts' poem. It is so–fresh and Russian. Send me a letter in cipher one day (numbers instead of letters), I will enjoy deciphering it. Here you are, for example (in old orthography):

/22'/9'7'3'31'/ 15'17'21'17'18'7'17'/ 4' /13'11'18'26'17'/,
/2'1'17'/20'23'/27'11'13'19'32'/21'3'19'17'20'17'4'/1'20'17'33'4'/,
/20'23'/27'17'27'32'18'27'1'20'32'/9'33'26'19'3'21'28'16'3'/
/4'/6'11'18'26'29'/,
/27'6'4'1'23'/2'33'26'7'29'4'/19'3'13'33'7'28'/–/27'33'13'28'/
/27'13'33'26'1'33'4'/.

The apostrophes separate letters, the slashes, words. I am curious whether you will guess this (a specific number always corresponds to the same letter, of course). We'll see, my Rollikins. If you are good, I'll send you a new little game in every letter. And have another picture taken of yourself! There is a great demand for such goods here. My sweet, I love you ... I am going to write a little story. Or maybe a poem. Will I get a letterlet tomorrow? Is it sitting now in a railroad car, in the

схожу [illegible]. Ужиналъ: яичница и ветчина. Сейчасъ
пять минутъ десятаго. Катышокъ, Катышокъ, райское
мое существо, что у тебя слышно? Будешь-ли
благоразумна и останешься-ли еще на двадцать-тридцать
дней въ St. Blasien'ѣ? Знаешь, мнѣ иногда
кажется, что я только теперь понялъ ~~какъ~~ я люблю
тебя, и какъ мы съ тобою счастливы... Мой Катышенокъ.
Стихи [illegible] сохрани. Такіе они — свѣжіе, русскіе.
Пришли мнѣ какъ-нибудь шифрованное письмо (цифры
вмѣсто буквъ) мнѣ будетъ пріятно его разгадывать.
Вотъ тебѣ, напримѣръ (по старой ороографіи):

|22'|9'7'3'31'|15'17'21'17'18'7'17'|4'|13'11'18'26'17'|,
|2'1'17'|20'23'|27'11'13'19'32'|21'3'19'17'20'17'4'|1'20'17'33'4'|,
|20'23'|27'17'27'32'18'27'1'20'32'|9'33'26'19'3'21'28'16'3'|
|4'|6'11'18'26'29'|,
|27'6'4'1'23'|2'33'26'7'29'4|19'3'13'33'7'28'|—|27'33'13'28'|
|27'13'33'26'1'33'7'|.

Маленькіе черточки раздѣляютъ буквы, большіе — слова. Интересно
догадаешься ли (опредѣленная цифра отвѣчаетъ всегда той же
буквѣ, разумѣется). Посмотримъ, мой Катышокъ. Если будешь
хорошей въ каждомъ письмѣ пошлю тебѣ новую маленькую
игру. Ты-же еще снишься! Тутъ большой спросъ
на этотъ товарикъ. Милое мое, я люблю тебя...
Собираюсь разсказикъ писать. А можетъ-быть стихи.
Будетъ завтра мнѣ письмецо? Сидитъ-ли оно сейчасъ
въ почтовомъ вагонѣ, въ темнотѣ, между письмомъ отъ
госпожи Мюллеръ къ своей кухаркѣ и письмомъ господина
Шварца къ своему должнику? Тема для стихотворенія:
мы всѣ — письма идущія къ Богу. Или нехорошо?
Катышь, маленькій мой, такъ давно нецѣлованный... В.

heat, between a letter from Mrs Müller to her cook and a letter from Mr Schwarz to his debtor? The subject for a poem: we all are letters going to God. Or is that no good? Rollik, my little one, so long unkissed ... V.

[ALS, 2 PP.]
[29 June 1926]

TO: Sanatorium, St Blasien, Schwarzwald

[Berlin]
29/VI–26

My darling,

You haven't written for ages. You haven't written for ages. You haven't written for ages. My darling ...

In the morning I went with Sh. to the Grunewald; I swam and ran. Very warm and nice. On the way back, crossing that segment of the roadway on the corner of Luther and Kleist, where there's an orgy of repairs going on, I met the effeminate Prof. Gogel, who said to me: 'and you will play Pozdnyshev. Yes-yes-yes ...' Thinking that he had taken me for someone else, I smiled, bowed and went on. Lunch: meatballs with stuffed tomatoes, and excellent blueberry jam. Paid the bill (54.80–with milk). Suddenly the maid comes in: 'A lady to see you.' Enter a lady with a briefcase. 'Gräger sent me to you. I sell cigarettes. My husband, an officer, was killed by a firing squad in Kiev.' I took a hundred–feeling that I was terribly betraying our little man. Before three I went off to the lesson with Kaplan. Around five went to tennis. On the way, my darling, I bought some stamps, sent you the newspapers with the story, and bought tennis shoes as well (4.45). Tomorrow, I'll pay Anyuta back thirty marks. I played well. I returned at half past seven, had some cold-cuts. Found a letter from Aykhenvald. The Board of the Journalists' Union is organizing a 'Pozdnyshev Trial'. They are asking me to play Pozdnyshev. I have just written to Aykhenvald, accepting. This will happen at the end of July. *Comment tu regardes sur ça? Rien à soi?* ('Good grief!') My darling, when you stop writing to me, I begin to panic a little. Maybe you are angry that I asked you to keep putting on weight in St Blasien? All the same—I implore you. As for these cigarettes, they are all right. The tobacco, I think, is better than the Maykapar kind. I will buy a hundred less from the little man. My darling, I am the only Russian émigré in Berlin who writes to his wife every day. But I won't send you a little game today—because you've been bad. It is half past nine. I will go out to post the letters—to Dubnyak and to you; and then I'll go to bed. In the mornings, the acacia by the wall in the courtyard bathes in its own lacy shadow, which rocks back and forth behind it on the wall and through its leaves, and interferes with the movement of the leaves: acacia in a shady peignoir. But now, the window's reflecting only my head in a Rembrandtesque light and the orange lamp. I love, I love you, my darling, my happiness ... I am afraid to write that there will be a letter tomorrow, because every time when I write this, it doesn't happen. My darling, I love you. My flight, my flutter ...

V.

[ALS, 2 PP.]
[30 June 1926]

TO: Sanatorium, St Blasien, Schwarzwald

[Berlin]
30/VI–26

My little one,

Today is the last of the pages you marked. Tomorrow it will be a month since you left.

This morning I took my time washing and dressing, then sailed off to the lesson with Mme Kaplan. For the last time (till August) I explained to her that St *Joan* is not Apostle John, but a young girl with a Bubikopf and warlike inclinations. After that I had lunch: fish and red currants. Then I went for a haircut. In the middle of the barber's shop, on the tallest stool, wrapped in a sheet hanging down almost to the floor, sat a very little girl, her golden-yellow little head bent down, wrinkling her whole face, closing her eyes in horror, as the barber trimmed her fringe and then sprayed at her from a huge bottle. As for me, I left there with a round, youthful little head—and went to tennis. I was on top form today. The sun was scorching. About seven I came home, changed, and went to exchange a book, then called in at Regensburger. There I had dinner and composed, with your father, a telegram to you. Around half past nine, I took the underground to Potsdamer Platz (on the way there, I read 'Rul'' and now send you the clipping. Amusing, no?) and from there sent the above-mentioned telegrammlet. Walked home and ate a second dinner (cold-cuts—sausage predominating. Mustn't forget two eggs and the oatmeal and the strawberry compote to which, in the absolutely incorrect genitive case ('can the electric power of the particle "not" be so strong as to affect a noun two or even three verbs later?' Pushkin used to say), Anyuta treated me), thinking that it's been a while since I last ate Kohler cheese and looking at Bushms among the bushes. Already a quarter to eleven now—but I still need to write to Mother (and enclose twenty-five marks: more won't be possible, my little one). I will write S. B., too. I have given Anyuta the money back.

My little one, be patient for just a bit more ... It's true that you need to get better ... And then, you can't count those two weeks which you ruined with all your relocations. I know that it is hard, my little one, but—have patience. E. L. told us how Peltenburg, flying from Moscow to Kovno on an aeroplane, entered a dangerous layer of fog. Lyusya: 'Well, I would like to know, well, what did he expeerience at that moment, anyway?' Anyuta (tearing herself away from the spirit stove): 'In any case, he had more courage in him then than you just listening to this.' Lyusya: 'What? But still, it'd still be interesting to know . . .' Your father likes my 'Fairy-Tale', but he finds that I 'specialize in risqué subjects'. True, the story is a bit frivolous.

My little one, how are you doing? I love you. The sky is starry now, with a warm wind blowing. The roses, fossilized by now, are still standing on my table. A whole month! My little one, I am kissing you all over. There was a letterlet today. What's that about the little monkey?

V.

[ALS, 2 PP.]

[1 July 1926]

[To: St Blasien]

[Berlin]

1/VII–26

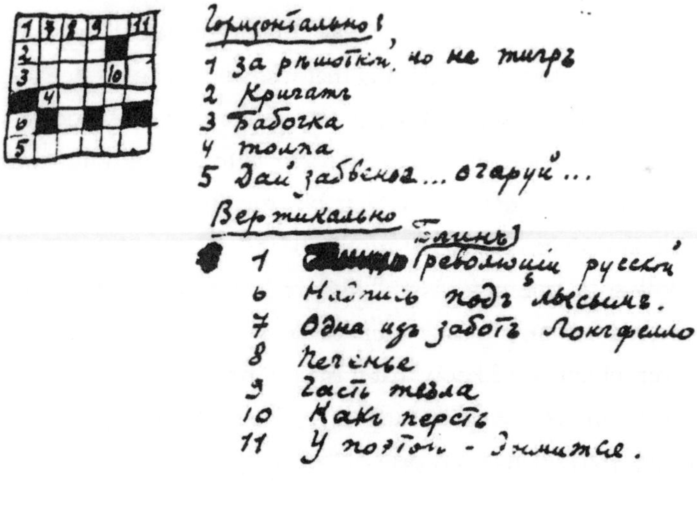

Across:

1 behind bars, but not a tiger
2 [They] shout
3 A butterfly
4 A crowd
5 Give me oblivion ... enchant ...

Down

1 The spoil of the Russian Revolution
6 An inscription below a bald man
7 One of Longfellow's cares
8 Biscuits
9 Body part
10 [...] as a finger
11 In poetry – it smokes

My Kitty-cat,

I forgot to enclose the clipping yesterday. Here it is. In the morning I met Sh. at the Charlottenburg station, we went to the Grunewald, but since the weather was very overcast, we didn't swim, just had a walk through the forest. On the way back, I got off the tram on Schillstr., – because a few days ago, I had noticed an entrancing purrypuss there – which I bought today. He is perfectly round, with a very sweet little snout and all in all no bigger than a grape. And he is intended for you. Only I don't know how to ship him – in a letter? No, he's too chubby for that. I'll consult with someone tomorrow and then send him. Only bear in mind that he is very, very sweet.

Had a veal cutlet and Regina Claudias compote for lunch, and a letter from Mother. She writes that she is very touched by all you write to her about Sergey. What exactly did you write? I had a lie-down after lunch, then changed and went to play tennis. On the way there I met Korostovets and on the way back I caught up with a gentleman walking and gesticulating strangely, mumbling something under his breath. As I passed him, I realized it was the actor Orlov. He was rather embarrassed at first and then started to chat about all kinds of nonsense. He told me that a couple of days ago he was invited to a private party to read my 'Fairy-Tale' to them, which is what he did ... I will be playing in a tournament next week. Bertman won a crystal carafe – I'm so envious. Ah, my Kitty-cat, I have just noticed that I have no more envelopes. I'll have to buy some tomorrow morning – before Sack – and write the address in the store. Annoying.

I got home around seven, read an idiotic French novel by the philistine Rosny jeune, then ate the usual cold-cuts. Yes, I forgot to write that (so as to get rid of Orlov) I had to stop at a pub, where I had a beer – and also bought a chocolate bar, which I had at home with some milk. Now a quarter past nine. I'll go to bed soon.

My Kitty-cat, I still do not know how you took our little telegram. You will find the promised little game, the *krestoslovitsa* (how gratifying to write a word I made up myself! It is almost two years old now) above. My Kitty-cat, send me another picture! Bushms is bored being alone ... And descriptions of butterflies you have seen. Mme Falkovsky took my poem 'The Room' to type up. It will probably come out on Saturday – I've already warned Hessen. My love, don't mope too much, keep adding your little pounds, a pound a day, so that by the time you arrive you'll have gained half a pood. My Kitty-cat ...

V.

[ALS, 2 PP.]

[2 July 1926]

TO: Sanatorium, St Blasien, Schwarzwald

[Berlin]

2/VII–26

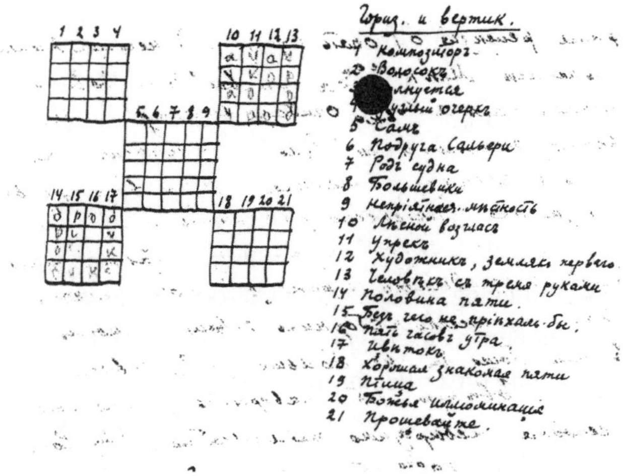

<u>Across and down</u>

1 Composer

2 A thin hair

3 Is waving

4 Roundish outline

5 Myself

6 Salieri's girlfriend

7 Kind of boat

8 Bolsheviks

9 Unpleasant locale

10 Sylvan exclamation

11 Reproof
12 Artist, compatriot of one
13 Man with three arms
14 Half of five
15 Wouldn't have come back without this
16 Five a.m.
17 Flower
18 Good acquaintance of five
19 Bird
20 Divine illumination
21 So long!

My love,

Right now a little dog is barking at an aeroplane: it's buzzing in its bass voice somewhere – the wall prevents me from seeing it – but the little dog is standing on a balcony and yapping at the sky.

This morning I had a great swim with Sh. in the Grunewald. A huge, hot sun. You squint at it, and a silver glitter trembles, a rainbow splinter. On the way back, I bought envelopes, ink (and, as always happens on the day I buy ink, I made a blot), sent off the letter. I had lunch (yes, I must let you in on a little secret: so far *I had my meals* either at the writing desk or – if I was working – at the bedside table. Both were extremely uncomfortable. But today one of the tenants left, and at last I got a comfortable table for *meals*. It's near the stove) – some kind of meat and wild strawberries – then went to tennis. I played so much and it was so hot, that I soaked through, like a mousch, and when I got back *I took a perfectly delicious cold bath*. Then I lay down for a while (Kaplan called: to say goodbye), thinking up a new little story. This will be an extensive review about (another ink-spill . . .) a non-existent 'literary almanac'. I think it will turn out to be rather amusing (have you noticed how deftly I'm skirting the puddle?), but it's not at all clear whether 'Rul'' will publish it. For supper – at the new table – I ate fried eggs and cold-cuts (here the word puzzle's showing through; I am curious whether you will solve it!). Now half past nine. *My love*, today is the thirtieth letterlet! Over sixty pages! A novel, almost! Had we published a little book – a collection of your letters and mine – there would have been no more than 20% of your share, *my love* ... I advise you to catch up – there's still time ... I love you unspeakably today. *My love*, the newspapers write that on the 29th, there was an earthquake across all of southern Germany – that 'houses shook' in Freiburg. Did you feel anything? When I was little, I always used to dream of an enormous flood: so that I could take a boat ride down Morskaya, make a turn ... Street-lamps are sticking out of the water, further on, a hand sticks out: I approach it – and it turns out to be Peter's bronze hand! *My love, do you miss me frightfully?* When you arrive, I'll meet you at the station alone – or not at all. In the 'almanac', there will be poems by a certain Lyudmila N., an imitator of Akhmatova. I will give you an example:

> I remember just your coldness
> and the diamond of the evening star.
> Ah, I won't touch up with mascara
> these tear-stained, wicked eyes of mine.

Amusing? And there will be short stories, articles ... But I don't want to talk about this in advance. *My love, I seal you with six kisses: eyes, mouth ... and the others I shan't tell you.*

V.

MY GREETINKS TO PUSS MINE TOO POOCH

[ALS, 2 PP.]
[3 July 1926]

TO: Sanatorium, St Blasien, Schwarzwald

[Berlin]
3/VII–26

Lomota, igumen, tyotka, Kolya, Maron
versifikator, Leta, chugun, tropinka
landysh, Ipokrena

Make ten new words out of the syllables of the words above, with these meanings: 1) A place where science meets ignorance 2) an engine 3) a city in Russia 4) a historic personage 5) a good woman 6) part of a cart 7) beatitude of the diaphragm 8) the first architect (see the Bible) 9) a lazybones 10) a woman's name.

My *grand ciel rose*,

This morning I went to the Grunewald on my own, lolled about naked on the sand from ten to one, then came back and had lunch (liver, apple purée). A postman arrived unexpectedly and handed me fifteen marks from one Lazarus (I suppose he is your student?). This was a godsend, since I had not a kopeck, and meanwhile the laundry had arrived (4.50) and the lady with cigarettes (2.50). But the little man, you know, has disappeared entirely! *A t'il eu vent de quelque chose?* I must tell you that I started to write this little letter around half past two; stopped; went to play tennis (again a beautiful heat). But around six there was a downpour, and I ran home *et je me regalai d'un bain froid*. I lay down for a while just in my bathing robe – and I suddenly noticed that the ink blotter which you, my pink sky, carried so carefully on that distant day, when we bought it, was still lying rolled up on the wardrobe.

I hurried to spread it out on the table, fixing it firmly in the corners with thumbtacks (*punaises*). Then I got dressed (everything new: the tie, the trousers, your shirt), and they have just brought me dinner. Stop.

I've had dinner: cold-cuts and macaroni. While I was eating, your dear, dear little letter arrived. 1) My little one, I beg you to hold out for two more little weeks or so … I can feel you getting better. As for the reason for your little fever – you know what it is, don't you … 2) I like Burns a lot, but do bear in mind that the line '*My dearest member nearly dozen*['*d*]' is extremely indecent. 3) I do not know exactly yet when I'll become Pozdnyshev. In any case, not before you get back. 4) The ciphered quatrain is 'I know coldly and wisely …' and so on. Great shame on you not to guess. I would have figured it out right away. I am sorry that my little games are not to your taste … I will send you one today, but not tomorrow … I have corrected my letter to Hanna – and I am refraining from reprimands …

Oh, my sweet, my own, eternally beloved … Such a sweet letterlet … How I love you … It's eight o'clock now. I have to get ready for the Tatarinovs. The rain has stopped. I love you. Stop.

I'm back. About two. The action took place at Kadish's, Danechka lectured on 'dance'. (Volkovysskу couldn't do it today). Tatarinov gave me an issue of 'Russkoe slovo' (Harbin) in which Aykhenvald's article about 'Mary' is reprinted in full. Delightful, no, my love? I have put it in the carton. I have eaten a lot of apricots, and I love you very, very, very much. And I forbid you to ponder whether I miss you or not!

The height of ignorance: to think that '*curriculum*' is Count Witte's little nickname. And at the soirée, one person there maintained that you can express anything through dance, that you can dance 'infinity'. I remarked that you couldn't dance without limbs. My darling, I am going to bed. It's rather late. I have been writing this letterlet in three steps. I love you, my Pussms, my life, my flight, my flow, darling pooch …

V.

[ALS, 2 PP.]
[4 July 1926]

TO: Sanatorium, St Blasien, Schwarzwald

[Berlin]
4–VII–26

Enter through A and exit through B
Labyrinthie 'Goat's Skull'.

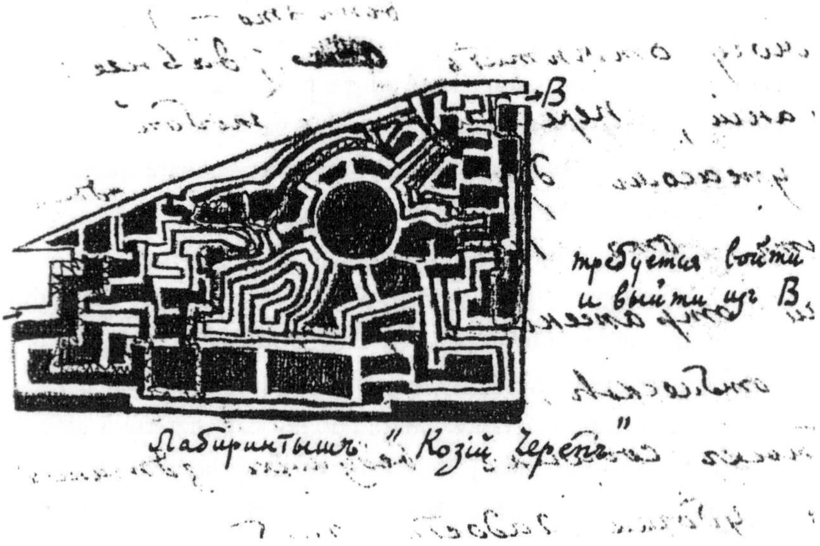

My darling,

There's been rain drumming down since morning – I went out only to post the letter, then spent the whole day at home. For lunch, there was veal gigot and apricot compote. The little cigarette man appeared – with a huge wet umbrella and terribly unshaven. I took a hundred from him. After lunch, I read, tried to write, but wasn't on form. Then I dozed off to the sound of the rain, and when I woke up – a pure blue sky was flying over the roof and in the puddles. Read again – and soon they brought dinner. Fried eggs and cold-cuts. Half past eight now. You see, my darling, what an interesting little day I've had. Maybe I'll go out for a little half hour stroll before bed . . . My darling . . .

My darling, I feel now especially sharply that from that very day when you came to me masked, I've been wonderfully happy, it's been my soul's golden age (ah, a clothes-moth is skipping over the page: don't you worry, it is not *pellonela* or *carpetiella*) and, really, I do not know what else I might need except you ... My darling, among the little side-wishes I can mention this one – an old one: to leave Berlin, and Germany, to move to Southern Europe with you. The thought of yet another winter here fills me with horror. German speech makes me feel sick – you can't live only on the reflections of street lamps in the asphalt – apart from these reflections, and blooming chestnuts, and angelic little dogs guiding local blind men, there's also all the squalid vileness, the coarse tiresomeness of Berlin, the aftertaste of rotten sausage, and the smug ugliness. You understand all this as well as I do. I'd prefer the remotest province in any other country to Berlin. My darling ...

My darling, I'm sending you a puzzle anyway today, too – a very sweet labyrinthie. I would have sent you a chess problem, if you'd had a chess set. You wouldn't be able to solve one on a diagram, would you?

Tomorrow is the Board meeting of the Union of Journalists (in the Liter. and Art. Circle) where we'll find out when the 'Trial' will take place, and the roles will be finally be assigned. (Aykhenvald is 'The Prosecutor'). All of this is rather silly, but its goal – to bolster the fund – is good.

I forgot to write to you yesterday: the Latin name of the cabbage white – *Pieris brassicae* L. (*Pieris* – is a pierid, *brassicae* is from *brassica* = cabbage, 'L.' is short for 'Linnaeus', who, in his 'System of Nature', first classified butterflies and gave Latin names to the most widespread). My love, I'm so pleased you're putting on the pounds. I love you utterly. I am kissing you, my head-spinning happiness, every little pound by itself . . .

V.

[APCS]

[5 July 1926]

TO: Sanatorium, St Blasien, Schwarzwald

[Berlin]

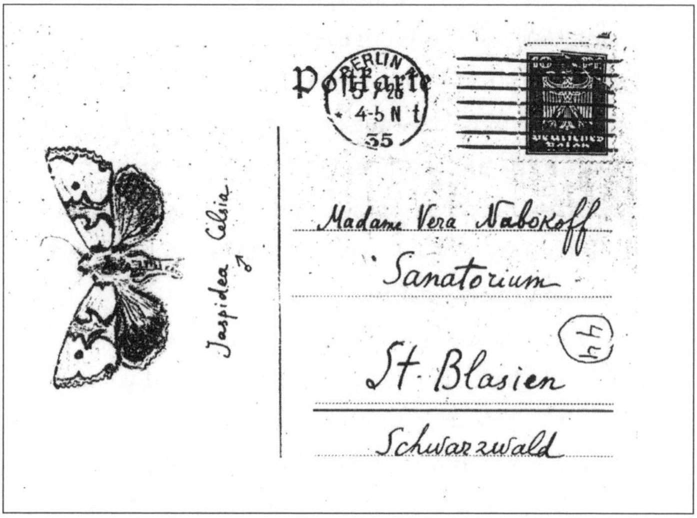

AEROPLANE

How it sings, how – unforeseen –
it flashed, a glassy spark,
flashed – and sings
there, above the roofs, in the deep
sky, where, with a shining side,
a cloud rises!

1926

On this peaceful Sunday morning,
its heavenly roar is a marvel,
    its thundering velvet . . .
And under a linden, by the grille
of a locked bank, a meek
    blind man listens.

Lips listen, and shoulders:
quiet human twilight
    turned all ear.
Unearthly sounds soar . . .
Nearby, his dog, from boredom
    snaps at a fly.

And a passer-by, money out,
frozen, head tilted back,
    watches as they glide,
wings, blue-grey, transparent,
through the azure, where big
    clouds shine.

V. Sirin
5–VII–26
noon

[ALS, 2PP.]
[5 July 1926]

TO: Sanatorium, St Blasien, Schwarzwald

[Berlin]
5–VII–26

A kind of epigram
on Aykhenvald

He judges nothing from above,
a lover of words and their beloved.
A Pushkin line hides in his name:
'The wide-noised oak grove . . .'

My Poundlets,

We received your exceptionally precious letterlet and are answering one point at a time. 1) Unfortunately, we are not endowed with any capital. At the moment, there are seventy three pfennigs in our pockets. We will talk to Anyuta, since we must pay for the shed tomorrow anyway. 2) About 'Rul'': in the letterlet of June 27th you write to us: 'Have you paid for July? Do not subscribe for August, because we have already subscribed from here.' Naturally, we immediately arranged for July. Your little letters, by the way, we know by heart. 3) We owe Anyuta only the old 29 marks. Tomorrow we will borrow 50 till the fifteenth. 4) We owe twenty marks to Tegel. 5) Gräger keeps mum. 6) We love you. 7) In those with holes.

I composed a new poem overnight, my Poundlets, and mailed it to you this morning. But I got up late: slept very little. Lunch: meatballs and chocolate jelly. I was half an hour late to Sack's (I had to be there at three o'clock) for the following reason: a husky Russian song rang out in the courtyard. I looked out. A short, stocky man was standing in the neighbours' courtyard – separated from mine by a fence – and was roaring 'Kalina' at the top of his lungs. Then he jerked his cap off and addressed the empty windows: 'And now you, brethren.' I put half a mark in a matchbox and tossed it. I hit the fence – the box, a little yellow square, still lay on my side of the fence. The man shouted that he would run around. I waited and waited, he didn't appear (later, when I returned, the little yellow square had disappeared. I hope he was the one who found it). Sh. and I went to play tennis. Around five, the sky turned black (I've never seen such a sheer black vista. Against that background, everything – houses, trees – seemed electrically pale) and such a downpour burst that in a few minutes the grounds turned into swimming-pools, where leaves, cigarette-butts, and even half a sandwich floated. We waited for ages in the pavilion, then ran across to a little pub (all this was happening near Kaiserdamm) and had a beer there. I got home looking quite wet – with 'The *Observer*' and 'Zveno' in hand (which I mailed to you. A comma there has ruined the first line of my poem). I had dinner (cold-cuts, fried eggs, a cold meatball) and then sailed off (after changing) to the Lit. Art. Circ., where they discussed the question of the 'Trial'. Apparently, they have no 'defence'. But they still hope to find him. My Pointlets, in 'Sovremennye zapiski' (Arbatov showed me this) there is an excellent large review of 'Mary' (by Osorgin) – one of the nicest reviews (I'll get a copy from 'Slovo'). And in the Warsaw newspaper 'Za svobodu' there is an exceptionally laudatory response to my reading at the Evening of Culture (I'll try to get this too). I got home at half past eleven and am now writing to you, my Kilogramling. You will soon be able to pack up for the trip back. Out of principle we do not write whether we miss you or not ... My Poundlets, my life ... Such a nice bee above the Arab's head! ...

V.

[ALS, 4 PP.]
[6 July 1926]

TO: Sanatorium, St Blasien, Schwarzwald

[Berlin]
6–VII–26

My dear life,

This morning (it was mother-of-pearly-overcast) I went to Sack's, read with him a story by Wells (about how a man, after an electric shock, had a very strange thing happen to his eyes: he saw an island in the antipodes – the seashore, the cliffs fouled by penguins – but only his eyes lived there – he soon realized that he himself was present where he had been before, in London, he could hear his friends' words, could palpate objects – but he saw only that shore and the penguins and seals, who, waddling, slid through him – and when he would climb, with his friends' help, up stairs in London, it seemed to him he was rising through the air, hanging over the sandy shore, over the cliffs). After reading, we ate gooseberries (like tiny soccer balls) for ages in the garden and then went for a stroll. I came home, had lunch (something like 'beef Stroganoff' and very delicious, sweet, fried eggs) and seeing the sun had come out, set off (with the 'Kreutzer Sonata') for the Grunewald. It was amazingly pleasant there, albeit crowded – and the water was awash with litter after the recent rains. A vendor walked by, carrying on his outstretched hand something like strings of colourful beads and shouting: 'a metre for a grosch'. This turned out to be – paper ribbons of hard candy! After about three hours in the sun I headed home, taking my time, on foot. In one place on the Hohenzollerndamm a house was being built. Through it, through the gaps in the brickwork, you could see foliage, the sun washed over the clean pine-smelling beams – and I don't know why, but there was some kind of antiquity, the divine and peaceful antiquity of ruins in the house's brick passages, in the unexpected pool of sunlight in a corner: a house, where life has not yet settled, looked like a house it had left a long time ago. And further on, in the depth of one of the side streets, an Oriental view – a real mosque, a factory pipe looking like a minaret, a dome (crematorium), cypress-like trees against a white wall and two goats lying on the yellow grass, among poppies. The enchantment was momentary– a truck dispelled it – and I couldn't reinstate it again. I walked further along, through Fehrbelliner Platz, where once upon a time, the big and beautiful one, along with the little ugly one, sat together on a bench – and through Hohenzollernplatz, where by chance I parted from such a dear, dear mask – in even more distant times. About distant times: in the Berlin 'Illustrated Newspaper' there's a reproduction of a drawing from a fashion magazine from 1880: the attire for lawn tennis. A lady is depicted standing somewhat sideways to the net (which looks like a fishing net), with the tiniest of rackets raised with such an affected movement – while a gentleman with the same affected racket stands behind the net, wearing a tall collar and a striped shirt. The lady is dressed thus: a very dark dress, a huge bustle, a belt strip around the lower part of her laced-up abdomen, a tight bosom and a row of countless buttons in the middle, from her chin down to her belly-button. A little foot on a high heel flashed modestly from beneath her fancy skirt, and, as I already said, the racket is raised – over a large wavy hat. In such a dress, probably, Anna Karenin (see the novel of the same title) played tennis. Shura and I saw this picture yesterday, when we were waiting out the rain at the pub – and we had a great laugh.

I carried on along Regensburg and stopped at Anyuta's. But no Anyutas happened to be there, and I sat down to wait for them in the not unknown café on the corner, where my last coins went on a glass of beer. Soon Anyuta sailed by (with packages) and I followed her. I sat with her for a while, had a little plate of raspberries, and arranged to stop by at the office tomorrow for some money. (Today I borrowed one mark from her.) Got home around eight, had dinner (cold-cuts and tomato salad). Mme Tatarinov phoned, told me that the funeral of Mme Usoltsev's mother will take place at Tegel tomorrow morning (it was a real tragedy: Usoltsev gave injections to his wife and his mother-in-law, and both developed blood poisoning. N. Ya. survived, but her mother died two days ago, after suffering for six weeks). Now half past nine. The sky is clear. It's warm. And I am writing to you, my dear life. My dear life, why don't you write me anything about your new acquaintance 'from Moscow'? Well? I am very curious ... Is he young and handsome? Well?

Stumpling, my sweet, I think, you'll come back in ten days or so. (But still, try to last till the twentieth ... It's very hard for me to tell you this, but truly, the longer you stay there, the better off you will be, my life.)

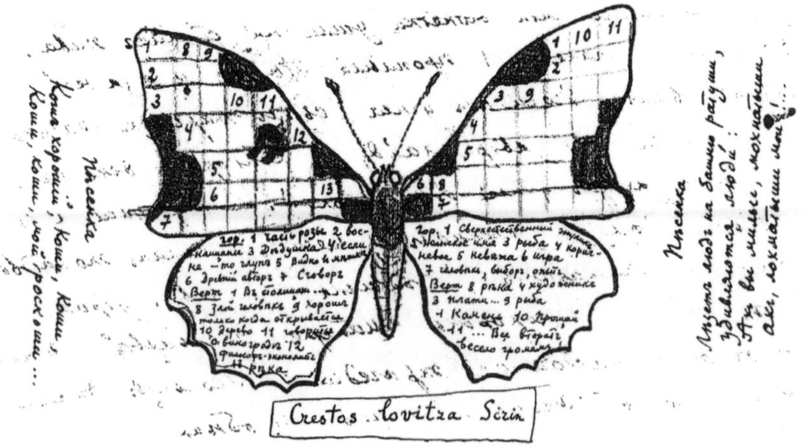

Isn't this a nice butterfly? I have struggled with it for two hours straight – but, after all, it's turned out nicely. My life, if you only knew how the cats are screeching in the courtyard! One of them screeches in a heartrending bass, another has a tormenting howl. If I had a revolver in hand at the moment, I'd've started shooting at them, I give you my word! This butterfly has really worn me out. My life, I love you. I read 'The Kreutzer Sonata' today: a rather vulgar little pamphlet – although once it seemed very 'powerful' to me. You will find a number of interesting things in the side compartments, too, my dear life.

V.

Acr. 1 part of a rose 2 exclamation 3 Grandfather 4 if not – then [he is] dimwit 5 can be seen in a sack 6 An ancient author 7 Accord
Down 1 In capital cities … 8 An evil person 9 Good only when it opens 10 a tree 11 said of grapes 12 a philosopher and economist 13 a river
Acr. 1 A supernatural trickster 2 woman's name 3 a fish 4 something brown 5 ruffian 6 a game 7 a man, a choice, and an experience
Down 8 a river 4 an artist 3 pay … 9 a fish 1 a rock 10 farewell 11 … All sings in cheerful tune with thunderclaps!

Crestos lovitza Sirin

A DITTY

Kit's so fit, Kitty, Kitty,
Kitty, Kitty, my splenditty.

A DITTY

Folk float up the town hall tower
flabbergasting folk:
Ah, my shaggies, how're
you, saggy-baggy sweet blokes?

[ALS, 2 PP.]
[7 July 1926]

TO: Sanatorium, St Blasien, Schwarzwald

[Berlin]
7/VI[I]–26

On Wednesdays, Mr Darling, the editor, has the day off, so there is no little puzzle today.

My sweet,

Today I've had a very pleasant day. In the morning, around ten, I rolled over to the Grunewald. It was overcast at first, then a marvellous shower fell, golden through and through (pierced with the sun), and after that the sun scorched to its utmost and I swam, did gymnastics, ran, lay about in the heat – till 4 o'clock! On the way back, I stopped in at the office and found your father there (he'd returned from Amsterdam this morning and is going, the day after tomorrow, to Bordeaux – and then back to Amsterdam via Paris), sitting in his office, looking very important in horn-rimmed glasses. Anyuta gave me (till the 13th) sixty marks and promised to send you something too. Awfully hungry, I returned home: they were all terribly agitated – believed I'd disappeared – they wanted to call the police. But they gave me lunch anyway: cold cherry soup (very delicious), meat swaddled in cabbage, and something that looked like sugar-frosted pineapple – this turned out to be turnip compote. And on the table, your dear letterlet was smiling its little white smile. My sweet, not 'ray mne', but simply 'op'yani', and, accordingly, not 'sukhari', but 'sukhar''. You want to know why 'arab' is Longfellow's 'concern'? But just remember this stanza from his poem: '. . . *and the cares that infest the day shall fold their tents like the arabs and as silently steal away.'* There you go! I will arrange everything – about the furs and 'Rul''. I solved your cipherlet without a key (I swear – es, double-u, ee, ay, er). *Same here, my sweet love...*

After I'd eaten I lay down and hit the hay for a whole hour. Woke up at six o'clock and went to tennis. At one corner, I saw two thick backs: Anyuta and Veryovkin, buying gooseberries from a tray. I played till eight. Had a magnificent shower, put on decent clothes, and around ten (after having dinner: sausages with potato salad, plus cold-cuts) set out for the Tatarinovs', for a meeting of the eight taking part in the 'trial', namely: Aykhenvald ('prosecutor'), Gogel (expert), Volkovyssky (second prosecutor), Tatarinov (representative of the press), Falkovsky (defence counsel), Kadish (chairman), Arbatov (secretary) – and little me (Pozdnyshev). Someone noted with amusement that there were the same number of Jews and of Russian Orthodox present. The 'trial' will take place no earlier than the middle of next week.

It's half past midnight now, my sweet, and I love you utterly. I am awfully glad at the thought that your weather is no doubt nice. My sweet, joy, love, my heart, my sweet heart, put on more pounds ... My elbow has completely healed from the sun – but this is temporary, of course. Kisses, my sweet, I kiss all possible and impossible little things – and then, very carefully – my Life!

V.

[ALS, 2 PP.]
[8 July 1926]

TO: Sanatorium, St-Blasien, Schwarzwald

[Berlin]
8–VII–26

Here's a new puzzle for you. But first an example, thus:

1	K	ai	r
2	u	ni	ya
3	d	e	d
4	a	d'	e
5	g	ashi	sh

In the first couplet I explain the whole—which is composed of the first and last letters of the given words (for ex. like here 'Kuda gryadesh'). Then, in a couplet, I explain the first word ('Kair'), then the second, and so on for all the words. Anyway, here's a puzzle like this for you.

THE WHOLE

A glade, a little hut among roses ... Bliss!
Here, my friend, we could have lived and thrived ...

1

A fruit wonderfully tasty, but no melon;
inside it, a Parisian goddess!

2

Great Tsar! Here's a denunciation concealed!
O, Tsar, look! here's an ear, and a nose.

Вотъ тебѣ новая задача. Сперва примѣръ, вотъ: ~~каиръ~~

1 | К аи р
2 | У нi я
3 | Д ѣ д
4 | А дь е
5 | Г аши ш

Первымъ двустишіемъ объясняю цѣлое — составленное изъ первыхъ и послѣднихъ буквъ заданныхъ словъ (напр. какъ здѣсь „Куда грядеши"). Затѣмъ объясняю двустишіемъ первое слово („каиръ) затѣмъ второе и такъ всѣ слова. Такъ вотъ тебѣ такая загадка.

Цѣлое

Поляна, домикъ въ розахъ... Благодать!
Вотъ тутъ-бы, другъ, и жить и поживать...

1

Плодъ чрезвычайно вкусный — но не дыня;
въ срединѣ-же — парижская богиня!

2

Великій царь! Здѣсь кроется доносъ!
О царь, вглядись: здѣсь ухо есть и носъ

3

Я въ нихъ ходить не очень-то люблю.
Предпочитаю хижину мою.

4

Копѣйка — входъ! Смотрите, шестипалый,
весь въ волосахъ, — но въ общемъ добрый малый

5

Тронь: острое! Я вижу, трепеща —
Толедо, ночь и блескъ изъ подъ плаща.

6

Не разъ царица оживляла ужинъ
уничтоженьемъ дюжины жемчужинъ.

Не трудно

Разгадай-ка!

3
I do not like to go there much.
I prefer my little hut.
4
Entrance one kopeck! Look, six-fingered,
Shaggy, but overall a good sort.
5
Touch this: it's sharp. I see, aquiver:
Toledo, night, and the gleam under a cape.
6
More than once the queen enlivened supper
by destroying a dozen pearls.

Try to solve this!

Roosterkin,

Ludwiga called me from 'Rul'' around nine in the morning: 'Come over, you have to do a translation into English for Hessen – a few lines. This is urgent.' Of course, I did not even think of going, since I had to meet Sh. around half past ten at Charlottenburg. And we met, and we went, my Roosterkin, to the Grunewald, where we had fun in the sun till one. Indeed, why not: the weather was wonderful, the sky – that blueness gone mad from the heat, and the sand, hot like cream of wheat. Still another shade of tan deeper, I came home and had lunch: veal cutlet and pudding with syrup. Then I napped for an hour and a half and went to play tennis. On the way back, I checked out a new book, came back and enjoyed a shower. I got a letter from S. B., very sweet. Thanks and regards. What did the doctor say on Wednesday? Then I had dinner – early, at seven – my Roosterkin, I ate fried eggs and the cold-cuts you know so well. After dinner, I flowed over to the Regensburgers and there had dinner all over again: salad with sour cream, an egg, tea with raspberry jam. Your father is leaving tomorrow. Anyuta, buying fabric with Sofa today, wanted to explain to Sofa why a fabric was no good, and for some reason, began to speak in dialect – so that the shopkeeper would not understand her. Lyusya sweated and coughed carelessly – spitting straight in my tea. Sofa demonstrated how tanned her arms were. Meanwhile, a sumptuous shower opened up, and I came home – at half past nine – under a borrowed umbrella and with a new, i.e. clean, Cambridge jersey under my arm (I am now wearing the grey pair and my new crêpe-georgette necktie). Overall, it was a very anyutish dinner – and I am mighty full now (besides, I am always full, don't you worry, my Roosterkin). The chambermaid here is very nice, but awfully familiar ('I'll tell Madame that you've gone out every evening' and so on) and nosey. It's now raining full tilt. With exactly the force of this downpour, with the same wet and sonorous force – I love you, my Roosterkin … I forgot to tell you that there is a letter for you from 'Lazarus', but there seems to be no need for me to forward it to you. I got a letter from Mother today: Olga was sick, she vomited, but everything's OK now. Sergey's friend has typhus. My sweet and multicoloured Roosterkin, don't rush your return too much, put on some more weight, Roosterkin … I suppose we'll never again in our life have such separations – but we do have to bear this one out to the end. My lovely, my warm little one, I can't tell you how piercingly and endlessly I think about you.

Good night, my Roosterkin …

V.

[ALS, 2 PP.]
[9 July 1926]

TO: Sanatorium, St-Blasien, Schwarzwald

[Berlin]
9–VII–26

Romans, satin, bufet, rama, lopukh
moshennik, zasov, tina, tishina
odinokiy, tura.

This is what you have to do: out of these eleven words (i.e. their syllables) make nine new ones: 5–Russian poets, 2–verse forms, a flower, a bird.

Kidlet,

This morning was overcast, I went to Sack's (by the way, he is going to take an extra 'class'–on Saturday. Shall I take money?), we ate gooseberries, read, then I went to 'Rul''. I cancelled the second copy. 'The Room' will come out tomorrow. Everyone congratulated me on the review in 'Sovr. Zap.' I came home on the top of the bus. Had lunch: liver and plum compote. I dozed for an hour, during which the sky cleared up. I looked out of the window and saw: a red-haired house-painter caught a mouse in his wheelbarrow and killed it with the stroke of a brush, then he tossed it in a puddle. The puddle reflected the dark-blue sky, quick black upsilons (reflections of swallows flying high) and the knees of a squatting child, who was attentively studying the little grey round corpse. I yelled at the painter–he didn't get what the matter was, took offence, began to swear ...ously. I changed and went to tennis. Played well: they all ...nted me. Unfortunately my left shoe began to gape: I will have to ...pairs tomorrow. And that's how things are, my Kidlet. ...hed, put on my black pyjamas, had dinner: fried eggs ..., the usual ham and sausage. Then I composed new 'magic words' for you and am now writing to you, my Kidlet. Twenty past nine. My adorable, your letterlets have stopped coming again ... I thought there would be one today, but no. I love you. I have lost count of my letters.

My Kidlet, soon the Apollo, *Parnassius apollo* L.,–a large white butterfly with black and red specks–must appear where you are. It flies above alpine meadows, its flight sluggish; early in the morning, it can be found sleeping on clover. If you see it–write.

My Kidlet, did you get my card with the new poem and drawing? I love you. I did not shave today–so my face crackles beneath my palm. I love you. Yesterday (as I walked to tennis), I bought a razor, matches and stamps at the new post office on Geisbergstr. (the Winterfeldt one has now shut down). I keep forgetting to stop by at the watchmakers'–and also–to call B. G. I love you. It is time to trim my nails again. I love you very much. My Kidlet, can you hear, I love you ... I need to buy a new writing pad. Love you. Good night, my Kidlet.

V.

[ALS, 2 PP.]
[10 July 1926]

TO: Sanatorium, St-Blasien, Schwarzwald

[Berlin]
10–VII–26

<u>For the month of June</u>

<u>Received</u>	<u>Spent</u>
288 Sack	55×5= 305 apartment
98 Kapl[an]	25+25=50 to Mother
27 my Life	25 Tegel
8 'Rul"	25 cigarettes

	10 laundry
	20 little things
——	——
421	435
	30 tennis
	——
	465
	10 *librairie*
	——
	475

They still owe me something at *Rul'* (not much).

On Tuesday, 13th I get 150. From that,
50 to Anyuta, 55 advance payment for the room (till 20th)
and 25 to Mother. (I don't have to pay
anything else for tennis).

Lovey,

In the morning, Sh. called off the lesson, so I took my time washing, shaving, dressing, then sat down to write. It was raining hard. Some oil got spilled in the courtyard puddle: at first, a huge steel-coloured oval formed, and in the middle, the most wonderful blot slowly bloomed, then slowly began to change colours. Imagine a continent on a map, where, let's say, mountains are of a glorious purple colour that turns tender-lilac at the edges, where wooded areas are marked by a malachite tint, plains are pink and plateaus orangey. Then, my Lovey, these colours slowly began to fade, the whole blot took on sandy and brownish tints, as if the vegetation had dried out and the continent had turned into a desert. But green and pink knots continued to linger here and there for a long time, so that the puddle looked like a huge dullish opal.

At first I wrote my 'review' (seems to be turning out entertaining), then got started on 'Pozdnyshev's speech' (I don't know how it'll turn out). They brought me the laundry – 4 marks (incidentally, I have to change my shirts almost every day – I'm sweating awfully). Then there was lunch: thick-skinned sausage and apple purée. The cigarette lady arrived. My aunt Wittgenstein was her husband's godmother. I sat down to write again. Received a letter from Véra Nabokov (she is quietly surprised at her husband's financial genius). Meanwhile, the weather cleared up, the acacia put on its shadowy peignoir. Yes. I also received a telegram from S. Kaplan from Biarritz, saying the following: 90 Pension Lefevre *cheaper possible too*. Ninety francs seems to be about nine marks. I carried on writing, then went to the library to get a new book. Ah, I must write out for you an enchanting bit from '*Le Martyre de l'Obèse*', – the love adventure of a fat man (a very talented book by Henri Béraud). Looking at his obesity: '*. . . mon tailleur ébahi en avalait ses épingles. Sans compter que mon cas épuisait ses euphémismes.*

– Monsieur est un peu fort, disait-il tout d'abord.

Puis il changea:

– Monsieur est fort . . . Monsieur est très fort . . . Monsieur est puissant . . .

Puissant, il s'en tint là. Après cela, il prit mes mesures en silence, comprenant, soudain, que d'un adjectif à l'autre, il en viendrait bientôt à me dire: "Monsieur est formidable . . . Monsieur est phénoménal . . . Monsieur est répugnant . . ."

Funny, don't you think? You can read it when you come back.

Cold-cuts for dinner. Now I am going to the Tatar., where Aykhenvald's talking on 'vulgarity'. You know all the ladies. Ah, do you know what just happened? I found Mr Darling (the editor of our 'puzzle' department), so tiny, in a wrinkled little frock-coat, sobbing in a wastebasket. I ask him: 'What's wrong, Mr Darling?' He sobs. I don't understand who could offend him so … Maybe you know? … I am mailing the letter now, so you'll get it sooner. Lots and lots of kisses and hugs, my Lovey.

V.

[ALS, 2 PP.]
[11 July 1926]

TO: Sanatorium St Blasien Schwarzwald

[Berlin]
11–VII–26

NIK. SEROV	E. T. IVANOV-SIRIN	M.M. SUKOTIN
How much older or younger than I is he?	What is his favourite aphorism?	Why does he write his last name without a hard sign?

Tigercubkin,

I'm out of letter-paper – I have to write on lined sheets and I can't range free.

This morning it poured. Oh yes: I haven't yet written about last night's meeting. So: Aykhenvald spoke delightfully but not convincingly on metaphysical vulgarity (proving that since man is 'divinity's original trait' and matter's supreme achievement, he falls rather between two stools – this is now my image – between the stool of matter and the stool of spirit, i.e. he is the golden mean, i.e. mediocrity, i.e. vulgarity. Man is doomed to vulgarity. There were also comparisons to Tyutchev's 'water-jet' and Derzhavin's 'god-worm'.) Raisa and I composed questions for the 'questionnaire', which I am sending you with a request to fill it in. By the way, before I forget: I have changed the last three lines of 'Aeroplane's' second stanza. It should read: 'And by the park grille, in his usual place, a meek listener, blind.' The 'bank' was doing nothing. So this morning, my Tigercubkin, it was pouring, and I decided to stay at home all day and write. By six o'clock, I finished the Pozdnyshev speech. Around two (lunch was as follows: veal and Claudia Regina compote), the little man stopped by – I took a hundred. The leaves on my acacia are already turning yellow and falling down, covering the ground with their golden tongues. But after the rain, a huge puddle gathered them up; some huddled together by the gutter grating, forming a brownish-yellow spot that looked like the slightly browned edge of an omelette. I read for a while, then had dinner: fried eggs and cold-cuts. Now it is ten to nine. Wonderful pink feathers of parallel clouds have just died out in the matt-blue sky – the ethereal ribs of heaven. The Pozdnyshev speech is my idea throughout. I will send it to you as soon as I read it out (my sweet, this will take place on Tuesday – I cannot tell you – and I should not tell you – how much I'd like you to be at that 'trial' . . . My sweet, only when you come back will I tell you how endlessly I longed for you – but now you should not know this – 'I am having a lot of fun without you' – and you must get a little better still. My sweet, the ginger little briefcase of mine gets fatter along with you – a poundlet for you, a letterlet for it. But the roses have disappeared off my table: they lasted there more than a month. For some reason I have been thinking now that life is the same kind of circle as a rainbow – but we can see only part of it, the colourful bow. My sweet . . .)

V.

<u>A questionnaire</u> for the immodest and curious
(not obligatory for anyone)

1. Name, patronymic, last name
2. Pen-name, or a preferred pen-name
3. Age and preferred age
4. Attitude to marriage
5. Attitude to children
6. Profession and preferred profession
7. What century would you like to live in?
8. What city would you like to live in?
9. From what age do you remember yourself; your first memory
10. Which of the existing religions is closest to your world-view
11. What kind of literature do you like the most? What literary genre
12. Your favourite books
13. Your favourite art
14. Your favourite artwork
15. Your attitude to technology
16. Do you appreciate philosophy? As a form of scholarship, as a pastime
17. Do you believe in progress
18. Your favourite aphorism
19. Your favourite language
20. On what foundations does the world stand?
21. What miracle would you perform if you had a chance
22. What would you do if you suddenly got a lot of money
23. Your attitude to modern woman
24. Your attitude to modern man
25. What virtue and vice do you prefer and disapprove of in a woman?
26. What virtue and vice do you prefer and disapprove of in a man?

27. What gives you the keenest pleasure?
28. What gives you the keenest suffering?
29. Are you a jealous person?
30. Your attitude to lies
31. Do you believe in love?
32. Your attitude to drugs
33. Your most memorable dream
34. Do you believe in fate and predestination?
35. Your next reincarnation?
36. Are you afraid of death?
37. Would you like man to become immortal?
38. Your attitude to suicide
39. Are you an anti-Semite? Yes. No. Why?
40. 'Do you like cheese'?
41. Your favourite mode of transportation
42. Your attitude to solitude
43. Your attitude to our circle
44. Think of a name for it
45. Ideal menu.

[ALS, 2 PP.]
[12 July 1926]

TO: Sanatorium, St Blasien, Schwarzwald

[Berlin]
12–VII–26

My unending love,

Today I don't feel like telling you how I rode to the Grunewald, how I had lunch, how I played tennis, how I read my 'speech' at the committee meeting (praise and more praise ... I am beginning to get sick of it: it even went as far as them saying I was 'subtler' than Tolstoy. Terrible nonsense, really) – I don't feel like telling you about all of this today, because I only want to say how I love you, how I wait for you. There won't even be a little puzzle today: Mr Darling has asked me to let him go to the Zoological garden, on business (little Show's aunt was delivered there; he doesn't know this yet. A terribly complicated and sad story. I will tell you the details some time). I don't want anything, anything in this letter, except my love for you, my happiness and my life. When I think how I will soon see you, hold you, I feel such excitement, such wonderful excitement, that I stop living for a few moments. During all this time I dreamt about you only once, and even then, very fleetingly. When I woke up, I couldn't remember the whole dream, but I felt there was something very lovely in it; like when you sometimes feel, without opening your eyes, that it is sunny outside – and then unexpectedly later, near evening, thinking again about the dream, I suddenly understood that the lovely, exciting thing that was hiding in it was you, your face, your very movement – flashing through my dream and making of it something sunny, precious, immortal. I want to tell you that every minute of my day is like a coin with you on the other side, and that if I hadn't remembered you every minute, my very features would have changed: another nose, different hair, another me, so that simply no one would have recognized me. My life, my happiness, my sweet marvellous creature, I implore you for only one thing. Arrange it so that only I am there to meet you at the railroad station – and more than that, that nobody knows that day that you've arrived – and announce yourself only the next day. Otherwise everything would be spoilt for me. And I want you to arrive very plump, and perfectly healthy, and perfectly untroubled by all sorts of silly, practical thoughts. Everything will be all right. My life, it is late now, I am a bit tired; the sky is irritated by stars. And I love you, I love you, I love you – and perhaps this is how the whole enormous world, shining all over, can be created – out of five vowels and three consonants. Good night, my joy, my unending love. I'm thinking now how you suddenly shudder when you fall asleep – and about much more, about the one thing that cannot be expressed by words.

V.

[ALS, 2 PP.]
[13 July 1926]

TO: Sanatorium, St Blasien, Schwarzwald

[Berlin]
13–VII–26

Mousie,

This morning, I Grunewalded with Sh., then on the way back had to make a few purchases: postage stamps, tennis shoes, 'Sovremennye zapiski' (which I will send you tomorrow morning – or maybe I shouldn't? Since you're coming soon, my Mousie, my sweet love . . .) I stopped by at the office – paid my debt to Anyuta (I still owe her 27 marks (the oldest), but I will pay ten more on Saturday (I'll get it from 'Rul'')). For lunch: magnificent blueberry soup, cold, and a veal cutlet. Then I went off to play tennis – and played rather poorly. I returned, sponged myself down, read till dinner (cold-cuts) and around nine sailed off to the Gutmann Saal. I wasn't wearing a tuxedo (it seems somehow inappropriate for a defendant to be in a tuxedo), but I had on my dark-blue suit, cream shirt, and greyish tie. Quite a crowd (Anyuta should have been there, but didn't show up for some reason), they played the *presto* from the Kreutzer Sonata (by the way, Mrs Shor and her husband besieged me – they very much want us to visit them; I had to give them our telephone number), then we sat down in this order:

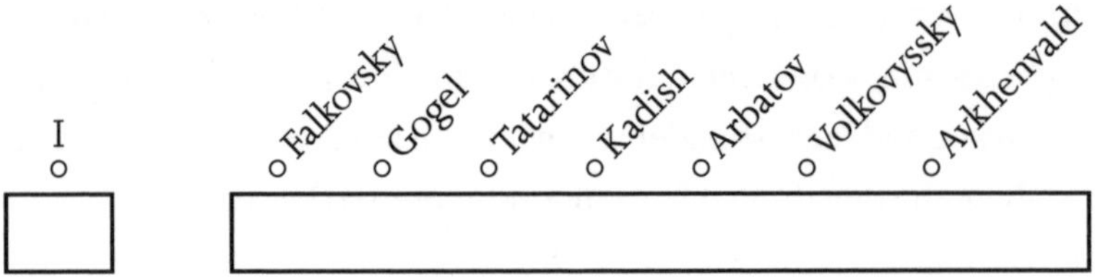

I was at a separate table, to the right of the main table. Arbatov read the indictment – rather poorly, Gogel – the expert – talked about crimes that can be forgiven – then the chairman asked me a few questions, I got up, and without looking at my notes, by heart, delivered my entire speech (which I am sending you). I spoke fluently and felt I was really on form. After that the case for the prosecution was given by Volkovyssky (who said: all of us, when we visited prostitutes . . .) and Aykhenvald (who said that Pozdnyshev committed a crime against both love and music). Falkovsky defended me – very well. Since I gave them a Pozdnyshev completely different from Tolstoy's it all turned out rather amusingly. Then the audience voted – and now I am already writing from jail. My Mousekin, when will you arrive? A roundish, very sweet purrypuss is waiting for you. I was afraid to mail it – they could have broken off his little feet. My Mousie, why don't you write to me? It's late now, I am terribly thirsty, I'm drinking all the time. Tatarinov and Aykhenvald are going to Wannsee tomorrow, they have invited me – but I don't know yet whether I'll go. My sweet, my joy, my life . . .

V.

[ALS, 2 PP.]
[14 July 1926]

TO: Sanatorium St Blasien Schwarzwald

[Berlin]
14–VII–26

Puss, Pussycat,

My adorable love ... Today about eleven we went to Wannsee. The Tatarinovs, Aykhenvald, Gurevich (a remarkably well-educated gentleman, my classmate at Tenishev), Danechka, Mlle Ioffe, and Tatarinov's former pupil – a plump, freckled, giggly girl. In general it was rather boring, but I sweetened the boredom by spending half of the time swimming – alone – and the other, talking to Aykhenvald. He is such a charming, gentle person ... By the way, the Prague Slonim is his nephew, so I am distantly related to him! The weather was delightful. Gurevich brought along two bottles of Sauternes; I've got even more of a tan. I was home around nine, had dinner (cold-cuts), and am now writing to you, my adorable love. How are you, do you love me, are you coming back soon? – after all, I don't know anything ... It is a mystery for me why you do not write, *mais je ne t'en veux pas* – if you don't feel like it – don't write: I love you in any case. My darling, the Tatarinovs' idea of an 'Ausflug' is sitting in a café. That's what they all did, but I went swimming, and Gurevich brought me, into the water, one glass of white wine after another. We rode the steamboat a few times and came back on the top of the bus, getting off at Zoo. I forgot my keys (i.e. I simply did not take them with me, because I left without a jacket, in white, I'd only brought along your speckled jumper, which I put on towards evening), and Mme Tatarinov called my place so they'd open the door for me. All this pleasure cost me around three marks. Was it fun? No.

Pussycat, I am sending you a clipping, an article from '*Observer*' about the discovery of Christ's appearance: 'A man of middle size, with a stooping back and a long face, a prominent nose, and with brows which grew together, with thinnish hair, but parted in the middle . . .' All of this is rather convincing, I think – and very interesting.

I must tell you one thing ... Hear me out attentively, try to consider it carefully, to understand it to the end. Maybe I have already told you this, but, just in case, I will tell you again. Pussycat, this is very important – please – pay attention. There are many important things in life, for ex.: tennis, the sun, literature – but this thing is simply incomparable with all of them – it's so much more important, deeper, broader, and more divine. This thing – Besides, there is no need for such a long foreword; I'll tell you directly what the matter is. Here: I love you.

Pussycat, Puss, yes, I love you, I'm waiting for you unbearably. And there is still another thing that I want to tell you – and this thing, please, you should also listen to carefully and remember well. I want to tell you ... No, please, consider it well – I want to tell you that I: love you without end.

V.

[ALS, 2 PP.]
[15 July 1926]

TO: Sanatorium, St Blasien, Schwarzwald

[Berlin]
15–VII–26

MAGIC WORDS

Tolpa, **stoy**ka, **chekh**arda, **ov**china, **go**ra, shcho**gol'**, podagra, biryuza, zanoza, Kain, gonchaya, gosudar', rama, mayak, sila, Minsk.

You musht täk zees zekshtain Wödz und tön zem into fortain azers, ze Meanink off witch ees: 1) russisch Rayter 2) ze saym 3) ze saym 4) a Paat off ze Sfinks 5) ze saym 6) a Trea 7) a Böd 8) a Paat off Veemin's Kloseez 9) Moofemint 10) Immobeelitee 11) Holeedai 12) a Kliff gloreefaid bai Puschkeen 13) Nekrazoff's Heeroeen 14) a schmoll Houl. Rezpektfulee, DARLINK

Fire-Beastie,

This morning, Sh. and I went to the Grunewald, the sun was wonderful, we sunbathed and swam for three hours. I came home (Mr Darling has got completely carried away – he wants to write this letter himself instead of me, he's jerking the pen out . . .), had lunch: schnitzel and apple compote. Imagine, Fire-Beastie, the whole façade of the house is covered with scaffolding, and today the workers have got into the courtyard too. I looked out the window – a ladder had serenely grown up there. There is chatter and clatter down below, they have piled up bricks, plaster is falling down, boards are clacking. Very jolly. Despite the noise, I had a lovely nap for an hour, and at four went to play tennis. It was unbelievably hot playing. I KAMM HOMM (I got up for a drink of water, and Mr Darling immediately seized the opportunity – quite intolerable!)

I came back home and found your precious letterlet. Mr Darling is asking me to SAIEE (no, don't grab, – I won't let you anyway!) that the artist is KORRO (Corot) which means that the 'exclamation' should be 'koo-koo'. In the 'myself' box there should be 'Sirin'. The butterfly wings are correct. Only one box is correct (ruka, udod and so on). And here is the acrostic:

A	nana	S	
N	avukhodonoso	R	
G	ost	I	*(angulus rides)*
U	ro	D	
L	ezvi	E	
U	ksu	S	

You've solved the 'magic words' well. After reading your letterlet, my Fire-Beastie, I began to wash myself in the *tub*, and at that moment the workers burst through the window and began (after some good-natured apologies) to fix the boards outside my windowsill. I continued to sponge myself placidly, then did gymnastics. They left after five minutes. I had dinner: fried eggs and cold-cuts. I was so thirsty that after dinner, I went to a café in Victoria Louise Platz and had a beer there, while Mr Darling (by the way, he has fallen asleep now, so it's much easier to write) composed these 'magic words' there. He insisted that I copied their 'meanink' exactly the way he pronounces it – but, between you and me, he lisps. The puzzle, however, is very difficult.

Got back at nine, and here I am writing to you, my Fire-Beastie. I am waiting, waiting, waiting for you. I can't keep you in St Blasia any longer. My happiness, my life ... It is very muggy – I'll get another drink of water I VOSS PREETENDINK TO SHLEEP MY GREETINKS DARL –

ah, he's unbearable: he tricked me again. My sweetheart, good night. Love you very much.

V.

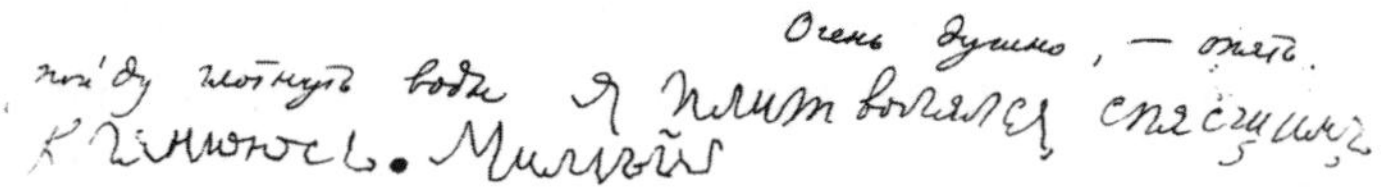

[ALS, 2 PP.]
[16 July 1926]

[To: St Blasien]

[Berlin]

You must find in this person

1) another face
2) a mouse
3) a bunny
4) a chick
5) a pony
6) Mrs Tufty in a new hat
7) a little monkey

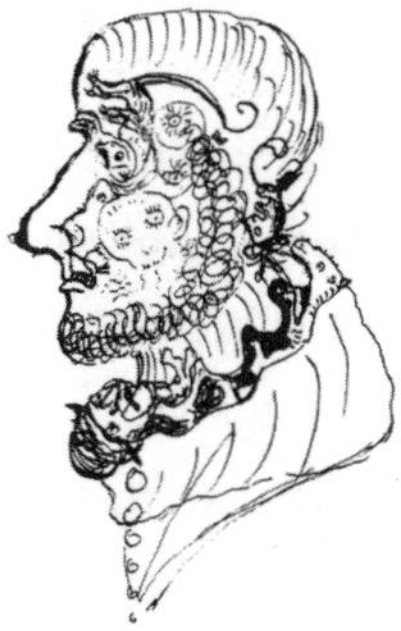

16–VII–26

My love,

This morning I went to the Grunewald with Sh., came home (the room's dark from the scaffolding, there's banging non-stop, unbearable), had lunch: liver and cherry compote. I had a lie-down (luckily, the stonemasons had left for lunch) then sat down to write. I didn't get anything done, though, because the work started up again, bits of plaster were crashing down from above, hitting the glass. The main thing's that I can't get them to tell me when this wretched work will be over, when they'll take the scaffolding down – I even think about moving (of course, if this lasts two or three days more, I can stand it. I'd prefer to stay here). It's a tiresome story all round. But the weather is wonderful, a cloud of fragrance under every linden, marvellous. And soon you'll be here, my love (only not in this room – if these nasty boards aren't taken off by then), you'll be here soon – that's such happiness I don't even know how I'll survive it ... Dinner: the usual cold-cuts, cheese, radishes. Nine o'clock now. In 'Sovremennye zapiski' there is a magnificent story by Bunin and a not-bad excerpt from Aldanov's verbiology. And an enchanting ballad by Khodasevich too. Perhaps I will send you the journal, after all – only I don't know how. I'll call in at Anyuta's tomorrow and decide with her. My love, when you arrive, I'll scold you terribly because you write to me so rarely and I'll boast terribly that I've written to you every day. Have you filled out the questionnaire? I've already done it, and tomorrow night, at the Tatarinovs', the answers will be disclosed. My finances are crying out. So, my love.

Kisses, my love, from your eyebrows down to your knees and back. What do you think of Mr Darling's work today? I don't think much of it, but I don't want to offend him. I badly need socks and eau-de-cologne. But I somehow always have plenty of shirts. My love, how about us going to Czechoslovakia for a week? Stars have already appeared between the boards. Good night my love. Terribly hot for sleeping. I sleep without pyjamas – and it's still hot. Love you.

V.

[ALS, 2 PP.]
[17 July 1926]

TO: Sanatorium, St-Blasien, Schwarzwald

[Berlin]
17–VII–26

Pussycat,

(the little critters seem to be repeating themselves, but I don't have a list of those I've already deployed, so not much I can do about this). This morning it smelled of turps, because the painters were spreading a reddish paint, sparkling in the sun, on to the balcony railings to the left of my windows. I dressed all in white and went to my lake. The sky was cloudless and covered me with another layer of tan. There I bought and ate a large, warty, crooked pickle. A man with an arm tattooed to his elbow was toting them around in a bucket, screaming: 'Sauer-jurken, sauer-jurken!' I came back, had lunch: meatballs and a nameless jelly (and clotted cream, left over from yesterday's milk). Then I wrote a letter to Mother, then sailed off to tennis. The heat was awful. I came back around six, treated myself to cold water, had a lie-down. In 'Rul'' there is a review of the trial performance. Raisa wrote it – and wrote it very nicely. I sailed off to Regensburg – wanted to have dinner there, so as to go to the Tartars' straight from there, but the landlady – looking, by the way, like an old gopher – informed me that no one was home. I wandered (I am wearing today, *faute de mieux*, lacework dance socks) through the evening streets, smoked in a public garden and, taking my time (around half past eight) set off for the Tatarinovs', where Gurevich was reading a long and rather entertaining paper about contemporary painting (the reading of the questionnaires will be on Saturday). The Landaus were there – she was wearing an utterly amusing dress made of a variety of patches: pink, white, lacy, with asymmetrical flower embroideries. Her little bird-like head with grey sausages of curls falling down her neck from behind was also very comical – but the most comical of all were the cape she put on when she left and the tall raspberry-coloured hat, like a layered helmet. A little old medieval fairy – take her or leave her. As for the question, 'What is your most memorable dream?' both Gurevich and I happened to write the same thing: Russia. Got back late – and although I'm very tired, all same (as Golubev says) I'm writing to you, my Pussycat. You'll be back soon! You'll be back soon! Mr Darling is already asleep, so there will be no little puzzle tonight. You'll be back soon! I love you. I'm waiting for you. My Pussycat I love you ... And why don't you write?

V.

[ALS, 2 PP.]

[18 July 1926]

TO: Sanatorium, St-Blasien, Schwarzwald

[Berlin]

Magic Words

Out of the seven days of the week and the words: lono, evrei, Sinay, parodiya, make 13 words with the meanings:
1) can't be divided in half 2) shrub 3) engine 4) rule over 5) what religion takes from entomology 6) dethrone! 7) the sun has them 8) fighter 9) undertaking 10) assistance 11) centre 12) part of the world 13) parts of a boat

18–VII–26

Puppykin,

The Tatarinovs organized another outflight today, but I refused to go, called them this morning to say I couldn't. I dressed late, I really wanted to sleep on. Had lunch: beef with green peas and Claudias – and by half past two I was already in the Grunewald, where I stayed till six. I came back, had dinner: fried eggs and cold-cuts – then put on my bathrobe and here I am writing to you, Puppykin. Raisa informed me today on the phone that she'd had a photograph from you (and was very touched by it). You seem to write to everyone except me. Is this fair, Puppykin? By the way, do you remember Baratynsky's verse:

> I have given her, out of affection,
> a capricious name,
> the fleeting creation
> of my childish tenderness –

– I'm not sure that the first two adjectives are correct and I can't remember the other stanzas. Do you? Quiet today, the painters and stonemasons are not to be heard, – since it's Sunday. They say this music will carry on for two more weeks. I really don't know what to do. Puppykin, don't come back without an Apollo! How is your acquaintance doing (from Moscow)? Will you be back soon? Puppykin, promise me that we will never, never, never have sausage for dinner. Promise? Thought I'd go to Anyuta's tonight, but I didn't – I became languid from the sun. There were so many people there today! I was lying with my eyes closed and thinking, as I listened to the wide sound, the human hubbub: I could be in the tenth century now – the same kind of din, splashing, heat from the sun, light creaking of the pine-trees, there's nothing in the sound around me that hasn't always been there, from the earliest cave eras. But I was mistaken. Right next to me, some kind of steady snuffling sound started up. Without opening my eyes, I tried to decide what it was. Finally I looked: it turned out to be a child playing with a bicycle pump. The same child later approached me, considered my cross carefully, and said: 'Christ'. It was very funny, Puppykin. It's a quarter to nine now. I love you. There'd better be a letterlet from you tomorrow, or 'I will have my revenge'. My beloved insecticle, today, by my count, I'm writing my hundredth page to you. And yours will make up no more than ten or so. Is this amiable? It's twelve minutes to ten. I'll go to bed now. I still have talcum powder, but the hair oil ran out long ago. I am waiting for replies from abroad from Bunin, Shakhovskoy, de Calry – up till now, not a single one of them has replied. And another too – from Uncle Kostya. Best wishes to you, Puppykin, kisses on your little paws.

V.

[ALS, 2 PP.]
[19 July 1926]

[TO: St Blasien]

[Berlin]
19–VII–26

My love,

This morning I received the sweetest little letter – with a description of the ant females. If you arrive on Wednesday, then of course this letter won't manage to get there before you leave, my love, but I am writing just in case – so you don't remain, longer than expected, one extra – and letterless – day. I took my time getting dressed, went to 'Rul'', where I picked up a small advance. The heat is terrible, I walk around without a jacket. I came back on the top of the bus. Had lunch – veal (I think) and apple mousse. Then I went to Sack's, we played tennis (by the way, the word 'tennis' comes from the French '*tenez*': this is what the server of the ball would shout – in the ancient game – indoors (Henry IV had a very powerful *service*), as now they shout (actually, only people in Russian dachas do this now – in

England this has stopped) '*play!*'). Mme Sack has come back from 'Maria's Estates', she brought me as a present a very nice silver pencil (which I plan to take to a pawn shop). On the way back I bought 'Zveno', the '*Observer*', and – because of some internal disorder – eight capsules of *Ol[eum] Ricini* – very beautiful, appetizing to look at, transparently glossy – and I can swallow them like oysters (it's now half past nine; at six, I swallowed four – following the pharmacist's advice – but they've had no effect so far). I had only an egg for dinner, and drank some tea. Spent time on chess. Elkin phoned and let me know that 1) Adamovich will still write about 'Mary' for 'Zveno' 2) He's brought me a letter – he'll forward it tomorrow – from 'Sovr. zapiski' with a request to give them a short story for the next issue. My love, are you really coming back? Will you really walk into my room if not today, then tomorrow? My love, all the little ones have gone crazy with happiness ... (I don't understand, why no effect? ...) I am sending you 'Zveno'. I love you. No stonemasons today, although the scaffolding is still all there. (Maybe I should take another one?) I love you endlessly and I am waiting for you. Send me a telegram. My love, my love, my love. My life.

V.

[ALS, 2 PP.]
[22 December 1926]

[TO: Berlin]

[Prague]

Mama will write to you tomorrow. Boxy is lying on his back, his stiff lip sticking out.

22–XII–26

Greetings, my greenikin,

My love and my happiness, my one-and-all. I had an excellent trip. The heater was right under my feet. They really turned our things inside out at the border. For a long time, the official couldn't understand 'what's that red thing', and it took my fellow-travellers a while to explain to him that it was 'peayamas'. Elena and her fiancé and Kirill met me at the station. Kirill is huge and speaks, not quite in a squeaky voice and not quite in a husky basso. Pyotr Mikhaylovich is pure enchantment. (I can't even describe what he has done for Mother . . .) Elena and he are awfully affectionate with each other – just a pleasure to watch. They will get married in February, and Olga and Shakhovskoy in the spring. Mother does not look bad, but she had a light asthma attack right before my arrival. Overall, they're not living badly. They put me in Mother's room, Mother sleeps with my sisters, and Skulyari with Kirill. They have a Czech maid, but she does not cook (the Epatievs hired her). My love and my happiness. Mother told me very interesting things about Sergey. I gave Pyotr Mikhaylovich one of the ties (the bow) as a present. They were all ecstatic about the gifts. The suit fits Kirill perfectly. And how is your dear health? I miss you so much ... I need you so, my greenikin. I get back on Sunday. Will bring the chess and my butterflies. Oh, my happiness ... They read my 'Terror' at one of the meetings here. And tonight I'll exhibit my little long poem. Somehow everyone already knows about the play – and rumours are circulating that the emigration is portrayed in it very non-emigraciously. It's rather chilly in our rooms. But you should write to me, my sweet. There's a little snow on the roofs. I love you much more now than during my first visits here ...

V.

[ALS, 2 PP.]
[23 December 1926]

TO: 12, Passauer Str., b/v. Dallwitz, Berlin

[Prague]

Aged, but respectable sir,

I have just received your letterlet. We get in on Sunday. We read our long poemlet yesterday. Both fiancés were there. I played chess with Olga's, won once, but lost the other time. Apparently, they inoculated Mother with Box's tail, because there are cases when a dog can cause asthma (in this case, it didn't help). P. M. calls Box 'Botya'. He's grown fat and old. On wet days, he crosses the street slowly-slowly. When he is wearing a coat they call him 'pauper', because the coat has a hole on one side (from his rubbing against the wall). Mother has mild attacks. She is very nervous. Skulyari gives her adrenalin injections. Overall the mood in Prague is not happy.

They mentioned me with a 'kind word' in 'Krasnaya nov''. It would be nice to get this issue (the latest). Some time ago, there was an evening of my poetry here. Someone named Bers recited (he also read 'Terror' and 'Beneficence'). Prof. Katkov with his son and Bobrovsky (whose wife is near her time) visited us yesterday.

Thank you for the marks, my sweet. I will buy the ticket today. My darling, how happy I am in you, with you. And why, how has Aykhenvaldo praised the pretentious thing aborted by Landau! I am healthy and cheerful. I am conceiving (but not writing) a short story (not about Horace).

How I hate celebrating the New Year in public! Hessen told me that he would print in 'Rul'' a highly unpleasant article against 'Put''. A response to 'Mr Dvurogin' (read 'Trigorin' = Volhkovysskу). I adore you.

V.

1929

[AL, 1 P.]

[18 April 1929]

[Le Boulou, Eastern Pyrenees]

CAUGHT A THAIS!

[ALS, 1 P.]

[TO: Berlin?]

[undated]

[Berlin]

My love,

call me at K.'s around 8.30. My gums, tongue, the whole left part of my mug are aching, and a gland on my neck has swollen up like a tumour – devil knows what it is!

I love you.

V.

1930

[ALS, 2 PP.]
[c. 9 May 1930]

[TO: Berlin]

[Berlin]

My sweet,

Here's my first letter. Old man Hessen phoned and asked me to take a package (books and a pair of–old–slippers) for his son. He will bring it to the meeting. Then the other old man (Kaminka) called and asked me to do a translation–which I will pick up between Mme Falkovsky and the meeting. Were there any letters? No, if one doesn't count the Sunday poets' circle. Mrs Walrus came in just now, enquiring whether I was taking the trunk (delivered yesterday) with me to Russia, i.e. she had thought that I was leaving for Russia tomorrow (that Mother lived in Russia). Charming. Secondly, for her daughter, she asked for 'one of the Ullstein books you received. My daughter likes reading Ullstein books.' Besides, she announced that yesterday, her husband's brother died. Give her K[ing], Q[ueen], K[nave], if we have a copy. I bought all I need. Now I will drop in on Anyuta and buy a few other things along the way. I have eaten, but not much–can't taste anything, because of my cold–which, by the way, is better.

So, my happiness. Kisses. I won't be back late.

V.

[APCS]

[12 May 1930]

TO: 27, Luitpoldstr., b/ von Bardeleben, Berlin

[Prague]

My darling,

I had a splendid trip, was met by Mother at the station: she looks great and is in great spirits. Boxy is old and fat, with a grey snout, and he paid no attention to me. Elenochka and E. K. have grown very pretty. I was allotted a small, very cosy little room. Elena's drawing posters for my evening. In general, everything's going very well. My darling, write to me.

V.

Dear Véra, I am very happy. Volodya is cheerful, merry, and not very thin. I am very happy, but we were all sad that you are not with us.

Kisses.

maman Hélène

[ALS, 2 PP.]

[12 May 1930]

TO: 27, Luitpoldstr., b/ von Bardeleben, Berlin W.

[Prague]

My darling,

I love you. I've just been sorting dusty books, will bring some of them, I have gorged myself on old issues of '*The Entomologist*'. I love you, my happiness. A stroke of luck – the first person who came to visit on Sunday turned out to be an entomologist: just imagine, my darling, how white hot we got; on Thursday, he will show me a famous collection of *Papilio* at the museum. He caught an absolutely black *podalirius* in Podolsk province – a *pendant* to the black swallowtail in Püngeler's collection. Tonight our whole family is going to the cinema, and tomorrow I'm invited to 'Skit Poetov'. My evening is on the 20th. I love you. Yesterday, a little old general came, who reminded me of Jan[n]ings in 'The Last Advent', and read his short story ('a marble foot looked out from under a satin blanket' and so on). Kirill is strikingly handsome and refined, reads a lot, is relatively well educated and very high-spirited. He tells me that my brother Sergey (who arrived stout, with a fat neck, looking like Shalyapin) asked where there was a café where men met and strongly advised him to sniff cocaine. Fortunately, Kirill is absolutely normal. I have not seen Olga yet, she's at the dacha with Petkevich. Elena is charming, while Petya 'in my presence' is very nice (E. K. and Mother slightly dislike him, and he says 'inflúenza' and 'enviáble'). I love you. Petkevich, it turns out, is one of the best local chess-players (another lucky break). My family have read 'The Eye' as if the hero died in the first chapter and his soul then transmigrated to Smurov. Apropos of the soul – I miss you very much, my darling. Boxikins looks at me with cloudy eyes and continues not to recognize me. Here they suppose he takes me for Seryozha come back. Mother is so full of pep I'm amazed. She's enthusiastic about 'Christian Science' (not nearly as much as Mrs Bliss, of course), and her asthma has gone, and her nerves are in order, so we can only very much approve it. She and E. K. prepared everything so nicely for me: the volumes of '*The Entomologist*' were lying on my bedside table, they specially bought stamps, new nibs, paper for my letters to you, my darling. I love you. There are two couples boarding here, and also the notorious Czech woman – a rather harmless and nice old maid. The weather is terrible, the saints are crapping. In the kitchen, Mother is asking Boxikin 'won't he go for a walk now with Volodya?', but he says nothing. My happiness, kisses, my sweet, my darling. Tell Anyuta that I love her very much. Keep your little ears pricked for reviews, Cossack choirs, and so on. Write to me, write, whether you are in good health, do you have pains, and all. 'The dog can't wait any longer,' I can hear from the kitchen. My happiness.

V.

[ALS, 2 PP.]

[TO: Berlin]

[16 May 1930]
[Prague]

My tender beast, my love, my greenikins,

Every new letterless day makes me sadder and sadder, that's why I didn't write to you yesterday and now greatly regret it, after reading about the mother swan and the ducklings, my enchantress, my beauty. For me, you are always, always Tiergarten-like, chestnutty, rosy. I love you. There are bedbugs and cockroaches here. Yesterday, as soon as I've turned the lights off, I sense a fidgety presence on my cheek, a soft whiskery touch. Lights on. Mrs Cockroach. The other day, I went to an evening of 'Skit Poetov'. Renewed friendly relations with Chirikov, Kadashev, Nemirovich-Danchenko. He, Nemirovich, is very old. I met a bald Jew (very carefully concealing his Jewishness), the 'famous' poet Rathaus. Eisner recited some poetry – in the style of Gumilyov, with 'red-mugged sailors', 'rum' and 'geographic map', full of the newest clichés, ringing out loudly; you'll understand in a word how vile it was.

And I had absolutely no idea what to say to Rathaus, it's awkward to talk to a man whose name now stands for bad poets. He said to me by the way: 'So they compare you to me . . .' Touching and revolting. Many young poets and poetesses read, so I felt the same as during our 'poetic' gatherings: it's all the same, nauseating. Kisses, my sweet, my darling. It occurred to me that Baudelaire never saw a '*jeune elephant*' in real life, did he? Well, of course there were all those 'present among us is . . . ', 'our dear guest . . .' etc. Which would make Kirill turn crimson. But more interesting to me than all the poets and writers was Fyodorov, yet another entomologist, very passionate and knowledgeable, and he and I immediately began to sing like nightingales, in unison, to a certain bewilderment among those around us. Just think, his large collection has been sold recently to recover debts, he's absolutely destitute. I don't know whether I will read 'The Aurelian' on Tuesday. I will definitely read the first chapter of 'The Eye' (Mama has it). Olga has not yet deigned to appear. I'll read a few poems. Kirill's studying well. He has no technical inclinations. He wants to be a natural scientist, to fight, for example, malaria in Africa. The whole family went to the movies, we saw the picture Sherman talked about so amusingly (the ring sliding off her finger, keeping pace with the woman's 'fall'). Mother confirmed to me in detail what Raisa told us about a certain old man and a certain old woman. Apparently, Mother kept the secret for fifteen years, and there was one very serious scandal in Berlin. General Dolgov (who read his story) says, like my grandmother, '*spleutni*'. Elenochka came in just now and asked, with an innocent face, where is Flemlandia. Ah, my happiness, how unbearable it is for me without you. You are my life. It will be hard to bear the approach to the Anhalter station. Did you get the money? My sweet, how I'm kissing you . . .

V.

[ALS, 2 PP.]
[17 May 1930]

TO: 27, Luitpoldstr., b/ Bardeleben, Berlin W.

[Prague]

Hello, my joy,

You can tell Gorlin that 1) I won't be performing at their evening – let them row their own boat 2) whether they publish the almanac in 'Slovo' or 'Petropolis' I won't participate anyway – I am not young and I'm not a poet. Tell Sherman that I loved his articles about Ivan Alekseevich very much. Greetings to our landlords. Buy, my love, Thursday's Pos. Nov. (from what's-his-name – but you know – I can't recall it at the moment). Yesterday I was at the museum, they showed me beautiful collections – of course, not nearly as full as in Berlin, but I cannot say this to the Czechs (now I remember – Lyaskovsky), and they have misnamed a lot. Fyodorov, about whom I wrote you, was just here, my happiness. He strongly recommends going to Varna, it is extremely cheap there and lots of butts. From here the trip costs 20 marks, so 40 in all from Berlin, for two persons or beasts – 80, there and back – 160, and one can get a room for 20 (for two beasties) a month, while food for two costs 1 mark a day – so in all we'll need about 250 marks (generously) for the trip and living expenses. We'll leave, I think, early in June. There are no snakes there, and Nem.-Danchenko will arrange a visa in two shakes.

I love you, – it is simply laughable how I miss you, my darling. Here there are bright-blue, round lanterns at the tram stops, a lot of slate-black houses, very narrow pavements, and one cannot smoke in the second carriage of the tram. In a day or two, we will be going to the Bobrovskys'. Kirill is educated, has a fine knowledge of literature, and is in love with a very sweet young lady. Mother remembers Massalsky from St Petersburg, no one here knows that he spent time in jail, so I am telling everyone about this, with details – tell Anyuta this. But indeed I keep silent as a fish or only say good things. Receptions continue at Kramář's house, but they do not talk to the hosts, they only stuff their faces, and recently Kiesewetter had a fight over aspic with another old man. In one Soviet almanac there were the memoirs of some commissar, and he recounts quite incidentally how things from our house were handed out and how he took for himself an iron Chinaman with a nodding head. I remember it so well, that figurine. Have you been to the Mishas', my beauty, what are you up to in general? The sea at Varna is marvellous for swimming. We'll catch *Papilio alexanor* there. Mme Fyodorov loves kissing caterpillars on the head, it's become downright normal for her. As soon as you get the money, send me something, let's say, ten-fifteen marks besides 20 for the road. I am now negotiating with a Czech publisher about 'Mary', but I am not sure it will work out (this is through the Czech woman who boards with Mother). Kisses, my sweet. How is your dear health? Yes, I love you, I love you endlessly. Please write to me, otherwise I'll have another fit of the spleen and stop writing. My love, my larentia, my *teplovata*.

V.

[ALS, 2 PP.]

[postmarked 19 May 1930]

TO: 27, Luitpoldstr., b/ v. Bardeleben, Berlin W.

[Prague]

I have received, my Bussa beast, your short and undertufty letterlet. I wrote to Fondamin that I agree (although I would have preferred – thinking of money – Pilgram to die in the basement of 'Poslednie novosti'). I also sent Fayard what I had to. Boxy keeps watching me with his dull eyes. Yesterday he produced 157 yelps in a row, we counted. The weather's decent today, we'll go for a walk. I am sad that you write so little, my endless happiness. Our finances here are sour, no money to buy stamps, I feel rather awkward.

I adore you.

V.

[ALS, 2 PP.]

[20 May 1930]

TO: 27, Luitpoldstr., b/ v. Bardeleben, Berlin W.

[Prague]

My love,

I don't know what kind of job you have, you write me very unclearly. How can we expose that nasty old woman? (Are you sure she was the thief – all kinds of tradesmen have been there recently – and where was the brooch?) Have you seen Adamovich's review in 'P. N.'? Shall I bring that issue? I'm reading today – prose and poems; I have to select enough for at least an hour and a half. I've already written you, my love, exactly what I'll read out. I will sort through the archive, and you try to find the recent issue of 'Za Svobodu', where Nalyanch writes something about me. This chasing up of articles about me is getting rather complicated, shouldn't we stop? After all, I am not an actress. My love, it feels more and more impossible for me without you. I get back on Sunday the 25th, at night – 11, I think – I'll write again with more detail. I confirm receipt of your honourable with the money. Now I'll write more often, my love.

Two days ago, we went for a walk, a wonderful pale-sunny day, we climbed the hill not far from us and could see a whole canvas town below – a wandering circus – and from there could hear the thick roar of tigers and lions, the merry-go-rounds sparkled (and there were ads on all fences: green tigers with bared teeth and, between them, a moustachioed braveheart with Brandenburgers). I was at the entomological museum again, and Obenberger – a very talkative beetle man – reviled Germany and said that Germans *sont pires que les juifs*. The Russian colony here, so they say, is also blackish. Olga hasn't yet appeared, but Shakhovskoy, who has married again, has. My darling, do you miss me? Kisses. Regards to Anyuta, please, and to the Mishas. Mama will write to you tomorrow. They are washing Boxy now. Mama looks younger, energetic, cheerful – when we were out walking, I kept admiring how well she walks and how elegant her legs are in their grey stockings. She insists it's all due to Christian Science. Yes, my happiness, I'll see you soon. Why don't you write me anything about Varna? *I thought you would jump at it* (seize it). Yesterday, I read '*Les Caves du Vatican*' by A. Gide, terrible nonsense, but well-written in places. I can't wait to sit down to a little novel again. I'm sending you an article, Mother copied it out. I'm very happy you exist, my beauty – but if your job is tiresome – watch out! I'm very happy; without you, my world has become a little pinched, but I still know you exist and therefore I'm happy anyway. How I'm kissing you!

V.

[ALS, 2 PP.]
[postmarked 22 May 1930]

TO: 27, Luitpoldstr., b/ v. Bardeleben, Berlin W.

[Prague]

My darling,

Very cheerfully, I'm writing to you again, although there is *neither rumour nor smell* of you. By the way, I'm copying the following from

Kipling for you: *Do you know the pile-built village where the sago-dealers trade.—Do you know the reek of fish and wet bamboo?—Do you know the steaming stillness of the orchid-scented glade when the blazoned, bird-winged butterflies flap through?—It is there that I am going with my camphor, net, and boxes,— to a gentle, yellow pirate that I know—To my little wailing lemurs, to my palms and flying-foxes, For the Red Gods call me out and I must go!* The '*flap*' is especially good. If tomorrow—and today is Thursday—there's nothing from you, I too will follow the Red Gods' call. And here about us: '*She was Queen of Sabaea—And he was Asia's Lord—But they both of 'em talked to butterflies When they took their walks abroad!*' We had lots of guests for dinner with us yesterday: [Countess] Panin and Astrov, the Gorns, the Kovalevskys, I read 'A University Poem', 13 of us in all. I'm leaving, my darling, on the 25th at 2.47 and will be at Anhalter at 10.15. I ask you to meet me—*solo*, of course.

I have not found the article about Volkovyssky in my father's papers. Wasn't it Sherman who promised to get that issue of 'Vozrozhdenie'? The workers opposite are filling the roof in with tiles very appetizingly. I love you very much, my darling.

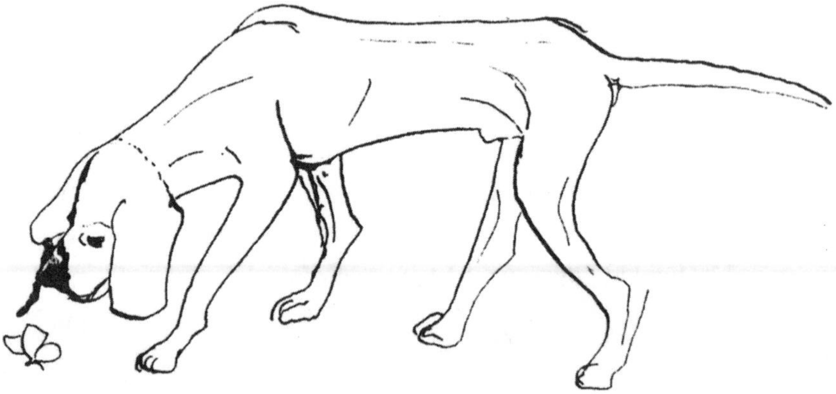

Its little face hasn't turned out very well. It's sunny today. Yesterday, I fell asleep at half past five, when the sparrows were already singing. We thought we'd go to visit the Bobrovskys in the country today, but we're not going. I've given three poems – old ones – to the local newspaper 'Nedelya' to feature in the article about my reading. Of people from Berlin, only Trotsky was there. I love you – unbearably and very, very tenderly.

V.

[AL, 2 PP.]
[postmarked 23 May 1930]

TO: 27, Luitpoldstr, b/ v. Bardeleben, Berlin W.

[Prague]

Hello, my darling. I love you. Neither when I was in Prague without you, nor when you were in St Blasien, has it been so unbearable without you as this time. This is probably explained by my loving you more and more. My reading was yesterday, a big crowd, I read 10 poems (all of them hits, of course), one chapter from 'The Eye' – the first one – and 'The Aurelian'. Meanwhile I drained two mugs of beer. Astrov spoke first about me, at length; later, he gave me an issue of 'Rossiya i Slav.' with Gleb's review, and there I recognized his phrases, since he'd marked them with pencil in the article – he'd drawn straight from it and then, evidently, forgot to erase. I met heaps of people, inscribed in albums, smiled, etc. Olga showed up at the reading with her husband, who, apparently, is one of the best chess-players in Prague. Overall, it was rather fun – but you weren't there, my darling. I met Avksentiev, who, unaware that Vishnyak had written me about discontinuing 'The Third Rome', said that Ivanov gave them just an 'excerpt'. He invited me insistently to Paris. Adamovich's article in 'P. N.' holds back as usual. But kind Sherman wrote charmingly. Thank him very much *de ma part*.

My warm one, you rarely write to me. On the whole I am offended by this, although I don't show it. Three and a bit days to go.

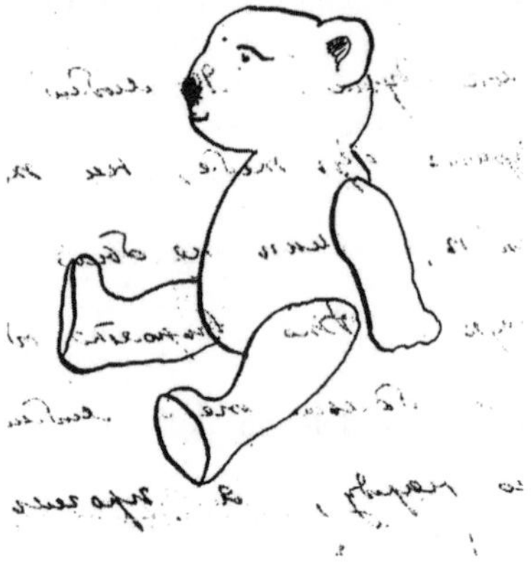

[AL, 2 PP.]

[c. 23 May 1930]

[TO: Berlin]

[Prague]

My little one,

This is the last little letter, I invite you to a date at 10.15 at the station on Sunday.

My little one,

I don't like your job, I'm cross, I don't like it at all. What I dislike most is that you have to get up so early, this must be awfully exhausting for you. As for your working from 9 to 5, you simply won't, I'll put my foot down (Anglicism), it's absurd. As soon as I arrive, I'll place an ad in 'Rul"—with my name and nickname—for lessons. My little one, my tender one, my weak one, working assiduously from 9 to 5, that's an impossible prospect. I will talk to Anyuta (by the way, big kiss for her little hand).

Izgoev was here yesterday—he'd come from Paris—and said the same as Nika. Ivanov is living with Zinaida. Today, Kadashev and Varshavsky will be here, and tonight, Olga and her husband—I'll play chess with him. Sergey Hessen and wife were here a few days ago, he asked a lot about his father's current relationship with Obstein. I told him all I knew and invented still more, to give it more shape. Kirill dreams poetry, has an excellent knowledge of literature, wrote a beautiful essay on Lermontov. He composes day in, day out—and has already been working on one poem for five days or so—and reads to me, while I rebuke him roundly. His English pronunciation is excellent and he knows English poetry well. Skulyari is honeyed as before and keeps cracking unfunny jokes,—but he's an excellent husband, and Elena an excellent wife. My relationship with Boxy is coolish, I keep waiting for him to recognize me. We eat well and plenty, they all have much better appetites than I do. See you soon, my love.

Bussa

[ALS, 1 P.]

[1930S ?]

[TO: Berlin?]

[Berlin?]

My darling,

Misha dropped by, invited us tonight, I said that I'd l let you know, but I couldn't reach you. You go to them. And I'll pick you up (from the Kaminkas') later (on my way from the Hessens).

I kiss your little hands.

V. Nabokov

1932

The originals of VN's letters to VéN from 1932 cannot now be located. In December 1984 and January 1985 VéN, willing to help BB's research for his biography of VN, but not prepared to let him read the parts of the letters she considered private, read as much of her letters from VN as she saw fit into BB's tape-recorder. These tapes now provide the only available evidence for the texts of the 1932 letters. The translations that follow present all that VéN chose to read out from that year's correspondence.

[VÉNAF]

[4 April 1932]

[TO: Berlin]

[Prague]

The first part of the trip was very pleasant. I read on and off and looked out the window at the childish spring sky [. . .]. Elena and Mother met me at the station. Mother is in excellent spirits. Very cheery, looks good, but thinner. Elena is dreamily disposed and very sweet. It turns out that Skulyari was not right for her [. . .]. So far, I like Kirill better than last time. His juvenility is superficial, slightly mischievous, to annoy Evgenia Konstantinovna. But he's a terrible idler. Olga's husband is as gloomy as always, but Olga herself has grown much prettier. Rostislav is extremely attractive and is already walking around the rooms. Evgenia

Konstantinovna has gone grey, but our poor Boxy has gone even greyer and half-blind. In a couple of days, Seryozha may come, and then all of us together will have our picture taken in exactly the same poses as one of our Yalta photographs. Boxy, too. My cold's still lingering. I sleep in Mother's room on a short narrow couch with a back. I won't go to any Paris. Send me, please, please, first of all, 'Lips to Lips' (I'll read it just to Mother, without a commentary), and secondly, my article on butterflies. You know, in spite of everything, you and I have a very comfortable life. Boxy is allowed to go to the loo and lift his leg by the porcelain pedestal (it's a pedestal for him).

[VÉNAF]
[5 April 1932]

[TO: Berlin]

[Prague]

Please pass on to Bertrand my thanks for his letter. As you can see, I have already written to Thompson. To my mind, this turned out very elegantly. Don't forget to send what I asked for. My cold is a little better. I am hearty, shaven and, in fact, I wanted to stop here, using the natural end of this little page, but then I thought that perhaps you've not quite understood my hints about the currants and the red-skins. Don't you think that his connection to Leskov's and Zamyatin's heroines is about as approximate as a beetle's connection to a grasshopper? Here we have solidity, slowness, even a certain stupidity, and there – light-heartedness, swiftness, elusiveness. Mother is at a lesson, Kirill was very keen to have Bertrand's postcard, but I did not give it to him. I too have my little album. Today, I made him have a shower. I am thinking of sitting down to start a new novel.

[VÉNAF]
[6 April 1932]

[TO: Berlin]

[Prague]

You've chosen the excerpts well. I will send 'Magda's Childhood' to *Poslednie novosti*, and her 'Visit', to *Rossiya i slavyanstvo*. I can't post them today, though. I'll do it on Monday. I have already spent about 20 crowns on myself (cigarettes, stamps). I feel quite embarrassed borrowing to post the excerpts, but I'll have to. Perhaps you could wire me 3–4 marks? Or is this too complicated? Bobrovsky's younger brother died because of Azef. Long before Azef was unmasked, he, the brother, had somehow discovered that Azef was an *agent provocateur*. This was in Karlsruhe, and he returned to Russia insane. Persecution mania. He decided that now Azef would kill him. He wouldn't talk to anyone, he ate almost nothing, and he went skating all day long. Once he tried to kill his elder brother with an axe. Soon after that he threw himself under a train. He got terribly mutilated and died. Pyotr Semyonovich, who came to dinner, has just told me this. And now it's near seven, and he's still sitting here.

Olga was crying today: her husband has lost the only little job he had. I gave my mite towards buying Rostislav something to wear. The only word he can say is 'yes', with lots of feeling and many times in a row: 'yes, yes, yes, yes, yes', affirming his existence. The weather is nasty and cold. Frantic clouds are rushing across the sky. I haven't gone out today, and my cold is almost entirely gone. I did not feel comfortable somehow today borrowing money to send things, but that's psychological. Conversations about the Petkeviches' situation and so on. But I'll do it on Monday. It was a mistake to leave myself only 20 crowns. I thought this would last for ages. You know what's funny: in the morning, Mother brings me your letters in exactly the same manner, with the same little grimace, as in *Glory*. By the way, write me in ink, because pencil rubs off and your little pages written in pencil look like grey moth wings with the dust falling off. Pyotr Semyonovich has promised to get me the issue of *Russkaya mysl'* where my poems were printed for the first time. Sorting out my extra notebooks, I found a poem I'd totally forgotten, but not so bad, written in Beaulieu, which starts 'Crosses, crosses . . .' If you don't know it, I will copy it out for you. I miss oranges terribly. I forgot to bring Kirill those little books of poems I'd promised him. There's a conversation going on in the room; it's hard to write. Here we all live in a mutual draught. I don't like *Camera*. By the way, I don't know the address of *Rossiya i slavyanstvo*, Kirill will find it out for me on Monday. Mother does not get it, nor *Nash vek* for that matter. *Nash vek* is boorish. I am re-reading *Bovary* for the hundredth time. So good, so good! Probably on Monday, I will be at Skit. There, to tell the truth, it's mediocrity on mediocrity, but it's curious all the same. Evgenia Konstantinovna is asking whether I want them soft-boiled or fried.

[VÉNAF]
[7 April 1932]

[TO: Berlin]

[Prague]

Today I am going with the Raevskys to look at the fresh little collection of butterflies at the museum, and from there, Mother, Kirill and I will go to Sergey Hessen's. By the way, where did I put the money? Ah, here it is, under the couch. I have already begun to doubt the epistolary merits of my letter yesterday to Thompson, but I want to believe you're in raptures over it, especially over the phrase about *fine, rich, warm, etc*.

Rostislav, in a pink jacket, blue pantaloons, and purple booties, is standing in the doorway, leaning over the lintel, and now he's set off walking, like a drunk, wanted to pick up a ball, dropped his little box, picked up the little box, dropped the ball, and smiled at me shyly. Box is awfully jealous of him; despite being deaf and blind, he starts to bark as soon as Evgenia Konstantinovna picks Rostislav up in her arms. Olga won't talk about anything but chess. Her husband is silent by conviction and so old-fashioned in his personal style that Olga, ricochet-like, says it's disgusting to use make-up, wear bright things, and so on. As a result she didn't take the lipstick, and he didn't need a safety razor, since he, of course, shaves with a regular razor. My cold has almost dried up, the weather is desperate. Icy wind, overcast. I've put on two pullovers. I'll bring Flaubert back, and the soccer boots. We'll go to Bulgaria this summer. It's settled. Please kiss Anyuta for me. I'm afraid that the landlady, taking advantage of my absence, is dropping in on you rather often to talk, talk, talk. Buy several 20 pfennig stamps at once and write. I would like to know, for instance, how your health is.

[VÉNAF]

[8 April 1932]

[TO: Berlin]

[Prague]

I can write to you too about birds and animals. Yesterday Raevsky and I went to the museum, but since a Pushkin exhibition has opened in one of the lower halls, my impressions have got somewhat muddled. Amateur photography – the foppish Gogol with a walking stick among Russian artists in Rome and a marvellous bird, *Pteridophora alberti*, about which I already wrote you two years ago. On paper of the same blue colour, the original of 'Odelia dear', and charming geometric views of old Petersburg, and a small flat blondish rodent with a straw roof on his back, *Chlamydophorus truncatus*. A mantle-clad lad. My cold is better, but the weather is rotten and cold. I read Gazdanov's story. It's very weak. I am very unhappy about the telegram about the galleys. I certainly sent them.

We didn't go to Sergey Hessen's. He's ill. We'll go on Sunday. Yesterday Kovalevsky and I, playing together, wiped out Boris Vladimirovich at chess. Mother has told me interesting things about her spiritualist séances with the Roerich family. In general life in Prague is wretched and dirty. But by some miracle, my sisters and my brother have preserved a surprising purity of soul. And Mother is in good spirits, and Evgenia Konstantinovna hasn't lost heart. I have just read in *Poslednie novosti* the stupidest and most vulgar article by Adamovich about the stupidest and most vulgar novel by Lawrence. One pederast writing about another. And now I will write to Anyuta. They're not letting me write today, so this has come out rather a mosaic of a letter.

[VÉNAF]
[11 April 1932]

[TO: Berlin]

[Prague]

We've been to Sergey Hessen's. The unbearably talkative Pletnyov and a very pleasant professor Karpovich from Harvard were there. All in all, Prague is a terribly ugly city. In its ancient monuments, in, let's say, some black, plucked-at, five-hundred-year-old tower, there is something crow-like. Churches here bear the burden of centuries without grace, and best to say nothing about the houses, all motley, the shops, and the mugs of its citizens. Last night there was an invasion again. The weather has warmed up, but the wind's still whirling. Dust. Soldiers playing soccer by the barracks. Sparrows hopping about the lawn in the public garden. The street traffic seems as if in a mirror for me. Know what I mean? Right seems left. At the tram stop there are large round bluish-purple street lamps, which I think I once wrote to you about. Listen:

'Twould ring the bells of heaven,
The wildest peals for years,
If Parson lost his senses
And people came to theirs,
And he and they together
Knelt down with angry prayers
For tamed and shabby tigers,
And dancing dogs and bears,
And wretched blind pit-ponies
And little hunted hares.

Ralph Hodgson. I tried to translate it, but so far it's not coming out very well. A sweet poem. I will bring back some books. My finger still hurts, and it's still pretty pregnant. I must have given it a good whack. I will also bring you the remnants of a very persistent cold. 'Za sobak i medvedey uchyonykh,/ tigrov unizitel'no ruchnykh,/ I petlyashchikh zaychikov i v shakhtakh/ loshadey slepykh.'

Yesterday we had a visit from Sikorski and another Ukrainian, Volkonsky, who's in torment from trying to propose. So far he hasn't dared do it yet. He took communion yesterday, but it didn't help. They've been fixing the electric doorbell. I will come back on Saturday night. At eleven, I think. I'll find out. Prepare a big supper for me. As soon as I'm back I'll sit down to the novel whose lines are just radiating out in my head. Write me a few words. An aquarelle's hanging on the wall in front of me – the Tsar's Trail between Miskhor and Yalta. Such divine smells there. There I caught *Libythea celtis* for the first time. And on the table, by the way, there's a round chunk of marble we stole from the Acropolis. What do you think, maybe it would be better, 'i slepykh loshadok-uglekopov,/ i zatravlennykh zaychikh'? Or maybe this way, 'za zhalkikh, priruchennykh tigrov,/ sobak uchyonykh, medvedéi,/ za malenkikh presleduemykh zaitsev/ i shakhtennykh oslepshikh loshadey.' Tell me what you like best. At 8 o'clock, Kirill and I are meeting at the museum to go to Skit.

[VÉNAF]
[12 April 1932]

[TO: Berlin]

[Prague]

Actually, I ought to be back in Berlin for the 20th: the Goethe evening, but I'll be glad to skip it. Tomorrow I will go to the police and find out whether I am allowed to stay another 4–5 days here. I have a visa to the sixteenth, and, if it's possible, I'll return on the twentieth or the twenty-first, but, in any case, no later. You should have seen how Mother beamed when I told her that I'd stay a few more days. Yesterday I was at Skit. A narrow stone staircase, Golovin's workshop. Doubtful works of sculpture along the walls, half-light, they all sit on some kind of low crates, tea, and little Bem by a small table, looking like a Tzadik. The reading was by someone called Markovich, a red-faced young man, a pretentious and feeble story. Example: 'She strained him through her eyelashes', 'A waiter who looks as if he has just swallowed a metre-stick' –

and chapter titles like, for instance, 'A Blonde on a Long Wave' or 'The Wind of Blue Romance'. The poor guy got a dressing-down. Then a poet, Mansvetov, long-haired, pale, eyeless, read his dim little poems with such little Pasternakian words as 'randomly', 'blindly', 'under wraps', 'ovations' and so on. After that, the poetess Alla Golovina read her graceful, toy-like poems in a tiny voice. And that was all. Khokhlov was there. He is going to Russia in the summer. The poetess Rathaus, the daughter of our best lyricist, who, by the way, has had a stroke (he's 64), asked me with a rapturous smile what I thought of Vicki Baum. I came back alone, because Kirill went to see home his friend Zhenya Hessen. Tonight, I'll read 'Lips' *en famille*. I'm going to the post office now to send off the excerpts. I could not get through Ivan Alekseevich's little masterpieces in *Poslednie novosti*. Could you? My cold is gone. It's cold. Windy. Now sun, now clouds. Do you know that in the days of Madame Bovary, cacti were in vogue, like now. Skulyari came to see us again yesterday. He brought us vodka, tea, a can of spiced sprats and told us how Americans had discovered a way of catching and collecting lightning. I play chess from time to time. It's hard for me to put off my coming, but you're right, I thought myself I'd stay (only a couple of days) extra.

[VÉNAF]

[14 April 1932]

[TO: Berlin]

[Prague]

How do you like the article in *Poslednie novosti*, the second one already, by the mysterious 'Average man'? I think it's rather nice. I've sent the excerpts. I read 'Lips to Lips' yesterday. They liked it.

I am writing to Dresden today. Mother and I are going to see Altschuler today, and tomorrow we'll go about the visa. I should say that Sikorski, who rides a motorcycle with a sidecar, earns half as little this year as last, although he rides all night long. Normally, no one rides during the day. The weather's gloomy and cold. I'm in two jerseys. I'm well, but my finger hurts. I'll have Altschuler look at it. Here's my old poem I told you about. Nothing special, but not bad, either.

Crosses, crosses, naked outlines
of graveyard crosses I saw in my dream.
No grief, no grief, but only anticipation
and the sweet wind with news of spring.
And from all over whispering sounds
were breathing, opening up like flowers,
while the crosses raised their arms slowly,
blooming trees, not crosses.

Beaulieu, 7–vi–23

You'll have to call Hessen and tell him I've had to stay in Prague and that therefore I will not be able to take part in the Goethe festival. *Ne précise pas la date de mon arrivée* since *il se peut* that I'll be back on the 20th, yes, definitely the 20th, but I do not want to dash from shore to ball.

Do this, please. And here is another old, very old little poem.

An India invisible I rule [. . .].

[VÉNAF]
[15 April 1932]

[TO: Berlin]

[Prague]

Seven years ago we went to the *Standesamt*. Today, too, I was in an office. I didn't get my visa extension. Some clerk in charge of this wasn't there. I'll have to go there again tomorrow morning. But in any event, a civil servant who'd refused to speak German to me on the pretext that we were, he says, both Slavs, was sceptical about the possibility of my further sojourn in his fatherland. If tomorrow too they try to put chocks in my clock wheels, I'll simply not bother, stay here till the 20th anyway, and then come what may. Maybe I'll have difficulties at the border because of this, but I'll get through. I ask you, how dare they, these rats, these perfectly inedible gentlemen, cause me such trouble.

Yesterday at the Altschulers', I got to know a charming affectionate black dachshund, belonging to his son, also a doctor. He is married to a Greek woman, with two girls. A wonderful apartment in a stylish area. His son has a huge practice. I showed the old man my sore finger. An inflamed joint. Night compress. We talked about this and that, about our Berlin acquaintances, our Crimean acquaintances. The dachshund wouldn't leave me alone. She demanded to be stroked. After that all evening I had the sensation of her smooth silky blackness on my palm. Sikorski came over yesterday, too, and Sergey Hessen, and the Kovalevskys crawled up from their apartment, too. He is pink, round-faced, youthfully bald, in a rimless pince-nez, in pyjamas, and also unwell (stomach ulcers). She is very beautiful, speaks with a burr, flirts with her eyes. I have written to Mulman, but I am afraid this is *peine perdue*. I will bring you the entire correspondence, Flaubert, and Gippius's 'Human Countenance'. It's a muddled poem, but it has amazing, very inspiring parts. For example, this stanza: 'If you still don't believe, let's go to sea, cast a net, a teeming catch of fish will answer. And like slaves, without arguing, we threw the net into the sea swell, and rejoiced that our net was heavy and thick and black with a teeming catch.' Don't you think it's good? I've enticed Mother with Joyce. But, unfortunately, you can't get him here. He is simply not in the public library. Except in Czech translation. I can imagine what nonsense that is. Aside from those I mentioned, we also had Vacek, a Czech old maid who used to live at Mother's, over yesterday, and Kirill's heartthrob, Irochka Vergun, was also supposed to come. But didn't show. I want to write a very harmonious, very simple book. But so far, I only see its large rays and get a pleasantly plaintive feeling. Ugh, how I'm going to catch it for poor *Camera*. And it will serve me right. Good God, how I crave oranges. They don't eat enough here, but the saddest thing is that while I am here, they eat better than usual. Evgenia Konstantinovna has now brought me a cup of coffee and a crescent roll and asks to send you her regards and says: 'Poor darling, she feels so sad without you today.' Mother is at her lesson now. Kirill's at the university. The weather's milder, but the sky's grey. You can't imagine how slovenly they are. If you don't keep an eye on her, she could, for example, wash the little boy's face in the same pot she uses for making soup and vice versa. The other day I came on this scene: Olga, on the couch, reading a disgustingly frayed volume of Herzen, while the child is on the floor, sucking dreamily on Box's tin bowl. If they suddenly move away or out, it's been decided that Rostislav will stay here.

[VÉNAF]
[16 April 1932]

[TO: Berlin]

[Prague]

The pupae never hang the way you've drawn them, and the smoke would not protrude like this from the very pleasant little house, but the young lion is very nice, as well as the bear-cubs. Of course I will be in Berlin on Saturday, so you can invite the Kozhevnikovs. I will be very happy to see Volodya.

The novel you ask about will deal with an exam. Imagine something like this. A man is preparing for a driving test on city geography. His preparation and conversations connected with it, and also, of course, his family, human environment, and so on, will be covered, in misty detail, you understand, in the first part. Then there's an imperceptible transition to the second part. He goes, enters the exam room, but it's not a driving test at all but, as it were, an examination of his earthly existence. He has died and they're asking him about the streets and crossroads of his life. And all of this is without a shadow of mysticism. He talks at that exam about everything he remembers from life, i.e. about the brightest and most lasting things in his whole life. And those who examine him are long-deceased, for example, the coachman who made a sledge for him when he was little, his old grammar-school teacher, some distant relatives whom he knew only dimly in life. This is my little embryo. I think I've told it to you badly. But it's hard. I have it, this novel, still at the stage of feeling rather than of thought.

My good friends and admirers are boors. Nothing to be done. But the optimist from Danzig is charming. Mother has caught a cold. She's in bed today. I am afraid it's bronchitis or flu. Her mood is awful. And that's understandable. It's no fun anyway, and now the cold as well. Her seventh since the autumn. In the morning Kirill and I went to the Commissariat, where we filled out some form where you figure as well (as they say in Czech), *zhonka*. I think this is generally called 'registering'. On Monday, they will extend my visa till Wednesday. That's charming. And here's my second poem. The first one (the very first) was published in *Vestnik Evropy* or *Russkoe Bogatstvo*, I don't remember. Don't remember the year either. I think in '16, winter. From *Russkaya mysl'* of, '17. It is very touching.

WINTER NIGHT

The silence in the winter moonlight night
seems the steady breath of the heavens.
In the air, the charm of pallid light.
Blessed by a lunar radiance,
the avenue, the field, and the wood slumber.
Springy skis sweetly squeak,
and my long blue shadow tags along.
Lindens sleep like black ghosts in a row,
sad, strange, hoar-frosted.
The moon softly lights the snowdrifts.
The regally round white flame
looks on the field, on its snowy smoothness.
From behind naked bushes, I frighten a hare.
Disrupting the smoothness with its triple footprints,
it disappears. And silence again.
I traverse the field – boundless –
kissing the crystal frosty air.
The sky is radiance, the earth silence.
In this hush of death and sleep
in my soul, clearly, I sense immortality.

V. V. Nabokov

All of this is very weak, but the entire magazine is also very weak, with some translations from the Norwegian, a novel by Mme Tyrkov, *The Plunder*, and such woman-writerish lines as:

> An elegant page with a smile of a fawn,
> a delicate page is going off to war.

Mother has just taken her temperature: 38.2° C. Flu, evidently. It's very gloomy here today. Don't forget to tell me about 'Lips to Lips'. I stay until Wednesday, for the sake of the rhyme.

[VÉNAF]
[18 April 1932]

[TO: Berlin]

[Prague]

So, I'll come the day after tomorrow, on Wednesday. Today, Kirill will find out the exact time my train arrives. We were again in that vile institution, where three boorish officials were idly smoking. My passport's still there. I will have to go and pick it up on Wednesday morning, and it will, probably, have some kind of a stamp. A loathsome and pointless affair. I am very sorry I started this process in the first place, but Mother was worried, thinking that they would turn me around at the border. She's feeling a little better today, but her fever's lingering. The other day, I re-read my translation of *Alice in Wonderland*. There are two or three places rendered well. I remember I was in a great hurry and made a few grammar mistakes. The illustrations are awfully vulgar. A wretched book.

Yesterday that idiot Petkevich got mad at the child for knocking over a cup and gave him a hard smack. Olga wept, repeating: 'I'd rather you thrashed *me*.' Evgenia Konstantinovna says this isn't the first time. A gloomy philistine. 'Children should fear their father.' A starched collar and dirty feet [nails?]. But I wish you could see the baby. He is tender, quiet, thoughtful. Shakhovskoy, who caught several rare butterflies over the summer with Fyodorov, wrote to me yesterday. Let's meet, he said, at the 'Hearth'. A normal *rendezvous* here. Olga found out about this and flew into a wild rage. I told her that if this was so unpleasant to her, then, of course, I wouldn't meet him. What can I do?

You remember I wrote to you about someone called Pletnyov. After he met Elenochka (they work at the library together), he said to her about me: 'Haughty, English type'. He is offended because I prefer Joyce to Dostoevsky and don't like Leskov. But she also says that Raevsky gets some kind of celestial expression on his face when he mentions my name. Tomorrow morning he and I are going to see a collection of fossil insects, or, rather, of the casts they've made. Following our good old Westphalia custom, I dropped a lamp the other day, and it had a cardiac arrest. I thought Seryozha would come, but there was a letter from him today, saying he couldn't. He has to economize. In other words, evidently, his boyfriend has to economize. Crisis. His boyfriend is a thickset, rather plump, forty-year-old man. Seryozha, when he was here last time, showed photos. And here's yet another poem for you: '*I hear a sudden cry of pain! There is a rabbit in a snare*. . .' That's a poem by James Stephens, but I won't copy it out.

I've decided not to take part in any more soccer matches, I'll only train. Funny: Kirill has just come in with letters from you and Anyuta and with *Poslednie novosti* with *Camera*. I'll have a talk with Olga's scoundrel, as we call him here. *Camera* has to be sent today. Not a word from

Mulmanovich. I shan't mislay Anyuta's letter. The Union won't perish if I don't read out Pushkin's 'Faust'. That's what Hessen should have been told. And if he thinks I intended to give a talk, then he's wrong.

[VÉNAF]
[19 April 1932]

[TO: Berlin]

[Prague]

Meet me at 10.25 p.m. tomorrow, Wednesday, at the Anhalter station. You know, we shouldn't have started that Dresden affair. They prefer to arrange the evening for this Saturday and so on. And although I feel sorry to disappoint them (the letter, let me repeat, is extremely cordial, with a promise of a warm welcome and lavish hospitality), I will not go to Dresden. All in all, this has turned out rather silly. This morning I was at the museum again. I saw the charming casts of dragonflies, cicadas, ants, centipedes, as well as insect mummies in transparent amber. Mother, in general, is better. Thank God, no asthma. Last night, because Kirill was away, I helped Evgenia Konstantinovna wash the kitchen.

[VÉNAF]
[13 October 1932]

[TO: Berlin]

[Kolbsheim]

You have a letter from Lisbet. Nothing interesting. And I have one from Fond, who will be back in Paris on the 14th or 15th. Everything here's just the same. But the weather! ... A story's ripening. You took that nail file with you after all. Kiss Anyuta and greetings to Dita. From Paris my letters will be long.

[VÉNAF]
[15 October 1932]

[TO: Berlin]

[Kolbsheim]

I'm forwarding you a letter I got today from Ullstein. They are taking 'The Doorbell'. Call Kreul, tell him I'm in Paris. Talk to doctor Jacob. Agree to the abridgement. That translation is a corpse anyway, you can hack it without regret. Only I don't know who should do the abridging. Kreul's letter is very nice.

Now, the second thing. Nika has put me in touch with a leading local bookseller, Hertz, who is on friendly terms with Grasset and Fayard. He's very 'interested' in me. He's promised to work something out. And in fact, he and his other book friends have founded a society of bibliophiles, which orders from the publisher a hundred extra *de luxe* copies – selected books for Alsace book-lovers. And he has promised to choose one of my books. And moreover to organize the advertising, to put up my portrait and a manuscript in his shop window, and so on. A foreign writer is exactly what he needs. By the way, he is asking for reviews. We should send him *Nouvelles littéraires*, but first I want to find out when my books are coming out. Send *Nouvelles littéraires* and also the one from *Mesures* here, to Nika. He'll pass it on. Besides, I urgently need the main points of my agreements with Grasset and Fayard. Write, I beg you. I am afraid to get all mixed up. I'm going to Paris tomorrow, on Thursday I'll be there (terrible pen) at 8 p.m. I have received a comparatively cheerful postcard from Mother. She asks me to see Seryozha, who's now in Paris.

One more thing. I got an offer from Brussels to come to read something, but the conditions don't appeal much. The Club of Russian Jews is organizing the reading, but it's Natasha's sister, Mme Malevsky-Malevich, who has written to me. She advises me to make a *contre-proposition* of 50% and travel there and back. Or a straight 75%. Apart from them, the Antwerp Russian circle has invited me. I'll write to her today. Will make this very counter-offer. My arrival in Brussels will have to coordinate with the reading in Strasbourg, about which Nika will be talking more to Hertz. And in general this all needs to be timed for my return from Paris. By the way yesterday, when I was in Strasbourg, I had my hair cut and my watch fixed. There was a huge poster featured prominently inside a tram car: '*Société Protectrice des Animaux*'. Which means we got upset for no reason.

Meanwhile, as I've been writing, it turns out that the head of the bibliophiles I mentioned will come to dinner on Thursday night, so I will go to Paris on Friday morning. An awfully businessy letter. Sunny today, and one battered *Io* basking on a battered aster. Such a wretched razor, if you happen to remember, please send me another in a letter, otherwise shaving is torture.

[VÉNAF]
[17 October 1932]

[TO: Berlin]

[Kolbsheim]

First, so I don't forget. The old lady's name is Mme Maurice Grunelius. In accordance with your request I will cross the streets in Paris very carefully, when I get there on Tuesday. I got a very nice letter from Denis Roche. He thanks me for my praise. Will be happy to meet me and so on. I think you didn't understand the photograph of Mungo and the snake. You see Mungo, or rather Mongoose, always kills the snake. It's his passion, duty and nature. In general, he's a very sweet and gentle little animal, but when it comes to snakes he turns furious, and then he celebrates his victory with a little dance. Inspiration's not coming. I'm afraid I won't write anything before I get to Paris. It's very cold here. You know, I seem to have misplaced Lisa's letter, but there was nothing important in it, was there? I'll look for it again. The Gruneliuses had a neighbour over for dinner. She asked a lot about you. I save mice, there are lots in the kitchen. The servant catches them: the first time she wanted to kill one, but I took it and carried it out into the garden and set it free there. Since then, all the mice have been brought to me with a snort: '*Das habe ich nicht gesehen.*' I've already set free three of them this way, or maybe it was always the same one. It'll hardly have stayed in the garden.

I don't understand why Mother's not writing. It's unbearable how much I want to sit down to write a story, but it's not all ripe yet. I am also thinking about the French of Russian noblemen, '*Ne parlez pas devant les genS*', *Bibliothèque Rose*, governesses, French poetry. I read, that is, re-read, Aleksandra Fyodorovna's letters to the Tsar. On the whole, awfully touching. They loved each other so much, but from the political point of view . . . By the way, you have probably read, lying prone or semi-prone on Anyuta's couch, about Blok in *Poslednie novosti*, about his letters. Did you know that Blok was of Jewish origin? A soldier Bloch in Nicholas's army. That pleases me mightily. I'll do all I can in Paris. Kiss Anyutochka.

[VÉNAF]
[22 October 1932]

[TO: Berlin]

[Paris]

The road from Strasbourg to Paris was absolutely enchanting in its picturesqueness. The hills are covered with rusty-red-and-green foliage. Curly like mignonette. I arrived at 5 p.m. Settled into Nika's small but charmingly comfortable apartment. I shaved, changed, went to a café, called Fondaminsky from there, and at half past seven I was already at his place. Zenzinov was there, too, but his wife was out. Then Kerensky arrived, looking like an old but still hearty actor. He speaks loudly, stares through a golden lorgnette that he presses to his left eye. We sat down and talked. A committee is being set up (Fond, Zenzinov, Aldanov and others) to organize my reading.

Fond had to go to a meeting of *Sovremennye zapiski*, and I saw him as far as Vishnyak's. There I saw Vishnyak (a monstrous accent, Acropolis schedules, 'let's talk about me'), quiet Rudnev, black Demidov, and Aldanov, who now looks *très en gros* like Sherman. Everyone is charmingly nice to me. *Camera* is having an absolutely unexpected success. According to Fond, even Zina liked it. Kerensky shook my hand, held the pause, and, in a dramatic whisper: 'Amazing'. Tons to do today. I'll have my coffee now, then call Supervielle, write to Cocteau, then *Poslednie novosti*, a meeting with Aldanov, and so on. Nika and Natasha are awful darlings. They secretly gave me all kinds of tasty things for the road. There's all I need here.

[VÉNAF]
[24 October 1932]

[TO: Berlin]

[Paris]

The wild activity continues. I called Supervielle yesterday and will visit him today at 11 a.m. It's very early now, a [. . .] Proustian morning. I sent off my letter to Cocteau. It's hard to get him by phone. The police are said to watch him to make sure he doesn't arrange opium orgies, so his phone lets in draughts. Yesterday I had lunch at a little Russian restaurant, where they sit on stools at the bar. Then I went to the editorial office. It was simply touching how they received me. I saw Ladinsky. He's very sweet, with a simple face. He works as a telephone boy. Aldanov and Demidov again. The three of us had coffee together downstairs. Polyakov, Volkov and so on. Then a rather pretty little lady showed up (the gaps between her protruding teeth spoil her, though), who turned out to be Berberova, and she and I went to a café. Her conversation is just a little philistine. She told me in detail about her break-up with Khodasevich. Hinted that some unruly grey eyes have turned up in his life. She said that my epigram on Ivánov was written in a special album by the 'Perekryostok' group, that she imagined me exactly this way, 'with a bit of tan'. A break, I had to get up. I went home. On the way I bought some pastries and so on in a Russian store. After dinner, I went to Don Aminado's evening. He had sent me a stage ticket. I sat with Aldanov. And the intermissions were announced by Rausch, in tails (hired, apparently, because of his tails and his title – awful), who, you remember, had come to see me. By the way, he offered me a room at his place. But the evening was nightmarishly boring. The audience exactly the same as in Berlin. The same ladies, among them Mme Adamov, who has invited me to her place. All this is very depressing. They wore us out with humour from old issues of *Poslednie novosti*, but of course, thank God, it was over early. This morning I began a letter to you and got two of yours. I will write a word of thanks to Frumkin. It's good that you have given S. G. a package for Mother. I haven't had a chance yet to see Zyoka. I am expecting news about Strasbourg and Belgium. I called Lizaveta today. We agreed I'll have dinner with them at 7 p.m. tomorrow. I like the poems of Limousin very much. I'm carrying on with the story. So, I was at Supervielle's this morning. He is lanky, looks like a horse. We talked about literature. He promised to introduce me on Friday to Paulhan, the editor of *Nouvelle Revue Française*. He was very obliging. I'll go to him again on Tuesday morning, with *Luzhin*. He talked about his own work eagerly and loftily, but, overall, very attractively. I walked back from Boulevard Lannes. Very agreeable weather. Russet-blue. I had lunch at a Russian restaurant and from there moved to a café, after remembering I needed to write to Nika. When they gave me some paper, it turned out to have *Rotunda* on it. At 3, I called in on Fond to talk about my evening. I met Amalia Osipovna and a very amiable colonel. My darling, what a cat they have! Something perfectly stupendous. Siamese, in colour dark beige, or *taupe*, with chocolate paws and the tail the same. Moreover, his tail is comparatively short, so his croup has something of a little dog or, rather, a kangaroo, and that's its colour, too. And that special silkiness of short fur, and some very tender white tints on its folds, and wonderful, clear-blue eyes, turning transparently green towards evening, and a pensive tenderness of its walk, a sort of heavenly circumspection of movement. An amazing, sacred animal, and so quiet – it's unclear what he is looking at with those eyes filled to the brim with sapphire water. Straight from there I called Lisbet, and when I sat down at the tea-table again, Amalia Osipovna, a plumpish old lady, very quiet and pleasant, silently handed me my letter to Stepun, about her translation of *Pereslegin* into English. *Tableau*. Stepun said that I did not know who had made the translation, and I pretended to be very surprised; everyone laughed in good spirits. So it's all turned out well. Around five, I went to Khodasevich's. A small, untidy, sour little apartment beyond the city limits. Khodasevich looks like a monkey or even like Acharya, and all those Hindu movements too, and jokes that aren't very funny, and he snaps words, and all this on a rather sad lining, and he is very thin, and he was terribly nice to me. And Berberova too was at the round table with its meagre little fare. Afterwards she said to me: 'Have you noticed how dirty it has become there since I stopped living there with him?' Terapiano and Smolensky are pleasant young men, in the style of our 'poets', and they speak like them, too. From there I went for dinner at Aldanov's. We dined *à trois*: his wife, corpulent and swarthy; I suddenly got drunk on two shots of vodka. Yes, I forgot, Khodasevich knows a few butterflies: *Antiopa*, *Io*, *Apollo*. On the whole, he's somehow quite touching. I liked him very much, much more than Berberova. Aldanov and I had a heart-to-heart conversation about my fate, one can have an apartment in Passy, 2–3 rooms, with all conveniences, for 5,000 francs a year. He showed me a whole bookcase of translations into fourteen languages, huge and very neat stacks of reviews, the desk where he writes, the scattered pages of a draft, an unfinished page, a folder with his notes. And it's as if he drinks in praise. Around 10, we went to Fond's. Kerensky was there again, he appropriated my matches (now I'm suffering from not smoking), called Aldanov '*M'sieur Aldanóff*'—a sample of his jokes—all this very loudly,—and spoke about Mussolini with a light trace of envy. The marvellous Siamese cat and the huge, fat, fat-fingered, Rutenberg, Gapon's murderer (he hanged him). He occupied himself with picking out coins, sous and francs, from a dog-shaped piggy-bank of Amalia Osipovna's, and Vishnyak told Aldanov, who drank in his words, what Gruzenberg had been writing about his things. And we drank wonderful tea. Anyuta will appreciate this. Tell her that I love and kiss her. Shortly after 11 p.m. I went home. I've become terribly tired in the course of the day and here I am lying down and writing to you. It's already half past one, I found a match in the lining of my jacket and have had a smoke. I haven't yet seen *Sovremennye zapiski*. No time. Tomorrow morning: Sergey and Milyukov. Andrey Sedykh is not Osorgin at all, as we thought, but Tsvibakh. He intends to interview me. Aldanov thinks my face looks like Osorgin's. Neither Adamovich – he is in Nice – nor Ivánov (he is sitting in Riga and waiting for the death of Odoevtseva's father) is here. 'My uncle has most honest principles . . .' Tomorrow, if I have time, I'll write something in French. The Fonds very much want me to come when they have the abominable Merezhkovsky couple over. But I have told him straight that I don't want to see them. Felsen, it turns out, is a great admirer of mine. I still need to see a thousand people. It's raining. See how much I have written you. During the dinner at Grunelius's, a button flew off my blue jacket, and everyone was in dinner jackets. Nika, true, compromised: a silk shirt, no waistcoat. But my button flew off, and Antoinette sewed it on. I am trying to avoid *gaffes* and so on, I'm gossiping within limits. Today, coming out of the metro to Supervielle's, I asked a passer-by, 'Where's Boulevard Lannes?' '*Oh M'sieur, c'est loin d'ici, c'est tout à fait de l'autre côté, devers les fortifications*.' We were both standing on Boulevard Lannes. This is the third such case. The most terrible one was in a pub, where there was a phone, when the owner explained to me the location of the *salle de vue* (Aminado's evening). He was sending me God knows where. Luckily I didn't listen to him but directed my steps according to my maps, with Fond's directions. I will probably read *Despair* to him, Khodasevich and Aldanov, and will give a chapter to *Poslednie novosti* after the reading, which will be on the 19th or 20th.

As Fond says, 'the campaign has started'. They tell me that Kuprin can't be invited. He gets dead drunk just on one glass. There are too many literary men here. *I've had my fill*. Aldanov does not always understand when I joke and when I don't. He looks at me with distrust, but Khodasevich understands right away. I said to Aldanov: 'I would not have written a single novel without my wife.' He responded: 'Yes, we've already heard how she helps you.' Weidle is very young. I have not seen him yet. He's away. It'd be much, much nicer to live here. Oh, it's so late.

[VÉNAF]

[25 October 1932]

[TO: Berlin]

[Paris]

Everything's going very, very well for me. I've already had time to become friends with Supervielle, who's awfully nice and talented. I spent the entire morning at his place. I read *Luzhin* to him, and he read me his poems. Some of them–wonderful–I've offered to translate into Russian. We had a very good and warm discussion. He went into raptures about the excerpts from *Luzhin*: the beginning and the chess match. He says the translation is not bad, just a bit clumsy in places. I'll be at his place again in a couple of days. Here's who he also reminds me of–Sergey Rodzyanko. I'm sitting in a café now, and just had an excellent lunch for 6 francs at *Procope*. It's a quarter past two. At 3, I must be at Henry Muller's (Grasset), and on Thursday, at Jean Fayard's. I arranged with both of them by phone yesterday. And tomorrow afternoon I'll be at Paulhan's, *Nouvelle Revue Française*. I'll offer translations of my stories to them and so on. Maybe Luzhin's chess match, as Supervielle advises. Yesterday afternoon I also called Lukash and

Milyukov (I've arranged a meeting) and Mme Adamov, who has promised to sell tickets. And I've written letters to Denis Roche, Kovarsky, and Frumkin, and signed that one for Kreul; I will see Levinson on Thursday at Fayard's.

I saw Sergey yesterday morning and had dinner at the Thompsons'. We didn't talk about my literature. He has some lessons here, Sergey does. That terrible glassy gaze and a certain aura of tragedy. And he says the obvious. But he said that he wanted to talk about the essential, to find out, apparently, my attitude to his life, and for that he'll call on me tomorrow, on Wednesday, at 3 p.m., after which I will go to *Nouvelle Revue Française*. I must write to Grasset now. A break. *L'addition, s'il vous plaît*. One coffee.

Now I'm home from Grasset. I had a lie-down, I must be at Fondaminsky's at half past six. They gave me a charming welcome at Grasset. Muller is a very nice young man, and, I think, a Jew, and another man, also very nice, is Tissen, who's specifically in charge of my novel. Muller and I had a very amusing and friendly conversation. He has promised to drop me a line in a day or two, to meet with me. Gabriel Marcel, the critic, strongly advised me to see Ergaz. He gave me addresses of some others as well. Tissen admitted to me that they bought *Camera* sight unseen or, to be more precise, they bought it thanks to the reports of Nemirovsky (!), Bryanchaninov (??) and Ergaz, who hasn't yet handed in her translations. They advised me to give her a push. I didn't say anything about the financial side there, if only because it would have been awkward without Kovarsky. I have a letter from Nika for Marcel, but the publisher's offices have a terribly dusty unpresentable look, like the old Logos warehouse. It's very agreeable and straightforward there, without all those German things, they sit on the tables, talk about cards, and so on. Some frayed, crumpled photos without frames on the wall. Among others, the bearded, thick-nosed

Lawrence with some young maiden at his side. Charming. They had thought that Nabokov was Sirin's representative. I think everything's working out excellently. – Touch wood.

Yesterday afternoon I wrote, letters that is, and telephoned, and then went to the Thompsons', having planned to buy *foie gras* on the way. I went to a dozen shops, without finding it, so wanted to buy flowers. Could not find any, either, and arrived pleading guilty. Told them in detail all that had happened. They thanked you very much for your attention. Treated me to a wonderful dinner with champagne and, in general, heaps of wine. But that's beside the point. They're both so sweet. He's so interesting. We had such a glorious conversation that I felt quite sorry to leave. He showed me wonderful old books. All the editions of 1001 *Nights*, a medieval anatomy textbook with skeletons striking nonchalant poses against the landscapes, wonderful English poets with authors' corrections, and a great deal more. And I'm quite on form now, meaning *en train*. Lisbet played the part of Yu. Yu. and said very touching things about you. And on Thursday I'm going, with the Thompsons, to a dinner at the American Club, where the playwright Bernstein will be talking. He seems to be a philistine, but it'll be interesting anyway. Tell Mme Tatarinov that I have called Romochka and that I'll see her. I'll slip her tickets. I'll meet with Lukash on Thursday, after the American Club. Tomorrow, I'll dash to the Shklyavers'. No matter who I call, everyone already knows I'm here. Outside, in the evening, whores strike up conversations with me in English. Yes, sir. Ah, Supervielle's so charming, and I recommended Thompson get Nicolas's music. He said he definitely would. I'm already less tired: getting used to it.

[VÉNAF]
[28 or 29 October 1932]

[TO: Berlin]

[Paris]

Yesterday, with the Tatarinov girls and women – Roma, Danya, Roma's sister Mme Adamov – and Roma's brother, who, actually, had invited everybody, I went to the gypsies, to a very pleasant Russian establishment, *Au Papillon bleu*. There we drank white wine and listened to the truly beautiful singing. Real gypsies plus Polyakova. This was my first carouse here, but not much of one. Then Klyachkin drove us all home (he's in Berlin this morning, by the way), I was at home by 1 a.m., very decent and sweet of me, but the running about and lack of sleep the last few days have taken their toll. I woke up at half past two. Luckily I had nothing on in the morning. And now it's near five. Soon I have to go to Denis Roche's. I've prepared a postcard for him with *Bac berepom* so that he can finally understand what it's all about. Paris is full of conversations about me already, and already they're coming back to me. They find me 'an Englishman', 'quality goods'. They say I always travel with a *tub*, in line with Martin, perhaps. And already my *bons mots* are coming back to me, too. So there you have me.

Have you read Osorgin's article and Adamovich's verbiage? They show, [in general, how pleasant....]. I can't conceal from you that I'm sitting in *Rotunda* again. It's very comfortable writing here. I am drinking coffee. Tomorrow and some of Sunday, I'll write. I feel great here. First of all, because I'm writing so comfortably, secondly, because my head's had a rest, and I sleep well, although not long. Don't forget to send me 'Music'. And if you can't find it, then I'll have to get it from *Poslednie novosti*. But then remind me when it was, approximately. I phoned the Shklyavers, but I didn't get them. Shall I call on Sonya? Ask the old man where Zyoka is. I phoned him, but they told me he was away or had moved.

There are so few dogs in the streets here! Yesterday, though, in some side-street, I petted the sweetest milky-eyed puppy. Tomorrow I will definitely write to Anyutochka. Tell her how fondly I think of her. I love her very much. I've caught two fleas already. Danya and Roma have barely changed. It seems they'll manage to sell lots of tickets. 'Once again a butterfly alights on the aster with its four coloured wings spread flat'. This is a poem about Kolbsheim. I've sent it to Nika and Natasha. I wrote twice to them, but they stay silent. I don't even know when they'll arrive, but I'm guaranteed a room at Rausch's, he's very nice.

[VÉNAF]

[29 October 1932]

[TO: Berlin]

[Paris]

Today, I was at Denis Roche's and at Danya's. Both live in the same building, in a very gloomy district, near the Boulevard Arago, where executions take place. Danya retells me her affair with a Frenchman. And Roche turns out to be a grey-haired gentleman with a long face, slightly old-fashioned. He says that he has yet to clean up and correct a lot in his translation. I'll call on him again on Tuesday night to look over a few places together. Znossko will be there, but today he had an old man over, who turned out to be the son of the artist Ge. Strictly speaking, I've already written you today, when I stopped at the café. But now, when I'm back home, I've found your double letter and feel like writing to you for the second time.

By the way, about the café. I stopped at the point when a five-year-old Russian girl walked in. Here's how it was. Across the little table from me (the table is located in front of a long settee), a heavy old gentleman in a black hat was sitting with a little Russian girl. [. . .]

[VÉNAF]

[31 October 1932]

[TO: Berlin]

[Paris]

Sunday evening.

It's around 11 now. I've just got home. Awfully tired by my day. So, yesterday, I had tea one-on-one with Fondik. He's really an angel, and everyone calls him an angel. One doesn't need a residence permit. In a couple of days, at Aldanov's, I'll meet an American professor who has become 'interested' in me. And if the Americans buy even one novel . . . Well, you understand. Gallimard still hasn't answered me about *Glory*. Maybe he'll take it. Besides, others too are also rosily doubtful. From there, I went to *Poslednie novosti*. There, in Demidov's office, sat Aleksandr Nikolaevich Benois; we greeted each other with a kiss. He has changed very little, only shaved off his little beard. But he's still as dark in the face, with a broad nose and a charming voice; he wears pince-nez and glasses over them. I'll call on him on Thursday night. I gave Demidov some biblio-biographic information. Talked with Aldanov and Tsvibakh, he'll interview me tomorrow morning and treat me to lunch. I had dinner at a restaurant and, around 8, I was already at home. I undressed, lay down, and was scribbling something till midnight. And then the wind wouldn't let me sleep. This morning I barely managed to get to the Thompsons' on time. Drank two cocktails straight on an empty stomach. They had quail for lunch. We had a very good and cosy conversation till 3 p.m. I'll go there again on Friday. At three, I went by electric train to

Meudon, and, from the station climbed up the hill. A very peculiar little town. At last I found Lukash. [. . .] Then Borman came, and I left after a while, barely making it to Khodasevich's place, where Berberova, Dovid Knut, Mandelstam, Smolensky, Weidle's wife, and some others whose names I didn't catch were sitting. Everyone read their poems. Me, too. Then they read epigrams from their notebooks. One was very sweet, on me, that I seduce old Social Revolutionaries with Magda's charms. Then everyone left around eight. I stayed with the very sweet Khodasevich, just the two of us. He cooked up a supper in his kitchen.

[VÉNAF]

[1 November 1932]

[TO: Berlin]

[Paris]

Tuesday morning

Yesterday I had an interview for *Poslednie novosti* and *Segodnya* with Tsvibakh. He asked idiotic questions and my replies weren't too sharp; it will come out terrible nonsense, I think. He is smallish, plumpish and philistine. I've finally got hold of Marcel. I'll call on him on Thursday afternoon. He has a thin little voice. I tried to write in the afternoon, it didn't work. Then I slept for an hour. In the evening I went to Roche's. He is now busy checking every phrase of his translation minutely, conscientiously and rather talentedly. He has already corrected many of the things you and I found there. And our proofs have gone to Levinson. He (Roche) has got hold of a thick volume – chess and other games – and is drawing his information from there. To me, he's an ideal translator, in that sense. *Luzhin* should come out not at all badly. As for 'lies' and 'lodges', he translated them as '*loge*' and '*l'auge*'. I had to give him my own copy of *Luzhin* with an inscription. Then the Znossko-Borovsky family came over: he, his wife and son. We drank some wonderful sweet wine and talked endlessly about *Luzhin* (they all remember it better than I do). Roche, after consulting with Znossko, corrected a few chess spots. All in all, I had an exceptionally pleasant evening. Now, Roche and I are trying to arrange for *Luzhin* to be published in a newspaper; we'll split the honorarium. I'll talk with Levinson about this, and with Evreinov about the chess film. I got home around 1 a.m., wrote a letter to Brussels, agreed to arrive on the 20th. I'm rather tired from all this running about. I simply have to write a story for the 15th and before then get a translation ready for N. R. F. But I don't get any peace. And Natasha is coming soon with the baby, and I don't know whether I should move to Rausch's or stay here. I've just got a postcard from Kyandzhuntsev, I'll call him. Buy a ticket and come here, why don't you? I will see Fond in the afternoon, then go back home, do some writing, and in the evening I'm at Berberova's.

It's twelve now, I must get up, I'm very hungry. Today, I think, is the first morning I've been able to have a long lie-in. I'll phone Levinson, Kaminka and others today. Oh yes, I phoned my brother, but he wasn't there.

[VÉNAF]
[2 November 1932]

[TO: Berlin]

[Paris]

Wednesday

I've just had lunch and returned home. Sergey will arrive at three, by five I must be at N. R. F. to see Paulhan, then at Kovarsky's, from whom I've received a polite, courtly letter. What place in my life did I stop at yesterday? Oh, yes, I remember: before the evening trip to Fondaminsky.

So then, at seven o'clock I rolled over to Fondaminsky's, where I caught the tea era still, and as part of it – thank God, already getting ready to leave – the Merezhkovsky couple. She is red-haired and deaf, he is small, looks like Bem, with the same kind of beard. We said hello, and a chill swept through (as Aldanov later said). I didn't talk to them at all, not even half a word. They soon left. After tea and still there for dinner (our supper) were Aldanov, Vishnyak (he is very likeable, funny and round), the invariable Kerensky, who also keeps cracking jokes with a remarkable Jewish intonation, and in general, has mannerisms a little like the old man Kaplan's. Zenzinov is very quiet, invisible (it was he who let Azef escape), and Mother Maria – a nun, fat, pink, very likeable, the former wife of Kuzmin-Karavaev. And when I, not knowing this, told how Hitlerites had beaten him up, she said with feeling: 'Serves him right!' After supper, Aldanov, Fondaminsky and Zenzinov discussed the organization of my reading – tickets, hall, etc. On Thursday the first announcement will appear in *Poslednie novosti* (Aldanov's doing this). They also want to bring in Osorgin, 'your great admirer'. All in all, it's going smoothly. Around nine, we all went together to a religious-political meeting, like this: into a small taxi-cab squeezed the plump Mother Maria, Ilya Isidorovich, Aldanov, Kerensky, who kept on teasing Aldanov saying that Gruzenberg, just like Kremenetsky, had diabetes. Aldanov felt really hurt. And me. And the jolly Vishnyak sat in front near the driver, who, of course, turned out to be Russian, and what's more with the name of Kremenetsky, and when we got out of the car, Vishnyak, with the air of a *conférencier*, introduced us one by one to the driver: just look whom you've given a ride to, and we all shook his hand, and he was embarrassed and beaming. It was all extraordinarily silly.

At the meeting, Struve spoke, as well as Kirill Zaytsev, Kartashev (he speaks wonderfully, with tight-shut eyes, with amazing force and imagery), Florovsky and Fondaminsky (who was terribly agitated: they had got at *Novyi grad*), with great spirit. And I, of course, was preoccupied not so much with the substance as with the form. I spoke to Lolly Lvov and to Zaytsev, to Pyotr Ryss, to a Russian journalist Levin, who, remember, used to exclaim 'I tell them in black and white', and I sat next to Berberova. She has wonderful eyes that seem enlivened and glazed in an artificial way, but she has an absolutely terrible promontory of rose flesh between her two big, wide-spaced front teeth. She told me that Felsen and another classmate of mine, I've forgotten his name, have found some lucrative business for me, almost an office job. Next Tuesday, I'll see them at her place. This all finished rather late, I barely made it to the métro. When I was leaving, Struve was yelling across the hall with a huge ridiculous gesture: 'Ivan the Terrible was scum, scum.' And Kartashev, in his speech, said about Tolstoy the thinker: 'A fool and a coachman.'

I fell asleep right away (I can't read before sleep now, sleep takes over), and this morning went to see Milyukov who lives right near me. A cheery old man, lots of papers on his desk, a piano, a radio, he is very polite and has promised to do all he can for the success of my reading. He didn't ask a single word about Mother, and I didn't say anything, either. I wrote very late yesterday, lying in bed after midnight, and the concierge has just woken me up: it's half past nine. At half past twelve there's the American Club, then Lukash, then Fayard, then Mlle Klyachkin. After Sergey left, I went to N. R. F., where Paulhan saw me right away and was very pleasant, promised to find out where things stand with *Glory*, and we agreed I will send him two or three short *nouvelles* for *Nouvelle Revue Française*. Oh, yes, by the way, I don't have 'Music'. How come? Where is it – not at Esther's or Anyuta's? If you find it, send it here. Meanwhile, I will be translating my 'Terra Incognita' for *Nouvelle Revue Française*, I want to do it and I will. Paulhan is small, swarthy, he looks like the owner of Teryuz. We talked about *Glory*, which goes on sale tomorrow, about its distribution, and about *Camera Obscura*. He will send me a copy of the agreement here in a day or two. I'll see him all the same, I have to go to sign copies of *Glory*. He'll send out twenty-five of them.

From there, I went to Aunt Nina's and saw Muma there. Aunt Nina is 72 years old, but she has kept her great liveliness and cheerfulness, while Nikolay Nikolaevich looks like a hearty old English Colonel. I brought her a copy of *Glory*, she'd already read it in *Sovremennye zapiski*. From her, I went with Muma to the Rausches'. They, especially he, have a reputation for being the kindest people on earth. They are touchingly sweet, I will definitely move in with them when Nika rolls up. He is great friends with Don Aminado. I recited poems, the young lady – plain, with braids, Mme Rausch's daughter from her first marriage – read out her productions to me: moon, birches, thunderstorms, waves. And Muma's last name is Zapolsky. He's a singer, now with the Russian opera in Italy. I stayed at Rausch's till half past twelve, went to sleep late. Time to get up.

[VÉNAF]
[2 November 1932]

[TO: Berlin]

[Paris]

Natasha and Ivan arrive on Friday, and I'll move to the Rausches'. Write to me at their address. It's morning, I'm lying in bed, drinking coffee brought by the concierge. Yesterday I told Fond that I had been to the Kyandzhuntsevs'. He said that Bunin's a great friend of theirs. Neither Saba nor his mother has changed a bit, but the sister I wouldn't have recognized. Beautiful eyes, but she's very plain. And they were so nice, so sweet, they know everything I've written down to the last line, and they remember you. I felt as if I'd just recently, the other day, been to see them on the Liteyny. On the wall there is a portrait of the elder brother, the one who died. Saba went to his room, rummaged around, and returned with long poems that I sent to him in Kislovodsk from St Petersburg on October 25 of 1917, i.e. on the first day of the Soviet era. I will certainly copy them for you. They know heaps about me, even the scene with Spiresco. Someone had told them: 'He, i.e. I, has such shoulders, such biceps',–so they thought a giant would come in. I'm having lunch with them on Saturday. Now *there* was a pleasant meeting.

From there, I rolled on to Berberova. She's very likeable, but so thickly literary, and she dresses terribly. I met Felsen at her place, we talked only about literature, and soon I began to get sick of it. I haven't had such conversations since my grammar-school years. 'And do you know this? And do you like *him*? And have you read *him*?' Terrible, in a word.

[VÉNAF]

[3 November 1932]

[TO: Berlin]

[Paris]

Thursday

There are all kinds of things to be sorted out. Yesterday afternoon I was at the Rausches', (I'll be staying with them from tomorrow), and at Fond's, who is busily occupied with distributing my tickets. I went with him to Aldanov's, where we ran into a Californian professor who turned out to be a Russian Jew, Khodasevich, Vishnyak, Zaytsev and one of Aldanov's relatives, through whom Aldanov wants to set you up at Hachette, but I have no idea whether you want it. The Californian has become very interested in my work, he's read some, and he invited me to lunch with him on Monday. Aldanov evidently invited everyone on his account, but it turned out no one talked to him. At first we discussed whether Bunin would receive the Nobel Prize and then, and up till the very end of the evening, a heated argument started up about the contemporary era and youth, in which Zaytsev uttered Christian banalities, Khodasevich literary banalities, and my very sweet and saintly Fondik very touching things of a social nature. Vishnyak from time to time threw in a phrase steeped in robust materialism, and Aldanov and his relative kept silent. I, of course, put into play my little thoughts about the non-existence of eras. Poor Aldanov was awfully glum, apparently he's being roughed up in the corridors of opinion. The press does not dare to [scold him], although in *Vozrozhdenie* Khodasevich put the knife in – took him to pieces for *The Cave*. In a little *aparté* Aldanov told me that his literary career, so they say, is over, that he's decided to stop writing and so on. Zaytsev invited me round. He has strange sunken cheeks and very prominent eyelids. Chukovsky wrote about him once that all of his heroes sleep a lot and in detail. I was too late for the métro and walked with Fondaminsky to Passy. He blamed himself and others that we hadn't asked the Californian a single question. It was awkward. I've got a letter here from Kulisher that the percentage is being raised to seventy-five and they have an exceptional advertising campaign, but they want me to come not on the 20th but on the 26th. On the 20th, Mme Damansky is arriving there. There was some kind of a mix-up; true, I answered them only the next day, but they'd asked for it immediately. I don't know whether I should agree to it now, especially since I don't know your plans and I don't know what to do with myself that week, from the 21st to the 29th. I don't want to spend it in Belgium at all, and in general I don't want you to go there. To hell with Belgium! Today's the *interview* in *Poslednie novosti*, written in a terrible style. Terrible vulgarity, and all beside the mark. And why my poor little coat had to suffer so much, I don't know. It's not all that bad, really. Especially nice is this little expression 'funny', in the sense of 'spare me'.

I had lunch today near the Luxembourg garden with Sergey and his husband. The husband, I must admit, is very pleasant, *quiet*, absolutely not the pederast type, with an attractive face and manner. But I felt somewhat awkward, especially when one of their acquaintances, a red-lipped and curly-headed man, approached us for a minute. From there, I went to *Rossiya i slavyanstvo*. Lolly again recalled the story with Tair, he invited me over. I'll have to go, it seems. That very Mme [Mlle?] Rachmaninov, it appears, will be there. Now I am sitting in a rather wretched little café, since I'm not far from Marcel's locale, where I need to be at 5. And it's 4 now. Not worth going home. In the evening I'm at Benois's. I don't know whether I'll write to you tomorrow. I'll be moving, and there's tons to do.

[VÉNAF]

[3–4 November 1932]

[TO: Berlin]

[Paris]

Thursday night

I've become very good friends with Gabriel Marcel. It turns out he has an excellent knowledge of my things, he has read K.Q.K. in German, he knows the storylines of my other three novels, terrible compliments and all that, and he absolutely wants K. Q. K. to come out in French. He is in charge of the foreign section at Plon, and says that when I was offering my things to them, they were going through a hard time and were wary. We arranged that in a day or two I'll have dinner at his place with others, including, by the way, the author of *Œil de Dieu*. Tomorrow I'm having dinner at Supervielle's with the Paulhan couple, and Grasset. The day after tomorrow, I—but why should I tell you all this if you think I'm doing nothing. Their refusal to publish *Glory* was not unexpected to me, alas, I knew but kept it quiet that their reader was the nasty Pozner, and Ehrenburg's evidently close to them too.

By the way, Roche told me that Plon's translation of Shmelyov's *The Sun of the Dead* was absolutely swamped by criticism, thanks to Soviet influence. Intrigues, intrigues, intrigues, as Maman Rouge used to say. I have just returned from a very pleasant evening at Benois's, lots of artists, I sold four tickets there. I am running around all day long, my tongue, red as a slice of ham, hanging out, and you say to me: 'Blunderer'. The fact they sent the letter to Berlin is their fault and not mine. Paulhan doesn't have a direct connection with Gallimard, but he has promised me to make enquiries. I couldn't demand more. I have decided to go to Brussels; I've had no news from Strasbourg. To tell you the truth, I am not keen to go there. All this would have to be arranged over again, the books will come out only in January, and then it's too tedious. I've got mighty tired, after all, and I want to write. Mme Damansky is already here, congratulate me, there's one I won't be losing any time over. My poor tattered time.

[VÉNAF]
[5 November 1932]

[TO: Berlin]

[Paris]

I'm already on such a footing with Paulhan that I can give a story to him at any moment, but for that I need that story, that is, a translation of it. Beside *Nouvelle Revue Française*, I have free access both to *Candide* and to *Nouvelles Littéraires*, not to mention other newspapers. Everyone here is connected to each other in one way or another, but, I repeat, I have to have the translations. Denis Roche, in principle, has promised me to translate, but he is too busy at work now. Mme Ergaz has been sick all this time. I will be at her place on Monday and offer her 'Music' to translate. I have begun to translate 'Terra' myself. I've written to Mme Lvovsky at last. Tomorrow I am at Levinson's, and there too I'll set something going. I can't do more than I'm doing. I began to write a story, but I have absolutely no idea if I'll finish it by the 15th. Yesterday I had dinner with the Paulhans. She's a woman of the simplish-socialist type, not very likeable, unbelievably dressed, in a short and, I think, knitted dress, but I did talk a lot to him, about literature. He wants to read *Glory*, but how he will read in Russian is unclear. I'll try to find out whom I should forward *Glory* to from Gallimard. Supervielle is as charming as before, we call each other *cher ami*. On Monday as well I'll have lunch with Kaun, and in a day or two I'm meeting Bradley. I'll also meet Evreinov at the Rausches', and I'll stay in Paris, in any event, till 23rd – 24th, because the evenings in Antwerp and Brussels are on the 26th and 27th. Nika thinks, correctly, that it's premature to advertise in Strasbourg a book that will come out only in January, so for the meantime the evening there won't happen. I think we ought to move here. And for that, go to the embassy, request a visa, talk to Wilhelm or Piquet. They gave you their recommendations for your getting a *permis* here till the first. And I will talk about this too to Maklakov, although there are jobs around with Russians, for instance, or with Armenians, where one can get by without a *permis*. And I could look up lodgings for us, and so on. Let me repeat, I do not want you to work, so I am giving this plan less attention. But, once again, I'm not going to insist on your coming. After all, this is all hard to resolve, so let everything be as you suggest. I will return to Berlin on the 28th or 29th, we will rewrite *Despair*, and in January we will move here. I have moved to the

Rausches', where I'm awfully uncomfortable. I sleep in the living room, at night they straggle around the entire apartment, there is no place to put up my towel in the bathroom, and so on. But they are infinitely sweet, so never mind.

Yesterday I had lunch at the Thompsons' and then went to see Avgust Isaakovich and Tsar Boris. Today I had lunch at the Kyandzhuntsevs, who bought 250 francs' worth of tickets from me. I'm not living off that money, of course. There's more from Fond, too, and tomorrow Vishnyak will give me some from *Sovremennye zapiski*. I spend very little. Everyone is surprised. I'll read 'Music'. Now I am going to see Natasha home. This evening I will write, if I can find a nook. I haven't borrowed money anywhere, this is all literary money. It's noisy here, hard to write. I am simply astonished at the multitude of things and connections I've done and set up on my own.

[VÉNAF]

[8 November 1932]

[TO: Berlin]

[Paris]

I'm carrying on yesterday's letter. Kaun, who has been, by the way, to Gorky's and to Bunin's, wants to take *Luzhin*, *K. Q. K.* and *Glory* to America to the publishers he's connected with. He doesn't know *Camera*. I'd like him to take it, it in particular, but I don't know whether we have a complete copy that we can send to him. Remember that we definitely have to send the ending of *Camera* to Ergaz, too, that is, minus what has been published already in *Sovremennye zapiski*. Besides, he has already got and will be taking with him 'Chorb', i.e., all the stories except 'Chorb'. He seems very businesslike and pleasant. He's already placed some books by Osorgin. Aldanov is conducting negotiations with him as well. A small, quiet person, elderly, with a trimmed moustache, in a tennis shirt. I met Max Eastman in his room at the hotel. He's a very well-known American poet and translator. Remember, Bunin asked me to find him? I have also met Eastman's Russian, *très soviète*, wife, and he himself is a half-communist, a Trotskyite, a huge, tanned man with wonderful, absolutely white hair, he looks like a cockatoo. Then Kaun and I went to a restaurant for lunch, and he took a picture of me, as I've already written, and we arranged to meet again. This is important: call *Slovo*, get them to send *Luzhin* and *K. Q. K.* to him, and maybe the German *K. Q. K.* as well, to the *Daily Times*. You mustn't put it off, because he plans to leave by the end of this month. From him I went to see Ergaz. She seems charming, and it turns out that she is so well provided for that she needs absolutely no honorariums, and, if I understood her correctly, she will give me her 45% back and, in general, is ready to translate my stories for free, but now, because of *Camera*, she cannot do it, although she is ready to correct someone else's translations and suggests, recommending him highly, Evgeny Shakh (an old acquaintance), to whom I'll give 40–50%. This, of course, relates only to the two stories I've given her ('A Bad Day' and 'Perfection', but not 'Music', as I had misinformed you, I think). Since then I'll make a rough draft myself, and she'll do the rest, or all of it, when she finishes *Camera*. She's a very obliging lady with huge connections through her rich lawyer-businessman husband. She suggests to me that she can go straight to the minister for your *permis*, which is almost guaranteed to come through. She has very elegant furniture and, imagine, she is acquainted with Lena but she says that they do not see eye to eye. Something unpleasant happened between them. In a couple of days, probably Wednesday, I'll have dinner at her place with Gabriel Marcel and other people. As you see, total success on this side, and it's nice, by the way, that she has offered to pay me 1,000 francs right now. I think I've already written about that. Send me a list of people I have to send *Glory* to. Do it without delay. You know, such a touching little thing. Next to me there now lies, neatly wrapped, your little brown dress with its colourful scarf. You, my little muddle-head, forgot it in Kolbsheim, and I picked it up just now from Natasha, where I had lunch. I told them to send it—you'll get it soon. I'm free this evening, I would have written, but, unfortunately, Koka's son has arrived, I'll be sleeping in the same room as him. All this is awful. So it's noisy here, and I am thinking of going out briefly with someone. I'll call the Thompsons now, I'm dining with them on Friday. Tomorrow I'll be at Kovarsky's (we need to send some people *Glory*) and I'll see Sergey. I'll see Evreinov on Saturday. You know, I am mighty tired of all of this. They are playing billiards here, it's noisy, I had a hot chocolate.

Goodbye . . .

[VÉNAF]

[Letter 2, 8 November 1932]

[TO: Berlin]

[Paris]

I had a letter today, and I'm no longer cross. Things are coming along rather well, details below. This is not ink, but diluted lilac, to put it kindly. Please, be careful, don't go out walking. Here they already imagine that there's a revolution in Berlin. I will find out when to apply for the visas, and will apply. In any case, in a day or two I'll be at Blackborough's. I don't remember whether I wrote to you that on Saturday I had lunch with the saintly Kyandzhuntsevs, that he was having his tuxedo altered for me, and so on. In the early evening I went to Natasha's, their fat German maid occupies one room, and Natasha and Vanya another. So that, in fact, there's nowhere to sit and it's quite a jumble. She and I went to a café in Montparnasse, and popped into some show booths, threw wooden balls; if you hit a particular point, a half-naked girl, turning upside down, suddenly falls out from the bed. In general harmless, except the girl has to lie in bed for hours before the eyes of all.

On Sunday, I had lunch at Muma's, who, according to Natasha, is performing with a group of women singers. She sang a few romances rather well. Then I went to Vishnyak's. I had tea there. He gave me 300 francs more towards the *Camera* payment, which will be enough for me till I leave. With the receipt of this it comes to (350+200+300) 850, of which this 300 is still almost intact. Besides, I am getting 1,000 francs on November 22 from Ergaz. Brussels and Antwerp will pay for my trip to Berlin and more, if I'm going to Berlin. I'm more and more inclined for you to come here. The evening will yield, according to Fond's estimates, 2,500–3,000 francs net. He is an optimist, but, it's true, the tickets are selling well. I didn't get especially involved in this, and I've already sold 690 francs worth, 480 of which I got in cash and submitted to Fond for accounting. From Vishnyak I went to the Levinsons', and here I must sharply change the tone of my narrative. An epic begins. In the midst of a luxurious apartment there sits in armchairs (note the plural form) the long-unshaven, fat-faced, big-nosed Andrey Yakovlevich, in a red dressing gown; he speaks through clenched teeth, savouring and weighing his words. Sometimes, the weighing lasts half or minute or so, during which time his face acquires the fastidiously haughty expression of some kind of well-fed Roman proconsul whose mother had once fallen into sin with a little provincial tailor. This continues, but the violin begins, namely, at a certain distance from him, from the idol, sits his wife, a lady of Krymov's wife's type, but, unlike her, unbearably talkative, she skips from word to word, as if detouring by swoops, quickly inserts the supposed answer in the mouth of an interlocutor, saying God knows what kind of nonsense, and, most importantly, she talks about her husband in his presence (whereupon his heavy lids lower ceremonially and benevolently) as if he were, for example, Leo Tolstoy. Andrey Yakovlevich says, or Andrey Yakovlevich wants to tell you, or, finally, Andrey Yakovlevich was very upset by the dry tone of your letters. In the background – homely, squashed by the greatness of the father and the energetic mother – the thin little Mlle Levinson, who told me on the staircase: 'I am your great admirer. Papa is waiting for you, M'sieur Sirin.' I was informed: 'Andrey Yakovlevich is your friend, yes, your friend.' He solemnly confirms it himself. Inside, I was dying from laughter. It was phenomenal and amusing. He talks about himself, too, as of an older friend. A little phrase goes on for five minutes or so. He is doing what he can: that is, for placing my stories in *Candide* and for printing *The Defence* in some newspaper. They both despise the émigré press like some emperor despises a small far-away rebellious country. *It was a rare treat*. I will call on them again in a few days. In the evening I was at Mme Adamov's, where I met Vadim Andreev.

[VÉNAF]

[10 November (?) 1932]

[TO: Berlin]

[Paris]

Somehow I didn't have time to write to you yesterday, although the day was relatively dull. I had lunch at the Kyandzhuntsevs', and dinner with Sergey, his boyfriend and Natasha, after which we went to the cinema.

But I began to work seriously on a new story yesterday. I definitely want – on this occasion re-read Ronsard's sonnet '*Je veux lire en trois jours*' – to finish this on Tuesday. So I'll try to seclude myself over these last few days, too, although they are already very much coloured in ahead with all sorts of tasks and meetings. I get terribly tired here. I'm absolutely confident that my career will thrive here, but all the same I'm afraid to summon you here completely decidedly and without question, that is, you should join your will to mine, and you haven't made up your mind either. Nika is arriving in a day or two. He'll take me various places. You know, when she was putting Vanya to sleep and pinning his clothes on him with a large safety pin, Natasha pierced his skin through and didn't notice, while he, of course, screamed; at last she suddenly thought, looked him over and then saw that his little tummy was neatly pierced and fastened with the pin. I have received a very sweet letter from Zyoka and another from Gleb in London. He is giving a whole lecture on me. I'm sending you the idiotic advertisement.

[VÉNAF]

[11 November 1932]

[TO: Berlin]

[Paris]

I'm carrying out your little instructions. I think that the translations will be ready in a day or two, and, of course, I'll deliver them in person. Yesterday in the metro I met the Elkins, who told me that in *Revue de Paris*, it's a journal, on the list of forthcoming books there is a *King, Queen, Knave*, but by another author. It may even be Giraudoux. The same happened to Aldanov. The book *Sainte-Hélène, petite île* came out, he met the author, who in his foreword mentioned the coincidence of titles. I'll find out the details of the case. Yesterday I was at Osorgin's: a youthful-looking, slender man with a hint of a mane, in some kind of a belted velvet jacket and an unbuttoned tennis collar. Our conversation was not very interesting, he hates Khodasevich and is friends with Otsup. He calls him a remarkable, decent man. From there I went to see the Zaytsevs: icons and patriarchs. They are rather nice, simple-hearted, and, among other things, they told me that Remizov is mortally offended by me. They have tons of Jewish friends, but, at the same time, Zaytsev likes to savour, now and then, a Jewish accent. And overall, there is something a little off in them, some rather unpleasant little quirk. I had tea with them and went to Lolly who happens to have a very likeable young wife with a hairdo in the mode of a Pushkin miss. I saw Mme [Mlle?] Rachmaninov there and the Pohl couple. It was hellishly boring. But then Rachmaninov took me home in her car. And I was simply collapsing from fatigue, since I also had supper at the Kyandzhuntsevs' and the Portnovs'. Today I wrote several letters to Yulia, poor Raisa, etc. And I was writing a story. At five I must call in on Fondaminsky, and from there go to dinner at the Thompsons'. I forgot last time to enclose in the letter to you the advertising flyer about *Glory*. And now I cannot find it.

I am sorry you had to retype the reviews. This was on Nika's advice. I have almost completely evened the score and dined with Natasha at a café, drank and so on. And Nika will be at my evening and, of course, I'll arrange seats for them. Yan Ruban still sings romances in my translations. She and Pohl, her husband, have come back from Saurat and even ate at that same hotel where, remember, it was so delicious, and he has landscapes from Saurat. He is a musician, an artist, and an occultist. But overall, he looks like that homeopathic doctor we once went to. Isn't that funny? Ruban is in the Society for Animal Protection;

she was very upset about the little ears. I am now sitting in the Rausches' tiny living room, where I sleep too. Portraits of his ancestors, and of Uncle Zhenya and Yurik are on the wall. Above the couch, where I sleep, hangs a guitar, all the chairs are so worn out you need to add a cushion when you sit down. They are very sweet people, and the children, Maria Vasilievna's daughter and Koka's son, are very sweet too, and are living in terrible poverty. I will soon call on the old man Kuprin. If you see Zyoka, tell him I'm writing to him. It is too late to put off 'the Belgians', and I think anyway I'll manage by the 26th to do everything I need to do.

[VÉNAF]
[12 November 1932]

[TO: Berlin]

[Paris]

On Sunday evening, I'm moving to the Fondaminskys' for three days, since I want to rest a little till Tuesday, and here, in spite of the Rausches' charm, resting is tricky. On Wednesday, their back room comes free, the tenant leaves, and I'll move in there till the end of my stay here. I am offering them to pay for it, but, so far, they've been saying no. But I think I need to talk them into it. Keep on writing to this address, or do the calculations right, I will get back here on Wednesday or Thursday, or there'll be a mix-up. I'll read, probably (still can't make a final decision), the first and, maybe, the second chapter of the novel. No, I will begin with poems, then the chapter, then a break, then 'A Dashing Fellow' and 'Music'. I've sent an invitation to the poor Yu. Yu. and Aunt Nina. Yesterday I was at Fond's, and from there—by foot—went to the Thompsons' along the charming rue du Docteur

Blanche, where the walls in the summer are covered in roses. Write a letter to Lizaveta, since you've written her only a few words. Today I had lunch with Natasha. I came back around four and will pop out only to post this letter and call in for a minute on Aldanov, who lives nearby. I feel extremely tired, but still I'm very sweet and cheery. I'm still writing in the same little living room. They're talking here too, and creating some kind of canvases on the table. I absolutely cannot concentrate. And everything here is very uncomfortable: the table, the chair, the pen. Tomorrow I will have dinner at the Evreinovs'. I am terribly annoyed that I won't finish my story for Tuesday. Let's see how it goes at Fond's. But here writing's impossible. This evening the Don Aminados and Muma and her husband will come to dinner. The letter today is somewhat scanty and a little sour. You can find quite a lot of vulgarity even in these *Nouvelles Littéraires* and *Candides* after all. I am very very sorry for old Mme Teisch. I haven't seen Berberova for quite a while.

[VÉNAF]

[14 November 1932]

[TO: Berlin]

[Paris]

What a wonderful sleep I had last night! What a great rest! In a charming room on rue Chernoviz, under a canopy of bookshelves, from 1 a.m. till two the next afternoon, and Fondik himself filled up my bath. I have finally settled on the programme. I will read six poems, those I usually read, then 'Music', and after the break, a chapter and a half of 'Despair'. I have just dictated four pages for Amalia Osipovna to type – to the point where he arrives from Prague and she makes eggnog for him. You'll have to retype these pages again anyway, if only because here they have no hard signs. The marvellous Siamese cat. His name is Zen-Zin (Zenzinov got him), he warms himself at the fireplace. It's quiet, cosy, nice. The pen writes beautifully. On Saturday night at the Rausches', Aminado with his wife and the Zapolsky couple, Muma with her husband, were there. They are all very good friends, they played guitar. Zapolsky lived in Siverskaya and courted Lyussya's sister, then he saw them in Poltava. A surprisingly funny combination. From the touching Thompsons I got an invitation to work, live and eat with them. I called them yesterday. I'll have dinner at their place on Wednesday. I was feeling disgustingly tired yesterday. I hadn't been sleeping enough for a week. I played chess with Koka, then took my suitcase off to the Fondaminskys', then dropped in to pick Muma up and we went to the Evreinovs'. Sofia Pregel and someone called Shaykevich were there, he an art connoisseur, director of the former Romantic Theatre. He spoke rather amusingly about the Armenian Gurdjieff, a Rasputin-like personality with huge hypnotic power. Overall a mystical-Freudian-Goyan spirit reigns in Evreinov's house. Not from 'goy', but from the Spanish artist. Mrs Evreinov, the author of the much-talked-of novel *Je veux qu'on se voit*, has excellent connections with the newspaper *Gringoire*, but she warned me that if I'm published in *Candide*, I can't be in *Gringoire*, and vice versa. She is 'from the merchants', as she says herself, emits torrents of words, is rather attractive, slender, near-sighted, with long earrings. We talked, of course, about Plaksin, while Pregel looked up Yuzya Bilig's telephone number, but I forgot to write it down. Evreinov himself is a person of a type absolutely alien to me, but very funny, and friendly and ardent. When he portrays someone or something, the result's talented and wonderful. But when he philosophizes, it's terribly crass. He said, for example, that all people can be divided into types, he's read a pile of some German, and that Dostoevsky is the greatest writer in the world. Rausch is a hopeless dreamer. [. . .] I'm going over what I'll be reading. It's already five o'clock today. At seven, I'll have dinner at the Kyandzhuntsevs'. A poor relative has come to see the Fonds now and brought teiglach. Aleksandr Fyodorovich has come and is already booming throughout the house.

[VÉNAF]
[16 November 1932]

[TO: Berlin]

[Paris]

Tuesday, 2 a.m.

Write to the Fonds' address. I'm sending 600 francs to Mother. In any event at Christmas we will have to be in Berlin for Mother's visit, so it probably makes no sense for us to move here and so on. But what a success! The huge hall was packed, I have three thousand already in my wallet, raptures, the love of the crowd, all in all, wonderful. Saint Fondik is literally jumping with joy. This morning I swotted up my poems and tried the same with the prose. At three I went to bed, that is, at three p.m., to sleep for a couple of hours before the evening. But as soon as I began to slide very sweetly into sleep, Rausch arrived and brought *your letter* from Boulevard Murat. It was wonderful, but he, unfortunately, came on another mission too. He sat at the foot of my bed for a solid hour and laid out his cinematographic plans in detail. But yesterday I talked to Saba, who'd been able to make enquiries, and found out that in *Vozrozhdenie*, for example, Rausch worked very muddle-headedly and awkwardly and, in general, it doesn't depend on him but on his companion to give him the job; moreover, the job Rausch might count on pays so little, and so on, but still, the main thing is that it's impossible to cool his ardour. No matter what I say to shrink or cool his prospects, he manages to turn everything for the best. In a word, he was full of energy–and talked and talked, and then I had to put on my dressing gown and lead him to the telephone, on which he called but did not reach some third person close to Kyandzhuntsev's companion. Terrible nonsense. Finally, he put on his poor gentilhommish coat with two buttons in the back, took his gloves and left, full of energy. I lolled about till six, heard in the distance the tiny voices of the Merezhkovskys, then again quiet footsteps. Afraid to wake me up, the Fonds and Kerensky were walking on tiptoe along the hallway to the office, to proofread some article or other, but right on the threshold they couldn't hold out any longer. An explosion, an argument about Mussolini, somewhere the door closed, but through it the booming and yellings of peremptory conversation continued. I had a great shave and began to dress. It turned out that the sleeves of my tuxedo were too short, that is, that the cuffs of the beautiful silk shirt of the same provenance stuck out too far. Besides, the belt was peeking out from underneath the vest when I stood up straight. So Amalia Osipovna quickly had, first of all, to make me those, you know, armbands, out of elastic and Zenzinov had to give me his suspenders. His trousers later kept falling down. He would hold himself around the stomach, since he couldn't use my belt. When all of that had been sorted, I looked very smart. Three of us sat down to dinner: Aleksandr Fyodorovich, Amalia and I; the rest had set out early. I had an eggnog, and the three of us went around nine, in a taxi cab, to rue Las Cases. I arrived–it was packed. There were no more seats or tickets. But people kept squeezing in, crowding forward. I won't list those we know–they were all there. And even before I began, those I knew and those I didn't were coming up to me endlessly. I was so tired of smiling I didn't even try any longer to establish whom, in fact, I was talking to. Fortunately, it soon began. I ran on stage like a fop, and, to the thunder of applause . . . Before I forget, I did send Mme Veryovkin an invitation, but I don't think she was in the hall. In the front row sat the Kyandzhuntsevs, Sergey and Natasha (I enclose Nika's telegram) and more relatives. The writers were all there, Adamovich, thousands of ladies, Mit'ka Rubenstein, in a word, everyone. A long, comfortable table, the cosiest of armchairs, a carafe with water. Taking my time I spread out all of my little things from the very nice briefcase I'd borrowed from Rudnev, felt myself completely *at home*, and, taking my time, began to recite my poems by heart. I recited 'To the Muse', 'Aerial Island', 'The Window', 'To an Unborn Reader', 'First Love', 'The Little Angel' and 'Inspiration, Pink Sky . . .' The most gratifying applause after every poem. I had a sip of water and began to *tackle* 'Music'. Magnificent acoustics. They listened marvellously. In a word, it all got to them. Again, thunder and then intermission. There they completely crowded me, and some dreadful woman, who reeked impossibly of sweat, turned out to be Mlle Novotvortsev, my Phalero girlfriend. God knows what she was saying. I got a glimpse of Denis Roche, of old Avgust, of some Tenishev old boys, of Aunt Nina, the Tatarinov girls, Khodasevich, Berberova, and many more I didn't know. The real enjoyment began, however, when I took up *Despair*. I read 34 pages. They got everything. I read, speaking modestly, absolutely remarkably. It's awfully silly to write about this, but I really was on form. And somehow, from the very beginning, there was a gleam of success, and the audience was good, simply wonderful. Such a big, sweet, receptive, pulsing animal, grunting and chuckling in the places I needed, and then obediently dying down again. It finished at half past eleven, and again—rapture. A handshake, Fondik's wonderful smile. In a word, all a vainglorious man could ask for. We crowded into a café, a large group of us. I gave a short speech, and so on. Finally, home. And there were we, the Fondiks and I, sitting down *à trois*. He counted the money. Tomorrow I'll send you 1,200 francs. He was so thrilled with every new hundred-franc bill. My share—that is, minus the expenses for the hall and the tickets – comes, as I have already said, to 3,000.

Suddenly something else has come up. Actually, I shouldn't be telling you this till I've looked into it properly. But anyway. I'll give you a general outline. One lady I don't yet know – Amalia Osipovna and I are going to see her in a few days – has offered you and me 3–4 months in her castle near Pau, and she'll not even be there, while we will have the servants, the car and so on at our disposal. I'll be at the Ministry of Foreign Affairs the day after tomorrow, where I am nudging our visas along. (Although could this be under the influence of Rausch and his wild imagination?) We will see, but how good it would be if something like this happened. I feel somehow quite joyful. *Touch wood*. I have a comfortable bed, I'm writing comfortably. But oh, how late it is, and tomorrow I've decided to go with the Fonds to the memorial service for Demidov's wife. I have to. He was awfully nice to me. In general, I'm just surprised by the charming, somehow selfless, tender relationship everyone has towards me. This was not an easy thing – to organize this evening. I'm enclosing another photo, I've found the advertisement.

[VÉNAF]
[18 November 1932]

[TO: Berlin]

[Paris]

It seems we will, after all, go to Pau for a few months. Amalia Osipovna and I wanted to go to visit this lady right away, but Fondik insisted that first, before accepting her offer, we find out who she is. So far we have found out that she is married to a Swede, Aschberg and not Amber, as I wrote, and she is not a relative of the Berskys, but their acquaintance, that her name is Olga Nikolaevna, that she is very, extremely, likeable, and that she has been nursing the thought of having us live in her castle for a long time. I am now at the Café de la Paix, where I am waiting for Aldanov, who has also promised to make enquiries. Then we will go to her, probably tomorrow, and I'll discuss everything. It would be, I think, not bad if we went there in January or at the beginning of February with the idea of first spending about two weeks in Paris and returning to Paris again in June, say, or going to Grasse or Saurat as well, and in the autumn, to Paris. I will write an ode for her, as Nika does. All of this is very amusing. Rausch has got hold of Kyandzhuntsev's companion, and it turns out that even the place of ticket-collector there is already taken. Tomorrow I am at Roche's. He told me the other day (yes, he was at my evening) that there's a hope of placing an excerpt from *Luzhin* in a newspaper. I must go to Ergaz's, too, about the translator.

[VÉNAF]
[Letter 2, 18 November 1932]

[TO: Berlin]

[Paris]

I found out from the Thompsons today that you called, but I happened to mix everything up and could not be with them on Wednesday. I think I won't be able to hold out and I'll call you. I've arranged things with the lady *en question*. I'll call on her tomorrow at half past three together with the saintly Amalia. I'm afraid that I've rather taken you aback with this trip, but I'm taken aback myself. And in any event I've firmly decided to accept her offer if there's nothing reprehensible in doing so. But I've generally relied on Fondik and Aldanov, who advise me to take the offer. I have placed *The Eye*. It will come out from Petropolis and *Sovremennye zapiski*. I have just spoken to Chertok. I'll add

'Pilgram' to it. And I was at Gallimard today, too. I took back *Glory*. All of them there are very obligingly waiting for my stories, but, alas, they're also flirting terribly with the Soviets.

Yesterday I dined at Aldanov's, and then had to go to the Rausches'. He invited two masons, Sheremetev and Obolensky. There were only four of us, but I, without hesitation, expressed all of my individualistic ideas and left early, having escaped their masonic enticements. The approach of poor Koka (who, by the way, is absolutely certain that sooner or later he'll convince Dastakiyan to hire him as head of the cinema), took this form: 'Don't you have any unresolved issues? It just can't be that you're not troubled by certain questions of a spiritual order.' I answered that I didn't care about such questions, and the masons looked at me, wide-eyed. No doubt this was embarrassing, that is, no doubt, Koka had told them with the same emphasis with which he talked about his cinematographic dream, developed and realized at one light touch, told them that look, gentlemen, Sirin would be there, and he's very interested in the masonic movement. He wants to join it and so on. And I was constantly turning the conversation towards the hockey match I was at on Wednesday night when you called. It was wonderful, we sat right by the ice, the Swedes were playing, and during intermissions Sonja Henie danced on the ice. As a matter of fact, I am describing Rausch in such a detail and not without relish, because I have a secret idea of reworking him, turning him into a story. Very tempting.

I am sitting in a café. I'll have a hot chocolate, and from here will leave for dinner at the Shklyavers'. 'The whole city' has been talking about my evening. Even an epithet beginning with a 'g', then 'e', then 'n', has reached me, so I'm puffing up, as the young Dostoevsky puffed up. The review in *Poslednie novosti* was written by Adamovich! And the one in *Vozrozhdenie* is Mandelstam's. Tsvibakh is offended because I have not thanked him for the interview. Today was again an awfully long day. I was at *Poslednie novosti*. Zamyatin didn't draw even a quarter of the audience there was at my evening. All in all, even old-timers don't remember . . . I'm ashamed to write about all this, but I want you to be in the know.

The story of the castle in Pau *is too good to be true*. It automatically decides the question of our moving to France. It's hard to write about Amalia and Fondik's attitude to me without tears. She herself fills up my bathtub, she's set up a special table with toiletries, with talc, eau-de-cologne and a wonderful soap ready for me. This is just one of a thousand examples of their unheard-of kindness. I often find Zen-Zin in my bed: warm, cosy, charming. Tomorrow's another hard day. Heaps of meetings. Well, I must go to the Shklyavers'.

[VÉNAF]
[21 November 1932]

[TO: Berlin]

[Paris]

I've started a whole new orgy of things to do and meetings, so I simply didn't manage to write to you yesterday. Listen, it's all settled. We're invited to Pau from the end of January or the start of February till June. And after that, Grasse. The thing is, we have to be in Berlin for Christmas, if Mother is coming. And in the beginning or the middle of January I want to be in Paris for when my books come out. Absolutely between us, in your little ear: I want to be in Pau precisely from February to June, because it corresponds to our stay, in the past, in Le Boulou and Saurat. And for me, you see, it's important to compare on a day-to-day basis the emergence of these or other butterflies in the east of the Pyrenees and the west. *Voilà*. So take a room for us for a month, close to Anyuta. I'll bring 300 marks. Besides, on Wednesday morning

I'll deliver, after sending a telegram (oh no, I haven't forgotten), the first chapter of *Despair* to *Poslednie novosti*, and from Berlin I will send them a story, which I won't have time to finish here.

Amalia Osipovna and I visited Mrs Aschberg. She is rather corpulent, fortyish, smartly dressed, agitated and uttered a few stupidities (to use an expression of Anyutochka's, whom I kiss on both cheeks and on the little forehead). Her husband, a Swede, is dead. The castle is near Perpignan, where Uncle Vasya's castle was: there's a coincidence. Two hours' drive from Biarritz. She has a summer cottage there, where we will go off to, too. She herself is going away to Italy. All in all, she is rather likeable, but very bourgeois. She's learning to sing, coloratura. Amalia Osipovna has invited her for tea on Thursday. Of course I was very, very polite. I thanked her and said when we would come. In my opinion, this unforeseen stroke of luck has already completely justified my trip. Why are you so worried about the stories? I've written to you that they're being translated and, when they're ready, they'll offer themselves to journals. On Wednesday evening I'll be at Ergaz's with Gabriel Marcel. An excerpt from *Luzhin* will appear in one newspaper to which Denis Roche has an 'in'. Grasset, Plon and Gallimard are waiting for *Despair*. A little conversation about *K.Q.K.*, *Glory*, and *The Eye*.

I repeat to you, it would be impossible to do more than I'm doing. I'm now going for lunch with Kaun, the American. He's got my books and is very happy. I won't talk to Saba about Rausch any more. I'm taking your advice into consideration. We'll send *Despair* to Berlin. Conversations are going on through Mme Struve, the wife of Pyotr Berngardovich, whom I've visited, about my evening in Belgrade: we will need to fix a date. In the last few days I've seen Roche, the Rausches, Natasha, Sergey, Ergaz, the Kyandzhuntsevs and others. And here's something funny: I'll bring you two long letters full of terrible curses against me from the abominable Mlle Novotvortsev. It's madly funny.

[VÉNAF]
[22 November 1932]

[TO: Berlin]

[Paris]

Not long now till we see each other. I'm off now to a party at Ergaz's, with Marcel and the Kuprins, and I've just been signing books for three hours, 24 copies, and writing addresses, sitting at the rather sweet Kovarsky's. I'm starting to get terribly tired again. This morning, I ran to the post office, wrote to Belgium, since they still won't give me a visa. But if they don't give it, I'll simply go with a transit visa. Then I had a restaurant lunch with Berberova, and now, before Ergaz, I have to find time to drop in on the Struves on the way.

Kovarsky told me that I've already earned 600 francs for *Glory*, but that the money hasn't come in yet, although 300 copies have been sold, which they consider very good. And actually my other books have woken up too. For some reason, everyone here loves *K.Q.K.* That's funny. Just think, in a month or a month and a half we'll already be packing for Pau. Yes, yesterday I went to the Slonim translation office. I said I'd give them a three-month option for the English *K.Q.K.*, but I'll do this once I'm in Berlin, because I'm afraid to confuse things. They want it badly. It seems there's a possibility of an English edition. Thank you for *Camera*. Last night I was at the Volkonskys'. The *beau monde* was there, and later we played *petits jeux*, and I was in my element. These days, I'm not managing to write to you very well, I'm constantly on edge, already dreaming of our quiet Berlin. I saw Sergey yesterday afternoon. We had a very calm and even warm chat. Tomorrow I'll send the wedding telegram and will try to catch Sonya. I must go.

[VÉNAF]
[25 November 1932]

[TO: Berlin]

[Paris]

Well, tomorrow Nikolay and I are going to *Feux croisés*, and the day after tomorrow, early in the morning of the twenty-sixth, I leave for Belgium. I anticipate being unbelievably exhausted. A reading that same night, and then a reading again the following night. On Tuesday, I was at the Struves'. I saw Yu. Yu., whose face has narrowed and who has grown dark (hair, eyelashes), but is still as mechanically talkative as ever. In the last couple of days, yesterday, I think, Gleb gave a lecture about me at the University of London. Four children, and the wife of Aleksey Petrovich, who looks very much like Gleb, has three. Do you know who she is? A Catoire. A musician, a cousin, and a childhood friend. From there I went to Ergaz, where I found Marcel, who's extraordinarily like Aykhenvald, but much younger, and – *en route* – the Kuprins, and Sergey, who gives Ergaz English lessons. The Kuprins speak almost no French. He's terribly nice, an elderly little peasant with narrow eyes. When we went outside later, the night was warm, just drizzling, everywhere yellow, brown, and still-green leaves were glistening on the pavement in the light of a street-lamp. He said to me: 'But what a marvellous – and short – thing life is.' Yesterday, on Wednesday, I was at his place again, but I lunched with the Thompsons. He is charming, just a fraction *gaga*. He went out for wine and brought back a bottle of red roughly wrapped in newspaper. He walks carefully and quietly, thrusting his face forward. Such a good, quiet smile. We sat at the table opposite each other, talking about French boxing, about dogs, about clowns, and about lots of other things. 'Ahead of you, there's quite some road.' By the way, he spoke about Jews in a somehow amazingly profound way – hard to convey this. But his daughter Kisa is rather unpleasant, a little actress with eyelids smeared in ultramarine, eyes like Ural gems, and a 'let's-talk-about-me' smile. Incidentally, Amalia Osipovna liked this expression so much she has been repeating it all the time. From there I went to *Poslednie novosti*.

1936

[APCS]
[postmarked 22 January 1936]

TO: Berlin–Halensee, Allemagne

4, rue Washington
[Brussels]

My adorable love, all went well (true, my journey was somewhat marred by the torturous talkativeness of a tailor from Kovno who got so friendly he offered me a foot-long kosher sausage as a present). It's morning now, I had a wonderful sleep. I just can't tell you how sweet Zina is. There's a cat sitting on each central-heating stand, and a twenty-day-old wolf puppy whining in the kitchen. And how is our puppy, I wonder? It was strange to wake up today without the little voice walking past my door in your arms. My dear love, it's awful to think that you'll be even more tired now. Somehow this pen's too thick. I am fighting an acute desire to smoke. Tell Anyuta I send her a kiss. The sandwiches were beautifully packed. If there were no time change, I am not sure by how much exactly, he would now be back from his walk and would be sticking out his hands. Today there's the Pen-Club affair. On the 27th I read in Antwerp. Zina thinks there is no need to have a performance for the students. And how's he stomping and banging without me? I feel great. You packed everything marvellously. They were very interested in my shoes at the border. My love and happiness, my dear eyes, my life!

V.

[ALS, 2 PP.]
[c. 24 January 1936]

[TO: Berlin]

[Brussels]

My dear love, they 'honoured' two others along with me, a Portuguese and a Peruvian, who, as soon as everyone had gathered in a touchingly ugly hall decorated with golden ivy, got out little papers and fired away in catastrophic accents. After which I said my three bare little sentences. Then they treated us to sweet wine, like Russian Orthodox communion wine. But I did meet wonderfully pleasant and interesting people. Now he is walking with the imperturbable Elli. I met, for example, P. de Reul, whose book about Swinburne I remembered well (Magda brought it over, when I was sick), several poets: René Meurant, Charles Plisnier, Paul Fierens, and later that night we had a reception at the home of the art critic of *Gringoire*, who said that, unfortunately, Franz Hellens could not come over because Zack is now painting him. A chandelier from Rome, with blue, pink and plain-ice pendants: very sweet, but possibly OK if diluted with sparkling water,—while Fierens's wife, Odetta, showed us a glass medallion belonging to her great-grandmother, Mme Roland ('*Liberté, quelles crimes . . .*') who was executed. I love you, my darling. Traces—palaeontological—of hairs remained on the glass, at one stage they'd been in the medallion, but were removed by the virtuous daughter of Mme R for moral reasons: they were hairs from her lover, Brisson, who also died a celebrated death. And suddenly with the unfinished portrait and the artist Zack in walked Hellens, an ageing gentleman with a remarkable, rather raptor-like clean-shaven face, and we immediately 'hit it off marvellously' (as Anyutochka–a kiss for her–puts it). He is married to a Russian, works as a librarian at the Parliament. And Zack turned out to be the brother of... Prof. Frank: very unexpected. In general the conversation was lively and varied, in a way I haven't been part of for a long time. Of course I passed around the photo of our boy, and the mistress of the house remarked: '*il a cinq ans–ou plus?*' The next morning I went for a walk with Zina in the local *Bois*, in the afternoon looked over '*Mlle O.*,' and in the evening Meurant and Plisnier visited, and again the conversation was about the arts, with forays into all the neighbouring districts. To avoid later embarrassments (as happened with my letters from Paris–when I re-read them) I now and henceforth absolutely refuse to quote all the direct and indirect compliments I receive. Zina has waged such a campaign here for '*C. O.*' and '*Course du F.*' that Fayard and Grasset should bow down at her little feet–where I've long been, because she's indescribably charming. How light and obedient their little puppy seems–yesterday he dived head-down in my side pocket where he got stuck, having burped a little blue milk. My joy, the shoes are fabulous. Please write me soon–I am here till the 28th.

At first I was put up in a large room, but yesterday a new tenant, a Persian, moved in there. The first thing he did was to place on the table a framed portrait of Greta Garbo–*c'est tellement typique*. As for me, I have moved to a no less cosy room under the roof–and sleep wonderfully. I have just sent Kirill news of my arrival. They say he's studying well–Zina completely pulls him apart, then puts him back together again: the sloppy attitude of course is still there, and the girls, and the muddle, and the giddiness–in other words, all his little traits, but still she maintains that he's studying. Walking through the park (where the trunks are just as green as the lawns), I told Zina everything I had to about the Peltenburg misses. P. N. reported that the Pen Club put on a lunch for me, but that's not true. Zina's husband and father-in-law are awfully sweet,–the husband Svyatoslav = Svetik (which is weird for me to utter, isn't it?) is also a Tenishev boy: he has now taken up writing a novel, showed me some excerpts, and it's not bad at all.

I will write to Mother and Fondaminsky from here. The servant here, Boronkin, has a melancholy face but he's very nice, fusses over the puppy and cooks wonderfully. I keep looking at babies–all the carriages here are on thick tyres. I woke up yesterday *en sursaut* utterly certain that my little boy had got into my suitcase and I had to open it up at once or he'd suffocate. Write me as soon as you can, my love. Boings, boings, boings against the highchair footstep in the kitchen each morning. I feel new words hatching there without me. Tell Anyuta that when, after the first conversation, the Persian left (to move in at night) without paying in advance, Zina exclaimed: if Mama been in my place, she would have twisted the money out of him so he didn't even notice. Remind me, you know, to tell 'Sovr. zap.' that I would like to write a little piece about 'Yakor'.' I speak French with suspicious lightness and eloquence. Don't know how my '*Mlle*' will go down today–I'm afraid it's long and boring. The very kind Aleksandr Yakovlevich isn't here yet, but I'll meet him in Paris and write to you all about him. It'd be nice, you know, to live here–a beautiful silence after our garages, a big garden outside the window, sparrows tickle one's ears all morning and sometimes a blackbird joins in–and those are the only sounds. The bathroom has that meekly and hopelessly dirty look all bathrooms have. Kisses, my dear love. I've stepped back a little from the picture and see it better, and see how pretty you are. Write me soon, my life.

V.

[ALS, 2 PP.]
[27 January 1936]

TO: 22, Nestor Str., Berlin–Halensee, Allemagne

4, rue Washington
[Brussels]
27–I–36

My dear love, I got your letter with the whirlwind trace of his little paw, and Mother's one too: I've already written to her about everything, by the way. I'm starting to miss you madly. The French evening went 'brilliantly', but there wasn't a big crowd–although all the 'elite' were there. That same evening Maurois was speaking and there was the premiere of a film about Anna Pavlova! Hellens (who calls me every day–and tomorrow I'm having lunch at his place) reckons I should give '*Mlle O*' to Paulhan (N. R. F.), but I think that a newspaper would pay more. I'll bring a report about the evening (in general, there are lots of little notices and articles,–I collect what I can, but you know how reluctantly I do this)–they compare me to Rilke who is now very much in fashion. The reading went well, because they listened marvellously. And yesterday was the Russian evening, lots of people,–and the room was charming, and 'everything got to them'. I went through the poetry first, then 'Lips to Lips' ... think he must be asleep now–my little sweetheart–or is purposefully throwing the ballast overboard–and the pillow's already lying on the floor, with the pacifier nearby, while he's standing upright and mumbling something ... anyway, they laughed a lot in the right places; in the second half I read the last three chapters of 'Invitation' (the night before, Zina had a tea-party, where I read the intermediate chapters, so now she knows the whole thing), and the result was such that I will now, of course, read these chapters in Paris too. After that there was supper at a restaurant. Now about Eleonora:

she was at my French reading, and was very successfully introduced there to Zina (who gets kinder and kinder all the time) and the next day (Saturday, that is) was invited by Zina to tea, and arrived first with a bunch of tulips. She and Zina have become beautifully close – they've already been walking with their arms around each other, for Zina *faisait de son mieux*, and after tea there was the reading itself – of the intermediate chapters – after which the guests (Auerbach and his wife, Mme Bazilevsky, Ilyashenko and someone else) left, but Eleonora (and Kirill) were kept back for supper (i.e., their dinner), after which we all went together to the cinema. And that's not all: when the rather poor film was over, we went to a little cellar pub (you know the usual vulgar dimness-tightness-cosiness, with a Spaniard playing the guitar, the haze of tobacco and pictures portraying headless dancers, collapsing houses, blood, freaks, bulls), and it was around half past one when we took Eleonora to her hotel; yesterday too she was there, but left in the evening (with a terrible mixture of 'Lips to Lips' and 'Invitation' in her head). As for Kaplan, he called on Zina twice, while I happily lunched at the Shcherbatovs', and then with his wife and car turned up at my reading at the Club, and although I tried hard to avoid this, slipped with wife and car into the restaurant where we were having supper, and he and Zina were making plans (till I stepped on her foot) about how to organize my reading in Eindhoven. I love you, my love, my dear darling – you're probably terribly tired, I think all the time about you and the teeny-weeny one. Sergey and the Shcherbatovs fuss touchingly over Kirill, who both sleeps and dines there; – and Sergey too has a little boy, a five-year-old, wonderful – it was so strange to lift him up off the floor. He has greatly changed for the better, Kirill, in every sense, Zina is very fond of him. During this time he managed to 1) fall off the marble stairs at the *Maison d'Art*; 2) trip over on the pavement in front of the restaurant where we dined yesterday. I have so far gathered only seven hundred Semyonlyudvigoviches. I am leaving for Antwerp tonight, but I just had lunch in the home of an absolutely charming publisher Masui who is married to ... Margarita. I got a letter from Mme Tatarinov with an invitation to a (French) soirée at her place on the 29th, so I'll leave here on Wednesday around one p.m. Sergey showed me marvellous engravings and portraits of Graun and other genealogical titbits. I did not know, for example, that we are relatives of the Shakhovskoys, and at the Shcherbatovs' they served a gigantic kulebyaka since there were fourteen at table and an atmosphere out of 'War and Peace'. *On a beaucoup admiré* my little boy and you. *Très svietski*.

And why hasn't 'Despair' come out? Greetings to Anyuta – please read to her about Eleonora, etc. *I did my best* – and both liked each other very much. Write to me again, my darling. The weather's warm here, at the end of the boulevard there's a little square with a black candelabra of araucarias, and the younger ones are thoroughly covered with pine – conifer camouflage. Kulisher divides all people into those from and those not from Kiev. Regina turned out to be a charming, youngish, somewhat greying lady, talented *au dire de Zina*. Zina's husband is an unusually forthright person and told me 1) he could not stand me because he thought I was a snob, like Nika 2) whom he can't stand because of his insincerity. Kirill's rather afraid of him. So, my joy, I have to write two postcards to Paris now, and then it'll be time to head for Antwerp. I love you very much. I kiss you very much. And this is for him:

V.

[ALS, 2 PP.]
[30 January 1936]

TO: Nestor Str. 22, Berlin–Halensee, Allemagne

130 av. de Versailles
[Paris]

What is Long's address?
30–I–36

My love, my joy, my precious creature, I've been so whirled around that I haven't written to you for two days. I think I stopped at the Antwerp reading. Yes. So, I went there and gave the reading, read two hundred and fifty Belgian pages, which, together with the earlier ones, amounts to nine hundred plus. Pumpyansky is unusually like an old parrot. It was rather boring. I read not 'Invitation' but 'The Aurelian'. During the intermission, and after the reading, and before the reading, a lethally tedious big black lady looked after me, while another of the organizers performed a magic trick – lighting paper without fire. I returned to Brussels around one a.m. and of course could not manage the lock, so poor Zinochka in her little grey robe had to ... Next day I had lunch at Hellens'. He's married to a Russian Jewess from Rostov-on-Don, three very sweet children speaking Russian better than French, a family atmosphere. They propose that we spend the summer where they do too, a first-class *pension* in the country, twenty francs a day, and for the three of us they'd make an even better price. It was very pleasant there. Bags under his eyes, aquiline nose, long teeth, a monocle. Both promised in general to consider 'my fate' thoroughly: he, as the foremost writer in Belgium, wields a lot of influence. In the afternoon Zina and I were at the Fierenses'. They will be in Paris in a week and will arrange a meeting for me with Jaloux – *not that I want it*. I also got on very well with them, and discussed my fate with them too. Hellens proposed writing to Paulhan about *Mlle O*, to place it in the journal: they pay three hundred French francs per page there. And here in Paris, *au dire de* Mme Tatarinov, Marcel and Ergaz and du Boz are all interested in it, so there'll most likely be a reading here, too. From the Fierenses' we went to a meeting of 'Thyrse', ageing Belgian men of letters greeted me with 'words of welcome'. A writer sitting next to me, his nose a net of purple veins, is famous, because as a youth he snacked on human flesh: his father was a railroad employee; some worker got run over; while they rushed for help, he, hurrying desperately, ate a piece of the half-severed leg – he wanted to try it: *une occasion comme celle-ci ne se présentera jamais plus* – the worker later filed a suit against him, although the leg got amputated anyway. A poet, he told me, should experience everything. That evening we visited the sculptor Le plaa. I've collected a small library of autographed books – most of them I've left at Zina's, since I'll stop for three days in Brussels on the way back, because the Club is counting on arranging another evening: in the first half I will read '*Mlle O*' (*qui commence à m'agacer*). The Shcherbatovs came up with a farcical project of my doing a reading with ... V. V. Baryatinsky (the uncle). Yesterday Zina saw me off at the station. From the Gare du Nord I went to av. de Versailles by metro, so that I arrived totally exhausted, with my gradually more and more stone-like and gloomy suitcases. All the tickets have sold already. In their announcements P. N. absolutely outrageously print me in big letters, and Khodasevich in small. A thousand five hundred each is already guaranteed. And other possibilities are popping up too. Here they've given me a very charming room in a beautiful apartment. Ilyusha and Zenzinov rival Zina as far as the tenderest kindness goes. Zenzinov told me in detail the whole story of A. O.'s illness. My heart constricts when I look at the cat, which has got darker and kindlier. As soon as I began to unpack – it was around half past seven – Bunin showed up, with his nasal voice, and, in spite of my fierce resistance, 'dragged' me to dinner at Korniloff's – there is such a restaurant. At first our conversation went absolutely nowhere – mainly, it seems, because of me – I was tired and angry – everything irritated me, his manner of ordering grouse, his every intonation, his little obscene jokes, and the exaggerated subservience of the lackeys, so that he later complained to Aldanov that I was thinking about something else the whole time. I was angrier (that I'd gone to dinner with him) than I had been for a long time, but towards the end, and then when we came out on to the street, suddenly sparkles of mutuality began to flash here and there, and when we reached Café Murat, where fat Aldanov was waiting for us, we had a great time. There too for a moment I saw Khodasevich, who's got very yellow; Bunin hates him, and he says about Fondaminsky: 'So! Ilyusha couldn't care less, but Zenzinov loved her (A. O.) for thirty years. Thirty years!' (and he raises a finger). Aldanov said that when Bunin and I talk with each other and look at each other, it feels as if two movie cameras are rolling non-stop. Iv. Al. recounted for me superbly how he was married in Odessa, how his six-year-old son died. He claims that the (figurative) features of 'Mitya Shakhovskoy' (Father Ioann) gave him the prompt to write Mitya's Love. He claims that – well, I'd better tell you in person. After the café the three of us had supper at the Aldanovs', so that I got to bed late, and slept poorly – because of the wine. My darling. How is my adorable little boy? A thousand things to do and I don't know where to start. Tell me, why is Despair still not out?

I will do with Long as you say. I love you, I love you.

V.

[ALS, 2 PP.]
[postmarked 2 February 1936]

TO: 22, Nestor Str.,
Berlin – Halensee, Allemagne

130 av. de Versailles
[Paris]

My sweet darling, my love,

you're silent; please, write; from time to time – on the street or in the midst of a conversation, a thought about you and our little boy pierces me right through (usually, when I think about him, there's a kind of heavenly melting inside my soul): write, my joy. I'm annoyed I forgot to write down Long's address, but I think I'll get it from you tomorrow and then will write to him right away, it's turned out awfully foolish. You know what, send me a copy of '*Mlle O!*' Vlad. Mikh.'s radio in the next room is playing 'yo, heave ho'. I received two 'Despairs' from you – it's come out not too badly – like a three-coloured banner. Will they send me more copies? And how about giving some to people we know? Whom shall we give them to? A list? I received a letter from Zina – she says they're taking the most active measures to settle us there. I have already seen tons of people. Two days ago (Thursday) I felt so disgusting that I thought I had flu, I could barely move; but then I had a really good sleep and yesterday and today I've been seething with activity. Dastakiyan turns out to be very likeable, blond hair and glasses, middle-aged and rather shortish; everybody loves him, he runs the Kyandzhuntsevs' cinema. They're the same as ever, as carefree and welcoming, I had dinner at their place and then went to that cinema of theirs, where Saba acted very much the boss, while Irina is as charming as she was (and she fell completely in love with the little boy's portrait). Behind us there sat (he – thinner, older, she – with a blind fox-terrier on her lap) …

Kalashnikov and his wife. I will have to see them (Ira immediately sold him two tickets). After the film the Kyandzhuntsevs left in their limousine, but Dastakiyan and I went to Café Murat to talk. We discussed things on the way, but met Aldanov and Kerensky in the café, so the business conversation did not happen. Kerensky was horrified that I am so apolitical. Today Dastakiyan came to see me, and I described my film (*Hôtel Magique*) to him in detail, he very much approved of it and in a few days will introduce me to Shifrin and someone else, we'll see (I'm trying very hard). Yesterday afternoon I was in the editorial office and told them about the disgrace I'm enclosing here, they promised me they'd come to their senses. I passed Matusevich's story on to Igor and refused the interview. Sherman, Vishnyak and Fedotov came to see me. The first interprets 'Invitation' beautifully and on Monday will give a talk about me. (Has *Despair* been sent to PN, it's important!). He also spits and holds his hand over his mouth. I will visit the Zeldoviches on Monday afternoon – I got a letter from her and phoned her. I wrote to Supervielle and D. Roche. What shall I do with the Dahls? The thing is, Girshfeld shares the bookstore with Neskin – this is why I am not very keen to go there (or shall I phone him?). Shall I send something to Mother? I am writing to Zyoka – I visited the old man today, Sarah has become much prettier. My dear darling, I even found time to work on '*Mlle* O' and visit Montparnasse, where after Poplavsky's death the poets wander around with the faces of meek martyrs. The Tenishev old boys have roused themselves. Spoke on the phone with Berberova. Tomorrow I am at Khodasevich's. Today there's a talk by Milyukov, to which I of course won't go. I live in the most marvellous conditions (the bathroom is better than ours) and I'm gradually feeling like myself again, I can't tell you how I felt in the first two days. My dear love, I'm writing this letter in great haste, somehow can't concentrate. In the métro it stinks like between the toes and it's just as cramped. But I like the slamming of the iron turnstiles, the flourishes ('*merde*') on the wall, the dyed brunettes, the men smelling of wine, the lifelessly sonorous names of the stations. You know, I'm thinking with pleasure about reworking '*It is me*'. Have you sent *Despair* yet? I love you and send lots of kisses for you and my boy.

Will write to Anyutochka in a day or two.

V.

[ALS, 2 PP.]

[postmarked 3 February 1936]

TO: 22, Nestor str., Berlin–Halensee, Allemagne

[Paris]

My dear happiness, I'm not arranging any kind of readings in Holland, that's the most utter nonsense. In Brussels there will probably be a French-Russian evening, on the 18th or 19th, after which I'll return to Berlin. I don't want to hear again about Kaplan's idiotic undertaking (actually it was Zina who prompted him out of kindness). What nonsense.

Don't forget to send me a copy of *Mlle O* (how could I give away my only copy to Hellens?). The evening (last Wednesday) at Raisa's fell through because her husband and daughter came down with the flu – they're better now and she'll have the same crowd again. I gave Zina two orchids, but, of course, she wouldn't take a *dédommagement*. Tell 'Petropolis' – we need 'Despair' to appear here in some quantity, they'll have to send it to both newspapers (personally – to both critics), because it'll sell well now in connection with my evening. Life is absolutely unbearable here for me without you and our little boy. Just now wet snow has been falling, the Seine is yellow, the dampness immediately takes the shape of one's feet, as soon as one goes out. So you say that he, my little one, dreams about me? My little darling.

Good Lord, I visited the Kalashnikovs – and won't set foot there again, ever (they live right around the corner – but they don't know that), the talk was exclusively about Corsica, Felix, and Bobby (whom I wrote from here, it turns out that he asked our mutual friends several times how he could get the books of mine he'd read about in the N.Y. *Times*, – Countess Grabbe told me this – I knew her when she was Beloselsky), Kalashnikov belched, talked a lot about his and others' sexual organs, about wealth (Tatyana has become wealthy), about a trepanation of the skull, which he's undergone twice, and advised me to read Claude Farrère. I lunched – yesterday – at the Kyandzhuntsevs', from there went to Khodasevich's: his fingers are bandaged – furuncles, and his face is yellow, like the Seine today, and his thin red lip curves poisonously (while his clean tight little dark suit is so glossy it hurts your eyes); his wife with beautiful, loving eyes and in general, to her waist (from the top down), quite pretty, but then all of a sudden her hips begin to burgeon; she guiltily hides them in the shifting planes of her gait, like a package of dirty laundry. Vladislav poured venom on all our colleagues the way they spray saplings against phylloxera, the Zaytsevs turn blue with terror when he approaches. He spoke rather wittily about 'Invitation' and his small nose moved between the lenses of his large glasses and the bandaged fingers bristled. Felsen was there, too, watching me with devoted eyes. In the evening I discussed with Sherman and Il. Is. what I should read and settled on the following: I'll read three short stories, all the same length: 1) Russian Beauty 2) A Slice of Life 3) Breaking the News.

I've set myself two tasks – to place *Mlle O* and 'Despair'. Will meet Shifrin about my film on Wednesday at three. Expecting calls from Supervielle and Denis. Will see Ergaz and Marcel on Wednesday. Tickets for the Khodasevich evening are selling unusually well, actually they sold out completely a long time ago, and now the reserve of extra chairs keeps growing. Tonight is Sherman's 'lecture' (he's in great form all round). Ilyusha is trying very movingly to 'influence' me in a religious way, for instance starting a conversation from afar – there are some outstanding priests around, wouldn't I want to hear just one short little sermon, and so on. A certain Mother Maria finds me somewhat 'starched'. Appreciate the tone *and the implication*. My happiness, write to me, I reread your last pale dear letter many times – my sweet, I can feel how tired you get, it's terrible; when I come back I'll look after our little one all day, you can rest. Awful draughts in this house, can't imagine how poor A.O. lived here, and there's never any sun, but the apartment itself is charmingly comfortable. I madly crave a smoke, but I think I'll preserve my virginity nonetheless. I wrote to Zyoka – have been to Vava's, saw the old man, there they're filming all those nudes, the whole apartment is covered with the hair of a shedding (and very lively) fox terrier. My love!

V.

[ALS, 2 PP.]

[postmarked 4 February 1936]

TO: Nestor Str. 22, Berlin – Halensee, Allemagne

130 av. de Versailles

[Paris]

Pussykins, and here is my reply to your dear letter of the 2nd.

I beg you, send the translation to Long without delay (enclosing or not, as you wish, the little letter I enclose here). The things noted and corrected – all of that means absolutely nothing – any Russian reader can find just as many birthmarks on any page of any of my Russian novels, and as your Englishwoman remarked, any (good) English writer allows himself just the same grammatical inaccuracies. Please, don't upset British majors and old maids, but send to England the copy I prepared, without inserting a single one of the corrections others have made (for example: she corrected '*compared with*' to '*compared to*', but Douglas always writes '*with*'; and I don't even want to talk about her prettifications). For this there'll be an exchange of letters (and improvements suggested and finally approved by me) between their *reviser* and myself. Please send it right away. I am writing to Long.

Now here's something for you: I have a great hope of placing 'Despair' here, and Marcel would like to read the English translation – this would greatly speed up and simplify everything. Maybe, my sweet, with Zyoka's help you could transfer the corrections from mine (except those five pages that I am keeping) to the copy and send it to me *as soon as possible* (and I could send this copy from here, after Marcel has acquainted himself with it, to Alta Gracia). This is very important I think.

Don't forget to send me a copy of '*Mlle O*', since I have arranged to meet Supervielle on Friday and would like to give it to him then. Raisa on the other hand is energetically trying to arrange a permanent job for me with a French newspaper (literary and theatre criticism).

My darling, how I miss you. My happy love. The little boy is now taking his bath (how do you manage?), my little darling. I saw a very red-haired B. G. yesterday and went for a walk with her along the boulevard, and in a day or two will visit her in the evening. Then I went to Editeurs Réunis (not on editorial business, but to see Parchevsky). Then I met with Mme Tatarinov and we discussed all sorts of things. In the evening there was a poets' meeting here: I think I made a mistake – Sherman's talk is next Monday – and yesterday Berdyaev gave a talk, interrupted by his own tongue. Alfyorov, Sofiev, Knut are very sweet and young. (The last of these looks more like a Hindu – small and crooked-legged – than a Jew.) Terapiano, greying, with a dark puffy face. Weidle, looking like Chichikov. Fedotov, quiet, slightly Asiatic. Sharshun, inarticulate, a chatterbox, – talked terrible drivel in a conversation with me. Yanovsky – curly, blond-haired, a belated *enfant terrible*. Mother Maria with two teeth. The poetess Chervinsky, a lippy, white-faced, painfully long girl with dark eyes and a lace collar over her entire bosom. Mochulsky – smiling, like Hepner in looks. Zenzinov was there, like Pushkin's nanny, Ilya was the chair, and Sherman the secretary. The talk was 'dedicated' to a philosophical analysis of the line: 'a thought once uttered is untrue', but it turned out that a thought once uttered is prattle. I had a busy and boisterous day today, but I'll describe it next time. Oh my joy, my sweet enchantment, my angel.

V.

[ALS, 2 PP.]
[postmarked 6 February 1936]

TO: Nestor Str. 22,
Berlin – Halensee, Allemagne

130 av. de Versailles
[Paris]

My life, my joy, I have had a very warm and high-powered talk with Marcel – he's cheerful, dancing, but also clumsy, with the *faux air* of Aykhenvald– and I can't wait to give him the English 'Despair' to read; what's more, he is terribly *alléché*, as he sweetly puts it, by the epigraph to 'Invitation'. He won't keep '*Despair*' for long. I will talk about the translation itself with Roche on Sunday (although another, livelier, translator would have suited me much better). The Fierenses arrive tomorrow, I will have dinner with them, but in the morning I'll talk with Jules Supervielle about '*Mlle O*'. In Brussels the French evening is on the 15th or the 17th, and the Russian on the 16th. My darling, I am very sorry to pile postal duties on to you, but I really need 'The Eye' in French, so that if you could send to Zina straight away that volume of *Œuvres libres*, that would be great (but hold on – I'll try to get one from Roche on Sunday, so wait, I'll write on Sunday), and yet I absolutely need a copy of '*Mlle O*' here – and '*Despair*'. I'll give Shklyaver a call, I hope to get Sofa's address from him, but first I'll look over your letters, maybe you wrote it down for me. I think not.

I went to Nina's. *Plus belle – osait-on dire*. Her husband is stocky, with big ears, of the 'Russian American' type, they live in a marvellous studio-like apartment. She says that all the pederasts were up in arms when they found out she's writing a life of Chaikovsky, their bum-buddy. She flashed her teeth, her eyes, her legs; but, all in all, something was not right – perhaps because her husband was present (one Makeev, the first husband of Osorgin's first wife). From there, having a free *après-midi*, I went to Le Cerf at the museum. There, that is, in the wonderfully cosy and for me agonizingly agitating entomological laboratory, they received me with the kind of warmth, to tell the truth, I'd only dreamt of.
Le Cerf showed me his latest discovery – still unpublished (the muscle moving the unusual jaws, already noted by Chapman, of a *Micropteryx* pupa and in front the rudimentary third pair of little wings – their tiny casings – a very ancient thing, from Carboniferous times). And a new species of *Ornithoptera*, just received, the male of which has on its yellow (hind) wings a remarkable aquamarine sheen, not encountered in a single one of the known species ... And an aberration of *rumina* – a unique specimen from Algiers, without the red spots and laughably like a Melitaea ... And a collection of Parnassians ... It was great, and if I lived here, I'd come every day and perhaps be set up there like Kardakov in Dahlem. Just think – Le Cerf worked with Oberthür.

Sarah photographed me (revoltingly, it seems), and then, with the old man, we set off for Aldanov's. There by the way I spoke with an Englishman (I don't know, rather lispy– but also rather funny), Haskell – remember, he wrote a book about ballet. Gubsky is his secretary; and there is also one Malcolm Burr, who apparently loves my work, a great connoisseur of Russian literature. I took careful note of all of this – and generally secured the 'connection' (nothing of real value, I think). He was with a pretty ballerina, a complete nincompoop. Loads of people showed up at the Aldanovs'; and again I had a longish – and rather laboured – conversation with a gloomy (Galina has left him!) Bunin. You know whom I liked much better than last time: Zaytsev. Unfortunate, jolly, red from wine, defenceless, tormented by Khodasevich.

Yesterday I had lunch with Shifrin at Dastakiyan's – very nice, large family – and today at five I'll meet with Shifrin again. Then I went to Marcel's with Raisa. Then out to the Kolomeytsevs' and found them the same as always, although she's already past 75. Nika had an affair with Grunelius in his youth. Aunt Nina is *au courant* with my writings, in detail, through Léon (whom I plan to see). At Aldanov's soirée and in general no matter where I am – the boy's photograph does the rounds of everyone there. I will probably get back in the afternoon of the 20th. My darling, do you remember me? And he, my little one? I just physically miss certain sensations, the wool of the breeches' straps, when I unbutton and button them up, the little ligaments, the silk of the crown at my lips when I hold him over the potty, carrying him up the stairs, the circuits of a current of happiness when he throws his arm across my shoulder. Don't forget to tell me whether I should send the books to Mother. I have written to the publisher. It is such a pleasure to hear how Sherman 'interprets' 'Invit. to a Beheading' – after all, interpreters usually only irritate me. I love you, my joy. Don't forget all my requests. I will arrange a rest for you when I get back. Kiss the teeny weeny one. I still want to write Anyuta a long letter, I have lots especially for her.

I kiss you, my adorable one.

V.

[ALS, 2 PP.]

[postmarked 8 February 1936]

TO: Nestor Str. 22, Berlin–Halensee, Allemagne

130 av. de Versailles

[Paris]

My love, what is this, why don't you write?

Today I have a reading and a cold. It'll be hard to read, I think. I called Lyusya, didn't get him, told them to pass on my telephone number *Aut.* 19-42. I spoke with Sofa [dear Anyutochka, this is for you. Here's how the conversation went. I'd begun by writing to her, and the telephone conversation too started from there–that she has, so to speak, a complimentary ticket. And then, embellishing her voice with a slight nasality and other tracery she took to explaining to me at length that, 'you see', she has important business with the director on Saturday evening and so does not know 'whether she can get out of it', but could I, 'just in case', leave the ticket for her, as she would be very happy, of course, to come, if 'she can after all'. I said: Sofa, decide now, because there are plenty of takers for a free seat. She suddenly got flustered, pretended she'd just remembered something, and said: anyway, I'll most likely be there. You know what, leave it for me at the ticket office.] I phoned Shklyaver, too, will call on them on Tuesday. Spoke for a whole hour with Shifrin in his office (huge nose, white eyelashes, puny, a pearl in his tie), and we agreed that I'll prepare a screenplay for him; he has explained his *requirements* to me in detail. I've already thought up something: the story of a boy, a king's son; his father is killed, just like in Marseilles, and he becomes a king – a Swiss tutor, *et tout ce qui s'en suit*. Then there is a revolution and he returns to his toys and his radio – it sounds rather flat, but one can make it very entertaining. Generally there's such a wild stirring in the portion of my brain in charge of muses, music and museums, such an itch, that I think I'll just write a story if I have even a single free day. My happiness, I love you. Zyoka writes that my little boy is talking a lot. I don't believe he exists, maybe it was all a dream, it's torture how much I want to feel him. Yesterday morning I was at Supervielle's, he's aged a lot, his nose has winey veins; we had a very friendly talk and he immediately got in touch with Paulhan about *Mlle O*. It turns out that Hellens – he's so kind – had already written to him about the same thing. At three I was already at the N.R.F. with my manuscript (having transferred the corrections to a separate page, so that I could write them in again when you send me another copy. Now I am left without everything, but I need to read it in Brussels). When I came, he wasn't there yet, but when he appeared he came in with Remizov, who had caught him on the stairs. Remizov looks like a eunuch and also like a chess figure already captured (*do you see my point*: it stands barely askew on the edge of a little table, immobile and sharply outlined). Fattish, short, in a tightly buttoned-up coat. He was very sweet with me. I explained to Paulhan everything I needed to about '*Mlle O*' and gave him the manuscript. If he doesn't take it (we agreed that he would give me an answer by the 14th), I'll pass it on to Fayard. From him I went to Slonim's and there got the manuscript of 'Pilgram' in French. If you also send me 'The Eye' in French, I'll have 'rich material' for the evening in Brussels. I had dinner yesterday (and what a dinner!) with the saintly Fierenses who had already sold forty tickets. We had a very genial conversation, he told wonderful stories. Today we met again at du Bos's, and on Monday will have lunch at Jaloux's. The conversation with Slonim was long, affectionate, but rather pointless. He introduced me to a man called Wallace from a Zurich newspaper. So, as things stand now: on Saturday the 15th the French reading in Brussels, on Sunday the 16th lunch at the critic Melo du d'y's (there's a name for you!), and the Russian reading in the evening. Zina rushed it a little in terms of time, I myself wanted to stay here till the 18th, since Mme Bataud (through Mme Tatarinov) is ready to organize a French evening for me here, and meanwhile the hall in Brussels is already booked and so on (but whether anything will happen after all with Bataud we don't know). I'm much less tired than on my last visit, since I'm living in wonderful comfort. They are such darlings, Zen-Zin and Nikolay. Elena Aleksandrovna talks to them in Amalia's voice. Write, my joy! Thank you for the two books – they have just arrived. Don't forget to reply to me about Mother and in general (shall I bring any books from Belgium?). My darling, I kiss you again and again. *I've been dreaming of you, my darling*. Tell me what to bring for Anyuta, any little thing. My little boy is taking a walk now. The old man has been tirelessly trying to place his memoirs here.

I love you, my happiness, my tired little one. You'll rest when I'm back, you'll see.

V.

[ALS, 2 PP.]

[postmarked 10 February 1936]

TO: Nestor Str. 22, Berlin – Halensee, Allemagne

130 av. de Versailles

[Paris]

My dear happiness, – so I don't forget, for God's sake send me '*Despair*', I've set everything in motion, have to give it to Marcel as soon as possible.

Forgive me, darling, for pressing you. And besides I will probably have to start getting ready for London, I've just received a letter from Gleb, they're offering to pay for my trip (so far he's only asking 'in principle' will I agree to come,—I've just replied Yes, but prefer to go at Easter, from Berlin), there will be an English-Russian appearance there. To get business over with: here they're trying hard to organize a reading of '*Mlle O*', but if it works out, it would be about the twentieth or twenty-first, so I will have to return here from Brussels, where I'm going on the morning of the 15th.

Yesterday afternoon I was at du Bos's (*très catholique*) and we discussed literature. He is emphatically affectionate; half English. All in all it was rather pleasant. The evening itself went perhaps even better than last time, a big crowd jammed the place (incidentally, they were jamming in while Khodasevich read, and he read a charming thing—a subtle concoction with a historical air and adorned with pseudo-antique poems). I was sitting with Bunin (in a coat and a cap, nose in his collar, he is insanely afraid of colds) and a plumper, powdered Adamovich (*qui m'a fait un compliment de pédéraste* 'you look even younger than before'). After the intermission I read: 1) A Russian Beauty 2) *Terra Incognita* 3) Breaking the News. For me it was all a huge pleasure, a *treat*. I gorged myself on candy, treated my cold with ointment and my voice generally behaved itself. The old man will tell you about the applause. Then a great crowd of us went to the café Les Fontaines and drank champagne there. The writers drinking: Aldanov, Bunin, Khodasevich, Weidle, Berberova, and others. All drank to Miten'ka's health. Across the table from Vladislav, sitting next to Nina, sat her husband, and across from Nina, his wife. *Ça m'a fait rêver*. It was all very jolly and lively (somehow this smacks of a schoolboy's essay about the holidays, but I didn't get a good sleep). Aldanov cried out that 1) 'you despise us all, I can see through you' 2) 'you're our leading writer' 3) 'Ivan Alekseevich, give him your ring.' Ivan, however, stood his ground, 'No, there's still some life left in us,' and addressed Khodasevich across the table thus: Hey you, Pole. Their nimbi still on, Ilyusha and Zenzinov sat quietly at another table. We got home after three a.m. My darling, what a pity you weren't at La Skaz – my darling, my love. The unavoidable Novotvortsev woman slithered over to me (having first sent me a note ending '*sans rancune*'. Isn't that splendid!). Sofa sat, I think, with the old man (who was darker than a cloud). Lots of ghosts from the past – you know, that not quite sure expression in their eyes – will the present accept me? Somehow I didn't notice Kalashnikov. Gave Denis a hug. Tenishev old boys. Ladies. V. Lolly. Poets. Khodasevich, who read first was in such a hurry (so as not to hold me up, very sweet of him) that Fondik sent him a note – slower. A full house. My love, I keep walking around in the letter you wrote on, on every side, I wander over it like a fly, with my head down, my love! Will write to Heath – yes, that's correct. Berta has put the squeeze on me, I can't wriggle out, will have to call on her. I saw Anna at the reading and had a long phone call with her. Haven't seen Lyusya yet. Now am going for lunch at Rudnev's. Then to Roche. Another performance in the evening, I'll read 'Lips to Lips' for the 'chosen'. My joy, how is my boy? My sweetie! This is for him.

Kisses, my love.

V.

[ALS, 2 PP.]

[postmarked 13 February 1936]

TO: Nestor Str. 22, Berlin – Halensee, Allemagne

130 av. de Versailles

[Paris]

Sherman implores you to send him the little snapshot of the boy (the one without a coat).

My love, my triumph, *elder-bush* means not 'a bush that is older' but elder; but still, have it your way, we will send from Berlin as soon as I get back (on the 23rd *au plus tard*); I will write to him – to Long, that is, as you advise. Around fifty tickets for the French evening in Brussels have already been sold at ten Belgian Semyon Lyudvigoviches each, and the evening at the club will also bring in something – so for our dear Grigory Abramovich it's very much worth it to go there. And here Grigory will read in French on the 21st – Doussia and Marcel and du Boz have been corralled by the energetic Raisa, while I have Supervielle and Jaloux. I am waiting for a letter from Struve, about the London performance: the 'Society of Northerners' wants to organize it – very cultured gentlemen. After numerous unsuccessful attempts I've finally arranged a meeting with Lyusya (on Friday). There, I think, are all the answers to the questions in your last little letter.

On the ninth I had lunch at Rudnev's with Kerensky and Vishnyak, and in the afternoon met with Roche – we drank chocolate at the hotel – I think he is a little gaga. He wants 'Despair' for some new magazine, and is asking me to translate into Russian his own novella which he, for family reasons, cannot publish in French! But first of all I will give (tonight – today is Wednesday, I think – yes, Wednesday – so, today) '*Despair*', which has just arrived, to Marcel, and on Friday I'll give Roche a Russian copy. At the evening here there was a good crowd (the writers were represented by Bunin, Aldanov, Berberova), and I read 'Lips to Lips' and then poems. We split up late – and automatically all gathered again at a café, so that we got home God knows when. We had quite an entertaining argument with B. about Tolstoy. How he, Bunin, looks like a wasted old tortoise, stretching its old sinewy grey neck with a fold of skin instead of an Adam's apple and chewing something and waving its dull-eyed ancient head!

On the tenth I was with the Fierenses at the Jalouxs': crystal, a whippet, a Negro maid, parquets, champagne for lunch. He is rather plumpish, amusing, fell off the chair trying to smash a nut with the chair leg – *tu va te tuer, Edmond* – his wife quietly said to this: beautiful, blue-eyed, half his age and half-Russian. The conversation was very dazzling – and in general it was thoroughly pleasant. He wants to write about 'Camera' and asked me to give it to him. In the afternoon I was – not for long – at Berta Grigor.'s. In the evening Sherman gave his talk about me. Adamovich (with sweet little eyes) and Terapiano (very repulsive to look at) directed devoted speeches at me. The overall tone was a mood of apotheosis, reconciliation. Sherman spoke with much wit, but overdid it a bit – *too much of the good thing*. Weidle is extremely agreeable. There were about twenty poets there. Varshavsky found that I resembled Stendhal. I will add him to the list of my imaginary teachers. Yesterday I had lunch at the Shklyavers' (see my description in 1932 – it was the same, point for point – even the appetizers), in the afternoon I corrected the French 'Pilgram' (the translation, overall, is beautiful, but there are lots of imprecisions, although they did try very hard. It was done by Slonim and Campaux), and in the evening I went to see Vava – learned that the old man had left very insulted because neither *Sovr. zap*, nor *Posl. nov.* had asked him for his memoirs. I will talk about this with Ilya and Aldanov. Today I was at Maklakov's; he's almost totally deaf but very *charmant* (Falkovsky imitates him). I am writing four, no, in fact five screenplays for Shifr. – incidentally, Dastakiyan and I will go in a day or two to register them – against theft. Aunt Nina brought three lovely little jackets and left a note: 'Let these little jackets warm your boy as you warmed my old heart that evening on February 8th.' I miss you madly (and my Miten'ka) and love you, my little darling, little darling mine. I will obtain *Aguet* from him – from Roche – and thanks to you for the corrections and shipments. You know who called me: Eva! 'How I regretted that I could not attend your paper (*sic*!).' I declined a meeting – although it'd be very curious. I kiss my little boy. I love you, write to me soon. Greetings to Anyuta.

V.

[APCS]

[postmarked 16 February 1936]

TO: Nestor Str. 22, Berlin – Halensee, Allemagne

[Paris]

3 p.m.

My love, I have been so rushed off my feet – a terrible mess getting a return visa here from Belgium, I wasted nearly ten hours on all kinds of prefectures. Now I am leaving for Belgium and will return here on the 18th. The evening here is on the 21st. Then I'll return to Berlin at once. I am writing to you so briefly because I'm out of time – I'll describe the last few days in detail from Brussels.

I can't tell you how I have missed you [and] my little one.

Had lunch with Lyusya.

Kisses, my love.

V.

[ALS, 2 PP.]

[postmarked 17 February 1936]

TO: Nestor Str. 22, Berlin – Halensee, Allemagne

[Brussels]

My love, my darling, the last days in Paris were dedicated mostly to arranging my French evening. Ergaz (who has filled out a little and divorced her husband) took to this very actively and introduced me to the lady (S. Ridel) at whose home it will all take place (the little hall has room for 80). And there are also great hopes of finding a French publisher for 'Despair'. I asked Supervielle to introduce my reading, but he said no, citing his workload and his shyness. They are now looking for another Frenchman (maybe Marcel). I was also at Roche's. He is still charming, but awfully lacking in sense. He is ready to translate 'Despair' if some literary newspaper he contributes to takes it (but I'm not worried: they won't take it, judging by the issue of the paper I was shown). But if Stock takes it, as Ergaz promises, I'd have to give it to her to translate – she wants to very much. I'm not all that keen. Now imagine me twice visiting government departments, twice waiting there for three hours each time, then putting together a request with Raisa's help, then twice visiting (an hour each time) the prefecture and finally receiving the return visa to Paris. I was twice at the Belgian consulate, too, where at long last they gave me only a transit visa, so at the risk of being late for the reading I had to get off at Charleroi (the train didn't go through Brussels) and switch to the electric train – anyway, I will tell you the details in person. The evening at the Fierenses' ('*Pilgram*' and '*Aguet*') was very stylish and successful, about 50 there, and they proposed I send the king a copy of '*Pilgram*', since he's interested in butterflies. Yesterday I had dinner at Masui's (where there was an 1872 Burgundy lying fast asleep in its bottle), and then I read at the Club – first '*Mlle O*' and then 'A Russian Beauty' – to a full hall. Today lunch at the Hellenses', then tea at Auntie Fierens', the most intelligent and sweet little old lady, who has seriously decided to tackle our moving here. Now (Monday, 8 p.m.) the twenty people Zina invited will start to flow in. *Elle est plus ange que jamais*. Kirill is preparing for a chemistry exam and behaving well. It's very hard for me to write on this paper – especially with nothing to put underneath. I will do all you write me about, my dear joy! I dreamt that my little boy was sick and stepped out of the dream as if out of hot salted water. I love you. Thousands of little trifles are getting through the holes in this sweep-net letter, I'm writing to you only about what's more or less important; I'll tell you about the *ambience* of good will, to put it modestly, after I come back. You would have liked Hellens awfully! He's Belgium's leading writer, but his books earn him nothing.

I think that my little darling is already sleeping. I love you. Tomorrow (18th) I return to Paris and right after the evening there, to Berlin. I received an offer to come back at Easter to give a lecture here about Russian literature, with my trip paid for first class. I do not doubt that either in Paris or here Grishen'ka and his family could settle down, but one has to decide on the move. I love you very much. The little puppy has grown up a bit, chews everything, adorable. What would I have done without my wonderful brunette – the black suit. But I could have left the blue jacket behind. I love you madly and miss you madly.

V.

[ALS, 2 PP.]

[postmarked 19 February 1936]

TO: Nestor Str. 22, Berlin – Halensee, Allemagne

[Paris]

My sweet love, my happiness, you know, the novel will have a different name – I am adding one letter to its original title and from now on it will be called 'The Gift'. Good, isn't it? I am having a terrible muse itch; I could plunge now into my private abyss – not to mention how much I want to work my way through '*It is me*' and '*Despair*' again. Last night I had a good trip back to Paris. The gathering at Zinochka's (two days ago) was very jovial – by the way, I got lots of addresses to send tickets to (here). Yesterday morning Zinochka and I went to buy a few little things – I am afraid someone's going to scold me. Grigory Abramovich has left the excess with her too, but Kirill does not know about this. I like him more and more – Grigory Abramovich. Sharp, businesslike, good-looking. I confess, I came second class, but I am old, my rump's bony, I'm tired from travelling. Again I saw the Eiffel Tower standing in lacy bloomers, with lit-up goosebumps running up her spine. And all this against the background of a marvellous sunset, addressed to God knows who and by and large utterly lost. My French reading threatens to be quite grand. The introductory speech, in front of ninety, will be delivered by Marcel (who is now busy reading '*Despair*'). My darling, this will be only on the 25th of this month, and on the 26th there is the same kind of reading, but in Russian, at the Kyandzhuntsevs', with an admixture of Bunins and Shik, so I'll get back on the 27th. I called Lyusya and told him this, because *mon premier mouvement* was to turn this all down since my visit here has now been extended, but apparently it is worth staying. Please write to me 1) Heath's address (I have written to Long) 2) shall I give copies of 'Despair' to good acquaintances or should I perhaps try to sell them off at the Russian evening 3) whether you still love me.

I have received copies of 'Glory' from Kovarsky. There is a fiancé for Mlle Peltenburg – arriving from the Congo, a Belgian man of Russian descent, Zina's cousin, well-to-do and decent. I get a little annoyed by Hellens's wife (Marsya Markovna) persistently drawing a parallel between her husband and me, right to the point that the wives are of the same nationality. But it's true that in his wonderful '*Naif*', which I am reading now, there is a paragraph almost literally corresponding to the place in '*Mlle O*' where I talk about '*fente*' or '*barre lumineuse*' (he has '*perche lumineuse*', which is much better!). And he, with his protruding eyes which seem to pop out from the sockets because his (morbidly sunken) cheeks are pressing on them, is very sweet.

Irina ~~Kyandzhu~~ Brunst (there's a rather banal slip of the pen) is trying with all her might to arrange an evening. She's zealously taking German language lessons – not from a Hellene, which pleased me, while Saba keeps asking about Kirill – without realizing, by the way, his boorishness then. Zenzinov was sick for the three days I was away and is still in bed, looking terribly like (since he is entirely surrounded by books and papers and is writing something with his bony knees propped up under the blanket) the German painting '*Arme Dichter*'. There is a medallion under his pillow – Amalia's.

My darling, *au fond* we could have moved now. In a few days I think the fate of '*Mlle O*' will become clear – I do not know whether to call Paulhan or wait for news from him. Have a look whether the middle eyelash is still longer than all the rest, as it used to be – we haven't been looking lately. You write to Zina about his new words, but I don't know them. My little paws. I might have lost the knack of dressing him up!

Balmont used to wander through the streets at night, curse Frenchmen as 'cochons', try to find a rosette to pick, get beaten up – and his friends would go around all the police stations looking for him. Now he is in a madhouse – and shows visitors a tree in which a yellow angel sits and sings. It's warm, drizzling, Nikolay the cat is asleep on my couch, his face buried in his tail, chewing something in his sleep, stirring a silvery whisker.

Somehow this letter has turned out uninteresting, but I love you very much, my sweet creature, my priceless, my little darling. *I would like you to come in just now*. I will overstay my visa.

My darling, Dastakiyan has come in, so I'm finishing.

I love you.

V.

[ALS, 2 PP.]
[postmarked 21 February 1936]

TO: Nestor Str. 22, Berlin–Halensee, Allemagne

130 av. de Versailles
[Paris]

My love,

nothing will come of the Russian evening, so I will get out of here myself on the evening of the 26th or the morning of the 27th–I'll let you know beforehand (for some smallish and warmish considerations of the meeting and greeting kind, I'd like to arrive in the afternoon!). The heart of the venture was Rabinovich, who turned out to be a sheer charlatan. He fussily set things spinning, directed everything, summoned the ladies, set up a ladies' tea at the Kyandzhuntsevs'–to which neither he nor the ladies, apart from two whom Ira knew personally, showed up. When they called him, he cited a swollen cheek and a muddled head. He even had the nerve to phone me and, without saying a word about his caddishness, invite me over. I politely declined. I have to say I had a feeling that he was a charlatan–and discouraged the Kyandzhuntsevs. Stupid.

But the preparations for the French evening are in full swing. I enclose a ticket. The whole *après-midi* yesterday went on the addresses given me in Belgium. I spoke with ~~Sofa~~ on the phone (set up a meeting) and offered her a ticket, but she said, 'you see, I still don't know, the thing is I have such a bad cold (?), and besides my director . . .' In the evening, when I dropped in at home to change and go to the Kyandzhuntsevs' for dinner (Elizaveta Samoylovna's birthday, I brought her carnations), I found a note–with traces of the excitement conveyed over the phone–that, lo, my ~~sister-in-law~~ asked me to call her urgently on very important business. I called, she was not there, I left the

Kyand[zhuntsevs'] number, she then called there to say I must not interfere in the situation with a certain Ratner whom ~~Sofa~~ is going to put in prison for her debts and who 'intends to appeal to me to influence her'. All terribly uninteresting, but so charmingly characteristic I had to describe it.

Long writes to me today that my intention to look through the manuscript once more '*is very wise*'. About a few other points in his letter I'll seek the advice of Lyusya, whom I'm meeting today at three. Don't forget: Heath's address! (I have re-read all of your letters, my love, because I thought you had already sent it to me—but no.)

There is a virtual parade-allée of my past passions here: Katherine Berlin called, whom I will see tomorrow at Léon's dinner. Two evenings ago (after I'd got free, with difficulty, of the very sweet, very kind, but rather importunate Dastakiyan,—having finally led him away,—. . .—and led him back to my place, since he accompanied me to all the shops I went into—and even to the elevator in a house I didn't know, which I entered in desperation so as to go up to see a non-existent acquaintance, who had to be urgently abolished, when Dastakiyan, beaming through golden glasses, ascended with me), Bunin phoned inviting me to dinner—together with Ald. and Zayts. to honour Küfferle, but I declined—and am very glad that I did so.

Oh my darling, I'll soon see you and my tiny one—show  this to him you know, I'm already having trouble imagining him, because I demand too much from imagination, which does not yield such high interest, and I myself reject lower rates, so, for example, I cannot reproduce my little boy on the inner velvet of my eyelid—as I can successfully do with you.

Ilyusha's household is badly run,—I try to use it as little as I can, since each *meal* is an untimely and accidental product of collective fantasy—itself collected casually—so that the most modest of dinners seems an inspired improvisation. Rain today—all the netting on the cast-iron lattice of the garden next door has identical pearls of rain, and somewhere sparrows are holding very sonorous and excited discussions. Today I will be at Khodasevich's, and this evening at Mme Kokoshkin's. Tomorrow, Fierens. I slept poorly after champagne at the Kyandzhun.s', my brows ache. I'll write to the old man now – this is an idea, isn't it? He thought that 'Sovr. zap.' (which by the way will be out in a few days) or 'P.N.' would be interested in his memoirs, – I spoke about this with Ilyusha, but to no effect, I think. I'd have to rewrite the French 'Pilgram' thoroughly for the Belgian king – I like this rather silly undertaking – the grassy lawn of tradition – nice to walk on, all the same, as it was for the Shakespeares and the Horaces and the Pushkins.

I am kissing you lots and very tenderly, my darling. Tell Anyuta to write to me! I've missed our home habits. But I don't know what to say to my little one – my little darling, he's now on his way back from his walk – he has probably grown up, just like Elli's belly. My sweet joy.

V.

[ALS, 2 PP.]

[postmarked 24 February 1936]

TO: 22, Nestor str., Berlin –Halensee, Allemagne

[Paris]

My darling, I am happy that our boysie is well, because somehow my thoughts about him were with a dot-dot-dot of worry. The life of my German visa – that lichen on the dilapidating wall of my passport – will last till May – if it hasn't completely disintegrated by then – I have glued it up, after they asked me at the Ministry *with pained surprise* (since it had split in two): '*c'est avec ça que vous voyagez?*' I am forwarding two letters to you – the American one is very important, for, as those in the know tell me, it's a good publisher, and generous; the Matveev proposal is a joke to which I should have replied: 'Unfortunately this does not suit us at all. By the way – which acquaintances do you mean?' (or maybe, indeed, I should send Matusevich to them? Think about that.) I think that we must immediately (McBride's letter of 10-XII!) send a copy of 'Despair' with my Berlin address on it to America – do it, my sweetheart.

The typesetter Aristarkhov told the Kokoshkins about *Camera Obscura* (which he was setting – and keeping them informed about its development): 'at first it was such a jolly story – who could have expected . . .' (and at this shook his head). I have met outstanding readers at the Kokoshkins' – *there* are people worth writing for. Two days ago I had coffee with Lyusya (I treated him) and a bit of a discussion. Then visited Khodasevich who was lying sick on an ottoman, strangely improved in his looks – perhaps even looking like (maybe because I was seeing him from a new angle) an Indian chief – dark, flat hair and thinness; – but some other likeness also tickled my imagination: wrapped in a plaid blanket, dishevelled and eloquent, 'with the seal of genius on his pale forehead', he suddenly reminded me of something old-fashioned, and the old-fashioned turned out to be Pushkin – I put side-whiskers on him – and believe me, he began to look like him (as some entomologist would look like a May-bug, or a cashier like a number). He was on top form and poured out for me his sparkling venom. Yesterday had lunch at the Kyandzhuntsevs, then went to the Louvre to a lecture by my dear old Fierens, with whom I am having dinner today. Walked with Irina in the Tuileries, then went to Léon's where I had dinner with Aunt Nina. Girshman is still very beautiful, but the younger (comparatively) Ekaterina has aged awfully. Léon has given me as a present (as far as I understood) several books by Joyce with his inscriptions, and suggested that we called on him after dinner, but surrounded the visit with so much fuss and caution that I finally refused, saying I didn't have the time (and the pointlessness of such a meeting. Joyce met Proust just once, by chance; Proust and he happened to be in the same taxi-cab, the window of which the first would close and the second open – they almost quarrelled). On the whole it was rather tedious.

About those new things of his: abstract puns, a masquerade of words, shadows of words, maladies of words. I parody him: *creaming at the pot of his Joyce*. Ultimately: wit sets behind reason, and while it is setting, the sky is marvellous, but then it's night.

My sweetheart, what if you wrapped our boy up and came here with him? We'll have enough to begin with, and then work will turn up. Well? I think such things should be decided at once, striking the iron while it *aurait chaud* (I'm still parodying him).

Yesterday I broke off the letter to go to Rudnev's for pancakes, and I had dinner with Fierens, – spent a lovely evening with him. Now it's morning. I will go for lunch with Sofa, then to Marcel's, then to Bunin's. If you dare not to come, then I'll head back on Thursday the 27th – today I will find out, if I have time, when the train arrives and let you know.

I think Anyuta has already remarked: there are no clocks at all at the métro stations, but there are all of two at the Trocadero station – one even with a pendulum. I once asked a conductor what was in the composition of the stone steps that sparkled so nicely – the sparks were like the play of quartz in granite, and at this he, with unusual eagerness – giving me *les honneurs du Métro*, so to speak, – started explaining to me and showed me where to stand and how to look to enjoy the glitter at its best: if I described this, people would say I made it up.

Kisses, my happiness ... You're somehow writing very briefly to me. Ilyusha hasn't had a single bath since I've been here.

Kissing you once more.

V.

Matveev's idiotic card won't fit in the envelope – I'll bring it.

[APCS]
[postmarked 26 February 1936]

TO: Nestor Str. 22, Berlin–Halensee, Allemagne

[Paris]

My love, my yesterday's *matinée* went marvellously, about a hundred came, it was lavish, lively–in a word, couldn't have gone better. Marcel spoke about me for about an hour (the day before, on top of everything he had read, I explained to him the idea of *Invitation*; besides he'd summoned Weidle, who crammed him full) and very, very intelligently. Every detail of '*Mlle O*' was greeted with waves of sympathy, smiles of approval–and a couple of times I was 'interrupted with applause'. I'm very pleased.

It seems we can consider solved the problem of placing '*Désespoir*' (Stock or Plon). The fate of '*Mlle O*' and '*Pilgram*' still hasn't been settled, I'll stay here for two more days, that is will leave on Friday–that's final. This evening there's a party at Marcel's. This little postcard is not part of my letter count, but just so you know how successful it was yesterday, my love. You know, after all our dear Grigory Abramovich has topped the previous trip. I'll see An. Nat. today.

My darling, I kiss you and my little one, *I am longing for you*.

V.

[ALS, 2 PP.]
[27 February 1936]

[TO: Berlin]

[Paris]

My love, my wonderful happiness, according to Cook I am leaving at

22.45 and arriving at Charlottenburg at 17.19, so if the weather is good and there are no little snuffles – well then, on Saturday, at nineteen minutes past five. On Monday (today is Thursday, evening), I had lunch with ~~Sofa~~ in a little Russian restaurant, she again talked with hatred about Ratner (who, in Raisa's words, in her own time, that is, about three months ago, had been obtaining and obtained money for ~~Sofa~~ herself; overboard, as old Joyce would've put it). I adopted the tone with her that you suggested in your letter. She said: 'all of that should have been told me when I was eighteen years old; now it's too late.' She didn't show up at my reading at Ridel's. After that I stopped by at Irina's and with her, in her limousine, made a formal call on Bunin, who received us in cherry-coloured pyjamas – bags under his eyes, with a cold, depressed – and treated us to Samosa wine. We sat down for a quarter of an hour (strictly speaking, the visit was meant for Vera Nikolaevna, but she wasn't there) and went to *Jones'* – that's a shop. When I got back I found Dastakiyan, whom I very promptly led off in the direction of Boulevard Murat, so I could invent a visit (to the Kaminkas). When I got back again I discovered the same society as was there last Monday, and the question for discussion was 'sacredness and creativity'. The sweetest of all was Ladinsky, like an old rooster that's lost its voice – a gentle rooster. Everyone left at half past two. On Tuesday there was the French reading, more than successful, and after that I went to bed at nine o'clock, impossibly tired (it lasted from three to eight, *tout compris!*). Yesterday I lunched at La Coupole with Mme Tatarinov; there too at three o'clock met Anna Natanovna, sat with her till four, after which appeared a very likeable but hopelessly red-haired Zeldovich, who walked me to the métro. In the evening there was a gathering at Marcel's: he read his new play, absolutely talentless, with a musical German émigré in the main role. At midnight we called in on the way back at a café where Kerensky, the Aldanovs, Teffi and many more had gathered. Today I spoke with Rudnev about 'Sovr. zap.': he definitely wants 'Chernyshevsky' for the next issue. He will write to the old man about the memoirs—he promised. I said goodbye to the Kyandzhuntsevs, then went to the Belgian Consulate. Then I bought some tulips and under the pouring rain, adorned with snow, called on Mme Ridel (she, by the way, is a cousin of Poncet, the ambassador), where I spent a very pleasant and useful hour. Tomorrow I will see Paulhan and Slonim and in the evening will set out on my return journey. I think of you with the most excruciating tenderness, my darling. And of my little one. It seems I will have to send this letter by airmail, or it won't make it. I want to be in Berlin. Got a letter from Long, everything's in order. It's raining, squelching in the garden outside the window; the rain's tired. Me, too.

There was a time when Teffi, corpulent and white-necked, would sit in the Stray Dog, in a décolleté for forty-eight persons, and approximately that many young gentlemen with parted hair would all latch on together to her shoulders, and now she's a haggish old woman with a face extraordinarily like a galosh. I hear Sherman's voice, he's come to Zenzinov. See you soon, my darling, I can't even tell you how much I'm kissing you.

V.

[APCS]

[postmarked 10 June 1936]

TO: bei Bromberg, Ehrensteinstr. 34-I, Leipzig N 22

Nestor str. 22

[Berlin]

My darling, thanks for the report. It was very sad to watch the little face floating by. I've just had dinner, not in a Russian, but in a German restaurant, since the Russian turned out too dear – more than a mark. A message has come from the Fid. Com. that the thing is finished and there will be money in two weeks; and Zeldovich writes that she has not received the books. I couldn't eat up all the rhubarb yesterday. The journal 'Krug' with Weidle's article about me has come. Frigid weather. Make sure he doesn't catch a cold. Today without him I'm as if I have no soul. Half past one now, I am writing in the post office, will return home and write. Tomorrow evening I am at Zyoka's. My love, stay longer without moving around.

Greetings to Anyuta and Elena Lvovna.

V.

[APCS]

[postmarked 11 June 1936]

TO: bei Bromberg, Leipzig N 22, Ehrensteinstr. 34-I

[Berlin]

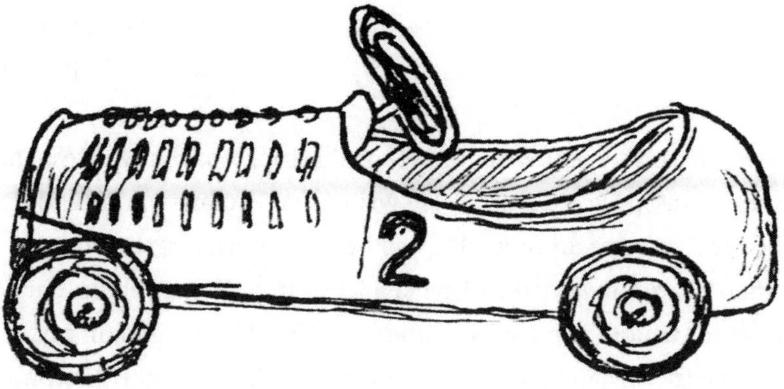

My love, a letter from Long. Having excused himself for the '*delay*', he carries on: '*up to the present, however, we have not made any plans for the publication of this book, the chief reason being that some of our Readers' reports have not been at all enthusiastic, especially in regard to your translation. In view of the latter, we are now writing to ask you whether it would be possible for you to get hold of the translation that the American publishers used?*' What shall I answer?

Nina P. phoned offering a job for you in the French *Verkehr* society: from 9 to 6, Fr. Germ. typewr. stenog., pay 150 marks. I said I'd write to you (but this is, of course, impossible to take).

Zhdanov sent the manuscript back.

At night I was composing a play and slept terribly. I love you, don't get too upset. I can imagine what kind of '*readers*' they have (which is not much consolation, all the same).

V.

[APCS]

[postmarked 12 June 1936]

TO: bei Bromberg, Leipzig N 22, Ehrensteinstr. 34-I

Nestor str. 22

[Berlin]

My love, make sure you write to me, or I'll stop, too. The sweetest and most touching postcard from F. He writes that Paulhan's number is 15–00. Everything is in order. He will be here himself at the end of summer. I have forwarded to Anyuta a letter in a long envelope. I am very bored without you and the little boy. Why does it smell in his room, persistently and amiably, of sour milk? I have been to Aksyonov's just now, and on the way spoke with princess Sh., whom I ran into. I received Adamovich's review of 'The Cave', where he very brazenly 'drew a parallel' between the precious M. A. and myself. Yesterday I 'dined' at home, and today, at the Russian deli on Pariser Str. *I love you, my darling*. Write.

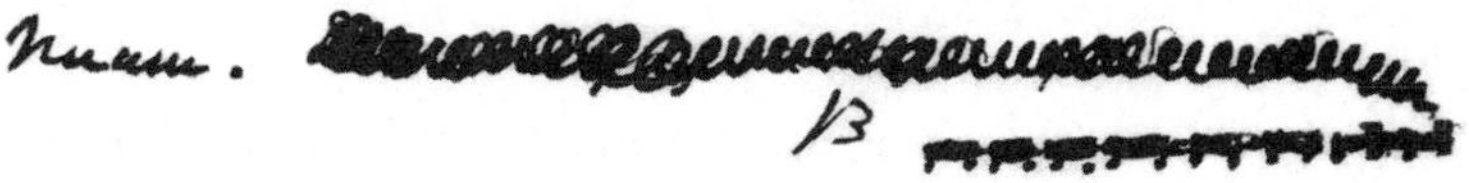

Greetings to Anyuta-anyuta ...

V.

[APCS]

[13? June 1936]

TO: bei Bromberg, Leipzig N 22, Ehrensteinstr. 34-I

Nestor str. 22

[Berlin]

My darling, I'm very happy that you're enjoying Leipzig. I received yet another article about myself (the third in three days!) – from Gleb, in the little Russian-English newspaper.

A letter from Mother, worried about K. (who foolishly wants absolutely to go to England for his holidays) and the apartment – not for the first time. The weather is marvellous today, I was in the Grunewald. 'Sovremennye' is coming out 1-VII. I must juggle a bit, so as not to spend more than a mark a day on everything.

Nika's mother has called. My darling, try to lie a little in the sun. When exactly will you come back? *I love you*.

V.

[APCS]

[14? June 1936]

TO: Leipzig N 22, Ehrensteinstr. 34-I, b/ Bromberg

[Berlin]

My love,

Nothing new, except a long thank-you letter from Mme Piotrovsky, I won't forward it to you. I'm waiting for Gertruda tomorrow. Was in the Grunewald today. The weather's so fine. Write me in more detail, when my son will be returned to me. Kissing you, my darling. Strange he's afraid of squirrels. Now I will make myself some cocoa.

V.

[APCS]

[postmarked 15 June 1936]

TO: Leipzig N 22, Ehrensteinstr. 34-I, b/ Bromberg

Nestor str. 22

[Berlin]

My dear darling, yesterday I spent most of the day in the forest, and today am having dinner at Hes.'s. By mistake I used the oatmeal caca-o and it turned out such slop that I almost threw up, and yet had to drink up three cups, so as not to waste the milk, which I was boiling at the same time, pouring 'caca-o' into it. Yesterday the radio of some loathsome neighbours (with the window open) thundered till midnight (of all inventions it's surely the most banal and foolish); I and somebody else yelled 'Ruhe!', but in vain: the red-checkered brown operatic voice continued at full tilt. Today it's overcast again. I miss you. *I love you*.

V.

I am forwarding two letters to Anyuta, whom I kiss.

[APCS]

[postmarked 16 June 1936]

TO: b/ Bromberg, Leipzig N 22, Ehrensteinstr. 34-I

[Berlin]

My darling,

a letter from Rudnev with a passionate plea to write for them on 'The Cave' – no one wants to do this. They need it for July first. Please, bring the book back.

I don't need your five marks yet, I'm still holding out. The old man asked me to read (re-read!) his 'memoirs' and mend where necessary. I am having dinner at his place today (which, to my mind, is somehow dimly-unconsciously connected with the editing) and in general he asks me to dine with him every day, *but I don't*.

I miss you very much, my love. Besides I am a bit irritated. Great that the little boysie has learned how to sit on the potty. Truda called in and brought him five eggs. I've forwarded two letters to Anyuta. *I love you*.

V.

The most cordial greetings to Elena Lvovna!

[APC]

[postmarked 18 June 1936]

TO: Leipzig N 22, Ehrensteinstr. 34-I, b/ Bromberg

[Berlin]

My darling, a letter today from Karpovich that he will be here on Sunday (so as to leave on Monday morning) and he proposes to call in here at 5 o'clock (but he'll be at Hessen's for the evening). I'll offer him tea.

Today on the lake I saw a pochard, who swam carrying his chick on his back – and envied him. Saw – and heard – a company of Russians, of whom one was, strictly speaking, a fat German, with pronunciation to match, so that when her husband asked her 'Pupusha, what are you sitting on there?' she replied 'On my ass'.

I haven't yet bought anything on the coupon at *Hemdenhalle*. Kisses to you, my love, and to him, him . . .

1937

[APCS]

[postmarked 20 January 1937]

TO: Nestor str., 22, b/Feigin, Berlin, Allemagne

[Brussels]

My darling, the snow on the carriage roof soon began to melt – and suddenly: the light bulbs started to drip, gradually drowning the compartment. At the border it turned out that Anyutochka was absolutely right: the official felt mortally insulted by the pins that fastened the inner belts, and there was an exchange of rough remarks finishing in a compromise: he unfastened the left one, and I – the right. In his rage, he ripped everything apart. Then lots of merry Belgian commercial travellers crawled in, and talked about the figures of ladies they know and about interest rates. *Pendant que l'avoine pousse, le cheval crèvera*, one remarked in some connection. It's wonderful at Zinochka's. I've slept well in a soft bed, in a marvellous room. Her yellow-eyed wolf keeps sniffing at me.

I wanted to write much more, but see I won't have time. I prefer to send as is. Love you, him. Kiss Anyuta.

V.

[ALS, 2 PP.]
[22 January 1937]

TO: 22, Nestor str., Berlin–Halensee, Allemagne

c/o Fondaminsky,
130, av. de Versailles
[Paris]
22–I–37

My darling, my dear love, I am writing to you on the train going to Paris, so there's a certain tremor in my handwriting. The French evening went even more successfully than last time, the big plush hall was jam-packed. In place of an introduction Jacques Masui spoke charmingly and intelligently about me. The old man de Rieux (who is now publishing a book about ... Lawrence, – not the colonel, but the lover), came up to me and remarked *qu'il n'aurait jamais cru* that Pushkin could have such a beautiful line as '. . . *l'étoile n'est plus là parce que l'eau se ride*'. The reading was drawn tight at the middle by a little belt of applause, and at the end there was a completely massive and heavy-duty din. Victor has earned a thousand francs for this kind of lecture, a fine fellow, isn't he? Eleonora was there, I kept her at my side all the time (why is she in such a hurry, express, jumps the gun), we were in a café together, and so on. By the way, they say that they didn't completely understand Aleksandra Lazarevna's mysterious hint (about the gift), but her father had guessed correctly to her. Kirill, alas, entirely conforms to the impression we already had of him (my darling, I already miss you insanely – and the little boyo – I am kissing you, my happiness), he is very thin and morose, completely lacking his former vivacity. I won't write about his 'light bulbs'. I retrieved his things for twenty-five francs (!), went myself with him to get them, because on his own he was afraid of the landlady. I will just say that among the armful of things we were wrapping up there was a teaspoon with leftovers of jam, and scissors rusted orange all over. Sergey and Anna are very kind to him, as well as Zina. How charming little Niki is! I couldn't tear myself away from him. He was lying, a red little thing, dishevelled, with bronchitis, surrounded with automobiles of all makes and sizes. I spoke with Margarita about Kir., her plan is to arrange a job at a toy store for him – in any case, she took it all very seriously. Fierens is in Paris. I was at Hellens's, he looked even more like a hungry condor than before. He was in a dressing gown, 'down with flu'. I have given him '*l'outrage*', and signed a dedication to it (remembering only later that in Russian this is, after all, dedicated to Bunin – so if it were published, it would turn out funny). He kept asking whether I had written his last name clearly enough, and then went ahead and scribbled it out himself, – that's what we're like. This little detail convinces me he'll really try to get the story out; but he advised me to give the lecture to Paulhan right away. I'm so tortured by my Greek, I'm dreaming about precipitation. I eat a lot, do not smoke, *ou presque*. It pains me to think, my joy, how tired you probably are now. Leonora insists you pay a visit to Holland. Why don't you go there earlier, i.e. before the final exodus?

Zina was thrilled by the amethysts. She and Svetik and Svyat. Adr. were absolutely heavenly-sweet with me. Turns out that Victor settled his accounts with her today and paid for his brother's card *d'identité*.

'*Mesures*' is rated the best French journal.

Thank you, my darling, for the news about Rudnev. The train's really flying. The fields are green, like in spring; I am sitting without a jacket. It's hard to write, my thoughts jump around with the jolting. More about Kirill: he's living now in an excellent, large, clean room, with a friendly and patient landlady who runs a pub downstairs. Only after she saw me did she really believe it was Kirill's brother pictured in the newspaper and now Kirill thinks his stocks have risen. Turovets (whose light bulbs he peddles) gave him a hat and a suit, on the whole he's dressed decently, but the shoes give him away. Thank god, this seems like a station. Yes. We're at the border. I keep showing everyone little snapshots. I am kissing him on the temple, my little one. Write me soon, my love. There was a lot I didn't tell you about the evening, but it would have come out cloying. Zina and Svetik were beaming. I am happy, because this augurs success in Paris too. Well, the train's moving again. Keep well, my love. *I kiss you a lot and very tenderly*.

V.

Greetings to Anyuta and tell her how exactly I 'conducted' all the conversations.

[ALS, 2 PP.]

[postmarked 25 January 1937]

TO: 22, Nestor str., Berlin–Halensee, Allemagne

c/o Fondaminsky,
130, av. de Versailles
[Paris]

Hello, my darling,

Last night there was a Russian reading (two excerpts from 'The Gift', the triangle and Bush). *It was quite a treat*. The tickets were all sold out, the public listened ideally, I read with a ten-minute break from ten till twenty to twelve (about 45 pp.). To start off, Khodasevich spoke a little, wittily and one-sidedly – mostly about 'devices', about how in what I write 'the devices live and work'. Lyusya laughed a lot when I read about Bush. Sofa informed me that the day before she had 'dictated to the secretary' all night. I saw Mme Morevsky. Saw scores more. Then, according to tradition, as a whole society, we relocated to a café, about twenty of us with the invariable Bunin, Aldanov, Berberova, Khodas. and so on. *On est très, très gentil avec moi*.

Tomorrow I'll be at Maklakov's. All my free time (and yesterday till half past three in the morning, since I have so little time free), I corrected the first chapter of 'The Gift' (since I have to rush to some deadline, when they raise the rate) and today, finally, submitted it all to Rudnev (who's charming with me). I've looked over the English galleys, except the part I'm expecting from you today – and then I'll send everything to Long.

I have already established contact with 'Tair', have talked about it all with Lol. Lvov, and, it seems, it might come out. I have been to Ergaz's, she's all red with a cold. Took her candy, it was all very nice. I have been to Raisa's (she's trying very, very hard), to the old man's, to Khodasevich's. On Wednesday I am having a serious conversation with Aldanov – the only person who has even the slightest influence on P. N. I have already been offered (Ilya) an apartment of three rooms with all mod. cons., in Boulogne (it's lovely there now, – I walked through on my way to Khodas.) for 300 fr. a month, and Sherman's offering another one for 400 fr., in a new house, etc. I met with Lyusya as soon as I arrived, brought him the boots and the dream. Everyone I see praises my 'Fialta'. I spoke with Teffi about London: her reading at Sablin's was remarkable, with the beau-monde and front-row seats a guinea, etc. Shouldn't I write to him from here? But what? Send me an outline!

On Friday I am having dinner at the Kokoshkins' with Fondam. and Zenzin. Irina has lost her good looks. With another Irina (Kyandzh.) I spoke on the phone, she gave birth to a girl about three weeks ago, I'll go there tomorrow. I've already spoken with Ilyusha's actors about the play. I will write it as soon as I have time. I've made arrangements with Paulhan for tomorrow.

My dear love, I miss you and him very much. His little snapshots produce raptures.

I'm very comfortable here, not an iota has changed since last time, I feel myself 'at home'.

Today I slept no more than three hours. In the afternoon I am at the old man's. It's now half past one, I haven't been out yet and haven't had lunch, it's raining, behind the door Jeanne is speaking to the cat: '*mon pauvre petit martyr!*'

Greetings to Anyuta.

My dear love!

V.

[ALS, 2 PP.]
[postmarked 27 [January] 1937]

TO: 22, Nestor str., Berlin–Halensee, Allemagne

[Paris]

My dear darling, my little sunshine,

I was at Maklakov's. He maintains there'll be no difficulties. But first of all, however, I have to extend my visa to 3 months with the right to return from London. Tomorrow I'll go there again about this. And in the morning, tomorrow, I'll be at Pavel's. Do you remember a certain *Calmbrood*? It turns out he has earned two thousand plus. I was at Paulhan's yesterday and gave him both things (he promised to be at the reading, but something that sparkled in his brown eye made me give him '*LeVrai*' right there, rather than put it away in the long drawer. He was unusually nice–and promises, in general, to help me). Two days ago, from Mme Damansky, I got several addresses of cheap pensions on the Riviera (20 fr. a day) and besides, she promised to write to her uncle in Beaulieu-sur-mer. Ilyusha, to whom I spoke about it all in detail, will take care of this, too. He thoroughly explained to me all the nuances (absolutely, by the way, in keeping with your and Anyuta's instructions) that I should stick to in my conversation with Milyukov. My plan is for you and the little boysie to travel in the middle (or the beginning?) of March through Paris straight to the south. It's obvious to me that Victor (he sends lots of kisses, my life, – he feels such a *longing for you, for your soft dear whiteness and everything. I have never loved you as I love you now*) will find a way to exist here. Aunt Nina visited me yesterday and brought – awfully touching – a whole dowry for the boy: a wonderful little dark-blue and pink bathrobe, two pink pyjamas, knitted jerseys, red leggings, white leggings, a little hat, little shirts, and lots more. Maybe you should drop her a line? 16, av. de la Grande Armée. Enclose a photograph.

On Monday night, there was a meeting of Christians and poets at Ilyusha's. Georg. Ivan. was there, too, a lisping little gentleman, his face looking like both a hoopoe and Boris Brodsky. I avoided a handshake. They discussed the topic of the sexual act in the light of Christianity, and Yanovsky, Mamchenko, Ivanov talked a lot of terrible and shameful nonsense, with Fedotov starting it (the speaker did not show up and Fedotov suggested the topic of 'frankness in literature').

I've done half of 'Despair' and have sent it (40 galleys) to Long. Yesterday I was supposed to have dinner with Bunin (along with Aldanov and Tsetlin), but there was a mix-up (I was at Paulhan's, and then had dinner alone in a little bar I know on rue Bonaparte – 6 fr. for everything), so from 7 to 11 they were calling Ilyusha. I had lunch yesterday at the Kyandzhuntsevs'. I saw Irina's little girl – dark-haired, in a huge pink baby carriage. Saba has a new car. He spent ages telling me his misfortunes in love. Irina isn't going back to Leipzig, and her husband's in England. I will call on Gaston Gallimard tomorrow, on

Paulhan's advice, and the day after tomorrow I'll have lunch with Sofa. Now I am sitting in a bar on my way to Mme Morevsky, where I will see Lyusya and give it to him. The watch is ticking in my coat. Marvellous weather, the Seine's like milk.

My Greek tortures me so much (I don't sleep at night because it's furiously itchy – and this greatly affects my mood) that I decided to see a doctor, since it gets even worse from the *précipité blanc*. This idiotic tar has affected me awfully. Mme Sablin (née Fomin, Yurik's former passion and Gogel's sister) is coming here any day, and I'll have a talk with her. Write me lots about Miten'ka. This is for him.

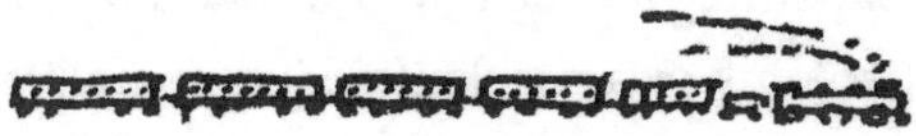

I am attaching a review from a Belgian newspaper. I have written to Mother.

My darling, I kiss you.

Greetings to Anyutochka. They haven't yet come for the things.

V.

[ALS, 1 P.]
[postmarked 28 January 1937]

TO: b/ Feigin, 22, Nestor str., Berlin – Halensee

c/o Fondaminsky,
130, av. de Versailles
[Paris]

My dear love,

Paulhan has just written to me that *Outrage* is '*délicieux, merveilleux, convaincant*' and that he's taking it for N.R.F. He wants to talk some more with me about '*Pouchkine*', so I am going to him again.

P. N. was extremely gracious with me. I reported everything to him – like a lesson – and received an A plus. Victor asked him for two thousand a month for three or four little articles. This will be decided in a day or two.

I was at Maklakov's again – rather, at N. M. Rodzyanko's, who's taking particular care of this and has filled out a long request. You don't have quite the right information about furniture: one simply needs to have a *permis de séjour* and then, with a note from the Fr. Consul in Berlin, it can be brought in without a tax.

My joy, write to me. I am kissing you and him, my darlings. I enclose Ald.'s very nice article.

V.

I have been to M.'s with Lyusya, and then to the doctor's. He suggests I get some kind of injections, twenty at twenty francs a time. I declined.

[ALS, 2 PP.]

[postmarked 1 February 1937]

TO: 22, Nestor str., Berlin – Halensee, Allemagne

Exp: Fondaminsky,
130, av. de Versailles
[Paris]

My darling, my love,

All the letters you ask about were written long ago – to Sablin and Zina, and to Long, and to Gleb, and to Molly, and to Gallimard (from whom there is still no reply; if there's still none, I'll phone). I live in something like concentric whirlwinds, moving from one to another. Paulhan is taking the *conférence* too, but he finds that the translations of the poems have no '*envolée*' and, after consulting with him, I have sent them to Melo du Dy, for feathering. On Thursday night I went with the Thompsons (and the chess – and very sweet) Bernstein to Rashel's. On Friday I had lunch with Sofa and Lyusya, and in the evening, with Ilyusha and Vlad. Mikh. (who won't part with my tie, which looks very good on him), had dinner at the Kokoshkin-Guadaninis', and returned along the gloomy and empty boulevards at 2 a.m. – and since then Ilyusha has been talking affectionately about Russian girls who make their living by giving haircuts to dogs.

On Saturday there was a very fancy and jolly reading at Ridel's (but Weidle *was not a success* since, as it turns out, he stammers – he clings to a word and cannot jump off and works on the spot for five seconds or so, and then it is smooth again, but overall he's very nice). In the evening I was at the Russian Theatre and then till morning we sat in a café with the actresses (and Ilyusha). Yesterday I was at the Bunins' (Ald. and Roshchin were there too), and today met with Polyakov in a café (the P.N. question has not been resolved yet), then I was at Gen. Golovin's and received from him a translation into English. Victor will be paid two hundred francs for ten pages. I had a visit from the Kazakh-Kirghiz Chokhaev, specially to talk about the circumstances of Godunov-Cherdyntsev's death, and he told me all I needed. I have been to Kanegisser's sister's (by the way: mentioning this name in my 'Gift' sounded – as Aldanov and Mme Tatarinov assured me – like a terrible gaffe), and gave her a film option for K.Q.K. Have been to the Louvre (for the work of Godun. Cherd., K. K., about butterflies in old still lifes), and tomorrow I am meeting with Zhdanov. I have been to Paulhan's again: if *Outrage* comes out in N.R.F., he won't give more than 40 fr. per page, and it will come out only in four months, so that he will try to place it in *Mesures*, and if not, then in N.R.F. I found a 'useful' man in Cambridge and several addresses in the South. My darling, get ready to leave! I won't tell you about the unbearable sufferings imposed on me by the Greek; the itchiness doesn't let me sleep, and all the linen is covered in blood – terrible. There is a good new salve, but I don't dare to use it, because it says on it '*Sali*[t] *énormément le linge*'. Yes, perhaps, I will go see Dynkin. Victor received around eight hundred from Ridel. I love you. Kisses to my little one. There were many other meetings, but I've got some things all mixed up. Have had lunch again at the Kyandzhuntsevs': Irina is divorcing her husband and says that he would cause scenes when they invited someone home. The little girl very sweetly *fait rotototo* after the bottle (a burp). My entire week is 'scheduled'. I enclose two reviews. Everything would be fine, if it weren't for the damned skin. I love you. The old man was stunned by the first chapter. My darling, I'm waiting for you so much. And him.

V.

[ALS, 2 PP.]

[postmarked 4 February 1937]

TO: 22, Nestor str., Berlin – Halensee, Allemagne

Exp: Fondaminsky,
130, av. de Versailles
[Paris]

My love, thanks to my heroic persistence I have made, in between all my other local visits, dealings and conversations, a most complicated technical translation into English – finished it yesterday around two. I've extended my visa for two months, that is, I'll receive it in London after this one expires. At the Ministry I met Ger. Abr., whom they didn't give a return visa. They came for the things. I met with poor Zhdanov, who'd come on the occasion of his father's death: the film possibility has arisen again, so I will meet with Kortn. first thing in London. My darling, how are you, what are you, I feel agonizingly empty without you (and without the little warm portable boy), I love you, my darling. I had lunch at the Berberovs' with Adamovich: we are very sweet to each other. She has a new '*Dawson girl*' haircut, but the same pink little isthmus of flesh between her front teeth. Today I see G. Marcel, who wants me to repeat the *conférence* (which he overpraises) to a Sorbonne audience: I think I'll have to agree, although they probably won't pay any money. I got a long letter from Sablin with a 'very polite' invitation to read at his place and with the practical advice to find a 'well-to-do' heir to the tsars who'd 'propagandize' the evening, since, as he says, they 'are more interested in Russ. literature than genuine Russians are'. From Struve – the absolute idiot – I received an offhand postcard that he considers a double reading 'inadvisable'. I wrote to Sablin, Grinberg, Mme Gavronsky, Long (I sent off the very elegant *title-page*), Mme Chernavin. Yesterday had lunch at Antonini's, he's very nice (if you don't count his nauseating snobbery). I need the contract with Long, to know how much he's paying. Send it without fail – or copy it out. Victor, as he tells me, spends piles of money, but he will write something for Lyusya. I think I'll end up choosing Rochebrune, cap. St Martin. As soon as I return from London, the visa will be sent to you. Not a line from Mother, I don't understand. The psoriasis is only getting worse. I will do something about it on my return from London. From time to time I have a dream: to cover myself with ointment from head to toe and lie in hospital for a month.

If it weren't for that everything would in general have been marvellous. *On me fête beaucoup*, I am surrounded by hundreds of very nice people. De-Monza said at Navashin's funeral: '*il y a cent ans, on a tué Pouchkine . . . Maintenant on a tué Navachine . . .*' Now I am going to have lunch with Roche, and then Ridel and I will go to Mme Chardonne's. In the evening I must see Khodasevich 'on business' in a café. My underwear is in such a state that it was too awkward to give it to Jeanne and I had to take it to a laundry, where washing a shirt costs almost three francs. Greetings to Anyutochka. My darling, I am beginning to count the days to March 15th. Write.

V.

They are trying to set me up here with a furnished apart., 3 r., all mod. cons, for 650 per m., through Zina.

[ALS, 2 PP.]

[postmarked 5 February 1937]

TO: 22, Nestor str., Berlin–Halensee, Allemagne

Exp: Fondaminsky,
130, av. de Versailles
[Paris]

My darling, my love, here are the answers to all your motleyish questions: I wrote about Kirill to Zina and Masui. I kicked Victor out. Bonnier and Jannelli have been written to. Zina will send the *Mercure*–if she has not sent it already. The business with Tair has not been clarified yet. Raisa took the belt rather indifferently. About Maurois: before the beginning Ridel had told me that '*mon grand ami Maurois n'a malheureusement pas pu venir*', and then, right there, after asking Weidle's advice, I crossed out the whole paragraph about 'Byron'. I do not know yet which of the two things Paulhan will place in N.R.F. and which in *Mesures*. It is very hard to catch Gallimard, but today I phoned N.R.F., reminding them that I am waiting for news from him (there is no other way), and his secretary there answered me that I will receive *un mot demain*.

It is impossible to find Shvarts, and I do not have time now for treatment, and if I went to Dynkin for advice, then he'd charge 75 fr. for this 'advice', but all the same I'll go to him after my return from London, but only if I haven't received free treatment at the hospital where Sherman works. I have asked several people today and they all said with one voice that 400 is very cheap and that it is, of course, *tout compris*, so that they all recommend that we grab it, as I do – although I'm still waiting for answers from *pensions* through Mme Schlesinger and others. Today out of curiosity I looked over the furnished apartment (3 rooms etc., magnificent, clean, spacious), which I was promised from Belgium through Zina, supposedly 650 a month *tout compris* (even that wouldn't work, of course) – but also it turned out to be not 650, but 800.

Cards: of course without any 'écrivain', but *tout court*. Lyusya has amassed a collection of three thousand butterflies – so far. Old man Paul has finally made me a proposal: two spots a month for 400, *c'est toujours quelque chose*, but I haven't yet agreed, I'll raise it. The old man is not stone, but cardboard. One spot, an essay or review, and the other, 'belles-lettres'. We are having wonderful spring weather all the time. Please, plan to set out in March.

Military duty cannot affect me in any way. I'll get a residence permit as soon as I return from London. Ilyusha does not need a wallet, but he was pleased. I handed over to the old man the books and vodka brought from Romania by El. Lvovna. I will write to Lisbet. And to Heath. Will write to Anyuta. I have received a desperate letter from Mother. *Au fond*, shouldn't I do this: I found out at the travel office that *aller et retour* to Prague costs five hundred and fifty (through Germany). Half I can earn back at an evening there. The other half I will use up anyway waiting for you. So: what if I went to Prague for ten days at the beginning of March? I have written to Ksyunin in Belgr., but still no reply. Advise me. Maybe this is a way out? Now Victor has appeared again! He complains that a lot goes on moving around, on food, on little things. Very much a business letter today. Yesterday I had an endless lunch with Denis Roche, and in the afternoon took tea with lots of ladies at Mme Jacques

Chardonne's. I received from Aunt Nina several 'society connections' in London, and the same from the Golovins, whom I visited today. In the evening I'm going to a party at Ergaz's. Kisses to my marzipanny, my engine-drivery, my dear one. I miss you madly, my love, my angel, my soul ...

Very true about Herzen. I love you. And the little man.

V.

[ALS, 2 PP.]
[8 February 1937]

[TO: Berlin]

[Paris]

My adorable love,

Not much from you lately, for some reason. The little boy's not sick, is he? Soon, I'll be able to think that I will see you in a month. My darlings ...

Feverish preparations are underway for my French reading – announcements in all the papers, sales of my '*Course*' and '*Chambre*' at the reading, endless phone calls. All of this is extremely lucrative for me, but of course there's a danger that those thirsting to hear the much-talked-about Hungarian writer won't be eager to listen to a substitute (as if a touring sword-swallower were to perform instead of Plevitskaya); but it's touching that many of those who were at Ridel's want to come again! Gallimard has finally arranged a meeting with me – on Thursday morning. There was a very successful evening at the Ergazes', and on Saturday night I read to the thirty 'knights' here, for which I chose 'Young Chernyshevsky', which left a painful impression on Vishnyak, Rudnev and Vlad. Mikh. (the last of these told me, bitterly: 'you have made him loathsome'), but which Ilyusha liked very much. The rest, apart from Aldanov, Teffi,

Pereverzev and Mme Tatarinov, simply did not get what it was about. Overall, it caused rather a scandal but went off very well. Yesterday I had lunch at the Etingons'–he can torture one to death with his Jewish jokes. Their son died in Berlin, from purulent appendicitis, at twenty. What can Anyuta say about them? I'm not asking this for nothing, but because they are very interested in my fate. But what about old man Pol! Eh? Four hundred francs ... *Je n'en reviens pas.* Yesterday I paid a visit to the very sweet and very deaf Maklakov. He showed me old photographs of his Moscow estate, through a stereoscope: every blade of grass seemed alive, but the people were flat.

I received, at the same time: a letter (charming) from Mme Chernavin, according to which I will 'huddle' on a couch in the same room as her son, and a letter from Lisbet, who suggests not locking their apartment (they leave on the 14th) so that I could stay there. I wrote her back right away, saying thanks but I'd live at Mme Ch.'s–and very much regret this, since I foresee I'll be diabolically uncomfortable in a room already inhabited–especially given my psoriasis (which absolutely poisons my existence, but I'm afraid to start treatment before leaving for London). My cheek almost puffed up, but Mme Adamov took out the rotting nerve, and in the métro, my mouth suddenly filled up with blood and pus–and everything cleared up miraculously; but, apparently, I'll have to have the tooth pulled out–but, again, I'm afraid to do this before Thursday. *Autrement*, I feel great. I talk to Lyusya on the phone almost every day, and I'll give him a few more journals before my departure. Today, I had a visit from one Isr. Kogan, with an offer to place short stories in American magazines. I gave him 'The Passenger' and 'Chorb' (in Struve's translations); but you should write to me <u>where</u> they've been published and, if possible, send me the review from the N. Y. *Times*. Bernstein sent him to me. Tonight, I am having dinner with Bunin and the Tsetlins.

I am expecting you both on March 15. Tell me your thoughts about the trip to Prague. Ilyusha is entrancingly, touchingly, and endlessly nice, but Vlad. Mikh. has turned glum after 'Chernyshevsky'. My darling, I embrace you over all your tender length. *I dreamt of you yesterday night.*

V.

[ALS, 2 PP.]

[postmarked 10 February 1937]

TO: 22, Nestor str., Berlin–Halensee, Allemagne

c/o Fondaminsky, 130, av. de Versailles

[Paris]

My love, my darling,

well, things turned out very successfully with the printing of '*Le Vrai*': it will appear in N. R. F. on March 1st. Today I am again going to visit Paulhan *qui est tout ce qu'il y a de plus charmant.*

I do not understand what you write about the south of France. It's absolutely decided that you'll leave in the middle of March (perhaps not even through Paris but through Strasbourg? Let's think more about this) to the place chosen (the choice will be made in 'the very near future'. About ten people are working on it). Please understand that if this isn't resolved now, then, again, nothing will come of it, we'll linger, put it off–in a word, tell yourself our Berlin life is over–and, please, get ready. Maybe we don't have funds for five years ahead, but we do for the summer. As soon as I come back from London, the visa etc. will be sent to you. Apart from everything else, I can't live without you and the little boy. I'll last one more month, but longer–no. Besides, my turning up again in Nestor str. borders on the grotesque. *Tu ne le voudrais pas.*

My psor is getting worse all the time–although in all other respects I feel splendid. Two days ago there was a literary dinner at Tsetlin's, and yesterday I went out of town to see my Kirghiz. Today I am having lunch at Léon's and will establish a connection with Polyakov in London. In the afternoon Lyusya and I will be at Sofa's. I'll write to Gubsky, of course. As for Czechoslovakia, I'm afraid you're right. I'm waiting for a reply from Ksyunin. There's a great buzz around my reading tomorrow. Marcel will start off again with a 'word' about me.

The reverberations from what I read ('young Chernyshevsky') are unusually loud. Vishnyak said that he'd quit the board of 'Sovr. zap.' if this is printed. It'll be interesting to see what happens when they read the whole chapter. But that's still a long way off.

I want to write! I was absolutely not made for the colourful life here – or, rather, everything would be fine if I could find, in the flashing landscape of each day, my little homeland – three or four hours to dedicate to writing. My darling, how I love you ... That's wonderful, the conversation with the little dog! My little one.

Mother is sick again. They live in one room so it'll be warmer. She is in despair that I'm not coming again, that there's disappointment once more. I just don't know what to do ...

I wrote the letter to Milyukov and gave it to Ilyusha, to whom Aldanov came today especially to talk about this problem. What are you doing now? (It is four o'clock, Wednesday. He probably didn't sleep and is now bustling around over something.)

Bunin phoned me now with an offer to find a place near Lavandou suitable for us and to settle down nearby. I'm having lunch with him on Saturday. The weather is what Pushkin's Laura imagines, thinking about Paris. But sparrows are twittering between the rains and the iron fences are glittering soothingly. I love you. I repeat: I expect you in the middle of March. If there is a permanent job – great, if just bits and pieces – never mind, I'll manage.

It's impossible to talk about Butler now, let's settle first the question of the newspaper. On Saturday afternoon I'm meeting Lady Fletcher. I *kiss you, my love.*

V.

[ALS, 2 PP.]
[postmarked 12 February 1937]

TO: 22, Nestor str., Berlin–Halensee, Allemagne

c/o Fondaminsky, 130, av. de Versailles
[Paris]

My happiness, my dear darling,

Yesterday's *matinée* was the most successful of my readings (although there were no more than 150 people–and crowds of local Hungarians returned tickets at the box office). In the morning, the translations, rather prettily plumed by Melot, arrived, so I read some of them in two versions. By the way, Joyce was present; we had a very nice talk. He's taller than I thought, with a terrible leaden stare: with one eye he can't see at all, already, while the pupil of the other (which he points at you in a special way, because he can't rotate it) is replaced with a hole, they had to operate six times before they managed to drill the pupil without causing a haemorrhage.

The letter to Mil. was rejected, and, probably, I'll have to see him again–or write another letter. I worked out a life-plan with I. I., but much depends on the London trip. One thing greatly cheers me up: the success of my little French pieces. Over the summer, apart from 'The Gift', I will definitely compose two *conférence*[s] and translate–or write directly–a story or two. We'll spend the summer in the south–and only in the worst case, if nothing at all comes out of the butterflies in London, will we have to settle near Paris. But, I repeat, I won't write today about all the details we've already discussed.

I arrived at Gallimard at noon, as arranged, and the telephone girl downstairs at reception, where I was the only visitor, said that a lady was with him, I had to wait. After a quarter of an hour, she (the telephone miss), humming, put on her little hat and went out to lunch. I stayed there as if in a desert. At half past, I went upstairs, asked someone there how to get to Gallimard's; the man said that G. was busy and let me into another, very elegantly furnished waiting room, with armchairs, ashtrays and a view of the rain, and there, in perfect silence, I sat for another half an hour–and probably would be sitting there still had I not guessed to go downstairs again. There I learned from a fleetingly glimpsed lady employee in a fur coat that Gal. had gone out to lunch. Then I said: '*c'est un peu fort*'. She offered to check anyway and at last in another part of the building we found Gal. already in a coat. It turned out no one had let him know. It turned out too that he cannot read English himself, but right away in my presence he made a note about '*Despair*', which Fernandez will read, and he'll give me an answer before the 15th (?). I've also asked Paulhan with whom I corrected *Le Vrai* the day before yesterday (he threw out the end so that now it ends with '*grenier*'–but I don't give a damn about these French excrements of mine! And instead of *poète anglais* I inserted '*allemand*') to talk again to Gal. and Fernand. There.

Sofa lives in a hotel room, with a lapdog and a double bed. As unbearable as ever. Today I had lunch at the Shklyavers': everything just the same as in '33 and '36, down to the menu. Now I'm going to Fletcher. I got a letter from Lisbet; they put their trip off for several days, so I'll see them. I wrote to her again. Sent the little books to Mother without touching Lyusya's. Slept well, in spite of the itch. The *matinée*, it seems, earned Victor nothing, i.e. Mme Tatarinov is writing to Földes asking for reimbursement for the losses. Everyone liked it so much that they decided to organize the same thing again–but on different conditions, of course.

Kisses for my little one! My kitten ... And you, my darling, I love infinitely and am waiting for you in agony.

V.

[ALS, 2 PP.]
[postmarked 15 February 1937]

TO: 22, Nestor str., Berlin–Halensee, Allemagne

c/o Fondaminsky, 130, av. de Versailles
[Paris]

My love, my dear love,

on the contrary–I read your letters very attentively–and even take notes, so I can reply to everything.

In London I will stay at the Tsetlins' apartment (her keys are already in my pocket). Here's the address: 15 Princes House 52 Kensington Park Rd c/o M. Zetlin. London W. 11. I'll be going there just a little later, in the evening of the 17th to be precise, since the reading at the Sablins' is on the 25th. Besides that, Gleb's arranging two whole English-Russian meetings, for one of which people will pay. I propose, in general, to read in English an excerpt from '<u>Me</u>' (a temporary title), since my French successes have greatly encouraged me. Pourtalès, author of many '*romancées*,' squirmed as I read about biographers' sins! A letter from Gleb–an unexpectedly sensible one. I wrote lots of letters to England, in keeping with the advice I got here. Léon, his wife and sisters are extremely obliging and sweet. I've received an invitation to Cambridge from acquaintances of Kan[n]egis.–will certainly go. Zhdanov is already in London, there he will 'hook me up' with K.; once again the hope of seeing *Cam. Obsc.* materialize flared up, but I don't much believe it will happen. I see thousands of people–the Kokoshkin-Guadaninis (*don't you dare be jealous*), Teffi, the Bunins, the Tatarinovs. Yesterday I was at Mme L. S. Gavronsky's, where a Persian did marvellous magic tricks, and then Berberova, driving very rhythmically, took me and Ilyusha home; incidentally, the little automobile broke down right near our house. Two more French readings have been announced, at the beginning of March. Please send Denis (who has worn me out) a copy of 'Spring in F'. (you will find an offprint in the trunk): he can't wait to translate it and plans to publish it together with '*Aguet*'. Besides that send (or tell Petrop. to send) a copy of 'Despair' to Antonini (6, rue Corot), he's writing about me. And one more thing I ask you to do, darling: send photographs of the boy to Mother. I can't part with mine. The story about the crows and the swallows had a resounding success here. My little darling!

I sent it off to Wilson. Yes, the cuisine's not great, it seems. I still believe all the same that we will indeed go south – but this will be decided when I'm back from London. I'm thinking of coming back here on February 27th. I often speak with Lyusya on the phone. *He is very nice, but rather impossible*. He invents complex cobwebs out of trifles and experiments with things he knows he has no intention of carrying out. Tomorrow I will see him and Mme Morevsky (who, by the way, was at Mme Gavronsky's). I'm still suffering terribly from the psoriasis: it has reached hitherto unseen dimensions, and it's particularly unpleasant that my face is blotchy, too. But the most awful thing is the itch. I dream madly of peace, ointment, sun ... Zen-Zin is sick today, and Vlad. Mikh. has bought him a chicken. I'll write to Mme Chernavin now, cancelling. A great relief, I must say.

I love you. A month's gone already ... I want so much to write, but I can't even think about it now.

Greetings to Anyuta, I will write to her again one of these days. Lyusya's not going anywhere on the 15th.

My darling!

V.

Do you have Khodas.'s article? If not I'll send it.

[APCS]

[postmarked 16 February 1937]

TO: 22, Nestor str., Halensee, Berlin, Allemagne

c/o Fondaminsky, 130, av. de Versailles

[Paris]

My love, so, tomorrow I'm on my way. I've written to everyone, got telegrams from Thompson and Gubsky, – and in general all's going well. I got the books from Paulhan. Wrote to Mother. Have you received '*Mercury*'? I met yesterday with Lyusya who's also planning to go to London. He'll now do thirty-one pages, and I have four more with me. As an author, I am pleased. I wrote five letters to Prague; but still no answer from Ksyunin. Yesterday was a quiet day; I went to bed early – while, in the dining room, 'Novyi grad' was holding a meeting. *My darling, I am afraid you are tired and lonely, but you have the little one with you at least, and I haven't*. Today I. I. and I will write a new letter to P. N. The whole time the weather has been wonderful, warm, damp. I overheard yesterday one conductor telling another on the métro: '*moi ce que j'aime chez Montherlant . . .*' *I love you, I love you*.

V.

[ALS, 2 PP.]
[postmarked 19 February 1937]
TO: 22, Nestor str., Berlin–Halensee, Allemagne
c/o Fondaminsky, 130, av. de Versailles
[Postmarked Paris, mailed from London]

52 Kensington Park Rd
Princes House 15
(you don't need anything else:
15 is the apartment number)
Tel: Park 79 74
19–II–1937

My darling, my love,

to the blue sleeping train they attached a single shortish third class car (where, however, there happened to be an empty compartment and a soft, narrow bench), and at half past one at night, in Dunkirk (we crawled for a long time past endless barrels and then by bridges, and the infrequent streetlights shone with a mean port light, carefully moving backwards, and the water, surprised, showed black every now and then) it was shamefully unhooked, so that the sleeping-cars, like somnambulists, streamed to the *ferry-boat*, while we (two Russian Jews, a lame Englishman, an old Frenchman and I) after a certain chilled stupor in a dimly, soullessly (I cannot pick the right adverb: it should smell immediately of all this material melancholy of the bare yellow custom houses at night) lit *douane* crossed without the car to the same *ferry-boat* and stepped down into a very comfortable saloon, where it was in any case better than in the luxurious coffins of the train, chained and nightmarishly, helplessly swaying along with the ferry, because: the tossing was terrible, for a long time they didn't dare go out to sea: the storm held us up for five more hours (and a strange thing happened to me: I was enjoying the tossing – from four to half past nine – and in the morning I saw something so poignantly familiar! the sea, very lightly touched up with blue and throwing itself at everything, and the seagulls, and the smudged horizon, and on the right, then on the left, then ahead the white-washed chiselled-off shores); the tossing continued to the very end, I ate an English breakfast (rather expensive), and then they tormented us (all of the same outcast little bunch) for more than an hour (passports, check-up) – and, finally, again in a soft empty compartment, we flew through Kent – and again the familiar: grey suede sheep on crumbly green meadows. At one I had to lunch with the Thompsons, but we arrived at Victoria at a quarter to: I rushed in an antediluvian cuboid cab (a cube of indigo, not just in shape), not recognizing anything, as if I had arrived for the first time: found your sweet darling letters on the table (and the room is ideal, with a huge bed hidden upright in a white closet, with a radio, with a live, human – not automatic – telephone and still-lifes by Mlle Avksentiev (a daughter from the first marriage) on the walls; and the bathroom is, of course, beautiful); I rang up the Thompsonovs, they sent an automobile for me from the restaurant in a quarter of an hour (I managed both to bathe and shave) – and six of us had lunch (with two *readers* – and I've already launched my 'autob', i.e. arranged to give it to her, the woman reader, and she'll try, through Curtis Brown, the old man, to get it to Gollan[c]z. Lisbet is still the same, animated, he chose the food, with the same terrible artfulness, and gorged; at a table nearby sat Fritz[i] Massari, tell Anyuta. Then we parted (tomorrow I'll dine at their place, again with some people). I called Struve and Molly: I'll see both tomorrow: with Molly I am lunching at Charing-Cross and I'll be taking from her the corrected '*autob.*' for Eileen Bigland – Curt. Br. – Goll.

I had dinner at a milk bar, it's now 10 o'clock, I'll finish writing and go to bed, I'm collapsing from fatigue, while the sounds of the city through my window are as insolently unfamiliar as before – I'll go and search tomorrow, it can't be that not a stone is left standing from the past!

I've written five postcards: Grinb., Budb., my aunt, Bourne, Mme Gavronsky. Tomorrow a few more. Will call Zhdanov and Gubsky in the morning. Will probably drop in to see Sablin. As for *copyright* – I'll find that out. A charming letter from Mme Chernavin, I'll be with them on Saturday. What precisely should I talk about with Heath? Write me! If I offered 'The Defence', then I'd have to give him a French copy, but I don't have one. Lyusya has received everything (and knew perfectly well that he would) and isn't going to L. for the time being. I brought books from Lolly for Gleb ('Tair' won't take 'Invitation', but offers to buy 'The Gift' instead, even if one chapter appears in 'Sovr. zap.' – but only one. Let's think about that.) Give Ridelius 'The Leonardo' or no, rather, 'The Adm. Sp.': there's an extra copy in the trunk. Will draw a little train some other time, I'm tired. *Radio Belge* hasn't invited me yet. I love you, my dears. The letter's turned out boring, but I am terribly exhausted. My darling, my dear love!

V.

[APCS]

[postmarked 22 February 1937]

TO: 22, Nestor str., Berlin – Halensee, Allemagne

[London, Notting Hill]

My darling, I am writing with gloves on, but burn this anyway, since I've caught a chill, am struggling successfully with the flu. Today at the Northerners, I will read in the thick blue jersey. By the way, the dinner jacket has turned out very well: I dined in it yesterday with the Thompsons and Sir Dennison Ross and his wife, we discussed lectureship possibilities, but all this is not serious. Molly has given me an excellently corrected 'autob.' and now I'm hurriedly transferring her corrections to my copy, so as not to be left without anything. After lunch with her, I rushed to see Struve (distances here are appalling, but seats in the underground are *moelleux*), saw the three children dog, cat, Yu. Yu., very plump but thin in the face. I wrote down the surnames of everyone I'll be meeting at the *parties* that have been set up.

It is windy and expensive here. I'm dreaming of France.

My hat (which lost all its shape after the first Paris rain) arouses astonishment and laughter, and my scarf trails along the pavement, having become, though, thin as a tape measure.

Don't worry about my flu, everyone here has colds. I'm living very comfortably. Love you, my darling. And I kiss him on his little temple. Greetings to Anyuta.

V.

[AL, 2 PP.]

[postmarked 22 February 1937]

TO: 22, Nestor str., Berlin–Halensee, Germany

52, Kensington Park Rd

[London]

My love, my happiness,

I'm already better today, my temperature fluctuates around 36.6–37, I'm lying very comfortably in bed. The very sweet Savely Isaak. appeared with lunch, fruit, thermometer and an offer to relocate to their place, but I declined the latter. I had to put off a few things today; I think tomorrow I'll be going out already. But last night it was terrible: full of quinine, whisky, port, with a high fever and a rasping voice, in a cold hall, I forced myself to read ('Fialta' and 'Breaking the News'), although it was an enormous success (but no big crowd, about a hundred). Gleb spoke superbly about me for half an hour – intelligently, imaginatively and articulately. During the night I 'tossed in delirium'.

Budberg telephoned me today that Wells is summoning me to lunch. By the way: having thought it over I chucked out one phrase about him in my thing, which I still don't know how to name: I've spent the entire day transferring the corrections to my copy, have just finished; it's now half past nine at night, the terrible silence of Sunday – but suddenly somebody whistled and, still whistling, hopped, to judge by the shadow of sound, on a bicycle that side-tracked my hearing – and that whistling and the auditory glimpses (all of that instantly) at once, as in the Proustian formula, have resurrected the England of my youth, completely!

If there's no invitation from Long tomorrow, I'll phone there. I have arranged to be at Sablin's at twelve. Baykalov is unpresentable and evidently not very bright. He was supposed to call me today about the result, but for some reason hasn't. At the soirée I saw Tatyana Vasilievna, Mrs Haskell (a trimmed down Mme Aldanov), Flora Solomon (Kerensky's ex-girlfriend) and many other not so interesting people (like, for example, the inevitable Wolf).

The young Tsetlin *a découché*, so I am completely alone here. In the pantry there are all sorts of unexpected goodies; I make forays there.

I talked to Grinberg today about possibilities here. He understands and wants to help. In a day or two he'll take me by car to Cambridge, we'll talk there with his and my former professors.

I love you, my darling. This paper, its format, marshals thoughts well and guides my style. If I don't sit down to the second chapter of 'The Gift' soon, I'll burst. What is my little one up to? I sometimes dream of him, but he's quite unlike himself. Why hasn't Anyuta answered my letter? *I am longing for you*, as soon as I get back to Paris I'll send you a visa and perhaps a ticket for the *Nord-Express, ne t'en déplaise*. I've written from here to Ilyusha, Rudnev, Mme Tsetlin. For some reason they don't understand me well at the post office. The rapidly ascending and just as rapidly (like an iron waterfall) descending staircases at the underground stations are very amusing.

So, my darling, now I will check it—and go to sleep. Thirty-six point nine. Write to me, my dear love.

[ALS, 1 P.]
[24 February 1937]

[TO: Berlin]

[London]
Notting Hill
24-II-37

My dear love, I've recovered and developed incredible energy. On Monday morning, I was at Sablin's. I had lunch with him (his wife is sick), we talked about everything. I'd got hold of and have given him a few more addresses for tickets. The reading is scheduled for the 28th. From there, I went to Solomon's office: she is a former publisher herself and with 'enormous connections' in the 'publishing world'. She gave me something 'from the circle of your admirers'. So the book will turn out rather long: eighty-four pages already, counting Lyusya's articles and The Northerners' three little pages. In the evening I was at the Grinbergs': his mother is leaving—on Saturday, I think—for Berlin and will bring the little train, tell the boy. My autob is being read now not by Thompson's readeress (*I thought better of it*), but by Frank Strawson (through Flora). On Tuesday, I lunched at Wells's, *à trois* (there also was a wonderful Irishman there, with bright yellow in his beard, a red face, and a grey crew-cut, a classmate of Joyce's and for that reason talking very amusingly about all those hints at the details, understandable and known only to those like him, hidden in 'Ulysses's' hold). The lunch was very animated and successful, in a remarkable mansion. Here too (as everywhere) I talked about a *lecturing-job*. From there (ah, I could've described lots, but I'm in a terrible hurry, must run again) I went to the Chernavins' (he, in a dressing gown, was drawing a salmon skeleton), then came home, where I changed into the tux and went with Struve to Mme Ridley (*née* Benkendorf); we had dinner there (tell Zyoka that my left-hand neighbour was Asquith's daughter), and then people gathered, about fifty, for my reading. I read the first chapter of '*Despair*' and the little sports chapter from Autob.—and they all were very pleased. Huntington (Putnam) and a literary critic from the *Observer*, Leslie Hartley, were there. The former has asked for the autob to read; I'll probably give him my second copy. Budberg was there. My God, I must dash! I was at Long's this morning, everything is perfectly all right. The book comes out on April 8th. I'll get it on Friday. My darling, I don't want you to be left without a letter, I'll finish off the details tomorrow.

I love you, my dear darling.

Just got your dear letter, luftpost.

V.

[ALS, 8 PP.]

[postmarked 27 February 1937]

TO: 22, Nestor str., Berlin—Halensee, Germany

52 Kensington Park Rd.

Princess House

[London]

My dear love, my sweetheart,

all strings, all springs are being pulled and pushed to get a *lecturing job*. I'm seeing thousands of people. In comparison with my wild activity here Paris seems a holiday, trifling. And the London *underground* is hell, even if well-organized, I have to spend around three hours every day underground, including the bother of the elevators and escalators.

But first let me add a few touches to my last hurried letter. Wells: he invited me to a banquet at the Pen-Club with the participation of and a presentation by ... Maysky, – so to my regret I had to refuse it, but this connection with the club is established. Budberg, a stately, unflappable lady with the remains of – hardly a former – beauty (is that clear?) – is his mistress: so they say.

Long: the translator has received (they sent it today) forty-five; out of this three will go to Molly. Mr Bourne (of whom, by the way, the very nice Claude Houghton, whom I saw today, reports very well) turned out to be an old man with a charming smile, very friendly and attentive (but has refused to raise to a pound). The book is coming out on April the eighth (and probably I'll come back here for then for a day or two to give a paid English soirée – there's already discussion about this). He plans lots of *publicity*. Even the galley-proofs will be sent to some people, such as Garnett, Hartley, Nicholson, Wells, and so on. As for 'Camera', only nine hundred and seventy copies have been sold, and we have to reach two thousand to cover the advance. He can take a *copyright* for America, but then, if after four months they don't buy the book there, anyone can publish a pirate edition. So that option's out. He says that my American agent should not worry: if the book *will be set* (typeset?) there, it's fine. We parted good friends; but I don't want to publish with them any longer: everyone advises me against it.

Regarding the autob: I've been flirting with four publishers of which *kommt in Frage*: Duckworth (very solid, today – at Mrs Allen Harris's cocktail party we agreed on a reading of the manuscript) or Putnam (the latter with a slight shade of the Baroness who wants to 'pass it on', although I spoke with the man himself and could have given it to him directly). Two other ways would be through Strawson (Solomon) and Bigland (Thompson). Everyone very much liked what I read from the autobi at Ridley's. I have no doubt that I will sell the manuscript, maybe not now but as soon as D. comes out. I've been to Aunt Baby's who gave me a few *tuyaux*–including an introduction to Vilenkin (Mark) with whom I will lunch on Sunday at the Liberal Club. He, and Flora S., and Haskell, and Mme Chernavin, and *scores of others* are trying to find something for me. Today I visited an organization (I think Frank wrote to them), which has written everything down in detail. At Cambridge I spoke about this with my tutor Harrison and the professor of French, Dr Stewart (both have promised to do all they can), while Grinberg meanwhile talked about the same thing with three of his professors.

I will see Pares on Monday–he's been away for the *weekend*. In general, my sweetheart, there are many people troubling themselves on my behalf (for instance, there's a project of a lectureship at a *public school* like Eton), but I absolutely don't know when this will happen–maybe tomorrow, maybe in a year, it all depends on good luck–and a responsive button.

I don't know whether I'd like to live in London. The city itself is awful, in my opinion. But the food, for example, is magnificent, smacks of freshness and good quality. But then, everything is very expensive (but one can buy flannel pants for five shillings). Today I've called in to the French Consulate for a visa, they've given it to me for two weeks. Victor, whom I also visited at the museum, has now accumulated a hundred and twenty-nine cases of butterflies–from the British fauna. Don't forget, by the way, to fetch mine. *It is quite settled, under these circumstance*[*s*], that we will spend the summer in the south of France. Necessary for you, the little boy and me (I don't want to write more about the Greek, who oppresses me endlessly and whom only the sun will get rid of). And I must write 1) a play (suitable not just for the Russian Theatre but also for Kortner, who gave me this commission today) 2) a novel 3) little things in French 4) translations. *I haven't done a spot of work since I left.*

From the Consulate, where in some totally incomprehensible fashion they gave me the visa for free, I took to one gentleman (an acquaintance of Grinberg's) a little package to be given to old Mme Grinberg (the only way to deliver it today), who's leaving for Berlin tomorrow – so call on her on Monday, she's at her daughter's, Pfalzb[urger] Str[asse], 83 (I think!). The nuts are for Anyuta. Then I went to have lunch at Mrs Haskell's, Gubsky was there too, rather likeable, a bit shabby, simple, but original. Her two-year-old little girl wouldn't let me hold her, started crying, and I was recalling my darling, my little one: – today he's been in my thoughts all day, on his knees, as you wrote, and drawing over my life, <u>over</u> all I have been doing today. My little sweetheart! By the way Gubsky told me that he had written twice to me (detailed, important letters) about the translation of 'Camera' (during the first raving of the translatress), but he sent them to me … through Otto K. No wonder I never received them! He would also like to get involved in the *placement* of my autobi – at Heinemann's. I'll meet him about that again, on Sunday.

From there I went to the organization (see above) and then to a meeting with Kortn. at Grosvenor House, but we didn't finish our talk there, since at six I had to go to a cocktail party (see above). There was a huge crowd there, all connected to literature. At nine I had a second meeting with Kort. – this time at the Carlton Hotel. He seems to be a perfect fool, but likeable. Read me two *versions* of 'Camera' – both horrifying to my taste. An oculist cures Kretschmar, but on his return he hides from Magda that he has his sight back and, pretending to be blind, catches the traitoress red-handed. Tomorrow I'm meeting him again, to reach a final decision on the conditions. He is very optimistic – but generally talked awful rot. I've just (well, not exactly so, I've been writing for about an hour) got back home, am writing in bed.

So this is a sample of my day – and if you keep in mind that the distances between appointments are extremely long and that during all of these talks (the party alone was quite a strain – the crowd, the sherry, *let me introduce you to Mr Sirin*) I had to keep cheery and upbeat, then you can imagine how tired I am. *I am rather fed up with the whole business*, and am desperate for peace, you, and my muse.

I get back to Paris only on Tuesday morning. There's no reason to stay any longer – and it's expensive – the shillings vanish. I still keep thinking about a trip to Prague. Think about it again, my sweet! Under great secrecy old Joseph told me that Avg. Is. is going to give a share of ten thousand francs from that business he's fussing about with my uncle to Elena Ivanovna and Victor. I don't know.

Oh yes, I haven't written you anything about Cambridge yet! We went there by car with the saintly Sav. Is. En route visited Aleksandr Blok – not the poet but a businessman (Kannegiser's former husband). It is hard, as they say, to convey what I felt on seeing this little town I haven't been in for fifteen years. What I preserved in my memory has lived, it turns out, its own life, has undergone, it turns out, an evolution not corresponding to any reality, and now

> … in confrontation
> with a chatty witness – with that
> reality, lying nonchalantly,

my poor memory was silent no matter how I tried to rouse her, taking her around familiar places. Everything now seemed smaller, greyer, simpler, everything lacked that harmonious soul that developed in it while it lived in me. I went into my former lodgings, automatically pushed a door to the right, found myself in the toilet, did a small business, and with tears in my eyes walked back into the little street (but before that I had been fingering, for a long time but with no result, a special little thing that would move in the entrance hall, a little board with the name of the tenant – at home and not at home – but the recollection was silent, my fingers could not feel the past). It was drizzling, in the side-street, right there, I met a man who once registered those having lunch in *Hall*, and he now recognized me at once, which somewhat shocked me. Then I plodded to the other side of the college, to the *Backs*. My God, how many poems I composed under these enormous elms! They have not changed

and in their nets – a movement of crows,
a sketch of a nest in a vellum gap;
not croaking, – but almost a cooing
and painted crocuses among the grass.

I looked at ditches I once jumped over, at the muddy water of the river – and a true Pushkinian mood began to work its iambic piston. I walked down the familiar road (the whole time, crows' cooing, and sparrows' – also melodiously moist sounds – and the ivy, and the boxwood, and the thuyas, and the old oaks) to the soccer field, there on the dark green a foursome were kicking near the goal, and one of the balls, like a dog who'd recognized a passer-by, ran over to me a few times, but although it was heavy and muddy, like in the old days, my foot could not get out of it the ring of the past. I returned to the college, walked in on Harrison, who hadn't changed a bit and who greeted me with no particular joy; I had tea with him, and he told me in the same expressions, with the same pause and smile, what he had told me at our first meeting in 1919 – how he was learning Bulgarian. He knows Swedish, too, – and begged me eagerly to send him the Swedish 'Defence' – so I'd ask you, my sweet, to do that: E. Harrison, Trinity College. This is important. From there I went to Stewart's, awfully old, but he recognized me at once. It would be good to send a French 'Defence' to him: Rev. Dr Stewart, Trinity College. By the way: in view of Solomon's unusual attentiveness to me could we ask Petropolis to send her two or three of my books, for example Despair, Defence and Glory? (There's someone else, besides her and Grinberg, who are also touchingly thoughtful and sweet: that's the Struve couple, all those parties – they arranged them – and took so much trouble – and he goes everywhere with my books, advertising me, and they call me every morning – charming!).

There seemed to be less traffic on Trinity Street – but then memory was thrusting at me the whole time some sum of former impressions, while that was just a share of a regular Cambridge day. The cut of jackets (and the colour – mostly chestnut) has changed, and now fashion dictates walking around with an umbrella! I had some more tea at a pastry-shop (described in 'Glory') and around six, joined with Grinberg again (who had visited his college on my behalf), we drove back to London. This visit was a good lesson – the lesson of the return – and a warning: we also need not expect life, heat, a wild awakening of the past – from our other return – to Russia. As a toy sold with a key, everything is already wrapped up in memory – and without it nothing moves.

I adore your letters, my happiness. Of course I have noticed the landscape from Bagrova's window (tell her that I called the hotel twice but could not reach him. But in fact I won't even call). Lyusya has not deigned to tell me from whom he got it. I haven't thought of a title yet, but something like yours. I won't draw a little train, since tomorrow a real one will arrive.

Sablin is pleasant, emphatically liberal, lives in a very elegant little mansion. A photograph of a bathing heir in combination with a book I read in Paris (about little Ludovic, in *Temple*) touches some creative string. I would very much like to write something. Sablin is actively occupied with my soirée – on Sunday. There's an advertisement for ink I really like: *permanently please people, pens, postmen and posterity*. Once sitting in *La Coupole*, in Paris, with Irina G., I suddenly noticed that the little cap of my pen, a present from Granny, was missing; after agonizing searches under the tables I found it in my coat pocket.

Today I will have lunch with the dear Lees, then will meet with Zhdanov-Kortner at the Hyde Park Hotel, then to Bar. Budberg's, then a cocktail at Lady Fletcher's, then dinner at the Thompsons' – and this is a comparatively easy day.

It is not a very interesting letter, I am afraid – but I have completely forgotten how to write, and was horribly tired – am writing this page on Saturday morning, since I couldn't finish last night for tiredness, but now I've had a good sleep. Nicholson has not returned from Africa yet, and I am sending a book with a letter to Baring. I can't tell you how much I love you and am kissing you. So on April first we will go south, till the autumn. Shall I send a book to Mother?

V.

[ALS, 2 PP.]
[1–2 March 1937]

[TO: Berlin]

Notting Hill
52 Kensington Park Rd
[London]
2-III-1937

My darling, now (8 p.m. Monday) I'm going to Paris. The soirée at Sablin's yesterday was extremely successful. I read fifteen little things.

Read from the first chapter of 'The Gift', and 'Music'. Had lunch yesterday at the Liberal Club (full of the shadows of Gladstone and Disraeli, but inhabited by white-headed elders; one of them marvellously nodded off after the meal, at coffee, his grey head bent to the side) and they offered to arrange a reading there, paid. Struve and Harris will arrange for me another English reading, paid (and besides, we might repeat at Sablin's). This will be scheduled for mid-April: I will come here again for three or four days (I've been invited to stay at Arnold Haskell's) for the publication of the book–this is very important. So. I think I've done splendidly. Now the second thing: I've had a very pleasant conversation today with Pares, and while I was with him he wrote a wonderful letter to Stephen Duggan in America, where he had recently placed another Russian and thinks he'll place me too: this is only the second time he's doing this, so our chances are good. Finally–perhaps the biggest success–I've been able to arrange so that we can move to England in the autumn, since they promise to provide for me for six months here, till I find a job (and no doubt I'll find lessons, good lessons, here to start off). So there's the general result of my trip, and now the plan is: we won't take any apartments in Paris, but will go south right away, on April 1st. I don't know exactly how much time we'll need to obtain the *identité*, but in any event we don't have to bring furniture. By winter we'll easily find an apartment here. *Darling, this is final*. In any case I'll start the *carte d'ident.* rigmarole right away. I want to spend this summer perfectly quietly, I need to write, and you and the boy need the sun, the sea–and we won't spend more than a hundred on such a summer. So only on April 15th I'll come here for 3–4 days, but I want you to be settled in the south <u>before</u> that.

I love you, my dearest, I am in a dreadful hurry, the train leaves in an hour, and I haven't packed anything yet, will write to Anyuta from Paris.

V.

1937

[AL, 2 PP.]
[postmarked 4 March 1937]
TO: 22, Nestor str., Berlin–Halensee, Allemagne
c/o Fondaminsky, 130, av. de Versailles
[Paris]

My love, my dear darling,

I spoke with Lyusya, and with another Ilya, and with some other people – and they all say that it makes absolutely no sense to bring the furniture – especially since we'll be settling down in London. I have been to Maklakov's about the *carte d'identité*. I'll have no trouble getting it, but it will take a minimum of a month from today. And you, my darling, should immediately submit a visa application to the French consulate, addressed to Maklakov, 57, *rue de l'Abbé Gruelt*, and to *Monsieur Eidel, Consul de France, Ministère des affaires étrangères*, and with a note that your husband is here. Apply for a month or two, this does not matter, because by that time I'll already have the *carte*. It would be risky to count that I'll have it by March 25th. – *Voilà*.

I'll remain here, of course, till your arrival. 1) This won't be inconvenient in the least for Ilya and V. M. 2) I was promised an advance of 1,000 fr. if I undertake a play, and it's very well set up for me to write here, and I have a marvellous idea – I'll write it in a month. And the play will work not only for the Russian Theatre, but also for Kort., and for the French (through Gabr. Marc. who has now brilliantly come out as a dramatist). 3) yesterday I began to translate my 'Music' for *Candide* – and it's turning out very well, very engagingly; I'll finish and submit tomorrow.

My '*Vrai and V-semblable*' has already come out in N. R. F. and is proving a success. I've written to Gallimard again, since he hasn't yet responded to me about 'Despair'. I have passed 100 pages in English on to L. Received a contract from Kort., signed by him.

It seems a place in the south has been found for us. Mme Schlesinger called today while I was out: everything has been set up and full room and board – the two of us and the boy – will cost us forty fr. (? and later we will find a little house.) I'll find out all the details tonight. I'm also keeping in mind Sasha Chorny's widow's *pension* in Le Lavandou. I want you to take the sleeper here and, after a day here, in the evening, take the evening sleeper south. Maybe I'll go there a day or two earlier and then, probably, it makes sense to go straight through Strasbourg. Lyusya strongly recommends that Anyuta too should come south for the spring and summer, tell her that. (In an hour I'm going to meet Valéry, while my lecture in *Feux croisés* – about 'women-writers' or 'exhibitions' – I haven't decided yet – is scheduled for May – I will come back here especially – in the General Franco sense, in any case, this will be a real success, with a guarantee). And here's what I think about the London trip in the middle of April (I have already arranged to go there and back for three pounds on a mail plane): two or three readings are promised me there – and I hope they will have more fat on them than those I've just done. I wrote seven letters to England from here yesterday. Probably there will be a reading at Teslenko's this month. I also must find out from Paulhan about 'A Bad Day'. He promised me.

It seems to me that all I have written and am writing to you is very consoling, my joy. For God's sake do not forget spreading boards, pins and boxes (one with the treasures, the other two empty). They need to be carried on in a suitcase, with you. To go to Brussels right now would be absurd, inconvenient and very expensive – you're wrong there, my love. I am ideally cosy here, after the horrendous London commotion. It seems I'll be able to set up a free lamp treatment of my Greek. I sent the book to Mother (and did you send the little photos?), so that altogether, nine hundred Czech pages have been set from my 'encyclopaedia'. I don't really understand what you write about Prague. You must find out about the French visa in Berlin, though, i.e. from Berlin they can, for instance, give them directions there to issue it, if a permission came from here. Write – this worries me terribly – the thought of Mother. On the whole, I am holding my tongue. Today I composed, with Ilya, a new letter to P.N.: am asking for a little more. If he agrees I will immediately give the excerpt (disguised) about the triangle inscribed in a circle. *I adore you. I adore the little one.* I expect you in 25 days. I wish it were sooner! Let's say, on March 20th!

I am writing to Altagracia.

[ALS, 2 PP.]

[postmarked 7 March 1937]

TO: 22, Nestor str., Berlin – Halensee, Allemagne

c/o Fondaminsky, 130, av. de Versailles

[Paris]

My darling, my sweetest love, my darling . . .

I must admit that Kort. and Zhdanov have somewhat pressured and hurried me. But what does Heath have to do with it? Does he really have an option? Kort. has no relation to him now whatsoever. As for Grasset – I'd love to see them dare ask for anything! (Besides Grasset himself has gone mad, everything has changed, Fisné left a long time ago – and, between you and me, *Camera* will come out under a different title if they film it. It seems that apart from the blindness nothing of it will remain). My cold's gone, but sometimes at night I start blowing my nose, madly and productively. I saw Lyusya, he is very cheerful. He called today asking to get him a free ticket to the Sovremennye zapiski evening at the furrier Kirkhner's 'salons'. We're meeting in two hours and going there together (Bunin will be there, the idiotic trio, and more). I got an offer from Heinemann to give them 'autob' to read (Putnam's reading it now). A letter from Struve with an action plan for the five or six days I'll spend in London in the middle of April. (Among other things there will also be Cambridge, Oxford and the French society). I am expecting from Budberg a translation of 'Fialta' being done for '*Hundred Russian Short Stories*'. A flowery note from Tsvetaeva. I have written to Mil.

You can congratulate me: last night I finished the French translation of Music (it has turned out, in my opinion, better than anything I've written in French) and tonight I'll give it to Ida for '*Candide*' (I will see her at K.'s). Yesterday at '*Feux croisés*', it was full, Raisa beamed, Valéry spoke (rather wanly) on Mallarmé. If it could be just as full at my reading in May . . .

The blue-haired and very nice Kogan-Bernstein, who also lives in this building, is giving me mountain sun. I'll start the play tomorrow. I work well here.

My love, I am in a hurry, am kissing you, my darling, and him, my little one.

V.

[ALS, 4 PP.]

[postmarked 10 March 1937]

TO: 22, Nestor str., Berlin–Halensee, Allemagne

c/o Fondaminsky, 130, av. de Versailles

[Paris]

My darling, my joy,

I have been scribbling away at the play, getting up late, going for the sun lamp every day at three: the mountain sun has already helped me, at least my little face, otherwise I looked thoroughly obscene. The itch on my neck has more or less gone – but how awfully I've suffered all these weeks, how my underwear looked – from the blood – I've never in my whole life been so *utterly miserable* ... This treatment costs me nothing. At the end of the sessions the doctor will also inject me with my own blood – it's supposed to help a lot. Either because I have been writing, or because of the lilac sun, or because I will see you in three weeks I am completely cheerful today.

I've been seeing actors, actresses (my *leading lady*, Bakhareva, is charming, yesterday we had dinner at her place with Ilyusha and V. M.), giving English lessons to Irina G. (fifteen), – there'll be one more lesson, but in general I'm sitting at home a lot: writing the play is torture (I told you its theme, – a cheerful, sweet young lady arrives with her mother at a resort – and all of that is only an *interv. luc.* – and ends – inevitably, with her returning to her ('theatrical') insanity). But in fact I began to write something else and nothing came of it – I furiously tore up the five pages. Now it's all right, though, rolling along – maybe I'll even lift my little wheels off the ground and a two-winged shadow, for which alone it's really worth writing, will start gliding across the page. Do you remember my letters from Prague, my life? Today I'm in the same mood again.

'Sovr. zap.' comes out in a day or two, and today Vadim Victorovich was offering his father a few hundred as an honorarium. The father will take it.

Tomorrow I will be dictating to Raisa, for *Candide*, '*Musique*', which Doussia has looked over. If they take it, I'll interrupt writing the play for a three-day translation into French of yet another story – it's turning out much easier and more fun than I thought.

A very sweet letter, today, from Bourne. He has already sent *advance copies* to Coulson Kernahan, Harold Nicholson, Hartley, Ralph Straus, David Garnett, Maurice Baring and Gubsky. It will appear on the fifteenth of April, by my request. About Gubsky: he's a very obliging person, but, in my opinion, rather talentless. He considers me 'arch modern' and himself as belonging to the line of deep and socially thoughtful Russian authors. I really enjoyed one of his phrases (in general, he is a pessimist and *blasé*): 'You know, even if they were translating – well, not your books or mine, but, let's say, "Anna Karenina", even then it would be difficult to find a *publisher* . . .' That's what we call: *le toupet*.

Bunin and Khmara got drunk at the Kirshner evening and swore rankly. Lyusya was in a dinner jacket and on the way there stopped several times, threw open his coat and in the gleam of the streetlight displayed himself so I could tell him if he looked good. He and I were inseparable that night. And yesterday I called him – and he swears he's written to Anyuta ('I have written differently now,' he told me) not to bring the furniture. You both know my opinion (and everyone's opinion), but you can act as you wish. But this (bringing it) is insane, and you'll regret it!

All in all, my puss, it's time you got ready to join me. Have you filed the application at the consulate? Why not come a little earlier, on the twenty-fifth, say? I'm expecting a letter from Roquebrune: they say it's a marvellous place and very quiet; some say it's better in a pension than subsisting on our own grub, but others recommend living in a pension first so we could look around and find a cabin of the Wilson kind.

In a couple of days I will give *Lucy* material for ten columns (about London). I'm now a little calmer, but yesterday I was very angry and still do not understand what the matter is: please explain. I thought everything was going very well. Re-read my letters.

I sent you N. R. F. today. I sent Gallimard an *advance copy* of *Despair* (i.e. the finished book, but in *bras de chemise* – in a brown-paper jacket) because it turns out (I pressed him really hard) that the *type-script* he got some time back . . . had been lost! I am also acting through their reader (Fernandez).

In the morning, when I take my bath, the cat (Zen-Zin) sits on the bath's marble edge, his nose against the heating pipe, and at night either he or the other (Nikolay) throws the whole weight of his body against my door, trying to thrust it open, so you get the impression an impatient and obnoxious man is forcing his way in.

I love you, my darling. Here I meet two kinds of ladies: those who quote me excerpts from my books and those who ponder the question whether my eyes are green or yellow. I have gathered lots of the good and likeable over this month and a half, but several buckets of vulgarity as well. The more I know I. I. and V. M., the more I love them.

My darling, *come soon! I can't live without you any more*. And my little one, my little one ... How wonderful that is – about 'you're smiling'!

Greetings to Anyuta – who never writes to me.

My love!. . .

V.

[APCS]

[postmarked 14 March 1937]

TO: 22, Nestor str., Berlin – Halensee, Allemagne

[Paris]

I will write a long one tomorrow.

My love,

What an enchantment he is in the dark little coat, and you have a nice smile too, my priceless happiness. No special news, I am writing my piece. 'Music' has gone to *Candide*. '*Despair*' has been handed on (besides Gallim.) to yet another – Ergaz's – publisher. I am in a rush now because today's Sunday and I want the postcard to leave before one. My joy, *come soon, come soon!* It seems at last that we're going to Roquebrune. Everybody recommends going straight through Strasbourg. Think about that! Find out about the ticket! We should certainly buy a tub, if only a little one for the little one. Yesterday I went to Aldanov's play *avec les* Kokoshkins. My darling, what you write about Italy and Abbazia is, alas, absolutely impossible. What would the trip alone cost us, and I have to be near the capitals. In a day or two I'll give Lyusya in my own words ten commissions or thereabouts. All is well, I am expecting you soon. For R you have to go through Menton. I am going to visit Mme Chorny – also about the boarding house. The widow of Sasha Chorn[y].

I love you, my own.

Poor Zamyatin! I was there for the carrying out of the body.

V.

[ALS, 4 PP.]

[postmarked 15 March 1937]

TO: 22, Nestor str., Berlin – Halensee, Allemagne

c/o Fondaminsky, 130, av. de Versailles

[Paris]

My love, my darling,

You make me anxious and cross, – what sort of a sentence is this, 'is it worth my travelling before your return from London?' Since (if I go at all, – for I'll go only if a reasonable profit from the evening or evenings is fully guaranteed) I'll be in London only during the fourth week of April (and no longer than four or five days – and I'll stay either at the Sablins', or at Haskell's, both of whom have invited me), your arrival would be delayed for another month, right? (This 'right' shows *how cross I am with you*). And since at the end of May I'll give my French lecture here (which will be called '*Lettres de femmes et femmes de lettres*'), then, perhaps, we can postpone till June as well, can't we? (*crosser and crosser*). Now listen.

I have just been to the very nice Maria Ivanovna Chorny and (in case I don't get a completely positive reply from Roquebrune which should come if not today then tomorrow) she and I have decided this: on Thursday she is going to her La Favière (it's at Lavandou station, Var) and offers to set us up at a boarding house she knows well (with central heating, by the way), a bit higher up, in a wonderful little town, among pine woods, Bormes, for April (it's a quarter of an hour by autocar from there to the beach), since it's nicer there in the spring than right by the sea. Full board should cost no more than 60 fr. *nous trois*. And then: in May she is leaving and offering us, if we like it, her little house (two rooms, two terraces, a garden) in La Favière (and this is right by the beach – so it's an ideal place for little ones). I think that this is all very seductive. So – if we decide on Bormes – I suggest the following: you and the boy take a ticket from Berlin to Toulon via Strasbourg (a 2nd class sleeper from Strasbourg) – which will certainly work out much cheaper than through Paris – and on Thursday, April first (a funny date, but what can we do) I'll meet you at the station in Toulon along with several podalirius (I'll arrive there on the same day as you) and from there, for 8 francs, an autocar will take us to Bormes. If I leave for a week at the end of April, then Maria Ivanovna has already promised to look after you. (She will write to me about the boarding house as soon as she arrives – so I can decide everything by the 23rd of this month).

How's the visa? See to the ticket a week before. I want an absolutely precise answer from you. To scramble after some unknown god in the back of beyond in Abbazia or Italy (where it won't be so cheap at all if we don't know what's what (– and if we start to find out, spring will pass, and summer, and two winters and eight more springs)) when it would be too far from here and from London anyway! In any case – whether we go to Roquebrune (it's near Menton) or Bormes (I am beginning to write like Chernyshevsky), you and the little one are leaving for Strasbourg no later than 30-III (and this is no longer a suggestion, my darling, but a statement).

I met with Wallace and gave him 'A Dashing Fellow' and 'Spring in Fialta' for Zurich. Send 'The Doorbell' to Vienna – the rest are too long. Or not – I've forgotten – how many pages are there in 'Chorb'? If ten or eleven, then it'd work. Send it, and I'll write to him. There's no point applying to Vinaver 1) I have enough people there thinking about me 2) he is rather repellent.

My poor tired little tim. You'll rest well and recover this summer. *I love you*, I'm waiting for you.

To Pavel I wrote only that, they say, Victor was paid that much and he can now submit his things only on the same conditions: all this was done under Ilyusha's strong pressure.

'*Eidel*' is correct, and '*repos*' is correct, too. It is wonderful, that you managed to send the collar to Mother! Why is Anyuta so stubborn in her silence – and is she planning to come to Paris? There were very few people at poor Zamyatin's funeral. He died from angina pectoris. Aldanov's play is far from bad, although local *beaux-esprits* rail against it terribly. The fifth performance will have a full house, and it's already playing in Prague and Riga. My writing's not coming easily. As soon as I receive an answer from '*Candide*' I'll translate another short story. Ergazikha had to correct almost nothing. Tell Anyuta that her teeth are real – I learned this from the lady dentist she goes to. In general she seems, on a very close inspection, the most timid and modest little creature. Both my Irinas are also very nice. Today I am having dinner at the Aldanovs'. Yesterday five of us went to the cinema: Ilyusha, V. M., Sherman, and Colonel Likhosherstov (about whom I wrote you back in 1933 – one of the most charming people on earth). I have been to Antonini's for pancakes. I see the Kyandzhuntsevs, the old man, the Tatarinovs. This essentially rather idle life has quite palled with me. I've sent the books to England. My Greek is better since every day I spend an hour lying naked under the mountain sun, while the doctoress sits chastely facing the window and entertains me with intelligent conversation. *People are tremendously nice to me*, I must say.

You know what I would like now: to embrace you, my happiness, kiss you from your lips to your little feet, my darling, my life …

V.

[APCS]

[postmarked 17 March 1937]

TO: 22, Nestor str., Berlin–Halensee, Allemagne

c/o Fondaminsky, 130, av. de Versailles

[Paris]

My darling, my love,

Had a reply from Roquebrune (two rooms and full board for three for 70 fr.), but we can find cheaper,–and on the whole Bormes is better, so we'll have to wait for a definite answer from there.

I went to the Pushkin exhibition yesterday. The day after tomorrow I have a meeting with the editor of *Le Matin*. I'm translating 'Breaking the News' into French. The play's creaky.

Maklakov reports that the processing's going well and will be finished soon. I'm meeting with Lyusya tomorrow. My darling, *I can't do without you any more* … thrushes are singing marvellously. Davydov (the traveller), whom I have been seeing here, says that a nightingale is a shallow soloist–coloratura, variety shows–but a thrush has a real soul and through its song tells about all it has seen in its flight. *C'est gentil?*

Kisses for you, kisses for my little one. My love!

V.

[AL, 2 PP.]
[postmarked 19 March 1937]
TO: 22, Nestor str., Berlin–Halensee, Allemagne
c/o Fondaminsky, 130, av. de Versailles
[Paris]

My darling, my life, my dear love. *I forbid you to be miserable, I love you and* ... there's no power in the world that could take away or spoil even an inch of this endless love. And if I miss a letter for a day it's only because I absolutely can't cope with the crookedness and twists of time I'm living in now. *I love you*.

Now down to business. I think it's crazy, this plan of yours. Both Fondaminsky and Lyusya, whom I have just seen, think the same. But do as you want and according to your–airmail–response, I'll write to Prague. First of all: if you need some special treatment (and you could have written to me about this in more detail), which one can receive at a special Czech resort (and here too you could have spelled things out more), then, of course, there is nothing to discuss–we must go there. But if you simply need to rest thoroughly and recover, then we won't find a better place than Bormes–and any doctor would tell you that. Secondly: do you seriously think that this would cost us less than life in the Bormes *pension* (and 60 fr. for three *avec tout confort* is cheap, everyone says that!). Thirdly: after all I've arranged with French publishers and journals–not to mention friends, who can help me in this way or that–it's utterly absurd to go that far off again (and in any case who goes to a Czech resort in April!). Apart from its being extremely complicated to get visas, I don't have a *carte* yet, and what is more I have to settle the trip to England. *One thing is definite:* I prefer to write to England that the trip is postponed (if there is no other way) to not seeing you for yet another month–and will write, if it does stand in the way–and yet I do not see how it could all be set up if we were to go to

Czechoslovakia on the first. The only sensible reason for Czechoslovakia is Mother, but I think that in any case it would be cheaper if I went there myself for a week. After all the efforts to get settled, *it is rather hard on me and everyone – Fondaminsky included* – for you to decide suddenly to go to a Czech resort where we will be again cut off from the world, where it will be cold, expensive and unpleasant. Now let's do this: if you decide after all to do as you write, then reply to me immediately and, so be it, I'll accept your decision and telegraph Mother right away to arrange the visa, so we can meet in Prague on April 1st. But I tell you absolutely decidedly that in May we must be in Favières (re-read my letter) – since I don't want to get stuck in Czechoslovakia, and it will, very likely, come to just that.

Worst of all is that you have already written to Mother about the visa! This is terrible ... Your plan has quite upset me. You should have thought about this earlier. I am convinced that in the south (for I'll be with the boy continuously, till you're thoroughly rested) you will recover – unless it is something special, that one can treat only in Czechoslovakia.

I love you, my only love. Answer quickly. Kiss the little one. I will send another little train.

I am hurrying terribly, to send it by air today.

[ALS, 2 PP.]
[postmarked 20 March 1937]

[TO: Berlin]

[Paris]

My darling, my happiness,

Yesterday I sent you an airmail reply, and I'm now writing to augment it. The more I think about it and consult with others the more ridiculous your plan seems. (And at the same time it's unbearable for me to think that Mother's peace is *en jeu*, – and that, all in all, according to some higher – or inner – law we should – in spite of everything – see her, show her our little one – it's all such torture, that I simply can't bear it – it's a sort of unending strain on the soul, but there's nowhere to lie down –). So do think over all I've written, all my reasons. Really after all this enormous effort spent on establishing a living link to London and Paris, must we scratch everything and go to the Czech backwoods where (psychologically, geographically, and in every way) I shall again be cut off from the sources and opportunities of earning a living? Because from there, we won't get ourselves out to any south of France, while my London trip at the end of April will become impossibly complicated. I assure you that at Bormes it'll be peaceful and restful for you, and there are doctors there who are no worse. Come to your senses, my darling, and decide. *Because if you go on like that I shall simply take the next train to Berlin* – that is, I will come after you, which will certainly be neither smart nor cheap. I find it hard to explain to you how important it is that we don't lose touch with the shore to which I have managed to swim, to put it figuratively but accurately – for, really, after your letter I feel like a swimmer who's being torn from the cliff he has reached, by some whim of Neptune, a wave of unknown origin, a sudden wind, or some such. I beg you to consider all this, my love. In a couple of days I should receive a letter from Mme Chorny. And on the first of April we shall meet in Toulon. *Incidentally, I am not particularly interested in the butterflies of that department – Var* – since I've already collected there and know them all, – so I will be with my little one all day and will write in the evenings. And in May we'll find something cheaper. I think this time common sense is on my side. (To one thing I shall definitely not agree: to put off our meeting for another month. I can't be any longer *without you and the little one*.)

Long writes me that Kernahan (a famous critic) to whom he sent '*Despair*', wrote back: *Reviewers who like it will hail it as genius ... Those who don't like it, will say that it is extremely unpleasant ... It is meant, I assume, to be the work of a criminal maniac, and as such is very admirably done*, and so on. Silly but flattering on the whole. Besides that he forwards me an enquiry from a publisher in America which I'm sending to the Old Grace.

My dear love, all the Irinas in the world are powerless (I have just seen a third one at the Tatarinovs – the former Muravyov). *You should not let yourself go like that*. The eastern side of my every minute is already coloured by the light of our meeting soon. All the rest is dark, boring, you-less. *I want to hold you and kiss you*, I adore you.

Don't forget the tub (or should I buy one here?). I gave the books to Lyusya yesterday. Had lunch at Petit's, with Aldanov, Maklakov, Kerensky, Bernadsky and my two. Write me in detail what the doctor said. I love you beyond words.

V.

[ALS, 2 PP.]
[postmarked 21 March 1937]

TO: 22, Nestor str., Berlin – Halensee, Allemagne

[Paris]

My darling, my love,

I've sent you two airmails and am waiting impatiently for an answer, but today's Sunday already, and there's still nothing. I love you. I continue to insist that my plan is the reasonable one.

I am afraid, my love, that you've again been left for two days without a letter, but this happened because two days ago I sent an airmail, waited for a reply yesterday, and today am sending this by regular mail – and, besides, – it's Sunday. It is already hard for me to grasp the happiness of seeing you and my little one. My darlings …

I got a reply from P. N.: he agrees very magnanimously to pay Victor ninety-three centimes per line – for some reason pointing out that Remizov receives eighty. I will give (passing them off as short stories) two little excerpts from 'The Gift' a month. *C'est toujours cela.*

The publisher Putnam, to whom I offered the autob, writes (after all kinds of compliments) that they are deciding not to publish it *in book form. 'On the other hand there is a possibility that parts of it might be* (I am writing in bed – hence the early-medieval perspective of my handwriting) *published in a literary magazine. If you would like to have me do so, I should be glad to consult an agent about such a plan.'* Write to me quickly whether I should agree to that or pass the manuscript on to the next publisher in line (Duckworth – and if they decline, too, – then Heinemann).

I have been to the Conciergerie, looked over it all. Very good and terrible. The bench on which Maria Antoinette sat while waiting for the fateful cart. The nauseating resonance of the stone slabs. Gorguloff was the last to sit there.

My happiness, I must get up, go to the mountain sun, then lunch at the Tsetlins. I can't tell you how bored I am with my 'society' way of life. I love you. Depending on your letter I may call you on the phone – all this torments and bothers me terribly – and, most important: Mother . . . Write sooner, my darling, *my dear one.*

V.

[APC]

[postmarked 22 March 1937]

TO: 22, Nestor str., Berlin – Halensee, Allemagne

[Paris]

My love, *the whole thing is a dreadful disappointment,* but if this is really necessary for you, then, of course, go. You will get better and Mother will see my little one—well, I will concentrate my thoughts on these two situations. To be another month without you (and without him)—it's a kind of nightmarish nausea and a burden, *I don't think I can stand it.* Don't write anything to Mother, but today I have already been to Maklakov, through whom I can get a Czech visa (tomorrow I will file an application at the consulate) without the necessity of troubling Mother. *My darling, what am I to do?* Had you been able to swear to me that on May 8th you would come from Prague to Toulon (i.e. if you made of this date something inviolable, like the sunrise) then I would have thought: should I give up the English trip (20-IV) and the reading in Paris (6-V). Raisa guarantees V. V. a thousand. *My love!* I will 'fix' the visa in any case, and then we'll see. I'm rather nonplussed now. Business is going well. I'll write next time. I'm in a hurry. Victor tells me he can count on six hundred a month in P. N. It would be unwise to quarrel. Now I'm worried about your health. *Yes, my dear love, go to F.* I am writing to Mme Chorny that we are taking her little cottage from early May! *I adore you and the baby!*

Greetings to Anyutochka!

We would certainly need a *tub*!

[ALS, 2 PP.]

[postmarked 24 March 1937]

TO: 22, Nestor str., Berlin—Halensee, Allemagne

[Paris]

My love, how funny and nice that we've written the same date. Yes, that's what I will be thinking, that it's postponed for just two weeks, since I'm going to London anyway in the second half of the month. *But I feel horribly lonely, sad, and fed-up, my dear sweet-love.* I am sick of being both busy and idle—of the ladies, of living in full view, of my own b o n s m o t s, of conversations about me. There is one joy: my Greek, thanks to the intensive light treatment, has almost disappeared (it's gone completely from my indecently tanned face), and now it's strange and creepy to recall how I suffered – bodily, from the monstrous itch (sometimes I simply thought I was losing my mind) never stopping for a minute (I slept through the itching) for two months – and no less in spirit, from constant thoughts about my bloody underwear, blotchy mug and the scales pouring down on the carpet. Only the sun – artificial, and better still, southern – can defeat this idiotic illness of mine. And the main thing: I didn't even have anyone to complain to. My sweet joy, how impatiently I want to see you – and my little one, my little one … Yesterday I was at Aleksey Struve's and patted on the head his very sweet, impish six-year-old son. I have more free time now, but somehow it's falling apart; the play's inching along. Sofia Grigorievna Petit is offering me a job, which, of course, I'll take: a translation of a French book into English. I am expecting responses from *Candide*, Michel, Lausanne (*Matin*), Paulhan, Gallimard. Soon I will have to sit down to write the French talk. I am translating 'Breaking the News' for '*Nouv. Lit.*' I received a long and sweet letter from P. N. M. (with an attached typewritten report of who gets what in the newspaper) with an offer of publishing six hundred lines a month at ninety a line. Two days ago I gave them 'The Present' (i.e. a little 'Gift' – or a present to the newspaper: that's what I called the episode about Yasha. Witty?). Sovrem. zap. comes out at the end of the month. I'm waiting for final news from England about my readings there. My dear darling, I am sending you this letter too by air, so that you don't have another day without a letter, since I keep miscalculating. Try, my happiness, to get to Czechoslovakia no later than the tenth, – or there'll be too little time for treatment. We will go to London by winter. I think that we could put the linen and books at Mme Morevsky's – she offered – but it's even simpler here, at Ilyusha's, plenty of space, and he offered himself. Rostovtsev isn't here yet. I've written to all the others. I am looking after *les petits gros chats*. I think that *with luck* Victor will manage to earn more, and the room and chow for one for the whole summer will be paid for by the columns in P. N. I repeat, that in that sense our perspectives are on the whole very rosy. Avgust is coming here in a day or two. Yesterday I went to the ministry about your French visa: there Eidel kicked up a fuss because he had been written down as guarantor when he was the one receiving the application. *My fault, sorry*. The visa has been sent to you, and pick it up without fail before you leave. And think whether you shouldn't buy the ticket from Prague to Toulon right then. The more I think, the more reckless it seems to me to leave France for the summer, so I am pleading with you (and you know doctors 'hold on to' you at such resorts) to be in Toulon on the 8th.

Tomorrow, it seems, *my little friend* is arriving. Had *meals* (alas!) been not as seductive (not in the gastronomical but in the economic sense, for eating at Ilyusha's makes me feel utterly uncomfortable – not so much because of the money but because of the bother it causes V. M-ch, who always tries to prepare something especially lush and tasty when I'm home), I would have declined all invitations, locked myself up and written. It's cold today, but in a spring way, and I love you. Try to arrange the typing of Inv. to a B. My darling, we can't do without a *tub*, keep it with you for what we discussed. Answer me about Putnam. Don't forget Filippov – regarding Tegel. I wrote to Mother that I'll hardly come, but I'm arranging the visa. I love you – and please, don't change the plans any more. Has the boy grown up? Don't forget – soccer. I am kissing you, kissing both of you. My tenderness ...

V.

[APCS]
[postmarked 26 March 1937]

TO: 22, Nestor str.,
Berlin–Halensee, Allemagne

c/o Fondaminsky, 130, av. de Versailles
[Paris]

My love, the boy isn't sick, is he? I had a dream along those lines–you know, a holey dream with a shadow. I am getting into rhythm with this postcard, so–enough aeroplanes. A little pussy comes to visit our cats, affectionate, blue-grey, she whimpers sweetly: no response. I have drawn that to Jeanne's attention. She, with a sigh: '*nos messieurs sont aussi comme ça* . . .' Tonight I'm going to the poets' evening, tomorrow I'm having dinner at Princess Tsitsianov's, the day after tomorrow is the première of Teffi's play. Denis Roche has finished his translation of 'Spring in F'. I have given two excerpts from the autob to Kogan for America and Holland. He hopes, besides, to place there *The* [*Door*]*Bell*, *Passenger* and Chorb. I had lunch at Mme Tatarinov's today and will have dinner at Aunt Nina's. *I love you, I am beginning to derive a certain pleasure from the thought* that Mother will see our boy, and that you will get better at F. Write to me: *what did the doctor say exactly*? And what will happen to the boxes of precious butterflies, the spreading trays and the pins? I will write to Anyutochka in a day or two–no, I won't write: I'm cross at her for her stubborn silence. I spoke with Lyusya on the phone, I'll see him. *I cannot tell you, how I love you and miss you*.

V.

[APCS]
[28 March 1937]

TO: 22, Nestor str., Berlin–Halensee, Allemagne

c/o Fondaminsky, 130, av. de Versailles
[Paris]

My darling, my love, I haven't had anything from you for three days. Today is the 28th, the fifteenth anniversary. I reminded P. N. about this in good time–but those philistines are invulnerable and have done nothing to mark it today (but then–they printed 'The Present'–and I am already preparing the next camouflaged excerpt). I am having a very 'society' Easter: yesterday was the première of Teffi's (horrendous) play, today I am having tea with Gr. Duch. Maria Pavl. at the *George V*, then a meeting with Bar. Budberg, then dinner with Vilenkin at the *Windsor Hotel*. But from Monday I'll lock myself up and write the play. *I love you, my sweet one.* I saw Zyoka for a moment this morning, he gave me what you'd asked him and told me how our little one, eyelashes lowered, mighty pleased and dreamy, was waiting for the automobile. I received a request from Chekhov in England to write a play for him 'which would reflect social and moral conflicts'. Upon a very close inspection Bunin turns out to be simply an old vulgarian–while Zaytsev, on the contrary, improves. Without you I am furiously bored–and dream about the trip to London as the next stage. My puss, don't write to me again, for God's sake, about some Italy or Belgium. I already have a written agreement about everything with Mme Chorny. Had a very pleasant conversation with the editor of '*Le Matin*'. Love you!

V.

[ALS, 2 PP.]
[postmarked 30 March 1937]
TO: 22, Nestor str., Berlin–Halensee, Allemagne
c/o Fondaminsky, 130, av. de Versailles
[Paris]

My love, what's going on, this is the fourth day I've had no letters. Is the little one well? Yesterday I took in my arms the three-year-old, red-locked, thoughtful-naughty nephew (also Dmitri and also called differently) of B. Budberg–and it reminded me to tears ... What an amazing toy store there is on Champs-Élys.–can't be compared to our Czech ones–such trains! (*'le plus rapide train du monde des jouets'* with a 'speed' locomotive and marvellously made dark-blue carriages). I know that there are a thousand chores, but still, write more often!

Denis Roche is translating 'Spring' excellently, it will be ready soon: yesterday he and I discussed various difficult spots. Budberg, however, has not coped with the translation, so either 'The Ret. of Chorb' will be included in the collection, or I will translate 'Spring' myself (or Struve–'Pilgram'): it must be submitted no later than in August. Putnam liked the autob-y <u>very much</u>, and everyone recommends agreeing to their launching it as a *'serial'* in a journal. I'll probably agree to it. Otherwise–the pace will be lost; and the size of the thing terribly complicates its publication as a book. It was she again (Budberg) who suggested to me today a meeting with Aleks. Tolstoy, but I will probably not go. Maria Pavlovna is a little lady with a cigarette and laryngitis; she kept ringing for tea and could not get it–on account of Easter. I spoke with her about lectures in America, she promised to help. Once somewhere remote she went butterfly hunting with Avinov. About Nika and Natasha she said that they were nice, but *snobs*–and this expression, coming from <u>her</u>, acquired a Proustian charm for me, while in relation to them, it took on a fresh and frightening power. I had dinner with Vilenkin who is now actively involved in arranging the evening in London and promoting my book. (By the way, absolutely indirectly I have learned that 'Luzhin' is having a big – they told me 'phenomenal' – success in Sweden.) Tomorrow I will be seeing Alma Polyakov and Mme Sablin. Today I am having dinner with six writers at some patron's house. 'The Present', which came out two days ago, turned out more than three hundred lines long – four hundred and twenty. Excellent. I'll call the next excerpt 'The Recompense' – and also squeeze in more lines than I have been allocated. Ah, my happiness, how I long to see you … It is entrancing to think about May. Zyoka says that he has grown even better-looking. Victor has lately, i.e. in one month, spent, all the same, more than 200 fr. In a couple of days I will be going to see Fayard, Lefèvre (*Nouv. Litr.*) and Thiébaut (*Revue de Paris*).

I adore you, it's very hard to live without you, please write me soon. It's 3 o'clock now, I am going to see the doctoress, then will try to write for an hour or two. Love you, my life …

V.

[ALS, 2 PP.]

[postmarked 2 April 1937]

TO: b/ Prof Geballe, 21, Osnabrücker Str., Berlin

c/o Fondaminsky, 130, av. de Versailles

[Paris]

My darling, strange to write to you to this new – and visually non-existent – address. How nice that our little one is all right. Next time I will send him another little train. It is impossible to get the permit immediately, things move at their own lawful pace, we can't speed them up, God willing I'll get it before the London trip, otherwise I will have to trudge to Eidel for a return visa. Boring and bothersome. I'm really starting to feel oppressed, the enervating charm of Paris, the divine sunsets (on the Arc de Triomphe, a fragment of the frieze suddenly comes to life – a pigeon taking off), the charm and the idleness, the outlines of time are wobbly, I can't write, I'm desperate for solitude with you and for Vlad. Mikhaylovich in the next room not to bother the wailing, lurching, mewing radio. *I am quite fed up with things.* We had a pleasant little party the other day, what can I say: tra-la-la, Aldanov in tails, Bunin in the vilest dinner-jacket, Khmara with a guitar and Kedrova, Ilyusha in such narrow trousers that his legs were like two black sausages, old, sweet Teffi – and all this in a revoltingly luxurious mansion ('they have white furniture' – Tatyana Markovna told me beforehand, enraptured), besides I had not taken the trouble to find out the hosts' name, and only when I got there did I recognize the mug of Mme Grinberg and her son; the first thing I said: 'And where is my *Oxford Book of Poetry*?' After dinner everyone – especially the ladies – had a bit too much to drink, Vera Nikolaevna *me faisait des confidences hideuses* and, as we listened to the blind-drunk Khmara's rather boorish ballads she kept saying: but my life is over! while Kedrova (a very sharp-eyed little actress whom Aldanov thinks a new Komissarzhevskaya) shamelessly begged me for a part. Why, of course, the most banal singing of 'charochka', a lonely vase with chocolates, the hostess's wail (about me): 'oh, he's eating all the chocolates', a view from the picture window onto the skeleton of the growing exhibition and the moon. *C'était à vomir*. Bunin kept impersonating my 'arrogance' and then hissed: 'you will die alone and in horrible agony'. A Mme Persky, a fat vulgar baba, lay on the shoulder of poor Ilya, who was desperately glancing at me and asking for some water to be brought to her, while people explained to him that it wasn't a fainting fit but a swoon of delight. And all of that – because they need money for the theatre. *Infecte.*

They have announced Sov. zap.'s next issue, with 'The Gift' in pride of place. Lifar seems to have taken offence at me because I didn't agree to give a lecture for nothing at his exhibition, but asked for a thousand. But then here's what I did, with great pleasure – wonderful revenge: there was an evening at Las Cases, a poetry reading, for the secret benefit of the very sick Terapiano (who once, if you remember, took to me in the foulest manner in 'Chisla') and I volunteered to read verse there (I read '*Inconnue de la S.*').

I have been to the cinema, to Aunt Nina's with a crowd of women, to the Zaytsevs', to the Kokoshkins' (often), to the Kyandzhuntsevs' and so on. The little purple sun continues to help me: I have completely recovered in that respect. My love, I can't even imagine now what you are doing at the moment since I don't know your new surroundings ... *My darling, my darling*, go to Czechoslovakia as soon as you can – *and whatever you do* go first of all to show yourself and the little one to Mother. It's now almost ten p.m., I'll go out and post the letter, then go to bed. No one understands why I have such a tan: they suspect a *clandestine* trip south.

In the next few days there should definitely be responses from the French journals. It's awful to think how tired you must be from all your efforts, my poor little one, my happiness!

V.

[APCS]

[postmarked 4 April 1937]

TO: c/o Prof. Geballe, 21, Osnabrücker Strasse, Berlin, Allemagne

c/o Fondaminsky, 130, av. de Versailles

[Paris]

My love, have you received the French visa? When are you going to Prague? Answer, my darling. I am writing from a not very comfortable position on the couch. Yesterday I saw Lyusya and Bromb. They were sitting on the terrace of a café, yellow and sad. They asked about Anyuta's plans, but I know nothing. A wonderful morning now, early, everything is motionless in blue milk, and the sparrows are singing all at once. My darling! I am going to a soccer match today with the Kyandzhuntsevs. How is my little one? To take him in my arms, to smell him, to kiss him–these are such heavenly sensations that I can even get palpitations. One more month. Write, my happiness, and answer the questions. I wrote heaps of letters yesterday, but the play's recalcitrant. *I love you dearly, I kiss you.*

V.

[ALS, 6 PP.]

[postmarked 6 April 1937]

TO: 21, Osnabrücker Str., b/ Prof. Geballe,
Berlin–Wilmersdorf, Allemagne

c/o Fondaminsky, 130, av. de Versailles

[Paris]

My darling, your muddle-headedness is absolutely killing me. What's really going on? Forgive me, my happiness, but honestly, this won't do.

Couldn't you figure out the currency question in advance? In the next letter you'll probably write to me that you are staying very peacefully in Germany, in a Bavarian resort. *I cannot tell how utterly depressing it is* (and yet you reproach me for thoughtlessness). It will be a terrible blow for Mother if now after all the plans and troubles (all for nothing, nothing ...) you do not go to Czechoslovakia. I knew we shouldn't have started any of this; and had you listened to me then you would already be sitting peacefully in Bormes. And now you write to me that you'll decide something or other 'in a couple of days'? What, precisely? And why these repeated and pointless confusions about what means we can count on? I have written to you about everything absolutely accurately and precisely and you must know perfectly well what's what, if you've read my letters. As I wrote to you, we'll stay first for a few days at the *pension* in Bormes, so as to take Mme Chorny's little cottage later, if we like it. If not, we'll find another place with no trouble, with her help. What's the matter, why does this perfectly simple plan cause you such indecisiveness, while the most difficult and absurd (as it turns out) journeys through Czechoslovakia seem pleasantly doable? My love, you have still not written to me for example whether you have received the French visa. *Do it at once, please*. By the way: my doctor, Kogan-Bernstein (the saintliest of women and an excellent doctor who gives me light treatment daily for an hour, which anywhere else would have cost a hundred francs per session, rather than nothing), says that Franzen[s]bad mud baths are perfectly replaceable – and even more than replaceable – by electric baths, which she would have administered, and she wittily decries the predilection for German-Czech spas. My darling, *it is unfair* (as I have already written to you) to talk of my thoughtlessness. I cannot write to you more than what Flora S. has told me about a six-month sojourn in England – you know it's impossible to produce an exact estimate – but she's a reliable and responsible person – everyone knows that. But let's not look that far, so don't you worry, but concentrate our thoughts on your arrival now in Toulon (of course you should buy the ticket there from Berlin). For God's sake, write to me at last exactly when and where you are going. Most importantly – I absolutely cannot be any longer without you – this half-existence, quarter-existence – is starting to get too much for me – and without the air which comes from you I can neither think nor write – I can't do anything. Our separation is becoming an unbearable torture, and all of these constant changes of mind and the ambivalence and swings and uncertainty you have (when everything is so wonderfully simple) only intensify the torture. No, I cannot work in this setting: a day interrupted by going out three or four times isn't a work day for me, you know that well, but when I do settle down to write, it's either Kerensky dictating nearby in his hysterical voice, or the radio, or Ilyusha's guests, –not to mention the telephone, which rings every minute. On the other hand, had I not been a dinner guest, I'd have spent much more than I'm spending – while I manage to spend mere trifles. Today I had lunch at the Tatarinovs', this evening I'll be at Dobuzhinsky's, yesterday I had dinner at a restaurant with the Rodzyanko couple and P. Volkonsky, the day after tomorrow there will be lunch at Mme Polyakov's and dinner at Bromberg's, and so on, and so on, and during the day there are trips to *Nouvelles Littéraires*, *Revue de Paris*, *Candide*, with their exhaustingly polite conversations. I beg you, my love, do not direct at me any more of these childish reproaches, *je fais ce que je peux* – and, after all, our future here has been arranged, if we decide not to go to London: with lessons alone I can easily find enough for us to live on, that's in the extreme case, if nothing else worked out, but help and possibilities come from everywhere – I think you absolutely cannot imagine the atmosphere towards me here.

I am terribly upset by your letter – and perhaps I should have calmed down first and then written to you. I'm insanely afraid that you'll offer me yet another 'plan'. Don't do that. Make every effort to travel to Czechoslovakia after all – that is for Mother – but, most importantly, get the visa and the tickets for the south.

I am bored and gloomy. 'Flowers do not please me . . .' – I am waiting for the final reply from London, since I still don't know where and when I will read. I wrote to Altagracia long ago. Have spoken with writers about *copyright* – and already reported to you about that. I did write to Putnam asking them to reply in more detail about publishing in a journal – and most importantly that it should be done right away. I will congratulate Thompson. I have written to Mme Chorny without binding us, and she herself also told me that she did not want to bind me without showing the house, and that she would rent it extremely cheap. The summer will cost (6–7 months) maximum ten thousand, tout compris, or more likely cheaper, and half of that I will certainly earn by writing so that not all the little centimes will go on that.

I read parts of your little card (about the move – terrible! I can imagine . . .) out loud to Ilyusha and Zinzin and they said they understood now who writes my books for me. Flattered? *I love you, my own one – and please don't be jealous of the* 'society' life I'm leading here. *People are very nice to me.* Here we go: two refugees from Russia have arrived and are talking loudly, emphasizing all their '*os*', with Aleks. Fyod. in the next room – about the price of bread, Stakhanovites, etc. How can I write a play? My darling, how much I'd give for you and my boy to come in right now. My little curly one! Please write to me quickly. Life is working out excellently, but you're still full of doubts (the tip of the pen has worn down, that's how much I've been writing). And again – Avksentiev has come in and is talking on the phone over me. No one there, which means that he'll pop back in five minutes. The young people are talking with relish about the new steamboats 'The Decembrist' and 'Lenin', while Kerensky's asking 'what is the local people's mood?' They reply: 'like a wolf's'. Sparrows are singing wildly in the garden, which has just turned green. I love you. If I write you short little letters it is because I feel myself empty, despondent and out of my sweet element, as well as not knowing how to manage my time. Avksentiev came back – and got an answer. They've told me about one gentleman who gulps down my work, and then, to alleviate the hangover, reads Leskov.

My darling, it is not a very nice letter, I'm afraid, but I am madly anxious about everything – your journey, and the boy, and your health ... Tomorrow I am at Maklakov's in the morning about the *identité*. And you, my darling, stop worrying yourself. Yes: we definitely need the tub, Mme Chorny has the sea but no bath. In a day or two I'll write to the *pension*, when I know exactly when we'll meet. Maybe before the 8th? I love you, my life.

V.

[ALS, 2 PP.]

[postmarked 7 April 1937]

TO: 21, Osnabrückerstr., b/ Prof. Geballe,
Berlin – Wilmersdorf, Allemagne

c/o Fondaminsky, 130, av. de Versailles
[Paris]

My love,

I resolutely refuse Belgium. I do not understand what's going on, why you are suggesting plans to me, one more ridiculous than the other. What's this nonsense that Var is more expensive and its climate worse than some kind of speculative, unheard of (how on earth will Zina 'search for it', I wonder) Belgian resort. The place in the south, which I proposed, is an ideal place for children (by the way, in the summer there it is cooler than in Nice) and, in general, for the weak and exhausted; the trip (i.e. that 'extra' we will have to pay compared with the travels around Belgium – *that hideously grey and cold country*) costs an utter trifle; and there, in the south, we will live first not at Mme Chorny's (with the *tub*), but higher, in the Bormes pension (*Hôtel Beau Soleil* with a bath). If – let us suppose – you knew today a specific treatment place in Belgium (like Fran-bad), and had a visa and could leave tomorrow – then OK, as a stage on the way south (i.e. the same combination as Czechoslovakia), it might have been fine, but since a month would go by just finding such a resort, it's simply not worth talking about. I dare say that by May 1st I'll be done with London, so I beg you to leave for Toulon by that date. *Darling, that is really my last word.*

I dreamt of you this night. I saw you with some kind of hallucinatory clarity, and, all morning long, have been going around in a sort of cloud of tenderness for you. I felt your hands, your lips, hair, everything – and if I'd been able to dream such dreams more often, my life would've been easier. You are my love.

I am going to Marcel Thiébaut's today. Yesterday I sat with Benois and Somov at Dobuzhinsky's: such a sweet man. Write to me, at last, have you received the visa? Victor sent his mother the fourth copy yesterday – in all one thousand two hundred pages of Czech translation over these two months.

I am preparing an excerpt for P. N. 'The Present' was a great success. Tomorrow, it seems, 'Sovremennye' is coming out.

I cannot tell you how your mental spinning around Central Europe torments me.

Greetings to Anyuta. Really, she could somehow write to me.

I kiss my little one. I *kiss you, my love.*

V.

[APCS]
[postmarked 9 April 1937]

TO: 21, Osnabrückerstr., b/ Prof. Geballe,
Berlin–Wilmersdorf, Allemagne

c/o Fondaminsky, 130, av. de Versailles
[Paris]

My love and my darling, of course, I'm very happy for Mother's sake if you go to Czechoslovakia after all. *Good luck, my darling.* But you know what, tell me in your next letter the doctor's diagnosis, in detail. I can imagine how exhausted you are, my darling, and how overstrung, but believe me, you will get much better over summer and you'll get a good rest. I'll be with the little one every moment, and I'll write at night. Regarding the passport: you don't realize at all *that my position is exceptional and that I haven't to bother about 'récépissés' etc. as other people* [*do*]. I told Rodzyanko and Maklakov about your worries: they are ridiculous, my darling. *I am afraid it's your cousin's panicky influence.* What I am getting here, by the way, is p e r m i s d e s é j o u r p e r m a n e n t. *Please, do not think any more about it!*

'Pilgram' has gone to *Revue de Paris*, '*Musique*' to *Candide*, '*Outrage*' to *Mesures*, 'Spring in F.' is promised to *Nouv. Lit.*

There's a letter from Putnam, he is trying to place '*English associations*' in a journal. Last night, I had dinner at Bromb.'s. The play is definitely not working, I've destroyed what I've written. *I love you, my sweet one and am terribly anxious about your health*, especially given that my boy is nervous and wild. *Hold out* just a little bit more, and everything will be fine. It's wonderfully warm. I am now going to Lefèvre then to Yablonovsk., Sergey. *My darling* …

V.

[ALS, 2 PP.]
[postmarked 12 April 1937]
[Paris]

TO: 21, Osnabrückerstrasse, b/ Prof. Geballe,
Berlin–Wilmersdorf, Allemagne

c/o Fondaminsky, 130, av. de Versailles
[Paris]

My sweet happiness, I'm still not sure whether you're going to Czechoslovakia, but now I hope passionately that you will. *Your last letter was lovely*.

I have sent Bourne a list of 25 names and addresses (of English critics and writers) to whom he should send the book as soon as it comes out. I compiled the list with the help of Budberg and Struve, from whom I have finally received a sensible letter: most likely, I'll go to London on the 20th. Besides the English evening, I'll also arrange a Russian one, again at Sablin's. The book has already been sent to Altagracia, but I'll discuss *copyright* again with people who know and then will write to him, although I already wrote to him clearly at the time what Bourne had told me. I've already received a little letter from Thompson in response to my congratulations. A very sweet invitation from *Mesures* to lunch on Wednesday. Yesterday I was at S. Yablonovsky's, had dinner at the Tsetlins', in the evening was at Berberova's, with Dobuzhinsky, etc. The last two days, my love, I have been working diligently on the arrest of Chernyshevsky, which, under the playful title 'The Reward', I must dictate to Mme Kovalyov today and send to P. N.

Today, in fact, the doctor was supposed to perform an experimental operation on me (to draw blood from one of my veins and to inject it in the other), but 'the students' (as Aleks. Fyod. calls Ilyusha and V. M.) are strongly dissuading me; besides, my Greek is getting wonderfully better from the sun. Yesterday I corrected proofs of my article about Amalia Os. On Tuesday, Sovr. zap. should come out.

On the morning of April first, celebrating this day religiously, I said to the 'students' that the evening before, at the Zaytsevs', they had told me that at night, while Bunin was partying, someone had robbed his apartment. The news spread very quickly, and the same day a reporter from P. N. set off for the – very angry – Ivan. It seems he has taken offence at me, when everything became clear. I don't see what's so offensive about this.

My darling, I love you, I love you, I love you! I kiss my 'person', my little one ... I will get rid of all the *conférences* by May fifth. On the eighth, we will meet in Toulon. How green everything is here, how warm, what grey pants I have from London for seven and sixpence!

I love you, my only happiness.

V.

[APCS]

[postmarked 14 April 1937]

TO: 21, Osnabrückerstr., b/ Prof. Geballe,
Berlin – Wilmersdorf, Allemagne

c/o Fondaminsky, 130, av. de Versailles
[Paris]

My love, I am tired of worrying about your trip to Prague – come what may, let destiny decide, but almost as much as I dream of seeing my little one, I dream of Mother seeing him. Regarding your little paragraphs: 1) we will manage 2) before renting the cabin we will, in any case, live at the pension for a while 3) the heat in those parts is considerably milder than in, say, Nice. Regarding A: '*Despair*' has been sent to him; besides, he will get another copy at once when it comes out. I won't get to London before the 25th. I'm in full contact with Struve, letters are flying back and forth. The publication of D e s p a i r is already announced in the Engl. newspapers. I dictated Chernysh all morning long today. At the last moment, I declined the operation I wrote to you about, and besides, said it was you who asked me not to do it: because I had gone too far with it, the doctor *was rather looking forward to that experiment*. It's pouring, the trees are getting greener before my eyes, I love you. A little over three weeks left. I'm almost afraid of the intensity of that happiness. Zenzinov finds my Chernysh, as before, 'disgusting'. Maybe I will stop by at the old man's tonight – it seems he is offended at me, and Zyoka too. Tomorrow I will have lunch with Paulhan and the lady editor of '*Mesures*'. I physically sense your fatigue, my darling, and endlessly, inexpressibly, chestnuttily love you.

V.

[ALS, 2 PP.]
[15 April 1937]

TO: 21, Osnabrückerstrasse, b/ Prof. Geballe,
Berlin – Wilmersdorf, Allemagne

c/o Fondaminsky, 130, av. de Versailles
[Paris]

My life, my love, it *is twelve years to-day*. And, today, '*Despair*' has come out and 'The Gift' is in S. Z.

Complete success with '*Outrage*'. It will appear in the May issue of '*Mesures*', and our Victor has already received a little thousand for it. Lunch at the villa of Henry Church (the publisher of '*Mesures*' – he's an American millionaire with a marvellous furuncle on his nape – old, silent, with a literaturizing wife of German stock) went remarkably well. The meeting point was Adrienne Monnier's bookshop, on the Odéon, and from there we went by car to the Churches', beyond St Cloud (everything is green, wet, almonds in bloom, gnats swarming). They really f ê t e d me, and I was on form. Among the writers was Michaux. I hit it off splendidly with Joyce's publisher, Sylvia Beach, a prim little lesbian, and through her I'll be able to do a lot to promote '*Despair*' and sort out arrangements for its French publication, in case Gallim. and Albin Mich. *ne marcheront pas*. After lunch, there was something like an editorial meeting of '*Mesures*', and a woman photographer took fifteen pictures of us. There was a conversation about how we could determine the sound of plants with the help of some kind of waves. I asserted that the poplar sings soprano, and the oak bass, but Paulhan asserted much more wittily than me that, no, the oak turns out to have the same kind of voice as a daisy – '*peut être parce qu'il est toujours un peu embarrassé*'. Tomorrow I will lunch with him, Cingria, Supervielle and Michaud on Montparnasse. My darling, I love you. The story about my little one ('for the shores') is entrancing. Zenzinov keeps laughing at it and tells it to everyone. *Your letter to* Ilyusha *is quite nice, my darling one.* Your passport will be extended in France, as soon as you arrive. I am terribly upset that Prague has fallen through again, but I didn't much believe it'd work out. I'm going to England for a week at the end of the month. Tomorrow at 5 I'll be at Mme Sablin's – settling arrangements for the Russian evening there. I won't go in any case till the 25th; I have to let the book wander around a little, as both Budberg and Struve write. I've sent Long the other addresses Sylvia Beach gave me. My 'Pushkin' is having a very agreeable success. I've grown fatter, more tanned, changed my skin – but I feel a constant irritation because I have no time and place to work. Tonight, I'm having dinner at the Kyands. I'll call the old man now.

My love, my love, how long since you stood in front of me in your prim little robe – my God! – and how much new there will be in my little one, and how many births (words, games, all kinds of little things) I've missed ... I wrote to Mme Chorny yesterday. My darling, see that you pack carefully, so there are no last-minute delays. How amusing – about Bardelebeness. Poor Ilf died, and somehow one thinks of separating Siamese twins. I love you, I love you.

My French stocks have risen much higher, Paulhan *est tout ce qu'il y a de plus charmant* and reminds me somehow – by his liveliness, his quick dark glance, his stature and his unshavenness – of Ilyusha. Greetings to Anyuta, I'm waiting for a letter from her.

I kiss you, my happiness, my tired little one ...

V.

TELEGRAM
[15 April 1937]
[Paris]

VERA NABOKOFF 21 OSNABRUCKER STRASSE BERLIN WILMERSDORF

CONGRATULATIONS MY DEAR LOVE++

[ALS, 2 PP.]
[postmarked 17 April 1937]

TO: 21, Osnabrückerstrasse, b/ Prof. Geballe,
Berlin – Wilmersdorf, Allemagne

c/o Fondaminsky, 130, av. de Versailles
[Paris]

My dear darling,

Thank you for the little journals. Tell me, shall I send you the issue of

Sovr. zap., or will it be an extra burden for your journey? Write to me definitively about the *tub* too: this is something absolutely necessary, *bath or no bath*. We can buy one here very cheaply.

I had a very pleasant lunch with my brother-writers – the French ones, *bien entendu* – I don't feel great love from my countrymen; – there were about fifteen of us – and it was rather a surprise for me that everyone paid for himself – which set me back thirty francs. Supervielle (whom I'll visit on Thursday) already looks so like an old horse – with a charming horsey smile – that I felt like giving him a large lump of sugar, all covered in strands of wool. I implored Paulhan to act on Gallimard, otherwise I don't know *où j'en suis* with '*Désespoir*'. Young writers from N.R.F. A syrup of compliments for the same old *Vraisemblable*. An exchange of addresses.

A little countertack: M., after reading my excerpt (the arrest of Chernysh), flew into a rage, stamped his feet and refused point-blank to publish. Ilyusha told me this today. A dilemma: should I refuse further collaboration with them or give them something else (the travels of G.-Ch., on which I've worked a little here). I'm inclined, alas, to the latter. But Ilya has offered me – if Rudnev doesn't want to publish the chapter about Chern. in Sovr. zap., – to place the one chapter, on the same conditions, in the new journal, 'Russkie zapiski'. I agreed.

I worked out with Mme Sablin about the evening and will write to her husband tonight. The persons I named have already received '*Despair*', but I haven't been sent a copy yet. Today, Denis Roch[e] is reading the final translation of 'Spring' to me – good man, he did it quickly. I will go to *Candide* in a day or two – since for some reason they're dragging their heels. There are two things I want more than anything else in the world now: for you to be (with him, my warm little one) next to me, near, *my sweet darling* – and to be able to carry on peacefully with my 'Gift' (not a single misprint in the first chapter – and, overall, it's presented very nicely). On Monday, I'll be at the English consulate. What do you think, shall I ask Bourne to send out the copies (mine) of '*Despair*' (to, say, Thompson, Solomon, Church, Harrison, and so on – ten to fifteen people altogether) or shall I do it myself from London? Answer all these questions right away, *my precious*. My happiness, I can't stand being without you any longer. – I kiss you, I kiss you – and I kiss you again.

V.

[APCS]
[postmarked 19 April 1937]

TO: 21, Osnabrückerstr., b/ Prof. Geballe,
Berlin – Wilmersdorf, Allemagne

c/o Fondaminsky, 130, av. de Versailles
[Paris]

My love, *is the little man all right?*

Today I received 6 copies of '*Despair*' in the familiar (abominable) binding, but with a charming jacket. Shall I send it to you? I'm going to the English consulate today for my visa, then to I. V. to listen to the next instalment of his memoirs ... The English evening, evidently, will be on May 3rd. Roche's translation was simply magnificent, but we went over it and corrected for 4 hours – and haven't completely finished; we'll have to meet again on Wednesday. I went, with Ira and Saba, to a music-hall, where pitiable women dance naked. I wrote five letters to England today. There is a notice from the post office that a package has come. Rudnev is asking for the next chapter by July 1st. Can it really be that in twenty days I'll see both you and him? *There are days when I adore you just a little more than a human being* *can* *adore – and today is one of them.* How are you feeling? My dear love ...

V.

[ALS, 2 PP.]
[postmarked 20 April 1937]

TO: 21, Osnabrückerstr.,
Berlin–Wilmersdorf, Allemagne

c/o Fondaminsky, 130, av. de Versailles
[Paris]

My only love, how nice, how charming's everything you write about the little man (and about the attic!) is, and, all in all, this was an especially dear letter (except for the 'vile rumours'). On Thursday morning I'll see Maria Ivanovna who has come to Paris from the south. She writes: 'I'll rent my little house to you with pleasure, from May on, if that suits you. I'll also give you detailed directions for installing yourselves in Favières, if you wish to settle down in a pension. It makes no sense to go to Bormes now, since it's already nice in Favières in May.' And how I am *looking forward* to his warmth, his new words, his sly little smile. *My darlings*! But I don't know how to arrange a flight here from Berlin–Maria Ignatievna cannot help us with this. She was, you know, the mistress of Gorky, of Lockhart, now–of Wells–*quite the mysterious adventuress type*. All in all, I don't know what would be better, whether you should go through Paris, which means a stopover, or through Strasbourg. The latter, I think. It'll be the last of your trials, this journey, my tired little one. In Favière I'll take him over from you completely. For the sake of the date (ours, as you know), I want to meet you in Toulon no later than May 8 (and out of coronation considerations too, one can't have an evening in London later than then). I'll send books to Mother from Paulhan's. I am preparing an excerpt for P. N. There will be no operation. I'm in touch with Zina, and at her request have asked *Nouv. Lit.* to send her back the Pushkin material she sent them earlier. I asked her about Kirill in two letters, but she hasn't responded yet.

The same rumours have reached me – and I didn't doubt that they would slither over to Berlin, too. The slippery mugs of those who spread them ought to be smashed! I heard another version, from the old man: that I'm having an affair with Berberova. I am indeed at the Kokoshkins' rather often – and both of them are very pleasant – I emphasize 'both'. My every act, pronouncement, gesture, facial expression is commented on minutely and malevolently in local literary and semi-literary circles. Here's an example, from among the most innocent. Once, between a meeting at the *Revue de Paris* and a dinner at the Kyandzh. or the Kokoshk., not knowing what to do with myself (a mighty spring rain was falling), I took a seat at a café on the Champs Elysée[s] and ordered a cup of hot chocolate. By chance Aldanov was there, we sat down together for a while and then went to the Place de la Concorde (I, under an umbrella, and he, in a bowler hat, the rain pouring down from the edges of the bowler), during which I asked him in detail about the historical associations of the square (about the place where they executed the king, about the buildings preserved from those times). The result: the next day a rumour reaches me: at night (!) Sirin out of snobbishness or perversion (!!) drinks chocolate in a café (i.e. not, say, Pernod or another aperitif, like an honest writer) and out of his haughty spite for everything ignores the sights of Paris. Ultimately I don't give a damn about the nasty things they say with relish about me, and I think you shouldn't give a damn either. I do and I will always care about you. In general, *I pull people's leg a good deal*, and they don't forgive me for that. My life, my love, *you are part of me and you know it perfectly well*. I kiss your hands, your sweet lips, your little blue temple.

V.

[APCS]
[postmarked 21 April 1937]

TO: b/ Prof. Geballe, 21, Osnabrückerstrasse,
Berlin–Wilmersdorf, Allemagne

c/o Fondaminsky, 130, av. de Versailles
[Paris]

My love, one cannot do anything from here, about the aeroplane, I mean; this should be done from Berlin; there is a comparatively cheaper *aller-et-retour*, but that won't do! *It is very complicated*–not to mention that perhaps on the 27th or 28th I'll be about to go to London, while today is already the 21st, so when will it all be and how can you live with the boy in Sofa's abominable hotel, while I find something here ... no, this won't work out! Your letter agitated me excruciatingly, for I know in advance nothing will come of this and I'll have to wait another 17 days. But here's something, perhaps: find out about the difference (monetary and hourly) between a trip to Toulon through Strasbourg and a trip to Toulon through Paris. If, in both cases, it's minimal, then go through Paris–now, so I could see you at least *entre deux gares*–and then go straight to Toulon–since it's better to expect me there from London, than in Paris. But it's only tomorrow that I will know the *pension* in Favière (and then I'll write you right away). *My love, I am terribly worried about your plight*, I can imagine what torture it must be staying at the scoundrels'. And yet I think you should not settle (without me) in Paris, but better go straight to Favière. I love you, life is meaningless without you, *and well, if you are plucky enough*, risk it, leave right away.

V.

Or maybe you can stay at Elena Lvovna's? Or at Anna Natanovna's? Shall I ask?

I replied to you about the aeroplane in my letter yesterday, so I am not sending this one by airmail.

[ALS, 2 PP.]
[postmarked 23 April 1937]
[Paris]

TO: 21, Osnabrücker Str., b/ Prof Geballe,
Berlin–Wilmersdorf, Allemagne

c/o Fondaminsky, 130, av. de Versailles
[Paris]

Thank you, my adorable life, for your little birthday greetings and for '*Mercury*' (by the way, did you read a charming little piece about Wagner in *Lit. Digest*?). This is how I'm spending my birthday: lunch at the Tatarinovs, then–sun, then I am going to see Sylvia Beach, then to *Candide* with Doussia, then to Léon, and if there's time, to Dobuzhinsky, who is painting my portrait, and in the evening I'll have to go to a reading by Ladinsky. I'm waiting for news from London, but only a draught of cold silence comes from there–I am afraid my little book is *anything but a best-seller*. Maybe reviews are out already, but I'm not buying English newspapers.

My love, regarding Favière: the die is cast, the house is rented (on the condition that if we don't like it there, the agreement will be annulled).

Voilà. It's surrounded by a vineyard and stands apart from the other cottages; from the south, a path goes down to the beach (5 minutes); from the north, there are hills and a pine forest. She is giving us bed linen, a <u>tub</u> (she says it's new), all the necessary dishes. The keys are with the farmer's wife next door, who will do our laundry (besides, she will

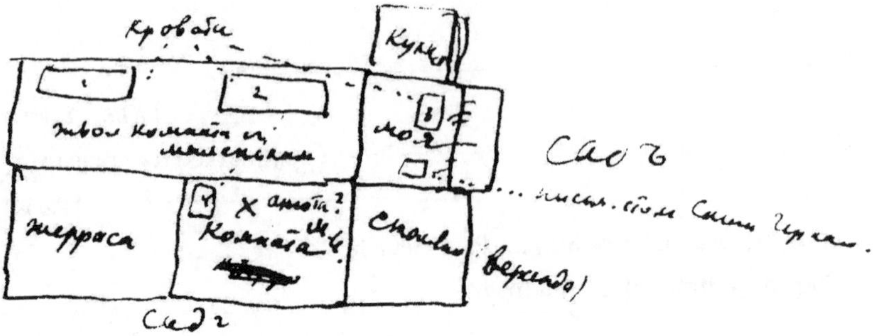

wash the sheets under Maria Ivanovna's name; she charges her half-price). The mattresses are new, especially for us. A butcher delivers meat twice a week, leaving it at the farmer's (Mme Angèle Montanard). We will probably be able to hire a girl from her as well to do the cleaning – although it will be very easy to clean there, a stone floor covered with straw mats. Everything is seaside-fresh from the sun and the sand. In general the house looks nice and clean. All groceries come from the Grudinsky's *épicerie*, on the beach. So: we can move in immediately (on May 8), but maybe, so that we don't have to worry about cooking for at least a week, in the first few days we can eat our meals at the pension of Elena Iv. Golde nearby, it's nice and cheap there. There is no electricity, but it does not get dark there (in May already) earlier than half past nine, we will go to bed early and get up early, as everyone does there. There is a large kerosene lantern on the terrace and several kerosene lamps in the house. On the corner verandah (the dining-room), there's a tap and as much water as we want. In the kitchen, we will have an oven, a primus and a spirit stove (in general, the absence of gas will be our only discomfort). For four months (i.e.

from May 8 to September 15), she is charging one thousand six hundred francs (which we can pay when and how we please); on the condition, though, that in July, she will come for two months and settle in the room marked with an X (*she is a very good soul*, adores children – and, all in all, we will only be more comfortable with her there). So now: we need to set aside another seven hundred francs' living expenses a month – according to her ample estimate, plus fifty more for wood and kerosene, so that *tout compris*, a month would cost us 1350–1400 fr. (at least half of which Victor will earn). A train leaves from here at half past nine in the evening and reaches Toulon at half past eight. An autocar takes us to Lavandou, and from there it's a quarter of an hour by taxi (25 fr. with luggage).

(No, here's how it's arranged: we hire a stove and a tank of gas ('*Buta-Gaz*' –absolutely harmless, by the way, since even if it leaks, it spreads over the ground in a thin layer). This costs 25 fr. a month; they bring it up from the city and set it up – so there'll be neither wood nor fuss.) My love, my dear – and already almost flesh-and-blood – love! Yes, on the 6th or the 7th I'll be here already – and if you think that it's less tiring for you to go through Paris, then let's meet here – but I still think it would be better for you to go straight to Toulon. By the way, I'll find out and write to you about the departure times of trains from Berlin, and the prices. Today's letter is strictly business, and I'm in a rush to send it. Remember that I won't tolerate any more changes, that the little house is rented, and that it's nice and cheap. You can't get cheaper anywhere, while the climate there is wonderful *and the little one will paddle to his heart's content*. I will write to Anyuta tomorrow. Won't she come with us? I kiss you without end, my happiness. I've bought you a wonderful lipstick.

V.

[APCS]
[postmarked 26 April 1937]

TO: 21, Osnabrücker Str., b/ Prof Geballe,
Berlin–Wilmersdorf, Allemagne

c/o Fondaminsky, 130, av. de Versailles
[Paris]

My dear love, the pictures are wonderful! *Thanks, my dear love.* I am sitting in our corner café, in the sun, and it drives me crazy and tortures me that you're not seeing with me that smiling linden tree, the shining of hobnails on passers-by, the ruby of my Dubonnet. Instead of a final decision, I received from Gleb today a foolish limp postcard informing me that he does not have two spare pounds to rent a hall; and Victor is simply afraid to send them to him, since he'll squander them. Alluding to the fact that not a single review of *Despair* has appeared yet, Struve hedges, ponders and proposes that I concentrate on Sablin, as a consequence of which I flew into such a rage that I almost sent him a letter to match. On the other hand, I have still not received an answer from Sablin–he must be fasting. My project of going there earlier, on the 28th, to reach a deal with the *Liberal Club*, has apparently fallen through utterly. I'll wait three more days and if there's nothing new, I will ask you to leave immediately, my happiness, so that by the first we could be in Favière. I'll write you about the trains. I am writing to Gleb today, to try seriously to organize at least the Russian evening, after getting in touch with Sabl., and on top of that an English evening in a private house, without renting any halls. *I feel quite miserable.* Most importantly, if England doesn't work out now, there'd be no need to postpone your visit so. I will talk to Mme Sablin again tomorrow. It seems to me that I can still make every effort so this trip to London happens.

I spent a very pleasant evening with Jules Superv. I was at Fayard, collected copies of '*Course*' and offered them '*Despair*' to translate. Jean was charming and promised me a quick reply. I have finished 'Fialta' with Roche – it's turned out magnificently. Dobuzhinsky has done my portrait – a good likeness, I think. I saw Lyusya, Sylvia, Ridel, Ergaz. My excerpt is in the Easter issue, and I have the right to give them three in May, since this month there was only one. My heart simply pounds when I think about our meeting. You. To you. With you. And I kiss my little boy, – and greetings to Anyuta.

My pen's gone on strike.

V.

[APCS]
[postmarked 26 April 1937]

TO: 21, Osnabrücker Str., b/ Prof Geballe,
Berlin–Wilmersdorf, Allemagne

c/o Fondaminsky, 130, av. de Versailles
[Paris]

My love, I had no need to send you that panicky postcard yesterday. Everything's sorting itself out. I have just received a very nice letter from Sablin, with the evening fixed on May 5, so that I could return as early as the 6th. Even if Gleb does not organize the English evening (on May 3), it's worth going anyway. I have sent them a list of addresses and written to all my friends in London. I will leave on the 30th or the 2nd. At Haskell's, I will have to live in the sitting room. All's well. I'm happy today, because I'll see you in less than two weeks, my love. And him. I wrote about Anna Nat. only because she suggested this to me herself, some time ago. If you still want to go through Paris, then by the 6th or 7th I'll try to find a room for you. *I want to get sea-and-sun things for you*, but I don't know your size etc.—that tortures me! Tonight there's an evening in memory of Zamyatin (I will read his 'Cave' in French there) at a private house—at the lady's to whom Gumilyov's 'Blue Star' is dedicated. What Lyusya has, remains untouched. I love you. Miracles of economizing. Only on correspondence do I spend a lot. They say I've grown fatter and tanned. How I dream of you getting some rest. Everyone praises it a lot—our little cottage. *I kiss you.*

Poor, poor Clem Sohn—Zyoka saw how he fell. *Ses ailes, ses pauvres ailes* . . .

V.

My dear Anyutochka,

I'm sad that you are not feeling well (even Anna Maks. wrote about this) and that there's so much fuss and discomfort. I am also upset that I don't know (and no one knows) your plans. I discussed in detail the question of the little cottage with Lyusya and then rented it. Will you come to France with Véra? How many stories I have for you! I hug you, be well, I've missed you a lot.

V.

[APCS]

[postmarked 27 April 1937]

TO: 21, Osnabrücker Str., b/ Prof Geballe,
Berlin–Wilmersdorf, Allemagne

c/o Fondaminsky, 130, av. de Versailles
[Paris]

My love, fine, I agree. I don't have the strength to continue this long-distance chess game—I give up. Your health, the meeting with Mother, and—why not admit it—the possibility of calmly composing 'The

Gift'—that's what I'm transferring to the forefront of my consciousness. But I feel madly sorry about Favière (I agreed with Mme Chorny to give her a final answer in writing, so it's not a problem). So now: fearing new re-decisions *de ta part*, I won't risk writing Mother today about the visa for me (I was at the Czech Consulate, and there they won't give me a visa without this, i.e. this takes 3 weeks). Therefore—if going to Czechoslovakia is decided on—immediately, right now (otherwise I won't get it before the 7th), write to tell her to go to the Ministry and to get them to send me the visa here. (Since we will soon have the *permis permanent* here, there's no need to worry about the passport—although, actually, it will probably have to be sent to Maklakov from Czechoslovakia). And you should leave without delay. *I am furious with you, but I love you very dearly.*

V.

I don't understand why we cannot live at Mme Chorny's, taking our meals at the pension nearby. I continue to think that this is the only sensible thing. This way there's no need for any special housekeeping. It's absurd to leave France when everything's going along so smoothly; this way I'll be forgotten here again and it'll all have to start afresh. For God's sake, think again. We will work out the housekeeping, I promise you. But do as you wish.

I won't bother about any other French resorts.

[APCS]
[postmarked 29 April 1937]

TO: 21, Osnabrücker Str., b/ Prof Geballe,
Berlin–Wilmersdorf, Allemagne

c/o Fondaminsky, 130, av. de Versailles
[Paris]

My love, my English trip has fallen through completely. Instead of an answer, Struve prattles limply about the English evening, while (after his definite invitation) Sablin changed his mind and informs me through his wife that it is risky to go: Easter and the coronation. I can't tell you what a state of irritation all these negotiations have driven me to. Damn. After all, this idiot has been giving me–and himself–the run-around for a month and a half. I'd never have thought about this second trip to London, had he not organized the first one so well. In fact then he did it for nothing, while now I offered him a share in the profits. Damn. I am curious what will happen next, that is, how long you will take to decide where to go and, in the case of your final and irrevocable (otherwise it would be criminal to agitate Mother again) decision to go to Czechoslovakia, how long I'll have to wait here for the Czech visa.

Tomorrow I will write you at more length–I am too worked up today and I'll calm down only when you (tonight, I hope) write that you are getting ready to go.

Still, I adore you, my sweet darling. I hug my little one.

V.

[ALS, 2 PP.]
[postmarked 1 May 1937]

TO: 21, Osnabrücker Str., b/ Prof Geballe,
Berlin–Wilmersdorf

c/o Fondaminsky, 130, av. de Versailles
[Paris]

My love and joy, I presume this at last is your final decision and that you really will be on your way the day after tomorrow. I am waiting for the visa and ready to take off. Will see Rodzyanko and Maklakov again about the passport,–but I assure you your worries are completely unnecessary. Before I forget: shall I take with me such things as the dinner jacket or the winter things (Aunt Nina's) for the boy? How about the crowd of books? Five copies of '*Despair*', two of '*Course du Fou*', three of 'Otchayanie'? And how many copies shall I take from Lyusya? Answer all of this.

I am wildly happy at the thought of seeing you–and him–(and Mother) so soon. Remember our dates: the 8th and the 10th. Will I get the visa by then?

The evening in Zamyatin's memory was high-style, crowded, and a little 'off'–as, by the way, Zamyatin himself was 'off'. I read 'The Cave' in French (a perfectly decent translation), while Bunin read in Russian the nastily cheap short story about a Red Army man (you know, he shoots old women, but feels sorry for the little–'itsy-bitsy'–sparrow: such orthodogged vulgarity). What a truly unpleasant gentleman Bunin is. He can more or less tolerate my muse, but he cannot forgive me my 'lady admirers'.

I paid a visit to Mme Ridel: the view from her window is on the Exhibition's grandiosely materializing, clownishly plaster (but illuminated by the disinterested spring sunshine) tastelessness. The Eiffel tower looms, watching over these mercenary and ephemeral constructions, like an old 'procuress over the romps of young whores'. And I, my happiness, have lately had a poem wandering in my head, but I cannot finish anything:

The blackness of the seductive Seine,
precious tears of lights;
leaves of lindens and green veins
in the theatrical silence of the streetlamps.

At the cinema, I saw the terrible, piercing fall of the 'bird-man' – and another reverberation for a long time gave me no peace.

Clem Sohn, Clem Sohn, how was the night before?
What did you dream in your hotel?
. . . London tomorrow, and Amsterdam in June . . .
Did you not count on this, Clem Sohn?

Besides this, a short story is revolving. Generally, I've been coming alive in this respect lately. The second chapter of 'The Gift' is thought through, down to the commas.

Ilyusha goes to church fervently (and for 57 days already – Vladimir Mikhaylovich marks every day on the calendar – has not taken a bath). He is offended (and horrified) at me, as at an atheist. I said I wouldn't go to the morning service if only because when I enter a church all the candles go out. Vera Nikolaevna doesn't call me anything else but 'the infidel'. *Tout ça est très rigolo.*

I continue to get letters from England, dissuading me from going there. Bourne sent me the form for the American *copyright*. I'll fill it out and send it back; you have to include 2 dollars. He has also sent me excerpts from seven reviews. '*Outstanding quality*.' '*Undoubted distinction*.' But one journal wrote that this novel ranks me among '*the small number of world humorists!*' This may be the truest thing ever written about me.

I am going to listen solo to the reading of the old man's memoirs, part two. He has already read one chapter from this second part to me once. All this time I have been haunting the thresholds of editors (*Candide, Revue de Paris, Nouv. Lit.*) – I'd like something at least to become clear before my departure. Shall I buy a butterfly net?

I love you. Yes of course, let's go to France after Czechoslovakia. Oh, my joy, I am afraid that your resort will be costly, rainy, and that we will regret the demise of Favière ... My darling, my darling! How much longer – a week? 10 days?

V.

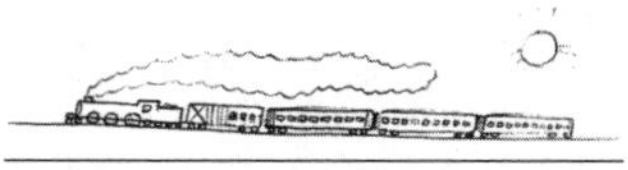

[APCS]
[postmarked 3 May 1937]

TO: 21, Osnabrücker Str., b/ Prof Geballe,
Berlin – Wilmersdorf, Allemagne

c/o Fondaminsky, 130, av. de Versailles
[Paris]

My darling, I have not received anything from you for days. Where are you? What's going on? According to my count, you've already left. In my next letter, I'll tell you in detail about the passport. It's very painful not to know even approximately when I'll get my visa. *I love you, my dearest.* You know, my excerpt (the journey through China) has had an absolutely 'exceptional success'. But then the vulgar cretin Pilsky has taken offence at my 'Gift' in a long-winded article, saying that 'he understood nothing in it' and 'cannot imagine who might understand'. The article in general is a pearl of stupidity. I am preparing a new masked little excerpt – the story featuring Pushkin. I have been eating an endless number of various paskhas – at Ilyusha's, the Tatarinovs', the Kokoshkins', the Rudnevs', the Vishnyaks', and so on. Once again the idea of the *tub* resurfaces. We should buy one, shouldn't we? Chestnuts are blooming – a whole illumination of flowers, – the lilacs are in bloom, too, a warm spell, mosquitoes, I've been going around coatless for ages. I would like to bring little pyjamas for you – I beg you, tell me your size! I have an insane longing to write and am insanely sick of living without you, without him. Write sooner! Do you know that people lose a lot of weight from mud baths and that after them one needs to 'regain weight' *ailleurs*? I kiss you, my darling …

V.

[ALS, 2 PP.]

[postmarked 5 May 1937]

TO: 21, Osnabrücker Str., b/ Prof Geballe,
Berlin – Wilmersdorf, Allemagne

c/o Fondaminsky, 130, av. de Versailles
[Paris]

My love, my sweet love, I note that in your last (*otherwise, delightful*) letter there is not a word about your departure.

About the passport: of course I am applying for the *permis* for both you and me (Rodzyanko, by the way, remembers Evsey Laz. well. He is a heavy man with broad shoulders, a beard, and black eyes, – he's Mar. Pavlovna's nephew). I am very worried that I haven't yet received the permit (which entitles me straight away to a 'French' passport), since I submitted the application back in February, and in March, I learned that the matter was in hand and proceeding well. Today, Rodzyanko went to the Sûreté over this, and tomorrow I'll have to talk to him about it again. Had we gone to Favière, as we were supposed to, i.e. had we resided in France, everything would have been very simple in general–we would have quietly waited for the *permis*. But if I don't get it before my departure, I'll need to send the passports back here from Czechoslovakia. On Friday, I will proceed to the Czech consulate (they tell me it's no big deal if the visa is two or three days past the deadline). I am insanely worried at not knowing where you are going, nor when, nor where nor when I should go (as you see, the 'nors' here are carrying a double load). Is it really possible we won't be together, not on the 8th, nor on the 10th? *Please hurry up, my love! I've had quite, quite enough of this separation*. Not a word from Mother–which also worries me greatly. I can see your meeting with Lena very clearly.

Tonight, I will dictate to Raisa at the typewriter '*Printemps à F.*' which Denis Roche has copied very diligently and illegibly, like an old Frenchman, by hand. To Gleb I wrote this, by the way: 'I am sincerely grateful to you for your energetic and far-sighted help.' The fool, I am afraid, won't be offended. My 'Gift' is reverberating. Rudnev created a little scene because I'd placed an excerpt without his permission. Will I manage to submit the second chapter to him by July 1? It all depends on when I can get out of here (since here I am absolutely unable to work, although I have heaps of ideas–and today too I will try to at least start a story I've thought up). Tomorrow I am meeting with Lyusya–who, as is his custom, will ask me questions whose answers he knows better than I do. Once he called me, asking if I couldn't meet him immediately, to lend him a hundred francs, which an acquaintance was asking him for, and then, a quarter of an hour later, he called again, to cancel–I did not really get what it was all about. *Some subtle move, I presume*. Fine, I won't buy the net, but the *tub*–definitely, right? I get breathless with happiness when I think I'll see you and my little one. I kiss my little one. I take my little one in my arms. My little one! My little darling! Three and a half centuries have gone by since I took him for a walk – down streets which I'll never in my life see again.

Demidov, that bearded maggot, is coldly polite with me, – but P. N. has somewhat 'got over' my last contribution – he had considered my Chernysh a personal insult, since he himself is working on that era now. (The telephone rang just now. Ivan. 'Although you, my dear man, have copied it all from somewhere – great work!') I see Zyoka very seldom. He is sour and somewhat lost. I took the little silver vase from Raisa. Handed the yellow shoes in to be repaired – they were gaping. I love you, my life.

V.

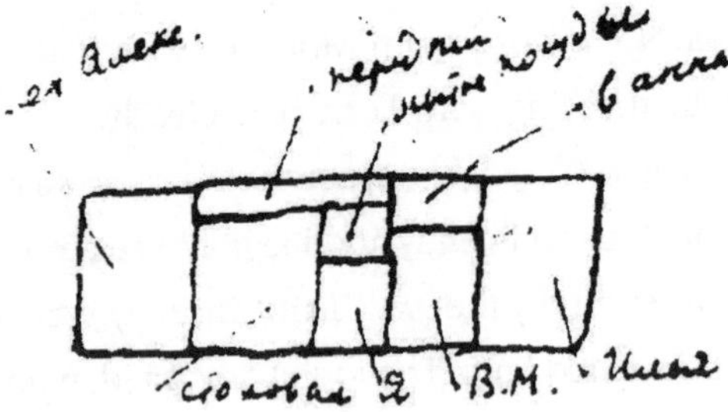

[APC]

[7 May 1937]

TO: 8, Koulova, Dejvici-Praha, Tchékoslovaquie

c/o Fondaminsky, 130, av. de Versailles

[Paris]

My darling, there is torture by water, but there's also torture by public office: after horrendous wanderings through one I have finally received a *carte d'identité*, by means of which I've also immediately acquired the French *aller et retour* visa (so that they will definitely give me the Czech visa now). However, as I should have expected, the Russian office made a mistake: the card is valid only for me [i.e. for you it is ready as well, but you must come in person to claim it] (and with it, I can immediately obtain a French Nansen passport). You will have either to—anyway, I'll write about this again—in any case, there is nothing for you to worry about (on Monday, I'll talk about this again to one special little man). If, however, we intend in general to move to France before July 7, then it's all utterly simple: a few days before expiration, they'll stamp yours with a French visa. We can also easily obtain Czech residence, as a springboard. I am insanely worried about how your trip went. My God, my happiness, how glad I am that you've got out! I received a very sweet letter from Anyuta and have sent you 500 cr. today.

For three days I have had an awful (awful) toothache. I had to go to the dentist to kill the nerve. I plan to leave for Prague on Wednesday or on Thursday. I'm waiting for a letter from you! Tomorrow is the eighth—and we're apart. Quick—I can't wait any longer! Will try the Czech consulate on Monday. How was the trip for my little one? *I am tremendously happy you are in Prague.* How do you find Mother? I kiss her. Till very soon, *my own darling* . . .

[ALS, 2 PP.]
[postmarked 10 May 1937]

TO: 8, Koulova, Dejvici-Praha, Tchékoslovaquie

c/o Fondaminsky, 130, av. de Versailles
[Paris]

My dear happiness, I was so worried, your little card arrived only today. I want details, how was the trip for my little three-year-old, how was his meeting with Mother, did he recognize her from the portrait . . . I don't even know where you are staying. How long, really, will it take to send me the visa? I would like to leave on Thursday. I am afraid that you'll get agitated about your passport, but I hope that through the *bonhomme* I'll see tomorrow, we will be able to sort that out somehow. In any event it's good that I have managed to obtain my *permis*. And in any case you should find out about Czech residency. Or are we coming back here before 7-VII?

I have simultaneously received news from Gallimard that they are reading '*Despair*' and very gratifying news from Albin Michel (through Doussia): their readers have given brilliant reports, so the chances are that Albin will take the book. Perhaps by writing that I have bumped luck's elbow and everything's already spilled. We'll see.

Endless fuss with 'Fialta': not only has Roche copied it out again very unclearly but he's also made new mistakes. I will hand the thing over only on Tuesday. This re-copying plus the prefecture plus a very nasty toothache, which even today (the nerve's battle with the arsenic) wakes up every now and then, stretching and shaking itself–have somewhat exhausted me. But most important I want to come to you as soon as I can, my love ... I'm so pleased that we have finally done with Germany. Never, never, never will I return there. Damn them, those foul scum. Never.

I am 'paying' farewell visits. Had dinner with the Bunins. What a boor he is! ('How can one not love you,'–Ilyusha says to me,–'if you spread it around everywhere that you are the best Russian writer.' I: 'What do you mean, how do I spread it around?!' 'How?–You write!') On the other hand Vera Nikolaevna, although a bit doltish and still craving for young love ('He is sometimes so rough with me–Lyonya,' she said to me with some foul wombish pleasure about Zurov), is always very kindly and has done me lots of the sweetest favours. But Ivan speaks with her like some boorish tyrant in a poddyovka, bellowing and nastily mocking her intonations–horrid, pathetic, bags under his eyes, tortoise neck, always a bit tiddly. But Ilyusha is mistaken: it's not my writing he's jealous of, but rather the 'success with women' that the gutter gossip attributes to me.

I've just been to Rashel's. Now it's after midnight. I'm utterly tired.

My sweet love, how I love your handwriting, that running shadow of your voice ... Tomorrow I'm expecting a long letter. I cuddle other people's children, – Ira B.'s very sweet baby, Mme Roshchin's lovely girl (he, Roshchin, is very nice – walked me to the dentist yesterday).

I saw Lyusya who totally wore me out with his talk about the *carte d'identité*. As far as I understand, in two months from now the furniture can head for Paris. Is that right?

If you only knew how much I want to write 'The Gift'. Lots and lots of kisses, my love. I'm tired, my pen is going blind and stumbling. Yesterday I looked in vain for a postcard with a train for the boy. In one of the shops the clerk said to me: 'I don't have any with trains, *mais si vous en voulez avec de jolies filles . . .*'. There are such red chestnut trees in bloom here!

V.

TELEGRAM
[10 May 1937]
[Paris]

NABOKOFF 8 KOULOVA DEJVICE PRAHA
MY LOVE TO THE LITTLE MAN +++++

[ALS, 2 PP.]
[postmarked 12 May 1937]

TO: 8, Koulova, Dejvici-Praha, Tchécoslovakei

c/o Fondaminsky, 130, av. de Versailles
[Paris]

My love, my visa has turned into a monstrous nightmare. I did not write that it was being issued – quite the opposite, I begged and am begging you to press them more energetically in Prague. No matter how much I pleaded with the Czech consul—I was there three times in all—they are not giving me the visa 1) without the request, which takes about two weeks 2) without permission, again from Prague, for the visa to be issued, in spite of the fact that my passport is valid for less than another two months. Just in case, I have put in an application to Prague (to the Min. of Int. Affairs), but it is definitely necessary to put pressure on them there—and, most importantly, explain about the expiration. I am attaching a note here, explaining where exactly to go and under which number. All of this is absolutely horrible. The main thing that worries me now is Franzen[s]bad. Darling, my love, I cannot stick around here any longer, this is becoming a torture chamber—this separation—and I want you to rest instead of becoming so upset. You can't really go to Fran-bad without me, on your own with the boy, that won't be a rest, but for you to continue living in Prague will probably be exhausting, too, as well as expensive. *I have set my heart on going to Prague and Fran-bad*—and now cannot and do not want to give it up. Please, do everything that you can in terms of putting pressure on in Prague, while I, for my part, will try all the same to get a Fren. Nans. pass., which cannot be issued before this vile one expires. *I cannot tell [you] how utterly miserable I am and how I long to see you*, my life. Only don't do anything silly and do not leave for France till there's absolute assurance that no power in the world can get me a Czech visa. I am sending you 500 more fr.—*I adore you*, all of this is so senseless and so painful as if fate *prend plaisir* in torturing us. My dear darling, my priceless, my sunshine, I beg you try to arrange for my visit!

Add to my condition my daily trips to the dentist. *Well, well, this hell must end soon, I suppose*. Write me sooner, my love.

V.

Kisses to Mother.

Tomorrow at the German consulate, I will try again to get an extension of my passport. If permission comes from Prague, it would be helpful for you to telegraph it here.

[APCS]

[postmarked 13 May 1937]

TO: 8, Koulova, Dejvici-Praha, Tchékoslovaquie

c/o Fondaminsky, 130, av. de Versailles

[Paris]

My darling, today I thrust my way to the Germans, but the only thing they could suggest was for me to travel to Czechoslovakia through Berlin and to extend my passport there—nonsense, of course. Tomorrow I am going, through Maklakov, to a French office for the immediate issue of a French Nans. passport. I'm waiting for news from you about the Czech visa. (I'm writing from a restaurant—for some reason, people are gradually ceasing to invite me, which will set me back 10 francs or so today). I seem never in my life to have been in such a state of irritation, despondency and agonizing indecisiveness. If it turns out that I cannot immediately get the French pass. and if, from the other side, they cannot send me my visa from Prague—without that idiotic reserve of 60 days—then I will ask you to come here. I have asked Lyusya for advice—he advises me to try again. *Cela devient ridicule*—our separation. I think my little boy won't recognize me now. As for you, I see you clearly only in my dreams, my love.

Tomorrow my tooth will be filled—and if there is time, I'll have to have two roots pulled out—my gum's swollen and rotting. Tonight, I'll be at Kalashnikov's, I met him in the métro. I can't tell you how passionately I want to come to Czechoslovakia. I sent you 750 crowns yesterday. My happiness . . .

V.

Kisses to Mother!

[ALS, 1 P.]
[postmarked 14 May 1937]

TO: 8, Koulova, Dejvici-Praha, Tchekoslovaquie
c/o Fondaminsky, 130, av. de Versailles
[Paris]

My darling, no need to write me these angry letters. I'm doing all I can to get out of here—but you too have to understand that without the permission from Prague, the Czechs won't give me any visa (not a resort one, nor the other kind). Maklakov has written to the local Czech big-shot asking if they can give me a visa anyway, but I won't get it all the same till Monday. *Je ne fais qu'* haunt the thresholds of bureaucratic offices, since I need 1) either the Czechs to give me a visa in spite of the insufficient expiration date—closing in every day—of my German passport (for I was issued the French *aller et retour* only within that date limit) 2) or to be issued the French Nans. passport—for which I will be at the *Sûreté* today. I implore you to remain patient for a few more days—and not to do anything foolish, like return to Berlin. If you go anywhere, then here, of course. But I am sure—at least they promised me this—that early next week I will, finally, get to Prague. Your letters only intensify my suffering. I am unbearably, in any case, worried by your plight—especially since you, evidently, are not going to Franzen[s]bad—and how could you go alone anyway. Our letters are turning into some kind of bureaucratic reports, full of red tape, but I adore you and am going crazy myself from this delay. Please do not write me that way, my love, my happiness.

V.

[ALS, 2 PP.]
[15 May 1937]

TO: 8, Koulova, Dejvici-Praha, Tchékoslovaquie

c/o Fondaminsky, 130, av. de Versailles
[Paris]

My priceless happiness – which, it now seems, I will finally be able to reach. The telegram arrived yesterday *avec une allure de* swallow. This morning at ten, I was already (they close earlier on Saturday) at the Czech consulate. It turned out that the visa hadn't yet arrived, although it had been sent. When it was sent, was there a note made about the insufficient duration of my passport? – since it was sent in response not to my special request on that account but to Mother's previous efforts? Or was it noted anyway? I asked them to note this specially and sent the file number. From the consulate, I rushed to the Czech *Legation* with a letter to the ambassador from Makl., which he had been writing for four days (!), but he also happened to be away, so I will see him and go to the consulate only on Tuesday morning – and if I get it, I will leave for Prague on Tuesday itself. I dreamt last night that my little one was walking towards me along the pavement, with dirty cheeks, for some reason, and in a dark little coat; I ask him about myself: 'Who is it?' and he replies: Volodya Nabokov, with a cunning little smile. I am done with my tooth today – a temporary filling for two or three months, but I have no time to pull out the roots. The swelling has eased a little through rinsing with chamomile. My dear darling, I have a very dim sense of your life in

Prague, I feel that you are awfully uncomfortable and uneasy – your comment about the bed-bug told me a great deal. My poor love . . . Yesterday I hung about the *Sûreté* for almost four hours and they promised to arrange the possibility of French passport by . . . Thursday, but, of course, if I get the visa on Tuesday, I won't linger another second here – besides, I do not trust their promises any more. I'm utterly worn out by all this senseless torture – and still more, by the thought of your worrying, your waiting. About the money: Lyusya has 3,100 fr. and 105 pounds. I have taken 1,100 fr. of that to send you, twice (I added from what I had). Besides that I have a silver pound and two hundred francs. I'll probably scrape what's needed for the ticket without touching the fund.

A clever review of 'The Gift' today by Khodasevich. He visited me the other day. Tonight I am going to the Russian Theatre to the first performance of 'Azef'. I have been working all these last days on '*Printemps à F.*', to get it perfect – and I think I have got there, but there were a million corrections and I had to do this three times. I continue to sun myself every day – and have, on the whole, recovered – you know, now I can tell you straight that because of the sufferings – indescribable – that I endured before that treatment, i.e. in February, I'd reached the border of suicide – which they wouldn't let me cross because of you in my luggage. My love, can it really be true that I will see you soon. Four days, if fate doesn't let us down. My dear love, I promise you that you will get a thorough rest and that our life in general will be easier and simpler. I've become still closer friends with Ilya and V. M. – they are wonderfully [sic]. And I cannot tell you how indebted I am to Kogan-Bernstein, whom I would have owed more than 5,000 fr. (!), had she charged me a cent (a session usually costs 100 fr.!) *Try not to worry too much, my love. We shall soon be together, any way*. Tell Mother that I kiss her and am not writing to her only because all of my epistolary strength is spent on you.

V.

TELEGRAM
[postmarked 15 May 1937]
[Paris]

NABOKOFF KOULOVA 8 DEJVICI =
SATURDAY NOT HERE YET TILL TUESDAY CLOSED +++

[APCS]
[postmarked 17 May 1937]
TO: 8, Koulova, Dejvici-Praha, Tchekoslovaquie
c/o Fondaminsky, 130, av. de Versailles
[Paris]

My darling, I have calmed down after your and Mother's postcard yesterday. Tomorrow is Tuesday at last–I am going for the visa as if it were an exam. For two days now I have been sorting my things–I'm overgrown with letters, manuscripts, and books–not to mention my complicated relationships with the laundress. Tonight, at the *Hôtel Meurice*, I have a meeting with Flora Grig., who's already going back to London tomorrow. The performance two days ago was super-bad. My darling, *how wildly happy I am to see you*. I kiss my little one.

V.

My dear Mummy,

If this nightmare tangle at last gets resolved tomorrow, then on Wednesday evening or Thursday morning I'll be with you. I simply can't believe I will see you so soon after all these years. Isn't he a fine little boy? I embrace you and E. K. and Rostik. Love you.

V.

TELEGRAM

[postmarked 18 May 1937]

[Paris]

NABOKOFF DEJVICI KOULOVA 8
= *VIZA OBTAINED STARTING WEDNESDAY* [E]*VENING* +++

[APCS]

[postmarked 19 May 1937]

TO: 8, Koulova, Dejvici-Praha, Tchekoslovaquie

c/o Fondaminsky, 130, av. de Versailles

[Paris]

My love, I will leave on Thursday at 10 p.m. and (via Switzerland and Austria) reach Prague on Saturday (!) at 6.20 (!!) a.m. It is impossible for me to travel otherwise—for reasons I'll explain to you later. How happy I am, my darling! Yesterday I darted between the ambassador and the consul—they tormented me till the very last minute—and today, between the Swiss consulate and the Austrian. Then Lyusya tormented me. I would have left tonight, but it wouldn't work. I had a very pleasant meeting with Flora. She offers 20 f. a month for six months, starting any time. (I am writing in a cheap, noisily cramped restaurant, very uncomfortable.) Still heaps of little errands. *I love you, I am happy, everything is all right*. Ida's husband just died in an automobile *crash*. Love you, my angel.

V.

The din, the miserable waiter sweating hailstones, the munching Frenchmen. And tomorrow the journey to you, to my little one, to Mother. Poor Aldanov is going round everyone and asking whether

Khodasevich's review is insulting to him. I'm leaving the dinner jacket at the Tatar. I've thought up a wonderful story.

[ALS, 2 PP.]
[postmarked 21 June 1937]

TO: Villa Busch, Marienbad

8, Koulova, Dejvice
[Prague]
Monday

My darling, I would've written earlier, but I didn't know where to, and was afraid that if I sent it to *Egerländer*, then the letter would boomerang back here. I was at Cook's, was (just now) at the Italian consulate. The best route, according to Cook's advice, is this: from Prague the 7.15 direct via Linz to Venice (5.35 the next morning), changing trains there and arriving in Nice at 8.23 p.m. Or we can do it this way: from Prague at 10.40 p.m., Venice at 10.15 p.m., Nice at 3.46 p.m. (i.e. two nights on the road). Both cost 840 cr. in second class and 550 in third. In my opinion, the first of these routes is in any case more convenient than yours, with an overnight in Vienna. Therefore I would suggest that you, my darling, come back here (on Thursday?), spend the night near the station, and set out in the morning (by the way, I have stupidly given my return ticket to the ticket collector in Prague). But here's the riddle: the transit visa (they almost stamped it on mine, but I decided to take the time to find out what you think) costs 188 crowns for both of us (i.e. the same amount as the entry visa). I will find out how much the Swiss one costs (we will have to pay for the Austrian visa anyway, no matter how much it is), and if it's the same, we would have to *s'exécuter*, although that would be abominably expensive – 188. On the other hand, if the Swiss visa is really cheap (in Paris, it cost me nothing), then it would be better for us to go through Paris–what do you think? Thiébaut, evidently, is an idiot; I would like to withdraw 'Fialta' from him as soon as I can and pass it straight on to Paulhan for *N. R. F.* or *Mesures*. Otherwise I will either have to send another copy from here (I have only three altogether), or write to Denis asking him to call in on *Rev. de Paris*, pick it up and pass it on to Paulhan (whom, unfortunately, he pestered with his own products, so of course this is risky, in view of Paulhan's fickleness). Maybe you are right about Doussia, I don't know ... but in any case I should fix this up too in person. I would give '*Musique*' to *Rev. de Paris*, if it turns out that *Rev. de France* hasn't taken it. How many days do you want to spend in Marienbad? Will you rest there? Shall I come to you? Won't it turn out too expensive? By the way, I've sat down to a short story, will finish it in three days (for Ilyusha, whom I'm writing to). The letter to Altagracia sailed off on the 'Hamburg'.

Because of a track repair, my train was an hour and a half late; so it was already eight when I got to the auditorium, without changing. You can imagine how worried Mother was! It was full. I read 'Fialta' and 'The Leonardo'. Then they treated me to beer.

I'm going to the dentist today. He still walks all over my soul as if it was his own bed, my darling, my little bunny. Such shiver and adoration ... *And I can[']t tell you how sorry I am that you were so miserable, my poor, sweet darling.* I love and kiss you and him. Write to me sooner whether I should get an Italian visa, and I'll let you know tomorrow how much the Swiss costs. Greetings to Anyutochka. Mother was very touched by the cigarettes, she thanks and kisses her ... The shoes fit the fat, rude, mad Olga well, although she hinted all the time that her foot was much smaller than yours. The gloves were right for Mother. How's your liver? I have acquired Kipling and Fargue for you. My darling ...

V.

[APCS]
[postmarked 22 June 1937]

TO: Villa Busch, Marienbad

[Prague]

My darling, a Swiss visa costs nothing (I did not get one all the same, to be cautious, fearing that otherwise the Italians won't stamp theirs), so you should decide now. I have 240 crowns in my pocket. I still need to pay Rubchik (or whatever his name is) 80 crowns and give the rest to Mother (I've given her 100). I've spent a lot on trifles, and the taxi cabs that crazy night cost heaps. And I still do not know how much an Austrian visa costs. Decide as soon as you can 1) what visa to get 2) whether I should go on Thursday (or even tomorrow) to Marienbad or wait for you here. I think that tonight, if you send yours express, I will receive a reply to my letter of yesterday and will know what to do. Will we have enough money for everything? I received a letter from Doussia today: *vous me voyez navrée*, but I have already sent your *contrat* to Franzen[s]bad (they have not forwarded it to me yet). If I sign it, '*je porterai les 2,000 fr à M'Feigin*'. She adds that before the book's published she will try to place the translation 'à la revue dirigée par Barbey'. So. I can't wait to see you and decide how, from where, and when we will travel. How much will a stopover in Vienna cost us? I can get all the visas in one hour. I kiss you, *my dear darling. And him*.

V.

1939

[ALS, 2 PP.]

[3 April 1939]

TO: Hotel Royal Versailles, 31, r. Le Marois, Paris XVI

5, Brechin Place, S.W. 7

[London]

3–IV–39

10 a.m.

My darling,

First of all, I adore you; secondly, I have had the pleasantest of journeys, although the sea was terrible, I couldn't stand on my feet, one little old lady was almost hurled overboard. But then, from Folkestone to London you travel in a magnificent Pullman car – I couldn't believe that this was IIIrd cl.

I have a charming room, the ceiling is painted with butterflies, the Sablins are very sweet – and I think I'll be able to stay here till the end. Konovalov, thinking I'd arrive by six, arranged for some kind of a dinner, I don't know exactly what, he'll have to call me again. I called Harris, talked to his wife Angelika Vasil., made arrangements for Wednesday, but she'll call me again since I asked her earlier. Mme Tsetlin called, she promises me a meeting with an 'influential' person, today at 3 p.m. I could not reach Mollie, but I will try again this morning. I ate almost nothing on the way because of the tossing, so brought a lot of it with me and used it to reinforce my breakfast, which here is 'continental', i.e. the *butler* (a regular Jeeves) serves one tea and toast with marmalade in bed. Braykevich also called; I am having dinner at his place tomorrow. It was pleasant to sink down into a real bathtub. My darling, your speaking eyes seem to be standing before me. Don't forget: 1) to contact Ilyusha about Berdyaev 2) to find out how to transfer money to Mother 3) to send to Priel. I will write to him either today or tomorrow. Jeeves is doing something to my hats, whose looks he wasn't happy with.

In 'Marianne', there are five thoroughly flattering and thoroughly nonsensical lines about '*Méprise*', I'll bring the newspaper, I don't know how to send it, but if I find out, I will. I kiss you, my love. And now I will print in capital letters:

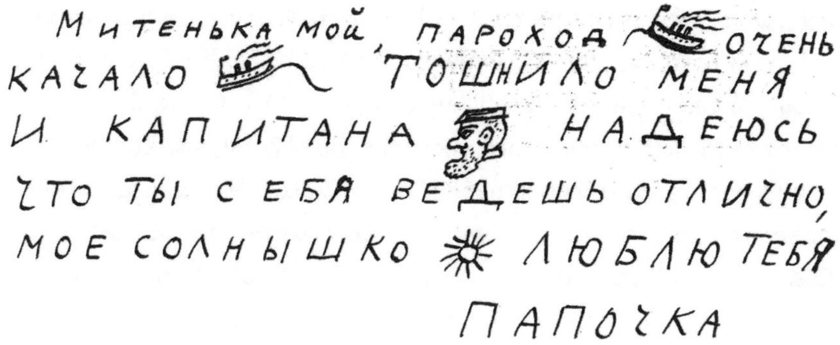
МИТЕНЬКА МОЙ, ПАРОХОД ОЧЕНЬ
КАЧАЛО ТОШНИЛО МЕНЯ
И КАПИТАНА НАДЕЮСЬ
ЧТО ТЫ СЕБЯ ВЕДЕШЬ ОТЛИЧНО,
МОЕ СОЛНЫШКО ЛЮБЛЮ ТЕБЯ
ПАПОЧКА

MY MITEN'KA, THE STEAMBOAT TOSSED A LOT, THE CAPTAIN AND I FELT SICK, I HOPE YOU'RE BEHAVING WELL, MY LITTLE SUNSHINE, LOVE YOU

DADDY

[ALS, 2 PP.]
[4 April 1939]

TO: Hotel Royal Versailles, 31, r. Le Marois, Paris XVI

5, Brechin Place
[London]
4–IV–39
10.30

My darling, my love,

I found the little photograph – it peeked out and smiled.

I was at Mme Tsetlin's yesterday – all three of them are leaving for Paris and have 'granted' me their – charming – apartment. I will move there if I become a burden on the Sablins: so, just in case. M. S., in an awfully sweet manner, made all the arrangements and gave me the key. Here, at the Sablins', it's pleasant and comfortable in the highest degree, so I won't move out unless compelled. With Mme Tsetlin, I went to Mrs Whale: an old intellectual Englishwoman, who once arranged lectures for my uncle, and wrote a book about the '*soul of Russia*', and knows various writers, etc. I'll go to her again on Sunday. At night, I met with the very nice and expansive Konovalov (he looks very much like Tolstoy's Pierre!) in a café, and he gave me lots of information of all kinds – showed me samples of references, applications, programmes – I wrote down a lot – in general he was extraordinarily eager to help. There will be a vacancy not only at Leeds, but also in Sheffield. Besides myself, there are two more candidates, one of them Struve, but K. says that Struve has the wrong information, i.e. he's counting on a larger salary than will in fact be offered, so it makes no sense for him to change London for Leeds. He believes that this will work out for me. At night, I set out the start of a Russian grammar for English speakers. Besides, paying heed to my persistent complaints, he promised to help me to get

1. The Nabokov family at Vyra, their summer estate in the St Petersburg countryside, 1907: the dachshund Trainy; Nabokov's mother, Elena; his sisters Elena and Olga, held by their grandmother Maria Nabokov; his father, Vladimir D. Nabokov; Vladimir, on the knee of his mother's aunt Praskovya Tarnovsky; and his brother Sergey.

2. The five Nabokov children in Yalta, November 1918: Vladimir (b. 1899), Kirill (b. 1910), Olga (b. 1903), Sergey (b. 1900), and Elena (b. 1906). (*See letter of 4 April 1932.*)

3. Vladimir Nabokov and Véra (presumably still Slonim), *c.* 1924, Berlin.

4. (*right*) Vladimir Nabokov and his pupil Aleksandr (Shura) Sack, during their hiking holiday, Constance, 1925.

5. Vladimir Nabokov, Berlin, 1926.

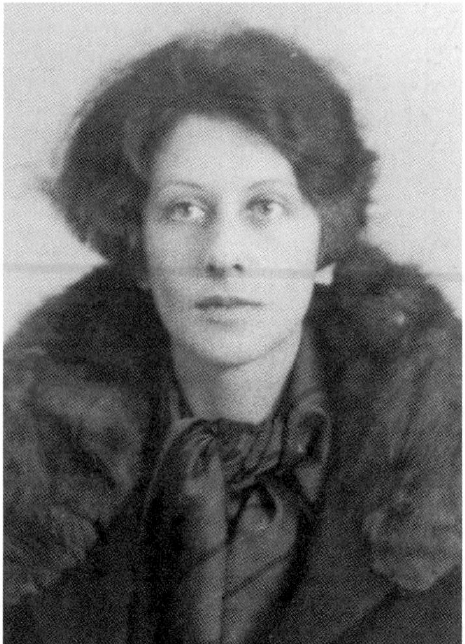

6. Véra Nabokov, Berlin, mid-1920s.

7. (*left*) Yuly Aykhenvald, émigré critic and friend, Berlin, 1920s.

8. (*above*) Ilya (Ilyusha, I. I., Fondik) Fondaminsky, one of the editors and chief financial support of *Sovremennye zapiski* (Paris), the leading literary journal of the Russian emigration, and Nabokov's close friend through the 1930s.

9. Savely (Saba) Kyandzhuntsev, Nicolas Nabokov, Irina Kyandzhuntsev, Vladimir Nabokov, Nathalie Nabokov, Paris, 1932.

10. Novelist, short-story writer and poet Ivan Bunin, the leading older writer of the Russian emigration. (*Foto Centropress Prague, Leeds Russian Archive*)

11. Vladislav Khodasevich, the foremost poet of the Russian emigration, Nabokov's closest literary ally, and a friend from 1932 until his death in 1939. (*Nina Berberova collection*)

12. Vladimir, Véra and Dmitri Nabokov, Berlin, summer 1935.

13. Elena Nabokov, Prague, 1931

14. Irina Guadanini. (*Private collection*)

15. Nabokov with the editorial board of *Mesures*, an offshoot of *La Nouvelle Revue Française*, at the villa of the journal's patron Henry Church, Ville d'Avray, on the outskirts of Paris, 1937. *Left to right*: Henri Michaux, Vladimir Nabokov, Sylvia Beach, Adrienne Monnier, Germaine Paulhan, Michel Leiris, Barbara Church, Jean Paulhan, Henry Church. (*Gisèle Freund*)

16. Vladimir, Véra and Dmitri Nabokov, Cannes, 1937.

17. Vladimir and Véra Nabokov, Wellesley, Massachusetts, summer 1942.

18. Vladimir and Véra Nabokov outside their rented home, 802 East Seneca Street, Ithaca, New York, 1951. There, Nabokov completed his autobiography and began *Lolita*.

19. Vladimir Nabokov dictating from index cards to Véra Nabokov, Montreux Palace Hotel, 1968 (*Time & Life Pictures/Getty Images*)

20. (*right*) Vladimir and Véra Nabokov, lepping (butterfly hunting), near Montreux, c. 1971 (*Horst Tappe*)

21. Vladimir and Véra Nabokov, Montreux, 1968. (*Philippe Halsman*)

subsidies. I will have to apply to Baring and the Duchess of Atholl with a letter signed by influential individuals – professors and so on – whom he'll round up – and to send the same letter to Bakhmeteff in America. In short, all of this is as unsure as writing on water, but water with the azure of reflected possibilities. Today I agreed on meetings with Gleb and the baroness, called Solomon because she asked me to do so (through Mme Tsetlin). Today I had lunch at the Polyakovs, and am meeting Mollie at Charing Cross and having dinner at Braykevich's. Yesterday I called O. Bromberg, didn't get him, left my number, but he did not call. I will try him again now. Jeeves tried to set out clean underpants for me and was surprised when he looked in the closet. I love you, my precious creature, write me, I kiss you.

V.

MY DARLING, HERE RED FAT DOUBLE-DECKER BUSES ARE REFLECTED UPSIDE DOWN IN THE WET ASPHALT. LOVE YOU DADDY

[APCS]
[5 April 1939]

TO: Hotel Royal Versailles, 31, r. Le Marois, Paris XVI

5, Brechin Place
[London]
5–IV–39

My love, it's time I got something from you. What shall I do about sending to Mother – there was another desperate letter from E. K. I have received an excellent *testimonial* from Berdyaev. Yesterday I had lunch at the Polyakovs' – he's the spitting image of Mussolini, there were lots of guests, I struck up a conversation with Lord Tyrrel about Nicholson, with no great success, since they are at fishknives drawn. Later I had tea with Mollie and her very charming husband. She brought me the play, well retyped, but in only one copy … Now I'll phone Rodzyanko. Then I had dinner at the very sweet old Braykeviches'; they have a wonderful collection of paintings, especially a whole seam of Somov, which I could not get my fill of. All of this means huge distances and rain, rain. In the evening, at the Sablins', I ran into Kasim-Bek, Billig and Shuvalov. K. B., a jaunty brunet with almond-shaped eyes, invited me emphatically to their teas in Paris. Now I am going to Budberg, then to Struve, then to Allen Harris, then my reading. I adore, adore you!

V.

MY MITEN'KA, SEND ME A LITTLE DRAWING. I KISS YOU

[ALS, 2 PP.]

[6 April 1939]

TO: Hotel Royal Versailles, 31, rue Le Marois, Paris XVI

5, Brechin Place

[London]

6–IV–39

My love, the evening went very well, I earned more than 20 pounds (there's still more expected to come in), Sablin gave an introductory speech, which ended that 'the crown on his (my) brow is not so much laurels as thorns'. I read 'Lik' and 'Museum'. During the intermission, a tiny shrill woman in a pince-nez approached me and asked: 'I want to know only one thing – did you receive my letter back then?. .'

(Remember–we received it in Menton), and when I confirmed this (with all sorts of additional cordial sounds), she added: 'I do not need anything else'–and stepped away with dignity. A photographer from '*Post (something)*' (a little magazine like '*Match*') took pictures of me, the audience, the paintings on the walls. Eva Lutyens was there, ugly, old, but a shadow of her '*chien*' remained. Bromberg was not there, although I had invited him.

Yesterday morning I visited Budberg–she treated all of my undertakings very crossly and shrewdly, outlined several plans and demanded 'Seb. Knight',–I gave her my second copy–she has an excellent publisher who likes exactly this kind of thing. At four I met Gleb. He explained frankly that if in Leeds they pay him more than in London (i.e. more than 450 pounds), then he will move there. Pares suggested two candidates to them–him and me. If this is so, then the London candidacy, mine, is supported by Pares as well. If the third candidate (the Englishman teaching at Sheffield) gets Leeds, then Sheffield will be free. In other words, it seems to work out that in any combination some position will be mine. I will see Pares in a couple of days. Struve isn't trying to fool me–more likely, Konovalov is. I have learned everything about applications, teaching, the course, and so on. Pares will get in touch with Leeds to set up an *interview* for me there (a procedure required for every candidate), since I am in London now, otherwise I would have had to come over from Paris just for that. At six, I was at the Harrises' *party*, gave him my '*Sebastian*', shined as well as I could–it was very nice and lively.

This morning, I spent two hours in the entomological section of the museum, where the people (whose every line I know from the '*Entomologist*') greeted me as one of them, invited me to work there when and as much as I wish, placed at my disposal all the collections, the whole library (all this is three times bigger and better than at Herring's), and I first of all sorted my Lycaenids out–finding out that my thing (the 'hybrid' race) is completely unknown, although everything is represented there, the 'Coridon' races alone occupy four boxes. Just now I had an elegant lunch at the Sablins' with the Polyakovs and a Chilean lady, Mrs Marshall. Now (it's near four) I must go to S. Rodzyanko's, with my play, and then I dine with Vilenkin.

I have just received your dear, blue letter, my enchantment, my tenderness! I'm writing separately to Miten'ka. I feel excellent. Thank you, darling, for the pyjamas and drawers – that would be wonderful. All *testimonials*, plus applications and the curriculum will be copied here as a separate brochure. I love you, love you, love you very much.

I will write to Anyuta tomorrow.

V.

[ALS, 2 PP.]
[7 April 1939]

TO: Hotel Royal Versailles, 31, r. Le Marois, Paris XVI

[London]
7–IV–39
2 p.m.

My dear love, I got another 10 guineas on top of those 21 pounds, but they're for Mother. Shall I send them to her from here (if possible)? And what is the situation with the transfer from Paris? It seems they expect more profits. There will be an English evening if Gleb does not get demoralized at the last moment. Yesterday I took my play to Rodzyanko, sat with him for a long time (in an enormous studio full of his – absolutely talentless and dead – paintings), we spoke warmly (and it became clear by chance – so typical – that he didn't have the slightest idea about the death of my father). He promised to do what he could, named five or six individuals he could turn to; in a day or two I'll meet his *belle-sœur*. I had dinner at Vilenkin's club,–he is a pathological chatterbox–it took him a solid hour to tell me, from various sides and ends, one and the same story (how in 1926, he got run over by a car), interrupting himself with the phrase '*to cut a long story short*', but since the phrase itself would remind him of this or that 'peculiarity of English life', it would lead him away down a new verbal side street, from where, via a roundabout route, he would return to the centre of the story. After dinner with him and an exceptionally amiable Major Crawford (who had known my father and has read '*Despair*') we went to a Music-Hall, where, by the way, there was a very good sketch involving Guitry. Today is *Good Friday*, everything's empty and quiet. Lee invited me to a soccer game this afternoon, and I'll have dinner at the Grinbergs'. This morning I went for a walk through Kensington Gardens (the museum–i.e. my department–is closed, alas, till Tuesday–it's as near me as Ilyusha is to us); it's strange, but on this trip I recall my past life here better than last time–maybe because I'm now living in the same district, a couple of steps from our former street–I went to look at the house, was looking round and stuck my heel in a greasy dog pile that I couldn't get rid of for a long time. In the park it was damp, an astringent lawny smell, bad-tempered swans were floating between toy sailing boats, and yellow pansies were blooming (more than anywhere else, they looked like little Hitler faces). I had to lunch in a restaurant, because the Sablins had been invited out. My little sunshine, how are you sleeping with my little one? Write me again, soon. I haven't had time to look Priel through to the end, I would have done it this morning, if it weren't for the strict ritual of cleaning the room each morning. Should I call Osya, who not only did not show up, but didn't get around to calling me, either? Lourie has made all the arrangements about the dinner–and, judging by the Sablins' hints, they will collect something for me there as well, i.e. I will probably have to read something there too. I am also reading at Mme Tyrkov's on Wednesday. There should be replies from Budberg and Harris by the middle of next week. I think I'll leave on the 15th—but only if I don't have to travel to Leeds. Not a word, not a whisper from Zina. My darling, I kiss you tenderly, I adore you, don't worry about anything, love you.

MY JOY, I SAW HERE ON THE POND BOYS LAUNCHING A TOY STEAM DREADNOUGHT.

I LOVE YOU. DADDY

[APCS]

[8 April 1939]

TO: Hotel Royal Versailles, 31, rue Le Marois, Paris XVI

5, Brechin Place

[London]

8–IV

My love, thank you for the lovely little letter—and the underpants. I write to you every day, but on Thursday (after the reading) morning I didn't have time, and at 11 a.m. I have to leave already—to let them clean up (I think I—yes, I did—went to the museum), so the letter went off in the afternoon. Today's a quiet day—I had lunch at Haskell's, came back just now (4.30)—she has lovely children—especially the little girl who answers as ours does, 'four and a quarter'. Yesterday I went to a soccer game with Lee, he picked me up in his car (a wonderfully nice man!) and later he drove me to the Grinbergs'. Savely wants very much to help me somehow—he asks me endlessly about my situation and so on. I phoned Struve, wrote to Pares, will be at Struve's on Monday to compose a circular letter (to Baring). I won't go out again today, will work on

Priel. I can't forgive myself for not bringing my butterflies with me – the wooden box. If anyone is coming here – send it to me! If you packed it very softly and wrote: *Très fragile! Very brittle! Papillons! Butterflies!* you could easily mail it, too. *J'essaye de faire mon petit Kardakoff.* It would be a pity to miss out. My cough's gone. My tenderness, my dear happiness, I kiss you.

V.

Denis Roche is right.

[APCS]
[9 April 1939]

TO: Hotel Royal Versailles, 31, rue Le Marois, Paris XVI

5, Brechin Place
[London]
A light grey-blue Sunday
9–IV
10 a.m.

My love, the last three days have been emptyish because of the holiday, but starting tomorrow, the barrel of the week will be loaded again. Today, there will be a fancy lunch for 10 persons at the Sablins'; at 4 p.m., I will be at Mrs Whale's; and at 6.30 p.m. Lourie will call to take me to the 'banquet'. I telephoned Flora in vain, and finally learned that her father has just died. Tell me quickly – shall I write her a few words? I think on Tuesday I'll get answers about *Sebastian* and then will immediately show up at Long's. Vera Markovna offers to introduce me to the publ. Heineman[n] (which is even better than Duckworth), whose *reader* her husband was, so if Harris and Budberg misfire, one of my copies would go to Heineman[n] and the other to Long. That's good – about Holland. According to yesterday's card from E. K., Mother is a tiny bit better – and very comfortable at the hospital – what a pity she didn't move there sooner ... I love you dearly, my precious. I've written to Bunin and will write to Pares.

I KISS MY MITEN'KA

A THOUSAND KISSES.

V.

[ALS, 2 PP.]

[10 April 1939]

TO: Hotel Royal Versailles, 31, r. Le Marois, Paris 16

[London]

10–IV Mon.

10 a.m.

My love and happiness (one more little card – the last one, I think – found in a tuxedo – which I put on for the first time yesterday – I didn't really have to wear it). Now someone's picking me up to go play tennis, with M. Sumarokov, whose legendary left hand I palpated with reverence yesterday at the club. Just think – he played with the immortals: Wilding, McLaughlin, Gobert, not to mention all his contemporaries. He is awfully nice, only 44, the secretary of the English-Russian Club. After the game they will take me to Mme Chernavin, where I'll have lunch, and from there, by 5, to Gleb's house, where I will probably spend the whole evening.

Yesterday we had a very pleasant Easter lunch here. For some reason I got along with the very nice C[ount] Shuvalov (who brought his little boy along – black-eyed and well-built – he is exactly the same age as ours!). Shuvalov (who serves as a decorator at Paramount) promised me a good theatrical agent, with whom I'll leave the play if nothing works out with Rodzyanko. I love you. There was a priest in an ultramarine cassock there, too, and Mme Tyrkov (wicked and whiskered), with whom I had a clear conversation about the possibility of subsidies and so on. I will see her on Wednesday. In the afternoon I visited Mrs Whale, who had already talked about me with Lady McDougall, to whom, we have agreed, I will write today, so I can meet her. She is an ultra-wealthy lady. I returned, found an interminable tea party at the Sablins', and at 7 p.m., Lourie called to pick up Nad. Iv. and me, and we drove to the club. It is a charming villa, with 4 tennis courts and a Russian barman like the Cap d'Antibes cook. Heaps of people were there, several speeches, a drinking song, and so on. Someone recited the poem: 'In the past, Mikhaylo Sumarokov beat everyone on the tennis courts, and now Nabokov beats everyone in prose, plays and poems.' With horror, I saw how I was being approached by a joyful-looking ... Nef, who adopted such a tone that everyone couldn't help thinking we were old friends from Berlin. But he was at the club for the first time (in other words specifically to see me) – while I, for my part, was at first sure that he was a regular there if not a board member, i.e. he pulled it off very well. When, after dinner, we (N. I. and I) went to drink tea at Lourie's, I told him what Nef's 'atmosphere' was; he was extremely shaken up and swore he'd find out how he had actually reached the club, i.e. who had brought him and who knew him. I love you, my tenderness. I have just received a postcard from Regina saying that, in view of 'the mood of the people', the evening in Brussels cannot go on. Shall I stay here longer, say, till the 18th? There are still a thousand things I need to bring to a close. So, my happiness. I must go. *I adore you.*

V.

I LOVE YOU, MY MITEN'KA
WRITE ME

[ALS, 2 PP.]
[11 April 1939]

TO: Hotel Royal Versailles, 31, rue Le Marois, Paris XIV

[London]
11–IV–39
3.30

My darling, my love, I will answer your little questions first: I had a long intimate conversation with Pares about what I wanted in 1937; besides, Mme Chernavin constantly reminded him about me (moreover, I had a correspondence with him about *S. F. Protection*), so he keeps me in mind; I cannot, however, take a *testimonial* from him, because he has already sent it to Leeds himself and it would be impossibly awkward to ask him for a 'proof'. In other words no matter whom he would like to advance on the sly, he has officially cast his vote for me—and I cannot demand anything else from him. Yesterday I tried just to drop in on him—he is a neighbour of the Chernavins, and she advised me to do so, being great friends with him; but it turned out that he had not yet returned from the country (the whole of London leaves for the country over Easter, which explains a certain pause in my activities—then again, the pause is imaginary, for I'm always bothering people, and if I go to the museum, it's only when I can't think up any other business at those times). The university opens tomorrow, so I will in any case see him. He has not yet replied to Gleb's letters (about how it would be good for me to use my presence in England to set up now the notorious *interview* at Leeds), i.e. they have probably not forwarded them to him. This morning I had great fun playing two sets with different couples at the club (I got everything there—white pants, shoes, etc.). Then I had a *double whisky* and was driven by Lourie to Mme Chernavin. She's so charming! She told me, by the way, that she especially responded to certain pages of 'The Gift' because her father was a (famous) botanist-explorer and she twice accompanied him (in the 20s) to the Altai, and so on, and then he disappeared, like mine, she was told in Tomsk that he had perished, but then it turned out he had been taken prisoner by some local rebels. Her husband works at the museum, several corridors away from me. Then I went to Struve's. Three of the children take after their father, very unpretty with thick freckled noses (the eldest girl is very *attractive*, though), but the fourth child, a boy of about ten years, also takes after his father, but a different one: he is absolutely charming, a very sweet appearance, with a haze, Botticellian, – quite lovely! Yulen'ka, chatty and dirty as in the old days, is carried away with Scouts, wears a brown jacket and a wide-brimmed hat with elastic. There was no tea when there should have been, while their 'dinner' consisted of Easter cake and a paskha (both dreadful) – that's all the children got, and not because of poverty, but because of lack of discipline. I secluded myself with Gleb and made him compose there and then the letter about which I told you (to Baring), then looked through all the textbooks he had. According to him my English evening will be on Friday, at Mme Shklovsky's, and, as far as I understood, people will pay. I don't know. I will call in at Rami's and give him 20 pounds for you. Sablin still has Mother's 10. I wrote to McDougall. Will visit Long in a day or two. Budberg has promised to talk to Wells, and I will see her tomorrow if not today. This morning I went to see Evans (a specialist on Hesperidae), a charming old man who knew Uncle Kostya well from India. We talked about everything, starting with the genitalia of Hesperidae and ending with Hitler. I will see him again the day after tomorrow. How I regret not bringing the (wooden) box with me. I had lunch at home, I'm waiting for the telephone number of Gubsky, whom I'm phoning and writing an application to. At 6 p.m., I will go to the Lees'. My darling, I do all I can, but I don't have talent or even a knack for such things. But how happy, how really happy Bubka would have been in the amazing parks here ... I love you endlessly. Have written to Pares. I kiss you, my darling.

HELLO, MY JOY, THANK YOU FOR THE LOVELY PICTURES – ESPECIALLY FOR THE SQUIRREL AND THE BIKE. LOVE YOU. DADDY

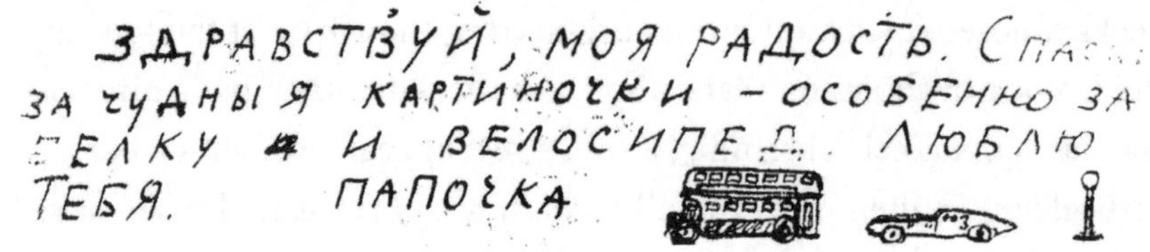
ЗДРАВСТВУЙ, МОЯ РАДОСТЬ. СПА
ЗА ЧУДНЫЯ КАРТИНОЧКИ – ОСОБЕННО ЗА
ЕЛКУ И ВЕЛОСИПЕД. ЛЮБЛЮ
ТЕБЯ. ПАПОЧКА

[ALS, 3 PP.]
[12 April 1939]

TO: Hotel Royal Versailles, 31, r. Le Marois, Paris 16e

5, Brechin Place
[London]
12–IV–39

My love, first of all, what are those half-crossed-out lines? What letter? What is all this nonsense? *I don't quite understand what you mean* – or *meant* – but I think that you genuinely cannot help feeling that *you, and our love, and everything is now always and absolutely safe*. Please, stop this, nothing exists for me except for you – and him. Nevertheless my response may be off, because I don't understand exactly what's got into your head – but whatever it is – it should leave, immediately and for ever. Now about my staying here: I cannot stay at the Sablins' longer than Sunday. On the other hand, I really should stay for three or so more days. If the Tsetlins don't come back, I would move to their place on the

17th—she left me the keys to her apartment. Today I spoke to Struve, and he vows that if I do 'get stuck' here, there'd be a big paid English reading on the 21st. This of course is the final deadline, because in any case (except for one thing—more below) I want to be at home on the evening of the 22nd. Meanwhile, I feel that the longer I stay here the better it is for my prospects, i.e. it would be good to wait for an invitation to a meeting at Leeds (and so, if, for example, I decided to stay up to and including the 21st and received that invitation at the very last moment, then I would have to stay here one day longer (it takes 6 hours to get there by bus, i.e. one can do it in a day)). All my other business—*Sebastian*, the play, the grant, the additional knotting up of connections also require more time. There was a letter from Zina today—the French reading isn't working out, either, so Belgium completely drops out. Yes, it seems I will have to stay till the 21st—which means I will see Vinaver here. See him too yourself on the 17th or the 18th. I have already written in detail about my situation: 1) I have prepared, and tomorrow will give to be copied out cleanly and attractively: an application, a curriculum, and three *testimonials*, plus names of the three *referee*[*s*]—Wells, Pares, Konovalov; 2) this can be mailed to the university only after the announcement; 3) the announcement may appear now, in April, or it may appear at the beginning of May; 4) I'm waiting for Pares so I can find out whether I could, before the announcement, i.e. right now, dash to Leeds for the *interview*—generally, this can be done, i.e. there is no strict dependence on the job announcement—but only they need to know there (through Pares) that I am here and that it would be more difficult to summon me from Paris; 5) three people are chasing Leeds: Struve and two English lecturers. a) Struve won't take it if it's less than 500 p[ounds]. b) Pares doesn't want to do without Morrison, who also won't take less than in London, where he teaches Polish, Serbian, and so on—and this is why, evidently, he offered them my candidacy. c)

B. . . . (I have forgotten his name) (no, I haven't–I've written it down–Birket) has the same position in Sheffield, for 250, it seems, i.e. he is my only serious rival, but then his chair will become free. This is all that I know so far, but maybe something else will become clear by the 17th. I talked about Hicks with Mrs Whale, and for Vinaver's contact with him I can ask her to write to him about this (in any case I will see her before my departure). I cannot write my 'work' now, of course,– that's unthinkable. But send me, just in case, '*Le vrai . . .*'–it is in my briefcase. Of course on my return all I'll do will be to write in English about Russian literature.

I was at the Lees' yesterday, it was very pleasant–I've made friends with him once and for all, while she, it seems, judging by several hints, is expecting a child. This morning I got phone calls from 1) Eva, with an invitation to dinner–I wouldn't have gone had she not given me 10 guin. for Mother; this will be a family dinner, of course (although she whispered insinuatingly that she was keeping my poems and 'will never part with them') 2) the very sweet Sergey phoned, he was very happy with the play, he gave it to Leslie Banks (a famous actor) and is expecting an answer tomorrow night. I'll visit him again. 3) Budberg phoned–saying that she was enraptured etc. by *Sebastian*, gave it to a publisher, thinks I have a very good chance, wrote to Walpole about me and wants to organize a dinner with him and me on the 20th–I said that I will give her my answer tomorrow about whether I am staying or not—; I'll go to her place tomorrow. 4) Gubsky phoned–I must go to see him now–and it seems I will have to break off the letter, my precious, my immeasurable love. My happiness.

This morning, I was at *Oriental Furs*, invited Osya (the other was not there) to a *bar*, treated him to beer and gave him 20 pounds, which will be sent to you immediately. Sablin offered to send the money to Mother, i.e. to Evg. Konst. from here, he can do this through his charity service record. The rate will be good: 1 p. = 22 marks. I had lunch at home. After Gubsky, I'll come back, Struve will come by, and we'll go to a lit. evening at Mme Tyrkov's, where I will read 'Tyrants'.

I will write to Priel – by the way, I would very much like you to see those gentlemen.

It's hot! I have been going around without a coat for three days now. Love you endlessly. When I come back from Gubsky, I will check whether I have written you everything, in the sense of answers to your questions and concerns – and if not, I'll add more tomorrow. I write to you every day – do you get everything? I kiss your dear eyes.

V.

MY MITEN'KA, MY DARLING!
DADDY

[ALS, 4 PP.]
[13 April 1939]

TO: Hotel Royal Versailles, 31, rue Le Marois, Paris 16e

5, Brechin Place, London S. W. 7
13-IV-39
3 p.m.

My love, my angel, congratulations: 14 years! One more week, and I will kiss you, my tenderness. Today, when I got up, I suddenly felt like dropping everything and coming back – especially since Gleb tells me sourly that the English evening at Mme Shklovsky's won't give me more than 3 pounds (however, I'll take my own measures too). I'll pay her a visit tomorrow to arrange everything with her in person. So, now: I have just sent a letter to Konovalov, at P. O. Euston, London (figuring that if he passes through there – though he does not know I'm here till the 21st–I'll see him again). I think he's still in Paris, at his father's. It is easy to find him through 'Posledn. nov.' I am asking him in the letter 1) whether I should send, with a reference to him, the copied-out application, *C.V.*, and *testimonials* directly to the Leeds vice-chancellor, without waiting for the announcement (which, by the way, sometimes doesn't appear at all, when the candidates are selected in advance); 2) whether he will let Leeds know that I am in England and can come to the required meeting (for it will be more difficult for me to do this from France). If you could catch him, that would be great. True, Gleb wrote to Pares especially about the second point and most likely, Pares has done it, but s i c h e r i s t s i c h e r. On the other hand, my candidacy has already been submitted (but, remember, we gave them the Saigon address, so if I'm still in England, I will receive the notice about the *interview* and so on from them by a roundabout route Saigon–Le Marois–5, Brechin–and with my luck, it'll happen right when I'm in the middle of my trip back), submitted by Konovalov and Pares (since I could (in Glebushka's words) be concerned that Pares only said he'd submitted it (with my curricul. composed by Gleb)), yesterday I went specially for this to the Gubskys', whose daughter is Pares' secretary, i.e. she knows his correspondence. She told me that he had indeed sent my candidacy and that they expect him any day. I arranged with her for her to let me know as soon as he comes back, so that I could immediately go to see him. I rang her today myself on the off-chance, but he is still not there. I need him, first and foremost, for the same thing I'm writing to Konovalov about. Gleb assures me that I'm worrying for nothing: 'that everything will happen in its own time', that 'they will let me know themselves' and so on, and can't understand that it's important for me to resolve all of this right away. But then, he wrote an excellent letter to Baring (6 copies made already), and I'll make sure he collects signatures quickly. All in all I have a feeling that something should come out of this, except that our destiny is a slattern and cares more for the soul than for the body.

Gubsky is just as apish and unlikeable as before – in his stoop-shouldered speech, in his gloominess with a little ironic edge, and even in his looks he is somewhat reminiscent of Achilles K. I got back from his place, changed, and with 'Tyr. Dest.' went to Mme Tyrkov's. About thirty people there, plus an Easter cake. Most were women, and I'm afraid, the impression was somewhat eerie – I judge that because, after the chain of usual compliments, Ariadna hinted that she feared for my reason. In a bleating chant, Gleb recited several poems about St Petersburg sent by an anonymous poetess from Russia. For my part, I was most interested in Elisabeth Hill, a lively, hefty, manly lady, with a wolf's jaw and burning eyes – a Russian lecturer at Cambridge (that very one). She told me in detail about her work, about 'wonderful youth', and invited me to give a lecture in Cambridge in October – a public one – about 19th century Russian literature. I won't get money for this, but they will cover all of my travel costs. I said yes, of course. In general, she fastened on me and wants without fail to organize the publication of '*Sebastian*' (all the same I don't have a free copy). She has to phone me today about our next meeting, and I had to give her two numbers, for where I will be tonight. She is unappealing. Energy, pressure, emphasis on *social life* (her students sing Russian songs – *you see what I mean*), but her Russian is excellent – she is the daughter of a Russian priest. Lionlike – and very much the lioness. This morning I was busy with Priel and throwing *au net* the papers for the university, then I bought one more (cheap, but wonderful) little toy for my little one, had lunch and now will go to Budberg's for 5, from there to Grinberg's for dinner (he promised 'to think of something', but he is also a ditherer, like Gleb), and from there to a friend of the Sablins, the actress Charova (old and fat – I mention this just in case, although even if she were young and slender, nothing would change – *I am only interested in one woman, – you*). The Sablins are extremely nice, especially him (under a wrapping of a certain pompousness). I announced to them at lunch today that I will stay in London till the 21st, but will move out of their place on the 17th. They did not object. I'm afraid that those three or four extra days will cost me more than all the previous ones. By the way: cigarettes cost a shilling a day, two trips underground (but I often have more than two – up to six or eight) are *sixpence* – if the distances are short, a stamp is 2½ and a London stamp is 1½ *pence*, and, well, there are other little expenses – for ex., I had to buy envelopes, so I spend a *minimum* of two shillings a day. I have money set aside for the ticket, of course.

I have written to Mme Solomon. Don't forget Vinaver and – Konovalov. How is the furniture? Are you moving? I am writing to Priel that I won't get back before the 22nd and that if worst comes to worst, my wife, etc. I had his old letter with me – the one about the manuscript.

Well, that's how things are, my darling. Everything that I do I do as if in the dark, gropingly, since I feel myself a cretin in cunning human connections. I'm ready to come back to Paris, having left the Leeds castle hanging in the lilac dusk an inch above the horizon, but if this happens, believe it, it won't be my fault – I'm doing all in my powers and possibilities. It seems the most important thing for me now is to get my papers to them and then to appear there in person. Struve is even more unreliable than Klamm's messenger.

Yellow-blue bus, I love you. I adore you.

V.

[ALS, 2 PP.]
[14 April 1939]

TO: Hotel Royal Versailles, 31, rue Le Marois, Paris XVI

5 Brechin Place
[London]
14–IV–39
morning, then 3 p.m.

My beloved (and a trifle silly) darling, I have prepared for you—a very small surprise, namely: when I went to the baroness's last time, I agreed with her that she'd write to her friend Jules Romain[s] to have me admitted to the Paris *Pen-Club*. Yesterday, when I was at her place, she showed me his reply, a very obliging letter—and there and then we composed something like an application, with my *curriculum* added, i.e. the official declaration of my wish to join; so there you are. I turned up around half past five, she was not there yet and arrived only an hour later, so I was hopelessly late for the Grinbergs, and feeling her leonine influence, I called the visit off (I'll see them another day). It turns out that Norman Douglas is a malicious pederast, who lives permanently in Florence. On the 20th, I will have *lunch* with Hugh Walpole. The reply about Sebastian will come any day. From there, I wandered off to Mme Charov's, whose husband's name is Shpunt, a thin gentleman in horn-rimmed glasses, constantly humming something. She is enormous and hospitable. The Sablins and Mme Vorontsov-Dashkov were there, too. Today I have another meeting with Elisabeth Hill (on the steps of the British Museum), tomorrow she is going back to Cambridge and wanted at all costs to see me again. The kitten knows well whose meat it has eaten. I'll spend the evening at Mme Shklovsky's.

Now another thing: I have managed to arrange for the English evening (on the 21st) to be hosted at Harris's, where there's lots of room and so on. I'm drawing up my list – and I think that we'll recruit those who can pay. I've written a long letter to Priel. Miss McDuggals hasn't replied to me, for some reason. On Monday, I'm going to some sort of vernissage with Rodzyanko (who called me today). I'm less sure than you about his ability to arrange anything. Gubsky has promised to obtain a translating job for me (i.e. somebody's book from Russian to English); it pays fairly well and is easy. Hill offered me the same thing.

I am moving to the Tsetlins' on the morning of the 17th. N. I. said perfectly plainly to me: 'you've stayed with us for two weeks, and that's enough.' I suggested moving to her a while ago, but she wouldn't let me go. *I don't want to hear any more, darling, of those dark hints of yours.* I have explained everything to you about Pares. He's not here yet. Wells is sick and not in London. After the signatures are collected (four will be quite enough – Sablin has already signed, and Mme Tyrkov too), the letter will go (probably the day after tomorrow) to Baring. It's typed in six copies, with no addressee, so another two of these will go to Wells and Hugh Walpole (that's not for sure, so perhaps to others). I will be at the baroness's again on Monday. On Tuesday I'll be at Long's – I have more or less figured out, with the help of good people, what his report means, but a lot of it is still unclear – I'll find out from him. I don't want to write how much money I'll bring because I am afraid to jinx it. I sent you 20, 10 has gone to Mother – we'll see about the rest. Do not write to me about '*don't relax*' and '*avenir*' – this only makes me nervous. I adore you, though. Lots of kisses, I want to see you madly, to kiss your eyes, I miss you and him more than ever.

V.

[illegible] just called me from Pares setting up a meeting, and Miss [illegible] several excellent bits of advice.

[ALS, 2 PP.]
[15 April 1939]

TO: Hotel Royal Versailles, 31, rue Le Marois, Paris XVI

[London]
15–IV–39
11 a.m.

My beloved and precious darling, I spent two and a half hours in a tea-house with Elizabeth Hill yesterday, and she, with unusual energy and concern, undertook to teach me how to land the Leeds position. On Monday, I arranged to meet with a very influential lady, Mrs Curran. Besides, yesterday I also wrote a long letter to Goudy in Cambridge, to whom I may even go (on Thursday, for example; the fare is cheap, only 5 shillings there and back! but besides, I will try to have Grinberg drive me). She is not without vulgarity, but marvellously knowledgeable and intelligent. Paid for the tea herself and took me home in a taxi. Pares will 'receive' me on Wednesday – he can't do it sooner! Hill, by the way, sees the situation in a somewhat different light, namely: if Birkett gets Leeds, then Sheffield and Leeds will merge (?) (like Birmingham and Oxford in Konovalov's case), and if Struve takes it, then his place will merge (?) with the 'Serbian-Polish-Albanian', which Morrison is currently in charge of. And still she thinks I 'have a good chance', in view of my lit. position and *testimonials*. I am ready – and you should be ready, too – to suffer defeat, but it will be a very bitter one. Remember, I'm doing all I can.

Last night, I was at Mme Shklovsky's, a very touching old lady, we made the final decision about the reading, and I gave Gleb 2 shillings for mailing the invitations. The reading will be at the Harrises', and there will be about 40 people. I love you, my happiness.

I am having lunch with Lourie, at four there will be tea here with tsar Vlad. Kir., and I'll have dinner at the Lutyens'.

I can feel now that there is alarm in the household because I'm in my room already, while they need to tidy it up. Nadezhda has reprimanded me twice already that I run down the stairs too fast and too noisily. In general there's plenty to say on the subject. Starting Monday, my address will be:

47, Grove End Gardens N.W. 8.

I am counting the days, my love, madly want to see you both.

Love you, love you, love you!

V.

By the way, Polyakov has given me a huge car for our kitten—I don't know how I'll transport it!

MY LITTLE KITTEN, MY LIFE, I KISS YOU!

DADDY

[ALS, 2 PP.]

[16 April 1939]

TO: Hotel Royal Versailles, 31, r. Le Marois, Paris 16[e]

5, Brechin Place

[London]

16–IV–39

Sunday

10.30 a.m.

My love, my life, today, luckily, is a free day—and, by the way, wildly windy, the windows are rattling, pimply young trees are fidgeting about. Yesterday, the Lourie couple (I think, I already wrote you that she is from the Vysotsky family, i.e. a sister of that sharp lady—they are all sharp in that family—who has such a chubby little boy—you saw them at Ilyusha's—*the aunt thinks he speaks beautiful Russian*) took me to the theatre—a very talentless and corny play—about how a pure soul (an ageing woman) tried to organize a school *in a Welsh mining village*, how there happened to be a genius among the coal children, and so on—but the old Sybil Thorndike acted amazingly well. Ah, there's something else: on Sunday, i.e. the 23rd, the Louries are going to Paris by car and they offer to take me along. I intended, in fact, to return on the 22nd, but I am tempted by the saving. We will leave from here at five or six a.m. and get to Paris toward seven p.m. It'll be rather exhausting, and I'll spend three quarters of my *birthday* without you, but I think it's worth doing.

I was late to tea with the tsar, i.e. came back home at half past six, changed and went to the Lutyens'. First of all, she showed me a rather fat leather book (which I would have never recognized as my album from 1917) with a good hundred poems (completely forgotten by me!) joined together under the title 'Transparency'—apparently, I intended to publish it all. They are about her, and about the revolution, and about Vyra—some are not really so bad, but mainly it's all very funny—that pervasive foreboding of certain unbelievable shocks, wanderings and achievements showing through everything. She's offering to have it retyped. The entire family assembled—the mother who's completely unchanged, the very sweet Hellers, Lutyens, with whom I recalled our Cambridge carouses and common friends—but he has lost them all, as I did. Everything there is very wealthy and problem-free. Eva explains that, 'you understand, my house (of fashion) is the same here as Chanel in Paris', and he is a flourishing architect. I talked in great detail to them about my situation and my dream of settling here (but without mentioning the university, or we will end up with a fatal set of nannies). I will visit the Hellers in a few days. Eva was saying 'rodnen'kiy' and 'smeshno!' Her boy is ten years old, very amiable and sweet-looking, but quiet and shy. She said: 'You see, you finally married a Jewess and a *timber-merchant*'s daughter, while I finally married a Christian and a man six years younger than me.' *Enfin* ... *Yes, she wants to send you some frocks* ... *I don't know.* Anyway, it was quite amusing.

I've rounded up, it seems, too many people for my English reading. Can you feel it, my sunshine, how I love you from here? You know, I think that even if Leeds doesn't work out, we'll move over here by autumn in any case – I know they will help me here. I kiss you, my dear thing. Today, it seems, I will be at home all day long, if nobody suddenly invites me.

V.

AS FOR YOU, MY LITTLE ONE, I AM TAKING YOU UP IN MY ARMS AND SAYING, LOOKING AT THE LAMP, 'A, A, A ....'
DADDY

[ALS, 2 PP.]
[17 April 1939]

TO: Hotel Royal Versailles, 31, rue Le Marois, Paris XVI

47, Grove End Gardens N. W. 8
[London]
Tel. Mai(divale) 70.83
16–IV–39
12 p.m.

My beloved darling, so, I have moved. A marvellous, elegant little apartment; a green view out the window ('parterre'), sparrows, clouds, daffodils. I got your dear letter with the little drawing (about the 15th, about the Romanian, etc.). The money situation is not particularly great: the reading yielded only £42 and some shillings (of which 10 have been sent to Mother and 20 to you), and on top of that I got £20 from Flora. In other words, I now have £30 and a few shillings on me. I don't know how much more the evening at the Harrises' will yield – in the worst case (i.e. if no one pays more than the entry fee, 2/6 – although on the invitation there's a hint to give more) – it will yield about 3 pounds. What the 'appeal' (to Baring, etc.) will bring in is also hard to say.

Yesterday I spent around two hours at Flora's, who had phoned me yesterday afternoon. I think she would never have invited me, had (as it later became clear from some of what she said) Eva (who does not know about my relationship with Fl.) not called her. I had tea at her place with a crowd of German émigrés – lucky ones – served by two – less fortunate – German émigré ladies. She decided to give up the past as a bad job and take me in hand all over again. She still advises me to move to London immediately, and when I explained to her that we had already taken an apartment in Paris (although if I could know for sure that I'd get a job here immediately – *reader*, cinema, anything – we could've sacrificed the apartment), her suggestions became more murky. She likes to see a person in front of her, under her arm, she has no inclination for forethought, but I think that if we really make up our minds and move over here in the autumn, then she will help. She also suggests that I should stick here on my own for three months, with the promise of finding me shelter, but (let alone that I am afraid and not even very happy to rely on her – her cold eyes and sugary little voice annoy me unbearably) this is nonsense, of course – I cannot live without you. This last week, beginning from today, is torture, I want to go home, to my own corner, my energy is running dry, I'm wildly tired, I can't stand it any more. The only thing that would have really made everything right would have been getting Leeds (yesterday, while

I was out, Pares came to the Sablins' and definitely told him that if, contrary to expectations – the expectations of Pares, who is utterly sick of Gleb – this is exactly how he explained it – Gleb, and not I, got the place at Leeds, then I, of course, will get the London place (this does not square with Elizabeth Hill's supposition about Morrison)). I will be at Pares's the day after tomorrow. It is very unfortunate that he called in by chance at Evg. Vasil.'s and I was not there. In answer to your two little questions: 1) Yes, Hill is taking it on herself to organize the Cambridge lecture – and I will bring you along 2) Gubsky's daughter is a large, corpulent, red-cheeked maiden with the rather empty eyes that maidens of her type usually have.

I spent the evening with the Sablins yesterday. She told me imperturbably how much I should leave for the servants: 10 sh. to Jeeves, 5 to the chamber-maid, and 5 to the cook, and since the only way to move with a suitcase and a large box (Bubka's automobile) from their place to here was to take a taxi, this morning (plus lunch, which I'm eating now) has cost me 25 shillings, after which, as I've already written, I'll have 30 poun. and several shill. left.

After lunch, I will do some work on Priel (I still can't finish it – I get so tired by the evening that I can't even read the newspaper), at 5.30 I will be at the baroness's, and at 8, at the Hellers'. *No,– emphatically, I'm not a man about town.* In June we'll go to the mountains. There.

I kiss you, my happiness, and I KISS YOU, TOO, MY MITEN'KA. THANK YOU FOR THE VERY SWEET DRAWING!

V.

Don't forget to give up the apartment when you move in, will you?

[APCS]
[18 April 1939]

TO: Hotel Royal Versailles, 31, r. Le Marois, Paris XVI

[London]
6 P.M. 18–IV

My darling, I am writing to you on my way home, from the post office, since I'm in such a sweat that if I put it off till home, I won't go out again. Yesterday afternoon I was at the baroness's – nothing new there, they are reading. I had dinner at the Hellers', met there with Misha Lubrz., all of them have very energetically taken my fate in hand, they have 'enormous connections', and so on. Tomorrow Heller has to call me about a specific move undertaken for Leeds. What a pen ... Today, I had lunch with Serg. Rodz. – there, too, they are 'reading'. From there I went to the City, passed on 25 pounds for you to Osya and called in to Spurrier (Long), who turned out to be an affected waxen young beau. It seems I will be able to sell 'The Defence', i.e. we have already talked about an advance – £60 (the translation, mine, is included). They promise to resolve this soon. My advances are not covered. Now I am going home, will have dinner with Osya who lives in the same building as me, he was very surprised by this. I will go to bed early, exhausted. I kiss you, my adorable thing; I think I have never missed you so much. Tomorrow too will be a difficult day.

I HUG MY MITEN'KA.

V.

[ALS, 2 PP.]
[19 April 1939]

TO: Hotel Royal Versailles, 31, rue Le Marois, Paris XVI

Grove End Gardens
[London]
19–IV
5 p.m.

My love, I've got both of your letters, addressed here directly and c/o the Sablins. Everything is all right, write me directly here, without c/o Zetlin. 47 is the number of my apartment, and the doorman already knows me well.

Here's my news: I have a feeling that I won't manage to settle my affairs this week. I am sorry I arranged with the Louries to go by car–it is awfully embarrassing to say no (he has already booked a place on the steamboat, and, in any case, he wouldn't have undertaken this journey with his wife and me, had he not wished to make '*a treat*' out of this for me, his wife, and himself–he would have travelled on his own by train). On the other hand, they are coming back, again by car, a week from now and are offering again to take me along with them. In other words, being away from here won't cost me anything (except for the new visa). But let me tell you about my affairs today first, so it's clearer:

Lubrzynsky called in the morning, and then Vera Heller, to say that 1) they will put pressure on Leeds through their connections 2) Eva through the numerous relatives of her husband is trying to organize for me in the meantime teaching Russian studies at a military or navy establishment 3) they are putting pressure on Dennison Ross, with whose nephew, it turns out, I was great friends at Trinity–I'd completely forgotten! And, finally, 4) M. Lubrzynsky is offering me financial help, if I stay here. In general, everyone tells me it's impossible to do anything in two or three weeks, I need to establish myself here. I went to fetch your little letter from the Sablins, and then had lunch with Konovalov. He told me nothing new, and he can't do anything about the papers. From there I went to Sir Bernard. In my presence, he dictated a letter to Leeds (in which among other things he said that '*If G. Struve leaves his post here, it shall be offered to Nabokoff*') about sending them my papers. The papers were enclosed, and the letter went off. He was extremely welcoming, I stayed with him for more than an hour. Besides, just in case, he also gave me a magnificent letter of recommendation to one of the 'big shots' at the University of Chicago, Professor Samuel N. Harper, who's here at the moment. On the way to Gubsky, with whom I am having dinner (with some lady writer Beausobre), I will drop this letter off at his hotel.

I am awfully anxious that I will have to return to Paris without resolving things, i.e. without waiting till the Leeds question is settled, but then again I cannot live any longer without the two of you.

Yes, we definitely need to move to London: give up the apartment and take back the deposit. I will now do the rounds for the visas – not through Budberg, but through the same old Lutyens (Eva, in one day, arranged for her brother a job with Sir Alfred Mond), but I will also talk to the Sablins and to Gubsky.

The *charwoman* was here. The day after tomorrow, I will call on Vinaver. They have moved Mother to the IIIrd class of the hospital, her condition's the same ... Send the money sooner – they owe 5,000 there ... I have written to the Romanian, and to the old man. Osorgin is right: there are too few moves for the queen to have nowhere to retreat ... I need to go, it's six o'clock. I adore you beyond measure and words.

V.

[APCS]

[postmarked 20 April 1939]

TO: Hotel Royal Versailles, 31, rue Le Marois, Paris XVI

[London]

12.30 p.m.

My dear love, I had dinner at the Gubskys' (they are very nice) with a woman recently escaped from Russia after having been through many jails (Beausobre). This morning at 10.30 I visited Sir Dennison Ross, who wrote about me to Leeds to his cousin, a professor of Orient. Lang. Everything's now going along swimmingly. Tomorrow or the day after tomorrow I will be seeing Gams about the visas. I am going out to lunch now (I am writing to you from the post office on the way) at Miss Curran's (*Secretary of Hist. Soc.*) who also *pulls strings*. Then I'll have tea at Piccadilly with Grinberg and have dinner at Halpern's. Tomorrow, at the Harrises', I will read chunks from *Sebastian*. Delightful sunny weather, everything shines and gets reflected. Blue taxi-cabs, passing by the red buses, turn purple for a moment. Ross was charming. I'm leaving on Sunday morning, at 6.30, so I think I'll be in Paris by eight. I love you. Overall, although there's still nothing concrete, *the outlook* in every respect *looks hopeful* – and Leeds or no Leeds we will move over here by autumn. But I will probably have to come back here in a week, with Lourie. I kiss you, my darling.

AND I KISS YOU, TOO, MY SPELLTACALL.

V.

[ALS, 2 PP.]
[21 April 1939]

TO: 59, rue Boileau, Paris XVI

Grove End Gardens, London N.W. 8
21–IV–39
4.30 p.m.

My love, today an absolutely tragic letter from Prague, Mother has an abscess on her lung, she has been transferred to the critically ill ward, where she's sharing a room with a dying woman. They are penniless, the Sablins' money can't have reached them yet, and what about your transfer from Paris? It's torture, torture that we can't speed it up. I absolutely do not know what to do! Solomon proposed one combination, I'll talk to her again. E. K.'s letter is utterly desperate. It's terrible ...

I am having a record day today in the sense of all sorts of tasks. Yesterday I had lunch at the *Historical Society* with its very obliging secretary, in a *hall* from some fabled century; I invited her to my reading today. From there I went to Piccadilly, where I had tea with Grinberg. He's very touching, offered me, embarrassed, 'ten pounds or so', I replied that I will borrow from him on occasion, long-term. Then I went home and chose what to read, the first three chapters from *Sebastian*. I love you. The day after tomorrow! Then I went to have dinner at Halpern's, who's not very pleasant and moves carefully, to avoid spilling himself, of whom he is full. All this means huge distances on huge buses. Today at ten a.m. I was at Prof. S. N. Harper's (who has at Chicago the same position as Pares here – but still more powerful). He turned out to be a large springy darling and said that from July first (remember the date) there'll be a chance of placing me in Chicago; he wants me to send him my papers by then. The day after tomorrow he is going to Russia. Parry works for him. In a word, there is hope here too. From him I dashed – had to take a cab – to Vinaver, who hasn't changed a bit in 20 years! We had a very friendly talk, he approved all I'm doing and promised to talk to Trofimov (a Russian lecturer in Manchester) so he could give 'a push of the shoulder' in Leeds. Besides at my request he wrote a letter to me (it will come to rue Boileau) 'with an offer to come to read in Manchester'. I asked for this to get the visa for here, since I can see I'll definitely have to come back with Lourie. The committee (that chooses candidates, etc.) will get together only at the end of next week and after that, I hope, there'll be an invitation to Leeds for the *interview*, at which they can ask you all kinds of unexpected questions (*what are your hobbies*, for ex.). Then I went to have lunch with the Sablins. If I get a place anywhere in England (by the way, there are other vacancies in the offing too), we will have no difficulties with the visa. In any case (i.e. just to move here by autumn, on the off-chance), I will see Gams again – whom yesterday and today I phoned in vain, he's hard to catch. Now I am going to the baroness, from there, to dinner with Haskell, and then, with her, to my reading at Harris's. It's wonderfully warm today, everything is green, and I've washed my hair with Silvikrin. Valya Tsetlin arrived this morning and is leaving tonight for the *weekend*. Till Sunday night, my love. Remember, it may happen that we don't get there by eight, but by ten or later (I don't think so). Will I have a place to sleep? I do not get nearly enough sleep here, although I go to bed relatively early. So: this is my last letter from here. I don't remember what our floor is at Boileau, pin up a card, since the concierge will be asleep if I arrive in the middle of the night. I adore you both.

MY JOY, MITEN'KA, I AM COMING!

V.

Vinaver asked to have 'Invit. to a Beheading' sent to him (for Trofimov). If we have one, send it! *Prof. E.Vinaver, The University, Manchester*.

[ALS, 2 PP.]
[1 June 1939]

TO: 59, r. Boileau, Paris 16^{e}

22, Hornton Str, London W. 8
Tel: Western 49-21
I–VI–39
11.30

My love, those three and a bit hours on the sea were terrible. Although the sun shone full strength, the sea was completely riven and upended by the wind, so the tossing was monstrous. I stayed on deck, roasting myself in the sun and washed every minute by the edge of a wave that would drench the less protected Englishmen. I have never seen so many people retching at the same time. A group of female sightseers made an especially pretty show–judging by the results, they had stuffed themselves full of oranges. The deck was all covered with streams of puke.

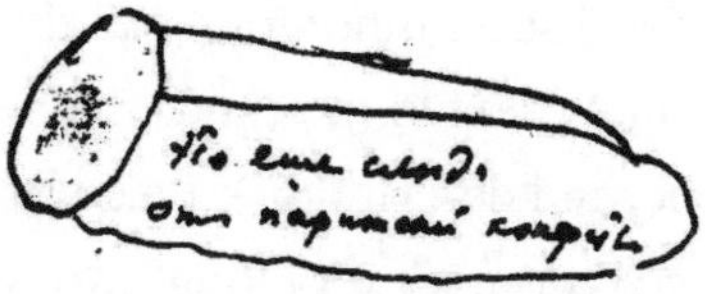

This is still a trace of Paris candy.

Here it's much nicer and cosier than it was at the Sablins'. Haskell is very sweet and interesting. They have already invited Politzer (Collins) to lunch on Saturday, and we'll have a focused talk on my book. You were so pretty, my happiness, at the station. Haskell, in general, *is very helpful*. I phoned the Tsetlins after dinner–will have dinner with them tonight–and I also phoned Lubrzynsky, whom I didn't get hold of, and Mme Solomon (I'll see her on Friday, and meanwhile she dictated me a letter which I should write to Colonel Clive Garsia about the possibility of getting a job of teaching Russ. lang. at *Staff College*), and the Gubskys (with whom I'll have lunch today), and Budberg's agent (Otto Thien, with whom I'll have tea today), and Gleb (who is dreamily talking about a reading evening and whom I will see tomorrow), and Eva, whom I dropped in on last night. She has been in bed for two weeks, heart weakness, her husband is sitting at her bedside, I'll visit them again on Sunday. In any event, I have again tuned up and set in motion the machine of visits and conversations and plans. Wait till tomorrow or the day after before sending your letter to Pneumothorax–I forgot the name! My God, how sickly and madly I crave butterflies. If I have nothing on tomorrow morning, I will drift to the museum (it's around the corner again).

It is very cosy and comfortable here. The three of us had b r e a k f a s t in dressing gowns, bacon and eggs, charming. Haskell graduated from Cambridge two years after me. He showed me very interesting shots of Australian animals and landscapes, *se pique de zoologie*. Today I'll have to do a few more telephonades. I still cannot forget a little boy who retched violently every five minutes next to me (and what was happening in the passengers' lounge is beyond description). I read last night Col. Lawrence's *Seven Pillars of Wisdom*, it's very long, two would have been enough–but wonderfully written in places. The weather is grey, slanting. It was very strange to sink into and stretch out in a real bathtub, after our sabot. My darling, *remember I adore you more than ever*.

HELLO, MY ROLLY! HOW'S CAPTAIN BELOV BEHAVING? I ADORE YOU.

V.

[ALS, 2 PP.]
[2 June 1939]

TO: 59, rue Boileau, Paris XVI

22, Hornton Str
[London]
2–VI
8.30

My dear love,

I had lunch at the Gubskys' yesterday, then sat in their tiny garden in the sun – the grapevine, having wound around the wall with its own hands, went off across the fence to the neighbours and will never return. I tried Gubsky about translations, he promised 'to do what he can', but hopes and plans are also capable of going off like vines. After an overcast morning, everything became very bright, the sky swift-moving, Whites were fluttering. He gave me his book, '*My double and I*', I read it on the tube, and to me it seems excellent – the beginning, at least. From there, having crossed an animated Thames, I went to Otto Thien: the little Budberg man I told you about, Dutch, looks like Silberman, and is, it seems, an American Jew. He couldn't give me any special news. Thinks that a final answer will come in a week. Moura gets back soon, I'll still have time to see her. Theis's wife, a journalist, works for '*N. Chronicle*'. On Monday, they're planning some kind of a *party*. From there, I went home – all this means enormous clattering distances – fetched Lyusya's bottle and went to the Tsetlins' (I left the bottle with the porter to be given to the Brombergs). It was very pleasant at the Tsetl[ins']. We spent the whole evening talking about my situation – she promises to get all the activity she can going, to organize a conference consisting of herself, Solomon, Vera Heller, Vera Markovna, etc. – in short, to get enough so we have money for the first months of a life in England, starting in October. Judging by the Thursday issue of Posl. nov. which I saw at their place, Pio has finally licked his way up to Adamovich's most delicious hole – this reciprocal shamelessness is enchanting.

I got home around twelve and read, till one, the very amusing 'Diary' of Arn. Bennett – all in all, there is an orgy of books here. I dreamed I clearly heard my boy's little voice, and woke up. I'm writing in bed, the chambermaid will call me to breakfast in a moment. Yesterday I phoned Grinberg (will see him on Saturday) and Mme Sablin (who is equally overwhelmed by the quitting of her cook and the wedding of one of the gr. pr. She asked me to phone her again, when her head will be clearer for the important decision, when to have me round. *Idiot*). Another series of calls this morning – to the Hellers, Mme Solomon, Rodzyanko, Aunt Bebesha. My happiness, I miss you two already. My day has not yet been completely divided up, at any event I will see Gleb and Misha L. *dans le courant* of the day. And yesterday, suddenly, it resolved itself with perfect lucidity that what I conceived when I was ill can and must be written in English – everything came together and clicked into place in an instant, – and now I very much want to lock myself up and lie down to write. I kiss your eyes, my happiness, lots of kisses.

V.

WRITE, MY LIFE, AND TAKE BIG STEPS, SLIDING, ONE-TWO, ONE-TWO . . . BANG!

MY JOY!

V.

[ALS, 2 PP.]
[3 June 1939]

TO: 59, rue Boileau, Paris XVI

22, Hornton Str
[London]
3–VI–39
8 a.m.

My darling, well, of course, yesterday morning (after abundant telephone exercises – I called Mme Solomon, where I will have dinner on Tuesday, Vera H., Mme Tyrkov, Mme Tsetlin – I will visit Mme Tyrkov on Thursday) I went to my museum. First I called on Capt. Riley (editor of the '*Entomologist*'). He looked at my *meladon* and said 1) *it is something quite new* 2) the only person *who may know* something *about the question* is Stempfer, who lives in Paris (and with whom Riley, in 1929, had a famous run-in over *carswelli-arcilani*, – you remember) 3) that I certainly must *publish it* in the '*Entom.*' and supply photographs of the beauty – normally it would cost me 2 pounds, but it seems I might be able to arrange it for free. Then I went to *Brigadier* Evans and for two hours straight he and I sorted out my Hesperidae, among which, again, there is one unknown, but for many reasons the question is so complicated (Evans himself suspected that yet another species flies with *alveus*, as well as *armoricanus* and *foulquieri*) that I'll have to work there some more. I had lunch with Vera Mark., *tête-à-tête*. It turned out that Politzer couldn't come to lunch on Saturday, but instead I'm invited to him, i.e. to Collins, on Monday morning. Lubrzhynsky, whom I phoned, maintains that they're eager for 'Sebastian'. I went to the *School of Slavonic Lang.* for 3.30 to see Struve and Sir Bernard. I had a rather platonic conversation with Gleb about arranging my reading, which he proposes arranging for the 3rd – but where, how and at whose place, who knows. The gossip about his getting a 'salary increase' is nonsense. Then I saw Yakobs. (at whose place I'll have dinner on Wednesday) and, with some difficulty, got through to Pares. He (perhaps feeling that he had been giving me false hopes and displaying – sincerely, it seems – indignation about the rejection from Leeds, which apparently did not even find it necessary to inform him about it) was extremely nice to me and immediately dictated two letters – one of them, putting pressure on Harper, the other … In a word, there is a very interesting new possibility at the *Intelligence Service*, which had applied to him for specialists. From the university Gleb and I went to the Harrises', who live nearby, and had tea there. I was at home at seven, had dinner, chatted, and went to bed early. I am dying to get down to the new book. My darling, write me a few words, I adore, I adore you. Today I am phoning Nadya, writing to Vinaver, Mme Chernavin, Mrs Hill, and someone else I have noted down, I will have tea at Mme Shklovsky's, and tonight I'm going, I think, with Arnold, to an *open air* Shakespeare performance. And here's the money situation for the moment. So far, I've got only 5 pounds (from Pares – a gift), but in any case, my trip has paid for itself. A funny joke: a private detective reports that he has climbed a tree to look through the window at a couple: '*first she played with him, then he played with her, then I played with myself and fell off the tree*'. My joy, I think that we shouldn't put off our trip till July first. I kiss you, lots of kisses, ten more days.

HOW ARE YOU, MY DOGGY-WOGGIES? ARRANGE THE BUTTERFLIES BY MY RETURN. I KISS YOU TWO.

V.

[ALS, 2 PP.]
[4 June 1939]

TO: 59, rue Boileau, Paris 16^{e}

[London]
4–VI–39
8 a.m.

My love, yesterday morning, of course, I was at the museum, where Hesperids suck me in (the fascination of butterflies, in general, is like some blessed velvet abyss), had lunch at home and after lunch wrote three–no, four letters–no, five even–to Vinaver, to Elizabeth Hill (with a plea for translating work), an answer to Colonel Garsia (who had invited me to tea tomorrow), a few words to Flora (who had asked me to inform her when Garsia responded), to the Lees, and to Mme Chernavin–from whom, ten minutes after my letter went, I received an invitation (and an offer of a small job, a translation)–I will visit her tomorrow. I set out around four to Mme Shklovsky's; while I was there she wrote a letter to a Mme Levitsky (a former flame of Milyukov's), who, Zin. Dav. assures me, will gladly provide an apartment for an English reading–a paying one, of course. From there I went to the Sablins',–she with a bad head cold, in blue glasses and a brown scarf; Vladimir Kirill. is staying with them in my place. At seven I had dinner and went with Haskell to the theatre–a Shakespeare open-air performance, *Much Ado about Nothing*–in every sense of the word. Imagine a little corner of a park (Regent['s] Park), files of green garden chairs (usually rented by black-clad old ladies) in the back rows and green deckchairs in front. They hand out plaids–but I wore two sweaters, an *overcoat* of my host's, and a beret. The stage was a freshly mown lawn surrounded by trees and blooming bushes, and by the 'footlights', a row of mounds of mowed grass wittily hiding microphones. A 'dazzling' although somewhat overbundled audience – and great actors. The weather was ideal, the day hung on for ages, and all that time the trees were settling down to sleep, along with the wind and the birds, one could hear thrushes, then pigeons, and the progression of that evening performance didn't correspond at all to the progress of the play – so that the sky and the park acted one thing and the people another – and later when night came the sky became completely purple, the lit-up trees became acid-green and exactly like some flat conventionally cut-out scenery. Lots of moths fluttered by, while next to us sat the amiable but supremely ungifted author of 'Magnolia Street'. I found your little letter, my happiness, upon my return home. 1) yes – *le grand-duc et le duc moyen* 2) *crottin* 3) 'the rain charged up' – any of them 4) translate literally, about the hard sign, and provide a footnote. There. This morning I'm going with Haskell to the Zoo, will have lunch at Vera Heller's, take tea at Eva's, have dinner at Grinberg's. They'll call me in a moment to b r e a k f a s t – all in dressing gowns, luckily. My darling, I love you, I kiss you, I'll be back soon, please get ready for our trip to the mountains.

MY MITEN'KA, MY LITTLE EARS, MY JOY!

V.

[AL, 2 PP.]
[5 June 1939]

TO: 59, rue Boileau, Paris XVI

22, Hornton Str., W. 8
[London]
8.45 a.m.
5–VI–39

My multi-coloured love, my Hesperid, *mihi*,

Yesterday morning I went with the very sweet Arnold (his face is very like a kangaroo's, which is remarkable – since he's crazy about Australia) and his youngest son (who looks like *Mus disneyi*) to the *Zoo*. An amazing green place – and the only zoo where the animals look, if not exactly gleeful, then at least not depressed. Of course we spent ages admiring the *Giant Baby Panda* (discovered by the missionary David in 1867 in the mountains of China). It's smoky-grey, with white patches and a large black spot around each eye, big-headed, soft as a toy animal the size of a bear – and generally looking like a bear. There was also a very interesting gentleman, an old man of the artist-naturalist type, with a small beard and tanned bald head, who amuses himself every morning with the wolves, i.e. he walks into their cage – rolls them around, lies down on them, under them, across them, kisses them on their teeth, pulls their tails, while they think about something else. Also good was a little island in the pond, as if completely unprotected, overgrown with flowers and swarming with various poisonous snakes. I had lunch with Vera Heller, from her went to Eva. Her son is very funny (he engaged me in an adult conversation). At both places, we discussed the question of my situation. I went off at five, leaving Eva another copy of the letter (I've got new signatures these last few days) which she wants to forward to someone she didn't name. Since it was still too early to sail off to Savely, I sat in Hyde Park for a while: hot sun, the glitter of radiators in the greenery. Savely was very touching. His parents were there – and his father discovered that we both were colleagues in terms of our visa and passport adventures. I was home by twelve. A little gap here: I didn't have time to finish the letter before b r e a k f a s t, and before lunch I must get to the bank and to Collins. After that I will have lunch at Mme Chernavin's, drink tea with the Colonel, at six, I will be at Otto's (a *party* in my honour), and tonight, a movie with the Haskells. The money situation is still poor. Besides the £5 from Pares, I received another £10 through Eva. It is true that Grinberg also offered me (not personally, but through his wealthy firm) to cover our costs here at first, from the beginning of October. He still doesn't know for how long – a month or longer, he has to call me. In any case I think you should definitely go to Tatishchev for your passport (phone Rodzyanko first, though, to make sure); and as soon as I come back, I will submit an application to the Eng. cons. for a month-long visa for us in October. To finish this letter, I took a seat at the edge of some monument (*Kensington Regiment something*), and it is not very comfortable writing, although the pen's behaving ideally. I think, my life, we can now calmly set out for Savoy on the 17th. For Heaven's sake, settle that. It is very hot and I adore you very, very, very much.

V.

MY MITEN'KA, WHY DON'T YOU WRITE? LOVE YOU.

[ALS, 2 PP.]
[6 June 1939]

TO: 59, rue Boileau, Paris 16e

22, Hornton str.
[London]
6–VI–39
8.30 a.m.

My love, yesterday's conversation with Collins was very pleasant. D z e *book is as good as* s o l d. Milton Waldman received me first, and then Collins himself joined us. They asked me all kinds of questions that reminded me of the *interview* at Leeds that never took place. It was important for them to know whether I had more books *dans le ventre*, whether I would write in England, etc. This morning I will take '*La Course du Fou*' there, it greatly interested them as well: Waldman has already baptized it '*The Fool's Mate*' (the fool's mate is in three moves, but also a punning 'translation' of the word 'fou'—very funny). Specifically, our conversation about Sebastian ended on this, that in a few days they *will make up their minds*—and I mine. There was a small change in the programme, i.e. Mme Chernavin has been moved to another day—so that my other visit was to the *Army and Navy Club*, to Col. Garsia. We sat in the billiard room, he drank tea and I whisky. He cannot do anything about the *Staff College*, if only because, in his words, there is no official teaching of Russian in any of the three military colleges. But he is a nice man. Thereupon, my darling, I went to Otto's—lots of people there—for example, Lovat Dickson, and I tried to sparkle. The book is at Macmillan's. Budberg, a while ago, asked me not to tell Otto that I had given another copy to Politzer (the representative of Collins), but Otto knows. If in the course of two weeks Collins makes a firm offer as suggested, and if Macmillan (which is generally worse than Collins) says no, then I'll withdraw the book from Otto. The situation now, however, because of the 'double game' (although I am my own agent in the negotiations with Collins—so I'm not really sinning against Otto) is slightly soapy.

I heard outstanding 'compliments' from Collins. Let me repeat, it was all very pleasant—and, for some reason, I keep thinking about my Ullstein-Meriks period. I had dinner at home (and lunch, at a *Milk Bar*,—it was too far to go back between the publisher and the colonel) and then the Haskells (with whom I have become very friendly—they are very sweet in every way) and I went to the cinema—an excellent French film '*Le Carrefour*'. This afternoon I am at Misha L.'s, but I'll have dinner at Mme Solomon's. My joy, do not forget to do what I asked you yesterday about the passport and Savoy. There is no need to be stuck in Paris till the first of July. We can stay in Savoy till September 1—I will bring at least 45 pounds, and besides that we can count on the sale of

'Sebastian'. And yet another monetary combination will become clear in a day or two. I adore you, my dear happiness, write to me.

MY DARLING, DO YOU LIKE THIS PICTURE? LOLOLOLOLOLOVELOVE YOU. WILL BE BACK IN A WEEK.

V.

[ALS, 2 PP.]
[7 June 1939]

TO: 59, rue Boileau, Paris 16e

22, Hornton str.
[London]
7.VI.39
11 a.m.

My love, why don't you write to me? The little laddie isn't sick, is he? You can always write a couple of words. *Pas gentil*.

Yesterday morning I took '*Course du Fou*' to Waldman and for the last, fourth, time, visited the museum. Brigadier Evans (Hesperids), with whom I've become very friendly since I've been here, gave me an important commission to Le Cerf in Paris – to bring *certain types*, which he will need in October, from the Paris museum – since to obtain something from a Frenchman by mail is almost impossible, as we all know. Besides he told me that *we are very understaffed here*, several collections need to be sorted out – and one should not rule out the possibility that they will give me work there when we move. I returned for lunch (it's hot, everything's hazy, the parks are full of sun-worshippers) and in the afternoon went to see Misha. He intends to champion my play seriously, he has his ways. From there I went to have dinner at Mme Solomon's. She had talked to two people, one in the Admiralty and another in the *Foreign Office*, and this morning I wrote both of them a letter each with my papers enclosed – curric., *testimonials*. By the way, I will soon need to send a copy to that – Harper, Samuel Harper. Today I will have lunch with the Haskells at Maria Solomoylovna's, then at 3.30 I'm meeting Molly at Victoria, then at six I must be at a *party* at Lovat Dickson's (a well-known publisher), then at the *Slavonic School*, and dinner at Yakobson's. What a day. Tomorrow evening I will be at Mme Tyrkov's. My darling, I'm wildly missing you and him. And most of all I'm worried that we won't get out of Paris on June 17th – this is necessary, I need (besides catching butterflies) to write – but a new fallow furlough in Paris will drag the business out. We should now have enough money for everything – not to mention one more source of help starting to take shape. Has there been anything from E. K.?; I will be writing to her on Friday after my meeting with Ariadna. This time I'm spending almost nothing here – the 45 pounds are intact. For God's sake write to St Thorax, if this has not been done yet. I told some people here that 'people we know are inviting my wife to the country, but she cannot go alone with the child, because this way it won't be a rest for her'. I called Sergey R., but he wasn't home. On Sunday, I'm playing tennis with Lourie. I feel well, but I'm dreaming of you and of peace (and of butterflies, *ça va sans dire*). It seems to me I'm managing all my affairs rather well, but I don't hear any praise from you. I kiss you, my beloved.

MY DARLING, I ADORE AND EMBRACE YOU. HOW'S THE CAPTAIN?

V.

[ALS, 2 PP.]
[8 June 1939]

TO: 59, rue Boileau, Paris XVI

20, Hornton str.
[London]
8–VI–39
8.30 a.m.

My darling, *I did not like your letter, it is quite off the point.* I want to go on the 17th. The 20th at the latest – it's the final limit – since I want to get hold of some first generations. Write to her. Next: 1) if I am 'having fun', then it's obviously because I have time: one cannot do any special business in London on a Sunday morning. 2) Lub[r]zynsky is taking care of the play. When there's only one copy, it is generally hard to 'do' anything. I've asked him in any case to get it copied 3) Mme Tyrkov was away – I couldn't see her before today, although I've already talked to her on the phone 4) Grinberg gave £30. I didn't tell you that it was for our settling permanently *mais c'est toujours quelque chose. Foolish and annoying.* 5) Collins didn't need any letters from Paris, since what they wanted was precisely a personal meeting. For Englishmen, the colour of an author's eyes can sometimes play a decisive role. 6) I wrote to Hill on Saturday – but this does not matter much 7) We should have excused ourselves from the Churches' absolutely meaningless invitation – *you don't know what those parties are – I do.* But I did write to them that 'my wife and I will be *delighted* to come, if only business doesn't keep me in London'.

11 a.m.

I began the letter before breakfast and was angry. Now it's over. So, my happiness, this is what my day was like yesterday. Mme Tsetlin apparently has already talked to some people. I have to call on her again on Monday. Then I will know for sure how much we can count on when we get here (besides Grinberg's, which of course I've not told anyone about). At 3.30 I was already at Victoria, where I drank lemonade with Molly. She said she was willing to check all my work in future too and so on, which is very sweet, *vu* that nothing has yet come of the play. At 5.45 I called in at Otto's and together with him went to Lovat Dickson (I suddenly realized – it was his magazine that once published '*The Passenger*'). There were lots of people there – I was on form – this sounds silly, but that's how I felt – spoke with Lovat for more than an hour (he's reading Sebast. for Macmillan), and everything went very well, the final response will come in a day or two. A new theory of literary creation flashed into my mind, which I immediately developed to him (however, I had already somehow thought about this: we don't look at a painting from left to right, but we take in everything at once; that's the principle a novel should be built upon, but because of the peculiarities of a book (pages, lines, and so on), it is necessary to read it through twice, and the second time is the real one). I had dinner with the Yakobsons. Serg. Iosif. suggested I see Thomson (in the committee for protection of *Science and Learning*), who has brought from America '8 places for Arians'. I'll see him. I hope *I shan[']t get into a mess* because Collins and Macmillan are both interested in 'Sebastian' at the same time. I'm asking Haskell for advice on this. I had lunch at Mme Chernavin's and this afternoon probably will go to *Fox Film Co.*, where as I was told they need *readers*; dinner at home, then to Mme Tyrkov's. This is beginning to bore me – especially after your letter. *But I love you tremendously*.

I KISS MY MITEN'KA.

V.

[ALS, 2 PP.]
[9 June 1939]

TO: 59, rue Boileau, Paris XVI

[London]
9–VI

My darling, my love, so, five more days and I'll be back. The more I think about it, the more I want to leave Paris on the 17th. Please let us not go to the Churches'! It's insanely far! It'll be wildly boring! It'll rain. I won't establish any 'contacts' there anyway. I implore you! This morning I was awoken by an unusually lively dream: Ilyusha (I think it was he) walks in and says that he'd been informed by phone that Khodasevich 'has ended his earthly existence'—word for word. Yesterday morning I was at (and then had lunch there) Mme Chernavin's. Got a translation,—a scientific article about determining the age of the mouse *Mus flavicollis* from its bones—30 pages of small print. I took it, because, after all, it works out at 7 and a half pounds, but I have to finish it in four days. I sat down to work around two in Kensington Park and then (when the sky clouded over) continued at home—I did almost a third—wildly hard and painfully written 5+10+30+7½ . . . . Then I went to Fox Film Co., a very nice lady said that they constantly need *readers* in Russian and French, she took down my address, etc. I continued the mouse, had dinner at home, then went to see Mme Tyrkov. As she'd already told me, she went to inspect cottages rented for refugees' needs 5 hours from London, but she says it's horrible there, earthen floors, damp, everything is beggarly—she wouldn't dare place E. K. and Rostik there. Now she'll make efforts to settle them in a Russian dorm here, where conditions are much better. She thinks something will come of this and overall she was very cordial.

Today I got letters from Hill (nothing useful), from Birch (I'll see him). I'll occupy myself with the mouse till 1, then lunch at Eva's, at 3 – no, Gubsky is tomorrow – it's Struve today. At 8 I'll have dinner at Politzer's. *I have had enough, I want my work.* Vera Markovna is enchantingly sweet, meticulously attentive – charming! Two days ago, in a wild rush between Lee and Lovat, in fierce heat, I sweated so much that in despair I walked into a *chemist's*, asked for *talc-powder* and an old lady there said: *you are the third gentleman today who wants me to sprinkle his back* – she sat me down on a chair and began to sprinkle talc down my collar. *My darling*, I am afraid I'll find you very tired and stressed. Let's send the Churches to the *chort* – please! It's quite cool today. I keep thinking what to bring you. Would you like gloves? Size? Or *shorts*? Waist? Or does none of this make any difference?

I hope to bring around 60 p. total. *I adore you, I kiss you so.*

DO YOU MISS ME, MY HAPPINESS? I WILL BRING A WONDERFUL AIR BALLOON ... JUST KIDDING!

V.

Thank you, my life, for your marvellous little letter, I will reply to the little boy tomorrow.

I beg you to leave no later than the 20th. I wrote to her I think on the 23rd, but write to her again. I love, I love, I love.

[ALS, 2 PP.]
[10 June 1939]

TO: 59, rue Boileau, Paris XVI

22, Hornton str.
[London]
10–VI–39
10 a.m.

My beloved darling,

Yesterday morning I worked on my mouse – tortuous work, I am sorry I took it, but I have to finish by Tuesday. Then had lunch at the Lutyens'; he is the subtlest and nicest of men, and in intelligence and flair many heads taller than his wife. She believes that the *grant* problem will be resolved before my departure – but I don't think so. In any case I finally reached the 'literary fund'. From there, I went to Struve's, who had written about me to Thomson to that very same *Union for Protection* I'd applied to before; but now after my candidacy at Leeds and Pares's efforts, I have a chance of getting the same kind of loan there as the young wooden Frank. From there, I went to have dinner at the Politzers', where there were the Haskells, Waldman and his wife, and the well-known bookseller Buchanan (who got plastered in the course of the evening and talked utter poppycock). Waldman (Collins's partner) invited me to the final discussions on Tuesday. Apparently we are talking about a contract. He very much liked *La Course du Fou*; it seems to me they want both books, the second in my translation. Politzer begged me to have nothing to do with *baroness Bugbear* or *Bedbug* (as he calls her), since her reputation sinks the books that he places. Haskell has composed a letter, which *je suis sensé* to send to Otto Theis (her partner). And in fact my discussion with her had only been about offering the book to Chatto and Windus (and I thought that Otto had introduced them). That he would simply go on placing the book and is now already offering it to Macmillan (Lovat Dickson) wasn't envisaged at all. All this isn't very pleasant – although everyone consoles me that all writers find themselves in such situations.

This morning I am going to Frank Birch, a rather famous man, about the *Foreign Office*. Then lunch with guests at the Haskells', and then I'll go to the Gubskys'. In the evening, the theatre. Between the Gubskys and the theatre I'll translate. My love, how I adore you today, and my little one, my little one … Get your little teeth seen to, I don't want to postpone our departure. Overall, the horizon's got a bit rosier – a delayed shade … Well, three more days, and I'll be back. By the 20th I can perhaps write the essay for Rudnev, it's ready in my head. And it's time to start the new book. And to kiss you, my enchantment.

THANK YOU FOR THE BUTTERFLIES, MY DARLING, AND FOR YOUR LETTER. I WILL BE BACK SOON!

V.

[ALS, 2 PP.]

[11 June 1939]

TO: 59, r. Boileau, Paris 16

[London]

11–VI

midnight

My love, when the value $t = \frac{D'}{mD}$ determines the actuality or non-actuality of the difference between the average of 2 samples … etc., etc. – thirty thickly-packed pages *of that stuff*. I have only five left to do.

Yesterday morning I called on Frank Birch, whom, it turned out, I had met more than once in Cambridge! He took a copy of my papers, proposed to make more and send them out to a list of persons he composed right away – so I could get a *job* at the *Foreign Office*. He was awfully sweet and said about my papers *that they are 'quite formidable'*. I had lunch with six people at Haskell's, then went to see the Gubskys, spent an hour there and by four had already sat down to this thrice-cursed translation, working till half-past eight, when we went to the theatre – an idiotic *revue, very topical*, terrible poshlost, and then we had supper at home. I played tennis at the club this whole morning, it was very jolly and pleasant, lunched there too, then visited Lourie and at five again glued myself to the translation. I worked without a break till 9.30, when they called me to supper. Vera Mark. was not there, but Haskell brought over 'a little dancer' – very pretty, with heavy legs and awfully shy. He was very proud at the theatre last night, because he was mentioned in one of the sketches: '*our Arnold*'. Straight after supper, I carried on working and am now totally exhausted. I hope to finish this tomorrow morning, then go to Aunt Baby, then lunch at Mme Tsetlin's, then Thomson, then dinner at the Harrises'. I am very, very tired. It seems that two letters are flowing into one, since I usually write in the morning, but today I've already described two days, my happiness. Tomorrow evening will be the last letter from here. One of my tennis partners was Fulda's son, the old man lives in Merana. I adore you and I can't wait to return. There's a lot that has to get resolved over the last two days, although it's already clear that 1) we can get through the summer no trouble and 2) we come here in October. *Lots of kisses, my sweet darling.*

AND HOW IS YOUR LITTLE SCHOOL, MY LITTLE ONE? I AM COMING ON WEDNESDAY. IT'S A RHYME. I LOVE YOU AND YOUR MUMMY.

V.

[ALS, 1 P.]
[12 June 1939]

TO: 59, rue Boileau, Paris XVI

[London]
12–VI–39
7 p.m.

My love, I've been so overburdened with work and errands today that I'll have time to write you only a few words. I've spoken about Rostik to many people, but it is impossible in many cases to mix these two plans, i.e. searching simultaneously for a *job*, etc., and asking to settle a nephew. Two people told me: 'Set up your son first'. In any case the question of our (first my, then your) move here has been settled. Mme Tsetlin promises to find the £100 needed for the first three months. I've just finished my translation and am taking it to Mme Chernavin tomorrow; Collins is tomorrow as well. No later than the 25th, my joy, remember! Or I'll go alone (Oh? So. Please – you can go completely on your own . . .) I am kidding, my dear happiness, and I love you very very much.

AND YOU, MY DARLING, MEET ME AT THE STATION ON WEDNESDAY AT FIVE FORTY-FIVE.

V.

1941

[ALS, 4 PP.]
[postmarked 18 March 1941]

TO: 35 West 87th Street, New York City

WELLESLEY COLLEGE
WELLESLEY, MASSACHUSETTS

My darling,

I've just received yours with the sweet postscripts from *miss* W. and L. and with Miten'ka's Chinese scribbles. Mansvetov is a fool and a scoundrel. I had a feeling that he, the philistine, would take fright. I love you. Boris Vasilyevich knows Borodin well, says that his face is rather like a swarthy backside and that he is a dark, pitch-dark character, all but a Communist provocateur, and for his boorishness was given a sharp kick out of the firm where they'd both been working. But how will you do without that 50 from Mansvetov? Any day now the editor of the '*Antlantic*' should get in touch with me, maybe he will take a piece, and then I'll immediately send you something. If there's a reply from *New Rep.*, send it on, I'd like to write an article here, lots of free time and a wonderful quiet room. At the Bogoslavskys' I found an ebbing wave of people (two or three American couples and a, rather pretty, Russian girl, whom Boris obviously fancies), played chess with him and thoroughly prepared my first two lectures. Went to bed early, took Bellofolit and almost immediately something unbelievable began in my stomach (all day till then I had had something weighing on my stomach, although I hadn't eaten any rich food) – and on top of that, wild shivering, fever, a temperature of forty to judge by the pulse, and nausea. The house was asleep, the rising wind bursting through the chinks in the window (so that the curtain was behaving as if the window were wide open), and my condition was such that I was already thinking with horror how tomorrow I would telegraph to *Wellesley* that I couldn't come. Piled on myself everything warm that I could get hold of and having finished the lectures (which already seemed nightmarishly useless) went to sleep around four a.m. In the morning woke up in soaked-through pyjamas ideally healthy, with a long-forgotten lightness in my stomach, which I still have. What was the matter? I think it was a real crisis, since the contrast between the night and the morning was utterly stunning – so stunning that I've got from it a rather marvellous thing that will go to fertilize one place in the new 'Gift'. And besides I love you, my darling, I'm kissing your little liver, and want so much for you to get well soon. Yesterday, as soon as I was ready, Boris Vas., who of course could not drive me in his car, informed me that actually in ten minutes the most, and the only, convenient train to Boston was leaving – and how I made it, I don't know. It took five hours or so, with many nonchalant transfers (Wellesley is one of the stations forming the idea of Boston), but I was feeling so wonderfully well that I just enjoyed the trip. Here the landscape is lovely, with hills and a lake, and college buildings reminiscent of Cambridge. B r e a k f a s t at 7.30, in a no-smoking common room. I sit at a separate table with five old-maid professors, and – what was her name, the owner of the Antibes house – with Miss Kelly who looks a lot like her, but who is very sweet. All utterly charming and comfortable.

Between today's two morning lectures (*Russian Novel, XIX century* and *Short Story Gorky-Chek[h]ov*) they hauled me off, naturally, to look over the treasures of their library, all sorts of first editions and tattered folios, which always make me queasy. But the very round little holes made by a worm in the first translation of Euclid, tiny holes as it were illustrating the rather less perfectly presented theorems, pleased me by their subtle mockery: 'can do better'. The lady librarian *rather misunderstood my delight* and dragged me off to the department of Italian manuscripts.

The lectures went very well. Miss Perkins (whom I twice called Miss Pinkley), a roundish, slightly Jewish-looking spinster, was there and was, I think, satisfied. The girls are all sporty-looking, down gloves everywhere, lots of pimples and lip colour, very pleasant all in all. Karpovich called, will go to see him on Saturday.

Am kissing you my dear love, be fit and strong, as my exile used to write.

V.

[ALS, 4 PP.]
[19 March 1941]

TO: 35 W 87, New York City

Trinity
~~WELLESLEY~~ COLLEGE
WELLESLEY, MASSACHUSETTS

19 III 41

My beloved darling,

Good news: today, the editor of the '*Antlantic*' called me from Boston – *We are enchanted with your story, it is just what we have been looking for, we want to print it at once*, and much more sweet talk. He asked for more and more. On Monday I'll have lunch with him in Boston. I wrote to Pertzov about this. It's made an impression here – a very lucky break.

And that's not even mentioning the lectures. Every time ('The Proletarian Novel' yesterday, and today was 'The Soviet Drama') there are more people and applause, and praise, and invitations, and so on. Both of my chaperones, Perkins and the very sweet Kelly, beam. How are you, my love? Write. I do not know yet how much the Antlantides will fork out – but the preliminary compliments should somehow be reflected in the lengthening of the figures on the lake of the price. I love you very much. Tomorrow's a free day, I'll polish the next lectures, on Saturday at 2 I am going to Karpovich's, will be back on Monday by 6. It's warmer today, the snow more sugary, the sky has a Menton tone, and everywhere in the building the sun is trying to draw circles or squares. *Et je t'aime*. I feel onderful (I had the cigarette holder between my teeth) – I feel wonderful, smoking less, because it's not allowed in most rooms here. I have written to Miss Ward, Chekhov, Dasha, Natasha, Lisbetsha. Today, I lectured in an especially large and full hall with an organ and a pulpit.

Miss Perkins picked up a strange infection in Constantinople, her head drops to the left, so that she keeps propping it up very skilfully and unobtrusively, now with a finger, now her purse, but I noticed it right away. Today, with her, I corrected the girls' English essays, and she accepted all my corrections (and at the same time I corrected one of her corrections). Yesterday I had dinner at the girls' club, 'you can imagine' how I pranced at the table surrounded by beauties and trying not to spit through the hole in my mouth. We began with academic conversations, but I very quickly lowered the level – in a word, *très bien, très beau parleur*, but Miss Perkins had warned me that I should stay till half past seven, but no longer. She will be in New York and wants to meet you. Judging by some little h i n t s and the genre of their questions, I have an impression that they may invite me for the autumn – I don't know.

It turns out that in the previous issue of the '*Atlantic*' (I've been writing it the whole time with an extra 'n', like incident) there were publisher's howls that they couldn't go on like this, that they needed real things, no matter about what, but real. *La rosse rousse sera bien enfoncée* (I have just had a conversation with a professor of French – it's contagious). I wonder what to translate next (in the same way, with P., with whom it's pleasant and easy to work), what do you think? 'Tyrants'? 'Breaking the News'? Or shall I write one LITTLE PIECE IN RUSSIAN – and then translate it? 'Living at Wellesley College, among the oaks and sunsets of peaceful New England, he dreamed of changing his American fountain-pen for his own incomparable Russian feather-pen.' (From 'Vladimir Sirin and His Time', 2074, Moscow). My Cambridge moods are somehow coming back to me. I kiss you, my darling, my incomparable little feather. Do write!

V.

[ALS, 3 PP]
[20 March 1941]

TO: 35 W 87, New York City

WELLESLEY COLLEGE
WELLESLEY, MASSACHUSETTS

20–III–41

From that night on, my stomach has been completely fine!

My love,

Today, I am quietly working on my lectures and translations from Pushkin. I'm afraid that I won't have time to write to you tomorrow: in the morning, there is a '*talk*' in the English style and composition class (in a word, in the department of English), for half an hour or so (not part of my programme, but I agreed), and then a lecture on S o v i e t S h o r t. After that—Boston.

I went for a walk this morning, the wind has turned towards spring, very distinctly, but it's still cold. The paper-white, indecently slender trunks of little American birches against the background of a young blue sky. The wrapping paper of dry oak foliage. The sharply bright, red, blue frames of girls' bikes (don't forget two things tomorrow: bike, Stein!) leaning against fir-trees.

I walked on my own. *Seul. Solus.*

Here, for example, is this:

[tempest nighing]
That sea-day with a storm impending—
how enviously did I greet
[dying]
the rush of tumbling billows ending
in adoration at her feet!

I wonder whether Miten'ka will get the point of the drawing I did for him.

Explain to him first that skaters trace out an 8 and that Romans wore such 'gowns'. *Ich hab gedacht dass ich bekomme ein Brief von Dir heute.* The local professor of German did not know who or what Kafka was.

The very sweet Miss Kelly now sends me a *plateau* with a luxurious breakfast in bed, having sensed that I won't be able to stand for long those common meals at a quarter past seven. The cook has sworn that '*we are going to put some fat on the bones of that man*' and now leans over backward to fry up as many kinds of sweet pastries as she can, which I hate. I adore you, my kitty.

V.

FOR MITEN'KA

A ROMAN EIGHT

[ALS, 3 PP.]
[24 March 1941]

[TO: New York]

WELLESLEY COLLEGE
WELLESLEY, MASSACHUSETTS

5 p.m., Mon.

My dear darling,

I've received only two letters from you, the first with postscripts by H. and L. and another, just now, from Musin'ka Nabokov. But was there anything in between?

I have just returned from the Karpoviches', where it was as agreeable as always, but also cosy in a new way – a very bright and light house, which has not yet managed (although it's starting to, in some corners) to blossom. The water in their tub was, as I told Tatyana, more like (warm) friendship than (hot) love. There were lots of guests yesterday – Evgeny Rabinovich (!), still as padded up and thick-legged as before, Pertsov's brother, Lednitsky – a yellowish-swarthy Pole who, when telling about his escape, always repeats: … 'well, I took along the little things I needed – eau d'cologne, toothbrush'. With dead eyes and ideally ungifted. Today I had lunch with Weeks – it turned out he is also a *Trinity College man*! He will send the galleys to me here. I think I'll now give him 'Spring in F'. One of the lady *readers*, who was also at the lunch, told me: '*I knew you would be distinguished, but I didn't know you would be fun.*' Dinner-time now. I love you. I still do not know how you feel. The bike is going tomorrow to New York straight to our apartment. I have two lectures tomorrow, '*Technique of Novel*' and a repetition of Chekhov-Gorky. Tonight, I will have to apply myself, some things still aren't done. It is damp, rainy, everything's runny like a watercolour that's too wet. This is my 4th letter.

I adore you.

V.

MY MUSIN'KA, THE BIKE IS RIDING TO YOU!
THIS IS WHAT IT LOOKS LIKE! Daddy.

[ALS, 3 PP.]
[postmarked 25 March 1941]

TO: 35 West 87 Street, New York City

WELLESLEY COLLEGE
WELLESLEY, MASSACHUSETTS

My dear love, I've received that in-between (and dear) letter, which I was already mourning. I'm happy you're feeling better. Yes, let's put off responding to Mr Dimwitsvetov. To Chairman Sedykh I am responding that I could, but I need to know how much they pay: it's not worth taking less than 50 for one lecture or 200 for five (and I can't do more than five). And I will offer to read my own work. Exactly fifty years ago Sergey Volkonsky was here and left the most vulgar description of *Wellesley* in his 'Wanderings'.

It's now midday, I have just returned from my two lectures: very successful. But I dare say that when they tell me '*it will be a tragedy when you go away*', this is the merest American courtesy.

Tomorrow morning – no, the day after tomorrow – I am going cap in hand before the President, whom I imagine as a queen bee or ant. Today I had my first lunch with a man here – a professor of English literature. You don't write to me how your other little health is. Absolutely between us: I want to go home. When I feel that my lectures will last less than 50 minutes, I gain time by writing in chalk the names of Russian writers on the blackboard. I had to speak several times without notes, though – explaining or answering questions – and it was rather easy.

Won't I really be able to draw something for Miten'ka before lunch? I still have a wonderfully pleasant impression of the *Atlantic* and of Weeks. I kiss you on the clavicle, my bird.

V.

MITEN'KA
CHUG CHUG CHUG CHUG
THE BIKE IS COMING
LOVE YOU

D.

[ALS, 3 PP.]
[postmarked 26 March 1941]

TO: 35 West 87th Street, New York City

WELLESLEY COLLEGE
WELLESLEY, MASSACHUSETTS

Wednesday
morning

My love,

I've just received the galleys of 'Cloud etc' and a very sweet letter from Weeks. Now I am leaving for lunch; I've been preparing in bed today's after-dinner lecture, the most important (the final part of '*Technique of Novel*': *Vosstorg and Vdakhnovenia*) and gone for a little walk: bright wind, strong sun, one can pump a *fountain-pen* straight from the lake; not a single butterfly. Yesterday I had dinner with Miss Perkins and three other sweet ruins. Brown told me – after I had complained that it was impossible to grasp the truth through the exaggerated compliments – that they really are extraordinarily pleased. The fountain spouts (or rather sputters) very audibly through the elephantine mound of ice completely covering it.

5 p.m.

Tatyana Nik. very opportunely came for the lecture (an open one today), then had tea in my room, and meanwhile your precious letter arrived, about the Anyuta situation. Karpovich has already received it and will do everything, but just in case I have arranged to stay with them from Saturday to Sunday (I am leaving for Ridgefield from Boston at 1 p.m.—which means on the 30th—and I think that on the 1st or 2nd I'll already be heading off to New York). The lecture was very grand and stood me in good stead. Just one is left, on Saturday morning (the repetition of *Sov. short*). Now they're taking me to a celebratory dinner, then to the theatre. I somehow did not manage to ask Weeks how much they will pay, but those in the know say that for an ordinary article of that size they pay 150 dollars. We'd better refanglicize 'Spring' pretty soon. Aldanov thrust a story on Pertzov, and he has agreed. I do not like it that you're still in your little bed. I kiss my Musin'ka Nabokov and you, my tenderness. Thanks to the Antlantic, we can easily scramble out of debts and there'll be something for a trip.

I love you still.

V

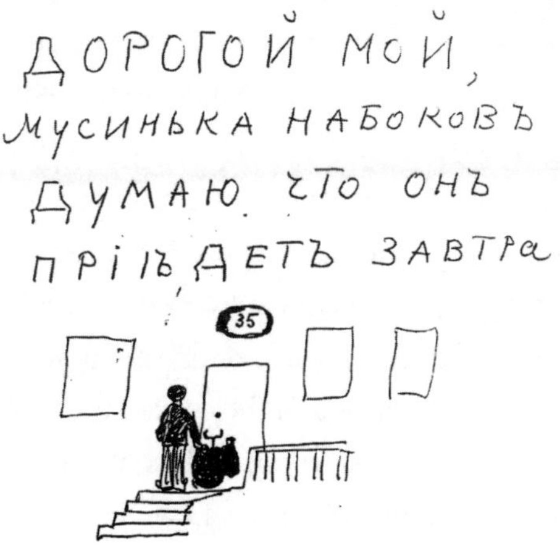

MY DEAR
MUSIN'KA NABOKOV
I THINK IT WILL
ARRIVE TOMORROW

[ALS 5 PP.]
[28 March 1941]

TO: 35 W 87, New York City

WELLESLEY COLLEGE
WELLESLEY, MASSACHUSETTS

28–III–41

My sweet love,

I've received a very warm letter from Dennis and have responded definitively to him, that I am ready to write an article of 3,000 for the *New Rep.*, '*Art of Translating*'. Yesterday, I slept and wrote. Today is March 28th. I have written to Bertrand, Schwartz, Wilson, Sedykh, Weeks, Bogoslovsky, Edgar Fisher, Lorrimer, Dennis, Aldanov, and sent off the p r o o f s. This evening, I was at a very boring concert by a certain Lilly Pons, an acrobatic soprano, tinted orange, like a sun-tan, in a white broad-skirted dress. A small dark Jewish flautist who looked like a shy satyr. There were so many in the theatre that they put a hundred or so on the stage – the elderly males and females of the *New Yorker* to a tee. I somehow did not think of going up to Koussevitzky. And last night there was a banquet – the entire *staff* of the English department and the brightest and most beautiful girls. After which they asked me to speak about Mansfield, Flaubert, Proust, and so on, and what came out was provoking and lively. It's now eight a.m., I love you. At 11 I am going to present myself to Mrs President, a young lady I have already g l i m p s e d at the concert.

On Sunday, April 20th, you and I will dine with Miss Perkins in the *Russian Tea-room*. Yesterday I suddenly realized whom she's strangely like – with her way of keeping a finger at her temple, her slight tic, her habit of bowing a tad when something. She is very *pointedly* interested in you (*Wellesley-rein?*). As far as I understand, Bobbs-Merr. is interested in a risky film venture, how about that?

Tomorrow after the morning lecture I'm off to the Karpoviches'. All in all, everything here was unusually successful (except for one *lapsus lingui* during the discussion yesterday: student: '*but don't you think that a reader must live with the characters?*' I: '*no, – with the author.*') The next, my bird, will probably be only on Monday from Ridgef. Love you.

V.

12 p.m.

I'm carrying on after my visit to Mrs President. I was told they were so pleased with me that they will pay 300 doll. (inst. of 250), which at least is concrete. At one I'll lunch at her place with dear Perkins and Kelly. I've just received your very sweet one. Yes, tomorrow I'll put firm pressure on M. M. I have no doubt he'll do everything. Today the weather is blue-greyish, very warm – and the seagulls have caught all the little goldfish in the pond. After a long argument, I've paid 2 doll. and 60 c. for the shipment of the bike. When I left, I had 6 or 7 dollars, I don't remember. The ticket to Darien cost a dollar. Yes, I had around five in Darien. The trip from Darien here cost more than six. I borrowed 10 from Bogoslovsky. Here almost every day they give or send a taxi cab for me, and each time it is 25 or 50 c. On top of that the bike, cigarettes and other little things. In a word, I don't have enough to go to Ridgefield and home – if I don't cash the cheque. Poor, poor old man H. Have you mailed my letter? They asked me: do I want a *permanent job*. Don't know, don't know – as Zyoka used to say. True, it's charming here – but all the trees are sprayed, so there are probably not many butterflies. I've already written to the Russian club for 50. Yes, on Thursday I should already be home. I am going through Norwork to Chekh. – not Norfolk. My God, I must run. I adore you, my kitty.

V.

MY DARLING,
SO, HAS THE LITTLE BIKE ARRIVED?
I WILL ARRIVE SOON MYSELF.

I KISS YOU ON MY FAVOURITE PLACE.

IT'S UNCOUPLING!

WELLESLEY COLLEGE
WELLESLEY, MASSACHUSETTS

Милый мой
постригли ли
тебя?
Ходишь ли въ
снѣжный паркъ?
Люблю тебя
папочка

MY DEAR
DID THEY CUT YOUR HAIR?
DO YOU GO TO THE SNOWY PARK?
LOVE YOU
DADDY

[ALS, 3 PP.]
[31 March 1941]

TO: 35 West 87th, New York City

[Ridgefield, Conn.]
31–III–41
morning

My fine love,

Because of all the travelling about, I absolutely couldn't fit in writing to you. The last lecture, on Saturday, seems to have been the most successful (*short story Sov.*–a repetition, but I revamped it). After it, I went with Miss Kelly to look at a famous butterfly collection in the private home I love you of the collector Denton–and, indeed, marvellous specimens, but with catastrophic labels and without *localities*. Then Tatyana arrived and we drove to their place. Poor M. M. has a boil on his head. He swore to me that on Monday, i.e. today, everything would be done. I put pressure on, said everything you had written, and I think it'll all be done.

Yesterday afternoon I set off for here–a six-hour ride, but now I'm already close to you. A charming hilly place rather like Vermont, crystal clusters in running streams, an absolutely lilac day, forest, thawed patches, but not a single butterfly. In the evening I had a four-hour-long conversation with Chekhov about Don Quixote, he liked my little piece a lot, and the changes he wants are simple and generally in tune. But this won't be my thing, of course. Christian revelations and so on. We'll work again tonight. I'll arrive on Wednesday the 2nd. They placed me in the actors' dorm (in the male wing I love you), much less comfortable than Wellesley (of which overall I've retained a simply charming and for me extremely flattering impression,–it couldn't be better in all senses). Sun, shadows, and Zhukovsky's paintings. Chekhov is part Lukash, plus genius. Now I am going to a rehearsal. In the afternoon I'll see Zhdanov and his class. When I was getting out of the carriage, the handle of my suitcase broke off. I adore you, my dear one.

V.

MY MITYUSHEN'KA
HOW DOES IT GO?
MY JOY!
D.

[AN, 1 P.]
[Undated. 1941–1942?]

My darling, Miss Perkins is begging me to come for tea in the *Faculty Room* (*Green Hall*), so I'll call in on Miss Kelly around 3.15 and around four will sail over with her to the *Fac. Room*. Come on over there.

1942

[AN 1 P.]
[May 1942 or later]
[Place unclear]

Vérochka,

Do for me in English first of all a typed list of all that Chichikov ate that day starting with breakfast (two) at Korobochka's and ending with dinner (p. 38–115) and what Plyushkin offered Ch III–VI.

Title this
Chic[hi]kov's diet during one day of 75 pages ()
(contrasted with what he did not eat at Pl[y]ushkin's).

[ALS, 2 PP.]
[3 August 1942]
c/o Mrs Bertrand Thompson, Commander Hotel, Cambridge Mass

West Wardsboro, Vermont
3. VIII. 42

My dear darling, only today did I get your little letter with the bears. I think there's no need for you to catch that bumpy ride with Newell on Thursday (and it's not clear whether he's going at all); it would be better to come on Saturday with the Derricks and Natasha. Mityushen'ka's behaving very well, and although I don't get a single line written, it's best to prolong this inactivity for two more days. The Karpoviches are driving to Cambridge on Wednesday, so you should call Mrs Levin to discuss the time and place of the Derricks' departure. I'll phone Lisbet tomorrow.

The landlady writes that if we move our things before 15-VIII, we won't have to pay for August. I enclose her letter and a letter from the Jewish Society. The Russian paper says today that 'the inspection of passengers (among whom "I. Feigin" is named) who arrived in Baltimore is proceeding very slowly. 175 people have been transferred temporarily from the steamboat to Baltimore's "Island of Tears"'. Maybe you should phone the Brombergs (she wrote here about Anyuta's arrival and that she had sent her a telegram to go to New York). I don't think it worth her dragging herself for ten days to Vermont.

He played ball marvellously today; spread five butterflies and signed the labels himself; built a new house with Marisha; bought a new Superman which I read to him at bedtime; he eats lots and falls straight to sleep.

The weather is vile: rather clear, a kind of convulsive sun and incessant wind. I love you. No moths – i.e. opening the window is impossible – it's blowing too hard. Overall, a rather useless summer, but it's doing him good. I read 'The Nose' to him. He laughed a lot, but prefers Superman.

Don't forget to bring: 1) rum 2) the box 3) pins (*medium*). Tell Banks that I miss the museum a lot.

You wrote me such a darling letter. If the apartment turns out to be good, but a tad expensive – take it. I'd rather groan over a payment than discomforts. These *Arctia virgo* flutter in like a Harlequin onto the stage (I have just opened the window a bit, to the lamp's great consternation). And don't forget about my room. I will have lots of work this winter.

The bank sent your cheques. Goldenweiser says he will pass on 50 doll. to Anyuta. I will write a Russian poem one of these days. He has suddenly understood how you need to catch and throw.

The little cart has not arrived yet; it'll probably come tomorrow. I kiss you my dear joy, my constant superdurable and marvellous joy.

V.

I am addressing this to Lisbet. Otherwise it will boomerang back here.

A letter from Anyuta arrived at the last moment. It's enclosed. Kissing you tenderly.

[APCS]

[postmarked 2 October 1942]

TO: 8, Craigie Circle, Cambridge, Mass.

[Hartsville, South Carolina]

Friday

Morning

My darling, just a few words to say that I adore you and that I arrived happily after various adventures at 6 pm, while the lecture (very successful) was at eight. I am now running to the next one (three in all). I will write to you in detail again today.

Kiss my Miten'ka and Anyuta.

V.

[ALS, 8 PP.]
[2–3 October 1942]

TO: 8 Craigie Circle, app. 35, Cambridge, Mass.

[Hartsville, South Carolina]
2-3-X
Friday and Saturday

My sweetheart,

a million butterflies and a thousand ovations (corrected for ardent Southern expansiveness).

But I had the vilest of trips. When I climbed into a sleeping-car in New York, it turned out that my berth was occupied by another horizontal passenger, who had been sold the same number as mine. He however took it meekly and we had a friendly chat in the atrium of the lavatory while the conductors solved our little problem. At last he was sent to another car and I scrambled up to my legitimate place–which happened around midnight. Couldn't sleep at all, since at the numerous stations the wild jolts and thunderings of the train cars' couplings and unlatchings allowed no rest. By day, lovely landscapes skimmed past–huge trees in a profusion of forms–with their somehow oily tint and iridescent greenery reminding me either of the image I have of the valleys of the Caucasus or of the sublimated vegetation of Potter (with a dash of Corot). Not the least trace of autumn and yet the softest 'enchantment of the eyes'. When I got off in Florence, I was immediately surprised by the heat and the sun, and the gaiety of the shadows–like what you feel when you reach the Riviera from Paris. The train was an hour late, and of course the bus had long since gone. I called *Coker*, and they replied that they would call back about a car. I waited an hour and a half, in a little restaurant, by the telephone booth, in a state of ever-increasing fatigue, unshavenness and irritation.

Finally a rich voice said to me on the phone that he was in Florence on business, that he was a professor (I didn't catch his name) at the college, that they had informed him about the situation, and that around six he would return – with me – to Hartsville. The lecture was scheduled for eight. I asked, in what must have seemed a rather pale voice, how he imagined I would wait there (there were three hours to go till six), and then he merrily said that he would come over immediately and take me to a hotel, he didn't say which, and I wasn't even sure whether I had understood him correctly. I headed for the *waiting room* nearby and began to wait for him. After a while I got a feeling that a young taxi driver, talking with someone on the taxi phone by the entrance (I had gone outside, bored by the hard benches and the stuffiness), had pronounced my name. I walked closer and asked whether it was my name he had said. It turned out to be a mistake – he had had a call from some Yellowater or something like that – something that was remotely similar in sound. But then, being talkative, he told me that his friend, who someone from some hotel had ordered to bring someone from the railroad station, wrecked his car when he hit a truck and asked him to take on the job. It sounded to me as if the name of the hotel was exactly the one mentioned by the rich voice, and I proposed, for his somewhat slow consideration, the question: perhaps I was the one he was supposed to pick up. It turned out that, indeed, the gentleman was to go to Hartsville, but his colleague told him neither my name nor the name of the man who had sent him, and now he was out of reach. As no one was coming for me and as I had absolutely no idea what to do (well, I could certainly get a car for ten dollars and just go to *Coker* – but I was afraid that the owner of the rich voice would search for me for ever), I decided for some reason that I was the person in question. When I was delivered with my suitcase to the Salmon Hotel, it turned out that no one there knew anything. The last weak link with

Hartsville represented by the driver who had delivered me disappeared (I had foolishly let him go), and I was sticking around the hall with a nightmarish feeling that everything was an utter misunderstanding, that I had been brought here instead of someone else and that the Voice was looking for me hopelessly at the railroad station.

Thinking it over, I decided to call the college again, at least, to find out the name of the Voice; at the same time I hadn't finished my big business on the train and had the urge to do that immediately. When I was approaching the office for the requisite information, I heard how one of the numerous people in the hall was saying to another that he could not understand what was the matter–why the taxi he had sent to the station hadn't returned. I interfered and asked rather desperately whether it was me he was waiting for. '*Oh no*,' he said, '*I am waiting for a Russian professor*.' '*But I am the Russian professor!*' '*Well, you don't look like one*,' he said with a laugh, and here everything became clear, and we embraced. He turned out to be Ingram by name, a professor of theology, very good-natured and just very nice. It was already around four, and he promised that having finished what he had to do he would pick me up around five to drive me (fifty miles!) to *Coker*. Feeling that I wouldn't have time to shave before the lecture (the dinner was fixed for 6.15) I set out (after the lavatory where I had awful diarrhoea) to a barber's. They shaved me horribly, leaving my Adam's apple all bristly, and since in the next chair a wildly screaming five-year-old child was fighting with the barber who was trying to touch the back of his head with the clippers, the old man shaving me was nervous, hushed the child, and finally cut me slightly under the nose.

Ingram arrived on time and just as we managed to get to our first corner a skinny lady called to us from the edge of the pavement. When we stopped, she was all embarrassed and said that she had taken our car for a taxi and (as everyone here is very talkative) added that she was trying to get to *Coker College*–where her daughter was a student–and was afraid to be late for a Russian writer's lecture. The day was obviously a day of whimsical coincidences, and so here were the three of us rolling along the highway, talking about Christianity and the war–a very good but somewhat tiresome conversation, lasting right to Hartsville. At six on the dot I was driven into a magnificent estate, to the magnificent multi-columned mansion of Mrs Coker (the *belle-fille* of the college founder, Major Coker, who lost a leg during the Civil War and who lived till he was 90), and here I remain as a guest till Tuesday. As soon as I barged in she told me that in ten minutes the guests invited in my honour would arrive, and at breakneck speed I began to bathe and tug at my dinner-jacket armour. I love you. The shirt came out so starched that the cufflinks would not go through the cuffs, and it ended with one of them rolling under the bed (to be discovered only today). Finally, seeing that it was already twenty past six, I shrugged off the cuffs and appeared downstairs 'without a trace of underwear'. Intuition prompted me to demonstrate the lack of cufflinks there and then, and someone else's cufflinks appeared at once, and to the approval of all, one of the ladies (but not the prettiest) attached them to my cardboard wrists. From that minute everything went smoothly and successfully.

The photograph had not been sent here, so it's no surprise that the college was expecting a gentleman with Dostoevsky's beard, Stalin's moustache, Chekhov's pince-nez, and in a Tolstoyan blouse. The books hadn't got here yet, either (they came on Friday–I have been writing this letter for two days, my darling–it's now 10 p.m. Saturday). For that reason President Greene introduced me to the large audience in rather smoky fashion. I spoke on '*common sense*' and it turned out–well, even better than I normally expect. After that there was the good old

Wellesley 'punch' and lots of girls. About ten I came home with Mrs Coker and, having noticed on the brightly lit columns of the façade some very interesting moths, spent about an hour collecting them into a glass with carbona. You can imagine how tired I was by that confused day – but then I had a marvellous sleep and the next morning lectured on the *tragedy of tragedy* (and to finish the lecture theme: today's, the third and final one – also in the morning, consisted of reading '*Mlle O*' – for all this I received a cheque today – for a hundred dollars – which I will cash on Monday).

In front of the house there is a huge garden, around it huge trees, various species of live oaks, and in one corner flower beds and the amazing caramel fragrance of 'tea olive' – this all in the blue of a Crimean summer – and masses of butterflies. I caught them there after the lecture, and after breakfast the college biologist (rather like McCosh) drove me in her car to the woods – or rather the coppices by the lake, where I caught remarkable Hesperids and various kinds of Pierids. Wanted to send my dear Mityushen'ka one of the broadest local *Papilio*, but they are tattered, so I will send a '*eubule*', the most striking butterfly here – I will soak and spread it for him when I get back. It is hard to convey the bliss of roaming through this strange bluish grass, between blossoming bushes (one bush here is in bright berries, as if dyed in a cheap Easter purple – an utterly shocking chemical hue, but the main tree in the area is some very tender pine). To the west, cotton plantations, and the prosperity of the numerous Cokers who seem to own half of Hartsville is founded on this very cotton industry. It is picking time now – and the '*darkies*' (an expression that jars on me, reminding me distantly of the patriarchal 'Yid' of western Russian landowners) pick out in the fields, getting a dollar for a hundred '*bushels*' – I am reporting this interesting data because it stuck mechanically in my ears. In the evening there was a dinner at some other Cokers' (I am absolutely lost among all the different daughters-in-law, sons-in-law, and so on, but the father of my *hostess* was a famous artist, and his rather academic paintings and his self-portrait – *Uncle Sam* beard, *Napoleon III* moustache – hang everywhere; her *beau-père*, a Major – but I've already written about the Major). Today after the '*tragedy of tragedy*' I went collecting again – and again it was marvellous, and after breakfast a *presbyterian minister*, Smythe, turned up, a passionate butterfly collector and son of the famous lepidopterologist Smythe whom I know a good deal about (he worked on Sphingids). The minister and I, both with nets, headed for a new locality several miles away and collected till half past four; I got something for Bankes there (*Chrysoptera* flies). At five, the college's best tennis player, a botanist, drove over for me, and we had a very pleasant game (the white shorts came in handy) till six, after which there was dinner (have had a dinner-jacket on for three days in a row) and then, at the college, the kind of academic reception we both know. By the way, the last visiting lecturer was the rather spooky Charles Morgan.

My room is wonderful, of course, the string-instrument sound of the crickets at night, a train puffing somewhere far away. I hope that at the next lecture stops there will be as many butterflies – but less hospitality and less whisky on the rocks. I haven't spent a cent here yet, and Fisher writes to me that in Valdosta they are ready to lodge me for as long as I like. Tomorrow, besides another Coker dinner at a nearby estate, I seem to have no other *engagements*, and will go further afield to collect butterflies. They have one large tailed Hesperid with some peacock fluff on her body – charming. A great many of the people here have read my little pieces in the *Atlantic* and *New Yorker* – and in general the atmosphere here is the same middle-brow one as at Wellesley. I have told all the same jokes and anecdotes which I've told at the gatherings there, and in general have been spreading the same tinsel glitter which I am sick of. The minister and I collected lots of interesting caterpillars which he will raise. I am thirsty. All the glasses have carbona.

Here, my sweetheart, is a full account of Thursday, Friday and Saturday. I hope you have already been to the museum. I will write to Banks in the next few days – to tell him that I will stay a bit longer than I had thought (by the way Fisher has not sent the next itinerary yet – only a card about Valdosta). I am already madly impatient to return to you and the museum, and only when I fight my way through the bushes for some Thecla do I feel that it was worthwhile coming here. Greene is awfully and very touchingly pleased, such a sweet, jovial, child-like gentleman. One lady who had been complaining about caterpillars in her garden and whom I told that tailed butterflies would come out of them, replied '*I don't think so. I have never seen them grow wings or anything.*' One of the Cokers told me that when he was seeing off his wife leaving for Europe on the Bremen, some German next to him was waving a kerchief for all he was worth and shouted to his wife who was waving back from the deck: '*Geh zu deine Kabine: ich bin müde!*' In the evenings, those who have children rarely go out because (despite their wealth) they have no one to leave the kids with – Negro servants never sleep over in the whites' homes – it is not allowed – and they cannot have white servants because they cannot work with blacks. There are Uncle Toms sitting at every corner here.

Write to me in detail about everything, too. Kiss Anyuta: I think about our life together with great pleasure – I hope it will continue for years. I want so badly to let in one Acidalia perched outside on the dark-as-night glass, but the mosquitoes here are Riviera-ish, brutal. They have washed one change of underwear here for me.

I am kissing you my dear sweetheart – and please do not imagine that I am running after Creole girls here. Here they're more the Miss Perkins type, and the younger women have fiery husbands; I barely see any girl students. I'm being heartily fed on. I'll let her in anyway.

V.

MY MITYUSHOK, GREY WAR PLANES ARE FLYING HERE, LIKE FISH.

[ALS, 1 P.]
[5 October 1942]

TO: 8, Craigie Circle, ap. 35, Cambridge, Mass.

[Atlanta, GA]
5–X–42
Monday

My love, I leave Florence for Richmond tomorrow by the afternoon train. Yesterday–Sunday–I collected butterflies in the morning; rested and read after lunch; and about four went canoeing with one of the Cokers along the charming water cypress groves,–i.e. remember what we saw somewhere on the way to New Mexico–a winding river (or, rather, 'creek', the sleeve of a lake) all overgrown with cypress and cedar–and all of that mixed up and re-reflected, with all kinds of tunnels and backwaters, and the trunks of trees deeply rooted in the water's dark glass widen towards the bottom, at the level of the water, and then narrow down, elongated by their reflection. Here and there you meet red-bellied turtles on snags–and one can glide along these water cypress labyrinths for hours, seeing nothing except them. A not quite tropical, not quite Tertiary sensation.

I dined again at the Cokers' (they are the couple Morgan stayed with and they know Weeks, Morrison, and other Bostonians of that kind well),—an enormous house, two cars, *swimming pool* and the other trappings of a factory owner, but we sat in the kitchen while he and she prepared dinner from cans (true, there was also cold pheasant).

It's now eight a.m., I'll go and cash the cheque, and then wander around with my net. Tell my Miten'ka that one child here calls a '*butterfly*' a '*flutter-by*'. I am sending him a jewel-like 'vanilla'. Kisses for him and you, my dear joy.

V.

[ALS, 1 P.]
[postmarked 7 October 1942]

TO: 8 Craigie Circle, a p. 35, Cambridge, Mass.

c/o President Read, Spelman College, Atlanta Georgia
Wednesday

My love,

I am writing you from a black Wellesley—a college for Negresses, where Fisher chased me on because there's a military black-out in Richmond and the lecture there's postponed. I am writing to him today that no matter how much these breaks are justified by the general situation and no matter what kind of hospitality I meet, I want to cut short the *tour* to be home by mid-November and not mid-December. I stay here till Tuesday, giving lectures for bed and board. The apartment's lovely and the woman president very nice indeed—and tomorrow I am going with a biologist (a third variant of Miss MacCosh) to collect butterflies in the vicinity—but ultimately my having a *good time* means wasting my time. I miss you, my darling, and my Mityushen'ka. Write me either here (if this letter arrives on Friday) or to Valdosta.

Monday I spent among Cokers and butterflies, but my head was already aching a little, and on Tuesday the ache was unbearable, with chills. It was hell to pack my suitcases, but I had some aspirin and took a *sleeping-car*. After an hour by Greyhound I reached the Florence railroad station around seven, completely done in, and waited for a train there till half past ten. Overnight a crying baby kept me awake (by the morning, he'd split in two – it turned out there had been two crying, one on the opposite berth and one on the berth next to mine), but by morning my illness was over and I arrived at college completely fresh. Lunch with Miss President and the dazzling sun. A tour of campus. At six thirty there will be dinner with the faculty. Before that, I'd like a nap. Kisses, my love.

V.

[ALS, 2 PP.]
[11 October 1942]

[TO: Cambridge, MA]

Saturday
11-X-42
Atlanta

My dear love,

too few butterflies here (about 1,000 feet above sea level), I hope that in Valdosta there will be more. As before, I haven't been spending a cent. My lecture about Pushkin (Negro blood!) was greeted with almost comical enthusiasm. I decided to end it with a reading of 'Mozart and Salieri', and since here not only Pushkin but music is also held in high regard I had the somewhat mischievous idea of sandwiching the violin and later the piano into those three places where Mozart (and the beggar musician) produces music. The desired effect – again, a rather comical one – was achieved with the help of a gramophone disc and a lady pianist. Apart from that I have been to a biology class, talked about mimicry, and two days ago rode with a lady professor and a group of very black young ladies, very intensely chewing mint bubblegum, in a wooden char-a-banc-cum-automobile to collect insects about twenty miles from here. Miss Read, the college headmistress, is a very likeable woman, round, with a wart by her nostril, but too ideological: every morning I breakfast at her place (with conversations about the Negro problem and telepathy) and every morning at 9 I am obliged to visit the *chapel* with her and sit with her on stage in an academic cloak facing four hundred maidens singing hymns amid the organ tempest. I have asked for mercy – saying that I am a heretic, that I hate any kind of singing and music, but she replied sternly: that's all right, you'll get to like it <u>here</u>. In my honour they choose prayers thanking God for '*poetry and the little things of nature; for a train thundering in the night; for craftsmen and poets; for those who take delight in making things and who make them well*'; as well as Lvov's music – God save the Tsar – arranged like an English hymn. This is all rather touching but difficult. Every evening there are dinners with various leading Negro figures – and no alcoholic drinks. I have two large rooms, and it is very strange to wake up around eight in the <u>semi-darkness</u> – for geographically here we are already in the West, but the time is Atlantic, so in reality it is not half past seven but rather five a.m. A couple of times I played tennis with a local lady professional. Am working on Gogol. Cloudless hot weather; and when I go after butterflies my trousers and shirt get covered with a green armour: clingy seeds like tiny burdocks. I am sad to have no letters from you, my darling. A hug to Anyuta. How IS MY PRICELESS ONE DOING? I HAVE LOOKED FOR POSTCARDS WITH TRAINS, BUT THERE AREN'T ANY. KISSING YOU, MY MITYUSHEN'KA.

It's four o'clock now, I am lying naked on the bed after a long walk. It's very difficult without you – in every sense. Stuff the boxes that are ready where my Lycaenids are – but to the left of them. I've caught several interesting flies for Banks, and will write him soon. Send a Russian magazine to me in Valdosta. The local Negro expert on Russian literature asked me – was it acceptable in Russia to talk about – and in general to admit – that Pushkin had Negro blood? I leave here on Tuesday morning. Have still to talk about '*tragedy*' – on Monday. My sweetheart, how is your little hip? Please write. Am kissing you lots.

V.

[ALS, 1 P.]
[12 October 1942]

TO: 8 Craigie Circle, ap 35, Cambridge Mass.

Atlanta, Spelman Coll.
Monday night

My dear darling,

I am sending Mityushen'ka a wonderful longtailed Hesperid, and you a cheque for a hundred dollars, which they rather unexpectedly gave me here in Spelman, although it was agreed that my eloquence would earn only room and board. In general I am surrounded here with the most touching respect, artists show me their purple canvases, sculptors their thick-lipped Madonnas, and musicians sing 'spirituals' for me. Miss President pays me a thousand charming kindnesses, she bought me tickets herself, sent a telegram to Valdosta, drove me around endlessly in her car when I needed cigarettes or razors – a very intelligent and refined old lady, we've become great friends. And, of course, all of my three daily meals with her featured special dishes and her endless endeavours to surround me with interesting people.

Thank you for your very dear little letter (its little financial wails notwithstanding). I will be done with Gogol in a day or two and want to write a short story. I assure you, all the fuss about the play will be hopeless, but if Bunny does turn up, give it to him to read, explaining that I didn't translate it myself, and that a lot of nuances have vanished. I'll write from Valdosta to Miss Kelly and Miss Perkins in the spirit you suggest. Most of all I want to be at Wellesley. I am ideally healthy but tired today after thousands of receptions, and I have to pack. I adore you.

V.

[ALS, 2 PP.]

[postmarked 14 October 1942]

TO: 8, Craigie Circle, apt 35, Cambridge, Mass

Valdosta
Wednesday

My love,

yesterday I sent you the Spelman cheque. Arrived here, on the Florida border, yesterday around seven p.m. and will leave for Tennessy on Monday morning. (I also stop overnight on the way at Spelman – Miss Read set this up.)

A lady professor who met me at the station drove me to the hotel, where the college has booked a beautiful room for me as well as paid for all my *meals*, so that here too I won't be spending anything before I go. They gave me a car, too, but I only look at it, not daring to drive it. The college, with a charming *campus* among pines and palms, is a mile out of town. It's very southern here. I took a walk down the only big street, in the velvet of the twilight and the azure of neon lamps, and came back, overcome by a southern yawn. Some gent, in the room next door, having climbed the stairs with me, suggested that I stop by for a cognac. He turned out to be a sugar producer from Florida and the conversation went accordingly. Completely by accident, looking for matches, I took out the box I carry with me in case of moths. Breaking off in mid-word (the conversation had been about the difficulties of finding workers – imagine how cross I was with myself for accepting the invitation) he remarked that in such boxes he puts, on excursions ... butterflies. In short, he turned out to be a passionate entomologist, a correspondent of Comstock's, and so on. It's the second time this has happened to me.

In the morning they came for me and drove me to the lecture. I talked on '*commonsense*'. The usual result. Then the corpulent and very likeable *president* took me to look over the library, the *swimming pool*, the stables, and so on. At one they drove me to lunch at the *Rotary Club*, where I also spoke (about the *war-novel*). After lunch I asked the president to drive me into the countryside, which he did. I collected charming butterflies for an hour and a half, and then he picked me up and brought me back to the hotel. I changed in a hurry and at four o'clock was delivered to a very funny and very vulgar Ladies' club where I read several verse translations. I'm just back; lying on the bed; have asked a *boy* to extract numerous thorns out of my trousers; I love you very much.

At seven they'll take me to a grand faculty dinner, but there should be no speeches on my part. All in all it is very pleasant here. I got your little letter that had wandered to Virginia. Where's Bunny's letter? I think that after my howl Fisher will either cut the tour short (I have asked him to free me in mid-November if he couldn't get more frequent lectures) or find me a large number of profitable talks. Tomorrow I'll write lots of letters. Oho, it is six o'clock now.

MITYUSHONOK, MY LITTLE MOUSE, IN MY ROOM THERE

IS A ROCKER AND AN ELECTRICAL FAN (ON THE LAMP)
R-R-R-R-R-R-R

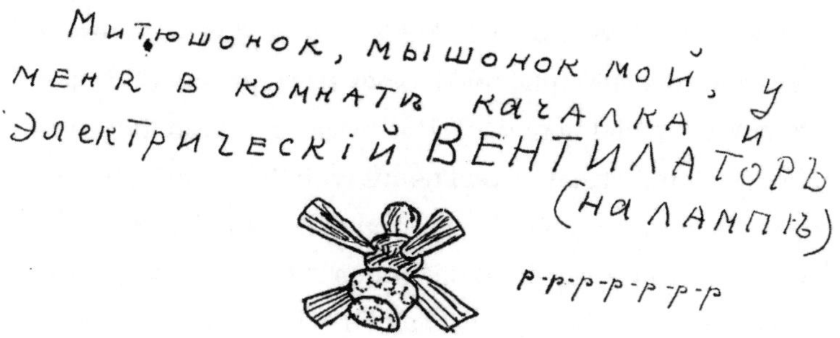

By the way, a small experiment in telepathy. Focus and try to tell me which two pictures are hanging in my room? Do it right away because I will tell you in my next letter. Give Anyuta my best. Part of the underwear has been left to be washed in Spelman, and I left the coat and hat too. Thank you for going to the museum, my sweetheart. Take up the *Pieridae* (*Pieris*, *Colias*, *Euchloe*, and so on – ask Banks) after you have repinned all the Satyridae. Love you, love you

V.

[ALS, 2 PP.]
[17–18 October 1942]

TO: 8, Craigie Circle, Cambridge, Mass.

17–18.X.42
Valdosta

My priceless darling,

I'm sending you a cheque for the lectures here. 150 all up (plus more than 80 in my wallet).

Your little letters, my love, keep coming from different places. I have filled in all the forms, had them retyped, and have sent them off already – it was a rather laborious procedure. I have described my future novel and referred to Bunny, Mikh. Mikh., and Miss Perkins. Yesterday I read *Mlle O*, and in the evening told biology students about mimicry. Today there was a meeting of the *Readers' Forum*, and I read Mozart and Salieri. Collected butterflies. Played tennis with President Reade. He's a perfectly brilliant man with Wilson's irrationality and Thompson's knowledge – today he analysed for an hour a short poem by Browning, and it was a delight to listen. He has evidently been sick for a listener, for here the level of professorship as well as maidenship is rather low. A huge gent looking – physically – like Kadish.

It's now 6 o'clock. The rewriting and so on of the documents has taken me three hours. At 8 there will be a grand dinner, tuxedoes. Tomorrow is a con ... here my pen ran out and I set the letter aside. After dinner was a concert, and today (it's now 11 p.m. Sunday) I was taken by the biologist (when the women biologists are mentioned always remember MacCosh's looks) to marvellous palmetto wilds and pine groves where I collected butterflies from ten till two. It was entrancing – flowers never seen before (one of which I am sending to Mityushen'ka), purple berries *Calocarpa americana*, *Myrica* bushes, palmettos, cypresses, scorching sun, enormous crickets and a multitude of the most interesting butterflies (among them one *Neonympha*). I got lost in those sunny thickets and am not sure how I got back to the road where the biologist was standing by the car knee-deep in the ditch water and collecting some sort of small water fry of her own. The only torture is all sorts of thorns that tear up the net and pierce my legs. We are right on the Florida border and the flora and fauna are the same, but I would very much like to get (about 150 miles) to the Gulf of Mexico, where it's even warmer. This was my best collecting.

Then I was taken to the Reades' cottage, where I lunched, rested, amused the guests, and had dinner – after which I was delivered back to the hotel. Tomorrow at 11.35 a.m. I am going to Atlanta, spending the night at Spelman and the next day go to Tennessee.

In spite of the butterflies, I'm missing you horribly; my dear joy. The hospitality in all three colleges I've been in so far amounts to their trying to afford me pleasure from morning till night, so that very little time is left for solitary work. I feel fine, but tired. Just now I asked for a sandwich to be brought, and it's full of little ants that have crawled over the room. One picture shows white cottages with red roofs across a river, the other a little girl looking at a little bird in the garden.

I am kissing you lots, my enchantment.

V.

Don't forget to pass my regards to Anyuta. You say that T. was looking at him with hatred?

[ALS, 2 PP.]
[20 October 1942]

TO: 8, Craigie Circle, Cambridge, Mass

THE DIXIE ROUTE
CHICAGO-FLORIDA

[Atlanta]
Tuesday
20–X–42

My love,

I'm writing to you on the way from Atlanta to Cowan – the train hasn't started yet. Please, write a few words to Miss Read – *my husband has been telling me so much about you in his letters that I almost feel as if I knew you* – something like that – and thank her for *all the kindness that you and your wonderful college showed him*. She gave me a real military compass for Mityushen'ka, and presented me with a huge print of details from an Egyptian fresco with butterflies, about which I'll write something. All in all, it's hard to describe how much attention she surrounded me with. She knows Moe well because previously she worked at the *Rockefeller Inst.*; she promised to write him about me. She is white.

I'm heading North again without much pleasure – and I still do not know where and when I will go further. The trains are packed, they are 2–3 hours late everywhere – but I get less tired than I expected. Yesterday I wrote a long letter to Miss Kelly. The train has just moved and is jolting my hand. I love you very much. I took a Pullman – only just over a dollar more, in this case.

MY MITYUSHONOK, THE TRAIN I'M ROCKING IN IS CALLED DIXIE FLYER. KISSES.

That's all, my darling. How're you keeping, my sweet? Good girl to have finished so many boxes. Greetings to the old man, I will write to him when I know when I'll get back.

V.

Big hello to Anyuta. I'll write to her separately.

[ALS, 2 PP.]
[5 November 1942]

TO: 8, Craigie Circle, app 35, Cambridge, Mass.

Chicago
station
5–XI–42

My dear love,

I had an ideal trip to Chicago and spent an ideal day at the famous local museum (*Field Museum*). I found my *Neonymphas*, showed how they could be reshuffled, chatted and lunched with a very nice entomologist (who somehow knew that I was completing a lecture tour – it seems to have been published in some museum journal). Now I'm in the very beautiful railroad station,

A VERY BEAUTIFUL RAILROAD STATION,
MY MITYUSHONOK,

where I have had my hair cut, and in half an hour I leave for Springfield. I feel great. The huge cloudy-wet spaces of the lakeside part of Chicago (where the enormous, absolutely marvellous museum is) reminded me somehow of Paris, the Seine. Warm but drizzly, and the grey stone blends with the turbid sky.

They charged me 2 dollars for the cut – terrible.

Kisses, I love you, my darling.

V.

[ALS, 2 PP.]
[7 November 1942]

TO: 8, Craigie Circle, Suite 35, Cambridge Mass

Springfield
7–XI–42

My love,

At the station in Springfield I was met (and then on the next day taken to see Lincoln's house and grave) by a secretary of the Club – a creepily silent melancholic of a somewhat clerical cast with a small stock of automatic questions which he quickly exhausted. He is an elderly bachelor and his profession consists of his doing secretarial work for several Springfield clubs. He livened up and flashed his eyes one single time – got awfully nervous having noticed that the flagpole by the Lincoln mausoleum had been replaced by a new, longer one. It turned out that his *hobby* – and even more, the passion of his life – is flagpoles. He breathed with relief when a watchman gave him the exact information – 70 feet – because the pole in his own garden is still 10 feet taller. He was also greatly comforted when I said that in my opinion the top of the pole inclined from the vertical. He felt it for a long time and looked up anxiously and finally came to the conviction that even 70 feet was too much and that the distortion was not an optical illusion but a fact. He's saving money for a 100-feet flagpole. Shpon'ka, judging by his dream, had the same complex, and Dr Freud could have said something interesting on the subject.

I spoke to a huge gathering. Got on very well with the director of the *State Museum* McGregor (really a charming museum with a decent collection of butterflies and undescribed fossil insects which will be sent to Carpenter at my museum) and with the director of the history library Paul Angle. Now I'm waiting at the Springfield station for the train, which is an hour late. I love you very much, my darling. Yesterday I again had an attack – but very short – of fever and pain between the ribs. It's not cold, but dampish. Lots of kisses for my Mityushonok.

V.

[ALS, 2 PP.]

[postmarked 9 November 1942]

TO: 8, Craigie Circle, Cambridge, Mass.

Monday

St Paul

My dear darling,

Fisher was right, after all, not us: the train from Chicago to St Paul turned out to be awfully expensive (tell Miten'ka that it was all steel, magnificently furnished, and rushed along at a speed of 100 miles an hour – it's called: *The Zephyr*). The very charming *president* Turck met me and drove me to the best (indeed very fancy) hotel. Yesterday (Sunday) I lunched with him and his elderly mother, and then he drove me out of the city to show me the countryside: a large lake looking somewhat like Annecy. The city of St Paul is big, cold, with a cathedral in the style of St Peter's in Rome on the hill, with a stark view of the Mississippi (behind which is the other *Twin Town* – Minneapolis). Today I spent the whole day at the university, looking over, talking and lunching with the faculty. To my horror it turned out that I had not brought along my lecture on the *Novel*, which they wanted from me at 10.30 – but I decided to speak without any notes and it came out very smoothly and well. Yesterday after the trip into the country I went, having got awfully bored, to the cinema and came back on foot – I walked for more than an hour and went to bed around eight. On the way a lightning bolt of undefined inspiration ran right through me – a passionate desire to write – and to write in Russian. And yet I can't. I don't think anyone who has never experienced this feeling can really understand its torment, its tragedy. In this sense the English language is an illusion and an ersatz. In my usual condition, i.e. busy with butterflies, translations, or academic writing, I myself don't fully register the whole grief and bitterness of my situation.

I am healthy, eating plenty, taking my vitamins, and read newspapers more than usual now the news is getting rosier. St Paul is a stupefyingly boring city, only owls at the hotel, a bar girl looks like Dasha; but my apartment is charming.

Fisher (who is somewhere near now and will probably be here tomorrow) has somewhat taken me aback with the news that in Galesburg there will be not two lectures but one, i.e. I will earn only 50 dollars there. The level of the intelligentsia here is significantly lower than in eastern universities, but everyone is very sweet and *appreciative*. It's now around five. At 6.30 I am having dinner at Turck's. Tomorrow I will find out about the train to Galesburg since it looks as if I will need to go back to Chicago and from there to Galesburg: something is mixed up in our schedule (I can also get to G. by changing *local trains*, without making a detour to Chicago – but that seems longer – in short, I will find out).

I love you, my darling. Try to be cheery when I come back (but I love you when you're low, too). If it weren't for the two of you – I have felt this perfectly clearly – I'd have gone to Morocco as a soldier: by the way there's a heavenly lycaenid in the mountains there – *Vogelii Obthr*. But how much more than this I would like now to write a book in Russian. The hotel is cotton-wool, rain outside the window, a bible and a telephone book in my room: for the convenience of communication with the heavens and the office.

V.

[ALS, 1 p.]
[11 November 1942]

TO: 8, Craigie Circle, Cambridge, Mass

Wednesday
11–XI–42
Galesburg
4 p.m.

My darling,

I arrived here this morning—with a swollen upper lip after the icy wind in St Paul. My lecture there in front of the audience of 900 people—*Commonsense*—went out on radio. Here is a small poem that I wrote:

When he was small, when he would fall,
on sand or carpet he would lie
quite flat and still until he knew
what he would do: get up or cry.

After the battle, flat and still
upon a hillside now he lies
– but there is nothing to decide,
for he can neither cry nor rise.

I've been put up here in a charming hotel–some wonderful golden-brown panels and lots of interesting g a d g e t s. I am buying the third newspaper today. Why are you not writing to me, my love? The university that I have just looked over is very pleasant. I'll talk there tomorrow evening. I want to be home, for a long time.

V.

MY SWEETHEART, MY JOY!

[AL, 1 P.]

[postmarked 7 December 1942]

TO: 8, Craigie Circle, app. 35, Cambridge, Mass.

[Farmville, Virginia]

Monday

My sweetheart,

I love you. Honours College has turned out to be charming and unusually elegant – in short, everything was very pleasant. In New York I managed to do everything I wanted. Saw Moe, and it became clear that Barbour is his closest friend. '*Well, you must be a jolly good man if Tom Barbour took you!*' It all turned out wonderfully well. Pierce took me to drink whisky, and we spent two hours in literary chit-chat. '*I keep getting letters telling me that you are my find of the season.*' (This flatters me much less now.) Saw Natasha who took me and an Armenian lady – whom you appear to know – to the cinema. An utterly trite Soviet film. Saw Aldanov to whom I had sent Zenzinov and Frumkin, and besides them there were the Kovarskys and Mansvetov with his poetess wife. Saw Dasha – took her out to a restaurant – she was awfully sweet and talkative. Saw Hilda – she won't take any money at all. Saw Comstock, Sanford, and Michener, who turned out to be a very nice young man (I discovered that it was he and not Comstock who made those magnificent drawings for me). I needed to prepare and draw the genitalia of my *Lysandra cormion*, but I found out that together with all other 'types' she had been transferred to the Entomological Institute fifty miles from New York. The next morning (a Saturday) she was brought to me from there, and I worked on her to my heart's content. Yesterday I arrived here after a killer of a trip. Had supper at Prof. Grainger's in an unheated country home in a pine forest and then was driven to a warm comfortable hotel. I have overslept – must get up quickly, goodbye, my love. Kisses for my Miten'ka.

1943

[APCS, 1 P.]

[postmarked 15 April 1943]

TO: 8, Craigie Circle, Cambridge, Mass

[New York]

My beloved darling – so: 18 years today. My joy, my tenderness, my life!

I have spent a very pleasant evening with Zyoka who has not changed a bit, except his nose is bigger – and lacquered. The doctor gave the affidavit (5 doll.) Then we went to Bunny's, other people arrived there, too, and Zyoka was completely overwhelmed. Now rushing to the museum, and from there to A. I kiss my boy. Adore you.

V.

1944

[APCS, 1 P.]

[5 June 1944]

TO: 250 W 104, app. 43, New York City

[Cambridge, MA]

5–VI–44

My darling,

I've spent two days without going out, writing, feeding on Roquefort and oranges. I have written eleven pages of my novel. If the i n s p i r a t i o n continues, I'll finish it before you get back. The *page-proofs* of Gogol and the milkman's bill have arrived. It's now Monday's morning, I'm going now to the museum. Fresh out, windy. Write how everybody is.

My Mityushen'ka, write me also when you can, my sweet, my f l y i n g f o r t r e s s.

I kiss you, my dears, greetings to Anyuta and Lyusya. *Very much.*

V.

[ALS, 1 P.]

[5 June 1944]

TO: c/o A. Feigen, 250 W 104 Street, New York City

8 Craigie Circle

Cambridge

Monday,

5–VI–44

5 p.m.

I am sending you, my darling, two bills, which evidently need to be paid. I have just got back from the mus. and found your and Mityusha's little postcard – saying that the operation will be on Wednesday. I can't wait for more information.

Had lunch at Wurst. H. with Carpenter. Loveridge greatly appreciated Mityushen'ka's letter.

Now I'll lie down and write.

I'VE THOUGHT UP A NEW AEROPLANE!

[ALS, 4 PP.]
[6 June 1944]

TO: c/o A. Feigin, 250 W. 104,
app. 43, New York City

[Cambridge, MA]
6–VI–44

My dear darling,

Yesterday was a day of extraordinary adventures. It started when, in the morning, the minute I was getting ready to go to the museum (with a tennis racket, since I'd arranged to play with Clark at 4.30), T. N. called, very agitated – she'd driven the sick M. Mikh. down from Vermont, and meanwhile the Dobuzhinskys had arrived and couldn't get into their house, since no one was at home (the Dobuzhinskys dropped out of view among the tribulations that followed, as you'll see in a moment). I agreed with her that after tennis I would drop in to check on M. Mikh., and left for the museum. Around one in the afternoon, still just as healthy and energetic, I had lunch at the Wursthaus, where I had *Virginia ham* with spinach and drank a coffee. I returned to my microscope around two. Exactly at 2.30, I suddenly felt an urge to vomit, had barely time to run outside – and there it began: an absolutely Homeric retching, bloody diarrhoea, spasms, weakness. I don't know how I got back home, where I crawled along the floor and poured myself out in the waste basket. Somehow or other I found the strength to call T. N., who summoned an ambulance, which took me to the truly horrendous hospital where you'd been with Mityushen'ka. An absolutely helpless brunette tried to pump my stomach through my nose – I'd rather not recall that – in a word, I asked, writhing from the spasms and retching, for them to take me quickly somewhere else. T. N., realizing that the doctor was there, drove me to their place. By then I was in a state of complete collapse. This doctor, very sweet (I don't remember his name), immediately made all the arrangements himself and himself drove, and carried, me to the hospital where you'd been. There they placed me in a ward with a terribly and raucously dying old man – and because of the groans I couldn't get to sleep. They poured a bottle of salt solution into my veins – and today, although the diarrhoea's still carrying on this morning, I feel great, am awfully hungry – and want to smoke – but they're giving me only water. I'm being looked after by a Dr Cooney.

He has just been here, the diarrhoea has stopped, he said I can be discharged the day after tomorrow, on Friday. They have just given me food for the first time (5.30) – and rather strangely, at that (but you know this): risotto, bacon, canned pears. I didn't eat the bacon. I'm writing you this because I am afraid that some misunderstanding might happen – I'm terribly worried about the little lad's surgery – how strange that today (Wednesday) we are both in hospital. A silly story, but all in all I am absolutely healthy now. I won't mention the living conditions here. Clean, but terribly noisy. I have been transferred to a public ward. *Enfin*. I dined in a very pleasant open gallery where they rolled me out and where I smoked my first cigarette.

The doctor says it was bloody colitis caused by food poisoning.

T. N. has visited me, she says that they haven't worked out what's wrong with M. Mikh., some kind of an allergy. She brought the mail.

The *New Yorker* (which hasn't received the story yet) is offering me 500 dollars for an option, i.e. for me to show them everything first.

In short, the bacilli had taken me for the *invasion beach*.

Don't come here under any circumstances: I've recovered.

How is my little boy? My dear! I love you both.

V.

Какъ поживаетъ мой мальчикъ? Мой дорогой!
Люблю васъ обоихъ

[APC, 1 P.]

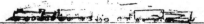

[postmarked 8 June 1944]

TO: c/o A. Feigin, 250 W 104, New York City

[Cambridge, MA]

Thursday

My dear darling,

I'm worried, I'm waiting for news!

I'm completely well today. Will write you a long letter about my funny hospital impressions as soon as I get out of here. This'll happen tomorrow. I'll probably spend the night from Friday to Saturday at the Karpoviches'.

I had *haemoraginal colitis*. Today, my bowels moved, I ate a lot, everything is well, I am thinking the novel through. How's my little boy? T. N. was a great help, and Carpenter was awfully touching.

Love you.

[APCS, 1 P.]

[9 June 1944]

TO: c/o A. Feigin, 250 W 104,
New York City

[Cambridge, MA]
Ward A. Friday
9–VI–44

My darling, I was so happy to find out that the operation went well. I will write to Dynnik as soon as I can get to an inkpot. I am leaving this weird place tomorrow morning (Saturday) and will spend the night at the Karpoviches'. I am completely healthy, today for the first time they allowed me to take a stroll down the gallery. I'm a little weak, but nothing serious. Write to me as soon as you can how Mityushen'ka is. I've been very worried about him. The doctor advises me to sue the restaurant. And the name of the doctor who brought me here is Magentanz. I think I have written to you that White is offering 500 for an option. I replied to her. Today is generally a much happier day. I kiss my little cloudy one. And you, my joy. Do not worry, everything's fine.

V.

[ALS, 2 PP.]
[11 June 1944]

TO: c/o Miss A. Feigin, 250 W 104,
app. 43, New York City

8, Craigie Circle,
Cambridge, Mass.
Sunday
9–VI–1944

My love,

It was a great comfort to hear your resonant little voice on the phone.

I feel unbearably bored without you and my little one. These few days have completely exhausted me physically, but in terms of i n s p i r a t i o n everything is going very well. Today's the first time my stomach has really worked properly, and if it weren't for the weakness in my loins, I'd feel excellent.

The public ward was utter bedlam. There was an endless unruly din consisting of the following elements:

1) the zoological sounds of an incessant radio set

2) the wheezes, groans, and roaring of the seriously ill

3) conversations across the whole enormous ward by the healthier, with guffawing and strolling around

4) the incredible noise produced by a sixteen-year-old idiot helping the nurses, the institutional fool. He grimaced, stomped, howled, deliberately banged every dish, cracked jokes – and imitated the moans of some of the old men who were in particular anguish, thereby arousing general goodhearted laughter.

The nurses constantly tried to pull open the curtains of my coop and got angry saying that since all the other curtains were pulled, my poor tabernacle was spoiling the general look of the ward. By the end of my stay I was in such a state of exasperation, that when on Saturday morning I saw from the gallery (where I had gone out for a smoke) T. N., who'd come for me, I jumped out through the *fire-escape* as I was, in pyjamas and a dressing-gown, rushed to the car – and we were already moving off, when the absolutely enraged nurses ran out – but they couldn't stop me.

Here I have been given Sergey's room, and I only got up today to have some tea with the Dobuzhinskys when they turned up. I don't know exactly what will happen next. Tomorrow Carpenter will drop by, he wants to take me to Lexington, but I still can't move at all. Here's what happened to him. That awful day when I was crawling out of the museum he wanted to escort me, but I refused. That evening he called; and of course having got no answer became worried and again came from Lexington to Cambridge, tried to force his way into our apartment, and didn't know what to do.

I have looked through and sent off the final *page-proofs* of Gogol. Looks very elegant. Barbour has arrived. Mikh. Mikh. is feeling better, but he's very sourish. The doctor says that I absolutely must file a complaint against the restaurant. I love you very much. I must confess there was a minute when I was lying there with no pulse thinking some rather funny thoughts. I wish you had seen the burly policemen summoned to Craigie by T. N. and wanting to know '*who is this woman?*' and '*what poison did you take?*' When do you get back? I adore you.

V.

MY DEAR ONE, HOW ARE YOUR LITTLE BELLIES? LOVE YOU BOTH!

[ALS 1 P.]
[postmarked 13 June 1944]

TO: c/o A. Feigin, 250 W 104,
New York City

8, Craigie Circle
Cambridge

My darling,

Yesterday, and just now, I crawled up to our apartment with difficulty, thinking that there would be a little letter from you, but there wasn't. The Russian departments we wrote to have replied very amiably and in great detail. I am forwarding you a bill from Grosya and a letter from Lisbet. My loins have grown terribly weak, I've been dragging myself as if up a hill. Tomorrow (Wednesday) I will move back home, and on Friday I will probably go for the *weekend* to the Carpenters. The Karpoviches are leaving for Vermont.

I still do not know any details about the operation, what the hospital is like, when you're planning to come back, or anything. I did stop by at the Wursthaus yesterday, and although I didn't intend to say to them anything offensive or damaging, a row erupted from the first words, thanks to the owner's rudeness, since, apparently, this was not the first complaint about his wretched ham. Tomorrow I think I'll drop in to the museum.

Kiss Anyuta, greetings to Lyusya. And write to me, my dear love.

V.

MY DARLING, CAN YOU LAUGH ALREADY?

1945

[APCS, 1 P.]

[postmarked 9 February 1945]

TO: 8 Craigie Circle, Cambridge, Mass.

[Baltimore, MD]

My darling,

I've just got here – at 1.30, with a delay because of the storm. The trip was very comfortable. They got me a room at the *Lord Baltimore Hotel* also in Baltimore. Not a great sleep. Now I'm going to lunch. Warm and foggy here, no snow at all, chocolate servants, a marvellous bristly shower.

And how is Miten'ka? How is Miten'ka? Ideal, isn't he?

Love you.

V.

[APCS, 1 P.]

[postmarked 10 February 1945]

TO: 8 Craigie Circle, Cambridge, Mass.

[Baltimore, MD]

My darling,

The lecture went <u>very</u> well. A charming school with a charming directress. Music is taught by one Mrs Bush, from Riga, who speaks Russian exactly like her namesake in 'The Gift' ('I interest me for Russian language'). In a few minutes I'll leave for New York. And how is Mityushen'ka, how is the little one, is he still ideal?

Love you.

V.

1954

[ALS, 1 P.]
[18 April 1954]

TO: 101 Irving Place, Ithaca, New York

Eldridge Hotel, Lawrence, Kansas

HUTSON HOTELS

18–IV–1954
6.30 p.m.

My beloved darling,

I've just arrived, now the Russian and the German profs are coming to pick me up.

I didn't sleep at all – so much rocking and tossing – but the berth was very comfortable. The p a r l o u r c a r was also all right, but the conductors, with nothing to do (all the trains were empty), turned on the radio. The hotel here is so-so, one needs to press for water, a showerless bathroom. Sticky heat, butterflies.

I love you very much. Has Mityushok phoned, I w o n d e r.

V.

[ALS, 2 PP.]
[20 April 1954]

TO: 101 Irving Place, Ithaca, New York

Eldridge Hotel, Lawrence, Kansas

HUTSON HOTELS

Tuesday, 20–IV–1954
10.45 *a.m.*

Hello, my darling,

yesterday was a very hard day, but I had had a great sleep (the hotel turned out to be very pleasant and quiet, with a predominance of 'p e r m a n e n t' little old ladies) and I had fun in my talks. At 10 *a.m.* I spoke for a whole hour about Tolstoy, then I had an hour free before lunch, I took your advice and retired to an empty room – where with a shy smile the professor in whose class I had just spoken brought me to read his typewritten memoirs. I had lunch with an old lady writer and a young author (who had written a novel apiece about frontier life in the beginning of the last century – 'from here you see') and I spoke in their combined class at 1 p.m. The class seemed bright to me, and I treated them to *Art & Commonsense* – and I think they understood more than their mentors. Meanwhile I was constantly in lively contact with Elmer, an agreeable sort and very circumstantial, passionate partaker in all kinds of conventions – you know what I mean; however not stupid (although he replies to everything with unnecessary details) and with humour. He found time to take me to see the university press, and then we rode around the campus. Everything is lilac and blooming Judas trees, and as the campus is on a hill, the impression is rather Ithacan – steep streets and awful difficulties with parking. I changed for tea, and by four was reading my English poems to a small but thoughtful group. As always, an unavoidable Pevzner couple, from Mogilyov, appeared, speaking Russian with sad tenderness, through a mist. The reading took place in a wonderful, elegant hall – in general, the beauties and comforts of the campus immeasurably surpass our poor Cornell. Around six I made it to the home of a young German couple, the Winters, where I had dinner: he'd been a translator in the German army and had reached Gatchina. Another supervisor of Russian classes, the very nice Andersen (former student of Cross), with two dachshunds, after dinner gathered a Russian group at his place, and I read my translations to them and showed how Herman[n] won, as well as how he pulled out the wrong card, because their mentors could not explain that (I didn't hurt anyone's feelings). Got home around 10 p.m., and fell asleep almost immediately – and again had a great sleep. Today entomology, and in the evening my Gogol talk. Adore you both, hug you both.

V.

1964

[ANS, 1 PP.]

[3 May 1964]

TO: Clinique Beaulieu, 22 ave. Beau-Séjour, Genève

[Montreux]
3rd May
1964

My love,

I wanted to send you orchids, but there weren't any.

I will come around noon.

A cheerful Mityusha phoned on Friday night. Hugs and hugs and hugs. My love.

V.

1965

[ANS, 1 P.]
[15 April 1965]

for Véra
40 flowers = years
V.

1966

[ALS 1 P.]
[2 October 1966]

TO: c/o Feigin, 250 West 104th St., New York City

[Montreux]
2–X–66
12:50 PM

My darling,

I got your telegram today, and yesterday, a charming postcard from Mityusha: he had an interview and a photograph in the local, Tulsa, newspaper. I also received from Minton adorable *end-papers* with a butterfly (surprisingly well hatched) on one side and a map of the Nabokovs' lands on the other: ask him for it, if you have a chance. No other interesting mail – except for the Grove edition of Miller's 'Tropic of Cancer' – the hilarious scheme of one Egorov, a Russian translator. I am writing awfully fast because I have just realized that if I do not send it off now (i.e. before Elena's and my journey for slippers on the 1.30 train to Lausanne), you won't get this letter. She is upset by Vladimír's affairs and slept poorly because they had put a board under her (they have taken it out today). She is now making an omelette for me, the weather's wonderful, I miss you unbearably.

V.

I don't know how to fold this thing ...

1968

[AN, 1 P.]
[8 June 1968]

Tomorrow morning

Please
write a confirmation *to Park* Hotel *and ask for theirs*
==
I will post it in the village

1969

[ANS, 1 p.]
[15 April 1969]
[Montreux]

Cymbidium lowianum
for *Vérochka*
from *VN*, *Ada* & Lucette
(*and* Dmitri)
15–IV–1969

[ANS, 1 P.]
[4 July 1969]
[Cureglia, Ticino, Switzerland]

4-VII-1969

How charming to hear your pure little voice in the garden from my balcony. Such sweet notes, such a tender rhythm!

cordially yours,

VN

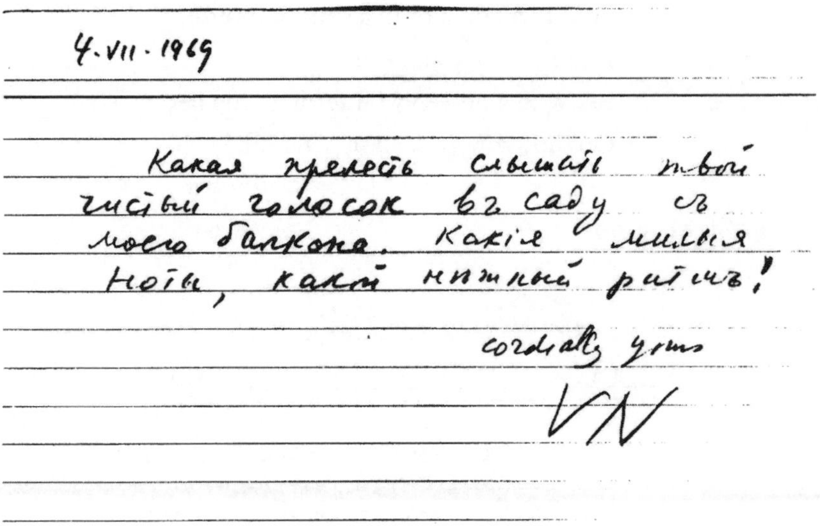
4·VII·1969

Какая прелесть слышать твой чистый голосок въ саду съ моего балкона. Какія милыя ноты, какой нѣжный ритмъ!

cordially yours

VN

[ANS, 1 P.]
[22 July 1969]
[Cureglia, Ticino, Switzerland]

To Vérochka

How I loved the poems of Gumilyov!
Reread them I cannot,
But traces have stayed in my mind,
Such as, on this think-through:

'. . . And I will die not in a summerhouse,
From gluttony and heat,
But with a heavenly butterfly in my net
On the summit of some wild hill.'

V. Nabokov

Cureglia (Lugano) 2. VII. 69

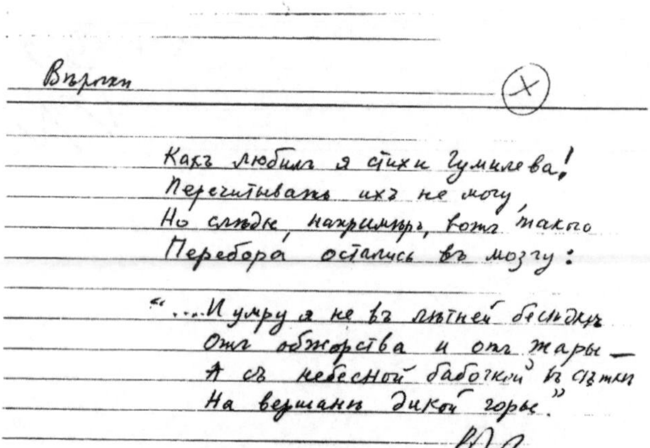
Вѣрочкѣ
Какъ любилъ я стихи Гумилева!
Перечитывать ихъ не могу,
Но слѣды, напримѣръ, вотъ такого
Перебора остались въ мозгу:
"...И умру я не въ лѣтней бесѣдкѣ
Отъ обжорства и отъ жары —
А съ небесной бабочкой въ сѣтки
На вершинѣ дикой горы."
В. Набоковъ
Cureglia (Lugano) 22.VII.69

1970

[ALS 2 PP.]

[6 April 1970]

TO: Montreux Palace Hotel, Montreux

SAN DOMENICO PALACE HOTEL

room 220

6–IV–1970

Taormina

Hello, my angel,

As I already reported to you and Mityusha da Monza on the phone yesterday, the overnight trip was fine and sleepless, in the same kind of uninteresting wagon-lit as the Montrome one. I told them to turn off completely the infernal heating in my compartment after which it gradually became horribly cold. In the middle of the night I called for wine, and the conductor brought me a half-bottle of half-good Ruffino. An emphatically old auto-charabanc from the hotel was waiting for me. The hotel is charming, i.e., rather, its charm very quickly grows through the fashionable shortcomings. The bed is marvellously soft, but the real masterpiece is a simply melting deep chair in golden silks. Your cell adjoins mine, slightly bigger. I suggest we agree on an apartment with a sitting-room.

A gift – half-a-dozen large oranges – in a fancy basket was waiting for me along with the most delicious business card of the director, Freddie Martini. I coughed up the last clot of Rome's black phlegm and immediately went for a four-hour walk. A chilly wind was blowing, but it was sunny and there were lots of butterflies flying. The little local *Euchloe ausonia* was skimming over the orange carpet of little wild chrysanthemums. Had dinner in an aura of embryonic friendship with the mercantile maître d'hôtel and went to bed at nine. I was woken around three by a very hungry, very lonely, very professional mosquito, which deftly disappeared into the white height of the walls, out of which one could cut two or three more such cells. The shutters opened more pliably than they were supposed to. I made it to the first performance of the apricot-and-blue dawn. Can see the sea and (from the little balcony) Etna, on which there is both snow and the familiar cloud-cap, don't forget to ask for a second blanket, while the Cyprian's silvery star shimmers in the pale azure, Russian prose-writers always loved to describe the beauties of the south. A great chirping in the picture-postcard garden; bring me without fail the book of European birds, it's next to the West-Americans on my 'kitchen' shelves, a little to the right and lowish.

Now I will shave and bathe, and at seven – they don't serve earlier – will phone for café complet to be sent up, after which I'll head for the hills beyond the city, not hills, not hills – slopes overgrown with olives between two villages. I miss you very much, my precious creature.

V.

[ALS 2 PP.]

[7 April 1970]

TO: Palace Hotel, Montreux

[Taormina, Italy]

SAN DOMENICO PALACE HOTEL

11 a.m.
Tuesday
7th Apr.

My love,

Yesterday it was cloudless and, in spite of the air's icy background, a lot of butterflies were flying in gullies and olive groves screened from the wind. I pottered about from eight in the morning till after noon trying to catch various quicker-flyers, and have already got some interesting stuff. I had a sandwich at a chance café. For two hours, I sat in the sun in our paradisiacal hotel garden, and then went out to buy little things, and on this occasion, I want to ask you, my darling, to:

¶ Bring me 1) three or four lavender sachets, the pharmacist knows what kind, with a picture of a lady on the sachet. They were foisting on me alternately either an insect repellent powder or an aromatic potion for the W. C. (a fool who understood English misunderstood my American *for the closet*); and 2) without fail at least one tube of *Mennen Brushless Shaving Cream*. Here one cannot get anything *brushless* except for the rather frightful *Noxzema, made in Italy*, judging by the literature on the tube: *Apply while your whiskers are warm and wet. Keep out of reach of children.* (Otherwise you will get what happened to Humbert). ¶

This morning, the Saturday issue of *Her. Trib.* triumphantly arrived (I read it in Rome), and it's raining. There's no wind, and the air seems to be a bit warmer, but disgustingly overcast, and I won't get out for a walk before lunch. I will try to locate our little restaurant, I couldn't find it yesterday – although I recalled a multitude of little details of the 'patterns of the past', as if it was very recent, and not ten years ago.

¶ Many, too many plump Germans. ¶

This is my second letter to you, you'll get the first one on Wednesday the 8th, the local optimists say, and this one on Thursday the 9th. Have you already booked your ticket for Tuesday the 14th [?].

I adore and embrace you.

V

[ALS 2 PP.]
[8 April 1970]

TO: Palace Hotel, Montreux

[Taormina, Italy]

SAN DOMENICO PALACE HOTEL

8–IV–70
Wednesday
7 *AM*

My a n g e l o,

I've finally found our restaurant, it is called *Chez Angelo*, and indeed, it is very pleasant. Yesterday morning (as you know from our pedant's Tuesday letter) was dolefully overcast, but suddenly the charming miracle from S. in Fialta occurred. I was between cannellini and coffee when I suddenly noticed a dimple of sunshine on the cheek of the day and, having cancelled coffee (but after finishing my beautiful red corvo), in three minutes I was at the foot of the Hotel Excelsior and caught one of the most delectable local enchantresses (*je m'excuse de ces mots un peu forts*), namely, the Thais *Zerynthia hypsipyle cassandra*. I am absolutely in love with Taormina and have almost bought a villa here (8 rooms, 3 bathrooms, 20 olive trees).

¶ A family of Americans at Angelo's; the mother calls the waiter: '*Où je peux laver le petit garçon?*' (*little boy wants to go to the bathroom*). An ancient old lady (rather for advertising purposes, it seems) brought over a basket of fresh eggs from her village. ¶

For some reason all Italian waiters who speak English pronounce 'vegetables' as if it rhymed with 'tables'. I went to bed at 8.30, took phanodorm, and slept from nine to six with one short break. For that reason, tell – or better not tell – Janits that the fresh little 'dacron-marquisette' used for sewing the net is now coloured – oh, not by the virgin blood of a young butterfly, but by my old man's blood, which was being sucked by a mosquitess who perished last night. I won't write on this foolishly thin paper again, it all shines through.

It's rained again since morning, like yesterday, layers of heavy clouds, the horizon in fog, the sea malachite at the shore, with capes of foam, palm-trees and araucarias stirring as they do in Galina Kuznetsova's diary. It was only 50°F in Milano, so I think your fur-coat has come in handy. I miss you awfully, my beloved! My 220 and your 221 are the last on one side of an enormous wide hallway or rather a prospect, with the doors facing each other. The door right opposite yours is a funny *trompe l'oeil*: it's fake, painted on, and from behind it a rather cheerful monk is sticking out his white-bearded head.

I will now shave and take a bath and then wait for the weather. I think it won't clear up before *lunch*. Lots and lots of kisses. I am waiting for a telephone call from you or a little note.

V.

[ALS, 2 PP]

[8–9 April 1970]

TO: Montreux Palace Hotel, Montreux

[Taormina, Italy]

SAN DOMENICO PALACE HOTEL

Wednesday 8–IV–70

6:00 PM

and Thursday 9–IV–70
6:00 *AM*

My love,

Today nevertheless the sun looked out, but not for long, and I collected for no more than about two hours in the valley behind the town, from eleven to one, then had a goat cheese sandwich and drank a glass of wine to your precious health. Be careful not to get sick! *Je tiens tremendously* that you're with me on the 15th.

I fell asleep rather stupidly in the afternoon, although I had slept marvellously at night, and at four went out for a haircut and to buy oranges, magazines, insoles for mountain boots: I am two steps away from remarkable places in the eastern spur of the Nebrodi Mountains where it would be a shame for us not to wander; we should, however, wait till the disgusting sirocco stops blowing, it tortures Taormina for three days running every spring (an old-timer tells me). I bought more oranges, I'm eating three a day, and walked into a very attractive bookshop. Apparently I had already been there, with my tail spread right out, ten years ago, since the owner recognized me as if in a dream and so on. Cars here still push their way through between tourists, but it's all still somehow cheerier and pleasanter in the spring; our garden is enchanting, our windows look out on it. You won't forget, my darling, the bird book, the shaving cream, and the lavender, the lavender, will you?

¶ They heat the place very well here. ¶

I haven't told you to give my greetings to Anyuta, that goes without saying. Won't I really get news from you? In a review of Lifar's new memoirs I read this phrase: '*Diaguiliev soon gave him up for his next new love, a schoolboy called Markevitch*.' Shall I tell Topazia about this? Anyway, she reads the 'Observer' where the review appeared. It's terrible.

¶ Have the journals been sent to me – *New Statesman, Spectator, The Problemist*, etc.? ¶

They have set aside for us a beautifully positioned little table.

This is the fourth letter. I am finishing it on Thursday – a wonderful morning! Thank you for your call yesterday, my radiance. Love you. Have you found my note in your box of *allenburies*?

V.

[ALS, 2 PP]

[10 April 1970]

TO: Montreux Palace Hotel, Montreux

[Taormina, Italy]

SAN DOMENICO PALACE HOTEL

10-IV-1970

Friday

7:00

My gold-voiced angel,

(can't get out of the habit of these endearments). Certain small inconsistencies in my letters are explained by my writing many things for future use, communicating with you several times a day, and finishing up my letter the morning after. This is the fifth, concluding, letter in this series, since I think you won't get anything after this in Montreux if you fly out on time.

On Thursday, the 9th, the weather remained cold but the sun was all ablaze and I took my first long walk (from nine in the morning till three in the afternoon) towards Castel Mola; but already at an altitude of 700 metres there were no butterflies and I spent most of the time in the immediate vicinity of Taormina (was I careful? I was very careful). A sweet detail: around one p.m. I walked into a trattoria, no one was there, I started calling in different languages, suddenly a shaggy dog appeared, rushed right out of the café, I stood there a moment, started to leave – and suddenly I saw: it was leading the owner back from a nearby shack. You can easily imagine the outcome. I returned, took my time sorting out the charming catches, at half-past four went out to drink some hot chocolate (wonderful!) in Café 'Macomba' where I will take you.

Alfred Friendly called, wanted (good God, this transparent paper again!), to come over on Saturday the 11th with his wife for two days, but I put him off, asked him to come around the 20th, which he will do. At dinner yesterday an American woman at a nearby table addressed her silent husband, pointing with her chin at a couple who'd walked in: '*He is something very important in coal*.' Another observation: in the square, where I was buying oranges again, a German with the most good-natured chuckle refused the souvenirs offered by a cripple and added: 'But to make up for it I will take a picture of you!' (I wish I remembered the exact *tedesko*-Italian phrase.)

I keep marvelling at the abundance of flowering plants on the slopes and some kind of elevated silence (as there was in the mountains of California), interrupted, though, either by the Puccinian radio on some farm or the awful, eternal sobbing of a donkey.

I am very pleased with your present – the knitted jacket.

Well, my sweetheart. The morning is sunny, but very fresh, with fleecy additions.

Now I'm waiting for you. I'm a little sorry, in one sense, that this correspondence is coming to an end, hugs and adoration.

Will note down the laundry, and then, around nine, go collecting.

V.

[ANS, 1 P.]
[15 April 1970]

TO: Mme Vladimir Nabokov, San Domenico Palace
[Taormina, Italy]

Forty-five springs!

V.

15–IV–70
Taormina

1971

[ANS, 2 PP.]

[15 April 1971]

TO: Mme Vladimir Nabokov, Montreux Palace

[Montreux]

To my darling,

For the forty-sixth year [anniversary].

V.

1973

[AN, 1 P.]

[postmarked 22 January 1973]

TO: E8 Chambre 831, Hôpital Cantonal, Genève

7.30 PM

Montreux

For you, my darling, here are
Twelve tens
Love you,
waiting for you

1974

[AN, 1 P.]
[5 January 1974]
[Montreux]

Mme Vladimir Nabokov

thumb hurts
Happy Birthday
my darling
1974
L'année d'Ada und 'Ada

[AN, 2 PP.]
[14 June 1974]
[Zermatt]

V e l' k o m tu Zerm, my darling,
The daily programme, etc.
B r e a k f a s t at my place. I eat cornfl. only. 7:30
Lunch around 1:00 at café of choice
(ham, local cheese)
The key to your fridge: blue
together with the door-key
Dinner at seven sharp
The stout porter in a frock-coat: M. Franzen
Other information: verbally

Cable car to Sch[w]arz[s]ee
Change at Furi
get out and go right
stairs and indication → Schwarz[s]ee

VN will be in cafeteria
(near Schwarz[s]ee station) 10:30–11
and then walk down to
Staffel-Zmutz-Zermat[t]
(at least two hours)

1975

[ANS, 1 P.]
[14 July 1975]
[Davos]

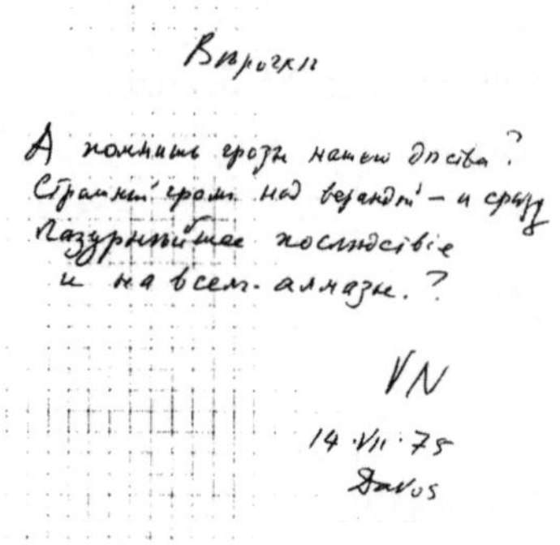
Верочке

А помнишь грозы нашего детства?
Страшный гром над верандой – и сразу
лазурнейшее последствие
и на всем – алмазы?

VN
14·VII·75
Davos

To Vérochka

And do you recall the thunderstorms of our childhood?
Frightful thunder over the verandah – and at once
The most azure aftermath
    and on everything – diamonds?

VN
14–VII–75
Davos

1976

[ANS, 1 P.]
[7 April 1976]
[Montreux]

To Vérochka

*

* *

In the desert a telephone rang:
I ignored the ring,
And soon it cut off.

V Nabokov
7–IV–76
Montreux

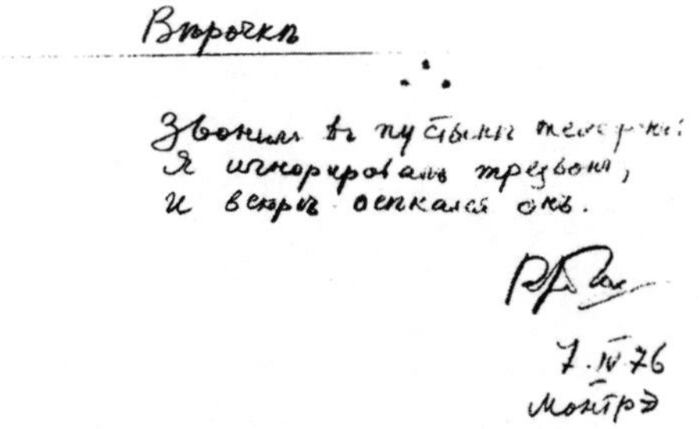

Вѣрочкѣ

∴

Звонилъ въ пустынѣ телефонъ:
Я игнорировалъ трезвонъ,
И вскорѣ осѣкался онъ.

7.IV.76
Монтрэ

Undated

[AN, 1 P.]

[Date and place unknown]

To Kitty Kitovich, Gold Petrovich.
Eat, my happiness,
This grapeppiness.

Appendix One: Riddles

In the summer of 1926 Nabokov attached to many of his daily letters to his wife – who was unwell and staying at a sanatorium – a diligently home-made word puzzle, meant not so much to baffle as to cause a smile. The puzzles are varied, inventive, light, jolly and mildly funny. With very few exceptions, Véra Nabokov seems to have solved them all by return post.

But what posed little trouble for Nabokov's wife in 1926, who likely had no reference books to consult, proved quite a challenge to his beGoogled editors next century. It took putting together three heads to crack these puzzles, with some solutions remaining questionable. It is idle, of course, to try to match wits with Nabokov the logopoet, who, incidentally, contributed all sorts of word-games to émigré periodicals in the mid-1920s, some of his own fabrication. Non-Russian readers are doubly disadvantaged here: to most of them, reading translations of the original Russian puzzles will be like watching a German film with Italian subtitles. But we place them here in the hope that at least the contours of the content of that labour of love will not be lost on them, as it surely was not lost on the original addressee. The gist of some foreign dialogues can be grasped by the facial expressions.

Gennady Barabtarlo

LETTER OF 1 JULY 1926

Crossword clues in Russian:

Across:

1 за решеткой, но не тигр

2 Кричат

3 Бабочка

4 Толпа

5 Дай забвенье ... очаруй ...

Down:

1 Блин революции русской

6 Надпись под лысым

7 Одна из забот Лонгфелло

8 Печенье

9 Часть тела

10 Как перст

11 У поэтов – дымится

Crossword clues in English:

Across:

1 behind bars, but not a tiger

2 [They] shout

3 a butterfly

4 A crowd

5 Give me oblivion ... enchant ...

Down:

1 The spoil of the Russian Revolution

6 An inscription below a bald man

7 One of Longfellow's cares

8 Biscuits
9 Body part
10 [. . .] as a finger
11 In poetry – it smokes

Answers in Russian:

Across: 1. кассир 2. орут 3. махаон 4. банда 5. опьяни
Down: 1. ком 6. oo [?] 7. араб 8. сухарь 9. стан 10. один 11. рана

Answers in transliteration:

Across: 1. kassir 2. orut 3. makhaon 4. banda 5. op'yani
Down: 1. kom 6. oo [?] 7. arab 8. sukhar' 9. stan 10. odin 11. rana

Answers in English:

Across: 1. cashier 2. [they] yell 3. [Papilio] machaon 4. a gang 5. intoxicate
Down: 1. kom 6. oo [?]7. Arab 8. rusk 9. torso 10. alone 11. a wound

LETTER OF 2 JULY 1926

Crossword clues in Russian:

Across and down:
1 Композитор
2 Волосок
3 Волнуется
4 Круглый очерк
5 Сам
6 Подруга Сальери
7 Род судна
8 Большевики

9 Неприятная местность
10 Лесной возглас
11 Упрек
12 Художник, земляк первого
13 Человек с тремя руками
14 Половина пяти
15 Без чего не приехал-бы
16 Пять часов утра
17 Цветок
18 Хорошая знакомая пяти
19 Птица
20 Божья иллюминация
21 Прощевайте

Crossword clues in English:

Across and down
1 Composer
2 A thin hair
3 Is waving
4 Roundish outline
5 Myself
6 Salieri's girlfriend
7 Kind of boat
8 Bolsheviks
9 Unpleasant locale
10 Sylvan exclamation
11 Reproof
12 Artist, compatriot of 1
13 Man with three arms

14 Half of five
15 Wouldn't have come back without this
16 Five a.m.
17 Flower
18 Good acquaintance of five
19 Bird
20 Divine illumination
21 So long!

Answers in Russian:

Across and down: 1. Гуно 2. усик 3. нива 4. окат 5. Сирин 6. Изора 7. ротор 8. ироды 9. Нарым 10. куку 11. укор 12. Коро 13. урод 14. Вера 15. ехал 16. рано 17. алоэ 18. муза 19. удод 20. зори 21. адио

Answers in transliteration:

Across and down: 1. Guno 2. usik 3. niva 4. okat 5. Sirin 6. Izora 7. rotor 8. irody 9. Narym 10. kuku 11. ukor 12. Koro 13. urod 14. Véra 15. ekhal 16. rano 17. aloe 18. muza 19. udod 20. zori 21. adio

Answers in English:

Across and down: 1. Gounod 2. a whisker 3. grainfield 4. circumference 5. Sirin 6. Isora 7. rotor [boat] 8. Herods 9. Narym 10. cuckoo 11. reproach 12. Corot 13. freak 14. Véra 15. travelled 16. early 17. aloe 18. the muse 19. hoopoe 20. dawns 21. adieu

LETTER OF 3 JULY 1926

Riddle in Russian:

Ломота, игумен, тетка, Коля, Марон, версификатор, Лета, чугун, тропинка, ландыш, Ипокрена

Из слогов данных слов требуется составить десять других слов, значенья которых: 1) Место свиданий науки и невежества 2) двигатель 3) город в России 4) историческое лицо 5) добрая женщина 6) часть повозки 7) благовест диафрагмы 8) первый архитектор (см. Библию) 9) бездельник 10) женское имя.

Riddle in transliteration:

Lomota, igumen, tetka, Kolya, Maron, versifikator, Leta, chugun, tropinka, landysh, Ipokrena

Riddle in English:

Aching, abbot, aunt, Kolya, Maro, versifier, Lethe, cast iron, little path, lily of the valley, Hippokrene

Make ten new words out of the syllables of the words above, with these meanings: 1) A place where science meets ignorance 2) an engine 3) a city in Russia 4) a historic personage 5) a good woman 6) part of a cart 7) beatitude of the diaphragm 8) the first architect (see the Bible) 9) a lazybones 10) a woman's name.

Answers in Russian:

1. университет 2. мотор 3. Кременчуг 4. Наполеон 5. матрона 6. дышло 7. икота 8. Каин 9. гуляка 10. Филомена

Answers in transliteration:

1. universitet 2. motor 3. Kremenchug 4. Napoleon 5. matrona 6. dyshlo 7. ikota 8. Kain 9. gulyaka 10. Filomena

Answers in English:

1. university 2. motor 3. Kremenchug 4. Napoleon 5. Matron 6. pole [of a carriage] 7. hiccups 8. Cain 9. idler 10. Philomena

LETTER OF 6 JULY 1926

Crossword clues in Russian:

Acr. 1. часть розы 2. восклицанье 3. Дедушка 4. если не–то глуп 5. видно в мешке 6. Древний автор 7. Сговор
Down. 1. В столицах ... 8. Злой человек 9. Хорош только когда открывается 10. дерево 11. говорится о винограде 12. философ-экономист 13. река

Acr. 1. Сверхъестественный жулик 2. женское имя 3. рыба 4. коричневое 5. Невежа 6. игра 7. человек, выбор, опыт
Down. 8. река 4. художник 3. плати ... 9. рыба 1. камень 10. прощай 11. ... Все вторит весело громам!

Crossword clues in transliteration:

Acr. 1. chast' rozy 2. vosklitsanie 3. Dedushka 4. esli ne–to glup 5. vidno v meshke 6. Drevniy avtor 7. Sgovor
Down. 1. V stolitsakh ... 8. Zloy chelovek 9. Khorosh tol'ko kogda otkryvaetsya 10. derevo 11. govoritsya o vinograde 12. filosof-ekonomist 13. reka

Acr. 1. sverkh"estestvennyi zhulik 2. zhenskoe imya 3. ryba 4. korichnevoe 5. Nevezha 6. igra 7. chelovek, vybor, opyt
Down. 8. reka 4. khudozhnik 3. plati ... 9. ryba 1. kamen' 10. proshchay 11. ... Vsyo vtorit veselo gromam!

Crossword clues in English:

Acr. 1. part of a rose 2. exclamation 3. Grandfather 4. if not–then [he is] dimwit 5. can be seen in a sack 6. An ancient author 7. Accord
Down. 1. In capital cities ... 8. An evil person 9. Good only when it opens 10. a tree 11. said of grapes 12. a philosopher and economist 13. a river

Acr. 1. A supernatural trickster 2. woman's name 3. a fish 4. something brown 5. ruffian 6. a game 7. a man, a choice, and an experience

Down. 8. a river 4. an artist 3. pay. . . . 9. a fish 1. a rock
10. farewell 11. . . . All sings in cheerful tune with thunderclaps!

Answers in Russian:

Acr. 1. шип 2. ура 3. мороз 4. далек 5. шило 6. Ювенал 7. антанта
Down. 1. шум 8. Ирод 9. парашют 10. олива 11. зелен 12. Конт 13. Аа
Acr. 1. маг 2. Ада 3. налим 4. какао 5. олух 6. короли 7. богатый
Down. 8. Обь 4. Коро 3. налог 9. окунь 1. малахит 10. адио (sic) 11. гам

Answers in transliteration:

Acr. 1. ship 2. ura 3. moroz 4. dalek 5. shilo 6. Yuvenal 7. antanta
Down. 1. shum 8. Herod 9. parachute 10. oliva 11. zelen 12. Kont 13. Aa
Acr. 1. mag 2. Ada 3. nalim 4. kakao 5. olukh 6. koroli 7. bogatyi
Down. 8. Ob' 4. Koro 3. nalog 9. okun' 1. malakhit 10. adio 11. gam

Answers in English:

Acr. 1. thorn 2. hurray 3. Frost 4. 'brightwit' 5. an awl 6. Juvenal 7. entente
Down. 1. din 8. Herod 9. parachute 10. olive 11. green 12. Comte 13. Aa
Acr. 1. magician 2. Ada 3. burbot 4. cocoa 5. fool 6. kings 7. rich
Down. 8. Ob' 4. Corot 3. tax 9. perch 1. malachite 10. adio 11. noise

LETTER OF 9 JULY 1926

Riddle in Russian:

Романс, сатин, буфет, рама, лопух, мошенник, засов, тина, тишина, одинокий, тура.

Требуется: из этих одиннадцати слов (т.е. из их слогов)

составь девять других: 5 – русских поэтов, 2 – формы поэтических произведений, цветок, птица.

Riddle in transliteration/ English:

Romans, satin, bufet, rama, lopukh, moshennik, zasov, tina, tishina, odinokiy, tura.

(Love song, sateen, cafeteria, frame, burdock, swindler, bar lock, slime, silence, lonely [man], rook.)

This is what you have to do: out of these eleven words (i.e. their syllables) make nine new ones: 5 – Russian poets, 2 – verse forms, a flower, a bird.

Answers in Russian:

Шеншин – Фет
Апухтин (more likely, as a joke, Опухтин)
Романов (possibly, also as a joke, Никрасов)
Никитин
Ломоносов
Ода
Сатира
Роза
Турман

Answers in transliteration:

Shenshin – Fet
Apukhtin (more likely, as a joke, Opukhtin)
Romanov (possibly, also as a joke, Nikrasov)
Nikitin
Lomonosov

Oda
Satira
Rosa
Turman

Answers in English:

Shenshin – Fet
Apukhtin (more likely, as a joke, Opukhtin)
Romanov (possibly, also as a joke, Nikrasov)
Nikitin
Lomonosov
Ode
Satire
Rose
Tumbler pigeon

LETTER OF 15 JULY 1926

Riddle in Russian:

Волшебные словечки

Толпа, **стой**ка, **чех**арда, **ов**чина, **го**ра, ще**голь**, подагра, бирюза, заноза, Каин, гончая, государь, рама, маяк, сила, Минск.

Их етих сесьнацати слоф тлебуйця зделять цецирнацать длюгих, снаценье католих: 1) люский писятиль 2) тозе 3) тозе 4) цасть Сфинкся 5) тозе 6) делево 7) пцица 8) цасть дямской одезды 9) движенье 10) неподзвизность 11) плязник 12) утёс, воз петый Пускиным 13) гелоиня Никлясова 14) маянькое отвельстие. С потьценьем МИЛЕЙШИЙ

Riddle in English / transliteration:

Magic Words

Tolpa, **stoy**ka, **chekh**arda, **ov**china, **go**ra, shcho**gol**', podagra, biryuza, zanoza, Kain, gonchaya, gosudar', rama, mayak, sila, Minsk.

(Crowd, counter, leapfrog, sheepskin, mountain, dandy, gout, turquoise, splinter, Cain, whippet, sovereign, frame, lighthouse, force, Minsk.)

You musht täk zees zekshtain Wödz und tön zem into fortain azers, ze Meanink off witch ees: 1) russisch Rayter 2) ze saym 3) ze saym 4) a Paat off ze Sfinks 5) ze saym 6) a Trea 7) a Böd 8) a Paat off Veemin's Kloseez 9) Moofemint 10) Immobeelitee 11) Holeedai 12) a Kliff gloreefaid bai Puschkeen 13) Nekrazoff's Heeroeen 14) a schmoll Houl. Rezpektfulee, DARLINK

Answers in Russian:

1. Толстой 2. Чехов 3. Мамин–Сибиряк 4. щека 5. лапа 6. чинара 7. гоголь/сойка 8. подол 9. гонка 10. стоп/заминка/стойка/поза 11. Пасха 12. Ая–даг 13. Дарья 14. щель

Answers in Transliteration:

1. Tolstoy 2. Chekhov 3. Mamin-Sibiryak 4. shcheka 5. lapa 6. chinara 7. gogol' / soyka 8. podol 9. gonka 10. stop / zaminka / stoyka / poza 11. Paskha 12. Aya-dag 13. Dar'ya 14. shchel'

Answers in English:

1. Tolstoy 2. Chekhov 3. Mamin-Sibiryak 4. cheek 5. paw 6. plane tree 7. goldeneye / jay 8. [skirt] hem 9. chase 10. stop / hesitation / hitch / pose 11. Easter 12. Aya-dag 13. Dar'ya 14. chink

LETTER OF 18 JULY 1926

Riddle in Russian:

Волшебные словечки

Из семи дней недели и из слов: лоно, евреи, Синай, пародия, требуется составить 13 слов значенье коих:

1) не делится пополам 2) кустарник 3) мотор 4) властвование 5) что религия берет у энтомологии 6) низложи! 7) Бывает на солнце 8) борец 9) занятие 10) помощь 11) центр 12) часть света 13) части корабля

Riddle in English / transliteration:

Magic Words

Out of the seven days of the week and the words: lono, evrei, Sinay, parodiya, make 13 words with the meanings:

1) can't be divided in half 2) shrub 3) engine 4) rule over 5) what religion takes from entomology 6) dethrone! 7) the sun has them 8) fighter 9) undertaking 10) assistance 11) centre 12) part of the world 13) parts of a boat

Answers in Russian:

1. нечет 2. тальник 3. ротор 4. царенье 5. воспарение 6. свергни 7. пятна 8. поборник 9. дело 10. субсидия 11. средина 12. Европа 13. реи

Answers in transliteration:

1. nechet 2. tal'nik 3. rotor 4. tsarenie 5. vosparenie 6. svergni 7. pyatna 8. pobornik 9. delo 10. subsidiya 11. sredina 12. Evropa 13. rei

Answers in English:

1. uneven 2. purple willow 3. rotor 4. reign 5. soaring 6. overthrow 7. spots 8. champion 9. enterprise 10. subsidy 11. middle 12. Europe 13. yard(-arm)s

Appendix Two: Afterlife

BRIAN BOYD

The first person other than Véra herself to be allowed to see any of Nabokov's letters to her was Andrew Field, who had begun to work on a biography of Nabokov at the end of the 1960s. In January 1971 Nabokov showed Field his letters to his parents and a few of his letters to his wife, with an occasional marginal identification. After her husband's death in 1977 (coincidentally the year Field published *Nabokov: His Life in Part*), Véra began to think about selling off his manuscripts. In 1979, after reading my Ph.D. thesis, she invited me to catalogue the archive for her, both as an inventory for a potential sale and simply to help her find materials for publication or to answer journalists' and researchers' queries. In 1981 she acquiesced in my starting another biography of her husband. After my repeated requests for access to his letters to her, she eventually agreed to read them into my tape recorder. On my trip during the New Zealand university summer vacation, in December 1984 and January 1985, she did read them out (she was now in her eighties), although she had developed a bad cold and had to croak and cough into my cassette recorder as I sat across from her at the small dining table in the living room of the suite at the Montreux Palace Hotel that she had shared with Nabokov since 1961. She had numbered the letters, but often not quite in the right sequence, and she picked up bundles haphazardly, so that the order was baffling. She had warned me she would not read everything – and indeed there were some she did not read at all – but, knowing her intense need for privacy, I was surprised that she read as much as she did between each announcement of a new '*propusk*' ('cut'). Occasionally, she would add a gloss. Later, when I was able to see the originals, I could see where she had marked '*ne chitat*' ('do not read') or 'NO' or '*chitat' ostorozhno*' ('read with care').

In December 1986, Field, who had heard I was working on a biography, published *VN: The Life and Art of Vladimir Nabokov*, largely a combination of his 1967 *Nabokov: His Life in Art* and his 1977 *Nabokov: His Life in Part*. The 1986 volume broke the story of Nabokov's affair with Irina Guadanini, of whom he heard from Zinaida Shakhovskoy (married name Malevsky-Malevich). Shakhovskoy, a staunch friend and supporter of Nabokov in the late 1930s and very warmly mentioned in the letters here, had turned against him and especially Véra by the end of the 1950s, perhaps partly because she resented that it was now Véra who handled almost all her husband's correspondence. That led to an article on Nabokov that he understandably disliked, and to his snubbing her when she approached him at the Gallimard party for the launch of the French *Lolita* in 1959. She blamed Véra for the snub (which had taken Véra herself by surprise) and was determined to get back at her. She did this in the first instance through her 1979 memoir *V poiskakh Nabokova* (*In Search of Nabokov*) – which she told me she had written 'against Véra. And if you say so, I will deny it'. Among her other ploys, she sent a transcription of Nabokov's last letter to Svetlana Siewert to the Library of Congress, where he had deposited many of his early manuscripts, and for good measure included another transcript in her own archive. She also took pains to ensure that the affair with Guadanini would be known. Immediately after reading Field's account of the Guadanini affair, Véra and Dmitri selected three letters to Véra from the time of the affair that make plain Nabokov's anxiety for Véra and Dmitri to rejoin him as soon as possible. The first of these, misdated by Véra 'Feb ~~19~~ 20 1937' (it was actually written on 20 March 1937), now bears Dmitri's note: 'translated on Dec. 20, 1986'. Despite their preceding Nabokov's arrival in New York in 1940, and the switch from Russian to English as his main language of correspondence, these three 1937 letters to Véra appeared in *Selected Letters, 1940–1977*, co-edited by Dmitri, in 1989.

In 1990 Véra had to move out of the Montreux Palace Hotel while it was renovated, and on Dmitri's advice bought two adjacent apartments on the slopes above Montreux and the hotel. She lived in the larger apartment and turned the smaller into an office, a guest room and the archive. On Véra's death in 1991, Dmitri took over the apartments. He sold the Nabokov archive to the Henry W. and Albert A. Berg Collection of the New York Public Library in 1992, but arranged to hold back some materials he wished to control, like his father's diaries, the manuscript of *The Original of Laura* and the letters to his mother. Dmitri had a New World openness that contrasted with his mother's Old World reserve, and later in the 1990s allowed Stacy Schiff and her Russian-speaking research assistant access to the letters to Véra for her biography of his mother, as he also permitted access to other researchers, journalists and documentary-makers. The Berg Collection administrators were anxious to receive whatever materials they had been promised, and in 2002 the letters to Véra were photocopied by Dmitri's assistants, with copies made for Olga Voronina and myself, and the originals sent to New York. We discovered the 1932 letters had not been photocopied, and then, with increasing alarm, that the originals had not been received in New York and could not be found in Dmitri's apartment or his basement, where photocopies of the rest of the archive were now stored. We translated the 1932 material from the tape recordings, which after more than twenty years had deteriorated in quality. In February 2011, on what turned out to be my last visit to Dmitri, a year before he died, he allowed me to rummage through every shelf, drawer and cupboard in the apartment and the basement, but the 1932 letters were nowhere to be found.

Notes

ENVELOPES FOR THE *LETTERS TO VÉRA* BY BRIAN BOYD

p. xxi: *'The years are passing . . .'*: *Conclusive Evidence: A Memoir* (New York: Harper and Brothers, 1951); revised as *Speak, Memory: An Autobiography Revisited* (New York: Putnam, 1967), p. 295. VN would later explain the autobiography's original title, *Conclusive Evidence*, in terms of the interlinked *v*'s at the centre, for Vladimir and Véra (interview with Pierre Dommergues, *Les Langues modernes*, 62 (January–February 1968), pp. 92–102, p. 99).

p. xxii: *'you and I are so special . . .'*: Letter of 13 August 1924.

'cloudless': SO p. 145: 'a cloudless family life'.

even in a letter to Irina Guadanini: VN to Irina Guadanini, June 14, 1937: fourteen years of 'cloudless happiness' ('yasnoe schast'e', Tatyana Morozov Collection).

p. xxiii: *'despite having lived . . . among former officers'*: BB interview with VéN, 20 December 1981.

samples of his verse she had clipped: As recorded in an album of Sirin's verse that VéN seems to have begun assembling later, along with other albums of his prose and of reviews of his work, when she became his archivist (VNA).

scooped the productivity stakes: The fact that this twenty-three-year-old could publish four books in four months shortly before meeting Véra gives the lie to claims such as these: 'Lawyers, publishers, relatives, colleagues, friends, agreed on one point: "He would have been nowhere without her"' (Schiff, p. xii).

p. xxiv: *'Zhemchug' ('The Pearl') in March*: Written 14 January 1923, published in *Almanakh 'Medniy vsadnik'* (Berlin, n. d., but advertised in *Rul'* on 18 and 25 March

1923), p. 267; reprinted in *Stikhi*, p. 76. Nabokov's sister Elena Sikorski, always very attentive to her brother's literary work and his love-life, identified it to BB as a poem written for Svetlana.

'V kakom rayu' ('In what heaven'), also in March: Written 16 January 1923, also published in *Almanakh 'Medniy vsadnik'*, as 'Cherez veka' ('Across the Ages'), p. 268. Also identified by Elena Sikorski as a poem written for Svetlana.

'Berezhno nyos' ('I carefully carried'): Written 7 March 1923 (VNA, Album 8, p. 36), published as 'Serdtse' ('Heart') under the group title 'Gekzametry' ('Hexameters') in *Rul'*, 6 May 1923, p. 2; reprinted in *Stikhi*, p. 94.

'Ya Indiey nevidimoy vladeyu' ('The Ruler': 'An India invisible I rule'): Written 7 March 1923 (VNA, Album 8, p. 37), published as 'Vlastelin' ('The Ruler'), *Segodnya*, 8 April 1923, p. 5; reprinted in *Stikhi*, 125; translated by DN in *SP*, p. 8. In *Stikhi* the poem is misdated '7.12.23' (7 December 1923); in VN's 1923 fair-copy verse album (VNA, Album 8) the 'III' of the month has a correction that makes it possible to read as 'XII', but the poem follows another of '7-III-23' and precedes one of '19-III-23'.

charity ball: *SO*, p. 127; *VNRY*, p. 558n.37.

p. xxv: *Véra wore that mask so that . . .* : BB interview with Elena Sikorski, 24 December 1981.

A day or two later: VN's fair-copy verse album (VNA, Album 8) records new poems often several times a week, often on consecutive days, but breaks off after 7 May until 19 August 1923.

one last forbidden farewell letter: There are transcripts of the letter to Svetlana in the Zinaida Shakhovskoy Papers, Library of Congress, and in the Zinaida Shakhovskoy Papers at Amherst Center for Russian Culture, Amherst College.

'as if licensed . . .': *VNRY*, p. 209.

A week later he wrote a poem . . . The Encounter: 'Vstrecha', *Rul'*, 24 June 1923, p. 2; reprinted in *Stikhi*, pp. 106–107; trans. BB. The epigraph comes from Aleksandr Blok's poem 'Neznakomka' ('Incognita', 1906). The 1 June 1923 date of composition derives from VN's manuscript, pasted by Nabokov's mother into one of the albums where she pasted or copied his verse: VNA, Album 9, pp. 48–9.

p. xxvii: *'Znoy' ('Swelter') . . . on 7 July . . . heat of a southern summer*: The poem (see p. 6) could be rendered 'Torridity' or 'Ardency', were the antique ring not wrong, and were not its point how subtly the speaker's sexual fire starts to infiltrate the literal seasonal heat. Never previously published, this poem was for a specific reader he already knew could read and understand his verse: could she also read and understand his desire?

p. xxviii: *another poem* . . . (*'Zovyosh'* . . .': *'You call* . . .'): Not published until *Stikhi*, p. 112.

this first letter: Letter of c. 26 July 1923, or later. In her biography *Véra* (*Mrs. Vladimir Nabokov*), Stacy Schiff begins with these first months but seriously confuses the evidence. She reports correctly the letter Vladimir wrote to Svetlana on 25 May, but then continues, referring to the first letter to Véra: 'Two days later he wrote to Véra Slonim . . . Was he still too preoccupied with Svetlana? . . . Forty-eight hours after telling Svetlana he will be changing continents the young poet felt compelled to return to Berlin, in part for his mother's sake, in part because of a secret, one "I desperately want to let out"' (p. 6). In fact Vladimir's first letter to Véra bears no date. Schiff has confused the date of the poem 'The Encounter' (May 1923 in Nabokov's posthumous selected Russian verse (*Stikhi*, p. 107), but correctly 1 June 1923 in his manuscript, in Album 9, pp. 48–9, VNA) with the date of the first letter to Véra, while ignoring that that letter encloses a poem ('You call . . .') not written until 26 July. Other elements of the first letter to Véra also indicate it could not have been written on 27 May 1923: the enclosed poem 'Swelter', written on 7 June (Elena Nabokov's transcript, in VNA Album 9, p. 54), and the letter's references to the plays *Dedushka* (*The Grandad*) and *Polyus* (*The Pole*), written on 20 June and 6 and 8 July 1923, respectively (see *Rul'*, 14 October 1923, p. 6, and 4 August 1924, p. 3).

Schiff suggests that Nabokov expresses unforgettable love to Svetlana in one letter, then writes with assured passion to Véra two days later. The record instead shows that he wrote a last farewell to Svetlana on 25 May, then a week later penned 'The Encounter', his response to that meeting with Véra three weeks earlier, which, as soon as it was published, constituted a direct appeal to her. Véra then responded to the appeal in several letters, as he then responded to *them* in two poems and his first letter enclosing the poems. Not two days for a swift switch of affections, as Schiff presents it, but two months of appeal and response.

p. xxix: *Tragediya gospodina Morna* (*The Tragedy of Mr Morn*): Published only in 1997 (*Zvezda*, 1997: 4), and in book form not until 2008 (VN, *Tragediya gospodina Morna, P'esy, Lektsii o drame*, ed. Andrey Babikov (St Petersburg: Azbuka-klassika, 2008)), and translated into English only in 2012 (*The Tragedy of Mister Morn*, trans. Anastasia Tolstoy and Thomas Karshan (London: Penguin, 2012)).

impressions of Prague . . . 'along that whiteness . . .': Letter of 8 January 1924.

first letter back to Véra . . . 'My delightful . . .': Letter of 13 August 1924.

sample letter, complete: 'I love you . . . ': Letter of 19 January 1925.

p. xxx: *a list of what made him suffer*: Letter of 19 June 1926.

p. xxxi: *Nina Berberova could respond*: Nina Berberova, *The Italics Are Mine*, trans. Philippe Radley (New York: Harcourt Brace Jovanovich, 1969), p. 318.

Bunin . . . commented: Quoted by Lev Lyubimov, *Novyi Mir*, 3 (March 1957); *VNRY*, p. 343.

p. xxxii: *the 'very sweet and saintly' Fondaminsky*: Letter of 3 November 1932.

p. xxxiii: *Stacy Schiff's apt phrase*: Schiff, p. 81.

p. xxxiv: *'forty-five springs!'*: Note of 15 April 1970.

p. xxxv: *rendered illegible . . . crossing out every word*: Except for one postcard of newlywed playfulness, which Véra may have preserved because Vladimir's words intermingle inextricably with hers. In their first winter of marriage, they skied at Krummhübel (then in Germany; now Karpacz, Poland). Several days after they returned, on 7 January 1926, Véra began a postcard to Nabokov's mother, but she reports (his words are italicized): 'Volodya's stopping me writing so much, that I'd better write another time, when he's not home. *I'm not stopping you.* That's not true. *It is true.* That it's not true.' Transcript, BB Archive.

p. xxxix: *Weather 'The trip went well . . .'*: BB transcript from original then in Montreux, current location unknown.

an anthology: *Kovcheg: Sbornik russkoy zarubezhnoy literatury* (*The Ark: Anthology of Russian Emigré Literature*) (New York: Association of Russian Writers in New York, 1942).

p. xl: *'Mme Kodryansky was here . . .'*: Ellipsis in VéN's citation of the original letter to Field. BB Archive. See p. xi. The children's writer and memoirist Natalie Kodryansky (Natalia Vladimirovna Kodryansky, née von Gerngross, 1901–1983) had arrived in New York from France in June 1940.

Perepiska s sestroy: VN, *Perepiska s sestroy*, ed. Elena Sikorski (Ann Arbor: Ardis, 1985).

p. xli: *'"You are voiceless . . ."'*: Letter of 12 January 1924.

'Don't you find . . .': Letter of 14 January 1924.

'Tufty, I think you write . . .': Letter of 9 June 1926.

'Will I get a letterlet . . .': Letter of 28 June 1926.

'*I am sad . . .*': Letter of 19 May 1930.

'*Won't I really . . . ?*': Letter of 8–9 April 1970.

'*I received today . . .*': Letter of 8 January 1924.

'*My sweetheart . . .*': Letter of 19 August 1925.

'*My love . . .*': Letter of 10 February 1936.

'*I read parts . . .*': Letter of 6 April 1937.

p. xlii: '*And all your letters . . .*': Letter of c. 26 July 1923.

'*I can't imagine . . .*': Letter of 8 November 1923.

'*I love you . . .*': Letter of 9 November 1942.

'*but why should I . . .*': Letter of 3–4 November 1932.

'*My darling, it is unfair . . .*': Letter of 6 April 1937.

'*I'm ready . . .*': Letter of 13 April 1939.

p. xliii: '*Do not write . . .*': Letter of 14 April 1939.

'*The Finnish president . . .*': Letter of 24 June 1926.

'*who's not very pleasant . . .*': Letter of 21 April 1939.

'*"let's-talk-about-me" smile . . .*': Letter of 25 November 1932.

'*as if he drinks in praise*': Letter of 24 October 1932.

p. xliv: '*praise and more praise . . .*': Letter of 12 July 1926.

'*To avoid later embarrassments . . .*': Letter of c. 24 January 1936.

'*wants me to repeat . . .*': Letter of 4 February 1937.

'*Don't know how . . .*': Letter of c. 24 January 1936.

'*I don't give a damn . . .*': Letter of 12 February 1937.

'*And he, with his protruding eyes . . .*': Letter of 19 February 1936.

'*I am surrounded . . .*': Letter of 4 February 1937.

'*He turned out to be . . .*': Letter of 21 April 1939.

'*I once asked a conductor . . .*': Letter of 24 February 1936.

p. xlv: '*I save mice . . .*': Letter of 17 October 1932.

'*what a cat . . .*': Letter of 24 October 1932.

'*How light and obedient . . .*': Letter of c. 24 January 1936.

'*There's a cat . . .*': Letter of 22 January 1936.

'*The servant here . . .*': Letter of 24 January c. 1936.

p. xlvi: '*I feel agonizingly . . .*': Letter of 4 February 1937.

'*And he, my little one? . . .*': Letter of 6 February 1936.

'How charming . . .': Letter of 22 January 1937.

'extremely attractive': Letter of 4 April 1932.

'I gave my mite . . .': Letter of 6 April 1932.

'Three of the children . . .': Letter of 11 April 1939.

p. xlviii: *'The teacher . . .'*: Letter of 2 June 1926.

'Now I'm floundering . . .': Letter of 14 January 1924.

p. xlviii: *'I'll go out to buy . . .'*: Letter of 11–12 June 1926.

'Semyonlyudvigoviches': Letter of 27 January 1936.

'The weather this morning . . .': Letter of 10 June 1926.

'You came into my life . . .': Letter of 8 November 1923.

'How he, Bunin . . .': Letter of 13 February 1936.

'my German visa . . .': Letter of 24 February 1936.

'In the métro . . .': Letter of 2 February 1936.

p. xlix: *singles Nabokov out as a case of amusia*: Oliver Sacks, *Musicophilia: Tales of Music and the Brain* (New York: Knopf, 2007), p. 102; *SM*, pp. 35–6.

'I read for an hour . . .': Letter of 27 June 1926.

'I went to the gypsies . . .': Letter of 28 or 29 October 1932.

p. l: *those to Edmund Wilson*: See Simon Karlinsky (ed.), *The Nabokov–Wilson Letters: Correspondence Between Vladimir Nabokov and Edmund Wilson, 1940–1971* (New York: Harper & Row, 1979), revised as *DBDV*, 1940–1971 (Berkeley and Los Angeles: University of California Press, 2001).

p. li: *'Now I'm waiting . . .'*: Letter of 10 April 1970.

'MY BELOVED AND PRECIOUS DARLING': TRANSLATING *LETTERS TO VÉRA* BY OLGA VORONINA

p. liv: *'I like to think . . .'*: Letter of 10 January 1924.

'The door right opposite . . .': Letter of 8 April 1970.

a good writer is also an enchanter: *LL*, pp. 5–6.

p. lv: 'Music': 'Music' seems to have been written in February 1932 and was published in *Poslednie novosti*, 27 March 1932, p. 2.

'Vadim Victorovich was offering . . . ': Letter of 10 March 1937. Since a patronymic is a derivative of one's father's name, the real Vadim Victorovich Rudnev appears to be Vadim, son of Victor – Nabokov's fictional creation and alter ego.

Gogol's knack: NG, p. 78.

transformation of the Belgian franc: Letter of 27 January 1936.

'Victor' . . . accumulates: 'Victor, whom I also visited at the museum, has now accumulated a hundred and twenty-nine cases of butterflies – from the British fauna.' Letter of 27 February 1937.

p. lvi: *'Journals' or 'books' . . . with 'pages'*: '. . . altogether, nine hundred Czech pages have been set from my "encyclopedia"' (Letter of 4 March 1937); 'Victor sent his mother the fourth copy yesterday – in all one thousand two hundred pages of Czech translation over these two months' (Letter of 7 April 1937).

Pooch, a relative of Poochums: Letters of 27 August 1925, 29 August 1925, 6 June 1926, 3 July 1926.

Mr Darling's crying: Letter of 10 July 1926.

to steal Nabokov's pen: Letter of 15 July 1926.

'life-generating' fiction: Nabokov writes about Gogol's 'life-generating syntax' in his essay on *Dead Souls* (LRL, p. 20).

with a 'sch' or 'shch': Letters of 4, 5, 7, 10, 15 June 1926.

p. lvii: *'Lolita, light of my life . . .'*: *Lolita* (New York: Putnam, 1958), p. 9.

p. lviii: *Russian translation of* Lolita: *Lolita*, trans. into Russian by VN (New York: Phaedra, 1967).

'disgrace': V. D. Nabokov, *The Provisional Government*, in *V. D. Nabokov and the Russian Provisional Government, 1917*, ed. and trans. Virgil D. Medlin and Steven L. Parsons (New Haven: Yale University Press, 1976), p. 100.

with a yat' . . . with a yer: In the spelling reform of 1917, the *yat'*, 'Ѣ', was replaced with 'e', already used in other semantic contexts, and the *yer*, 'Ъ', 'hard sign', was eliminated in most environments.

p. lix: *'it was not the snow . . .'*: 'The Visit to the Museum', *SoVN*, p. 284.

'"Living at Wellesley . . ."': Letter of 19 March 1941.

charmingly antiquated: Modern spelling: 'галстук', *galstuk*, necktie; 'шофер', *shofyor*, chauffeur; 'прийти', *priyti*, to arrive.

p. lx: *dropping the final 'a' in 'Anna Karenin'*: *LRL*, p. 137.

1923

Letter of c. *26 July 1923*

Date: Though undated, the letter encloses the poem 'Evening', dated 26 July 1923 in Nabokov's mother's album (VNA), and must be written on or shortly after that date.

masquerade trick: VN first met Véra Slonim on 8 May 1923, at a Russian émigré charity ball, where she wore – and did not lower – a masquerade mask.

Ronsard: Pierre de Ronsard (1524–85), French poet, whom VN had translated the previous year ('Sonet (iz P'era Ronsora)' ('Quand vous serez bien vieille'), *Rul'*, 13 August 1922) and would allude to later, most memorably in *Lolita* (Pt I Ch. 11).

It was strange: The thoughts expressed here find an echo in the second part of the two-part poem 'Provans' ('Provence'), 'Slonyayus' pereulkami bez tseli' ('I wander aimlessly from lane to lane', written on 19 August 1923, just after he arrived back in Berlin), published *Rul'*, 1 September 1923, p. 2. VN translated it in *PP*, p. 27, where he retrospectively misassigned it to 'Solliès-Pont, 1923'.

Mother: Elena Ivanovna Nabokov (née Rukavishnikov, 1876–1939), to whom VN was very close: see *SM*, Ch. 2.

Evening: Published (without title) in *Stikhi*, p. 112; dated 26 July 1923 in EN's album of VN's verse, VNA. VN's sister Elena Sikorski understood this poem, with its 'You call', as her brother's response to Véra's first letters to Domaine-Beaulieu (interview with BB, 24 December 1981).

Swelter: Unpublished. Dated 7 July 1923, Domaine-Beaulieu, in EN's transcript in her album of VN's verse, VNA, and marked in VN's hand for inclusion in *Stikhi*, but not included there.

'The Granddad': *Dedushka*, written 30 June 1923, published *Rul'*, 14 October 1923; trans. by DN in *MUSSR*.

'The Pole': *Polyus*, written 6 and 8 July 1923, published *Rul'*, 14 August 1924, pp. 2–3, and 16 August 1924, pp. 2–3; trans. by DN in *MUSSR*.

'Gamayun': Gamayun, one of the three prophetic birds in Russian mythology, the other two being Sirin and Alkonost', gave its name to a short-lived (1922–23) Berlin émigré publishing house, which published only seven books before folding, including VN's verse collection *Grozd'* (*The Cluster*, 1923), and his translation of *Alice's Adventures in Wonderland*, *Anya v strane chudes* (1923).

'Russkaya mysl': *Russian Thought*, literary and political monthly founded in 1921, in Sofia, then published intermittently, first in Prague, then in Paris. Its lapse between 1924 and 1927 presumably explains the eventual publication of *Polyus* in *Rul'*.

Letter of 8 November 1923

je patauge: Fr. 'I'm floundering about'.

(Your face betw): The start of the abandoned draft sits at right angles to the text of the letter, which skirts around it.

turned out to be fat: The words translated 'full of knights' can also be read, grammatically, as 'plump knights'.

some other American: Presumably VN had in mind the American Elisha Gray (1835–1901), who invented a telephone in 1876, rather than the better-known Scots-Canadian Alexander Graham Bell (1847–1922), who also invented the telephone, and won the American patent for it, in the same year.

Yes . . . flight . . . : These lines break the text of the letter vertically in two.

Letter of 30 December 1923

en trois quarts: Fr. 'in three-quarter view'.

our trip . . . awful: EN with her younger children relocated to Prague, where she was offered a modest pension by the Czech government. VN came to help with the move.

Kirill: Kirill Vladimirovich Nabokov (1911–64), VN's youngest brother and godson.

twelve (. . . with an 'e'): VN ironically refers to the Russian spelling of the word for 'twelve', 'двенадцать' (*dvenadtsat'*) which, in pre-revolutionary orthography, was spelled 'двѣнадцать'.

Kramář's house: Karel Kramář (1860–1937), Czech nationalist statesman and Czechoslovakia's first prime minister (1918–19). A Russophile, and married to a Russian (Nadezhda Nikolaevna Kramář-Abrikosov, née Khludov, 1862–1936), he strongly disliked Bolshevism and welcomed prominent Russian émigrés into Czechoslovakia and to his Prague home.

the twenty-third (old style): On 5 January 1924 (New Style), Véra's twenty-second birthday.

Morn sat down here with me: The hero of the five-act play *Tragediya gospodina Morna*, which VN began in December 1923 and completed in January 1924, and was published only posthumously, in *Zvezda* (1997: 4), and, in book form, TGM and in English as TMM.

Letter postmarked 2 January 1924

Date: VN's date looks like '3-XII-23' (although the '3' appears to rework or overwrite another numeral). The postmark of the envelope with which VéN kept this letter is '2.1.24' (that is, 2 January 1924). VN *may* have written '31-XII-23'; the letter certainly follows the previous, whose own probable '30-XII-23' also has an unclear first digit, which *could* be '2' rather than '3', but VN seems to have been in Berlin until late December 1923 (*Rul'*, 8 January 1924, p. 5). If we take the previous letter as correctly dated 30 December 1923 and the '2.1.24' postmark as belonging to this letter, 31 December 1923 seems the least unlikely.

my father: Vladimir Dmitrievich Nabokov (1870–1922), criminologist, liberal statesman, journalist and editor, and patron of the arts. VN admired him boundlessly (see SM, Chs. 1 and 9) and set great store by his moral, political, literary and artistic judgement. In 1923, he was still deeply affected by his father's assassination in March 1922; almost a quarter of a century later, he could still write of the 'very special emotional abyss' caused by his father's death (SM, p. 191).

Tatarinov: Vladimir Evgenievich Tatarinov (1892–1961), journalist and regular contributor to *Rul'*.

Rul': *The Rudder*, liberal Russian-language daily published in Berlin between 1920 and 1931, founded by VDN and his two close pre-revolutionary colleagues,

Avgust Kaminka and Iosif Hessen; the dominant Russian newspaper in Berlin, which until 1924 was the dominant Russian émigré centre. While *Rul'* lasted, VN published there (under the pen-name Vladimir Sirin) scores of poems, stories, plays, reviews, essays, chess problems and crossword puzzles.

Buffon: Georges-Louis Leclerc, Comte de Buffon (1707–88), French naturalist and encyclopaedist.

Monte Cristo . . . you and me: Le Comte de Monte Cristo (1844–5) by Alexandre Dumas (1802–70). When Monte Cristo asks Berticcio about visiting cards, he expects the cards to be made; Berticcio tells him that one of them has already been delivered and the rest are waiting on the mantelpiece in his bedroom.

Tatarinovs: Vladimir Tatarinov and his wife Raisa Abramovna Tatarinov (née Fleyshits, pen-name Raissa Tarr, 1889–1974), Sorbonne-educated lawyer, and decades later, a well-known French writer. Raisa Tatarinov was known for her remarkable talent at bringing together the Russian émigré writers, artists and thinkers she regularly invited to her apartment in Berlin.

Struves: Gleb Petrovich Struve (1898–1985), a friend of VN's, especially in the 1920s, and his wife Yulia Yulievna (née André, 1902–91). Before the October 1917 Revolution, Struve's father Pyotr Berngardovich Struve (1870–1944) had been, like VDN, a leading liberal opponent of the Tsar, and, in emigration, was a political spokesman and editor of influential Russian periodicals. Gleb had been a student at Oxford while VN was at Cambridge, and both lived in Berlin through much of the 1920s; he would become the first literary historian of the Russian emigration.

1924

Letter of 8 January 1924

Date: The envelope bears a Berlin postmark, '12.1.24' on the verso (therefore not the initial postmark); the stamp, with its Czech postmark, has been cut off. VéN has dated the letter on the envelope, under the absent stamp, '8-I-24'.

Moldau: The German name for the Czech Vltava, the river bisecting Prague.

Lukash: Ivan Sozontovich Lukash (1892–1940), prolific writer, journalist, literary critic. In the early 1920s, before he left Berlin for Riga, he and VN were close friends and collaborated on several projects, including the pantomimes *Agasfer* (*Ahasuerus*) and *Voda zhivaya* (*The Living Water*).

Sergey Makovsky: Sergey Konstantinovich Makovsky (1877–1962), poet and art historian.

gymnasium: Traditional high school, emphasizing classics.

Aldanov: Mark Aleksandrovich Aldanov (Landau) (1886–1957), former chemist, a historical novelist since just before the First World War and especially successful in the emigration.

Voloshin: Maksimilian Aleksandrovich Voloshin (1877–1932), prominent Russian (but not émigré) poet. VN, who met him in Crimea in 1918, thought highly of his poetry and appreciated his mentoring.

Sirin: VN adopted 'Vladimir Sirin' as his regular pen-name in January 1921, partly to distinguish himself from his father, also Vladimir Nabokov, who edited and contributed to *Rul'*, where most of VN's work was then appearing.

fiancée: VN's fiancée since 1922, Svetlana Romanovna Siewert (married name, Andrault de Langéron, 1905–2000), broke off their engagement on 9 January 1923.

'The Wanderers': *Skital'tsy*, a short two-act play VN wrote in October–November 1921; published *Grani*, 2 (1923), pp. 69–99. VN first sent it to his parents as his translation of a work by an English playwright, Vivian Calmbrood (a near-anagram of Vladimir Nabokov).

Letter of 10 January 1924

my sister: His favourite sibling, his younger sister Elena Vladimirovna Nabokov (married name Sikorski, 1906–2000).

Madame Bertran: Very private by nature, VéN assumed the name 'Madame Bertran' on envelopes and in messages to VN in the early days of their relationship, in Berlin and Prague.

Mr Lermontov's famous line: The motif of parting (*razluka*) is central in the poetry of Mikhail Yurievich Lermontov (1814–41), but VN here in fact reworks a famous two lines from 'Razgovor Knigoprodavtsa s poetom' ('Conversation between a Bookseller and a Poet', 1824) by Aleksandr Sergeevich Pushkin (1799–1837): 'Chto slava? – Yarkaya zaplata / Na vetkhom rubishche pevtsa' ('What is fame? – A bright patch / On a bard's tattered cloak').

punch lollipops: Hard candy on sticks, made of punch or toddy.

Matter must decay . . . :, TMM, Act V, Scene 1, pp. 128–9. Italics mark differences between this draft and the published translation.

a note in Rul': L. L. [Lolly Lvov], review of 'Agasfer, a Pantomime', *Rul'*, 8 January 1924, p. 5.

Mme Landau: Unidentified.

Ahasuerus: *Agasfer*, a pantomime VN composed with Ivan Lukash to music by V. F. Yakobson. In late December 1923, VN and Lukash recited their play to a small audience at a friend's home.

Letter of 12 January 1924

'voiceless': Could also be translated 'verbless' if VN means to evoke the famous poem 'Shopot, robkoe dykhan'e . . .' ('Whisper, timid breathing . . .', 1850) written by Afanasy Afanasievich Fet (1820–92) without a single verb.

u. s. w.: Ger. 'and so on'.

magic lantern show: See SM, Ch. 8, for VN's reports of the magic lantern shows of his childhood.

'Grani': The 'almanac' (literary miscellany) *Grani* (*Facets*), Book 1, published in 1922, in which VN's poem 'Detstvo' ('Childhood') and his essay 'Rupert Bruk' ('Rupert Brooke') appeared. It is unclear what VN refers to: 'Slonim' does not

feature on the cover. *Grani* was published by a Russian press of the same name, founded in 1921 in Berlin by Sasha Chorny (Aleksandr Mikhaylovich Glikberg, 1880–1932), poet, satirist and friend of VDN; in 1923 it had published VN's collection *Gorniy Put'* (*The Empyrean Path*).

Kadashev-Amfiteatrov: Vladimir Aleksandrovich Amfiteatrov-Kadashev (1888–1942), poet; member of the 'Brotherhood of the Round Table', a literary group VN and others formed in 1922.

'veterinary' instead of 'Virgin Mary': In the original: *bogoroditsa* ('Mother of God'), *pugovitsa* ('button').

Nemirovich-Danchenko: The writer Vasily Ivanovich Nemirovich-Danchenko (1844/5–1936) lived in Berlin before emigrating to Prague in 1923.

'Spolokhi': *Northern Lights*, Russian literary journal founded in Berlin in 1921 by the émigré writer Aleksandr Drozdov (see note to next letter).

'paddle the horse!': In the original: *sedlay konya* ('saddle the horse'), *sdelay konya* ('make a horse').

You will leave . . . : TMM, Act IV, p. 107. Italics mark differences between this draft and the published translation.

Letter postmarked 14 January 1924

Date: Berlin postmark on verso; the original Prague postmark, presumably a day or more earlier, has disappeared with the stamp, cut off the envelope.

my boss: Probably Yakov Davidovich Yuzhny (1884–1938), director of Berlin's Bluebird cabaret, who paid VN for sketches, especially in late 1923 and 1924.

Drozdov: Aleksandr Mikhaylovich Drozdov (1896–1963), writer, translator, founding editor of the journal *Spolokhi*, editor of the literary miscellany *Vereteno*, to both of which VN contributed. During the course of 1923, he had denounced the emigration and *Rul'* in a way that prompted VN to consider calling him out to a duel (*VNRY* 203); in December 1923, he returned to the Soviet Union.

Letter of 16 January 1924

Date: Found in an envelope postmarked 26 January 1924; but VN's date and the reference to 17 January show it was written earlier.

those elders: Presumably the notorious anti-Semitic hoax *The Protocols of the Elders of Zion* (1903), which purported to document Jewish plans for world domination and was popular among conservative Russian émigrés.

Nilus: Sergey Aleksandrovich Nilus (1862–1929), religious writer, published *The Protocols of the Elders of Zion* as part of his book *Velikoe v malom i antikhrist, kak blizkaya politicheskaya vozmozhnost': Zapiski pravoslavnogo* (*The Great within the Small and Antichrist, an Imminent Political Possibility: Notes of an Orthodox Believer*, 1903).

Krasnov: Pyotr Nikolaevich Krasnov (1869–1947), general in the Russian and Cossack armies, novelist and publicist.

c'est tout dire: Fr. 'that says it all'.

A Vision: The poem ('Videnie') is written on the back of the letter. Published *Rul'*, 27 January 1924, p. 2; *Stikhi*, p. 126.

Letter of 17 January 1924

Frost and sunshine: Echo of the poem 'Zimnee utro' ('A Winter Morning', 1829), by Pushkin.

Sadko: A hero of the Novgorod epics. In the opera *Sadko* (1897), by Nikolay Andreevich Rimsky-Korsakov (1844–1908), the hero enchants the daughter of the sea king with his music, and descends into the Volkhov to find treasure and save his honour.

I will Amerigo: In Russian, *ameríknu*.

Flaubert ... 'Madame Bovary': Gustave Flaubert (1821–80), *Madame Bovary* (1857). VN kept his high opinion of Flaubert, whose *Madame Bovary* he taught at Cornell and Harvard (LL).

lacrimae arsi: *Lacrimae* – 'tears'; *arsi* – 'I burned'. A pun on Latin *ars*, 'art' (although 'tears of art' would be *lacrimae artis*).

'The scarlet ribbon ...': From Lermontov's long poem 'Demon' (1829–39), Canto X, ll. 5–6: '*Luchom rumyanogo zakata / Tvoy stan, kak lentoy, obov'yu.*'

Letter of 24 January 1924

frustrations flock: In the Russian, *khlop'ya khlopot*, 'flakes of troubles'.

Asta Nielsen: Danish silent-film actress (1881–1972).

'The Living Water' ... 'Sinyaya ptitsa': *The Living Water*, which VN co-wrote with Lukash, ran for more than a month (January–February 1924). 'Bluebird' ('Sinyaya ptitsa') was a Russian cabaret club in Berlin.

Medes: Ancient Persian people. One of the main characters in TMM is called Midia.

my estate: VN inherited the Rozhdestveno estate from his uncle, Vasily Ivanovich Rukavishnikov (1872–1916), the 'Ruka' of SM (especially Ch. 3).

Lenin is dead: Vladimir Ilyich Lenin (Ulyanov) (b. 1870), leader of the Bolshevik Revolution and Soviet Premier, died on 21 January 1924.

Marina Tsvetaeva's: Marina Ivanovna Tsvetaeva (1892–1941), a leading Russian poet, and an essayist and playwright, emigrated in 1922 to join her husband, then a student at Prague University. From 1925, she lived in Paris until her departure for Soviet Russia in 1939.

Letter of 13 August 1924

Date: VN appears to have mistakenly written 'VII' for 'VIII' (as in the next letter); this and the next three, the last two dated 'VIII', seem in fact to cover just over a week in Prague and the Czech resort of Dobřichovice. VN has returned to Prague after seven months in Berlin with VéN.

Letter of 17 August 1924

Date: see note on date of previous letter.

Chirikovs: Evgeny Nikolaevich Chirikov (1864–1932), writer, member of several Russian literary unions in Prague.

Olga: The older of VN's two sisters, Olga Vladimirovna Nabokov (1903–78), to become Shakhovskoy by her first husband, Sergey Sergeevich Shakhovskoy, and Petkevich by her second, Boris Vladmirovich Petkevich.

her grant: To which she was entitled as a member of the family of a Russian émigré scholar or writer (her father) and living in Czechoslovakia.

your cousin: Probably Véra's cousin Anna Lazarevna Feigin (1890–1973), to whom she was very close, who had a cousin, Herman Bromberg, in Leipzig.

Tegel: Berlin suburb, in whose Russian cemetery (the Russisch-Orthodoxer Friedhof) VDN was buried. VN sent money there for the upkeep of the grave and for memorial services.

'Prayer' … and 'Rivers': 'Molitva' ('Prayer'), *Rul'*, 24 August 1924, p. 2, and *Stikhi*, pp. 140–41; 'Russkaya reka' ('Russian River'), *Nash mir*, 14 September 1924, pp. 264–6, and as 'Reka' ('River'), *Stikhi*, pp. 97–100.

whether anything's appeared in 'Segodnya': *Today*, émigré daily, published in Riga (Latvia was independent between the wars) from 1919 to 1940. The poem 'Gadanie' ('Fortune-Telling') would appear in *Segodnya* on 26 August 1924, p. 11.

Letter of 18 August 1924

hope (with a small 'h'): Nadezhda (Hope) is a common name for a woman in Russian.

Mokropsy (there is such a hamlet): To a Russian ear the name sounds like 'wet dogs'.

lots of new English words: VéN already knew English well enough to give lessons in it, but wanted to expand her vocabulary.

Korostovets's: Vladimir Konstantinovich Korostovets, until 1930 Berlin-based Russian correspondent of the *Westminster Gazette* and *The Times*, who paid VN well to turn his articles into English.

Letter of 24 August 1924

my youngest sister: Elena, who was eighteen.

Vrubel: Mikhail Aleksandrovich Vrubel (1856–1910), Russian painter famous especially for his dark, intense images illustrating Russian literary and folk themes.

Alkonost: In Slavic mythology, a bird of paradise with the head of a woman, whose beautiful song makes mortals forget everything else. Alkonost is often portrayed together with Sirin, another prophetic bird, as in the famous painting *Sirin i Alkonost: Pesn' radosti i pechali (Sirin and Alkonost: Song of Joy and Grief*, 1896), by Victor Mikhaylovich Vasnetsov (1848–1926). (See the note on Gamayun to the first of VN's letters to VéN, c. 26 July 1923.)

faithlessness (is this witty?): *Vera* in Russian means 'faith'.

Kresty: 'The Crosses', a prison in St Petersburg.

Vyborg Appeal: After Tsar Nicholas II unexpectedly dissolved the First Duma in July 1906, many of its deputies (representatives) travelled from St Petersburg the next day to nearby Vyborg, Finland, and there issued a proclamation exhorting the populace to such civil disobedience as resisting military service and taxation. VDN, a leader in the Duma, helped draft the appeal and signed it, for which he was sentenced to three months' imprisonment.

bread-and-salt: A Slavic greeting of welcome for an honoured guest.

1925

Letter of 19 January 1925

Date: The date is marked on the back of the envelope, in pencil, by VéN. The stamp is missing.

Letter of c. *March–April 1925?*

Date: Undated letter in an unstamped envelope.

Letter of 14 June 1925

Date: A note written on the front of a small envelope, dated on the back, in pencil, in VéN's hand '14.VI.25'.

I *Love you*: In Russian, the capitalized and carefully aligned first letters of words *Lyublyu* ('I love'), *Obozhayu* ('I adore') and *Radost'* ('joy') form the word LOR ('LAUR[A]'?) when read vertically.

Letter postmarked 19 August 1925

Zoppot: A Pomeranian beach resort town in the then Free City of Danzig; now Sopot, Poland.

Shura: Aleksandr (Shura) Sack, whom VN tutored in Berlin and was escorting to Zoppot.

S.A.: Sofia Adamovna Sack, Aleksandr's mother.

Postcard of 27 August 1925

Bol[l]: Boll, a hamlet a mile north of Bonndorf, into which it would be incorporated in 1971, between Bonndorf and Reiselfingen (see next letter).

Postcard of 28 August 1925

20 versts: A verst is two-thirds of a mile or just over a kilometre; twenty versts = thirteen miles.

Bad-Bol[l]: Not to be confused with Bad-Boll, a well-known town over a hundred miles away. A small Bad-Boll stood near the Boll now incorporated into Bonndorf, although only a few traces remain.

Postcard of 29 August 1925

We passed through here: Inscription over the image on the picture side of the postcard, a photograph of a steam locomotive crossing the well-known railway bridge Ravennaviadukt across the Black Forest valley of Höllental. There is a caption at the bottom of the card: 'Höllental — bad. Schwarzwald. Ravennaviadukt'.

Postcard postmarked 30 August 1925

We'll spend . . . St Blasien: Written on the picture side of the postcard, across the sky of a landscape captioned 'Zastlerhütte'.

Postcard 1 of 31 August 1925

Shura suggests . . . plant: The date was written first; the top two lines were written around this point, after the postcard and the poem had been finished.

The Summit: The poem ('Vershina') is inscribed on the other side of the card. Published, *Rul'*, 19 September 1925, p. 2; trans. by VN as 'I Like That Mountain' in *PP*, p. 35.

Postcard 2 of 31 August 1925

Pension Zeiss . . . little card: VéN had just written to say she had rented a room at Pension Zeiss in Konstanz.

Postcard of 1 September 1925

Säckingen: Bad Säckingen am Rhein.

follow the route we covered today: The route is marked on the map of Todtmoos and St Blasien on the picture side of the postcard.

Postcard 1 of 2 September 1925

Postcard, captioned 'Wehr (Baden)' with an image of the little town as seen across the railroad tracks.

in your namesake: i.e. in Wehr (in Russian the phrase for 'in Wehr' sounds, and is spelled, like 'in Véra').

30 versts: About twenty miles.

Postcard 2 of 2 September 1925

my song: A reference to the picture side of the postcard: a gentleman in theatrical 'Renaissance' dress, pressing a similarly dressed lady to his heart, and holding a trumpet in his left hand; his horse is behind them. Below the image there is a caption in verse, from the 1853 poem by Joseph Victor von Scheffel (1826–86), set to music in, for instance, the opera *Der Trompeter von Säckingen* (1884) by Victor Ernst Nessler (1841–90): 'Behüt' dich Gott. / Die Wolken flieh'n, der Wind saust durch die Blätter, / Ein Regenschauer zieht durch Wald und Feld, / Zum Abschiednehmen just das rechte Wetter, / Grau, wie der Himmel, steht vor mir die Welt' ('God protect you. / The clouds fly, the wind whistles through the leaves / A rainshower drifts through wood and field, / Just the right weather for leavetaking. / The world stands before me grey as the sky').

1926

Letter of 26 April 1926

Ivan Vernykh: Manuscript of abandoned short story (VNA, Box 1) that turns into a letter to Véra. The '1.' at the beginning indicates that this was to be the first section of a multi-section story. *Vernykh*, 'true' or 'faithful', shares a root with *vera*, 'faith'. Thanks to Gennady Barabtarlo for reminding us that this story becomes a 'letter to Véra'.

Letter of 2 June 1926

Date: VéN left her husband a letterpad on which she had written the day and month (from 2/VI to 30/VI); VN added the year. See start of letter of 30 June 1926.

I don't even know where you are: In the summer of 1926, VéN spent two months at several health resorts in southern Germany with her mother, Slava Borisovna Slonim (1872–1928). VN remained in Berlin in a Russian pension in Nürnberger Strasse.

Gotter-knows-where: Pun on 'God-knows-where', using a mistransliterated German *Götter* (gods).

'Zveno': *Zveno* (*The Link*), a Russian weekly edited in Paris from 1923 to 1928 by Pavel Milyukov and Maksim Vinaver.

a song: my dress is blue, blue: 'Blau, blau, blau sind alle meine Kleider', a German children's song.

Albertine: *Albertine disparue* (also *La Fugitive*; *Albertine Gone*), the sixth volume (1925) in *À la recherche du temps perdu* (*In Search of Lost Time*, 1913–27), by Marcel Proust (1871–1922).

Kaplan's: Sergey Kaplan was a regular pupil of VN's in 1925–6, his mother an occasional one.

Regensburger Str.: VéN's parents separated in 1924. Her cousin Anna Feigin joined her father, Evsey Lazarevich Slonim (1865–1928), and others, in an apartment in Regensburger Strasse.

Sofa: Sofia Evseevna Slonim (1908–96), VéN's youngest sister.

Arctia hebe: The arctiid moth *Arctia (hebe) festiva*, the Hebe Tiger Moth.

Daphnis nerii: The sphingid moth, the Oleander Hawk Moth, present in parts of Africa and Southern Asia all year round and in summer in much of Europe.

livornica: The sphingid moth *Hyles livornica*, the Striped Hawk Moth, found in Africa, Southern Europe and Central and East Asia.

celerio: The sphingid moth *Hippotion celerio*, the Vine Hawk Moth, permanently present in Africa and Southern Asia and a migrant in Europe.

niceae: The nymphalid butterfly *Stibochiona nicea*, the Popinjay, occurs usually in the Australo-Indomalay ecozone.

Aporia crataegi-augusta: The pierid butterfly *Aporia crataegi*, the Black-Veined White, a rather large white with prominent dark veins. The sub-species *Aporia crataegi augusta* was named in 1905 by Eurilio Turati (1858–1938), after whom VN named Luzhin's opponent in his fateful last chess game (*The Defence*).

Shura's: The home of VN's pupil, Aleksandr Sack.

Sofia Ad.: Sofia Ad[amovna?], possibly Mme Sack, Aleksandr's mother.

B. G.: Spelled out in letter of 21 June 1926 as Berta Gavrilovna, otherwise unidentified.

my own club: One of the best tennis clubs in Berlin, where VN played almost for free thanks to his strong game.

Finanzamt: German tax office, here trying to collect the mandatory 'Church Tax'.

pusschen: For the next few months, VN often adds diminutive suffixes 'ch', 'sch' or 'shch' to his endearments and other nonce words, possibly in imitation of the German diminutive '-chen' suffixes.

Letter of 3 June 1926

Observer: The world's oldest Sunday newspaper, founded in London in 1791.

Anyuta's: Anna Feigin's.

Letter of 4 June 1926

Stein: Semyon Ilyich Stein (1887–1951), half-brother of VN's close friend Georgy Iosifovich Hessen. See next note but one below.

'Mary': VN's first novel, *Mashen'ka* (*Mary*), published in Russian (Berlin: Slovo, 1926). In German it would appear as *Sie kommt – kommt sie?*, trans. Jakob Margot Schubert and G. Jarcho (Berlin: Ullstein, 1928).

'Slovo': Slovo (The Word), a Berlin publishing house established in 1920, on the suggestion of VDN and his friends Iosif Hessen and Avgust Kaminka, as a branch of the major German publisher, Ullstein. VN published with Slovo his translation of Romain Rolland's *Colas Breugnon* (*Nikolka Persik*, 1922), his novels *Mary* (*Mashen'ka*, 1926) and *King, Queen, Knave* (*Korol', dama, valet*, 1928), and his collection of short stories *The Return of Chorb* (*Vozvrashchenie Chorba*, 1930).

Gräger: Unidentified.

and no Spaniards: May combine a pun on *marok*, the genitive case of 'marks' and a homophone of 'Maroc', the French for Morocco, and an echo of a line ('and no Spaniards') from 'The Fifth International' (1922), by Vladimir Vladimirovich Mayakovsky (1893–1930), which had quickly become a catchphrase.

the book of short stories: No volume of Nabokov short stories would appear in German until *Frühling in Fialta: Dreiundzwanzig Erzählungen*, ed. Dieter E. Zimmer, trans. Wassili Berger, Dieter E. Zimmer, Renate Gerhardt and René Drommert (Reinbek bei Hamburg: Rowohlt, 1966).

Evsey Lazarevich: Slonim, VéN's father, consulted here for his business sense.

By some miracle I received 'Rul'': Despite his having changed addresses and not informed *Rul'*'s delivery service.

composing a poem about Russia: He hoped to have a new poem to read for his performance on Russian Culture Day, 8 June.

'il est evidang': Mispronunciation of '*il est évident*' (Fr. 'it is obvious').

'Ouna lettra por vous, mossieu': Provençal Fr. 'A letter for you, sir.'

Letter of 5 June 1926

Slava Borisovna: VéN's mother. Referring to others by the initial letter of first name and patronymic is standard Russian practice.

Ladyzhnikov's: A Russian bookstore and lending library in Berlin (Rankestrasse 33).

Zoshchenko: Mikhail Mikhaylovich Zoshchenko (1895–1958), master of short satirical fiction, whom VN would later come to appreciate more.

Sergey K.'s: Kaplan's.

E. L.: Evsey Lazarevich (Slonim).

Mlle Ioffe: Unidentified.

Freud – pleasant topic: VN would become famous for his dislike of Sigmund Freud (1856–1939) and his baiting of Freudians.

Day of Culture: Russian Culture Day, 8 June (in honour of Pushkin's birthday), the most important cultural fixture in the émigré calendar.

Letter of 6 June 1926

Tartars: The Tatarinovs, whose name means 'of the Tartar'.

Karsavin: Possibly Lev Platonovich Karsavin (1882–1952), religious philosopher and historian of medieval culture.

trying to prove: The dispute took place on 14 February at the Press Ball held by the Union of Russian Writers and Journalists.

Aykhenvald: Yuly Isaevich Aykhenvald (1872–1928), literary scholar and critic, and friend; the first major critic to hail VN as a writer of the first rank.

Purishkevich: Vladimir Mitrofanovich Purishkevich (1870–1920), high-ranking Russian right-wing politician and anti-Semite, who had been a friend of Aykhenvald (a Jew) during their student years. Aykhenvald's article 'Purishkevich' appeared in 1926.

Grif: Unidentified, and if his article was published, it remains untraced.

Kadish: Mikhail Pavlovich Kadish (1886–1962), journalist, writer and translator.

some Spaniard: Presumably the Spanish Jesuit, José de Anchieta (1534–97), who travelled to Brazil as a missionary in 1553.

Leonov's 'Badgers': *Barsuki* (*Badgers*, 1924), a novel about post-revolutionary transformations in Russian peasant life, by the Soviet writer Leonid Maksimovich Leonov (1899–1994). VN was studying Zoshchenko, Leonov and others for a talk on Soviet fiction for the Tatarinov circle; he would complete his draft on 11 June.

Seyfullina's 'Vireneya': The Soviet writer Lidiya Nikolaevna Seyfullina (1889–1954), author of ideologically correct but artistically lame fiction. Her novel *Vireneya* (1925) tells of a peasant woman caught up in the revolutionary turmoil.

Letter of 7 June 1926

A clipping of an announcement of *Volya Rossii* with a review of Sirin's *Mary* is enclosed (the review would appear in the May 1926 issue, pp. 196–7). VN drew a line from the 'N. M. P.' initials of the reviewer, to her name above: 'N. Melnikova-Papoushek' (Nadezhda Fyodorovna (Filaretovna) Melnikov-Papoushek (Papoushkova), 1891–1978). Also enclosed is a page with the poem 'Tikhiy shum' ('Soft Sound'), written in ink with minor corrections and, on the other side, the draft of the same poem in pencil.

Wells: H. G. Wells (1866–1946), English writer whom VN's father had hosted at his house in St Petersburg for dinner in February 1914, and whose fiction VN always esteemed highly.

'Volya Rossii': *Volya Rossii* (*Russia's Will*), a Russian émigré periodical published in Prague between 1920 and 1932. Initially a daily, from 1922 it became a monthly literary and political journal.

E. L.: Evsey Lazarevich (Slonim).

S. B.: Slava Borisovna (Slonim).

out of S. B.: St Blasien; perhaps a reference to VéN's chilly relationship with her mother.

your reprimand: VéN's reply (in German) to the letter from the Finanzamt that VN forwarded to her on 2 June.

'Soft Sound': Poem ('Tikhiy shum') enclosed both as a draft and a final copy; published *Rul'*, 10 June 1926, p. 4; trans. by VN in *PP*, pp. 59–61, where he mistakenly hazards place and date of composition as 'Le Boulou, 1929'.

Letter of 8–9 June 1926

success: VN's reading at Russian Culture Day.

'Moskva': 'Moscow', a Russian bookstore in Berlin.

wrapping the thing – not Anyuta, but the coat: The Russian form '*eyo*' (here translated as 'the thing') in this sentence would at least as often mean 'her'.

Lena's: A present for VN from Elena Evseevna Slonim (1900–1975), VéN's older sister, whose later married name would be Massalsky.

Weisskäse: Ger. curd (cheese).

Sergey Gorny: Pseudonym of Aleksandr Avdeevich Otsup (1882–1949), writer, humourist.

Kardakov: Nikolay Ivanovich Kardakov (1885–1973), entomologist, in Berlin from 1921, first at the German Entomological Institute, then the Natural History Museum; had participated in entomological expeditions in the Altai and the Russian Far East as well as in Indochina and Ceylon.

Lyaskovsky: Aleksandr Ivanovich Lyaskovsky (1883–1965), historian of literature.

Vl.Vl.: Vladimir Vladimirovich, VN's first name and patronymic.

Yasinsky: Ieronim Ieronimovich Yasinsky, pen-name Maksim Belinsky (1850–1931), writer and journalist.

Zaytsev: Kirill Iosifovich Zaytsev (1887–1975), literary critic, historian, political commentator, and in later life a theologian, archimandrite Konstantin.

Ilyin: Ivan Aleksandrovich Ilyin (1883–1954), Russian Orthodox philosopher.

'The Jubilee': Comic sketch, *Yubiley* (1876), by Anton Pavlovich Chekhov (1860–1904).

Ofrosimov Group: Gruppa, a theatrical troupe organized by Yury Victorovich Ofrosimov (1894–1967), director and theatre critic. In 1927 VN's play *Chelovek iz SSSR* (*The Man from the USSR*, 1927) would be premiered by Gruppa.

immediately the applause exploded: The previous year, at the first of what would become the annual Russian Culture Days, VN had read his poem 'Exile', 'which conjures up an image of Pushkin as a member of the emigration' (*VNRY*, p. 242).

Hessen: Iosif (Joseph) Vladimirovich Hessen (1865–1943), prominent member of the Constitutional Democratic party, member of the Second State Duma, political commentator, publisher (with Slovo) and co-editor of *Rul'*.

print the poem in Rul': Where it appeared on 10 June 1926, p. 4, with a report on its reception and on Russian Culture Day.

'It's Not Always Shrovetide for the Cat': *Ne vsyo kotu maslenitsa* (1871), a play by Aleksandr Nikolaevich Ostrovsky (1823–86).

Panchenko: Unidentified.

K.: Kaplan's.

Letter of 9 June 1926

street of winter fields: Winterfeldtstrasse, Berlin.

Kaminka: Avgust Isaakovich Kaminka (1865–1941?), a close friend and colleague of VN's father, business manager of *Rul'*; supported EN after the death of her husband in 1922, and personally subsidized *Rul'* after the economic crisis of the mid-1920s made it no longer self-sustaining.

Gladkov's 'Cement': *Tsement* (1925), by the Soviet writer Fyodor Vasilievich Gladkov (1883–1958), was considered a model of Socialist Realist literature. Nabokov quotes Gladkov's sentences exactly but runs absurd examples even more absurdly together.

Lalodya: One of their named 'Littlies' (little figurines).

Letter of 10 June 1926

Hôtel Pension Schwarzwaldhaus: The postman crossed out the old address, 'Sanatorium St-Blasien Todtmoos', and wrote this one above.

Dipod: In Russian, *tushkan* (*tushkanchik* means 'jerboa'); jerboas form most of the family *Dipodidae*.

fastbreak: VN's word in Russian is not the usual *zavtrak* but the nonce-word *postolom*, which merges *post*, which can mean 'a fast', or specifically 'Lent' (but with echoes of 'postal service'), and the root of the verb *lomat'*, 'break': so, a Russian 'break fast' also breaking the fast in his mail from VéN.

Fedin: Soviet writer Konstantin Aleksandrovich Fedin (1892–1977). His novel *Goroda i gody* (*Cities and Years*, 1924) was his most important to this date.

'The Fight': 'Draka', written late June/early July 1925, published *Rul'*, 26 September 1925, pp. 2–3.

'Beneficence': 'Blagost'', written in March 1924, published *Rul'*, 27 April 1924, pp. 6–7.

'The Seaport': 'Port', written early 1924, published *Rul'*, 24 May 1924, pp. 2–3.

chessboard ... compose a problem: VN had begun to compose chess problems by at least 1917, and published his first in 1923. He would collect some of his best, along with thirty-nine Russian and fourteen English poems, in *Poems and Problems* (1970): 'Chess problems demand from the composer the same virtues that characterize all worthwhile art: originality, invention, conciseness, harmony, complexity, and splendid insincerity' (*PP*, p. 15).

'V. Sirin recited ...': VN quotes from *Rul'*, 10 June 1926, p. 4, where 'Soft Sound' was prefaced: 'below we print V. Sirin's poem, read by the author yesterday. The poem had an enormous success, and the unending applause of the audience forced the talented poet to recite his composition twice.'

Letter of 11–12 June 1926

Hôtel Pension Schwarzwaldhaus: The postman crossed out the old address, 'Sanatorium St-Blasien Todtmoos' and wrote this above.

wasted two marks on 'Volya Rossii': For the review signed N. M. P., '[Review.] Sirin, 'Mashen'ka', *Volya Rossii*, May 1926, pp. 196–7. Melnikov-Papoushek was an occasional contributor to Russian émigré periodicals.

Melnikov-Papoushek (whose papa ushered no good news in): A play in Russian on her surname *Papoushek*: *ey papa ushek ne dral* ('papa didn't shake her by the ears'): he didn't discipline her enough to make her a good writer.

lecture: 'Neskol'ko slov ob ubozhestve sovetskoy belletristiki i popytka ustanovit' prichinu onogo', MS, VNA; published in *Diaspora*, 2 (2001), pp. 7–23, ed. Alexander A. Dolinin.

June 12th : VN had written 'July'.

Golubev-Bagryanorodny: Leonid Nikolaevich Golubev-Bagryanorodny (1890–1934), Russian avant-garde artist famous for his pencil drawings of the Russian émigré community and Berlin cityscapes.

Bunin: Ivan Alekseevich Bunin (1870–1953), major novelist, short-story writer, poet, in 1933 would become the first Russian to win Nobel Prize for Literature.

Uncle Kostya: Konstantin Dmitrievich Nabokov (1872–1927), brother of VN's father, Russian diplomat, former Counsellor of the Russian Embassy in London.

Letter of 12 June 1926

Katyusha: From Katya, a Russian woman's name.

Squire, Steps to Parnassus: *Steps to Parnassus: And Other Parodies and Diversions* (1913), by poet, writer and editor John Collings Squire (1884–1958).

Henry James, The Outcry: The last completed novel (1911) of Henry James (1843–1916).

Sofa: Sofia Slonim, VéN's sister.

E. I.: Unidentified.

E. L.: Evsey Lazarevich (Slonim).

K.'s: Sergey Kaplan's.

Volkovysky: Nikolay Moiseevich Volkovyssky (1881–after 1940), journalist. VN sometimes spells his name with one *s*.

Mme Falkovsky: Probably the wife of the lawyer and journalist Evgeny Adamovich Falkovsky (1879–1951).

Letter of 13 June 1926

'Rooms'. Or even 'A Room for Rent': Apparently never written as a story, but these thoughts result in the poem 'Komnata' ('The Room'), written on 22 June 1926 (see below).

Tegel: For the upkeep of VN's father's grave and for memorial services: see note to letter of 17 August 1924.

Letter of 14 June 1926

Hotel-Pension St Blasien: The postman crossed out VN's words 'Schwarzwaldhaus' and 'Todtmoos' and added the new address.

about the Maid with Madame K: About Joan of Arc with Madame Kaplan.

the Walrus and the little saintly Nuki: Perhaps a nickname the Nabokovs gave a neighbour who walked his dog near where they lived, or a fantasy game involving the little creatures VN describes in his letters of this period.

Grunewald: The largest municipal forest in Berlin, predominantly Scots pine and relatively unkempt, almost the only place in Berlin VN (and Fyodor in *The Gift*) liked.

Veryovkin: A friend of Anna Feigin and the Nabokovs, otherwise unidentified.

Sergey K.: Kaplan.

'Ways to Strength and Beauty': 'Wege zu Kraft und Schönheit' (1925) by Nicholas Kaufmann (1892–1970) and Wilhelm Prager (1876–1955).

Letter of 15 June 1926

Hotel-Pension Schwarzwaldhaus: Across the front of the envelope there is a typewritten inscription: 'abgereist nach St Blasien Sanatorium' ('moved to St Blasien Sanatorium').

Bobby de Calry: Count Robert Louis Magawly-Cerati De Calry (1898–?), VN's fellow student and friend at Cambridge.

Sergey: Sergey Vladimirovich Nabokov (1900–1945), VN's brother, a year younger than him. Theirs was a complicated relationship: 'For various reasons I find it inordinately hard to speak about my other brother . . . I was the coddled one; he, the witness of coddling . . .' (*SM*, p. 257).

Lena: Perhaps Elena Evseevna Slonim, VéN's sister.

'*Odd (A Fairy-Tale)*': 'Odd' in the sense of 'Uneven'; under the title 'Skazka' ('Fairy-Tale'), published *Rul'*, 27 June 1926, pp. 2–3, and 29 June 1926, pp. 2–3; trans. DN with VN as 'A Nursery Tale', *TD*.

frivolous Hebe: A reference to the poem 'Vesennyaya groza' ('Spring Thunderstorm', 1828), by Fyodor Ivanovich Tyutchev (1803–73): 'Ty skazhesh': vetrenaya Geba, / Kormya Zevesova orla, / Gromokipyashchiy kubok s neba, / Smeyas', na zemlyu prolila!' ('You will say: it was the frivolous Hebe, / Who, while feeding Zeus's eagle, / Laughing, spilled the thundering and boiling cup / From heavens to earth.').

Je ne dis que cela: Fr. 'I'll say no more.'

Letter of 16 June 1926

Hotel-Pension Schwarzwaldhaus: The words 'Hotel-Pension Schwarzwaldhaus, Todtmoos' are crossed out by the postman, and the letter readdressed: 'St Blasien Sanatorium/ b Fr Slonim'.

Winter Palace . . . purple: The Winter Palace was ochre-coloured for more than a century, until Nicholas II decided to paint it terracotta-red. After the Revolution, it would be painted grey in 1927 and other colours over the next few years.

Librairie: Fr. 'bookstore'; in this case, a bookstore–lending library, probably Ladyzhnikov's.

note-pad you arranged for me – with dates: In June–July 1926 VN wrote his letters on a note-pad numbered by VéN. He would sometimes add a year to the date, but almost all the dates at the top of the letters' first pages were written in VéN's hand.

Letter of 17 June 1926

Hotel-Pension Schwarzwaldhaus: 'Schwarzwaldhaus, Todtmoos, Schwarzwald' is crossed out, and the letter readdressed 'St Blasien Sanatorium'.

L.: Probably Ilya ('Lyusya') Feigin, Anna Feigin's cousin.

E. L.: Evsey Lazarevich (Slonim).

Sofia S.: Unidentified.

Letter of 18 June 1926

Hotel-Pension Schwarzwaldhaus: 'Hotel-Pension Schwarzwaldhaus, Todtmoos' is crossed out, and the letter readdressed 'St Blasien Sanatorium'.

composed the whole poem: A fair copy of the poem 'Pustyak . . .' ('A Trifle') (see below) is enclosed, on a separate sheet.

Terijoki: A Finnish resort thirty miles to the north of St Petersburg; from 1940, part of the Leningrad region; in 1948 renamed Zelenogorsk.

Bubikopf: Page-boy cut.

A Trifle . . . : 'Pustyak, – nazvan'e machty, plan, – i sledom', published Zveno, 4 July 1926, p. 7, and in Stikhi, p. 183; trans. DN, as 'A Trifle', SP, p. 25.

Letter of 19 June 1926

Hotel-Pension Schwarzwaldhaus: The words 'Hotel-Pension Schwarzwaldhaus, Todtmoos' are crossed out, and the letter is readdressed 'St Blasien Sanatorium bei Frau Slonim'.

'Odd': Working title of story 'Skazka' ('A Nursery Tale').

S. K.: Sergey Kaplan.

Danechka: A former girlfriend of VN's; maiden name unknown; she later married Vladimir Tatarinov's younger brother.

Rusina: Mme or Mlle Rusin, unknown.

Trotsky: Ilya Markovich Trotsky (1879–1969), journalist, Berlin correspondent of the newspaper Russkoe Slovo.

Zvezdich: Pyotr Isaevich Rotenshtern, pen-name Zvezdich (1868–1944), journalist and translator.

the story. . . the poem: His most recent works: the story 'A Nursery Tale'; the poem 'A Trifle'.

like a rooster in soup: Kak kur vo shchi ('like a rooster in soup'), a play on the proverbial kak kur v oshchip ('like a rooster to be plucked').

Poletika: Vladimir Ivanovich Poletika (Waldemar von Poletika, 1888–1981), geographer, statistician and agronomist.

That's Pushkin: From Pushkin's letter to Pavel Voinovich Nashchokin, 23–30 March 1834: 'They say that unhappiness is good school: perhaps. But happiness is the best university. It finishes the education of the soul capable of the good and the beautiful, like yours, my friend; like mine, too, as you know.' VN would cite the aphorism in an interview at Wellesley College, 'Vladimir Nabokov – A Profile', *The Last Word* (April 1943), pp. 19–21.

'I walk on a carpet . . .': A joke, compounding the pun in Chekov's 1898 story 'Ionych': 'Ya idu po kovru, ty idyosh', poka vryosh" ('I walk on carpet; you walk, while you tell lies'). *Po kovru*, 'on carpet', sounds the same as *poka vru*, 'while I tell lies'; *poka vryosh'*, 'while you tell lies', no longer resembles the Russian for 'on carpet'. The pseudo-German *Teppich, teppst du* would be a weak pun on the German *Teppich* (carpet) pretending to be a verb, and meaning something like 'If I tep, you tep too.'

Letter of 20 June 1926

Hotel-Pension Schwarzwaldhaus : 'Hotel-Pension Schwarzwaldhaus, Todtmoos' is crossed out, and the letter readdressed 'St Blasien Sanatorium bei Frau Slonim'.

the poem: 'A Trifle': see letter of 18 June 1926 above.

My brother: Sergey Nabokov.

review: Konstantin Mochulsky, 'Roman V. Sirina' ('Novel by V. Sirin'), *Zveno*, 168, 18 April 1926, pp. 2–3.

Elkin: Boris Isaakovich Elkin (1887–1972), lawyer, political commentator and publisher, member of the editorial board of *Slovo*.

Mochulsky: Konstantin Vasilievich Mochulsky (1892–1948), literary critic, professor of literature at the Sorbonne (1924–39).

Letter of 21 June 1926

Berta Gavr[ilovna]'s: See note to letter of 2 June 1926

Shura: Aleksandr Sack.

Bavarian square: Bayerischer Platz.

Konoplin: Ivan Stepanovich Konoplin (1894–1953), writer, poet, journalist and contributor to *Rul'*.

Taboritsky and Shabelsky-Borg: Sergey Vladimirovich Taboritsky, (1895–?) and Pyotr Nikolaevich Shabelsky-Bork (1893–1952), Russian right-wing monarchists, who in 1922, while trying to assassinate one leading Russian liberal, Pavel Milyukov, killed another, VN's father.

E. L.: Evsey Lazarevich (Slonim).

Letter of 22 June 1926

Two pages from VN, two from EN to VéN, and on a separate page a fair copy of VN's poem 'Komnata' ('The Room'), which has mutated from a story project (letter of 13 June 1926).

to take a lot off: Pun on two meanings of the Russian verb *snimat'*: 1) 'to take pictures'; 2) 'to take off clothes'.

floridithy: From *vit'evatiy*, 'florid' or 'ornate'.

owlthy: The provenance of VN's nonce-endearment *syshch* is not very clear. It could be from *sych* ('owl'), *sytiy* ('full', 'sated'), or even *sushchiy* ('existent, real').

This poem: 'Komnata' ('The Room'): see below.

The Room: 'Komnata', *Rul'*, 11 July 1926, p. 2, and *Stikhi*, pp. 184–5.

18–VI–26 / Dear Véra: EN's letter, enclosed in VN's letter to VéN.

Ev. K.: Evgenia Konstantinovna Hofeld (1884–1957). From 1914, governess to Olga and Elena Nabokov, she remained for the rest of her life very close to the Nabokov family, especially VN's mother, and was buried next to her. She stayed in Prague for the rest of her life, supporting Olga's son Rostislav Petkevich and was herself supported financially by VN and Elena Sikorski. VN had tried to get his sister Elena and her family, as well as Evgenia Hofeld and Rostislav Petkevich, to America after the war.

K.: Kirill Nabokov.

Letter of 23 June 1926

Mme K.: Kaplan.

Lena: Elena Slonim.

F.: Unidentified.

Letter of 24 June 1926

Martin du Gard: Roger Martin du Gard (1881–1958), French writer, who would win the Nobel Prize for Literature in 1937.

pales or aphirape: Sub-species of the fritillary butterfly *Brenthis ino* (*borealis*).

Letter of 25 June 1926

S. B.'s: Slava Borisovna (Slonim)'s.

Uncle Kostya: Konstantin Nabokov.

Letter of 26 June 1926

proofs: Of 'Skazka' ('A Nursery Tale').

Ludwiga: Unidentified *Rul'* staff member.

Uncle K: Kostya (Konstantin Nabokov).

Shakhovskoy: Dmitry Alekseevich Shakhovskoy (1902–89), translator and poet; from August 1926 he would be a Russian Orthodox priest (Father Ioann), rising to Archbishop; brother of Natalia Shakhovskoy, who in 1927 would marry VN's cousin Nicolas Nabokov.

'*Blagonamerenny*': *The Loyalist*, shortlived Russian émigré journal, published in Brussels in 1926, edited by Shakhovskoy.

Pirandello: Luigi Pirandello (1867–1936), Italian dramatist.

at least like Anyuta: Anna Feigin was chubby.

Letter of 27 June 1926

Hercules bridge: Schillstrasse ends at the Herkulesbrücke, which crosses the Landwehrkanal, which in turn flanks the Berlin park, the Tiergarten.

'*Real*': *Yav'*, a title that rhymes with the well-known Russian periodical *Nov'* (*Virgin Soil*) and outdoes in its brevity (in Russian, three letters rather than four) this and titles like *Rech'* (*Speech*) and *Rul'* (*The Rudder*). VN invents a Soviet journal, *Red Reality* (*Krasnaya yav'*), in 'The Christmas Story' ('Rozhdestvenskiy rasskaz,' *Rul'*, 25 December 1928).

Letter of 28 June 1926

really is a Hoffmann Street: As in 'A Nursery Tale'. Named in VN's fictionalized Berlin, as in the real city, after E.T.A. (Ernst Theodor Wilhelm) Hoffmann (1776–1822), German writer of fantasy and horror fiction.

books have been sent: Copies of *Mary* for Bunin and for Konstantin Nabokov.

to Zoo: The Zoo train station.

an absolutely charming poem: A clipping from *Slovo* No. 189 is enclosed, containing a poem by I. Perts, 'Teterevinyi tok' ('The Lek of a Black Grouse'), under the heading 'Young Poets'.

Adamovich: Georgy Victorovich Adamovich (1892–1972), poet, and the most influential literary critic in the emigration.

thorough scolding: Adamovich regularly published, under the pseudonym 'Sizif' (Sisyphus), a column in *Zveno* called 'Otkliki' ('Comments'), usually caustic responses to contemporary, especially Soviet, literature. Nabokov refers here to the column of 27 June 1926, pp. 4–6.

/22'/9'7'3'31'. . . : VN sends VéN his solution to this riddle in his letter of 3 July below.

Letter of 29 June 1926

Prof. Gogel: Sergey Konstantinovich Gogel (1860–1930), lawyer and law professor at the Russian Academic Institute in Berlin.

Pozdnyshev: The main character in the novella 'The Kreutzer Sonata' (1889), by Lev Nikolaevich Tolstoy (1828–1910). See below.

Comment tu regardes sur ça? Rien à soi? ('Good grief!'): VN appears here to offer comically lexical (not even literal) and unidiomatic French translations of Russian idioms, *Kak ty na eto smotrish'?* ('How do you look on that?') and *Nichego sebe!* (lexically in English 'Nothing to self', but idiomatically expressing surprise: 'Good grief!').

Maykapar: 'Maykapar' was the name of a tobacco factory, founded by a Karaim family in Riga in 1887.

Dubnyak: Aykhenvald. *Dubnyak* means 'oak wood'; its German translation is *Eichenwald*, of which 'Aykhenvald' is the Russian transliteration. VN plays with the name's origin in the epigram on Aykhenvald at the start of the second letter of 5 June 1926.

Letter of 30 June 1926

pages you marked: See note to letter of 2 June 1926.

send you the clipping: VN forgot to enclose the clipping; see next letter.

Pushkin used to say: From Pushkin's 'Oproverzheniya na kritiki i zamechaniya na sobstvennye sochineniya' ('Refutation of the Criticism and Comments on My Own Works', 1830, partly published for the first time in 1841). 'What does grammar say? That the acting verb ruled by a negative particle demands not Accusative, but Genitive case now. [. . .] Is it possible that the electric power of a negative particle must go through this entire chain of verbs and resonate in the noun? I don't think so.'

S. B.: Slava Borisovna (Slonim).

E. L.: Evsey Lazarevich (Slonim).

Peltenburg: Leo Peltenburg (?–1955), Dutch business partner of E. L. Slonim and a good friend of the family.

Lyusya: Ilya Feigin.

'Fairy-Tale': The story later translated as 'A Nursery Tale'.

Letter of 1 July 1926

Crossword: See Appendix One: Riddles, p. 525.

Give me oblivion . . . enchant: Perhaps a paraphrastic extract from the romance 'Pod charuyushchey laskoy tvoeyu . . .' ('Under Your Enchanting Caress') which included the line 'Akh, potseluem day zabven'e' ('Oh, give me oblivion with a kiss'), attributed to composer Nikolay Zubov and poet A. Mattisen.

The spoil of the Russian Revolution: 'Blin revolyutsii russkoy'; a distorted echo of the Russian proverb *Pervyi blin komon* (literally 'The first pancake will turn out just a lump'; a rough English equivalent would be: 'You must spoil before you spin').

clipping: A review of an art exhibition in which Tatyana Siewert, the sister of VN's ex-fiancée Svetlana, took part.

Regina Claudias: A kind of plum.

Orlov: Unidentified.

Bertman: Unidentified.

Rosny jeune: J. H. Rosny jeune (Séraphin Justin François Boex, 1859–1948), French science fiction author.

krestoslovitsa . . . two years old: In 1924 VN coined a Russian equivalent for 'crossword', *krestoslovitsa*, which, however, would lose out before long to the straightforward transliteration *krossvord*. See below, note to letter of 6 July 1926.

half a pood: A *pood* is 16.8 kg or about 37 pounds.

Letter of 2 July 1926

Across and down: VN's crossword puzzle for VéN: see Appendix One: Riddles.

word puzzle: Unsolved.

Morskaya: The Nabokovs' St Petersburg house was at 47 Bolshaya Morskaya Street. His dream may have been influenced by the name of the street: *morskaya* means 'of the sea'. In the description that follows he refers to Pushkin's poem 'The Bronze Horseman' (1833), which not only famously describes the disastrous flood of 1824 but also presents Tsar Peter the Great (1672–1725) as a supernatural being capable of overcoming, if not controlling, the elements. The landmark bronze statue of Peter the Great on horseback – commissioned by Catherine the Great and sculpted from 1770 to 1782 in a team led by Étienne Maurice Falconet, and a central character in the poem – stands on Senate Square, about a quarter mile from the former Nabokov home.

Akhmatova: Anna Akhmatova (Anna Andreevna Gorenko, 1889–1966), poet, translator, literary critic, memoirist.

'I remember just your coldness . . .': The story did not materialize (but see letter of 10 July 1926), but a version of Lyudmila N. turns up much later in *Pnin* (1957) as Liza Bogolepov, Pnin's manipulative ex-wife, formerly the narrator's ex-mistress: 'A few days later she sent me those poems; a fair sample of her production is the kind of stuff that émigré rhymsterettes wrote after Akhmatova: lackadaisical little lyrics that tiptoed in more or less anapaestic tetrameter and sat down rather heavily with a wistful sigh . . . A prose translation would go: "No jewels, save my eyes, do I own, but I have a rose which is even softer than my rosy lips. And a quiet youth said: 'There is nothing softer than your heart.' And I lowered my gaze . . ."' (*Pnin*, pp. 180–81).

MY GREETINKS . . . : Written in a mixture of capital and small letters: VN imitates an unsteady hand, like that of a child who has not yet mastered writing but is trying to write neatly.

Letter of 3 July 1926

Lomota . . . : Aching, abbot, aunt, Kolya, Maro, versifier, Lethe, cast iron, little path, lily of the valley, Hippocrene. For solution, see Appendix One: Riddles.

grand ciel rose: Fr. 'great pink sky'.

A t'il eu vent . . . : Fr. 'Did he get wind of something?'

et je me regalai . . . : Fr. 'and I treated myself to a cold bath'.

'*My dearest member* . . .': Line 6 of 'Epistle To James Tennant of Glenconner' (1789) ('My dearest member nearly dozen'd') by Robert Burns (1759–96).

'*I know coldly and wisely* . . .': VN's poem, commenting on VéN's habit of carrying a gun in her purse, written on 1 September 1923: 'Ya znayu kholodno i mudro, / chto v sumke lakovoy tvoey – / v sosedstve zerkal'tsa i pudry / spit chornyi kamen': sem' smertey' ('I know, coldly and wisely, / that in that lacquered purse of yours, / next to a mirror and a powder-case / sleeps a black stone – seven deaths': VN manuscript album, January–October 1923, VNA). VéN's handgun, a Browning, held seven bullets. These lines were published in a different translation in Schiff, p. 56, and with an incorrect date, p. 388.

Hanna: Unidentified.

'*Russkoe slovo*': *The Russian Word*, a Russian émigré periodical published in Harbin, Manchuria, from 1926 to 1935.

Aykhenvald's article: Yuly Aykhenvald, 'Literaturnye zametki' (review of V. Sirin, *Mashen'ka* and P. P. Veimarg, 'Kornet Korsakov'), *Rul'*, 31 March 1926, pp. 2–3.

Count Witte's little nickname: VN's pun on 'curriculum vitae'. Count Sergey Yulievich Witte (1849–1915), Russia's Minister of Finances (1892–1903) and first Prime Minister (1903–1906).

couldn't dance without limbs: Pun: *beskonechnost'* ('limitlessness, eternity') is nearly homophonic with *bez konechnostey* ('without limbs'): the letter transliterated 'z' is here unvoiced, so sounds like 's'.

Letter of 4 July 1926

pellonela or *carpetiella*: *pellonella* is *Tinea pellionella*, the case-bearing clothes-moth (from Latin *pellis*, 'hide' or 'skin', which VéN would recognize via French *pelisse*, a long fur coat); *carpietella* is VN's joke name for the carpet moth, *Trichophaga tapetzella*.

Postcard 1 of 5 July 1926

Jaspidea Celsia: *Staurophora (Phalaena, Calotaenia, Jaspidea) celsia* L. 1758, a Noctuid moth found in central Europe. After catching a specimen of this species on a Berlin street, VN wrote to his mother on 28 September 1925 that he had found 'a wonderfully rare moth – the dream of German collectors (it's rather large, with soft-emerald forewings marked with brown)' (*N'sBs*, p. 119).

Aeroplane: 'Aeroplan', published, with some changes, *Rul'*, 25 July 1926, p. 2.

Letter 2 of 5 July 1926

A kind of epigram . . . oak grove: Ger. *Eiche*, 'oak', *Wald*, 'forest'; *Eichenwald*, 'oak grove'. 'Shirokoshumnaya dubrova' ('wide-noised oak grove') echoes, in the last line of this epigram, the last line of Pushkin's 'Poet' ('The Poet', 1827).

new poem: See Letter 1 of this date, above.

'Kalina': 'Kalinka' (1860), by writer and folklorist Ivan Petrovich Larionov (1830–89).

ruined the first line of my poem: 'A Trifle': see letter of 18 June 1926: *nazvan'e, machty* ('a name, masts') should have been *nazvan'e machty* ('a mast's denomination').

Pointlets: VN's wordplay: *funtiki* ('poundlets'); *punktiki* ('pointlets').

'Sovremennye zapiski': *Sovremennye zapiski* (*Contemporary Annals*), the Russian emigration's major literary and political journal, published in Paris, 1920–40. VN had published three poems in the journal in 1921 and 1922 but nothing since; his days of being the major fiction-writer in the journal, from 1929, still lay ahead.

Arbatov : Zinovy Yurievich Arbatov (1893–1962), writer, journalist.

Osorgin: Mikhail Osorgin, 'Rets[enziya]: *Mashen'ka*. Berlin. Slovo, 1926', *Sovremennye zapiski*, 28 ([early June], 1926), pp. 474–6.

Za svobodu: *For Freedom*, Russian émigré daily, Warsaw, 1921–32.

Letter of 6 July 1926

story by Wells: 'The Remarkable Case of Davidson's Eyes' (1895).

grosch: *Groschen*, a small coin worth 10 pfennigs.

'Illustrated Newspaper': *Berliner Illustrirte Zeitung*, weekly, founded in 1891.

Anna Karenin . . . tennis: See 'A special note on the game of tennis' in VN's essay on *Anna Karenin* (*LRL*, p. 234). The note is accompanied by VN's drawing of 'a tennis costume such as Anna wore in her game with Vronski'. In the drawing, the racket is lowered and the hat is small.

Mme Usoltsev's: Unidentified.

butterfly: See Appendix One: Riddles.

Acr. 1 part of a rose: The lower part of the left wing.

can be seen in a sack: A reference to a Russian proverb, 'One cannot hide an awl in a sack' ('Shila v meshke ne utaish'').

In capital cities . . . : From the poem 'V stolitsakh shum, gremyat vitii, / Kipit slovesnaya voina' ('There is a din in the capitals, orators thunder, / A war of words is seething', 1857) by Nikolay Alekseevich Nekrasov (1821–78).

Acr. 1 A supernatural . . . : The lower part of the right wing.

All sings . . . thunderclaps!: A line from Tyutchev's poem 'Vesennyaya groza' ('Spring Thunderstorm'): 'S gory bezhit potok provornyi, / V lesu ne molknet ptichiy gam, / I gam lesnoy, i shum nagornyi – / Vsyo vtorit veselo gromam' ('A swift stream runs from the hill, / The din of birds in the forest does not still, / And the forest din and the noise on the hill – / All sings in cheerful tune with thunderclaps').

Crestos lovitza Sirin: *Krestoslovitsa* is the Russian word VN invented to render the English word 'crossword'. (Crosswords, developed in their modern form in 1913, became a craze only in the 1920s.) In this letter, while inscribing the crossword puzzle in a shape of a butterfly, VN spells it as 'Crestos lovitza Sirin' – like a Latin binomial, as if it were a butterfly he had named, with 'Sirin' in the place of the first describer's name. The spacing also draws attention to the Russian *lovitsa* ('can be caught'), hidden in the inscription.

A ditty: Kit's . . . : Written vertically to the left of the butterfly drawing. The original reads: 'Kosh khoroshiy, Koshi, Koshi, / Koshi, koshi, moy roskoshi' (literally: 'Good kitty, Kitty, Kitty, / Kitty, kitty, my luxurious').

A ditty: Folk . . . : Written vertically to the right of the butterfly drawing. The original reads: 'Lezet lyud na bashnyu ratushi, / Udivlyayutsya lyudi: / Akh vy milye, mokhnatyshi, / Akh, lokhmatyshi moi!' (literally: 'People are scrambling to the city hall tower, / People are surprised: / Ah, my sweet shaggies, / Ah, my dishevelled ones').

Letter of 7 July 1926

On Wednesdays: Written at the top of the page, near and a little below the date.

Mr Darling: His identity is explained in the letter of 10 July 1926.

'rai mne' . . . *'sukhar'*: VN is correcting VéN's answers to the crossword puzzle of 1 July. *Rai mne*: 'heaven to me'; *op'yani*: 'intoxicate' (imperative); *sukhari*: dry bread, rusks; *sukhar'*: a rusk.

'and the cares . . .': From 'The Day is Done' (1845), by Henry Wadsworth Longfellow (1807–82), final stanza (ll. 41–4): 'And the night shall be filled with music, / And the cares, that infest the day, / Shall fold their tents, like the Arabs, / And as silently steal away.'

healed from the sun: VN suffered from psoriasis, which would become acute in early 1937 (see below). He would write amusingly about the condition in *Ada*, Pt. 1 Ch. 21.

Letter of 8 July 1926

puzzle: VN drew two vertical arrows pointing down along the column of words/letters: from 1 to 5 and from 'r' to 'sh'. Across: 1 Cairo; 2 union; 3 grandfather; 4: adieu; 5: hashish. Down: *Kuda gryadesh* (*Lat. Quo vadis*, 'Whither goest thou?', the question St Peter asks of Jesus, John 13: 36).

a puzzle like this: VN provides a solution to this puzzle in his 15 July letter.

S. B.: Slava Borisovna (Slonim).

Lazarus: See letter of 3 July 1926.

Letter of 9 July 1926

Romans . . . : Love song, sateen, buffet, frame, burdock, swindler, bar lock, slime, silence, a lonely [man], rook. See Appendix One: Riddles.

new post office on Geisberg str.: 7–9 Geisbergstrasse, Berlin-Schöneberg.

Letter of 10 July 1926

$55 \times 5 = 305$: Miscalculation. VN probably multiplied 50 by 5 and added 55.

27 *my Life*: Presumably income sent on from VéN from language lessons she has been giving.

puddle: The image of a spectacular puddle that seems a window on to another world recurs in *Bend Sinister* (1947), which begins: 'An oblong puddle inset in the coarse asphalt; like a fancy footprint filled to the brim with quicksilver; like a spatulate hole through which you can see the nether sky' (p. 1).

wrote my 'review': See letter of 2 July 1926 and n.

My aunt Wittgenstein: Elizaveta Dmitrievna Sayn-Wittgenstein (née Nabokov, 1877–1942), widow of Prince Heinrich Gottfried Chlodwig (Genrikh Fyodorovich) Sayn-Wittgenstein (1879–1919).

'Le Martyre de l'Obèse' . . . Béraud: *The Martyrdom of the Obese Man* (1922) by Henri Béraud (1885–1958) won the 1922 Prix Goncourt and would be made into a 1933 film (same title in French, *Fat Man's Worries* in English), directed by Pierre Chenal (1904–90).

'. . . mon tailleur . . .': Fr. '. . . my flabbergasted tailor swallowed some of his pins. Without realizing that my case exhausted his euphemisms. – Monsieur is rather strong, he said first of all. Then he changed: – Monsieur is strong. Monsieur is very strong . . . Monsieur is powerful. Powerful, he was satisfied with that. After that, he took some of my measurements in silence, realizing, suddenly, that, from one adjective to the next, he would soon reach the point of telling me: "Monsieur is formidable. Monsieur is phenomenal . . . Monsieur is repugnant."'

'vulgarity': Aykhenvald's lecture was on *poshlost'*, a concept that VN famously explained to non-Russians in 'The Art of Literature and Commonsense' (*LL*), *NG* and *SO*, and enjoyed depicting in his fiction.

Letter of 11 July 1926

Enclosed is also a four-page carbon copy of a typed questionnaire.

Nik Serov . . . : *Nik. Serov: rovesnik* ('peer'); *E. T. Ivanov-Sirin: in vino veritas; M. M. Sukotin: kommunist* ('communist', and therefore a follower of the 1918 Bolshevik reform 'simplifying' Russian orthography, which most émigrés resisted).

'divinity's original trait': A line from the ode 'Bog' ('God', 1784), by Gavriil Romanovich Derzhavin (1743–1816): 'Ya svyaz' mirov povsyudu sushchikh, / Ya kraynya stepen' veshchestva; / Ya sredotochie zhivushchikh, / Cherta nachal'na bozhestva' ('I am the ubiquitous connection of worlds, / I am the extreme stage of matter; / I am the concentration of the living, / Divinity's original trait') (ll. 81–4).

Tyutchev's 'water-jet': From Tyutchev's 'Fontan' ('Fountain', 1836): 'O smertnoy mysli vodomyot, / O vodomyot neistoshchimyi! / Kakoi zakon nepostizhimyi / Tebya stremit, tebya myatyot? / Kak zhadno k neby rvyoshsya ty! . . . / No dlan' nezrimo-rokovaya / Tvoy luch upornyi, prelomlyaya, / Svergaet v bryzgakh s vysoty' ('Oh water-jet of mortal thought, / Oh inexhaustible water-jet! / What inscrutable law / Speeds you, agitates you? / How greedily you rush towards the sky! . . . / But an unseen fateful hand / Refracting your persistent ray, / Throws it, in a spray, down from above').

Derzhavin's 'god-worm': *Bogocherv'*, a word VN fashioned from Derzhavin's ode 'God': 'Ya tsar' – ya rab – ya cherv' – ya Bog! / No, buduchi ya stol' chudesen, / Otkole proisshol? – bezvesten; / A sam soboy ya byt' ne mog' ('I am tsar – I am slave – I am worm – I am God! / But, being such a wonder, / Where am I from? – unknown; / But just from myself I could not be').

Raisa: Tatarinov.

the last three lines of 'Aeroplane's' second stanza: See letter 1 of 5 July 1926.

took a hundred: Cigarettes.

life . . . rainbow . . . colourful bow: An echo of 'Abt Vogler' (1864), by one of VN's favourite poets, Robert Browning (1812–89), l. 72: 'On earth the broken arcs; in the heaven, a perfect round.'

A questionnaire: Enclosed typescript on two separate pages.

'Do you like cheese': From 'Epigram No. 1' (1854) by Koz'ma Prutkov, a fictitious author invented by the writers Aleksey Konstantinovich Tolstoy (1817–75) and the three brothers Aleksey Mikhaylovich (1821–1908), Vladimir Mikhaylovich (1830–84), and Aleksandr Mikhaylovich Zhemchuzhnikov (1826–96).

Letter of 12 July 1926

'subtler' than Tolstoy: The writer Lev Tolstoy. A pun, based on the literal meaning of *tolstiy* ('thick', 'fat') and *tonkiy*, the Russian word for 'subtle' as well as 'thin'.

five vowels and three consonants: In original Russian: 'out of five vowels and five consonants': 'я тебя люблю' (*ya tebya lyublyu*).

Letter of 13 July 1926

Gutmann Saal: VN's mistake. The trial would take place at the Schubert-Saal, Bülowstrasse 104.

Mrs Shor: Possibly Nadezhda (Nadiva) Rafailovna Shor, wife of Evsey Davidovich Shor (1891–1974), philosopher, art historian, journalist.

from jail: In Tolstoy's story, Pozdnyshev was acquitted.

Letter of 14 July 1926

Gurevich: Aleksandr Gurevich, perhaps the son of Vissarion Yakovlevich Gurevich (1876–1940), member of the Socialist Revolutionary party, political commentator and, in emigration, professor of Russian law in Prague.

Tenishev: The liberal private school VN attended in St Petersburg from 1911 to 1917; he writes about it in Ch. 9 of SM.

the Prague Slonim: Mark Lvovich Slonim (1894–1976), political activist, literary critic, journalist and translator; in 1922–7 he lived in Prague, where he edited the 'Literary Diary' and 'Literary Chronicle' at the literary-political daily *Volya Rossii*.

mais je ne t'en veux pas: Fr. 'But I don't hold it against you'.

'Ausflug': Ger. 'outing'.

article . . . Christ's appearance: Rev. George H. Box, 'The Appearance of Christ. Testimony of Josephus. Dr Eisler's "Reconstruction".' The clipping was enclosed.

Letter of 15 July 1926

Magic Words: See Appendix One: Riddles.

Tolpa . . . : Crowd, counter, leapfrog, sheepskin, mountain, dandy, gout, turquoise, splinter, Cain, whippet, sovereign, frame, lighthouse, force, Minsk.

You musht . . . DARLINK: The word puzzle and parts of the letter are written in distorted Russian, with a stage-German accent. Some words, including the signature 'Darlink', are written in a childlike handwriting, bigger than VN's normal cursive (they are capitalized throughout the letter), perhaps with his left hand.

acrostic: PineapplE, NebuchadnezzaR, GuestS, An ugly persoN, A bladE, VinegaR, which, if read vertically in Russian, spells the Latin phrase ANGULUS RIDES

angulus rides: VN gives '*angulus rides*' as the answer to his puzzle, although the Latin phrase he has in mind is presumably *angulus ridet*, from 'Ille terrarum mihi praeter omnes angulus ridet', in the *Odes, Book* II, no. vi, line. 13, of Horace (65–8 BCE): 'That *nook* of the earth *smiles* for me more than any other.'

Letter of 16 July 1926

story by Bunin: 'Solnechnyi udar' ('Sunstroke'), *Sovremennye zapiski*, 28 (July 1926), pp. 5–13.

Aldanov's verbiology: 'Zagovor' ('Conspiracy'), *Sovremennye zapiski*, 28 (July 1926), pp. 73–134. VN's coinage *mnogologiya* manages to include *mnogo* ('much', 'a lot'), *monolog* and elements equivalent to 'verbose trilogy'.

ballad by Khodasevich: 'John Bottom', *Sovremennye zapiski*, 28 (July 1926), pp. 189–96, by Vladislav Felitsianovich Khodasevich (1886–1939), leading Russian poet, literary critic and biographer, who would become VN's literary ally and friend in the 1930s.

Letter of 17 July 1926

Sauer-jurken: Ger. *saure Gurken* ('pickles'), in the Berlin dialect *saure Jurken*.

Raisa: Tatarinov.

faute de mieux: Fr. 'for lack of better', 'since there's no choice'.

Landaus: Grigory Adolfovich Landau (1877–1941), philosopher, political commentator, contributor to *Rul'*, and his wife.
Golubev: Possibly the artist Leonid Golubev-Bagryanorodny.

Letter of 18 July 1926

Magic Words: See Appendix One: Riddles.
lono . . . : Bosom, Jews, Sinai, parody.
outflight: VN uses the Russian *vylet*, a literal translation ('outflight') of the German word *Ausflug*, 'outing', 'excursion'.
Baratynsky's verse: Compare VN's quotation ('Svoevol'noe nazvan'e / dal ya miloy v lasku ey / mimolyotnoe sozdan'e / detskoy nezhnosti moey') and the original ('Svoenravnoe prozvan'e / Dal ya miloy v lasku ey / Bezotchotnoe sozdan'e / Detskoy nezhnosti moey'), the opening lines of 'Svoenravnoe prozvan'e' (1832) by Evgeny Abramovich Baratynsky (1800–44), which VN would translate into rhyme, about 1949, under the title 'To His Wife': 'I have given her a nickname / just a fanciful caress, / the unconscious inspiration / of my childish tenderness' (*V&V*, p. 225).
an Apollo: See letter of 9 July 1926.
replies . . . from Bunin . . . : To his sending complimentary copies of his first novel, *Mashen'ka* (*Mary*).

Letter of 19 July 1926

'tennis' . . . 'tenez' . . . Henry IV: Real tennis was not played in England at the time of Henry IV; Henry VIII was a famous enthusiast for the game; but perhaps VN is thinking of this response from Shakespeare's Henry V, also, as Prince Henry, the hero of *Henry IV Parts 1 and 2*, to the French ambassador's gift of tennis balls, a sneer at the King's past reputation as a playboy: 'We are glad the Dauphin is so pleasant with us; / His present and your pains we thank you for. / When we have matched our rackets to these balls, / We will in France, by God's grace, play a set / Shall strike his father's crown into the hazard. / . . . tell the pleasant Prince this mock of his / Hath turn'd his balls to gunstones; and his

soul / Shall stand sore charged for the wasteful vengeance / That shall fly from them' (*Henry V*, Act I, Scene 2, ll. 259–84).

'*Maria's Estates*': Marienbad.

Ol[eum] Ricini: Castor oil.

Letter of 22 December 1926

Mama will write . . . : Written upside down at the top of the first page.

Pyotr Mikhaylovich: Pyotr Mikhaylovich Skulyari, fiancé and then first husband of Elena Nabokov (by her second marriage, Sikorski).

Shakhovskoy: Prince Sergey Sergeevich Shakhovskoy (1903–74), entomologist, first husband (until c. 1930) of Olga Petkevich (née Nabokov).

'*Terror*': The story 'Uzhas', published in *Sovremennye zapiski*, 30 (1927), pp. 214–20; trans. DN with VN, *TD*.

my little long poem: 'Universitetskaya poema' ('The University Poem'), written late 1926, published *Sovremennye zapiski*, 32 (December 1927), pp. 223–54; trans DN, *SP*.

the play: *The Man from the USSR* (*Chelovek iz SSSR*), written in the fall of 1926. Act I was published in *Rul'*, 1 January 1927, pp. 2–3; trans. by DN in *MUSSR*. First published in full in Russian in *TGM*.

Letter of 23 December 1926

23 December 1926: VéN had later placed the date '1928' on the letter, but its content clearly indicates 1926.

P. M.: Pyotr Mikhaylovich (Skulyari).

mentioned me . . . in 'Krasnaya nov'': The Soviet journal *Krasnaya nov'* (*Red New Soil*) (1921–41), which had first written of 'Sirin' in 1924 (N. Smirnov, 'Solntse myortvykh: Zametki ob emigrant. lit.' ('The Sun of the Dead: Notes on Émig. Lit.'), *Krasnaya nov'*, 3 (20), pp. 250–67, discussing Sirin on pp. 264–5). No later reference is known.

also read 'Terror': 'Uzhas' ('Terror') would not be published until January 1927 (see previous letter). Had Bers received a typescript copy via VN's mother?

Katkov: Georgy Mikhaylovich Katkov (1903–85), then professor of philosophy and Indology at the University of Prague.

Bobrovsky: Pyotr Semyonovich Bobrovsky (1880–1947), a Menshevik, member of the Crimean Regional Government in which VDN was Minister of Justice.

Aykhenvaldo ... Landau: Aykhenvald positively reviewed Grigory Landau's book of aphorisms, *Epigraphy* (*Epigraphs*) (Berlin: Slovo, 1927). 'Literaturnye zametki', *Rul'*, 22 December 1926, pp. 2–3.

'Put'': Presumably the monthly journal *Put'* (*The Way*), published in Paris from 1925 to 1940.

Mr Dvurogin: A semi-transparent deformation of the name 'Trigorin' (*tri* ('three') to *dva* ('two'), *gorin* to *rogin*), a character in Chekhov's play *Chayka* (*The Seagull*, 1896). Trigorin is a popular writer, morally unscrupulous and aware of the limitations of his talent.

1929

Note of 18 April 1929

Le Boulon: In VéN's hand, on the margin: 'Boulon?'

Thais: The papilionid butterfly *Thais rumina* (now *Zerynthia rumina*), the Spanish Festoon. 'Further on towards Las Ilas, in a ravine near a stream, a greasy-looking butterfly that floated low above the ground turned out to be a small, slightly faded female of *Thais rumina* var. *medesicaste*, but no more were to be found', 'Notes on the Lepidoptera of the Pyrénées Orientales and the Ariège', *Entomologist*, 64 (November 1931), p. 255, reprinted in *N'sBs*, p. 130.

Undated note (1929?)

Date: There is nothing to indicate a date for this little note, except that VéN kept it in the 1928–30 sequence, unless the 'K.' refers to Kramář and therefore to 1924, rather than to 1930, when he was also in Prague.

1930

Letter of c. *9 May 1930*

Date: Dated '1926' in VéN's hand, incorrectly, since VN mentions the German translation of his novel *King, Queen, Knave* (*König, Dame, Bube*) as already published by Ullstein; this was in fact serialized in Ullstein's *Vossische Zeitung* from 15 March to 1 April 1930 and presumably appeared in book form almost immediately thereafter. VN sent his first letter from his only 1930 trip to Prague on 11 May. It seems that he left this note for VéN to find on her return, just before he himself made a final round of visits and returned to complete packing his trunk, before heading for the train to Prague.

his son: Sergey Iosifovich Hessen (1887–1950), philosopher and political commentator, lived in Prague from 1924 to 1935.

Mrs Walrus: VN's nickname for his landlady, Frau von Bardeleben.

Postcard 1 of 12 May 1930

Elenochka: His sister Elena, by then surnamed Skulyari.

E. K.: Evgenia Konstantinovna Hofeld.

Dear Véra: Added by EN, below VN's message.

Letter 2 of 12 May 1930

'The Entomologist': British entomological journal, which VN read avidly even as a child. As early as ten or so, he tried to publish there a description of what he thought a new species (SM, pp. 133–4); he eventually published there, the first of four times, 'A Few Notes on Crimean Lepidoptera', *Entomologist*, 53 (February 1920), pp. 29–33.

Papilio: A genus in the Swallowtail family, Papilionidae; the Latin for 'butterfly', and the genus in which Linnaeus originally placed all butterflies.

podalirius: The Scarce Swallowtail, *Papilio* (now *Iphiclides*) *podalirius*.

Püngeler: Rudolf Püngeler (1857–1927), district court councillor in Aachen and lepidopterist, who identified about 300 new species, mostly moths.

'Skit Poetov': 'The Poets' Hermitage' (1922–40), a Russian émigré literary group founded in Prague by literary critic Alfred Bem.

a little old general: Presumably the General Dolgov of the 16 May 1930 letter.

Jan[n]ings in 'The Last Advent': German-Austrian actor Emil Jannings (1884–1950) in his most famous role, as a hotel doorman in F. W. Murnau's film, *Der letzte Mann* (*The Last Laugh*, 1924).

Shalyapin: Fyodor Ivanovich Shalyapin (1873–1938), famous opera bass.

Petkevich: Boris Vladimirovich Petkevich (?–1965), engineer. VN's sister Olga and her first husband, Sergey Shakhovskoy, had divorced by 1930, when she married Petkevich.

Petya: Pyotr Mikhaylovich Skulyari.

'The Eye': *Soglyadatay* (*The Eye*), written December 1929–February 1930, published in *Sovremennye zapiski*, 44 (November 1930); trans. DN with VN (New York: Phaedra, 1965).

Apropos of the soul: 'Darling' here is *dushen'ka*, a diminutive of *dusha*, 'soul'.

Mrs Bliss: Unidentified.

Letter of 16 May 1930

Rathaus: Daniil Maksimovich Rathaus (1868–1937), poet.

Eisner: Aleksey Vladimirovich Eisner (1905–84), poet and literary critic.

Gumilyov: Nikolay Stepanovich Gumilyov (1886–1921), Russian Acmeist poet whom VN regarded highly in his youth.

'So they compare you to me . . .': In an article hostile to 'Sirin', the poet, translator and critic Georgy Vladimirovich Ivanov (1894–1958) pointedly compared Sirin as a poet to Rathaus and other second-rate poets (review of *Mashen'ka*, *Korol', Dama, Valet*, *Zashchita Luzhina* and *Vozvrashchenie Chorba*, in *Chisla* (*Numbers*), 1 (1930), pp. 233–6). See note on Nalyanch, letter of 20 May 1930.

Baudelaire . . . 'jeune elephant': 'Le serpent qui danse' ('The Dancing Snake'), in *Les Fleurs du Mal* (1857), by Charles Baudelaire (1821–67), ll. 21–4: 'Sous le fardeau de ta paresse / Ta tête d'enfant / Se balance avec la mollesse / D'un jeune éléphant'

('Under the burden of your idleness / Your childlike head / Sways with the softness / Of a young elephant).'

Fyodorov: Possibly Vasily Georgievich Fyodorov (1895–1959), short-story writer, member of 'Skit Poetov'.

'*The Aurelian*': 'Pilgram', story written March 1930, published *Sovremennye zapiski*, 43 (July 1930), pp. 191–207; trans. VN with Peter Pertzoff, *Atlantic Monthly*, November 1941, pp. 618–25.

Sherman: Savely Grigorievich Sherman, pen-name A. A. Saveliev (1894–1948), writer, critic, *Rul'* contributor and friend.

Raisa: Tatarinov.

General Dolgov: Unidentified.

'*spleutni*': *Spletni* ('gossip'), with a (French?) distortion.

Flemlandia: *Flamandiya*, Elena's back-formation from *flamandsky*, 'Flemish'.

Letter of 17 May 1930

Gorlin: Mikhail Genrikhovich Gorlin (1909–44), poet, whom in 1927 VN taught English and prosody; founded a Young Poets' Club (1928–33) in Berlin.

'*Petropolis*': Publishing house founded in St Petersburg in 1918; in 1922 a branch was opened in Berlin, which became independent in 1924. In 1931 Petropolis published the first anthology of the Poets' Club, *Novoselie: sbornik stikhov berlinskikh poetov* (*House-Warming: Collection of Poems by Berlin Poets*).

Ivan Alekseevich: Bunin.

Pos. Nov.: *Poslednie novosti* (*The Latest News*, 1920–40), Russian daily published in Paris; Georgy Adamovich's review of *The Defence* appeared there on 15 May 1930.

lots of butts: VN writes *i mnogo babok*, where *babok* stands for *babochek*, 'butterflies'.

Nem.-Danchenko: Vasily Nemirovich-Danchenko was not only a writer but also a board member of the Czech-Russian Union (the former Czech-Russian Committee, 1918–39).

Massalsky: Prince Nikolay Massalsky, husband of VéN's sister Elena Slonim.

Kiesewetter: Aleksandr Aleksandrovich Kiesewetter (1866–1933), historian, political activist and commentator, professor of Russian history at the University of Prague.

Chinaman with a nodding head: See *The Gift*, p. 14: 'a small bare-bellied idol of almatolite', identified by Alexander Dolinin as agalmatolite, a stone from which souvenir figurines are carved out in China: see his '*The Gift*: Addendum to Commentary', *Nabokov Online Journal*, 1, 2007, http://etc.dal.ca/noj/articles/volume1/DOLININ.pdf

the Mishas: Possibly VN's close friend Mikhail (Misha) Avgustovich Kaminka (?–1960?), son of VDN's friend Avgust Kaminka, and his wife, Elizabeth.

Papilio alexanor: The Southern Swallowtail, butterfly.

my larentia, my teplovata: *Larentia*, a genus of geometrid moths; VN invents the species name *teplovata*, from Russian *teplovatyi* – 'tepid, lukewarm'.

Letter postmarked 19 May 1930

Bussa: A nickname the Nabokovs shared in the 1930s.

undertufty: Mrs (or Miss) Tufty (Tuftikins) is a character VN invented in 1926, when writing to VéN in Schwarzwald.

Fondamin: Ilya Isidorovich Fondaminsky, pen-name I. Bunakov (1880–1942), prominent Socialist Revolutionary leader, a founder and co-editor of *Sovremennye zapiski*, a close friend and supporter of VN in the 1930s.

Pilgram to die in the basement: The main character of VN's story 'Aurelian', dies from a heart attack on the threshold of his home. *Podval*: both 'basement' and 'lower part of a newspaper page'.

Fayard: Librairie Arthème Fayard, French publishing house, founded in Paris in 1857. Fayard would publish VN's first book translated into French: *La Course du fou* (from *The Defence*), 1934.

Letter of 20 May 1930

Date: Undated. Postmark is torn off, '1930' added on the envelope by VéN. The 20 May date of the reading is announced in letter of 12 May 1930.

Adamovich's review: Of *Sovremennye zapiski*, 42 – which serialized *Zashchita Luzhina* (*The Defence*), from Ch. 10 to the end – in *Poslednie novosti*, 15 May 1930, p. 3.

Nalyanch writes something: Sergey Ivanovich Nalyanch, pen-name of S. I. Shovgenov (1902–79), poet and literary critic. His article is 'Poety "Chisel"' ('On the poets of *Chisla*'), *Za svobodu*, April 28,1930, p. 3 (on the notorious attack by poet, critic and novelist Georgy Ivanov, a longtime literary ally of Georgy Adamovich and foe of Khodasevich and Nabokov, in the first issue of *Chisla* (*Numbers*), March 1930, on VN's four most recent books and on VN's poetry); see note to Rathaus, letter of 16 May 1930.

of your honourable: VN writes *tvoyo pochtennoye*, punning on the fact that he highly esteems (*pochitaet*) VéN's letter, which arrived by post (*pochta*).

Brandenburgers: Ornamental braid trimmings used on uniforms.

Obenberger: Jan Obenberger (1892–1964), Czech entomologist, professor at the National Museum in Prague.

sont pires que les juifs: Fr. 'are worse than the Jews'.

blackish: As in 'Black Hundred', a number of political groups and parties that joined the anti-revolutionary movement after the Revolution of 1905, with agenda based on anti-Semitism, monarchism and Orthodoxy.

the Mishas: Possibly Mikhail Kaminka and family.

'Les Caves du Vatican' by A. Gide: The satirical tale *Les Caves du Vatican* (1914), translated as *The Vatican Cellars* and as *Lafcadio's Adventures*, by André Gide (1869–1951).

Letter postmarked 22 May 1930

the following from Kipling: stanza 3 of 'The Feet of the Young Men' (1898), by Rudyard Kipling (1865–1936).

She was Queen of Sabaea: From Kipling's poem 'There was never a Queen like Balkis', included in *Just So Stories* (1902).

[Countess] Panin: Countess Sofia Vladimirovna Panin (1871–1956), before the Bolshevik Revolution, leading Constitutional Democrat; the Nabokovs had been given refuge on her Crimean estate, Gaspra, in 1918.

Astrov: Nikolay Ivanovich Astrov (1868–1934), before the Bolshevik Revolution, leading Constitutional Democrat; in emigration, chair of the Union of Writers and Journalists of Czechoslovakia (1930–32).

Gorns: Vasily Leopoldovich Gorn (1876–1938), Zemstvo official, an émigré lawyer and journalist.

Kovalevskys: Evgraf Petrovich Kovalevsky (1865–1941), member of the Third and Fourth State Dumas, Commissar of Education in the Russian Provisional Government of 1917.

'Vozrozhdenie': *Vozrozhdenie (Renaissance)*, conservative daily with nationalist and monarchist tendencies, published in Paris, 1925–40. VN was interested in Vladimir Weidle's recent review of *The Defence*: 'Rets. Sovremennye zapiski. Kn. 42'. *Vozrozhdenie*, 1930, 12 May, p. 3.

Its little face: the dog in the drawing.

'Nedelya': A Russian-language newspaper *Nedelya* (*Týden, The Week*), published in Prague in 1928–30.

Letter postmarked 23 May 1930

Gleb's review: Gleb Struve, 'Zametki o stikhakh', *Rossiya i slavyanstvo* (*Russia and Slavdom*, Paris daily, 1928–34), 15 March 1930, p. 3.

Olga . . . with her husband: Olga (née Nabokov) and Boris Petkevich.

Avksentiev: Nikolay Dmitrievich Avksentiev (1878–1943), before the Bolshevik coup, a Socialist Revolutionary politician; in the emigration, one of the publishers of *Sovremennye zapiski*.

Vishnyak: Mark Veniaminovich Vishnyak (1883–1976), Russian politician, lawyer, Socialist Revolutionary; in emigration, one of the editors of *Sovremennye zapiski*.

Ivanov gave them just an 'excerpt': Georgy Ivanov's novel *Tretiy Rim* (*The Third Rome*), started in 1926, began to be published in *Sovremennye zapiski*, 39 and 40, in 1929; the last instalment ('Excerpts from Part Two of the novel') appeared in *Chisla*, 2–3, 1930, pp. 26–54.

Adamovich's article in 'P. N.': Adamovich, review of '"Sovremennye zapiski", kniga 42' (which included an instalment of *The Defence*), *Poslednie novosti*, 15 May 1930, p. 3.

Sherman wrote charmingly: A. Saveliev (Savely Sherman), review of '"Sovremennye zapiski", kniga 42', *Rul'*, 21 May 1930, p. 2.

de ma part: Fr. 'from me'.

Letter of c. *23 May 1930*

Date: Undated. No envelope; the letter is inscribed in Véra's hand 'From Prague 1930.'

Izgoev: Aron Solomonovich Lande, (pen-name Aleksandr Samoylovich Izgoev, 1872–1935), lawyer, prominent Constitutional Democrat and political commentator.

Nika: VN's cousin, the composer Nikolay (Nicolas, Nika) Dmitrievich Nabokov (1903–78).

Ivanov is living with Zinaida: VéN has footnoted at the bottom of the page: 'Gippius?' Zinaida Nikolaevna Gippius (1869–1945), poet, literary critic, playwright, married since 1889 to poet and novelist Dmitry Sergeevich Merezhkovsky (1865–1941), both founders of Russian literary Symbolism and central figures in St Petersburg's literary circles before the Revolution.

Varshavsky: Possibly Sergey Ivanovich Varshavsky (1879–1945), journalist, lawyer, professor at the Russian law faculty in Prague, or (although he lived in Paris by now) his son, the writer and critic Vladimir Sergeevich Varshavsky (1906–78).

Obstein: See letter of 4 June 1926 for VN's conversation with Stein, who peppered his speech with the idiosyncratic filler 'obli'.

Undated Letter (1930s?)

Misha . . . Kaminkas: Mikhail Kaminka and his wife Elizaveta moved to France early in the 1930s.

1932

Headnote

cannot now be located: See Appendix Two, especially p. 539.

Letter of 4 April 1932

sky [. . .]: The words 'and so on' here on the tape were probably added by VéN, as she tried to edit the letter while reading it aloud. Here and below, her words are replaced with ellipses and, in some cases, supplied in a note.

Rostislav: Rostislav Borisovich Petkevich (1931–60), son of VN's sister Olga.

Seryozha: Sergey Nabokov, VN's brother.

one of our Yalta photographs: The photograph of the five Nabokov children, taken in Yalta in November 1919, reproduced in SM, facing p. 224. Elena holds Box, the family's dachshund. See Plate Section, photo 2.

'Lips to Lips': 'Usta k ustam', a short story completed on 6 December 1931. The story transparently critiques the way writers behind the Paris journal *Chisla* – Nikolay Otsup, Georgy Adamovich and Georgy Ivanov – had shamelessly exploited the literary ambitions of a wealthy but untalented writer, Aleksandr Pavlovich Burd-Voskhodov, pen-name Burov (1876–1957), so that he would bankroll the journal. *Poslednie novosti* accepted the story, even set it in type, but once it recognized the targets, refused to publish. The story first appeared in *Vesna v Fial'te* (New York: Chekhov Publishing House, 1956); in English, trans. DN with VN, RB.

my article on butterflies: 'Notes on the Lepidoptera of the Pyrénées Orientales and the Ariège'.

Letter of 5 April 1932

Bertrand: Clarence Bertrand Thompson (1882–1969), management consultant and author of books on management, sociology and economics; American husband of VéN's close friend Lisbet Thompson. VN first met him in 1926, and continued to think him one of the brightest people he knew (*VNRY*, 393–94).

Thompson: A joke. VN has written to Thompson, but he is asking VéN to thank Bertrand, i.e. to pass on his thanks to the very person he has just written to.

Leskov's and Zamyatin's: Nikolay Semyonovich Leskov (1831–95) and Evgeny Ivanovich Zamyatin (1884–1937). Zamyatin emigrated in 1931, after Soviet ideologists reacted to his anti-utopian novel *We* (1920) and viciously ostracized its author. VN may be comparing Leskov's anti-nihilist novel *Na nozhakh* (*At Daggers Drawn*, 1870–71) to *We*, drawing a parallel between one of Leskov's female characters, perhaps Glafira Akatov, and Zamyatin's revolutionary heroine I-330.

to start a new novel: Not the novel he would in fact next write, *Otchayanie* (*Despair*), which he would begin composing in June, complete in first draft in September, and finish revising in December.

Letter of 6 April 1932

'Magda's Childhood' . . . 'Visit': Excerpts from VN's novel *Kamera obskura*, finished May 1931, serialized in *Sovremennye zapiski*, 49–52 (1932–3), published in book form in 1933 (Berlin and Paris: Parabola and Sovremennye Zapiski); translated by Winifred Roy as *Camera Obscura* (London: John Long, 1936) and by VN as *Laughter in the Dark* (Indianapolis: Bobbs-Merrill, 1938). For the excerpt VN calls 'Magda's Childhood', see 'Kamera obskura (Glava iz romana)' ('Camera Obscura (Chapter from a Novel)'), *Poslednie novosti*, 17 April 1932, pp. 2–3. If an excerpt appeared in *Rossiya i slavyanstvo*, it has not been located.

Azef: Evno Fishelevich Azef (1869–1918), agent provocateur, secret agent of the Russian imperial police, and an early member of the Socialist Revolutionary party, for whom he organized assassinations. After being exposed in 1908, Azef escaped abroad.

Pyotr Semyonovich: Bobrovsky.

Glory: *Podvig*, published in *Sovremennye zapiski*, 45–8 (1931–2), and in book form (Paris: Sovremennye Zapiski, 1932); translated DN with VN (New York: McGraw-Hill, 1971); see *Podvig*, p. 150 (ch. 31), *Glory*, p. 126 (ch. 30): 'He saw in the mirror . . . that special expression on his mother's pink, freckled face: by the fold of her lips, tightly compressed but ready to spread into a smile, he could tell there was a letter.'

issue of Russkaya mysl' where my poems: VN's poem 'Zimnyaya noch'' ('Winter Night') had appeared in *Russkaya mysl'* in March–April 1917; in fact he had been published previously in a journal (apart from earlier school journal publications) – the poem 'Lunnaya gryoza' ('Lunar Reverie'), which appeared in *Vestnik Evropy* (*The Messenger of Europe*), July 1916, p. 38.

a poem . . . written in Beaulieu: Domaine-Beaulieu, the farm near Solliès-Pont and Toulon, France, where VN worked in 1923 and from where he wrote his first letters and poems for Véra.

I don't like Camera: VN had been checking the proofs of his *Kamera obskura*, the first instalment of which would appear in late May in *Sovremennye zapiski*, 49.

Nash vek: *Our Age*, a weekly Russian newspaper published in Berlin from 1931 to 1933, in the wake of the demise of *Rul'*, and edited by some of VN's acquaintances, such as Yury Ofrosimov and Savely Sherman.

Skit: 'Skit Poetov' ('The Poets' Hermitage'): see note to letter 2 of 12 May 1930.

Letter of 7 April 1932

Raevskys: Nikolay Alekseevich Raevsky (1894–1988), entomologist and Pushkin scholar, deported to the Soviet Union after the Second World War. He wrote a memoir, 'Vospominaniya o Vladimire Nabokove' ('Recollections of Vladimir Nabokov'), *Prostor*, 2 (1989), pp. 112–17; an excerpt in English appears in *N'sBs*, p. 147.

Letter of 8 April 1932

Pushkin exhibition: 'Pushkin and His Time' exhibition organized by the Národní muzeum (National Museum) in Prague in 1932.

Pteridophora alberti: The King of Saxony bird of paradise.

the original of 'Odelia dear': Adèle Hommaire de Hell (1817[?]–1871[?]), French traveller; author, with her husband, geographer Xavier Hommaire de Hell (1812–48), of a travel memoir, *Les steppes de la mer Caspienne, le Caucase, la Crimée et la Russie meridionale* (Paris, 1843). She became the central subject of a literary mystification by Pavel Petrovich Vyazemsky (1820–88), son of Pushkin's friend, the writer Pyotr Andreevich Vyazemsky. Vyazemsky first wrote about her in his article 'Lermontov i gospozha Gommer de Gell v 1840 godu' ('Lermontov and Madame Hommaire de Hell in 1840'), *Russkiy arkhiv (The Russian Archive)*, September 1887, pp. 129–42. In 1933, an 'all-inclusive' edition of Vyazemsky's *Pisma i zapiski Ommer de Gell (Letters and Memoirs of Hommaire de Hell)* was published by M. M. Chistyakova (Leningrad: Akademia, 1933). The 'letters' mentioned Pushkin and described, among other things, an affair between Hommaire de Hell and Mikhail Lermontov. After its publication, in May 1934 the Pushkin scholar N. O. Lerner denounced it in a paper at the research institute Pushkinsky Dom ('The Pushkin House'), where he revealed Vyazemsky's authorship. Shortly thereafter, P. S. Popov published a more detailed essay demystifying Hommaire de Hell in 'Mistifikatsiya' ('A Mystification'), *Novyi mir*, 1935, No. 3, pp. 282–93.

Chlamydophorus truncatus: Correctly *Chlamyphorus truncatus*, the Pink Fairy Armadillo. VN plays in the next phrase on the Greek *chlamys* and Russian *khlamida*, 'cloak, mantle'.

Gazdanov's story: Gayto Ivanovich Gazdanov (1903–71), Russian émigré writer and literary critic, whose story 'Schast'e' ('Happiness') appeared in *Sovremennye zapiski*, 49 (May 1932), pp. 164–202, in the same issue as the first chapters of VN's *Camera Obscura*. Georgy Adamovich reviewed 'Happiness' and *Camera Obscura* in one essay, noting the brilliance of style shared by both writers (*Poslednie novosti*, 2 June 1932, p. 2). In 1935–6, reviewers continued to compare VN and Gazdanov: see, for example, Adamovich's review of *Sovremennye zapiski*, 58, where he says that 'reading Gazdanov after reading Sirin is a true relaxation: everything resumes its place, we are no longer in jail, in a madhouse, in a vacuum, we are among normal people . . .' (*Poslednie novosti*, 4 July 1935, p. 3).

Boris Vladimirovich: Petkevich.

Roerich: Nikolay Konstantinovich Roerich (1874–1947), Russian painter, mystical philosopher, explorer. In 1900, the Roerich family, including his son Yury Nikolaevich, began to conduct spiritualist séances in their home.

article by Adamovich about the . . . novel by Lawrence: Adamovich reviewed the Russian translation of D. H. Lawrence's novel *Lady Chatterley's Lover* (1928) (trans. T. I. Leshchenko; Berlin: Petropolis, 1932): 'O knige Lorensa' ('On Lawrence's Book'), *Poslednie novosti*, 7 April 1932, p. 3.

Letter of 11 April 1932

Pletnyov: Rostislav Vladimirovich Pletnyov, pen-name Daniel, (1903–85), literary scholar, critic and professor at Charles University in Prague.

Karpovich: Mikhail Mikhaylovich Karpovich (1888–1959), former political activist and member of the Socialist-Revolutionary party, then a historian of Russia and professor of history at Harvard. After the Nabokovs' arrival in the US in 1940 they would become good friends with the Karpoviches.

an invasion: Of bed-bugs.

Ralph Hodgson: Ralph Hodgson (1871–1962), English poet: 'The Bells of Heaven' (*Poems*, 1917).

'*Za sobak . . .*': Here and below, VN inserts his translation of Hodgson's poem into Russian in the text of the letter.

Sikorski: Vsevolod Vyacheslavovich Sikorski (1896–1958), a pre-revolutionary Russian army officer, who would marry Nabokov's sister Elena in May 1932.

Volkonsky: Unidentified.

to propose: To Elena Nabokov, who had by then divorced her first husband, Pyotr Skulyari.

aquarelle ... Miskhor and Yalta: Miskhor, now part of Koreiz, on the Crimean Riviera about a mile west of Gaspra, itself to the south-east of Yalta. Probably a landscape painted by Vladimir Pohl (see below, note to letter of 11 November 1932), and later inherited by Elena Sikorski from her mother.

Libythea celtis: The European Snout butterfly.

Acropolis: In 1919 the Nabokovs, after fleeing the Crimea, stayed in Greece during April and May before departing for London, where they settled for a year before the parents and younger children relocated to Berlin.

Letter of 12 April 1932

Goethe evening: On 20 April 1932, the Union of Russian Writers and Journalists in Berlin celebrated the 100th anniversary of Goethe's death.

Golovin's workshop: Aleksandr Sergeevich Golovin (1904–68), sculptor.

Bem: Professor Alfred Lyudvigovich Bem, literary scholar, founder of 'Skit Poetov' (1886–1945).

Tzadik: 'A righteous man' in Judaic tradition.

Markovich: Vadim Vladimirovich Morkovin (1906–73), fiction writer and poet, historian of literature.

Mansvetov: Vladimir Fyodorovich Mansvetov (1909–74), poet, journalist. In 1939, he would emigrate to the US and from 1940 to 1943 work for *Novoe Russkoe Slovo* (*The New Russian Word*, the Russian daily newspaper published in New York from 1910), and later for *The Voice of America*.

such little Pasternakian words: *Naobum*, *vslepuyu*, *pod spudom*, *ovatsii*. Boris Leonidovich Pasternak (1890–1960), poet, novelist, translator.

Alla Golovina: Alla Sergeevna Golovina (née Baroness Steiger, 1909–87), poet, wife of sculptor Aleksandr Golovin.

Khokhlov: German Dmitrievich Khokhlov (1908–38), poet and literary critic. After returning to Russia in 1934 he would be arrested and executed as 'a member of a terrorist organization'.

poetess Rathaus: Tatyana Danilovna Klimenko-Rathaus (1909–93), poet and actress.

Vicki Baum: Vicki Baum (1888–1960), bestselling Austrian novelist, most famous for *Menschen im Hotel* (*People in a Hotel*, 1929, filmed as *Grand Hotel*, 1932, which won the Best Picture Academy Award). VN parodied the *Grand Hotel* formula in *The Real Life of Sebastian Knight* and critiqued it in a still unpublished Cornell lecture ('ghastly stuff') (VNA).

Zhenya Hessen: Evgeny Sergeevich Hessen (1910–45), poet, member of 'Skit Poetov', ('The Poets' Hermitage'), grandson of Iosif Hessen.

Ivan Alekseevich's little masterpieces: Bunin's short stories 'Kostyor' ('Bonfire') and 'Nadezhda' ('Hope') (*Poslednie novosti*, 10 April 1932).

catching and collecting lightning: May reflect experiments by Nikola Tesla (1856–1943), Serbian-American physicist and inventor, who had appeared on the cover of *Time* magazine in July 1931.

Letter of 14 April 1932

'*Average man*': In 1932, *Poslednie novosti* published several chapters of the novel *Sivtsev Vrazhek* by Mikhail Andreevich Ilyin, pen-name Osorgin (1878–1942), in which he tells the story of the Russian intelligentsia's survival after the Revolution. The excerpts were signed 'Obyvatel'' ('An average man, a philistine').

Altschuler: Isaak Naumovich Altschuller, a doctor friend of VN's mother.

sidecar: Sidecars were often used as cheaper alternatives to taxicabs.

my old poem: published, with mistakes, in Maria Malikova, ed., *Stikhotvoreniya*. VN called the poem 'Crosses' in a letter of 19 June 1923 to his mother. See letter of 6 April 1932.

Hessen: Iosif Hessen.

Ne précise pas . . . : Fr. 'don't specify the date of my arrival . . . it's possible'.

dash from shore to ball: 'S korablya na bal', one of the many proverbs originating in the comedy *Gore ot uma* (*Woe from Wit*, 1823, published 1833) by Aleksandr Sergeevich Griboedov (1795–1829).

An India invisible . . . : VéN's commentary: 'This poem was published. And so on. It gets worse later.' See n., p 544.

Letter of 15 April 1932

Date: VéN recorded the date as '17 April 1932', but the first sentence suggests VN wrote the letter on 15 April.

Standesamt: German Civil Registration Office. VN is writing on their wedding anniversary.

his son, also a doctor: Grigory Isaakovich Altschuller, son of I. N. Altschuller.

Mulman: Unidentified.

peine perdue: Fr. 'a wasted effort'.

Gippius's 'Human Countenance': Vladimir Vasilievich Gippius, pen-names Vl. Bestuzhev, Vl. Neledinsky (1876–1941), poet, prose-writer and critic, taught VN literature at Tenishev School in St Petersburg; *Human Countenance* (*Lik chelovecheskiy*), a narrative poem (Berlin: Epokha, 1922).

Joyce: James Joyce (1882–1941), Irish novelist. Nabokov always admired *Ulysses* and even wrote to Joyce in 1933 offering to translate it into Russian (letter of 9 November 1933, James Joyce – Paul Léon Papers, National Library of Ireland).

Dostoevsky: Russian novelist Fyodor Mikhaylovich Dostoevsky (1821–81). Nabokov continued to think little of Dostoevsky, even when lecturing on him at Cornell and Harvard (*LRL*).

Vacek: Unidentified.

Irochka Vergun: Irina Dmitrievna Vergun, daughter of Dmitry Nikolaevich Vergun (1871–1951), literary scholar, political activist and professor at several universities in Prague.

how slovenly they are: In VéN's voice: 'I don't know about whom.' In fact, VN is writing about his sister Olga and her husband Petkevich.

Letter of 16 April 1932

Volodya: Vladimir Kozhevnikov, a university student at the time, had been VN's and VéN's pupil in 1928 in Berlin.

zhonka: Czech, 'wife', 'Mrs'.

my second poem: 'Zimnyaya noch', *Russkaya mysl'* 3–4 (March–April) 1917, p. 72.

The first one: 'Lunnaya gryoza'.

Russkoe bogatstvo: *Russia's Riches*, journal, St Petersburg, 1876–1918.

Mme Tyrkov: Ariadna Vladimirovna Tyrkov-Williams (1869–1962), writer, member of the Central Committee of the Constitutional Democratic party and deputy of the First Duma. Mme Tyrkov's novel *Plunder* (*Dobycha*) was published in *Russkaya mysl'*, 6–7 (June–July), 1917.

38.2° C: 100.8 degrees Fahrenheit.

Wednesday, for the sake of the rhyme: *Priédu v srédu* rhymes in Russian.

Letter of 18 April 1932

my translation of Alice in Wonderland: Lewis Carroll (Charles Lutwidge Dodgson, 1832–98), *Alice's Adventures in Wonderland* (1865); *Anya v strane chudes*, trans. Vladimir Sirin, with illustrations by S. Zalshupin (Berlin: Gamayun, 1923).

Olga . . . flew into a wild rage: Sergey Shakhovskoy had been the first husband of Olga Petkevich (née Nabokov).

Pletnyov: See letter of 11 April 1932.

Seryozha: VN's brother Sergey.

'I hear a sudden cry': The opening lines of 'The Snare' (1914), by James Stephens (1882–1950), Irish novelist and poet.

Poslednie novosti with Camera: 'Kamera obskura (Glava iz romana)' ('Camera Obscura (Chapter of a Novel)'), *Poslednie novosti*, 17 April 1932; Ch. 3 of the novel.

Camera has to be sent today: Presumably the proofs for *Sovremennye zapiski*.

Mulmanovich: Earlier mentioned as Mulman. Unidentified.

mislay: In Russian, *valyat'*.

Union: The Union of Russian Writers and Journalists in Berlin.

Pushkin's 'Faust': Pushkin, 'Stsena iz Fausta' ('A Scene from Faustus', 1825).

Letter of 19 April 1932

that Dresden affair: On 7 May, VN did read his work in the cellar of a Russian church in Dresden (*VNRY*, p. 379).

Letter of 13 October 1932

Kolbsheim: In early October 1932, VN's cousin Nicolas Nabokov, his wife Nathalie (Natalia Alekseevna, née Shakhovskoy, 1903–88), and their son Ivan (1932–) were invited to vacation at a friend's house in Kolbsheim, near Strasbourg. They invited VN and VéN, who spent two weeks with them. After his wife's departure for Berlin, VN stayed behind for a few days to go to Paris for a reading and to establish contacts.

Lisbet: Thompson.

Fond: Fondaminsky.

Dita: Unidentified.

Letter of 15 October 1932

Ullstein . . . 'The Doorbell': 'Zvonok', *Rul'*, 22 May 1927, pp. 2–4; and in *VC*. The German translation, if it was published, has not been located.

Kreul: Or Krell? Unidentified: possibly an editor at Ullstein.

doctor Jacob: Unidentified.

Nika: Nicolas Nabokov.

Hertz: Paul Hertz (1900–?), owner, with his wife Suzanne, of the Librairie de la Mésange, Strasbourg. The bookstore was famous for the owners' knowledge of both its books and its customers; a familiar haunt of local faculty and students, it often staged lectures and art exhibitions (Raymond Aubrac, *Où la mémoire s'attarde* (Paris: Jacob, 1996), p. 46).

Grasset and Fayard: The French publishers Éditions Grasset, founded in 1907, and Librairie Arthème Fayard.

Nouvelles littéraires: André Levinson, 'V. Sirine et son joueur d'échecs' ('V. Sirin and His Chess Player'), *Nouvelles littéraires*, Paris, 15 February 1930, p. 6. VN would meet Levinson on 6 November 1932.

also the one from Mesures: Although VN would publish in *Mesures* in 1937, it did not yet exist as a journal. He apparently had in mind a critical article by Gleb Struve, 'Les "Romans-escamotage"' ('Novels of Conjuring'), *Le Mois*, Paris, April–May 1931, pp. 141–52. (Trying to make out the text here, VéN reads: '*Mesures* or something, don't know.')

Seryozha: VN's brother Sergey.

Malevsky-Malevich: Princess Zinaida Alekseevna Shakhovskoy (1906–2001), writer and literary critic, married to Svyatoslav Svyatoslavovich Malevsky-Malevich (1905–73). Mme Shakhovskoy would be a friend and staunch supporter of VN in the 1930s but became hostile to him and especially VéN in later years. See Appendix Two, p. 540.

'Société Protectrice des Animaux': Fr. 'Society for the Protection of Animals'.

Io: *Inachis* (*Vanessa*) *io*, the Peacock Butterfly.

Letter of 17 October 1932

Mme Maurice Grunelius: The Grunelius family lived in Kolbsheim for generations. The Nabokovs stayed on the property of Alexandre and Antoinette Grunelius.

Denis Roche: Denis Roche (1868–1951), French writer and translator from Russian into French of *The Defence*, *The Eye* and 'Spring in Fialta'.

Mongoose: A mongoose is the title character of Rudyard Kipling's short story 'Rikki-tikki-tavi' in *The Jungle Book* (1894).

'*Das habe ich nicht gesehen*': Ger. 'I see nothing', in the idiomatic English sense that the servant prefers to ignore how VN saved the mice she had caught.

'*Ne parlez pas devant les genS*': Fr. 'Don't talk in front of the servantS' (with the last letter pronounced by the Russians, as it would not be by the French).

Bibliothèque Rose: A series of children's books in French published by Hachette since 1856. VN mentions some volumes in the series, such as *Les Malheurs de Sophie*, *Le Tour du Monde en Quatre Vingts Jours*, *Le Petit Chose*, *Les Misérables*, *Le Comte de Monte Cristo*, in *Speak, Memory* (SM, p. 105).

Aleksandra Fyodorovna's letters to the Tsar: Tsarina Aleksandra Fyodorovna (1872–1918), wife of last Russian Emperor Nicholas II (1868–1918). VDN translated their letters from the original English into Russian: *Pis'ma Aleksandry Fyodorovny k imperatoru Nikolayu II* (Berlin: Slovo, 1922).

about Blok in Poslednie novosti, about his letters: A first volume of Blok's letters to his family, *Pis'ma k rodnym*, had been published in 1927; the second volume had just appeared, ed. M. A. Beketova and Vasily Desnitsky (Moscow, Leningrad: Academia, 1932).

Nicholas's army: Tsar Nicholas I, born 1796, ruled 1825–55.

Letter of 22 October 1932

Zenzinov: Vladimir Mikhaylovich Zenzinov (1880–1953), a leading Socialist Revolutionary and a friend of VDN's while in Russia. After emigrating, he lived first in Prague, then Paris, where he served on the editorial board of *Sovremennye zapiski*, and finally, from 1939, in the US.

his wife: Fondaminsky's wife, Amalia Osipovna Fondaminsky (née Gavronsky, 1882–1935).

Kerensky: Aleksandr Fyodorovich Kerensky (1881–1970), socialist politician, Prime Minister of the Second Provisional Government (1917), in emigration from 1918.

Rudnev: Vadim Victorovich Rudnev (1879–1940), formerly a prominent Socialist Revolutionary leader and friend of VDN, now an editor of *Sovremennye zapiski*.

Demidov: Igor Platonovich Demidov (1873–1946), politician, journalist, deputy of the Fourth Duma, deputy editor of *Poslednie novosti*.

très en gros: Fr. 'writ very large'.

Zina: Zinaida Gippius, who had warned VDN in 1916, as VN recalls, 'to tell me, please, that I would never, never be a writer' (*SM*, p. 238).

Supervielle: Jules Supervielle (1884–1960), French poet, novelist, short-story writer and dramatist.

Cocteau: Jean Cocteau (1889–1963), French poet, novelist and playwright.

Letter of 24 October 1932

very early now: In Véra's voice: 'I can't make it out.'

a [. . .]: Word unclear.

his phone lets in draughts: i.e. his phone is tapped.

Ladinsky: Antonin Petrovich Ladinsky (1896–1961), poet.

Polyakov: Aleksandr Abramovich Polyakov (1879–1971), journalist, secretary and later deputy editor of *Poslednie novosti*.

Volkov: Nikolay Konstantinovich Volkov (1875–1950), formerly member of the Constitutional Democratic party, deputy of the Fourth Duma and, in Paris, managing director of *Poslednie novosti*.

Berberova: Nina Nikolaevna Berberova (1901–93), writer and journalist.

break-up with Khodasevich: The civil union of Khodasevich and Berberova lasted ten years. They separated in 1932.

epigram on Ivánov: VN allegedly recorded his epigram on Georgy Ivanov in Khodasevich's album and then posted it to Gleb Struve and Fondaminsky in the spring of 1931 (*VNRY*, p. 370; Malikova, pp. 512, 616n). The epigram, transliterated, appeared in Andrew Field's *Nabokov: His Life in Art* (Boston: Little and

Brown, 1967, p. 379): '"–Takogo net moshennika vtorogo / Vo vsey sem'e zhurnal'nykh shulerov!"' / "Kogo ty tak?" "Ivanova, Petrova, / Ne vsyo l' ravno . . ." "Postoy, a kto zh Petrov?"' with VN's free translation: '"No greater crook exists among the sharpers / Of the whole magazine fraternity!" / "Whom are you cursing so?" – "Oh, Johnson, Smithson, / What do I care . . ." – "But Smithson – who is he?"'

the 'Perekryostok' group: 'Crossroads', a literary group founded in Paris by poets closer to Khodasevich than to the circle of Georgy Adamovich and the 'Paris Note' school of poetry he epitomized. The poets Vladimir Smolensky, Dovid Knut, Yury Mandelstam and Georgy Raevsky belonged to 'Perekryostok.' In 1930, the group published a collection of their poetry: *Perekryostok: Sb[ornik] stikhov* (Paris: Ya. Povolotsky, 1930).

Don Aminado's: Aminodav Peysakhovich Shpolyansky, pen-name Don Aminado (1888–1957), satirical poet.

Rausch: Baron Nikolay Nikolaevich Rausch von Traubenberg (1880–1943), a relative of VN's (VN's paternal aunt Nina Dmitrievna Nabokov had married his uncle, Baron Evgeny Aleksandrovich Rausch von Traubenberg in 1880). Before the Revolution, he had served at the Russian court.

Mme Adamov: Possibly Nadezhda Konstantinovna Adamov (1880–1955), doctor of medicine, wife of Mikhail Konstantinovich Adamov (1858–1933), a lawyer, a relative of the Tatarinovs (see letter of 28 or 29 October 1932).

Frumkin: Yakov Grigorievich Frumkin (1880–1971), lawyer, had been a friend of VDN. In 1940, as chair of a Jewish rescue organization in New York, he would help the Nabokovs obtain passage on a refugee ship from St Nazaire to New York.

S. G.: Perhaps Sergey Hessen ('Gessen' would be a strict transliteration of the Russian name) or Sofia Grigorievna Hessen, second wife of Georgy Hessen. VN referred to her as S.G. in his correspondence with the Hessens (see V. Yu. Gessen, ed. Pis'ma V. V. Nabokova k Gessenam', *Zvezda*, 4, 1999, 42–45).

Zyoka: Nickname of VN's close friend, Georgy Iosifovich Hessen (1902–71), translator and movie reviewer, after arrival in US a simultaneous interpreter; son of Iosif Hessen.

Lizaveta: Lisbet Thompson.

Limousin: Presumably the Limousin troubadour Bertran de Born (c. 1140–c. 1215) and others like Bernart de Ventadorn (1130s–1190s). VN had studied medieval French literature at Cambridge.

Paulhan: Jean Paulhan (1884–1968), French novelist, literary critic and publisher.

Nouvelle Revue Française: Leading French literary magazine, founded as a monthly in 1909.

Luzhin: *Zashchita Luzhina* (*The Defence*), serialized in *Sovremennye zapiski* and *Poslednie novosti* in 1930; published in book form in Berlin by Slovo, 1930.

Boulevard Lannes: Supervielle lived at number 47.

Amalia Osipovna: Fondaminsky, wife of Ilya Fondaminsky. After her death from tuberculosis, VN would contribute a memoir in *Pamyati Amalii Osipovny Fondaminskoy* (*In Memory of Amalia Osipovna Fondaminsky*, Paris: privately printed, 1937).

Stepun: Fyodor Avgustovich Stepun (1884–1965), philosopher, novelist and editor, with Ilya Fondaminsky and Georgy Fedotov, of the Paris-based literary-religious journal *Novyi grad* (New City) (1931–9).

Pereslegin: *Nikolay Pereslegin* (1927), a philosophical and autobiographical novel by Stepun.

Acharya: Nabokov's friend Magda Maksimilyanovna Nakhman-Acharya (1889–1951), artist, painter, married M. P. T. Acharya (1887–1951), one of the founders of the Communist Party of India.

Terapiano: Yury Konstantinovich Terapiano (1892–1980), poet, memoirist and translator.

Smolensky: Vladimir Alekseevich Smolensky (1901–61), poet.

Antiopa, Io, Apollo: *Nymphalis* (*Vanessa*) *antiopa*, the Camberwell Beauty; *Inachis* (*Vanessa*) *io*, the Peacock Butterfly; *Parnassius Apollo*, the Apollo.

Rutenberg: Pyotr Moiseevich Rutenberg (1878–1942), engineer, politician and businessman.

Gapon: Georgy Apollonovich Gapon (1870–1906), a Russian Orthodox priest, organizer of a workers' strike and a peaceful demonstration to the Winter Palace that was met by gunfire from government troops on 'Bloody Sunday', 9 January 1905. In April 1906 Gapon was executed by activists of the Socialist Revolutionary Party on the grounds of his being a government agent, traitor and provocateur.

Gruzenberg: Oskar Osipovich Gruzenberg (1866–1940), lawyer, contributor to *Sovremennye zapiski*.

Milyukov: Pavel Nikolaevich Milyukov (1859–1943), liberal politician, leader of the Constitutional Democratic party, historian and journalist. In the emigration, he wrote books on Russian history and edited *Poslednie novosti*. In 1922, at a public lecture Milyukov was giving in Berlin, VDN tried to wrest the gun from a monarchist who had shot at Milyukov and was himself shot by his accomplice.

Tsvibakh: Yakov Moiseevich Tsvibakh, pen-name Andrey Sedykh (1902–94), writer, journalist and secretary to Ivan Bunin.

Odoevtseva: Iraida Gustavovna Heineke, pen-name Irina Vladimirovna Odoevtseva (1895–1990), poet, novelist and memoirist; the wife of Georgy Ivanov.

'My uncle has . . .': A reference to the first line of Ch. 1 of Pushkin's *Eugene Onegin*. VN translated the first stanza: 'My uncle has most honest principles: / when he was taken gravely ill, / he forced one to respect him and nothing better could invent. / To others his example is a lesson; / but, good God, what a bore to sit by a sick person day and night, not stirring / a step away! / What base perfidiousness / to entertain one half-alive, / adjust for him his pillows, / sadly serve him his medicine, / sigh – and think inwardly / when will the devil take you?' (*EO* [1964], I, p. 95).

Merezhkovsky couple: Dmitry Merezhkovsky and his wife Zinaida Gippius.

Felsen: Nikolay Berngardovich Freidenstein, pen-name Yuri Felsen (1884 or 1885–no later than 1943), writer and literary critic.

Antoinette: Mrs Grunelius.

'Oh M'sieur . . .': Fr. 'Oh, Monsieur, it's a long way from here, right on the other side, towards the fortifications.'

salle de vue: Fr. 'viewing room'.

Despair: VN began to write *Despair* in June 1931, finishing the first draft by September. He brought the manuscript of the novel to Paris to revise.

Kuprin: Aleksandr Ivanovich Kuprin (1870–1938), Russian novelist and memoirist.

Weidle: Vladimir Vasilievich Weidle (1895–1979), literary scholar, historian of the Russian emigration and poet.

Letter of 25 October 1932

Sergey Rodzyanko: Sergey Nikolaevich Rodzyanko (1878–1949), deputy of the Fourth Duma, member of the Octobrist party. His uncle, Mikhail Vladimirovich Rodzyanko (1859–1924), had been chairman of the State Duma and during the February Revolution of 1917 had worked closely with VDN while preparing the Tsar's abdication documents.

Procope: Le Procope, the oldest restaurant in Paris, rue de l'Ancienne Comédie, Paris 6.

Henry Muller: Henry Muller (1902–80), French writer and journalist, from 1923 a reader for Grasset.

Jean Fayard: Jean Fayard (1902–78), French writer and journalist, winner, in 1931, of the Prix Goncourt. He was director of Librairie Arthème Fayard, the publishing house founded by his grandfather. In 1934, VN would publish with them Denis Roche's translation of his novel *The Defence*, *La Course du fou* (Paris: A. Fayard, 1934).

offer translations of my stories to them and so on: These hopes did not materialize. VN's first publication with *Nouvelle Revue Française* would be the essay 'Pouchkine, ou le vrai et le vraisemblable' (1937).

Kovarsky: Ilya Nikolaevich Kovarsky (1880–1962), doctor, member of the Socialist Revolutionary party, and, in 1917, assistant to Vadim Rudnev, then mayor of Moscow; in 1919 he emigrated to France, in 1940 to the US. In Paris he practised medicine, and founded the publishing and bookselling company, Rodnik (Spring). He seems to have played a key role in the publication of the book version of *Podvig* (*Glory*) by the Sovremmenye Zapiski Publishing House (Paris, 1932).

Levinson: Andrey Yakovlevich Levinson (1887–1933), literary and theatre critic, professor at the Sorbonne. His essay, 'V. Sirine et son joueur d'échecs', *Nouvelles littéraires*, February 1930, was a major early overview.

L'addition . . . : Fr. 'The bill, please.'

Tissen: Or Thyssen, Tiessen. Unidentified.

Gabriel Marcel: Gabriel Marcel (1889–1973), French Christian-existentialist philosopher, playwright, literary and music critic of *Nouvelle Revue Française*.

Ergaz: Ida Mikhaylovna Ergaz (1904–67), known as Doussia; French translator, later VN's continental agent.

Nemirovsky: Irina Lvovna (Irène) Nemirovsky (1903–42), French writer. By the time VN came to Paris, she had five novels published with Fayard and Grasset.

Bryanchaninov: Possibly Aleksandr Nikolaevich Bryanchaninov (1874–1960), publicist and right-wing political activist.

Logos warehouse: A booksellers' warehouse in Berlin, associated with the publisher Slovo, and run by Iosif Gessen.

en train: Fr. 'in good spirits'.

Yu.Yu.: Most likely, Yulia Yulievna, wife of Gleb Struve.

Bernstein: Henri Bernstein (1876–1953), French playwright.

Romochka: Roma (Romochka) Klyachkin (Kliatchkine, 1901–59), translator, active in émigré community, one of VN's pre-Véra girlfriends.

the Shklyavers: Georgy Gavrilovich Shklyaver (1897–70), lawyer and professor of international law at the University of Paris.

Nicolas's music: VN's cousin, the composer Nicolas Nabokov.

Letter of 28 or 29 October 1932

Date: VéN dated the letter 19 October, but the correct date is probably 28 October, since Osorgin's review, mentioned in the letter, appeared on 27 October.

Danya: See note to letter of 19 June 1926 (Danechka).

Mme Adamov: Presumably Nadezhda Adamov (see letter of 24 October 1932).

Polyakova: Anastasia Alekseevna (Nastya) Polyakova (1877–1947), famous performer of Gypsy songs.

Klyachkin: Perhaps 'Roma's brother' mentioned above.

Bac berepom: A reference to a note found in Luzhin's pocket by two drunken Germans in *The Defence*. They misconstrue a two-word fragment in Russian cursive ('Вас вечером', *Vas vecherom*, 'you tonight'), reading it as meaningless characters in Roman script (*The Defence*, p. 147).

travel with a tub, in line with Martin: A reference to VN's *Glory*, whose hero, Martin Edelweiss, always baths in his own rubber tub.

Osorgin's article: Mikhail Osorgin, '[Review] 'Podvig'. Paris: "Sovremennye zapiski", 1932', *Poslednie novosti*, 27 October 1932, p. 3.

Adamovich's verbiage: G. V. Adamovich. '[Review] "Sovremennye zapiski". Kn. 50-ya. Chast' literaturnaya', *Poslednie novosti*, 27 October 1932, p. 3: 'Sirin's novel *Camera Obscura* is as entertaining as before, deftly constructed, and superficially brilliant. It is difficult, of course, given the productivity the young author shows, to expect new masterpieces all the time. [. . .] Outwardly, the novel is successful, that's unarguable. But it is empty. It is exceptional cinema, but rather weak literature.'

how pleasant [. . .]: VéN here said 'No!'– meaning that she was breaking off this sentence to move on to the next.

'Music': The short story 'Muzyka', written early 1932, published *Poslednie novosti*, 27 March 1932, p. 2; and in *Soglyadatay* (Paris: Russkie Zapiski, 1938).

Sonya: VéN's sister, Sofia Slonim.

Ask the old man . . . Zyoka: Ask Iosif Hessen about his son Georgy (Zyoka).

a poem about Kolbsheim: These three previously unpublished verse lines can be read as a finished poem, although VN may have written a longer text, now lost.

Letter of 29 October 1932

Danya: Unidentified.

Znossko: Evgeny Aleksandrovich Znosko-Borovsky (1884–1954), chess-player, author of books on chess, literary and theatre critic. VN repeatedly spells his name as 'Znossko'.

Ge: Nikolay Nikolaevich Ge (1857–1940), son of the Russian painter Nikolay Nikolaevich Ge (1831–94); he taught Russian at the Sorbonne and promoted his father's legacy in Europe.

a little Russian girl. [. . .]: VéN: 'All of that is of no interest to you.'

Letter of 31 October 1932

Fondik: Fondaminsky.

American professor: Alexander Kaun (1889–1944), Russian-born professor of Russian Literature at the University of California at Berkeley.

Benois: Aleksandr Nikolaevich Benois (1870–1960), artist, art historian and art critic, one of the founders of the Mir Iskusstva (World of Art) circle and the journal *Mir Iskusstva*, a friend and colleague of VN's father.

Lukash. [. . .]: VéN: 'I will omit everything about Lukash.' Ivan Lukash, writer, friend and occasional literary collaborator of VN in the latter's early years in Berlin. VN recalled him as 'a good friend, and a remarkable writer' (*TD*, p. 142).

Borman: Unidentified.

Dovid Knut: Duvid Meerovich Fiksman, pen-name Dovid Knut (1900–1955), poet, member of 'Perekryostok'.

Mandelstam: Yury Vladimirovich Mandelstam (1908–43), poet, literary critic and member of 'Perekryostok'.

Weidle's wife: Lyudmila Victorovna Baranovsky (1904–?), Vladimir Weidle's second wife.

Magda's charms: Magda is the hero's passion and downfall in *Camera Obscura (Laughter in the Dark)*. Many of the editorial board of *Sovremennye zapiski*, which published all VN's Russian novels in serial form from 1929 to 1940, were former Socialist Revolutionaries.

Letter of 1 November 1932

interview for Poslednie novosti and Segodnya: 'U V. V. Sirina' ('At V. V. Sirin's'), *Poslednie novosti*, 3 November 1932, p. 2, reprinted as 'Vstrecha s V. Sirinym' ('A Meeting with V. Sirin'), *Segodnya*, 5 November 1932, p. 8.

'lies' and 'lodges': In the Russian, *lozh'* and *lozh*.

Evreinov: Nikolay Nikolaevich Evreinov (1879–1953), renowned director, playwright, theatre critic and philosopher.

Kyandzhuntsev: Savely (Saba, Sava) Kyandzhuntsev, VN's classmate at Tenishev School.

Letter 1 of 2 November 1932

Bem: Alfred Bem.

the old man Kaplan's: Father of Sergey Kaplan, VN's pupil in Berlin.

Mother Maria: Elizaveta Yurievna Skobtsov (née Pilenko, Kuzmin-Karavaev in her first marriage; Mother Maria, St Mary of Paris; 1891–1945), poet, memoirist and theologian, canonized by the Constantinople Patriarchy in 2004.

Kuzmin-Karavaev: Dmitry Vladimirovich Kuzmin-Karavaev (1886–1959), a lawyer, who in 1920 converted to Catholicism and in 1922 was exiled from Russia. Headed the Russian Catholic Mission in Berlin (1926–31) and later served in France and Belgium.

my reading: The Sirin evening would take place on 15 November 1932 at the Musée Sociale, 5 rue Las Cases.

Ilya Isidorovich: Fondaminsky.

Kremenetsky: Semyon Isidorovich Kremenetsky is the main character of Mark Aldanov's trilogy *Klyuch* (*The Key*, 1929), *Begstvo* (*Escape*, 1932), and *Peshchera* (*The Cave*, 1934–6).

Gruzenberg: Oskar Gruzenberg, see letter of 24 October 1932.

conférencier: Fr. 'master of ceremonies'.

Struve: Probably the father of Gleb Struve, Pyotr Berngardovich Struve (1870–1944), first a Marxist, then a liberal politician, deputy of the State Duma, political thinker and editor.

Kartashev: Anton Vladimirovich Kartashev (1875–1960), Russian Orthodox historian.

Florovsky: Georgy Vasilievich Florovsky (1893–1979), Eastern Orthodox priest, theologian, historian, who taught at the St Serge Institute of Orthodox Theology in Paris.

Lolly Lvov: Lolly Ivanovich Lvov (1888–1967), journalist, member of the editorial board of *Rossiya i slavyanstvo*.

Peter Ryss: Pyotr Yakovlevich Ryss (1879[1870?]–1948), historian, political commentator and secretary of *Poslednie novosti*.

Russian journalist Levin: Isaak Osipovich Levin (1876–1944), historian, publicist and journalist.

Felsen and another classmate of mine: Felsen was not VN's classmate; VN here means: other than Savely Kyandzhuntsev.

forgotten his name: Probably Savely Grinberg.

about Mother: Who had been widowed in 1922 when VN's father came to Milyukov's defence against his would-be assassins. Mutual friends of the Nabokovs and Milyukovs repeatedly wrote to the Milyukovs, who were comfortably off, beseeching them to help relieve the desperate plight of EN, but to little avail (Nadezhda Rodionova, 'Uchastie Milyukovykh v sud'be sem'i V. D. Nabokova posle ego gibeli' in M. Yu. Sorokina, ed., *Myslyashchie miry rossiyskogo liberalizma: Pavel Milyukov (1859–1943)* (Moscow: Dom Russkogo Zarubezh'ya im. Aleksandra Solzhenitsyna and Bibliothèque Tourguéniev, 2010), pp. 214–25).

Mlle Klyachkin: Roma (Romochka) Klyachkin.

nouvelles: Fr. 'stories'.

Esther's: Unidentified.

'Terra Incognita': The story 'Terra Incognita', *Poslednie novosti*, 22 November 1931, pp. 2–3; collected in *Sog*, *RB*. No early translation into French appears to have been published.

Teryuz: Unidentified.

aunt Nina: Nina Dmitrievna (née Nabokov, 1860–1944), sister of VDN; from 1888 to 1910 Baroness Rausch von Traubenberg, then Nina Kolomeytsev.

Muma: Maria Sergeevna Zapolsky (née Nabokov, 1900–1972), VN's cousin.

Nikolay Nikolaevich: Former Vice-Admiral Nikolay Nikolaevich Kolomeytsev (1867–1944). See SM, pp. 189, 193.

Rausches: Nikolay Rausch von Traubenberg, his wife Maria Vasilievna (1884–1970, née Menzelintsev, by first marriage Obolensky), and their two children.

the young lady . . . Mme Rausch's daughter by her first marriage: Maria Nikolaevna Obolensky (1914–46). VN had written 'Aunt Nina's daughter,' but VéN, reading out the letter into BB's tape recorder, corrected to '[Mme] Rausch's daughter.'

He's a singer: Muma's husband, Vladimir Evgenievich Zapolsky (1898–1982).

Letter 2 of 2 November 1932

Natasha and Ivan: Nathalie Nabokov and her son Ivan.

the sister: Irina Kyandzhuntsev.

Liteyny: Liteyny Prospect in St Petersburg.

long poems: 'Pegas' ('Pegasus'), written 25 October 1917, published in Gennady Barabtarlo, *Aerial Views: Essays on Nabokov's Art and Metaphysics* (New York: Peter Lang, 1993), pp. 248–50. The Kyandzhuntsev family kept the manuscript of the poem until the late 1960s, then passed it on to Zinaida Shakhovskoy.

Spiresco: Kosta Spiresco, a Romanian violinist in Berlin who apparently drove his wife to suicide by abusing her physically, then escaped punishment and continued to perform and enjoy the admiring attention of other women. On 18 January 1927, VN and Mikhail Kaminka came to the restaurant where Spiresco worked, in order to administer their own punishment. VN, a sometime boxing coach, drubbed him, while Kaminka fought the orchestra (see *VNRY*, pp. 271–2).

Letter of 3 November 1932

Californian professor: The Berkeley professor Alexander Kaun.

Zaytsev: Boris Konstantinovich Zaytsev (1881–1972), writer, translator and literary historian.

and one of Aldanov's relatives: Khodasevich, in his 'Kamer-fur'erskii zhurnal' ('Chamber-Courier's Journal') mentions all the people whom VN notes, adding as also present Ilya Fondaminsky and Yakov Borisovich Polonsky (1892–1951), a bibliographer and bibliophile, who co-edited an almanac of the Society of Friends of the Russian Book. Polonsky was the husband of Aldanov's sister, Lyubov' Aleksandrovna Polonsky (née Landau, 1893–1963).

Hachette: French publisher, founded in Paris in 1826.

whether Bunin would receive the Nobel Prize: Bunin did indeed receive the Nobel Prize in 1933.

took him to pieces for The Cave: *Peshchera*, a novel being serialized in *Sovremennye zapiski*, it would be published in book form in two volumes, 1934 and 1936. V. Khodasevich, 'Knigi i lyudi. Sovremennye zapiski, kn. 50', *Vozrozhdenie*, 27 October 1932, p. 3. In the same review, Khodasevich praised the latest instalment of VN's *Kamera obskura*.

aparté: Fr. 'aside.'

Chukovsky: Korney Ivanovich Chukovsky (1882–1969), literary critic and children's writer.

Kulisher: Aleksandr Mikhaylovich Kulisher (1890–1942), lawyer, historian, sociologist and journalist who worked for *Poslednie novosti* in Paris.

Mme Damansky: Avgusta Filippovna Damansky (1877–1959), writer, poet and translator.

interview in Poslednie novosti: A. Sedykh, 'U. V. V. Sirina'. *Poslednie novosti*, 3 November 1932, p. 2.

my poor little coat: Sedykh called VN's suit 'good quality but rather baggy', adding that 'in Paris almost no one wears such a mackintosh with a button-up lining'.

'funny': The word 'funny' is attributed to VN, who, responding to his interviewer's question about the influence of German writers on him, allegedly said: 'How funny! Yes, they've accused me of being influenced by German writers whom I do not know. Generally speaking, I read and speak German poorly.'

his husband: Hermann Thieme.

Tair: Tair (1920–35), a publishing company founded in Paris by the composer Sergey Vasilievich Rachmaninov (1873–1943). The company's name took the first syllables of the names of the composer's daughters, Tatyana and Irina, who were expected to run the company. Tair published music and music criticism as well as fiction (by, for instance, Ivan Shmelyov and Aleksey Remizov).

Mme [Mlle?] Rachmaninov: Possibly Natalia Aleksandrovna Rachmaninov (née Satin, 1877–1951), the composer's wife; more likely, though, it was one of his daughters, Tatyana Sergeevna Konyus (1907–61) or Irina Sergeevna Volkonsky (1903–69).

Letter of 3–4 November 1932

Plon: Plon, French publishing company founded in 1852.

Œil de Dieu: *Eye of God* (1925), a novel by Franz Hellens (pen-name of Frédéric Van Ermengem, 1881–1972), a writer VN greatly admired and would consistently champion.

Pozner: Vladimir Solomonovich Pozner (1905–92), poet and critic, who in 1932 or 1933 became a member of the French Communist Party.

Ehrenburg: Ilya Grigorievich Ehrenburg (1891–1967), prolific poet, novelist, playwright, journalist and political commentator. Although a Soviet citizen, Ehrenburg lived and worked in Europe as a correspondent for *Izvestia* (1923–39).

Shmelyov's The Sun of the Dead: The novel *Solntse myortvykh* (*The Sun of the Dead*, 1923) by the Russian writer and religious thinker, Ivan Sergeevich Shmelyov (1873–1950); in its French translation, Ivan Chméliov, *Le Soleil de la mort*, translated by Denis Roche (Paris: Librairie Plon, 1929).

Letter of 5 November 1932

Candide: French literary and political weekly founded in Paris in 1924.

'Terra': 'Terra Incognita'.

Mme Lvovsky: Unidentified.

the Paulhans. She's: Presumably his first wife, Sala Prusak; he divorced her in 1933 to marry Germaine Pascal, with whom he had had an affair for many years.

Bradley: Unidentified.

Maklakov: Vasily Alekseevich Maklakov (1869–1957), former lawyer, politician, publicist, member of the Central Committee of the Constitutional Democratic party and deputy of the Second, Third and Fourth Dumas; in Paris, chair of the Russian Émigré Committee at the League of Nations.

Avgust Isaakovich: Kaminka.

Tsar Boris: Grand Prince Boris Vladimirovich Romanov (1877–1943), grandson of Alexander II.

Natasha: Nathalie Nabokov.

Letter 1 of 8 November 1932

Gorky: Aleksey Maksimovich Peshkov, pen-name Maksim Gorky (1868–1936), Russian writer, playwright and founder of Socialist Realism in literature. From 1921 to 1932 Gorky lived abroad, mostly in Sorrento, Italy.

Camera . . . Sovremennye zapiski: To date Chs. 1–7 and 8–17 had been published in *Sovremennye zapiski*, 49 (May 1932) and 50 (October 1932) respectively. The rest of Chs. 17–26 and Chs. 27–36 would appear in issues 51 (February 1933) and 52 (May 1933) respectively.

'Chorb': From the collection *VC*.

Max Eastman: American writer, poet, political activist and supporter of socialism (1883–1969).

Bunin asked me to find him: In 1931 Bunin had asked VN and others to help him contact Eastman, whom he wanted to translate his novel *Zhizn' Arsen'eva* (*The Life of Arsen'ev*, the first four parts published in 1927–9, the last part in 1939). See 'V. V. Nabokov i I. A. Bunin. Perepiska' ('V. V. Nabokov and I. A. Bunin. Correspondence'), ed. R. Davis and Maxim Shrayer, *S dvukh beregov. Russkaya literatura XX veka v Rossii i za rubezhom* (Moscow: IMLI RAN, 2002), pp. 197–9, 214.

Eastman's Russian, très soviete, wife: Elena Vasilievna Eastman (née Krylenko, 1895–1956), painter and graphic artist, sister of Nikolay Vasilievich Krylenko (1885–1938), devoted Bolshevik, member of the central committee of the Communist Party (1927–34) and organizer of mass terror campaigns and political show trials.

Daily Times: Possibly the *Los Angeles Daily Times* (as it was once known); or perhaps VN, confused by the distinction between the daily London *Times* and the *Sunday Times*, had in mind the *New York Times*.

Evgeny Shakh: Evgeny Vladimirovich Shakh (1905–?), poet, member of 'Perekryostok.'

'A Bad Day': 'Obida', written in Berlin in the summer of 1931, pp 2–3, published in *Poslednie novosti*, 12 July 1931, and in *Sog*.

'Perfection': 'Sovershenstvo', written in June 1932, published in *Poslednie novosti*, 3 July 1932, and in book form in *Sog*.

Lena: VéN's elder sister, Elena Massalsky.

Maria Vasilievna's daughter and Koka's son: Maria Obolensky and Aleksandr Nikolaevich Rausch von Traubenberg (1909–65), son of Nikolay Rausch (family nickname Koka) by his first marriage to Olga Aleksandrovna Eveling (1885–1928, divorced in 1915).

Letter 2 of 8 November 1932

imagine . . . a revolution in Berlin: In the German general elections of 6 November 1932, the National Socialist Party lost 34 seats in the Reichstag but the Communist Party gained 11, which must have seemed alarming to the Russian émigré community in Paris.

Blackborough's: Unidentified.

Vanya: Ivan, Son of Nicolas and Nathalie Nabokov.

Muma: Maria Zapolsky.

[I don't know what]: VéN's words.

his wife: Lyubov' Shlemovna Levinson (née Sharf).

Krymov's wife's type: Berta Vladimirovna Krymov, wife of Vladimir Pimenovich Krymov (1878–1968), Russian entrepreneur, publisher and writer.

the thin little Mlle Levinson: Maria Andreevna Levinson (1914–?).

Vadim Andreev: Vadim Leonidovich Andreev (1903–76), writer, one of the organizers of the Union of Young Poets and Writers in Paris; the son of the writer Leonid Nikolaevich Andreev (1871–1919).

Letter of 10 November (?) 1932

Sergey, his boyfriend, and Natasha: His brother Sergey, Sergey's partner Hermann Thieme, and Nathalie Nabokov, wife of his cousin Nicolas.

a new story: Apparently not completed.

'Je veux lire en trois jours': 'Je veux lire en trois jours l'Iliade de Homère' ('I want to read Homer's Iliad in three days', 1560), from *Les Amours*: until he finishes reading, Ronsard wishes for no interruptions from anyone, even the gods – unless someone should come from his Cassandra.

Nika: Nicolas Nabokov.
the idiotic advertisement: For *Podvig* (*Glory*) in book form (Paris: Sovremennye Zapiski, 1932).

Letter of 11 November 1932

Elkins: Boris Isaakovich Elkin (1887–1972), lawyer, and one of the founders of the Berlin publishing house Slovo, and his wife Anna Aleksandrovna.
Revue de Paris: French literary magazine, founded 1829.
a King, Queen, Knave, but by another author: Perhaps *Un roi, deux dames et un valet* (Paris: L'Illustration, 1935), a play in four acts by François Porché (1877–1944).
Giraudoux: Jean Giraudoux (1882–1944), French novelist, essayist, playwright and diplomat.
Sainte-Hélène, petit île: Mark Aldanov, *Sainte-Hélène, petit île* (*Saint Helena, Little Island*) (Paris: Povolozky, 1921); Albéric Cahuet, *Sainte-Hélène, petit île* (Paris: Fasquelle, 1922).
Otsup: Nikolay Avdeevich Otsup (1894–1958), poet and critic, brother of Aleksandr Otsup (Sergey Gorny).
Zaytsevs: Boris Zaytsev and his wife, Vera Alekseevna Zaytsev (née Oreshnikov, 1879–1965).
Remizov: Aleksey Mikhaylovich Remizov (1877–1957), writer, artist and literary critic.
Lolly: Lvov.
Mme [Mlle?] Rachmaninov: Either the composer's wife Natalia Rachmaninov or one of his daughters, Tatyana or Irina.
Pohl: Vladimir Ivanovich Pohl (1875–1962), pianist and composer, one of the founders and professor at the Russian Conservatory in Paris, and his wife, Anna Mikhailovna, née Petrunkevich stage-name Yan-Ruban, (*c.* 1890–1955), concert singer. VN first met them on the estate of Gaspra in the Crimea, where his family lived in 1918–19. Vladimir Pohl tried to interest young VN in mysticism; VN's poem sequence 'Angels' is dedicated to Pohl (written 1918; published in *Gorniy put'* (Berlin: Grani, 1923); one poem, 'Arkhangely' ('Archangels'), was selected for *Stikhi*, pp. 14–15). In 1919, Pohl set to music VN's poem 'Dozhd' proletel' ('The Rain Has Flown', 1917): *VNRY*, pp. 138,

143–4, 152–6; Z. A. Shakhovskoy, 'V. I. Pohl' i 'angelskie stikhi' Vl. Nabokova', *Russkii almanakh / Almanach russe*, ed. Z. Shakhovskoy, René Guerra and Evgeny Ternovsky (Paris, 1981).

Portnovs: Unidentified.

Yulia: Yulia Struve.

Raisa: Tatarinov.

writing a story: Possibly abandoned, or the beginning of 'The Admiralty Spire', which nevertheless seems to arise out of VN's meeting with and letters from a former girlfriend, Mlle Novotvortsev (see letters of 16 and 21 November 1932, below), and which he was working on when he left Paris (see letter of 21 November 1932, below).

Saurat: The village in the Ariège, France, where VN and VéN spent late April–late June 1929.

Ruban . . . upset about the little ears: Possibly a reference to Bonzo, the little flop-eared dog who was the subject of a worldwide craze in the 1920s and early 1930s and who inspired the popularity of 'Cheepy', a cartoon guinea-pig whose cute humanized images begin in the cartoonist's mind with thoughts of vivisection, in Nabokov's *Camera obscura*. See BB, 'On the Original of Cheepy: Nabokov and Popular Culture Fads', *The Nabokovian*, 63 (Fall 2009), pp. 63–71.

uncle Zhenya: Baron Evgeny Aleksandrovich Rausch von Traubenberg (1855–1923), first husband of VN's aunt, Nina Dmitrievna Kolomeytsev.

Yurik: Baron Georgy (Yury, Yurik) Evgenievich Rausch von Traubenberg (1897–1919), son of E. A. and N. D. Rausch von Traubenberg, VN's favourite cousin (see SM, especially Ch. 10).

Maria Vasilievna: Maria Rausch von Traubenberg.

Koka's son: Aleksandr Rausch von Traubenberg.

Letter of 12 November 1932

the novel: His new novel, *Otchayanie* (*Despair*), still not completely revised in its later sections.

'A Dashing Fellow': 'Khvat', a short story written between 20 April and 5 May 1932, published in *Segodnya*, 2 and 3 October 1932; in book form in *Sog*.

Yu.Yu.: Yulia Yulievna Struve.

Lizaveta: Lisbet Thompson.
won't finish my story for Tuesday: That is, for his public reading.
Mme Teisch: Unidentified.

Letter of 14 November 1932

to the point where he arrives from Prague: Ch. 1 and part of Ch. 2 of *Despair*.
no hard signs: The Fondaminskys may have been using a typewriter already adhering (unlike émigré publications) to the Soviet orthography which, after the reform of 1918, eliminated four letters as 'unnecessary'. The hard sign was not eliminated, but Ѣ (*yer*), which looked similar, was.
Siverskaya: A town near St Petersburg, on the river Oredezh, close to the Nabokov estates.
Lyussya: 'Lyussya' was the nickname of Nabokov's first love, Valentina Evgenievna Shul'gina (1900–?), the 'Tamara' of SM, whom he met near his family's country estate, in the Siverskaya area, in the summer of 1915. She had three sisters, Natalia, Anastasia, and Irina. After the Revolution she lived in Poltava.
Sofia Pregel: Sofia Yulievna Pregel (1894–1972), poet.
Shaykevich: Anatoly Efimovich Shaykevich, pen-name Ash (1879–1947), lawyer, theatre critic, screenwriter, musician, and one of the organizers of the Russian Romantic Theatre in Berlin (1922–6).
Gurdjieff: Georgy Ivanovich Gurdjieff (1868?–1949), occultist, psychoanalyst, organizer of a dance theatre that performed in Paris (he wrote music for the performances).
Rasputin-like: VN compares Gurdjieff to Grigory Efimovich Rasputin (1869–1916), a notoriously licentious Russian Orthodox 'healer' and spiritual adviser to Tsar Nicholas II and his wife, Tsarina Aleksandra.
Spanish artist: Francisco Goya (1746–1828).
Mrs Evreinov: Anna Aleksandrovna Kashin-Evreinov (1898–1981), actress and writer.
Je veux qu'on se voit: Fr. 'I want us to see each other.' Her novel *Khochu . . .* (*I want . . .*) was published in Paris in 1930.
Gringoire: Right-wing French political weekly, founded in 1928, notable for its high-quality literary pages. VN cannot have known at this point of the newspaper's anti-semitic bent.
Plaksin: Boris Nikolaevich Plaksin (1880–1972), former state councillor and jurist, memoirist and occasional poet.

Yuzya Bilig: Unidentified.
dreamer. [. . .]: VéN: 'And so on, I am skipping this.'
teiglach: Jewish honey and nut cookies for Rosh Hashanah.
Aleksandr Fyodorovich: Kerensky.

Letter of 16 November 1932

Saba: Savely Kyandzhuntsev.

gentilhommish: From Fr. 'gentilhomme', a gentleman.

tuxedo . . . shirt of the same provenance: Savely Kyandzhuntsev had lent VN a tuxedo and silk shirt.

Aleksandr Fyodorovich: Kerensky.

Mme Veryovkin: A friend of the Nabokovs in the late 1920s (in VéN's words), otherwise unidentified.

Sergey: VN's brother.

Natasha: Nathalie Nabokov.

Mit'ka Rubinstein: Dmitry Lvovich Rubinstein (1876–1936), merchant, lawyer and patron of the arts.

'To the Muse' . . . : 'K muze', *Rul'*, 24 September 1929; 'Vozdushnyi ostrov', *Rul'*, 8 September 1929, and *Stikhi*; 'Okno', *Nedelya*, 5 May 1930, and *Stikhi*, translated as 'The Muse', *PP*, p. 57; 'Budushchemu chitatelyu', *Rul'*, 7 February 1930, and in *Stikhi* under the title 'K nerodivshemusya chitatelyu' ('To the yet unborn reader'); 'Pervaya lyubov', *Rossiya i slavyanstvo*, 19 April 1930, and in *Stikhi*; probably 'Sam treugol'nyi, dvukrylyi, beznogiy', *Poslednie novosti*, 8 September 1932, and in *Stikhi*; 'Vecher na pustyre', published untitled, *Poslednie novosti*, 31 July 1932, and in *Stikhi* with a dedication to VN's father, as also in VN's translation, 'Evening on a Vacant Lot', *PP*, pp. 68–73.

Mlle Novotvortsev: Otherwise unidentified.

old Avgust: Kaminka.

One lady I don't yet know: Olga Nikolaevna Aschberg, wife of Olof Aschberg (1877–1960), a Swedish banker and leftist sympathizer whose banks helped the Bolshevik government in the 1920s. VN is obviously not yet aware of the origins of their wealth.

Demidov's wife: Ekaterina Yurievna Demidov (née Novosiltsev, 1884–1931), deceased wife of Igor Demidov, deputy editor of *Poslednie novosti*.

Letter 1 of 18 November 1932

Berskys: Unidentified.

her castle: Not the Château du Bois du Rocher at Jouy-en-Josas, near Versailles, which Aschberg also owned.

Grasse or Saurat: Towns in south-east and south-western France, respectively: Grasse (Alpes Maritimes), popular with Russian émigrés; Saurat (Ariège), where VN and VéN had spent time in 1929 – VN writing and collecting butterflies.

Letter 2 of 18 November 1932

The Eye: The collection *Soglyadatay* (*The Eye*), which, as eventually published (Paris: Russkie Zapiski, 1938), would consist of the novella 'Soglyadatay' and a number of short stories, some at this point not yet written: 'Obida' ('A Bad Day'), 'Lebeda' ('Orache'), 'Terra Incognita', 'Vstrecha' ('The Reunion'), 'Khvat' ('A Dashing Fellow'), 'Zanyatoy chelovek' ('A Busy Man'), 'Muzyka' ('Music'), 'Pilgram' ('The Aurelian'), 'Sovershenstvo' ('Perfection'), 'Sluchay iz zhizni' ('A Slice of Life'), 'Krasavitsa' ('A Russian Beauty'), 'Opoveshchenie' ('Breaking the News').

Petropolis and Sovremennye zapiski: Sovremennye Zapiski as a publishing house (it published the book versions of *Podvig* in 1932 and *Kamera obskura* in 1933). In fact, only VN's next novel, *Otchayanie* (*Despair*), would be published by Petropolis (Berlin: Petropolis, 1936). The collection *Soglyadatay* would not be published until 1938 by Russkie Zapiski (as a publishing house rather than a journal allied to *Sovremennye zapiski*).

Chertok: Lev Chertok, bookseller and publisher; in 1921–8, one of the senior staff at the Berlin publishing company Grani; also worked at the publisher Dom Knigi in Paris.

Sheremetev: Count Dmitry Aleksandrovich Sheremetev (1885–1963), mason from 1922, member of the 'Astrea' lodge, founder of the 'Golden Fleece' lodge, and master of the 'Northern Lights' lodge.

Obolensky: Prince Vladimir Andreevich Obolensky (1869–1950), politician, member of the Central Committee of the Constitutional Democratic party in 1913–16, and member of the Supreme Council of Russian Masons.

Dastakiyan: Savely Kyandzhuntsev's business partner, otherwise unidentified.

Sonja Henie: Norwegian world champion ice-skater, later a Hollywood movie star (1912–69).

Dostoevsky: Dostoevsky's head was famously turned by the fulsome praise for his first novel, *Bednye lyudi* (*Poor Folk*, 1846)

review in Poslednie novosti . . . by Adamovich: Unsigned, 'Vecher V. V. Sirina' ('V.V. Sirin Evening'), *Poslednie novosti*, 17 November 1932, p. 3.

Mandelstam's: M., 'Vecher V. V. Sirina' ('V.V. Sirin Evening'), *Vozrozhdenie*, 17 November 1932, p. 4.

Letter of 21 November 1932

our stay . . . in Le Boulou and Saurat: In 1929. See VN, 'Notes on the Lepidoptera of the Pyrénées Orientales and the Ariège', *Entomologist*, 64 (November 1931), pp. 255–7; reprinted in *N's Bs*, pp. 126–34, and *VNRY*, pp. 288–90.

the first chapter of Despair to Poslednie novosti: 'Otchayanie', *Poslednie novosti*, 31 December 1932, pp. 2–3.

a story: Apparently 'Admiralteyskaya igla' ('The Admiralty Spire'), *Poslednie novosti*, 4 June 1933, p. 3, and 5 June 1933, p. 2.

Her husband . . . dead: Incorrect: Olof Aschberg did not die until 1960.

uncle Vasya's: Vasily Rukavishnikov.

excerpt from Luzhin: From the French translation of *The Defence*, *La Course du fou*. Unlocated and perhaps not published.

Mme Struve: Antonina (Nina) Aleksandrovna Struve (née Heard, 1868–1943).

Natasha: Nathalie Nabokov.

Sergey: Nabokov, VN's brother.

Letter of 22 November 1932

the Kuprins: Aleksandr Kuprin and his wife, Elizaveta Moritsovna Kuprin (née Heinrich, 1882–1942).

600 francs for Glory: From the sales of the edition of *Podvig* (*Glory*) published by the Sovremennye Zapiski publishing house on 6 November 1932.

Slonim translation office: The Agency for Placing Foreign Translations of Books by Russian Writers ('European Literary Bureau').

Volkonskys: Possibly at the home of Irina Volkonsky (née Rachmaninov).

petits jeux: Fr. 'parlour games'.

Sonya: Sofia Slonim, VéN's sister.

Letter of 25 November 1932

Feux croisés: A lecture in the series ('Crossfire') organized by Gabriel Marcel, in association with the international literary book series of the same name that he directed for the Paris publisher Plon. See letters of 5 February and 4 March 1937.

Yu.Yu.: Yulia Yulievna Struve.

Aleksey Petrovich: Aleksey Petrovich Struve (1899–1976), bibliographer, antiquarian, brother of Gleb Struve; his wife was born Ekaterina Andreevna Catoire (1896–1978).

Kisa: Ksenia Aleksandrovna Kuprin, stage-name Kissa Kouprine (1908–81), actress and painter; she would return to the USSR in 1958, where she helped organize the Kuprin Museum in Narovchat.

1936

Postcard postmarked 22 January 1936

Zina: Zinaida Shakhovskoy.

our puppy: Their son, Dmitri Vladimirovich Nabokov (1934–2012).

Letter of c. *24 January 1936*

Date: No envelope; VéN has added later 'ca. 20–I–36', but this must follow the preceding letter.

they 'honoured': At the Belgian Pen Club (Brussels) reading mentioned in the previous letter.

Elli: A nanny for DN, apparently, and pregnant (see letter of 21 February 1936).

P. de Reul: Paul De Reul (1871–1945), professor of English at the University of Brussels, literary historian and critic.

book about Swinburne: *L'Œuvre de Swinburne* (Brussels: R. Sand, 1922).

Magda: VN's friend Magda Nakhman-Acharya.

René Meurant: René Meurant (1905–77), poet and translator.

Charles Plisnier: Charles Plisnier (1896–1952), Marxist Belgian writer.

Paul Fierens: Paul Fierens (1895–1957), art historian and critic, professor at Liège University, poet. In 1945, he would become Curator-in-Chief of the Royal Museum of Fine Arts (Musée Royal des Beaux-Arts) in Brussels.

art critic: VN drew a two-pointed arrow, connecting 'Paul Fierens' to 'critic'.

Franz Hellens: The Belgian novelist, poet and critic, whom VN was to have met but did not, in Paris in 1932.

Zack: Léon (Lev Vasilievich) Zack, pen-names Chrysanth, M. Rossyansky (1892–1980), artist and poet.

Mme Roland: Manon (Marie-Jeanne Phlippon) Roland (1754–93) and her husband, Jean-Marie Roland de la Platière, supported the French Revolution as Girondists. She was executed during the Reign of Terror.

'Liberté, quelles crimes . . .': Madame Roland is famous for crying, as she stepped up to the guillotine, 'O Liberté, que de crimes on commet en ton nom!' ('Oh Liberty, how many crimes are committed in your name!').

Brisson: Jacques (Jean) Pierre Brissot (1754–93), a leading Girondist.

Prof. Frank: Semyon Lyudvigovich Frank (1877–1950), philosopher, theologian and psychologist. After Frank's father died, his mother married Vasily I. Zack, by whom she had Lev.

'il a cinq ans . . .': Fr. 'He's five – or more?' In fact DN was only twenty months old.

Bois: Fr. 'wood'.

'Mlle O.': 'Mademoiselle O', VN's memoir about his French governess, his first narrative written entirely in French, *Mesures*, 2:2, 15 April 1936, pp. 145–72, trans. VN with Hilda Ward, *Atlantic Monthly*, January 1943), and revised as Ch. 5 of *Conclusive Evidence* (New York: Harper & Bros, 1951) / *Speak, Memory* (London: Victor Gollancz, 1951).

'C. O.': *Chambre Obscure* (*Camera Obscura*), trans. Doussia Ergaz (Paris: Grasset, 1934).

'Course du F.': *La Course du fou* (*The Defence*), trans. Denis Roche (Paris: Fayard, 1934).

Greta Garbo: Swedish film actress and celebrated beauty (1905–90).

c'est tellement typique: Fr. 'That's so typical'.

Kirill: Kirill Nabokov, VN's youngest brother, now a student in Louvain.

Peltenburg misses: Vera and Leonora, daughters of Leo Peltenburg, Evsey Slonim's Dutch business partner; VN and VéN tried to play the role of matchmakers for them.

Svyatoslav: Svyatoslav Svyatoslavovich Malevsky-Malevich (1905–73), businessman, diplomat and artist.

Svetik . . . weird for me to utter: Svetik was also the nickname of VN's fiancée Svetlana Siewert, who broke off with him at her parents' insistence in January 1923.

en sursaut: Fr. 'with a start'.

'Yakor'': *The Anchor*, ed. G. V. Adamovich, M. L. Kantor (Berlin: Petropolis, 1936), an anthology of Russian émigré poetry; reprint, eds. O. Korostelev, L. Magarotto and A. Ustinova (St Petersburg: Aleteya, 2005).

Aleksandr Yakovlevich: Unidentified.

Letter of 27 January 1936

French evening: At La Maison d'Art, 185 Avenue Louise, Brussels.

Maurois: André Maurois (1885–1967), popular French novelist.

Anna Pavlova: Anna Pavlovna (Matveevna) Pavlova (1881–1931), foremost ballerina of her time.

N. R. F.: *Nouvelle Revue Française*.

Rilke: Rainer Maria Rilke (1875–1926), Bohemian-Austrian poet who wrote in German.

Russian evening: On 26 January, VN gave a reading to the Club of Russian Jews in Belgium, at 65 rue de la Concorde, Brussels.

'Invitation': The dystopian novel *Invitation to a Beheading* (*Priglashenie na kazn'*), written June–December 1934, serialized in *Sovremennye zapiski*, 58–59 (1935) and 60 (1936); in book form, Paris: Dom Knigi, 1938.

Eleonora: Leonora Peltenburg.

faisait de son mieux: Fr. 'was doing all she could'.

Auerbach: Unidentified.

Mme Bazilevsky: Wife of Pyotr Georgievich Bazilevsky (1913–93), agrarian engineer and entomologist.

Ilyashenko: Possibly Vladimir Stepanovich Ilyashenko (1884–1970), poet.

Kaplan: Possibly Sergey Kaplan, VN's former pupil in Berlin.

Shcherbatovs: Prince Pavel Borisovich Shcherbatov (1871–1951), aide-de-camp of Tsar Nicholas II, and his wife, Anna Vladimirovna (née Baryatinsky, 1879–1942), who settled in Brussels and are buried there. One of their eight children, Anna Pavlovna Shcherbatov (1909–2010), had married VN's cousin Sergey Sergeevich Nabokov (1902–98) in 1929.

Sergey: Sergey Sergeevich Nabokov, VN's cousin.

a little boy: Nicolas (Nikolay Sergeevich) Nabokov (1929–85).

Semyonlyudvigoviches: Francs: from here on, VN, apparently fearing that his letters might be scrutinized, refers to his earnings outside Germany in various coded forms, possibly to avoid tax penalties upon his return. The Belgian franc becomes Semyon Lyudvigovich Frank, the philosopher and theologian he mentioned in his previous letter.

Masui: Jacques Masui (1909–75), French writer.

Margarita: Otherwise unidentified.

Graun: Carl Heinrich Graun (1704–59), German composer, especially of Italian opera, 'the great-grandfather of Ferdinand von Korff, my grandfather' (SM, p. 54).

genealogical titbits: Cousin Sergey would remain a passionate genealogist and contribute to the information VN drew on in his 1951 autobiography and its 1966 revision.

out of 'War and Peace': In *War and Peace* (1863–9), Lev Tolstoy features *kulebyaka* – a pie of sour or pastry dough with multi-layered savoury stuffing – served at the name-day party of Natasha Rostov (I.i.xv).

On a beaucoup admiré: Fr. 'They much admired'.

Très svietski: Combines the French 'very' and, in Roman letters, the Russian word for 'high-society', as if in the manner of a French-speaking nineteenth-century Russian aristocrat.

'Despair': The novel *Otchayanie*, serialized in *Sovremennye zapiski* (54–6) in 1934, would not appear in book form (Berlin: Petropolis) until 20 February 1936.

Kulisher: Presumably Aleksandr Kulisher.

Regina: Unidentified.
au dire de Zina: Fr. 'according to Zina'.

Letter of 30 January 1936

Long's: London publisher John Long Ltd, who published *Camera Obscura*, trans. Winifred Roy, in '1935' (actually January 1936) and would publish Nabokov's own translation of *Despair* in 1937.
Antwerp reading: For the Cercle Russe (Russian Circle), at the Brasserie de la Bourse, 19 rue des XII mois, Antwerp, on 27 January 1936.
two hundred and fifty Belgian pages: VN refers to the Belgian francs he earned in Belgium.
Pumpyansky: Leonid Semyonovich Pumpyansky, journalist and poet.
married to a Russian Jewess: Maria Markovna Hellens (née Miloslavsky, 1893–1947).
Jaloux: Edmond Jaloux (1878–1949), French novelist and critic.
au dire de: Fr. 'according to'.
du Boz: Charles Du Bos (1882–1939), French critic and essayist.
'Thyrse': *Le Thyrse*: *Revue d'art et de littérature*, a French journal published in Brussels, 1899–1944.
une occasion . . . : Fr. 'an opportunity like this will never be offered again'.
Le plaa: Unidentified.
the Club: Russian Jewish Club in Belgium.
qui commence à m'agacer: Fr. 'which is starting to annoy me'.
V. V. Baryatinsky: Prince Vladimir Vladimirovich Baryatinsky (1874–1941), journalist, playwright, political commentator, brother of Anna Vladimirovna Shcherbatov (née Baryatinsky) and uncle of Anna Pavlovna Nabokov (née Shcherbatov), the wife of VN's cousin, Sergey Sergeevich Nabokov.
av. de Versailles: VN would stay at 130 Avenue de Versailles, the apartment of Ilya Fondaminsky, where Vladimir Zenzinov also lived.
P. N. . . . print me in big letters, and Khodasevich in small: There was a long-standing feud between poet and critic Georgy Adamovich, who ruled the literary sections of *Poslednie novosti*, and poet and critic Khodasevich, who wrote a literary column in Paris's rival émigré daily, *Vozrozhdenie*. Despite Adamovich's antipathy towards

VN too, he appears to have relished still more the chance to needle Khodasevich.

Ilyusha: Fondaminsky.

A. O.'s illness: Amalia Osipovna Fondaminsky died in 1935 of tuberculosis.

Kornilov's: Restaurant 'Chez Kornilov', 6, rue d'Armaillé, Paris 17.

Iv. Al.: Bunin.

how his six-year-old son died: Bunin married Anna Nikolaevna Tsakni (1879–1963) in Odessa in 1898. Their only son, Nikolay, died of meningitis at the age of five. In summer 1918, Bunin and his new, 'civil' wife Vera Nikolaevna Muromtsev (1881–1961; they married in 1922) left Moscow for Odessa, then occupied by Austrian troops. They did not flee in April 1919, when the Red Army approached the city, but stayed in Odessa and experienced the terror and starvation of the Civil War. After reaching France, Bunin recorded his Odessa experiences in *Okayannye dni* (*Cursed Days*) (Paris: Vozrozhdenie, 1926).

'Mitya Shakhovskoy' (Father Ioann) . . . Mitya's Love: *Mitina lyubov'* (*Mitya's Love*, 1924) tells the story of a young man's obsessive love for an actress; Katya's unfaithfulness and his own spiritual turmoil lead to Mitya's suicide. By 1936, Dmitry Alekseevich Shakhovskoy (Father Ioann), brother of Zinaida Shakhovskoy, had served for ten years as a Russian Orthodox priest in France and Germany; in May 1937 he would become archimandrite.

Letter postmarked 2 February 1936

Vlad. Mikh.'s: Vladimir Mikhaylovich Zenzinov's.

'yo, heave ho': '*Ey, ukhnem*', the song of the Volga boatmen, also known as 'Dubinushka' ('The Cudgel').

two 'Despairs': *Otchayanie* (Berlin: Petropolis, 1936).

Zina: Shakhovskoy.

Kalashnikov: Mikhail Kalashnikov, with whom VN first shared rooms at Trinity College, Cambridge, in 1919–20, then lodged with nearby until 1922. In 1921 Kalashnikov introduced VN to Svetlana Siewert, his cousin, who became VN's fiancée the next year. VN later felt uncomfortable at having been on friendly terms with someone he had come to think a philistine vulgarian.

Ira: Irina Kyandzhuntsev.

my film (Hôtel Magique): Never realized.

Shifrin: Semyon Savelievich Shifrin (1894–1985), engineer, producer, manager of France Libre film studio, co-owner of Grand Production Cinématographique, and from 1928 director of Sequana-film.

Matusevich's: Iosif Aleksandrovich Matusevich (1879–1940?), artist, writer and playwright; on editorial board of *Poslednie novosti*.

Igor: Possibly Igor Platonovich Demidov.

Fedotov: Georgy Petrovich Fedotov (1886–1951), historian, philosopher, translator and co-editor, with Stepun and Fondaminsky, of the Paris journal *Novyi Grad*.

Zeldoviches: Berta Grigorievna Zeldovich (1882–1943), translator.

the Dahls: Most likely, VN's four-volume set of *Tolkovyi slovar' zhivogo velikorusskogo yazyka* (*Explanatory Dictionary of the Living Great-Russian Language*, 1863–6, 1880), by Vladimir Ivanovich Dahl (1801–72).

Girshfeld: Unidentified.

Neskin: Unidentified.

Zyoka: Georgy Hessen.

the old man: Zyoka's father, Iosif Hessen.

Sarah: Sarah Yakovlevna Hessen, first wife of Georgy (Zyoka) Hessen.

Poplavsky's: Boris Yulianovich Poplavsky (1903–35), promising young poet, whose mysterious death from poisoning was much talked about. VN later reproached himself for 'the ill-tempered review in which I attacked him for trivial faults in his unfledged verse' (SM, p. 287).

'merde': Fr. 'shit'.

'It is me': One of several titles VN was considering for an autobiography he had written (recently?) in English. It remains unclear how much of its material he used for the autobiographical sketches he published in the late 1940s and early 1950s and integrated into *Conclusive Evidence* (in the US) and *Speak, Memory* (in the UK) in 1951.

Have you sent Despair: Apparently, the typescript of VN's English translation, to John Long (see letter of 4 February 1936).

Letter postmarked 3 February 1936

Kaplan's idiotic undertaking: His attempt to organize a Sirin reading in Eindhoven (see letter of 27 January 1936).

Raisa's: Added in VéN's later hand: 'Abr[amovna] Tatarinova (Tarr)'.

dédommagement: Fr. 'compensation' (for the cost of keeping him).

both critics: Presumably Georgy Adamovich at *Poslednie novosti* and Vladislav Khodasevich at *Vozrozhdenie*.

Felix: Unidentified.

Bobby: Count Robert de Calry, VN's friend at Cambridge.

the books of mine he'd read about in the N.Y. Times: *Camera Obscura* (in a review by Alexander Nazaroff, 'New Russian Books in Varied Fields', *New York Times Book Review*, 17 December 1933, pp. 8, 20) and *Despair* (in a review by Nazaroff, *New York Times Book Review*, 'Recent Books by Russian Writers', 18 August 1935, pp. 8, 18), both reviewed on the occasion of their serial appearance in *Sovremennye zapiski*.

Countess Grabbe: Countess Elizaveta Nikolaevna Grabbe (1893–1982), married in 1916 to Prince Sergey Sergeevich Beloselsky-Belozersky (1867–1982).

Tatyana: Tatyana Siewert, sister of Svetlana Siewert, VN's ex-fiancée, and Kalashnikov's cousin.

Claude Farrère: Frédéric-Charles Bargone, pen-name Claude Farrère (1876–1957), novelist, winner of the 1905 Prix Goncourt, but soon out of favour.

his wife: Olga Borisovna Margolin (1899?–1942), who in 1933 became Khodasevich's fourth wife.

Zaytsevs: Boris Konstantinovich Zaytsev and his wife Vera Alekseevna.

'Invitation': *Invitation to a Beheading*.

Il. Is.: Ilya Isidorovich Fondaminsky.

1) Russian Beauty . . . 3) Breaking the News: 'Krasavitsa' ('A Russian Beauty'), *Poslednie novosti*, 18 August 1934, p. 3; 'Sluchay iz zhizni' ('A Slice of Life'), *Poslednie novosti*, 22 September 1935, p. 3; 'Opoveshchenie' ('Breaking the News'), *Poslednie novosti*, 8 April 1934, p. 2; all appeared in *Sog*.

Denis: Roche.

the Khodasevich evening: The VN–Khodasevich double bill on 8 February.

Ilyusha: Fondaminsky.

Mother Maria: Elizaveta Yurievna Skobtsov (Pilenko, Kuzmin-Karavayev, Mother Maria), whom VN met in 1932.

A.O.: Amalia Osipovna Fondaminsky.

Zyoka: Georgy Hessen.

Vava's: Vladimir Iosifovich Hessen (1901–82), writer and memoirist, son of Iosif Hessen.

the old man: Iosif Hessen.

Letter postmarked 4 February 1936

translation: *Of Despair*.

Douglas: British novelist Norman Douglas (1868–1952), whose *South Wind* (1917) VN greatly admired.

Marcel: VN wrote in his later hand 'Gabriel' before 'Marcel' and 'the philosopher' after, indicating that this was a letter shown to Andrew Field in January 1971 as part of his research for *Nabokov: His Life in Part* (New York: Viking, 1977).

Alta Gracia: Altagracia de Jannelli, VN's American agent.

Raisa: Tatarinov.

B.G.: Berta Grigorievna Zeldovich.

Editeurs Réunis: Not the conglomerate of French publishers printing bestsellers, but the leading Russian bookstore in Paris, also a publisher.

Parchevsky: Konstantin Konstantinovich Parchevsky (1891–1945), lawyer, political commentator and journalist.

Berdyaev: Nikolay Aleksandrovich Berdyaev (1884–1978), philosopher.

Alfyorov: Anatoly Vladimirovich Alfyorov (1903–54), writer and literary critic.

Sofiev: Yury Borisovich Sofiev (1899–1975), poet.

Chichikov: Hero of *Myortvye dushi* (*Dead Souls* 1842), by Nikolay Vasilievich Gogol (1809–52).

Sharshun: Sergey Ivanovich Sharshun, pen-name V. Mirnyi (1888–1975), Dadaist artist and writer.

Yanovsky: Vasily Semyonovich Yanovsky (1906–89), writer and doctor.

Chervinsky: Lidiya Davydovna Chervinskaya (1907?–88), writer, poet and literary critic.

Hepner: Benno (Bruno) Pavlovich Hepner (1899–?), lawyer, historian and sociologist.

Pushkin's nanny: Arina Rodionovna Matveev (née Yakovlev, 1758–1828), of whom Pushkin was very fond and to whom he dedicated several poems.

Ilya: Fondaminsky.

'a thought once uttered is untrue': A line from Tyutchev's poem 'Silentium' (1830?), which VN translated into English in 1941–3, *V&V*, p. 237.

Letter postmarked 6 February 1936

faux air: False air.

alléché: Fr. 'enticed'.

by the epigraph to 'Invitation': Which, being in French, he could read: 'Comme un fou se croit Dieu, nous nous croyons mortels' ('As a madman believes he is God, we believe ourselves mortal'), attributed to the invented Pierre Delalande's *Discours sur les ombres* (*Discourse on Shades*).

that volume of Œuvres libres: *L'aguet: nouvelle inédite*, trans. Denis Roche, *Œuvres libres*, 164 (February 1935).

Sofa's: Sofia Slonim.

Nina's: Berberova's.

Plus belle – osait-on dire: Fr. 'Better looking – dare I say it'.

Chaikovsky: Pyotr Ilyich Chaikovsky (1840–93), Russian composer; Nina Berberova, *Chaikovsky, istoriya odinokoy zhizni* (*Chaikovsky, History of a Lonely Life*) (Berlin: Petropolis, 1936).

apres-midi: Afternoon.

Makeev: Nikolay Vasilievich Makeev (1889–1973), journalist, artist, philosopher, historian and member of the Socialist Revolutionary party.

Le Cerf: Ferdinand Le Cerf (1881–1945), leading French lepidopterist, at the Musée National d'Histoire Naturelle in Paris.

Chapman: Thomas Algernon Chapman (1842–1921), British physician, expert on butterfly biology.

Micropteryx: A family of very primitive moths with functional mandibles.

thing: VN has written *vest'*, 'news', but may have intended *veshch'*, 'thing'.

Ornithoptera: A genus of the Birdwing butterflies of India, Southeast Asia and Australia.

rumina: The papilionid butterfly *Zerynthia rumina*, the Spanish Festoon.

Melitaea: A genus of the Checkerspot butterflies Nymphalidae, a completely different family.

Parnassians: A genus of papilionid butterflies.

Kardakov in Dahlem: Kardakov became head of the Lepidoptera Section of the German Entomological Museum and Institute in Dahlem, southwest Berlin, in 1934.

Oberthür: Charles Oberthür (1845–1924), French lepidopterist, with whom Fyodor's father in *The Gift* is said to have worked.

Sarah: Hessen.

the old man: Iosif Hessen.

Haskell: Arnold Haskell (1903–80), ballet and theatre critic.

Gubsky: Nikolay Mikhaylovich Gubsky (1889?–1971), writer.

Malcolm Burr: Writer, translator, entomologist (1878–1954).

Galina: Galina Nikolaevna Petrov (née Kuznetsov, 1900–1976), poet, translator, memoirist and Bunin's mistress. From 1927 to 1942, she lived from time to time with the Bunins in Grasse, in the Alpes Maritimes.

Kolomeytsevs: The family of VN's Aunt Nina.

Grunelius: Possibly Alexandre Grunelius. VN and VéN spent a vacation with Nicolas and Nathalie Nabokov at the home of the Gruneliuses in Kolbsheim in 1932.

au courant: Fr. 'up to date'.

Léon: Pavel (Paul) Leopoldovich Léon (1893–1942), lawyer, historian of literature and James Joyce's secretary; husband of Lucie (Elizaveta Matveevna) Léon Noel (née Ponizovsky, 1900–1972), the sister of Aleksandr Matveevich Ponizovsky (?–1943), VN's friend at Cambridge. In 1939, Lucie Léon Noel would help VN copy-edit his first novel in English, *The Real Life of Sebastian Knight*.

Letter postmarked 8 February 1936

Lyusya: Ilya Feigin.

Anyutochka: Anna Feigin.

just like in Marseilles: The assassination of King Alexander I of Yugoslavia (1888–1934), on 9 October 1934 in Marseilles. Alexander's son Prince Peter (1923–70) inherited the throne when he was nine years old. The regency was established, with King Alexander's cousin, Prince Paul of Yugoslavia, serving as a regent from 1934 to 1941. The heir seized the throne after a coup d'état, becoming King Peter II of Yugoslavia.

et tout ce qui . . . : Fr. 'and all that follows from that'.

Zyoka: Georgy Hessen, now living in Paris but visiting Berlin.

N.R.F.: *Nouvelle Revue Française*.

Slonim's: Mark Slonim, who ran an agency for placing books by Russian writers in translation. See letter of 22 November 1932.

Wallace: Unidentified.

Melo du d'y: Robert Mélot du Dy (1891–1956), Belgian poet and prose writer, a colleague of Hellens.

Mme Bataud: Unidentified.

Zen-Zin and Nikolay: Fondaminsky's cats.

Elena Aleksandrovna: Possibly Elena Aleksandrovna Peltser (née Kovalyov, 1898–1983), a good acquaintance of the Fondaminskys. VN dictated some of his work to her in April 1937.

The old man . . . his memoirs: Not published in fact until long after his death: I. V. Hessen, *Gody izgnaniya: Zhiznennyi otchyot* (*Years of Exile: A Life Record*) (Paris: YMCA, 1981).

Letter postmarked 10 February 1936

'Despair': The typescript of VN's translation into English.

Gleb: Struve.

The evening itself: A Sirin–Khodasevich double bill, 5 rue Las Cases, 8 February 1936.

a charming thing – a subtle concoction: Khodasevich read 'Zhizn' Vasiliya Travnikova' ('The Life of Vasily Travnikov'), a literary hoax, dedicated to the life and poetry of an invented early nineteenth-century Russian poet. The essay was published in *Vozrozhdenie*, 13, 20, 27 February 1936.

qui m'a fait . . . : Fr. 'who gave me a pederast's compliment'.

The old man: Iosif Hessen.

Miten'ka's: DN's.

Vladislav: Khodasevich.

Nina: Berberova.

Ça m'a fait rêver: Fr. 'It felt like I was dreaming'.

give him your ring: Aldanov, calling on Bunin, refers to the story of the leading eighteenth-century Russian poet, Derzhavin, welcoming Pushkin in 1815 as the next great Russian poet. According to a popular legend, Pushkin, who read a poem in Derzhavin's honour and in his presence at a public exam in his school, the Lyceum, received a ring from the old man. In his own account Pushkin does not mention the ring ('Derzhavin', 1835–6).

Pole: Khodasevich's father was Polish.

La Skaz: The reading took place in a hall on rue Las Cases; perhaps a pun on Russian *skaz*, 'tale'.

'sans rancune': Fr. 'without bitterness'.

the old man: Iosif Hessen.

Denis: Roche.

Lolly: Possibly Lolly Lvov.

Heath: A. M. Heath and Co., authors' agents in London.

Berta: Zeldovich.

Anna: Unidentified.

Letter postmarked 13 February 1936

au plus tard: Fr. 'at the latest'.

ten Belgian Semyonlyudvigoviches each: Decoded, this means 'at ten Belgian francs apiece'.

Grigory Abramovich: VN invents this new character to report to VéN in coded form about his own earnings abroad.

Doussia: Ergaz.

du Boz: Du Bos.

'Society of Northerners': The most influential Russian émigré cultural group in England (full title, 'Society of Northerners and Siberians of Great Britain'), founded in 1926. It published the newspaper *Russians in England*, in which Gleb Struve's article on Sirin would appear on 15 May 1936 ('O V. Sirine', *Russkie v Anglii*, p. 3).

'Despair': The typescript of the translation into English.

tu vas te tuer, Edmond: Fr. 'you're going to kill yourself, Edmond'.

Berta Grigor.'s: Zeldovich.

Varshavsky: Vladimir Varshavsky.

Stendhal: pen-name of Marie-Henri Beyle (1783–1842), French novelist whom VN did not care for.

'Pilgram': 'The Aurelian'.

Campaux: Mark Slonim's ex-wife Suzanne Campaux (1904–?).

Vava: Vladimir Hessen.

the old man: Iosif Hessen, who lived in Berlin.

Falkovsky: The lawyer and journalist Evgeny Falkovsky, whom VN had met in Berlin in the 1920s. In 1938, Falkovsky moved to Paris, where he served on the Russian Émigré Committee, chaired by Vasily Maklakov.

Shifr.: Shifrin. Nothing of these appears to have survived.

Nina: VN has absentmindedly written 'Kita'.

Aguet: *The Eye* in French.

Eva!: Eva Efimovna Lutyens (née Lubrzynska (Lubryjinska), 1894–1963), VN's girlfriend in St Petersburg in 1917 and London in 1919.

Letter postmarked 17 February 1936

S. Ridel: Unidentified.

Stock: French publishing firm, founded in Paris in 1708.

'Pilgram' and 'Aguet': French versions of 'The Aurelian' and 'The Eye'.

the king: Belgian King Leopold III (1901–83), amateur entomologist, reigned from 1934 until his abdication in 1951.

the Club: The Russian Jewish Club, 65 rue de la Concorde, Brussels.

Elle est plus . . . : Fr. 'She's more of an angel than ever'.

very hard . . . to write on this paper: The ink shows through badly from the other side.

Grishen'ka: Grigory Abramovich, VN's alias.

Letter postmarked 19 February 1936

the novel will have a different name: VN had planned to call his novel *Da* (*Yes*); adding the letter 'r' turned it into *Dar* (*The Gift*). He began researching the novel in 1932 and completed its composition in January 1938. *The Gift*, except for Ch. 4, was serialized in *Sovremennye zapiski*, 63–7 (1937–8). Its first book form and first full text was *Dar* (New York: Chekhov Publishing House, 1952); trans. Michael Scammell and DN with VN, *The Gift* (New York: Putnam, 1963).

Zinochka's: Zinaida Shakhovskoy.

Grigory Abramovich: VN's alias.

has left the excess with her . . . : Decoded: VN left some of his earnings with Zinaida Shakhovskoy, without telling his brother about this.

Shik: Aleksandr Adolfovich Shik (1887–1968), lawyer, journalist and translator.

mon premier movement: Fr. 'my first impulse'.

'Glory': *Podvig* (*Glory*) (Paris: Sovremennye Zapiski, 1932).

'Naif': 'By Hellens' added in VéN's hand, indicating this was a letter shown to Andrew Field in January 1971 for his *Nabokov: His Life in Part*. Franz Hellens, *Le naïf* (Paris: Éditions Émile-Paul, 1926).

'fente' . . . 'barre lumineuse' . . . 'perche lumineuse': Fr. 'chink', 'bar of light', 'pole of light' ('Mademoiselle O', *Mesures*, 15 April 1936, p. 161).

Brunst: Apparently, the married name of Irina Kyandzhuntsev (who later became Irina Komarov).

Hellin: Unidentified.

'Arme Dichter': Carl Spitzweg (1808–85), *Der arme Dichter* (*'The Poor Poet'*, 1839), Neue Pinakothek, Munich.

au fond: Fr. 'after all'.

Balmont: Konstantin Dmitrievich Balmont (1867–1942), prominent Symbolist poet, translator, literary scholar and memoirist.

'cochons': Fr. 'pigs'.

Letter postmarked 21 February 1936

Rabinovich: Unidentified.

Ira: Irina Kyandzhuntsev.

~~Sofa~~: Thickly crossed out, like the two later references, in VéN's later hand.

Elizaveta Samoylovna: Elizaveta Samoylovna Kyandzhuntsev, Savely's mother.

Ratner: Unidentified.

Katherine Berlin: Ekaterina Leopoldovna Berling (née Leon), a former girlfriend of VN's. See next letter.

Ald. and Zayts.: Aldanov and Boris Zaytsev.

Küfferle: Rinaldo Küfferle (1903–55), writer (including a novel about the Russian emigration, *Ex Russia*, 1935), essayist and translator from the Russian.

Mme Kokoshkin's: Vera Evgenievna Kokoshkin (1879–1968), first marriage to Yury Ivanovich Guadanini (?–1911); second marriage to Vladimir Fyodorovich Kokoshkin (1874–1926), youngest brother of the prominent member of the

Constitutional Democratic party, Fyodor Fyodorovich Kokoshkin (1871–1918), who was an acquaintance of VDN.

Kyandzhun.: Kyandzhuntsevs.

the old man: Iosif Hessen.

'*P. N.*': *Poslednie novosti*.

Letter postmarked 24 February 1936

my passport: VN and VéN each had a 'Nansen passport', an identity card issued to stateless refugees by the League of Nations; a sheet of paper folded in half, it could easily tear.

'*c'est avec ça . . .*': Fr. '*That's* what you travel with?'

the American one: Possibly Bobbs-Merrill, with whom VN would sign a contract for *Laughter in the Dark*, his reworking of *Kamera obskura*, in September 1937.

Matveev: Unidentified.

McBride's: Unidentified.

Aristarkhov: Otherwise unidentified.

Kokoshkins: Vera Kokoshkin and her daughter Irina Yurievna Guadanini, pen-name Aletrus (1905–76), a poet, who lived with her mother and earned an income as a dog-groomer. In the first half of 1937 Nabokov would have an affair with Irina.

Pushkin . . . he began to look like him: Khodasevich was a Pushkin scholar as well as a poet very much inspired by Pushkin's clarity and command of form.

Léon's: Paul Léon, Joyce's secretary, and his wife Lucie Léon Noel.

Girshman: Henrietta (Evgeniya) Leopoldovna Girshman (née Léon, 1885–1970), collector, artist and wife of art collector Vladimir Osipovich Girshman (1867–1936).

Ekaterina: Ekaterina Berling (the 'Katherine Berlin' of the previous letter), sister of Henrietta Girshman.

creaming at the pot of his Joyce: Screaming at the top of his voice; becoming over-rich (turning to cream, or floating like cream) in his Joycean word-pail. VN parodies Joyce's *Work in Progress*, the working title of the advance portions of *Finnegans Wake*.

aurait chaud: Fr. 'it would be warm'. VN puns on the sound of the Russian proverb 'Kuy zhelezo poka goryacho' ('Strike the iron while is hot'). *Aurait chaud* vaguely resembles *goryacho* in sound and sense, but sounds still more like Russian *khorosho*, 'good' or 'nice'.

les honneurs du Métro: Fr. 'the honours of the metro' (instead of the usual *les honneurs de la maison*, 'the honours of the house').

Postcard postmarked 26 February 1936

Date: Postmark not fully legible ('26-[II?]-36') but sequence and the 'stay here for two more days, that is will leave on Friday' suggest the letter was written on Wednesday 26 February.

matinée: At Mme Ridel's, 12 Quai de Passy.

'*Désespoir*': The French version of *Despair*, trans. Marcel Stora, would in fact be entitled *La Méprise* and be published by Gallimard, but not until 1939.

Grigory Abramovich has topped the previous trip: Meaning that VN has earned more than on his last trip.

An. Nat.: Anna Natanovna. Unidentified.

Letter of 27 February 1936

Date: No envelope. VéN later dated the first page '26? Febr 36', but since the letter was written on a Thursday, it must be 27 February 1936.

Cook: Thomas Cook, the travel agency.

~~*Sofa*~~: See VN's letter of 21 February, where the same name is similarly crossed out.

Raisa: Tatarinov.

overboard: Since *za* can be both 'for' and 'over', *za bort* puns: she obtained money for Sofia Slonim to pay 'for [room and] board' but was then thrown out, 'overboard'.

Irina's: Kyandzhuntsev.

Vera Nikolaevna: Muromtsev-Bunin.

tout compris: Fr. 'altogether'.

Teffi: Nadezhda Aleksandrovna Buchinsky (née Lokhvitsky), pen-name Teffi (1872–1952), popular writer of humorous, satirical fiction.

definitely wants 'Chernyshevsky' for the next issue: In fact Rudnev would turn down the 'Life of Chernyshevsky', Ch. 4 of *The Gift*, considering it an insult to Russia's radical intelligentsia and one of its idols, the writer Nikolay Gavrilovich Chernyshevsky (1828–89).

Poncet: André François-Poncet (1887–1978), French ambassador to Germany (1931–1938).

Stray Dog: 'Brodyachaya sobaka', cabaret in St Petersburg, a meeting place of artists and writers from 1911 to 1915.

Postcard postmarked 10 June 1936

Fid. Com.: Fiduciary Committee of the Supreme Court (Fideikommisssenat des Kammergerichts) responsible for setting the inheritance from the Graun estate that VN unexpectedly received in the summer of 1936.

Weidle's article about me: Review, 'Otchayanie. Berlin: Izd. Petropolis', *Krug* (*The Circle*), 1 (July) 1936, pp. 185–7.

Elena Lvovna: Elena Lvovna Bromberg, Anna Feigin's cousin.

Postcard postmarked 11 June 1936

'. . . this book . . .': *Despair*.

'. . . the translation that the American publishers used?': The translation was VN's own, and he had not sent it to an American publisher, let alone had it published there.

Nina P.: Nina Alekseevna Korvin-Piotrovsky (née Kaplun, 1906–75), wife of Vladimir Lvovich Korvin-Piotrovsky (1891–1966), poet, playwright and member, with VN, of the Poets' Club (1928–33).

French Verkehr Society: society for Franco-German Exchange.

Zhdanov: Georgy Semyonovich Zhdanov (1905–98), actor and director, closely associated with theatre director Mikhail Chekhov.

the manuscript: Unidentified. No evidence suggests Nabokov wrote any dramatic work between *Chelovek iz SSSR* (*The Man from the USSR*) in 1926 and *Sobytie* (*The Event*) in 1937. Perhaps a prose fiction that offered dramatic possibilities?

composing a play and slept terribly: Possibly the first inklings of what would become *Sobytie*; although he did not write this play until November–December 1937, he could talk over his plans with actors in January 1937 (see letter of 25 January 1937).

can imagine what kind of 'readers' they have: John Long Ltd had a strong detective fiction list.

Postcard postmarked 12 June 1936

F.: Presumably Fierens.

Aksyonov's: Unidentified.

princess Sh.: Anna Leonidovna Shakhovskoy (née von Knienen, 1872–1963), mother of Zinaida Shakhovskoy and Nathalie Nabokov.

Adamovich's review of 'The Cave': 'Po povodu "Peshchery"' ('On the Occasion of "The Cave"'), *Poslednie novosti*, 28 May 1936, p. 2.

M. A.: Mark Aldanov or Mark Aleksandrovich [Aldanov]; Mark Aldanov, *Peshchera* (*The Cave*) (vol. 1, Berlin: Slovo, 1934; vol. 2, Berlin: Petropolis, 1936).

Postcard of 13(?) June 1936

Date: Stamp removed and postmark date therefore absent.

another article . . . from Gleb: Gleb Struve, 'O V. Sirine' ('On V. Sirin'), *Russkie v Anglii* (*Russians in England*), 15 May 1936, p. 3.

K.: Kirill Nabokov.

Nika's mother: Lydia Eduardovna Falz-Fein (1870–1937).

Postcard of 14(?) June 1936

Date: Undated, postmark illegible.

letter: Something is crossed out, probably by VN as he writes.

Mme Piotrovsky: Nina Korvin-Piotrovsky.

Gertruda: Unidentified.

Postcard postmarked 15 June 1936

the forest: Grunewald.

Hes.'s: Hessen's.

caca-o: Instead of *kakao* (cocoa), VN writes *kakoe*.

'Ruhe!': Ger. 'Quiet!'

Postcard postmarked 16 June 1936

passionate plea to write for them on 'The Cave': VN obliged: 'M. A. Aldanov. Peshchera. Tom II. Izd. Petropolis. Berlin. 1936' ('M. A. Aldanov. The Cave. Vol. II. Petropolis Press. Berlin, 1936'), *Sovremennye zapiski*, 61 (1936), pp. 470–72.

The old man: Iosif Hessen.

Truda: The Gertruda of the 14(?) June 1936 letter.

1937

Postcard postmarked 20 January 1937

Pendant que l'avoine . . . : Fr. 'While the oats grow, the horse will die.'

Letter of 22 January 1937

The French evening: VN read on 21 January at the Brussels Palais des Beaux-Arts, at an evening commemorating the hundreth anniversary of Pushkin's death.

de Rieux: Paul de Reul, author of *L'Œuvre de D. H. Lawrence* (Paris: Vrin, 1937).

Lawrence, – not the colonel . . . : In other words, novelist D. H. Lawrence (1885–1930) (*Sons and Lovers*, 1913; *Lady Chatterley's Lover*, 1928), not autobiographer Lieutenant-Colonel T. E. Lawrence ('of Arabia', 1888–1935).

qu'il n'aurait jamais cru: Fr. 'that he would never have believed'.

l'étoile . . . : Fr. 'the star is no longer there because the water ripples'.

Victor: Another invented proxy VN uses to camouflage references to his earnings abroad. VN reports he was almost baptized 'Victor' by a priest who misheard his parents, so that at the ceremony he was a 'howling, half-drowned half-Victor' (SM, p. 21).

Eleonora: Leonora Peltenburg.

Aleksandra Lazarevna's mysterious hint (about the gift): Apparently another veiled message about money, with Anna Lazarevna Feigin disguised as Aleksandra Lazarevna.

Sergey and Anna: VN's cousin, Sergey Sergeevich Nabokov, and his wife Anna.

Niki: Their son Nicolas.

Margarita: Wife of Jacques Masui.

Kir.: Kirill Nabokov.

'l'outrage': His story 'Obida' ('A Bad Day'). No published 1930s translation into French located.

the lecture: 'Pouchkine, ou le vrai et le vraisemblable', *Nouvelle Revue Française*, 48 (1937), pp. 362–78; 'Pushkin, or the Real and the Plausible', trans. DN, *New York Review of Books*, 31 March 1988, pp. 38–42.

my Greek: His psoriasis – as if it were a character in Greek tragedy.

ou presque: Fr. 'or almost'.

Zina . . . and Svetik and Svyat. Adr.: Zinaida Shakhovskoy, her husband Svyatoslav Malevsky-Malevich, and her father-in-law, Svyatoslav Andreevich Malevsky-Malevich.

Victor settled his accounts . . . : Veiled talk about money: decoded, VN paid back Zinaida Shakhovskoy and paid for Kirill's identity card.

'Mesures': Where 'Mademoiselle O' had been published.

Turovets: Unidentified.

Letter postmarked 25 January 1937

Russian reading: Solo 'Sirin' reading, 5 rue Las Cases. VN read parts of Ch. 1 of *The Gift*, dealing with the suicide of Yasha Chernyshevsky and a literary meeting at the Chernyshevskys' where Hermann Ivanovich Bush reads his vacuously pretentious play in broken Russian.

'the devices live and work': See Vl[adimir] Khodasevich, 'O Sirine', *Vozrozhdenie*, 13 February 1937, p. 9; trans. Simon Karlinsky and Robert Hughes, 'On Sirin', *TriQuarterly* (Evanston, Ill.), Winter 1970, pp. 96–101.

Mme Morevsky: Unidentified.

On est très, très gentil avec moi: Fr. 'People are very, very nice to me'.

Maklakov's: As chair of the Russian Émigré Committee, Maklakov could help VN obtain a French residence permit.

the English galleys: *Of Despair* (London: John Long, 1937).

'Tair': VN offered 'Tair' *The Defence*, but they wanted to take *The Gift* instead: see letter of 19 February 1937. The publication never occurred.

Lol.: Lolly.

the old man's: Iosif Hessen's.

P. N.: *Poslednie novosti* or perhaps its editor, P. N. Milyukov. VN wanted to sign a contract with the newspaper to write for it on a regular basis.

Boulogne: The Bois de Boulogne district in the West of Paris.

'Fialta': Short story 'Vesna v Fial'te' ('Spring in Fialta'), written April 1936, published *Sovremennye zapiski*, 61 (1936), pp. 91–113.

Sablin's: Evgeny Vasilievich Sablin (1875–1949), diplomat, Russian chargé d'affaires in London (1919–1921). In 1915, as First Secretary of the Russian embassy, he served under K. D. Nabokov, VN's uncle.

with Ilyusha's actors about the play: The actors of the Russian Theatre, sponsored by Ilya Fondaminsky. The play may be *Sobytie* (*The Event*), written by VN for the Russian Theatre, although indications in May are that the play he has been writing has not gone well and he may be abandoning whatever concept he was working on.

the old man's: Iosif Hessen's.

Jeanne: Fondaminsky's housekeeper.

'mon pauvre petit martyr!': Fr. 'my poor little martyr'.

Letter postmarked 27 [January] 1937

Pavel's: Milyukov's.

Calmbrood: Vivian Calmbrood, a near-anagrammatic literary alias that VN first used when he published the play *Skitaltsy* (*The Wanderers*) as a translation of the invented Calmbrood's work. He revived the name in 1931, 'Iz Kalmbrudovoi poemy "Nochnoe puteshestvie"' ('From Calmbrood's Long Poem "The Night Journey"'), *Rul'*, 5 July 1931; *Stikhi*. Here VN uses the name as another decoy when he reports his earnings.

both things: The Pushkin talk, 'Pouchkine, ou le vrai et le vraisemblable', and the French translation, 'L'Outrage', of the story 'Obida' ('A Bad Day').

Victor: Again VN refers to himself.

a meeting of Christians and poets: Perhaps a meeting of *Novyi grad* (*The New City*, 1931–9), a philosophico-religious journal edited by Fondaminsky, Fyodor Stepun and Georgy Fedotov.

Georg. Ivan.: Georgy Ivanov.

Boris Brodsky: Boris Yakovlevich Brodsky (1901–51?), journalist.

Mamchenko: Victor Andreevich Mamchenko (1901–82), poet, one of the organizers of the Union of Young Poets and Writers.

Tsetlin: Mikhail Osipovich Tsetlin, pen-name Amari (1882–1945), writer, poet, literary critic, editor and publisher, poetry editor at *Sovremennye zapiski*.

Gaston Gallimard: French publisher (1881–1975), founded *Nouvelle Revue Française* in 1908 and the publishing house Librairie Gallimard in 1919.

see Lyusya and give it to him: VN will leave his earnings with Anna Feigin's cousin Ilya Feigin.

précipité blanc: Fr. 'white precipitate'.

Mme Sablin: Nadezhda Ivanovna Sablin (née Bazhenov, 1892–1966), wife of Evgeny Sablin. VN errs in saying her maiden name was Fomin. Yurik is VN's cousin, Georgy (Yury) Rausch von Traubenberg.

Gogel's sister: Actually the sister of S. K. Gogel's wife, Aleksandra Ivanovna (née Bazhenov). Sergey Gogel took part with VN in the 1926 mock 'Pozdnyshev Trial' in Berlin.

review from a Belgian newspaper: R. D[upierreux], 'Conférence de M. Nabokoff-Sirine', *Le Soir*, 23 January 1937.

Letter postmarked 28 January 1937

Outrage: French 'Obida' ('A Bad Day'). It would be accepted by *Mesures* for its May 1937 issue (see letter of 15 April 1937) but apparently would not be published there either.

'délicieux, merveilleux, convaincant': Fr. 'delicious, marvellous, convincing'.

P. N.: Pavel Nikolaevich Milyukov.

Victor: VN refers to himself.

N. M. Rodzyanko's: Nikolay Mikhaylovich Rodzyanko (1888–1941), former General Secretary of the Russian Émigré Committee, chair of the labour department of the Central Russian Office in Paris, and son of Mikhail Rodzyanko, a politician and colleague of VDN.

permis de séjour: Fr. 'residence permit'.

Ald.'s very nice article: Mark Aldanov, 'Vechera "Sovremennykh Zapisok"', *Poslednie novosti*, 28 January 1937, p. 3.

M.'s : Mme Morevsky's.

injections: For his psoriasis.

Letter postmarked 1 February 1937

Molly: Molly Carpenter-Lee (1911–after 1973), one of Gleb Struve's best students, who would help check VN's translation of *Despair* into English.

conférence: Fr. 'lecture', 'talk': 'Pouchkine, ou le vrai et le vraisemblable.'

'*envolée*': Fr. 'lift', 'take-off.'

Melo du Dy: Robert Mélot du Dy. The essay included translations of several Pushkin poems: 'Dans le désert du monde' ('Tri klyucha', 'Three Springs'); 'Ne me les chante pas, ma belle' ('Ne poy, krasavitsa, pri mne', 'My beauty, do not sing for me'); 'Je ne puis m'endormir' ('Mne ne spitsya, net ognya', 'I cannot sleep, the light is out'); 'Pourquoi le vent troublant la plaine' ('Zachem krutitsya vetr v ovrage', 'Why does the wind swirl in a ravine'), *Nouvelle Revue Française*, 1 March 1937, 25 (282), pp. 362–78.

Bernstein: Presumably chess grandmaster Osip Samoylovich Bernstein (1882–1962).

Rashel's: Unidentified.

Vlad. Mikh.: Vladimir Mikhaylovich Zenzinov.

haircuts to dogs: Irina Guadanini earned a living as a dog-groomer.

Ald.: Aldanov.

Roshchin: Nikolay Yakovlevich Fyodorov, pen-name Roshchin (1896–1956), writer, journalist and literary critic, lived with the Bunins from the mid-1920s to the 1940s.

Polyakov: Aleksandr Polyakov, deputy editor of *Poslednie novosti*.

Gen. Golovin's: General Nikolay Nikolaevich Golovin (1875–1944), military historian and writer.

Victor: VN refers to himself.

Chokhaev: Mustafa Chokaev (1890–1941), before the Revolution lawyer and journalist, secretary of the Muslim Faction at the State Duma, worked in Paris as proofreader at *Poslednie novosti*.

told me all I needed: VN was checking his account of his character Konstantin Godunov-Cherdyntsev's apparently fatal last lepidopterological expedition to Central Asia, in *The Gift*, Ch. 2.

Kanegisser's: Leonid Ioakimovich Kannegiser (1896–1918), amateur poet and member of the Party of People's Socialists; he killed Moisey Uritsky (1873–1918), head of the Petrograd Cheka (security police), for which he was shot.

sister's: Elizaveta (Lulu) Ioakimovna Kannegiser.

mentioning this name . . . a terrible gaffe: In the serial version of *The Gift*, VN characterized Yasha Chernyshevsky's poetry, 'replete with fashionable clichés', as 'a mixture of Lensky and Kannegiser' (Lensky, in Pushkin's *Eugene Onegin*, is a mediocre Romantic poet) (*Sovremennye zapiski*, 63 (1937), p. 45). In the eyes of many, VN sullied the memory of Kannegiser, a man whose self-sacrifice was much admired by the Russian emigration. In the later book versions of the novel (*Dar*, p. 46; *The Gift*, p. 50), he cut 'a mixture of Lensky and Kannegiser'.

K.Q.K.: *King, Queen, Knave*.

for the work of Godun. Cherd., K. K., about butterflies: Although VN did not get Konstantin Kirillovich Godunov-Cherdyntsev to write this essay, he would think of doing so himself in the late 1940s ('A very interesting piece might be written on the whole subject (with illustrations) about butterflies in art beginning with the species figured in 1420–1375 B.C. by an Egyptian under Tuthmosis IV or Amenophis III (British Museum no. 37933). I am a pioneer in this subject,' letter to George Davis, 10 November 1949, in *N'sBs*, p. 449), and would start a projected *Butterflies in Art* in the mid-1960s.

the Greek: Psoriasis.

'Sali[t] énormément le linge': Fr. 'soils linen terribly'.

Dynkin: The Fondaminskys' family doctor.

Victor: VN's alias for fiscal matters.

two reviews: Of VN's readings on 21 and 24 January. Not in the archive. Probably M. (Yury Mandelstam), 'Vecher V. V. Sirina' ('V. V. Sirin Evening'), *Vozrozhdenie*, 30 January 1937, p. 9; and possibly G. Fischer, 'Un écrivain russe parle de Pouchkine' ('A Russian Writer Speaks on Pushkin'), *Le Thyrse*, 34, 1937, p. 41.

The old man: Iosif Hessen.

the first chapter: Of *The Gift*.

Letter postmarked 4 February 1937

Ger. Abr.: Misspelled Grig[ory] Abr[amovich], one of VN's decoy aliases.

Cortn.: Fritz Kortner (1892–1970), actor, film and theatre director, with whom VN discussed a film based on *Camera Obscura*.

conférence: Fr. 'lecture' or 'talk': 'Pouchkine, ou le vrai et le vraisemblable'.

Struve: Gleb Struve.

Grinberg: Savely Isaakovich Grinberg, VN's former Tenishev schoolmate.

Mme Gavronsky: Lyubov' Sergeevna Gavronsky (1876–1943), widow of Boris Osipovich Gavronsky (1875–1932), elder brother of Amalia Fondaminsky.

Mme Chernavin: Tatyana Vasilievna Chernavin (née Sapozhnikov, 1890–1971), museum curator, formerly with the Hermitage Museum. In 1932, she was able to flee from the USSR, after helping her husband escape from the Gulag.

Antonini's: Giacomo Antonini (1901–83), journalist and literary critic, who had reviewed *La Course du fou* and *Chambre Obscure* in 'Russische Romans 1934', *Den Gulden Winkel*, December 1934.

the contract with Long: The contract for the English *Despair*.

Victor: VN refers to himself; since he deposited most of his earned income with Ilya (Lyusya) Feigin, 'writing' for Lyusya means making more money.

Rochebrune, cap. St Martin: He means Roquebrune-Cap-Martin, between Monaco and Menton, as a place for them to settle.

On me fête . . . : Fr. 'They make a great deal of me'.

De-Monza: Anatole de Monzie (1876–1947), former Minister of Education and Fine Arts; from 1935, President of the Committee for the Publication of the French Encyclopaedia.

Navashin's: Dmitry Sergeevich Navashin (1889–1937), lawyer, financier, writer, journalist and mason; worked in Soviet banks in Paris, absconded in 1931, and was killed under unresolved circumstances in the Bois de Boulogne.

'*il y a cent ans* . . . ': Fr. 'A hundred years ago, Pushkin was killed . . . Now Navashin has been killed.'

Mme Chardonne's: Wife of Jacques Boutelleau (1884–1968), pen-name Jacques Chardonne, French writer, who won the Grand Prix of the Académie Française in 1932 for his novel *Claire*.

Jeanne: Fondaminsky's housekeeper.

Letter postmarked 5 February 1937

Bonnier: Swedish publishing group based in Stockholm. Nabokov's *Zashchita Luzhina* (*The Defence*) had been published by Bonniers in 1936, as *Han som spelade schack med livet* (*He Who Plays Chess with Life*), trans. Ellen Rydelius.

Mercure: The literary magazine *Mercure de France*.

Tair: See letter of 3 November 1932 and note.

Maurois: As well as novels, André Maurois wrote fictionalized biographies, including *Don Juan ou la vie de Byron* (1930), of the type VN scorned in his 'Pouchkine, ou le vrai et le vraisemblable'.

'mon grand ami . . .': Fr. 'unfortunately my great friend Maurois wasn't able to come'.

the whole paragraph about 'Byron': Presumably paragraph three, where VN writes of a madman he knew (read: invented), who thinks he was present at many moments in the distant past, a past constructed in his imagination only from the banalities he has read: commonplaces like 'Byron's melancholy, plus a certain number of those so-called historical anecdotes historians use to sweeten their texts, provided, alas, all the detail and colour he needed' ('Pushkin, or the Real and the Plausible', trans. DN, *New York Review of Books*, 31 March 1988, p. 39; 'Pouchkine, ou le vrai et le vraisemblable', p. 363). The next two paragraphs directly attack *biographies romancées*, 'fictionalized biographies'.

un mot demain: Fr. 'a word tomorrow'.

Shvarts: A doctor VéN recommended.

tout compris: Fr. 'all included'.

Mme Schlesinger: Fanni Samoylovna Schlesinger (?–1959), co-founder of the Friends of Russian Writers committee, chaired by Bunin, which provided material assistance to writers.

'écrivain' . . . tout court: Fr. 'writer'; 'plain'. Presumably business cards for VN.

Lyusya has amassed: VN refers to his earnings kept at Ilya Feigin's, 'butterflies' here meaning 'francs'.

Old man Paul: Pavel Milyukov.

c'est toujours . . . : Fr. 'it's still something'.

to the old man: Iosif Hessen.

El. Lvovna: Elena Lvovna Bromberg.

Lisbeth: Lisbet Thompson.

Au fond: Fr. 'after all', 'fundamentally', here 'when it comes down to it'.

aller et retour: Fr. 'a round trip'.

Ksyunin: Aleksey Ivanovich Ksyunin (1880?–1938), journalist, writer and publisher of the Belgrade weekly newspaper *Vozrozhdenie* (*Resurrection*), not to be confused with the Paris daily of the same name.

Belgr.: Belgrade.
Victor: VN's alias.

Letter of 8 February 1937

[8 February 1937]: Undated, no envelope. The references to the dinner at the Tsetlins' in this letter and in that of 10 February confirm that this was written on 8 February.
my French reading: At the Salle Chopin, 11 February. Gabriel Marcel had suggested that VN replace Hungarian writer Jolán Földes (1902–63), who had fallen ill at a late hour, in the Feux Croisés lecture series he organized.
my 'Course' and 'Chambre': *The Defence* and *Camera Obscura* in French.
much-talked-about Hungarian writer: Jolán Földes's 1936 novel, *A halászó macska utcája*, in French *La Rue du Chat-qui-pêche* (*The Street of the Fishing Cat*), after the name of Paris's shortest street, had been a prize-winning international success.
Plevitskaya: Nadezhda Vasilievna Plevitskaya, née Vinnikova (1884–1940), popular singer of Russian folk songs.
Vlad. Mikh.: Zenzinov.
'you have made him loathsome': VN's 'Life of Chernyshevsky' mockingly depicts the Russian liberal thinker and philosopher Nikolay Chernyshevsky as a would-be grand reformer who was at the same time inept at coping even with his own life, and a committed realist who was unable to see or understand the concrete world around him.
Pereverzev: Pavel Nikolaevich Pereverzev (1871–1944), lawyer, in Russia a Socialist Revolutionary member of the Fourth State Duma.
Etingons: Possibly Max Eitingon (Mark Efimovich (Yakovlevich), 1881–1943), Russian-born psychiatrist, and his wife Mira Yakovlevna (née Burovsky, 1877–1947), actress. Khodasevich mentions 'Eitingons' in his 'Chamber-Courier's Journal' (record of 24 January 1937).
old man Pol!: Pavel Milyukov.
Je n'en reviens pas: Fr. 'I can't get over it'.
Mme Adamov: Nadezhda Konstantinovna Adamov, doctor of medicine, whom VN had seen in 1932.
Autrement: Fr. 'otherwise'.

a few more journals: In fact, money for safe-keeping.

Isr. Kogan: Israel Cohen or Kogan, unidentified.

'The Passenger' and 'Chorb' (in Struve's translations): 'Passazhir', *Rul'*, 6 March 1927, and in *VC*, 1930; trans. Gleb Struve, 'The Passenger', *Lovat Dickson's Magazine*, 2: 6 (June 1934), pp. 719–25; 'Vozvrashchenie Chorba' ('The Return of Chorb'), *Rul'*, 12 November 1925, pp. 2–3 and 13 November 1925, pp. 2–3, and in *VC*; trans. Gleb Struve, 'The Return of Tchorb', *This Quarter*, 4:4 (June 1932).

the review from the N. Y. Times: Al. Nazaroff, 'Recent Books by Russian Writers', *New York Times Book Review*, 18 August 1935.

Tsetlins: Mikhail Tsetlin and his wife, Maria Samoylovna Tsetlin (née Tumarkin, by her first marriage Avksentiev, 1882–1976), former Socialist Revolutionary, hostess, publisher.

Vlad. Mikh.: Zenzinov.

Letter postmarked 10 February 1937

qui est tout . . . : Fr. 'who is as charming as could be'.

Tu ne le voudrais pas: Fr. 'You wouldn't want it'. VéN, after all, had insisted that VN leave Germany after Sergey Taboritsky, one of the assassins of his father, was appointed second-in-command to Hitler's head of émigré affairs, General Biskupsky.

my Kirghiz: Chokhaev, to glean information about Central Asia for the second chapter of *The Gift*.

Polyakov: Probably Solomon Lvovich Polyakov (pen-name Litovtsev, 1875–1945), journalist, writer and playwright; former employee of the Russian Embassy in London where he worked under VN's uncle Konstantin Nabokov.

Gubsky: Nikolay Gubsky, Haskell's secretary.

what Pushkin's Laura imagines: From Act 2 of Pushkin's *The Stone Guest* (*Kamennyi gost'*) (*Little Tragedies* (*Malen'kie tragedii*), 1830), where Laura says: 'A daleko, na severe – v Parizhe – / Byt' mozhet, nebo tuchami pokryto, / Kholodnyi dozhd' idyot i veter duet ('And far up north – in Paris – / Maybe the sky's covered with clouds, / A cold rain is falling, and the wind is blowing'.)

Butler: Richard ('Rab') Austin Butler (1902–82), Conservative British politician, then Under-Secretary of State for India, whom VN knew at Cambridge; the 'Nesbit' of *SM*.

Lady Fletcher: Possibly Mary Augusta Chilton, Lady Aubrey-Fletcher, wife of Sir Henry Aubrey-Fletcher (1887–1969), a crime writer under the pen-name Henry Wade.

Letter postmarked 12 February 1937

Yesterday's matinée: At the Salle Chopin, as part of the Feux Croisés programme.

plumed by Melot: VN's translations of Pushkin poems into French, edited by Robert Mélot du Dy.

Mil.: Milyukov.

I.I.: Ilya Fondaminsky.

conférence[s]: Fr. 'lectures', 'talks'.

the butterflies in London: VN hints at the possibility of making a living in London. In a letter of 27 February 1937, he refers to the money earned in London as his 'butterflies'.

'c'est un peu fort': Fr. 'this is a little much'.

Fernandez: Ramon Fernandez (1894–1944), philosopher, novelist and an editor at Éditions Gallimard.

now it ends with 'grenier': Fr. 'garret': 'No, the so-called social side of life and all the causes that arouse my fellow citizens decidedly have no business in the beam of my lamp, and if I do not demand an ivory tower it is because I am quite happy in my garret' ('Pushkin, or the Real and the Plausible?', p. 42).

poète anglais . . . 'allemand': Fr. 'English poet . . . German': 'I have had occasion to find some rather curious items in these accounts of eminent lives, such as that biography of a famous German poet, where the contents of a poem of his entitled "The Dream" was shamelessly presented *in toto* as if it had actually been dreamt by the poet himself' ('Pushkin', p. 39).

Sent the little books . . . without touching Lyusya's: VN means that he sent his mother money without touching the fund accumulating at Ilya Feigin's.

writing to Földes asking for reimbursement for the losses: On 11 February, VN read in place of Jolán Földes who had suddenly fallen ill; there was not enough time to advertise his reading sufficiently widely and thus to sell enough tickets to cover the expenses.

Letter postmarked 15 February 1937

'Me' (*a temporary title*): A title for an early autobiography, mentioned in the letters of 2 and 19 February 1936 as 'It is Me' and already being revised. Since no manuscript survives, it is unclear how much of it VN wrote in the mid-1930s, and how much he retained in his published autobiography, successively called *Conclusive Evidence* (1951), *Speak, Memory* (1951) and *Drugie berega* (*Other Shores*, 1954).

Pourtalès: Guy de Pourtalès (1881–1941), French writer.

K.: Kortner.

Denis: Roche.

'*Aguet*': *The Eye* in French.

Petrop.: Petropolis.

Wilson: Unidentified.

Zen-Zin: Fondaminsky's cat.

cancelling: Cancelling his acceptance of Mme Chernavin's invitation to stay with her family in London (see letter of 8 February 1937).

Khodas.'s article: Khodasevich's 'O Sirine': see letter of 25 January 1937 and n.

Postcard postmarked 16 February 1937

[Illustration]: Inscription: 'from PAPA'.

got the books from Paulhan: VN means he got paid by *Nouvelle Revue Française*.

Mercury: Perhaps the article in *American Mercury*, 29 (July 1933), discussed in n. to letter postmarked 23 April 1937.

met yesterday with Lyusya . . . : Apparently, when decoded, not in fact that Ilya Feigin was going to London, but a reference to VN's earnings. Perhaps a 'page' here means 'a hundred francs'.

I.I.: Fondaminsky.

P. N.: Pavel Nikolaevich Milyukov.

'moi ce que j'aime . . .': Fr. '*what I like about Montherlant* . . .' Henry de Montherlant (1895–1972), French novelist, dramatist and essayist.

Letter postmarked 19 February 1937

130, av. de Versailles: This Paris address appears on the envelope.

52 Kensington Park Road: London address appears at the top of the letter's first page.

19–II–1937: In VéN's (later?) hand.

douane: Fr. 'customs house'.

cuboid cab (a cube of indigo . . .): Here VN is simultaneously punning and alluding. '*Kubovyi*', meaning both 'cube-shaped' and 'indigo' in Russian, derives from '*kub*', an alliterative relative of 'cab'. In *Petersburg* (1913), a novel VN esteemed highly, he misremembered (as is clear from a letter he wrote to Khodasevich on 26 April 1934) that Andrey Bely (Boris Nikolaevich Bugaev, 1880–1934) had written '*kubovyi kub karety*' ('an indigo cube of a carriage'), thus bringing together the form, the colour and the sound in one striking image. Ableukhov's cab in *Petersburg*, however, was black–an inconsistency Alexander Dolinin notes in 'Kubovyi tsvet. Iz kommentariya k slovaryu Nabokova', in Lazar Fleishman, Christine Gölz and Aage A. Hansen-Löve, eds., *Analysieren als Deuten. Wolf Schmid zum 60. Geburtstag* (Hamburg: Hamburg University Press, 2004), p. 565.

Mlle Avksentiev: Aleksandra Nikolaevna Pregel (née Avksentiev, 1907–84), painter and illustrator; daughter of Mme Tsetlin.

Curtis Brown: Albert Curtis Brown (1866–1945), literary agent who founded the Curtis Brown literary agency in London in 1905.

Gollan[c]z: Victor Gollancz (1893–1967) founded the British publishing house Victor Gollancz Ltd in 1927.

Fritz[i] Massari: Fritzi (real name Friederike) Massary (1882–1969), Austrian operetta soprano and film actress, one of the most famous divas of her time, left Germany because of her Jewish heritage in 1933.

Molly: Carpenter-Lee.

Eileen Bigland: English biographer and travel writer (1898–1970).

Budb.: Baroness Maria Ignatievna (Moura) Budberg (née Zakrevsky, by first marriage Benckendorff, c. 1891–1974), adventuress, agent of GPU and British intelligence service, mistress of the British diplomat Sir Robert Hamilton Bruce Lockhart (1887–1970), literary secretary and mistress of Maksim Gorky, later mistress of H. G. Wells.

my aunt: Aunt Baby, Nadezhda Dmitrievna Wonlyar-Lyarsky (née Nabokov, 1882–1954), VDN's sister.

Bourne: H. J. Bourne, the manager of the publisher John Long Ltd.

L.: London (see previous letter).

Lolly: Lvov.

'Tair': The Rachmaninovs' publishing house.

Ridelius: Ellen Rydelius, who had translated *The Defence* into Swedish in 1936.

'The Leonardo': 'Korolyok', *Poslednie novosti*, 23 July 1933, p. 6, and 24 July 1933, p. 2; and in *VF*.

'The Adm. Sp.': 'Admiralteyskaya igla' ('The Admiralty Spire').

Letter 1 postmarked 22 February 1937

successfully with the flu: VN inserted 'but burn this anyway' in pen as he was writing, and added 'successfully' later in pencil.

Northerners: Society of Northerners.

Sir Dennison Ross: Sir Edward Denison Ross (1871–1940), linguist, specialist in the Near East, director of the British Information Bureau for the Near East.

moelleux: Fr. 'soft'.

Yu. Yu.: Yulia Struve.

Letter 2 postmarked 22 February 1937

On the envelope, in VN's hand: 'I am well!'

36.6–37: degrees Celsius; 97.9–98.6 degrees Fahrenheit.

Savely Isaak.: Savely Isaakovich Grinberg.

Budberg: See letter of 19 February 1937 and note.

still don't know how to name: VN's autobiography, which he refers to around this time as 'autobi', 'autob.' or 'It Is Me'. In *SM*, VN writes about his father's meetings with H. G. Wells, whom, in 1919, 'it proved impossible to convince that Bolshevism was but an especially brutal and thorough form of barbaric oppression – in itself as old as the desert sands – and not at all the attractively new revolutionary experiment that so many foreign observers took it to be' (*SM*, p. 255).

Baykalov: Anatoly Vasilievich Baykalov (1882–1964), writer, journalist, regular contributor to *Poslednie novosti*, editor of the newspaper *Russians in England*.

Tatyana Vasilievna: Chernavin.

Mrs Haskell: Vera Markovna Haskell (née Zaytsev, ?–1968).

Mme Aldanov: Tatyana Markovna Landau-Aldanov (née Zaytsev, 1893–1968), Vera Haskell's sister.

Flora Solomon: Flora Grigorievna Solomon (née Benenson, 1895–1984), influential Zionist, champion of workers and children, publisher, and widow of the scion of a London stockbroking firm.

Wolf: Unidentified.

a découché: Fr. 'stayed out all night'.

ne t'en déplaise: Fr. 'don't be cross about it'.

Thirty-six point nine: 36.9 degrees Celsius or 96.8 degrees Fahrenheit.

Letter of 24 February 1937

Date: No envelope. In VéN's hand, 'Notting Hill 24·II·37'.

eighty-four pages already . . . : 'the book' apparently indicates VN's earnings to date during this trip; 'Lyusya's articles' may mean the money he has already given Ilya Feigin in Paris; and the 'three . . . pages' from 'The Northerners' probably refers to three guineas he made from the reading in London.

Frank Strawson:. Frank Strawson, partner and company secretary of the publishing firm Victor Gollancz Ltd.

Ridley (née Benkendorf): Natalia Aleksandrovna, Lady Ridley (née Benckendorff, 1886–1968), wife of Sir Jasper Nicholas Ridley (1887–1951).

Asquith's daughter: Lady Violet Bonham Carter (née Asquith, 1887–1969), the only daughter of Herbert Henry Asquith, 1st Earl of Oxford and Asquith (1852–1928), British prime minister (1908–16).

Huntington (Putnam): Constant Huntington (1876–1962), editor-in-chief of the London office of the American publisher G. P. Putnam's Sons.

Leslie Hartley: L. P. (Leslie Poles) Hartley (1895–1972), British novelist, short-story writer and critic.

The book: *Despair*.

Just got your dear letter, luftpost: Written vertically along the left edge of the letter.

Letter postmarked 27 February 1937

Maysky: Yan Lyakhovetsky (Ivan Mikhaylovich Maysky, 1884–1975), historian, writer, member of the International Affairs committee of the Bolshevik government and, from 1932 to 1943, Soviet ambassador to Great Britain.

the translator: VN himself.

Molly: Molly Carpenter-Lee, who helped check VN's translation of *Despair*.

Claude Houghton: British writer, author of metaphysical thrillers (1889–1961).

The book: *Despair*.

Garnett: Constance Clara Garnett (1861–1946), well-known British translator of Russian fiction.

Nicholson: Sir Harold George Nicolson (1886–1968), British diplomat and writer, author of works on Verlaine, Tennyson, Byron and other poets.

kommt in Frage: Ger. 'is possible'; here, 'the prospects are'.

Duckworth: Gerald Duckworth and Company, founded in London in 1898.

Mrs Allen Harris's: Angelica Vasilievna Allen Harris.

D.: *Despair*.

Aunt Baby's: Nadezhda Wonlyar-Lyarsky's.

tuyaux: Fr. 'leads'.

Vilenkin (Mark): Mark Vladimirovich Vilenkin (1891–1961), lawyer, worked on the liquidation of old Russian banks with assets in England.

Flora S.: Solomon.

Frank: Victor Semyonovich Frank (1909–72), literary critic and historian, whom in his letter of 10 June 1939 VN will mention in association with the 'Society for the Protection of Science and Learning' that he probably refers to here.

Harrison: Ernest Harrison (1877–1943), whom VN describes, SM 259, 268, 273.

Dr Stewart: The Reverend Dr Stewart, Trinity College, Cambridge, not further identified.

Pares: Sir Bernard Pares (1867–1949), distinguished British historian of Russia, director of the School of Slavic and East European Studies at University College London; an acquaintance of prominent Russian liberals, including VN's father.

Victor ... a hundred and twenty-nine cases of butterflies: VN means that from his trip to Britain he has garnered £129 in all (donations, entrance fees, advance).

the Greek: Psoriasis.

Otto K.: Klement. Literary agent who sold *Camera Obscura* and *Despair* to Hutchinson & Co..

Heinemann's: London publishing house founded in 1890 by William Heinemann (1863–1920).

Kortn.: Kortner.

old Joseph: Iosif Hessen.

Avg. Is.: Avgust Isaakovich Kaminka.

Elena Ivanovna: EN, VN's mother.

Victor: VN.

Sav. Is.: Savely Isaakovich Grinberg.

Aleksandr Blok–not the poet: Unidentified. Not Aleksandr Aleksandrovich Blok (1880–1921), the leading Russian poet of his time.

Kanegisser's: Elizaveta (Lulu) Kannegiser.

its iambic piston: The poem in the making here, but never developed, reverberates with references to one of Pushkin's most famous poems 'Vnov' ya posetil . . .' (1835), translated by VN c. 1947 as 'The Return of Pushkin' ('I have seen again . . .'), *V&V*, pp. 200–205.

the Swedish 'Defence': *Han som spelade schack med livet*, trans. Ellen Rydelius (Stockholm: Bonniers, 1936).

Bagrova's: Maria Vasilievna Znosko-Borovsky (née Nerpin), stage-name Filaretova-Bagrova (1882–1946), actress.

tomorrow a real one will arrive: The present on its way for DN.

a book . . . (about little Ludovic, in Temple): Georges Lenôtre, pseudonym of Louis Gosselin (1855–1935), *Le Roi Louis XVII et l'énigme du Temple* (Paris: Perrin, 1936), tells the story of the dauphin Louis-Charles (1785–95), son of Louis XVI and Marie-Antoinette, who was imprisoned in the Tour du Temple, raised by a cobbler and died in prison of tuberculosis.

permanently please . . . posterity: Advertisement for Stephen's Ink.

Irina G.: Guadanini.

Granny: Maria Ferdinandovna Nabokov (née von Korff, 1842–1925), VN's paternal grandmother.

the dear Lees: Molly Carpenter-Lee and her husband.

was horribly tired: The word 'was' added later.

Baring: Maurice Baring (1874–1945), playwright, writer, poet and translator; reported from Russian side of Russo-Japanese War, 1905; accompanied H. G. Wells to Russia in 1914 and with him visited the Nabokovs in St Petersburg.

Letter of 1–2 March 1937

[*1 March 1937*]: No envelope; date of 2 March added in VéN's hand, but VN's 'Monday' indicates the letter must have been begun on 1 March.

Stephen Duggan: Political science professor, College of the City of New York, a founder of the Institute of International Education and its first president (1870–1950). After arriving in the United States in 1940, VN did undertake lecture tours for the Institute, in 1941 and 1942.

Letter postmarked 4 March 1937

Monsieur Eidel: Unidentified.

Kort.: Kortner.

Gabr. Marc.: Gabriel Marcel.

L.: Lyusya (Ilya Feigin). VN means the British pounds he has earned in England and given to Ilya Feigin for safe-keeping.

(*? and later . . . little house*): The parenthesis and its contents added above the line.

Sasha Chorny's: Aleksandr Mikhaylovich Glikberg, pen-name Sasha Chorny (1880–1932), poet, satirist and children's writer.

widow's: Maria Ivanovna Glikberg-Chorny (née Vasiliev, 1871–1961).

Valéry: Paul Valéry (1871–1945), French poet, essayist, playwright and philosopher.

in the General Franco sense: Perhaps as General Francisco Franco (1892–1975) came back to Spain from Morocco with his Spanish Army of Africa forces on 20 July 1936, just after the beginning of the unsuccessful coup that started the Spanish Civil War on 17 July 1936.

Teslenko's: Nikolay Vasilievich Teslenko (1870–1942), lawyer, deputy of the Second and Third Dumas, and from 1931 chair of the Committee for Aid to Russian Writers and Scholars.

find out from Paulhan about 'A Bad Day': VN had given him the translation 'L'Outrage': see above, letters of 27 and 28 January 1937.

nine hundred Czech pages . . . : VN means that 900 Czech crowns have been sent to EN.

P. N.: Pavel Nikolaevich Milyukov.

the excerpt (disguised) about the triangle inscribed in a circle: Part of Ch. 1 of *The Gift*.

Altagracia: De Jannelli, his new American literary agent.

Letter postmarked 7 March 1937

Kort.: Kortner.

Fisné: Unidentified.

the furrier Kirkhner: Unidentified. In the letter of 10 March 1937, the name is 'Kirshner' (Kirchner).

'*Fialta*': 'Vesna v Fial'te' ('Spring in Fialta').

'*Hundred Russian Short Stories*': No such book appears to have been published.

Mil.: Possibly abbreviated 'Milyukov', with the dative *yu* ending added.

French translation of Music: Story 'Muzyka'. VN's translation is not known to have been published.

Ida: Ergaz.

K.'s: Presumeably at Kortner's or at Kirkhner's, where *Sovremennye zapiski* were giving a party that night.

Mallarmé: The poet Stéphane Mallarmé (1842–98).

Kogan-Bernstein: Elena Yakovlevna Kogan-Bernstein, physician.

the play: To judge by the next letter, not yet *Sobytie* (*The Event*), the next play he would complete.

Letter postmarked 10 March 1937

Bakhareva: Princess Maria Aleksandrovna Tsitsianov (née Bakharev), stage-name Bakhareva (?–1962).

its theme . . . insanity: Not the plot of any known VN play or story.

interv. luc.: Lucid interval.

'*Sovr. zap.*' *comes out in a day or two*: Number 63 of *Sovremennye zapiski*, with the first instalment of *Dar* (*The Gift*) in pride of place, pp. 5–87.

Vadim Victorovich . . . father will take it: Vadim Victorovich Rudnev, editor of *Sovremennye zapiski*. VN deploys Rudnev's patronymic (Victorovich = the son of Victor) for one of his coded messages about Victor (the decoy alias he uses to talk about his own earnings), who here gets paid by Rudnev, his 'son', for a publication in the journal.

'*Musique*': No publication in French known in VN's lifetime.

advance copies: Of the English *Despair*.

Coulson Kernahan: British novelist and essayist (1858–1943).

Ralph Straus: British novelist, bibliographer, biographer (1882–1950).

David Garnett: British writer (1892–1981).

on the fifteenth of April, by my request: The eleventh wedding anniversary of VN and VéN.

le toupet: Fr. 'nerve'.

Khmara: Grigory Mikhaylovich Khmara (1882–1970), actor, director.

Lucy: Ilya Feigin. VN means, apparently, that he gave Lyusya for safe-keeping £10 of his earnings in London.

N. R. F.: The 1 March 1937 issue, with VN's essay 'Pouchkine, ou le vrai et le vraisemblable'.

bras de chemise: Fr. 'shirtsleeves'.

Postcard postmarked 14 March 1937

'Music' has gone to Candide: But apparently was not published there.

Aldanov's play: 'Linia Brungil'dy' ('The Line of Brunhilda'), *Russkie zapiski* (*Russian Annals*), 1 (1937), pp. 9–92.

avec les: Fr. 'with the'.

give Lyusya ... ten commissions: Another coded reference to earnings VN has left with Ilya Feigin.

R: Roquebrune.

Zamyatin: The writer Evgeny Zamyatin died on 10 March 1937.

Letter postmarked 15 March 1937

'Lettres de femmes et femmes de lettres': Fr. 'Women's letters and women of letters'. VN seems never to have written or given this lecture.

nous trois: Fr. 'for the three of us'.

podalirius: *Iphiclides (Papilio) podalirius*, the Scarce Swallowtail, one of Europe's few Swallowtail butterflies. Having already spent time in that area (in 1923), VN knew what butterflies would emerge when.

to write like Chernyshevsky: Nikolay Chernyshevsky, the Russian writer whose clumsy style VN parodies in Ch. 4 of *The Gift*.

'The Doorbell': 'Zvonok', *Rul'*, 22 May 1927, pp. 2–4; in *VC*.

Chorb: 'The Return of Chorb'.

Vinaver: Evgeny Maksimovich Vinaver (1899–1979), literary scholar, son of Maksim Moiseevich Vinaver (1862–1926), one of the founders of the Constitutional Democratic party and a friend of VDN. In 1933, Evgeny Vinaver became professor of French language and literature at Manchester University.

Pavel: Milyukov, as editor of *Poslednie novosti*.

beaux-esprits: Fr. 'wits'.

an answer from 'Candide': About whether or not they will take 'Music'.

Ergazikha: A somewhat scornful rendering of Doussia Ergaz's surname.

Both my Irinas: Kyandzhuntsev and Kokoshkin-Guadanini.

Likhosherstov: Aleksandr Aleksandrovich Likhosherstov (1874–1958), colonel, commander of the Kiev militia during the First World War, from 1927 to 1940 in office of *Poslednie novosti*.

about whom I wrote to you back in 1933: In fact, VN wrote about Likhosherstov in his letter of 24 October 1932.

the old man: Iosif Hessen.

Postcard postmarked 17 March 1937

the Pushkin exhibition: 'Pouchkine et son époque' at the Salle Pleyel, on the centenary of Pushkin's death. Organized by Sergey Mikhaylovich Lifar (1905–86), it opened with great fanfare on 16 March 1937, the day VN visited.

Le Matin: A popular French daily newspaper (1883–1944).

Davydov: Konstantin Nikolaevich Davydov (1877–1960), zoologist; he travelled to Syria, Palestine, the Arabian peninsula, India and China.

C'est gentil?: Fr. 'Isn't that nice?'

Letter postmarked 19 March 1937

avec tout confort: Fr. 'with all modern comforts'.

Letter of 20 March 1937

Date: No VN date or envelope; dated by VéN 'Feb ~~19~~ 20 1937' and with DN note: 'translated on Dec. 20, 1986', in other words immediately after the publication of Andrew Field's *VN: The Life and Art of Vladimir Nabokov* (New York: Crown, 1986), with its first public account of VN's affair with Guadanini. Published in SL. VéN's date (and therefore that in SL) is wrong: the context and continuity show it was written the day after the 19 March 1937 letter above.

en jeu: Fr. 'at stake'.

the Old Grace: Altagracia de Jannelli.

the former Muravyov: Possibly Irina Nikolaevna Ugrimov (née Muravyov, 1903–94), theatre set and costume designer.

gave the books to Lyusya: Another encoded reference to earnings left with Ilya Feigin.

Petit's: Famous Paris literary salon of Eugène Petit (1871–1938), French lawyer, and Sofia Grigorievna Petit (née Balakhovsky, Sophie Petit-Balachowsky, 1870–1966).

Bernadsky: Mikhail Vladimirovich Bernatsky (1876–1943), economist, Minister of Finance in 1917 Provisional Government and professor of economics in Paris.

my two: Fondaminsky and Zenzinov.

Letter postmarked 21 March 1937

P. N.: Pavel Nikolaevich Milyukov, as editor of *Poslednie novosti*.

Victor: As the decoy alias of VN.

C'est toujours cela: Fr. 'It's better than nothing'.

Conciergerie: A former palace, also a prison, on the Île de la Cité.

Gorguloff: Pavel Timofeevich Gorguloff (1895–1932), a Russian émigré guillotined for assassinating the French president Paul Doumer (1857–1932).

Postcard postmarked 22 March 1937

May 8th: The anniversary of the day they met, which the Nabokovs always celebrated.

V.V.: Vladimir Vladimirovich, i.e. VN.

Victor: VN's alias.

F.: Franzensbad.

Greetings to Anyutochka!: Added above.

We would certainly need a tub!: Added vertically on the right.

Letter postmarked 24 March 1937

six-year-old son: Nikita Alekseevich Struve (b. 1931), future literary scholar, translator.

Michel: Publisher Les Éditions Albin Michel, founded in Paris in 1900.

Lausanne (Matin): Stéphane Lausanne, editor of the Paris *Le Matin*.

'Breaking the News': No 1937 French translation has been located.

'Nouv. Lit.': *Nouvelles littéraires*.

P. N. M.: Milyukov.

'The Present': Part of Ch. 1 of *Dar* (*The Gift*), 'Podarok' ('The Present') – the title contains the word *dar* ('gift'), the title of the whole novel – was published in *Poslednie novosti*, 28 March 1937, p. 4.

Rostovtsev: Mikhail Ivanovich Rostovtsev (1870–1952), authority on ancient and classical history, archaeologist, formerly member of the Central Committee of the Constitutional Democratic party; taught at Yale from 1925 to 1939. VN had previously asked Rostovtsev if he could help him find 'any kind of work at all' (*VNRY*, p. 430).

les petits gros chats: Fr. 'the little big cats'. VN may be referring to his major earnings, saying that he wouldn't spend the money in Paris. *Grosha* (Russian for 'small coin', with an irregular masculine plural ending *-a* added, as in *domá* (houses), *veká* (ages)) is a homophone of Fr. *gros chats*.

Victor: VN's alias.

Avgust: Kaminka.

my little friend is arriving: VN apparently refers to the toy car he was sending to DN in Berlin with Georgy Hessen.

V. M-ch: Vladimir Mikhaylovich Zenzinov.

Inv. to a B.: *Invitation to a Beheading*.

Filippov: Unidentified.

Tegel: Presumably regarding payments for the upkeep of VDN's grave at the Tegel cemetery in Berlin.

Letter postmarked 26 March 1937

Jeanne: Fondaminsky's housekeeper.

'nos messieurs sont aussi comme ça . . .': Fr. 'our men are like that too'.

Princess Tsitsianov's: the actress Bakhareva, see letter postmarked 10 March 1937 and note.

Teffi's play: *Moment sud'by* (*The Moment of Destiny*, 1937), premiered on 27 March at the Russian Theatre.

'Spring in F.': The story 'Spring in Fialta'.

The [Door]Bell, Passenger, and Chorb: The stories 'Zvonok' ('The Doorbell', 1927), 'Passazhir' ('The Passenger', 1927) and 'Vozvrashchenie Chorba' ('The Return of Chorb', 1925).

F.: Franzensbad.

Letter of 28 March 1937

the 28th, the fifteenth anniversary: Of VN's father's assassination.

P. N.: Milyukov. VDN was murdered in 1922 at Milyukov's public lecture, when he tried to defend his friend from the first would-be assassin to fire and was shot by a second.

Gr. Duch. Maria Pavl.: Grand Duchess Maria Pavlovna of Russia, Duchess of Södermanland, Princess Putyatin (1890–1958).

Bar.: Baroness.

Chekhov: Mikhail Aleksandrovich Chekhov (1891–1955), famous Russian and American actor and theatre director; nephew of Anton Chekhov.

Letter postmarked 30 March 1937

Champs-Elys: The Avenue de Champs-Élysées, Paris's famous street of luxury and speciality shops.

'le plus rapide train du monde des jouets': Fr. 'the fastest train in the world of toys'.

'The Ret . . .': 'The Return of Chorb'.

the collection: 'A Hundred Russian Short Stories'.

translate 'Spring': translate 'Spring in Fialta' into English.

Aleks. Tolstoy: Count Aleksey Nikolaevich Tolstoy (1882–1945), famous and prolific Russian writer, lived in Paris and Berlin between 1919 and 1923, then returned to Russia. VN was hostile to his pro-Bolshevik sympathies.

Avinov: Andrey Nikolaevich Avinov (1884–1949), Russian-born American lepidopterologist, from 1926 to 1945 curator at and then director of the Carnegie Museum of Natural History in Pittsburgh.

Alma Polyakov: Anna (Alma) Eduardovna Polyakov (née Reiss, ?–1940), actress, philanthropist.

'The Present' . . . came out two days ago: *Poslednie novosti*, 28 March 1937, p. 4.

'The Recompense': 'Voznagrazhdenie'. No excerpt from *The Gift* appeared with this title; the next would be 'Odinochestvo' ('Solitude'), *Poslednie novosti*, 2 May 1937, pp. 2, 4.

he has grown even better-looking: DN, whom Georgy Hessen saw in Berlin.

Victor: VN's alias.

Lefèvre (Nouv. Litr.): Frédéric Lefèvre (1889–1949), editor-in-chief of *Nouvelles littéraires*.

Thiébaut (Revue de Paris): Marcel Thiébaut (1897–1961), literary critic and translator.

Letter postmarked 2 April 1937

a pleasant little party the other day: According to the diary of Vera Muromtsev (Bunin), it was a dinner in honour of Teffi.

Kedrova: Elizaveta (Lilia) Nikolaevna Kedrova (1909–2000), theatre and movie actress; Grigory Khmara's first wife.

Tatyana Markovna: Aldanov.

Mme Grinberg and her son: Possibly Sofia Maksimovna Grinberg (née Vinaver, 1904–64), lawyer, wife of antique-book dealer and bibliophile Lev Adolfovich Grinberg (1900–1981). Their son Mikhail Lvovich Grinberg (Michel Vinaver b. 1927), future dramatist, novelist and translator, was then ten years old.

Vera Nikolaevna: Muromtsev (Bunin's wife).

me faisait des confidences hideuses: Fr. 'confided frightful things to me'.

Komissarzhevskaya: Vera Fyodorovna Komissarzhevskaya (1864–1910), famous Russian actress.

'charochka': Russian drinking song. A *charochka* is a small cup of wine.

the growing exhibition: Paris's *'exposition internationale des arts et techniques dans la vie moderne'*, 25 May–25 November 1937.

C'était à vomir: Fr. 'It was enough to make you sick.'

Mme Persky: Dominique Desanti (née Dominika Sergeevna Persky, 1914–2011), journalist, writer.

Infecte: Fr. 'vile'.

Lifar: Sergey Lifar, dancer and choreographer; organizer of the 'Pouchkine et son époque' ('Pushkin and His Era') exhibition.

Terapiano (who once . . . took to me . . . in 'Chisla'): 'V. Sirin. "Camera Obscura", Izd. Parabola, 1933', *Chisla*, 10 (June 1934), pp. 287–8.

'Inconnue de la S.': 'Inconnue de la Seine'. Published as 'Iz F. G. Ch.', *Poslednie novosti*, 28 June 1934, p. 3, as if by Fyodor Godunov-Cherdyntsev, the poet and protagonist of *The Gift*; trans. VN as 'L'Inconnue de la Seine', *PP*, pp. 82–5.

Postcard postmarked 4 April 1937

Bromb.: Possibly Herman Bromberg, the owner of a fur-trading business and cousin of Anna Feigin, whose sons Iosif and Abraham VN and VéN chaperoned in Binz, on the Baltic Sea, in July 1927.

Letter postmarked 6 April 1937

Flora S.: Flora Solomon.

Dobuzhinsky: Mstislav Valerianovich Dobuzhinsky (1875–1957), famous graphic and theatre artist, painter and illustrator; VN's art teacher in the boy's late childhood.

the Rodzyanko couple: Nikolay Mikhaylovich Rodzyanko, secretary of the Russian Émigré Committee, and his wife, Lidia Erastovna Rodzyanko (née de Hautpic, 1898–1975).

P. Volkonsky: Possibly Prince Pyotr Petrovich Volkonsky (1872–1957), diplomat and historian.

je fais ce que je peux: Fr. 'I'm doing what I can'.

'Flowers do not please me . . .': Aleksandr Blok, 'Nad ozerom' ('Over the Lake', 1907), ll. 100–102: 'Ya vsya ustalaya. Ya vsya bol'naya. / Tsvety menya ne raduyut. Pishite . . . / Prostite i sozhgite etot bred . . .' ('I am utterly tired. I am utterly sick. / Flowers do not please me. Write . . . / Forgive me and burn this nonsense . . .').

Altagracia: De Jannelli.

tout compris: Fr. 'all included'.

Ilyusha and Zinzin: Fondaminsky and Zenzinov.

Aleks. Fyod.: Kerensky.

Stakhanovites: Those engaged in the movement of competitive over-achievement in individual productivity started in the Soviet Union in 1935, and named after Aleksey Grigorievich Stakhanov (1906–77), an extremely productive coal miner.

Leskov: Nikolay Leskov, whose folk-inspired Russian fiction had rich Orthodox undertones.

Letter postmarked 7 April 1937

with a bath: Added above the line.

Somov: Konstantin Andreevich Somov (1869–1939), Russian painter, one of the founders of the 'World of Art' movement.

one thousand two hundred pages of Czech translation: VN means he sent his mother a fourth money transfer from France, apparently 1,200 Czech crowns.

excerpt: From *The Gift*.

Postcard postmarked 9 April 1937

'récépissés': Fr. 'receipts'.

permis de séjour permanent: Fr. 'Permanent residence permit'.

'Pilgram' . . . Nouv. Lit.: None of the stories appeared in these journals, despite (in the case of 'Outrage') the payment mentioned in the letter of 15 April 1937.

'English associations': An excerpt from VN's proto-autobiography. His published autobiography would include, as Ch. 4, 'My English Education' (especially his family's Anglophilia and his English governesses); Ch. 13, 'Lodgings in Trinity Lane', would cover his Cambridge years.

Bromb.'s: Bromberg's.

Yablonovsk., Sergey: Sergey Victorovich Potresov, pen-name Yablonovsky (1870–1953), writer, journalist and literary critic.

Letter postmarked 12 April 1937

the book as soon as it comes out: *Despair* (London: John Long, 1937).
will write to him: VN supposed for some time, despite the ending of the name 'Altagracia', that his New York agent was male.
'The Reward': 'Nagrada' not accepted by *Poslednie novosti*: see letter of 17 April 1937.
Mme Kovalev: Unidentified.
Aleks. Fyod.: Kerensky.
my article about Amalia Os.: In *Pamyati Amalii Osipovny Fondaminskoy* (*In Memory of Amalia Osipouna Fondaminsky*, Paris, 1937), pp. 69–72.
conférences: Fr. 'lectures'.

Postcard postmarked 14 April 1937

A: Altagracia de Jannelli (VN still supposed she was male).
dictated Chernysh: The section on the arrest of Chernyshevsky, from Ch. 4 of *The Gift*, intended for an excerpt in *Poslednie novosti*, but not published there.
the old man's: Iosif Hessen.
Zyoka: Georgy Hessen.
the lady editor of 'Mesures': Adrienne Monnier (1892–1955), poet, bookseller, publisher, and administrative editor of *Mesures*.

Letter of 15 April 1937

twelve years to-day : Since they were married.
'Despair' has come out and 'The Gift' is in S. Z.: *Despair*, trans. VN (London: John Long, 1937); 'Dar: roman v pyati gl[avakh]: Glava 1' ('The Gift: A Novel in Five Chapters: Chapter 1'), *Sovremennye zapiski*, 63, April 1937, pp. 5–87.
Victor: VN's fiscal alias.
already received a little thousand: Nevertheless it did not appear in *Mesures*.
Henry Church: American-born writer, publisher and patron (1880–1947).
literaturizing wife: Barbara Church (1879–1960).
Michaux: Henri Michaux (1899–1984), French artist, poet and writer.
Sylvia Beach: Nancy Woodbridge (Sylvia) Beach (1887–1962), American-born bookseller, publisher and patron of James Joyce.

ne marcheront pas: Fr. 'don't work'.

woman photographer: Gisèle Freund (1908 (1912?)–2000), German-born French photographer who specialized in photographing writers and artists.

'peut-être parce qu'il est toujours un peu embarrassé': Fr. 'perhaps because it is always a little embarrassed'.

Cingria: Charles-Albert Cingria (1883–1954), Swiss novelist.

Michaud: Michaux.

Kyands.: Kyandzhuntsevs.

the old man: Iosif Hessen.

Bardelebeness: Frau von Bardeleben, their landlady from 1929 to 1932, 27 Luitpoldstrasse, Berlin; landlord, Albrecht von Bardeleben.

Ilf died . . . one thinks of separating Siamese twins: Iehil-Leib Arnoldovich Faynz, pen-name Ilya Ilf (1897–1937), Russian satirical novelist, wrote as one half of the duo Ilf and Petrov, the other half being Evgeny Petrovich Kataev, pen-name Evgeny Petrov (1903–42). Their novels *Dvenadtsat' stuliev* (*The Twelve Chairs*, 1928) and *Zolotoy telyonok* (*The Little Golden Calf*, 1931) were among the very few literary works by writers who emerged in the Soviet Union that VN admired.

est tout ce qu'il y a de plus charmant: Fr. 'is as charming as can be'.

Telegram of 15 April 1937

Congratulations: On their twelfth wedding anniversary.

Letter postmarked 17 April 1937

bien entendu: Fr. 'of course'.

a large lump of sugar, all covered in strands of wool: As a mitten-clad child in the Russia of VN's childhood might have offered a horse after a winter ride.

où j'en suis: Fr. 'where I am'.

Vraisemblable: VN's Pushkin talk.

M: Milyukov.

my excerpt (the arrest of Chernysh): VN's excerpt for *Poslednie novosti* came from Ch. 4 of *The Gift*, the mocking biography of Nikolay Chernyshevsky, which the editors of

Sovremennye zapiski had refused to publish in advance of the rest of the novel and would continue to reject even in its correct sequence.

G.-Ch.: Godunov-Cherdyntsev.

in the new journal, 'Russkie zapiski'. I agreed: But it was never published there.

Postcard postmarked 19 April 1937

I.V.: Iosif Hessen.

Ira and Saba: Irina and Savely Kyandzhuntsev.

the next chapter: Of *The Gift*, for *Sovremennye zapiski*.

Letter postmarked 20 April 1937

Maria Ivanovna: Chorny.

Maria Ignatievna: Budberg.

the date (ours . . .): 8 May, the anniversary of their first meeting, in 1923.

out of coronation considerations: The coronation of King George VI (1895–1952) was to take place on 12 May 1937.

send books to Mother from Paulhan's: That is, VN will send money to his mother from the payment he has received from Paulhan.

an excerpt: From *The Gift*.

rumours: Rumours about VN's affair with Irina Guadanini.

I asked him . . . about the historical associations of the square: Aldanov was the right friend to ask: among his most celebrated works was a tetralogy, *Myslitel'* (*The Thinker*) set in the French Revolution and Napoleonic times: *Devyatoe Termidora* (*The Ninth Thermidor*, 1923), *Chortov most* (*The Bridge of Devils*, 1925), *Zagovor* (*The Conspiracy*, 1927), *Svyataya Elena, malenkiy ostrov* (*St Helena, Little Island*, 1926).

Postcard postmarked 21 April 1937

allez-et-retour: Fr. 'round trip'.

entre deux gares: Fr. 'between two stations'. The Berlin–Paris train arrives at the Gare du Nord, the Paris–Toulon train leaves from the Gare de Lyon.

Elena Lvovna's: Bromberg.

Anna Natanovna's: Unidentified.

I replied . . . : Written on the margin of the address side of the card.

Letter postmarked 23 April 1937

'Mercury': Possibly an article from their files, by Albert Parry, 'Belles Lettres among the Russian Émigrés', *American Mercury*, 29 (July 1933), pp. 316–19, which singles out VN's work for high praise and seems to be the first discussion of his work in English.

piece about Wagner in Lit. Digest: 'Parade', *The Literary Digest*, 13 March 1937, p. 13: '"I hate Wagner," commented Vernon Duke [Vladimir Dukelsky], composer ("April in Paris"). "It is a phobia with me, a Wagner phobia. I feel he brought all sorts of extraneous things into music. He robbed it of its natural life."'

regarding Favière: the house rented in Favière. The notes on the house plan read: 'your and the little man's room'; beds'; 'mine; Sasha Chorny's desk'; 'the terrace'; 'M. I.'s room; Anyuta?'; 'the dining-room (verandah)'; 'garden'; 'kitchen'. 'M.I.' stands for Maria Ivanovna Chorny.

Maria Ivanovna's name: Chorny.

épicerie: grocery.

Iv.: Ivanovna.

the absence of gas . . . : The word 'gas' is marked with an X. And an arrow is drawn from it to the paragraph below, in square brackets.

tout compris: Fr. 'altogether'.

Victor: VN's earning self.

Letter postmarked 26 April 1937

Victor: VN's financial alias.

Superv.: Supervielle.

'Course': *La Course du fou* (*The Defence* in French).

Jean: Jean Fayard.

finished 'Fialta' with Roche – it's turned out magnificently: No French publication around this time known.

Sylvia: Beach.

My excerpt is in the Easter issue: 'Odinochestvo' ('Solitude'), from Ch. 2 of *The Gift*, *Poslednie novosti*, 2 May 1937, pp. 2, 4, the Orthodox Easter, and not 'Podarok', the first excerpt, published on 28 March 1937, which happened to be the Western Easter.

My pen's gone on strike: In pencil.

Postcard postmarked 26 April 1937

Anna Nat.: Anna Natanovna, surname unknown.

Zamyatin (... his 'Cave'...): The story 'Peshchera' (1923).

to whom Gumilyov's 'Blue Star' is dedicated: Gumilyov's poetic cycle 'Sinyaya zvezda' ('Blue Star', published in 1923, after the poet's death) is dedicated to Elena Karlovna du Bouche, whom he met in Paris in 1917. It is unclear whether the meeting took place at her house or at a house of another woman who claimed the fame of the 'Blue Star'.

Poor, poor Clem Sohn: Written upside down along the top edge of the card. Clements Joseph Sohn (1910–37), American airshow dare-devil, died on 25 April 1937 in Vincennes, France, before a crowd of 100,000. He jumped from an airplane in a home-made wingsuit and opened his parachute only a few hundred metres above ground. This time, neither his main nor his emergency parachute opened.

Ses ailes, ses pauvres ailes ... : Fr. 'his wings, his poor wings'. An echo of 'Histoire morale d'un serin de Canarie' ('The Moral Tale of a Canary'), by Alphonse Karr (1808–90), in his *Menus Propos: Mélanges Philosophiques* (*Small Talk: Philosophical Miscellany*, Paris: Michel Levy Frères, 1859), p. 16: 'il bat joyeusement ses ailes, ses pauvres ailes engourdies!' ('he joyfully beats his wings, his poor swollen wings!').

Anna Maks.: Anna Maksimovna, surname unknown. Unidentified.

Postcard postmarked 27 April 1937

de ta part: Fr. 'on your part'.

I don't understand ... : On the other side of the card.

I won't bother ... : Written vertically along the left edge of the card.

Postcard postmarked 29 April 1937

Easter and the coronation: 2 May 1937, the Orthodox Easter; 12 May 1937, the coronation of King George VI.

Letter postmarked 1 May 1937

'Otchayanie': *Despair* in Russian.

how many copies . . . : VN asks how much of the money he keeps at Ilya Feigin's should he take?

our dates: the 8th and the 10th: 8 May, anniversary of their first meeting; 10 May, Dmitri's third birthday.

the nastily cheap short story: Zamyatin, 'Drakon' ('The Dragon'), 1918.

Red Army man: The Red Army soldier in Zamyatin's story stabbed a man whose face looked too intelligent.

an old 'procuress over the romps of young whores': From Pushkin's 'Delvigu' ('To Delvig' 1821): 'Tak tochno, pozabyv segodnya / Prokazy mladosti svoey, / Glyadit s ulybkoy vasha svodnya / Na shashni molodykh <blyadey>' ('That's how, having today forgotten / Pranks of her youth / Your procuress looks with a smile / At the romps of young <whores>').

a short story is revolving: The next story he would publish (in November but with a 25–6 June 1937 date of composition) would be 'Ozero, oblako, bashnya' ('Cloud, Castle, Lake').

has not taken a bath: As part of an unusually severe interpretation of the penitence for Lent.

Vera Nikolaevna: Muromtsev, Bunin's wife.

Tout ça est très rigolo: Fr. 'This is all quite comical'.

seven reviews: Apart from the three about to be cited, these were *News Review*, 15 April 1937, *Tribune*, 16 April 1937, *Public Opinion*, 23 April 1937, and *Sunday Times*, 25 April 1937.

'Outstanding quality': *Birmingham Sunday Mercury*, 18 April 1937.

'Undoubted distinction': *Edinburgh Evening News*, 20 April 1937.

'the small number of world humorists!': *Reynolds News*, 25 April 1937.

the old man: Iosif Hessen.

Postcard postmarked 3 May 1937

my excerpt: 'Odinochestvo' ('Solitude').

Pilsky: Pyotr Moiseevich Pilsky (1876?–1941), journalist, head of the literary department of the Riga *Segodnya*.

long-winded article: Review of '"Sovremennye zapiski", kniga 63', *Segodnya*, 29 April 1937, p. 3.

a new masked little excerpt – the story featuring Pushkin: This excerpt, also from Ch. 2 of *The Gift*, would end up not being published separately.

paskhas: An Easter dish in the shape of a pyramid made of curds and butter, with sugar, eggs and other rich ingredients added for flavour. In 1937 the Orthodox Easter fell on 2 May.

ailleurs: Fr. 'elsewhere'.

Letter postmarked 5 May 1937

Allemagne: This address is crossed out and another hand has written the new one over it: '8 Koulova / Praha-Dejvici / Tschékoslovakei'.

Evsey Laz.: Evsey Lazarevich Slonim, VéN's father.

Mar. Pavlovna: Grand Duchess Maria Pavlovna.

Sûreté: The detective branch of the French police force; the police in general.

Lena: Elena Sikorski, VN's sister.

'Printemps à F.': 'Spring in Fialta' in French.

placed an excerpt: In *Poslednie novosti*. As secretary of the editorial office of *Sovremennye zapiski*, Rudnev may have objected in general to the small newspaper pre-serializations (in the case of Ch. 1, about one ninth of the total) ahead of serialization in their own journal, or perhaps only to the failure to obtain permission for each excerpt.

Demidov: Igor Demidov, deputy editor of *Poslednie novosti*.

P. N.: Pavel Nikolaevich Milyukov.

working on that era now: In his capacity as a historian.

Ivan: Bunin.

'have copied it all from somewhere – great work!': Ch. 2 of *The Gift* depicts Konstantin Godunov-Chernyntsev's lepidopterological explorations through Central Asia, as imagined by his son, Fyodor, who wanted to accompany him on his last expedition, from which he never returned. Fyodor, and VN, imagine Count Godunov's travels in brilliant detail by drawing inspiredly on a plethora of sources, identified and reproduced in Dieter E. Zimmer, *Nabokov reist im Traum in das Innere Asiens* (Reinbek bei Hamburg: Rowohlt, 2006).

Illustration: Plan of the Fondaminsky apartment, marking up the following locations: 'dining-room'; 'I'; 'V[ladimir] M[ikhaylovich]'; 'Ilya'; 'bathroom'; 'dishwashing'; 'entrance hall'; 'Elen[a] Aleks[androvna Peltser]'.

Postcard of 7 May 1937

aller et retour: Fr. 'round trip'.

the card is valid only for me: From the word 'me', VN drew an arrow to the top edge of the card, where he added: 'i.e. for you it is ready as well, but you must come in person to claim it.'

cr.: Crowns.

Letter postmarked 10 May 1937

three-year-old: Dmitri turned three on the day VN wrote this letter.

bonhomme: Fr. 'fellow'.

Gallimard . . . reading 'Despair': *Despair* would be published as *La Méprise*, trans. by Michael Stora (Paris: Gallimard, 1939).

Never, never, never: He kept his word.

Vera Nikolaevna: Muromtsev, Bunin's wife.

Zurov: Leonid Fyodorovich Zurov (1902–71), writer, art critic; Bunin's secretary.

Ivan: Bunin.

poddyovka: A man's long tight-fitting coat, worn among the lower-middle classes in pre-revolutionary Russia.

Rashel: Possibly the Rashel mentioned in the letter of 1 February 1937.

Ira B.'s: Probably Irina Brunst's (Kyandzhuntsev's sister's).

mais si vous envoulez avec de jolies filles: Fr. 'but if you would like some with pretty girls . . .'

Telegram of 10 May 1937

THE LITTLE MAN: DN, on his birthday.

Letter postmarked 12 May 1937

prend plaisir: Fr. 'takes pleasure'.

this hell must end soon, I suppose: See SM, p. 276: Russian émigrés' 'utter physical dependence on this or that nation, which had coldly granted us political refuge, became painfully evident when some trashy "visa", some diabolical "identity card" had to be obtained or prolonged, for then an avid bureaucratic hell would attempt to close upon the petitioner and he might wilt while his dossier waxed fatter and fatter in the desks of rat-whiskered consuls and policemen. *Dokumentï*, it has been said, is a Russian's placenta. The League of Nations equipped émigrés who had lost their Russian citizenship with a so-called "Nansen" passport, a very inferior document of a sickly green hue. Its holder was little better than a criminal on parole and had to go through most hideous ordeals every time he wished to travel from one country to another, and the smaller the countries the worse the fuss they made.'

Postcard postmarked 13 May 1937

Cela devient ridicule: Fr. 'This is becoming ridiculous'.

Letter postmarked 14 May 1937

Je ne fais qu': Fr. 'All I do is'.

Letter of 15 May 1937

avec une allure de: Fr. 'with the speed of a [swallow]'.

Makl.: Maklakov.

review of 'The Gift' today by Khodasevich: ' "Sovremennye zapiski", kniga 63', *Vozrozhdenie*, 15 May 1937, p. 9.

'Azef': A play by writer, journalist and playwright Roman Borisovich Gul' (1896–1986), about the agent provocateur Evno Azef.

'Printemps à F.': 'Spring in Fialta'.

Postcard postmarked 17 May 1937

Flora Grig.: Flora Grigorievna Solomon.

performance: *Azef* at the Russian Theatre.

E. K. and Rostik: Evgenia Konstantinovna Hofeld, EN's companion, and Rostislav Petkevich, son of VN's sister Olga, who left him in the care of her mother.

Postcard postmarked 19 May 1937

6.20 (!!) a.m.: VN added 'Don't meet me, of course!!' along the top edge of the card and drew a line from the word 'a.m.' to it. Below '6.20' he wrote 'Wilson' (the name of a train station in Prague).

Flora: Solomon.

Ida's: Ida Ergaz.

The din . . . : Written on the other side of the card.

a wonderful story: Presumably 'Oblako, ozero, bashnya' ('Cloud, Castle, Lake'), which would be dated 25–6 June 1937 on its first publication.

Letter postmarked 21 June 1937

Cook's: Thomas Cook's, the travel agency.

s'executer : Fr. 'cough up'.

Thiébaut: Editor of *Revue de Paris*.

for Ilyusha: For Fondaminsky, i.e. either for *Sovremennye zapiski* or for *Russkie zapiski*, its sister journal from 1937 to 1939, of both of which he was an editor and both of which he supported. The latter would publish the story.

Olga: Petkevich, VN's sister.

Fargue: Léon-Paul Fargue (1876–1947), French poet.

Postcard postmarked 22 June 1937

Rubchik: Unidentified.

vous me voyez navrée: Fr. 'you see me heartbroken'.

'*je porterai les 2000 fr à M. Feigin*': Fr. 'I will take the 2,000 francs to M. Feigin'.

'*à la revue dirigée par Barbey*': Fr. 'in the review edited by Barbey'. *La Revue hebdomadaire*, founded in Paris in 1892; Bernard Barbey (1900–1970), Swiss writer.

1939

Letter of 3 April 1939

Konovalov : Sergey Aleksandrovich Konovalov (1899–1982), Slavist, professor at Birmingham University (1929–45), would become chair of the Russian Division of the New School (Oxford University, 1945–1968) and editor of Blackwell's Russian Texts, the series of Russian Classics published at Oxford.

Vasil.: Vasilievna.

Mollie: Molly Carpenter-Lee.

Jeeves: Reginald Jeeves, character from 1915 to 1974 in the fiction of P. G. Wodehouse (1881–1975): the valet of Bertie Wooster, a wealthy but inept British aristocrat, whom Jeeves saves from various misadventures.

Braykevich: Mikhail Vasilievich Braykevich (1874–1940), former engineer, economist, member of the Constitutional Democratic party, art collector and patron of the arts, closely associated with the World of Art group.

Berdyaev: The philosopher Nikolay Berdyaev was to write VN a letter of recommendation for the position of Russian professor at the University of Leeds.

Priel: Jarl Priel (1885–1965), writer, French translator of VN's *Invitation to a Beheading* and *The Event*.

'Marianne': French intellectual weekly, founded by Gaston Gallimard, published from 1932 to 1940.

'Méprise': *La Méprise* (*Despair*).

Letter of 4 April 1939

Mme Tsetlin's . . . all three of them: Mikhail and Maria Tsetlin and their son Valentin.

M. S.: Maria Samoylovna Tsetlin.

Mrs Whale: Winifred Stephens Whale (née Sophia Charlotte Winifred Stephens, 1870–1944), English author and translator.

'soul of Russia': *The Soul of Russia* (London: Macmillan and Co., 1916).

like Tolstoy's Pierre: Pierre Bezukhov, the tall, fat, bespectacled protagonist of Tolstoy's *War and Peace*.

Struve: Gleb Struve, then lecturer at the University College London's School of Slavonic Studies.

Duchess of Atholl: Katharine Marjory Stewart-Murray, Duchess of Atholl (1874–1960).

Bakhmeteff: Boris Aleksandrovich Bakhmeteff (1880–1951), engineer and businessman, professor of civil engineering at Columbia University; until June 1922, ambassador of the Russian Provisional Government to the United States.

the baroness: Budberg.

Polyakovs: Possibly the family of journalist and writer Solomon Polyakov-Litovtsev.

O. Bromberg: Iosif (Osya) Bromberg, a relative of Anna Feigin's.

Postcard of 5 April 1939

Lord Tyrrel: William George Tyrrell, 1st Baron Tyrrell (1866–1947), Permanent Under-Secretary of State for Foreign Affairs (1925–8), British ambassador to France (1928–34).

Nicholson: Harold Nicolson

her very charming husband: Asher Lee (born Asher Levy, 1909– after 1973), air intelligence officer.

the play: Perhaps a translation of *Sobytie* (*The Event*), written in November–December 1937, published *Russkie zapiski*, 4 (April 1938), pp. 43–104 trans. DN, MUSSR); or of *Izobretenie Val'sa* (*The Waltz Invention*), written in September 1938, published *Russkie zapiski*, 11 (November 1938), pp. 3–62 trans. DN with VN (New York: Phaedra, 1966).

Rodzyanko: Possibly Sergey Pavlovich Rodzyanko (1895–1979), son of Pavel Vladimirovich Rodzyanko, whom VéN's father, Evsey Slonim, used to represent in court (Schiff, p. 22).

Somov: Braykevich became Somov's closest friend and, after the artist's death in his arms in Paris in May 1939, the executor of his estate.

Kasim-Bek: Aleksandr Lvovich Kasem-Bek (1902–77), leader (1923–37) of the political group of Russian émigré monarchists 'Mladorossy' (Young Russians), founded in 1923 in Munich.

Billig: Possibly I(osif?) M. Billik, translator and journalist whose articles appeared in *Novaya rossiya* (*New Russia*). VN mentions Yuzya (Iosif) Bilig, an acquaintance of Sofia Pregel's, in a letter of 14 November 1932.

Shuvalov: Count Pavel Aleksandrovich Shuvalov (1903–60), film set designer.

Letter of 6 April 1939

'Lik' and 'Museum': 'Lik' ('Lik'), *Russkie zapiski*, 14 (February 1939), pp. 3–27, and in *VF*; 'Poseshchenie Muzeya' ('The Visit to the Museum'), *Sovremennye zapiski*, 68 (March 1939), pp. 76–87, and in *VF*.

'Post (something)': Presumably *Post* (or *Post Magazine and Insurance Monitor*), founded in London in 1840.

'Match': A Paris sporting weekly founded in 1926, which became a news weekly in 1938 and would be reborn as *Paris-Match* in 1949.

'chien': Fr. 'charm', 'fascination'.

Bromberg: Iosif Bromberg.

'Seb. Knight': VN's first novel in English, *The Real Life of Sebastian Knight* (New York: New Directions, 1941), written end 1938–January 1939.

museum: At that time officially the British Museum (Natural History), but also then informally, and now formally, known as the Natural History Museum, Kensington, London.

'*Entomologist*': *The Entomologist*, in which VN had published in 1920 and 1931.

Herring's: Erich Martin Hering (1893–1967), German entomologist, curator of the Zoologisches Museum (now Museum für Naturkunde) in Berlin.

my thing (the 'hybrid' race) is completely unknown: The butterfly specimens VN caught above Moulinet, in the Alpes-Maritimes, on 20 and 22 July 1938, and would later name *Lysandra cormion*, in 'Lysandra cormion, A New European Butterfly', *Journal of the New York Entomological Society*, 49:3 (September 1941), pp. 265–67.

'*Coridon*': Local varieties of the butterfly *Lysandra* (now *Polyommatus*) *coridon*. Although VN published a new species name, *Lysandra cormion*, for the butterflies he had caught, he was aware they could prove to be hybrids between *Lysandra coridon* and *Meleageria* (now *Polyommatus*) *daphnis*, as was shown conclusively to be the case in 1989, by Klaus G. Schurian, in *Nachrichten des Entomologischen Vereins Apollo*, N.F. 10:2 (1989), pp. 183–92 and 12:3 (1991), pp. 193–5.

Mrs Marshall: Unidentified.

curriculum: Curriculum vitae.

Letter of 7 April 1939

belle-sœur: Fr. 'sister-in-law'.

Major Crawford: Unidentified.

Guitry: Sacha Guitry (1885–1957), French actor, playwright, film director and scriptwriter.

as near me as Ilyusha is to us: As Fondaminsky's apartment is to that of the Nabokovs in Paris.

our former street: In 1919–20, VDN, EN and their children lived in London, at 6 Elm Park Gardens in Chelsea.

to look Priel through to the end: Priel's translation into French of *Invitation to a Beheading*.

Osya: Iosif (Osya) Bromberg.

Lourie: Unidentified.

Mme Tyrkov: Ariadna Tyrkov-Williams.

Postcard of 8 April 1939

Lee: Asher Lee.

on Priel: I.e. on Priel's translation into French of *Invitation to a Beheading*.

J'essaye de faire mon petit Kardakoff: Fr. 'I'm trying to do my little Kardakoff'. Nikolay Kardakov, entomologist.

Denis Roche is right: VN's confirmation of the spelling of the name of another of his translators into French. Written vertically, along the card's right margin.

Postcard of 9 April 1939

the holiday: Easter.

Flora: Solomon.

father has just died: Businessman Grigory Iosifovich Benenson (1860–1939), on the board of the former Russo-English Commerce Bank.

Vera Markovna: Haskell.

her husband: Arnold Haskell.

Letter of 10 April 1939

M. Sumarokov: Count Mikhail Nikolaevich Sumarokov-Elston (1893–1970), in the 1910s Russia's most famous tennis champion.

Wilding, McLaughlin, Gobert: Anthony Frederick Wilding (1883–1915), Maurice Evans McLoughlin (1890–1957), André Gobert (1890–1951), tennis champions.

his little boy: Aleksandr Pavlovich Shuvalov (b. 4 May 1934, six days before DN) would become director of the London Theatre Museum.

Lady McDougall: Unidentified.

Nad. Iv.: Nadezhda Ivanovna Sablin.

like the Cap d'Antibes cook: The Nabokovs had lived in Cap d'Antibes from late August to mid-October 1938.

Nef.: Unidentified.

N.I.: Nadezhda Ivanovna Sablin.

Regina: Unidentified.

Letter of 11 April 1939

S. F. Protection: Society for the Protection of Science and Learning, founded in 1933 in Britain to assist refugee scholars.

botanist-explorer: Vasily Vasilievich Sapozhnikov (1861–1924), Russian botanist and geographer.

like mine: Konstantin Godunov-Cherdyntsev, the father of Fyodor, the protagonist of *The Gift*, is a lepidopterist who explores in the Altai and other parts of Central Asia; Fyodor imagines accompanying him on his last voyage, from which Count Godunov-Cherdyntsev never returns.

Her husband: Vladimir Vyacheslavovich Chernavin (1887–1949), professor of ichthyology; escaped the Gulag in 1932 with his wife Tatyana Vasilievna and son Andrey.

Three of the children . . . the fourth: Gleb Struve's four children: Marina, Andrey, Nina and Danila.

Yulen'ka: Yulia Struve, Gleb Struve's wife.

Mme Shklovsky: Zinaida Davydovna Shklovsky (?–1945), editor and political columnist, widow of Isaak Vladimirovich Shklovsky, pen-name Dioneo (1864–1935), journalist, ethnographer, writer.

Rami: Unidentified.

Wells: H. G. Wells.

Evans (a specialist on Hesperidae): Brigadier William Harry Evans (1876–1956), lepidopterist, British army officer, served in India; Hesperidae, the family of typical Skipper butterflies.

Uncle Kostya: Konstantin Nabokov.

Bubka: DN.

Letter of 12 April 1939

Sebastian: VN's novel *The Real Life of Sebastian Knight*, for which he was trying to find a publisher in London.

the play: *The Event* or *The Waltz Invention*.

Morrison: Unidentified.

Birket: George Arthur Birkett (1890–1954), professor at the University of Sheffield, and author, with Raymond Beazley and Nevill Forbes, of *Russia from the Varangians to the Bolsheviks* (1918).

Hicks: Possibly John Richard Hicks (1904–89), economist, then professor at the University of Manchester (1938–46), where, from 1933, Evgeny Vinaver taught French language and literature.

Vinaver's contact with him: VN drew an arrow connecting 'him' to 'Hicks'.

Eva: Lutyens.

Sergey: Sergey Rodzyanko.

the play: An English translation of *The Event* or *The Waltz Invention*.

Leslie Banks: Leslie Banks (1890–1951), actor; in the 1930s starred in several films directed by Alfred Hitchcock.

Walpole: Sir Hugh Seymour Walpole (1884–1941), prolific British novelist.

Osya: Iosif Bromberg.

Tyrants: 'Istreblenie Tiranov' ('Tyrants Destroyed'), *Russkie zapiski*, 8–9, August–September 1938, pp. 3–29; reprinted in *VF*; translated by DN with VN in *TD*.

Priel: Who was translating *Invitation to a Beheading* into French.

Letter of 13 April 1939

14 years!: 15 April was the anniversary of their wedding.

his father's: Aleksandr Ivanovich Konovalov (1875–1949), politician and statesman, businessman, pianist.

sicher ist sicher: Ger. 'sure is sure' ('better safe than sorry').

the Saigon address: Previously, the Nabokovs lived at 8 rue de Saigon, in Paris; they moved to the Hotel Royal Versailles in February 1939.

Le Marois: Hotel Royal Versailles, 31 rue Le Marois.

Glebushka's: Gleb Struve.

Achilles K.: Unidentified. 'Akhill K.' in Russian.

Ariadna: Tyrkov-Williams.

Elisabeth Hill: Dame Elizabeth Mary Hill (1900–1996), Russian literature and Slavonic studies scholar, from 1936 at Cambridge.

au net: Fr. 'into fair-copy form'.

Charova: Vera Sergeevna Charova (?–1971), actress, theatre director, founder of the London Russian Theatre Group of Drama Actors.

Klamm's messenger: In *Das Schloß* (*The Castle*, 1926), by Franz Kafka (1883–1924).

Yellow-blue bus: Plays on the sound of the Russian *ya lyublyu vas* ('I love you'), which follows.

Letter of 14 April 1939

Jules Romain[s]: Jules Romains (1885–1972), French novelist, playwright, poet and essayist.

Shpunt: Unidentified.

Mme Vorontsov-Dashkov: Countess Lyudmila Nikolaevna Vorontsov-Dashkov (née Zeidler, 1885–1943), second wife of Count Illarion Illarionovich Vorontsov-Dashkov (1877–1932).

British Museum: On Great Russell Street.

Miss McDuggals: VN spelled the name 'McDougall' in previous letters (10 and 11 April 1939). Unidentified.

N. I.: Nadezhda Ivanovna Sablin.

'*avenir*': Fr. 'future'.

Letter of 15 April 1939

Mrs Curran: Minnie Beryl Curran, secretary of the Royal Historical Society.

Goudy: Alexander Porter Goudy, former lecturer in Russian at the University of Cambridge. When Goudy retired in 1936, Elizabeth Hill took over his position.

tsar Vlad. Kir.: Grand Prince Vladimir Kirillovich Romanov (1917–92), from 1938 head of the Romanov House in exile.

Letter of 16 April 1939

from the Vysotsky family: Unidentified.

a very talentless and corny play: *The Corn is Green* (1938) by George Emlyn Williams (1905–87), premiered at the Duchess Theatre, London.

Sybil Thorndike: Agnes Sybil Thorndike (1882–1976; Dame Sybil from 1970), British actress.

Hellers: Vera Heller (née Lubrzynska), Eva's sister and business partner, was a clothing designer at their fashion house in London.

Lutyens: Robert Lutyens (1901–72), architect with his father, the famous architect Sir Edward Lutyens (1869–1944).

we will end up with a fatal set of nannies: Following the Russian proverb, 'A child with seven nannies has only one eye'.

'rodnenkiy' and 'smeshno!': Rus. 'My very own'; 'funny'.

Letter postmarked 17 April 1939

Date: 16–IV–39 was a mistake on VN's part. He had written and posted a letter on 16 April from the Sablins' in Brechin Place; *this* letter is postmarked and was written on 17 April, the day he moved to the Tsetlin apartment.

Mai(divale): Maida Vale, a residential district in West London.

the Romanian: Rostislav Donici, translating *Kamera obskura* for the Romanian publishing firm Vremea. The outbreak of war appears to have prevented publication.

Flora: Solomon.

Evg. Vasil.'s: Evgeny Vasilievich Sablin.

baroness's: Budberg.

Postcard of 18 April 1939

baroness's: Budberg.

they are reading: Presumably this means the publishers' readers are still reading *The Real Life of Sebastian Knight*.

Misha Lubrz.: Mikhail Efimovich Lubrzynsky, brother of Eva Lutyens, and VN's Cambridge classmate.

What a pen: The postcard is written thickly, with a blunt post-office pen.

Serg. Rodz.: Sergey Rodzyanko.

Osya: Iosif Bromberg.

Spurrier: Unidentified.

Letter of 19 April 1939

Hotel Royal Versailles . . . : The address is crossed out.

Zetlin: VN's spelling here; an alternative transliteration for 'Tsetlin'.

Dennison Ross: Sir Edward Denison Ross, linguist, with whom VN had dined in February 1937.

Sir Bernard: Pares.

Samuel N. Harper: Samuel Northrup Harper (1882–1943), professor of Russian (1906–43) at the University of Chicago.

Beausobre: Julia de Beausobre (née Yulia Mikhaylovna Kazarin, 1893–1979), later Lady Namier, first married to the Russian diplomat Nikolay de Beausobre. After his death in 1932, she was interned in a Soviet concentration camp; on her release in 1935 she came to England, where she married Lewis (later Sir Lewis) Namier, the historian, in 1947. Her memoir, *The Woman Who Could Not Die*, was published in 1938.

Sir Alfred Mond: Sir Alfred Moritz Mond (1868–1930), from 1928 Baron Melchett, British industrialist, financier and politician.

the Romanian: Donici.

the old man: Iosif Hessen.

Postcard postmarked 20 April 1939

his cousin: Alan Strode Campbell Ross (1907–80), linguist, lecturer in English language at the University of Leeds (1929–40).

Gams: Unidentified.

Halpern's: Aleksandr Yakovlevich Halpern (1879–1956), lawyer, former chargé d'affaires of the Russian provisional government in 1917.

SPELLTACALL: This word (*sel'takat'*) presumably echoes some word which DN has invented and VéN has reported to VN.

Letter of 21 April 1939

terrible: EN died at the hospital on 2 May 1939.

Parry: Albert Parry (1901–92), Russian-born scholar of Russian history, who had discussed 'Sirin' in an early overview of Russian émigré literature (see letter postmarked 23 April 1937). After earning a Ph.D. from the University of Chicago in 1938, he founded the Department of Russian Studies at Colgate University, New York.

Trofimov: Mikhail Vasilievich Trofimov (?–1948), lecturer in, then professor of, Russian (1919–45) at Manchester University.

Silvikrin: Medicinal shampoo.

Valya Tsetlin: Valentin Mikhaylovich Tsetlin (Valentine Wolf Zetlin, 1912–2007), future psychoanalyst.

Letter of 1 June 1939

Politzer: Ronald Politzer, publicity director at Collins, British publisher founded in 1819.

Lubrzynsky: Mikhail Lubrzynsky.

Colonel *Clive Garsia*: Lieutenant-Colonel Willoughby Clive Garsia (1881–1961), lecturer at the Staff College, Camberley, Surrey, near London.

Otto Thien: Otto Theis (1881–1966), American-born, London-based editor and literary agent. VN spells his name variously as Thien, Theis, Theiss.

Pneumothorax: VN was hoping to spend part of the summer in the Savoy Alps. Apparently, he and VéN had discussed renting in the village of Seythenex, which he transforms into 'Pneumothorax'.

se pique de zoologie: Fr. 'prides himself on his zoology'.

Col. *Lawrence's Seven Pillars of Wisdom*: Lieutenant-Colonel Thomas Edward Lawrence, whose autobiographical classic *Seven Pillars of Wisdom* (1922) recounts his experiences during the Arab Revolt against the Ottoman Turks in 1916–18.

Letter of 2 June 1939

Whites: More generally, butterflies of the Pieridae family; more specifically, the white butterflies in the sub-family Pierinae, like the familiar Large (Cabbage) White, *Pieris brassicae*, and the Small (Cabbage) White, *Pieris rapae*.

'*My double and I*': Nikolay Gubsky, *My Double and I: Sentimental Adventures* (London: William Heinemann, 1939).

Thien: Theis.

looks like Silberman: Silbermann, a quirky character in *The Real Life of Sebastian Knight*, Chs. 13–14, 'a little man with bushy eyebrows . . . big shiny nose . . . shiny smile . . . bald brow . . . bright brown eyes'.

Moura: Baroness Maria (Moura) Budberg.

Theis's wife: Louise Morgan (1883–1964), American-born journalist.

N. Chronicle: *News Chronicle*, British daily formed by the merger of the *Daily Chronicle* and the *Daily News* in 1930, and absorbed into the *Daily Mail* in 1960.

Vera Markovna: Vera Haskell.

Pio: Korvin-Piotrovsky.

Adamovich . . . reciprocal shamelessness: Georgy Adamovich, 'Literatura v "Russkikh zapiskakh" [No. 17]', *Poslednie novosti*, 1 June 1939, p. 3: Piotrovsky is 'a poet, rarely appearing in our local press, very skilful and demanding of himself . . . His mode is something like [Aleksandr] Blok, dried off and cleaned up a little, as if checked by Pushkin.' VN was a long-time opponent of what he saw as Adamovich's favourable reviews for sale, for the price, say, of a restaurant dinner (see *Pnin*, p. 54: 'selected among the Parisian Russians an influential literary critic, Zhorzhik Uranski, and for a champagne dinner at the *Ougolok* had the old boy devote his next *feuilleton* in one of the Russian-language newspapers to an appreciation of Liza's muse on whose chestnut curls Zhorzhik calmly placed Anna Akhmatova's coronet').

Arn. Bennett: Arnold Bennett (1867–1931), prolific British novelist and journalist. His diaries have not been published in full; VN may refer to Bennett's bestseller, *How to Live on 24 Hours a Day* (1910), or his *Self and Self-Management: Essays about Existing* (1918).

gr. pr.: Grand Prince Vsevolod Ioannovich (1914–73), next in line to the Russian throne after Grand Prince Vladimir Kirillovich. On 31 May 1939 he married morganatically Lady Mary Lygon (1910–82), thereby invalidating his claim to the throne.

Aunt Bebesha: Nadezhda Wonlyar-Lyarsky, known as 'Aunt Baby'.

Misha L.: Lubrzynsky.

dans le courant: Fr. 'in the course of'.

lie down to write: Exactly what is not clear. After *The Real Life of Sebastian Knight*, finished in January 1939, VN did not begin any new fiction in English until *Bend Sinister*, started perhaps in October 1941. Since this novel seems to have been sparked by Hitler's invasion of the Soviet Union in June 1941 (prompting VN, for all his hope that the Soviets would defeat the Nazis, to conflate and critique German and Russian totalitarianisms) and reflected the strain of trying to extricate VéN and DN from Europe after the war had broken out, it seems unlikely to have been the work he anticipates writing here. His next major fictions in Russian would be the novella 'Volshebnik' ('The Enchanter'), a prototype of *Lolita*, written in October and November 1939, and the abandoned novel *Solus Rex*, a forerunner in some ways of *Pale Fire*, begun some time late in 1939, but there is too little information to know which, if either, of these fictions VN thinks here of treating in English.

ONE-TWO, ONE-TWO . . . BANG!: Possibly a reference to DN's learning to roller-skate.

Letter of 3 June 1939

Vera H.: Vera Heller.

Capt. Riley: Norman Denbigh Riley (1890–1979), British entomologist, Keeper of Entomology at the British Museum (Natural History). Much later VN would review L. G. Higgins and N. D. Riley's Collins guide, *A Field Guide to the Butterflies of Britain and Europe*: 'Rebel's Blue, Bryony White', *Times Educational Supplement*, 23 October 1970, p. 19; reprinted in SO, pp. 331–5.

meladon: His 1938 Moulinet catch, *Lysandra cormion*, now known to be a cross between *Polyommatus (Lysandra) coridon* and *Polyommatus (Meleageria) daphnis*: see note to letter of 6 April 1939.

Stempfer: Henri Stempffer (1894–1978), French lepidopterist.

a famous run-in over carswelli-arcilani: In 1926 the amateur lepidopterist Morris Carswell (1862–1942), after catching a butterfly in Murcia new to him, passed it on to Stempffer, who identified it as a new sub-species, which he named in Carswell's honour, '*Cupido minimus carswelli* TTTS', *Soc Boll. FRCS. Ent.* (1927), p. 247. The same year, Riley named it as a new species, *Cupido arcilasis* Riley, from specimens in the same locality collected by Carswell's friend Cooke: 'A New European Lycaenid: *Cupido arcilacis*', *Entomologist*, 60 (1927), pp. 269–76. The next year, Stempffer, after a detailed morphological examination of the butterfly and its congeners, concluded it was a new species, in 'Contribution à l'etude de *Cupido carswelli* Stempffer', *Encycl. Ent. Ser. B. III Lep.*, 3 (1928), pp. 105–15. Riley responded in '*Cupido carswelli* Stempffer = *Cupido arcilacis* Riley', *Entomologist*, 61, pp. 38, 91, but his species name was ultimately invalidated. The specific status of *Cupido carswelli*, often in dispute, was eventually resolved in Felipe Gil-T., '*Cupido carswelli* (STEMPFFER, 1927): morphology of its chrysalis and genitalia compared with those of *Cupido minimus* (FUESSLY, 1775) and *Cupido lorquinii* (HERRICH-SCHÄFFER, 1847) (Lepidoptera, Lycaenidae)', *Atalanta*, 37 (1/2) (September 2006), pp. 150–60.

Hesperidae: A large family of small to medium butterflies, the skippers, taxonomically difficult because many species are very close to one another.

alveus, as well as armoricanus and foulquieri: *Pyrgus alveus*, the Large Grizzled Skipper, distributed through most of continental Europe; *Pyrgus armoricanus*, Oberthür's Grizzled Skipper, also through continental Europe; *Pyrgus foulquieri*, Foulquieri's Grizzled Skipper, central and southern France, northern Italy and Spain.

Vera Mark.: Vera Markovna Haskell.

Sir Bernard: Pares.

Yakobs.: Sergey (Sergius) Iosifovich (Osipovich) Yakobson (1901–79), lecturer at King's College, University of London, and at Oxford and Cambridge; from 1934 to 1940 head of the library of the School of Slavonic and East European Studies at the University of London; later director of the Slavic and East European Division at the Library of Congress. His brother, Roman Osipovich Yakobson (Roman Jakobson, 1896–1982), was the famous linguist and literary scholar.

Nadya: Presumably, Nadezhda Sablin.

Arnold: Haskell.

Letter of 4 June 1939

Flora: Solomon.

Mme Levitsky: Possibly Aglaida Sergeevna Shimansky (née Levitsky, 1903–95), poet, novelist and literary critic.

Zin. Dav.: Zinaida Davydovna Shklovsky.

Vladimir Kirill.: Grand Prince Vladimir Kirillovich.

ungifted author of 'Magnolia Street': Louis Golding (1895–1958), the author of the novel *Magnolia Street* (1932).

le grand-duc et le duc moyen . . . crottin . . . : VN's response to queries in translating into French the story 'Poseshchenie muzeya' ('The Visit to the Museum'): 'a pair of owls, Eagle Owl and Long-eared, with their French names reading "Grand Duke" and "Middle Duke" . . . frass' (*SoVN* 274). No French translation of 'The Visit to the Museum' published in or soon after 1939 is known.

translate literally, about the hard sign, and provide a footnote: At the end of the story, the émigré protagonist steps out of the museum, in a French provincial town, in which he has become mysteriously lost, into a street where Russian shop signs are spelled without a *yer* (hard sign), a detail that makes him realize with horror that he has somehow resurfaced in Soviet Russia.

Letter of 5 June 1939

mihi: Lat. 'for me'.

Arnold: Haskell.

Mus disneyi: i.e. Mickey Mouse.

the missionary David: Father Armand David (1826–1900), French Catholic priest, missionary, zoologist and botanist, received a giant panda skin from a hunter in 1869. The first live giant panda was brought to the West, to Brookfield Zoo in Chicago, in 1936; in 1938 five giant pandas were sent to London Zoo.

amuses himself every morning with the wolves: Douglas Stuart Spens Steuart (1872–1949), fellow of the British Zoological Society, known as 'the wolf man of the London zoo'.

Savely: Grinberg.

the Colonel: Garsia.

Otto's: Theis's.

Tatishchev: Count Boris Alekseevich Tatishchev (1877–1949), formerly General Consul of the Russian Embassy in France.

Rodzyanko: Nikolay Rodzyanko, whom VN had already contacted about visas in 1937.

Kensington Regiment something: The Prince Louise's Kensington Regiment monument, in Iverna Gardens, off Kensington High Street.

Letter of 6 June 1939

Dze book is as good as sold: Echoing the mock-Germanic English of the oddly sanguine Silbermann in *The Real Life of Sebastian Knight*, the book in question.

Milton Waldman: publishing consultant, editorial adviser (1895–1976).

dans le ventre: Fr. 'in the womb'.

'La Course du Fou': The French translation of *The Defence*.

punning 'translation' of the word 'fou': French fou means 'madman', but also 'bishop' in chess, so *La Course du fou* means both 'the bishop's move' and 'the madman's course'. *The Fool's Mate* picks up on the sound of *fou* and anticipates the virtual 'sui-mate' of Luzhin in *The Defence*.

Otto's: Theis's.

Lovat Dickson: Horatio Henry Lovat Dickson (1902–87), Canadian-born British publisher and writer.

my Ullstein-Meriks period: VN's first two novels, *Mashen'ka* (*Mary*, 1926) and *Korol', dama, valet* (*King, Queen, Knave*, 1928) were published in German by Ullstein, in 1928 and 1930 respectively, translations for which the not-yet-established author was handsomely paid. Perhaps *Meriks* is a fusion of the start of the titles of *Mary* and *King, Queen, Knave*?

'Le Carrefour': Directed (1938) by Curtis Bernhardt (1899–1981).

Misha L.'s: Lubrzynsky's.

DO YOU LIKE THIS PICTURE?: The manuscript original has an outline of a peeled-off sticker at the bottom of the page. Judging by its contour, the sticker could have featured a car.

Letter of 7 June 1939

Pas gentil: Fr. 'not nice'.

types: A *type*, in taxonomy, is the specimen after which the published 'original description' of a species has been made, and is therefore the prized standard and reference for future work on the species. See also letter of 7 December 1942.

Misha: Lubrzynsky.

champion my play seriously: Presumably to arrange for the staging of either *The Event* or *The Waltz Invention*.

curric.: Curriculum vitae.

Maria Solomoylovna: Maria Samoylovna Tsetlin. Samoylovna and Solomonovna are distinct patronymics, but VN's regular contact with Flora Solomon seems to have caused a slip of mind and pen.

fallow furlough: VN is using the Russian word *mezhmolok*, which refers to the period of milklessness, when a cow cannot be milked.

Ariadna: Tyrkov-Williams.

St Thorax: The village of Seythenex in the Savoy Alps, where they planned to spend their summer vacation.

Sergey R.: Rodzyanko.

ça va sans dire: Fr. 'That goes without saying'.

Letter of 8 June 1939

first generations: First generations of butterflies that summer.

mais c'est toujours quelque chose: Fr. 'but it's still something'.

vu: Fr. 'in view of the fact'.

Otto's: Theis's.

once published 'The Passenger': 'Passazhir' (1927) became VN's first short story translated into English, by Gleb Struve, as 'The Passenger', in *Lovat Dickson's Magazine*, 1:6 (June 1934), pp. 719–25.

Thomson: David Cleghorn Thomson (1900–?), secretary and councillor (1938–54) of the Society for the Protection of Science and Learning (1933–87).

Letter of 9 June 1939

Khodasevich 'has ended his earthly existence': Vladislav Khodasevich had cancer. When VN had visited his ailing friend in Paris in late May, Khodasevich was already too ill to see him. He died on 14 June.

5+10+30+7½ ...: The number of pounds he has earned on this trip.

Rostik: VN's nephew Rostislav Petkevich and the former governess of VN's sisters, Evgenia Hofeld, now his guardian.

Birch: Francis (Frank) Birch (1889–1956), British cryptographer, served in the Navy. In VN's days at Cambridge, Birch was a Fellow of King's College (1915–34) and a university lecturer in history (1921–8).

Vera Markovna: Haskell.

Lovat: Dickson.

send the Churches to the chort: Chort means 'devil' in Russian (and is used as an expletive like 'Damn!'). VN is punning, spelling the Russian word in Roman script.

Letter of 10 June 1939

Frank: Victor Frank.

Buchanan: Unidentified.

Pollizer: Polizer.

baroness Bugbear or Bedbug: Budberg.

je suis sensé: Fr. 'I'm supposed'.

the essay for Rudnev: An essay, 'O Khodaseviche' ('On Khodasevich'), *Sovremennye zapiski*, 69 (July 1939), pp. 262–4, to which VN had agreed on 29 May (Russkiy Arkhiv Literatury, MS 1500/7, details supplied by Andrey Babikov, personal communication). Khodasevich did not die until 14 June, but the émigré literary community in Paris knew the operation scheduled for him at the end of May was well-nigh hopeless.

Letter of 11 June 1939

Vera Mark.: Vera Markovna Haskell.

Aunt Baby: Nadezhda Wonlyar-Lyarsky.

Fulda's son: Possibly Ludwig Anton Solomon Fulda (1862–1939), German writer and poet. Fulda, however, committed suicide in Berlin in March 1939, which his son would have known about. Or perhaps German lepidopterist Oscar Fulda, who ran a famous butterfly store in New York from 1904 to 1945.

Merana: In the Italian Piedmont.

COMING ON WEDNESDAY. IT'S A RHYME: *V sredu priedu* in Russian.

Letter of 12 June 1939

Rostik: VN's nephew Rostislav Petkevich, then in Prague.

1941

Letter postmarked 18 March 1941

WELLESLEY COLLEGE . . . : Letterhead. On 15 March, VN began a two-week series of guest lectures at Wellesley College.

miss *W.* and L.: Hilda Ward, whom he was tutoring in Russian in New York, and Lisbet Thompson.

Mansvetov: Vladimir Mansvetov.

Boris Vasilievich: Boris Vasilievich Bogoslovsky (1890–1966), former officer in the White Army; in emigration, Columbia-educated philosopher and educational theorist. In 1935–45 he taught at and was one of the directors of the progressive Cherry Lawn School in Darien, Connecticut.

Borodin: Unidentified.

'Antlantic': VN's persistent misspelling, for a time, of the Atlantic Monthly, an American magazine of literature and culture, founded in Boston in 1857. It was edited from 1938 to 1966 by Edward Weeks (1898–1989).

New Rep.: The New Republic, an American magazine of politics and the arts, founded in New York in 1914, at that time published weekly. Through his new friend, the prominent literary and social critic Edmund Wilson (1895–1972), long-time writer for the magazine and briefly, in late 1940, its editor, VN had published book reviews in it four times since mid-November 1940.

Bogoslavskys: Boris Bogoslovsky and his wife, Christina Staël von Holstein (1888–1974), who was the co-principal and then principal of the Cherry Lawn School (1935–65).

Bellofolit: Probably Bellafolin, medicine used as an anti-spasmodic.

temperature of forty: 40 degrees Celsius; 104 degrees Fahrenheit.

telegraph to Wellesley: In 1940, VN joined the New York-based Institute of International Education, through which he had been invited to lecture at Wellesley College.

the new 'Gift': After VN finished *The Gift* in January 1938 (published, except for Ch. 4, in *Sovremennye zapiski*, 63–7 (April 1937–October 1938)) the novel continued to reverberate in his imagination. Probably in the spring of 1939, he added to it another significant piece, first published in English in DN's translation as 'Father's Butterflies: Second Addendum to the Gift' (*N'sBs*, pp. 198–234); 'second addendum' because the 1934 story 'Krug' ('The Circle') was a first 'addendum' (LCNA, Box 6, fol. 5; for the Russian, see also 'Vtoroe dobavlenie k *Daru*', ed. Aleksandr Dolinin, *Zvezda*, 2001: 1, pp. 85–109). A folder survives, apparently begun no earlier than September 1939, marked '*The Gift*, Part II' with other materials apparently being considered for a second volume of the novel (LCNA, Box 6, fol. 4). At one stage the second volume was to conclude with the completion, by Fyodor Godunov-Cherdynstev, protagonist of *The Gift*, of Pushkin's unfinished verse drama, *Rusalka*, which VN ended up publishing under his own name in *Novyi zhurnal*, 2 (1942), pp. 181–4. Where the new idea expressed in this letter would have fitted into the fluid plans for the continuation of *The Gift* remains impossible to say without more evidence.

Boris Vas.: Boris Vasilievich Bogoslovsky.

Cambridge: Cambridge University.

Miss Kelly: Amy Ruth Kelly (1882–1962), associate professor of English composition at Wellesley College.

two morning lectures (Russian Novel . . .): While living in New York in 1940–41, VN prepared hundreds of pages of lectures on Russian literature for teaching in the US. Some of this material was presumably used for the 1941 guest Wellesley lectures, and later reworked for Russian literature courses at Wellesley (1946–8), Cornell (1948–58), and Harvard (1952), and published in *LRL*, where he discusses Gogol, Turgenev, Dostoevsky, Tolstoy, Chekhov and Gorky.

Miss Perkins: Agnes Frances Perkins (1877?–1959), professor of English literature at Wellesley, who was VN's hostess and friend at Wellesley College. She was near retirement age when VN arrived at Wellesley.

Karpovich: Mikhail Karpovich, a professor of history at Harvard University and, from 1942 on, editor of *Novyi Zhurnal*. VN first met Karpovich in 1932 in Prague, but became close friends with him only after moving to the United States.

be fit and strong: VéN had been 'in bed with a crippling case of sciatica' (Schiff, p. 113).

my exile: Nikolay Chernyshevsky, exiled to Siberia, whose epistolary style VN mocks in Ch. 4 of *The Gift*.

Letter of 19 March 1941

the editor of the 'Antlantic': Edward Weeks of the *Atlantic Monthly*.

your story: 'Cloud, Castle, Lake' (translated from the 1937 story 'Ozero, oblako, bashnya'), *Atlantic Monthly*, June 1941, pp. 737–41. It is one of VN's best stories, but its strongly anti-totalitarian and specifically anti-Nazi themes help explain the particular enthusiasm recorded here and later in the letter.

Pertzov: Pyotr Aleksandrovich Pertzov (1908–67), Russian-born, Harvard-educated translator of VN's short stories, 'Cloud, Castle, Lake', 'The Aurelian' and 'Spring in Fialta'. See Maxim Shrayer, 'Nabokov: Letters to the American Translator', *AGNI*, 50 (October 1999), pp. 128–45.

the lectures . . . 'The Soviet Drama' . . . applause, and praise, and invitations: Since the Treaty of Non-Aggression between Germany and the Soviet Union, signed in August 1939, had made it feasible for Hitler to invade Poland and precipitate the Second World War, VN's frank and vivid anti-Sovietism made him particularly appealing at this time to an American audience lending support to, if not yet joining, the Allies.

on the lake of the price: VN echoes the lake and its reflected cloud, a vision of elusive happiness, in 'Cloud, Castle, Lake', and puns: the Russian *ozero* ('lake') suggests that he hopes another zero may be added to the *Atlantic Monthly*'s usual rate.

Karpovich's : In Cambridge, Massachusetts.

a Menton tone: The Nabokovs had lived in Menton (or Mentone), France, from October 1937 to July 1938.

Et je t'aime: Fr. 'and I love you'.

Chekhov: Mikhail Chekhov, the theatre director. In late 1940 VN had written to Chekhov (by then running a theatre studio in Connecticut), suggesting he produce an adaptation of *Don Quixote* which VN would write for him. Chekhov was interested, although the project was never realized.

Dasha: Dorothy Leuthold.

Natasha: Nathalie Nabokov.

Lisbetsha: Lisbet Thompson.

très bien, très beau parleur: Fr. 'a very fine, very glib speaker'.

La rosse rousse sera bien enfoncée: Fr. 'The Russian rotter will be thoroughly smashed up'. An allusion to the beating the Russian émigré receives at the hands of German excursionists in 'Cloud, Castle, Lake'?

P.: Pertzov.

what do you think?: After completing his translation of 'Cloud, Castle, Lake', Pertzov would translate 'The Aurelian'.

Tyrants: 'Tyrants Destroyed' (1938 story).

Breaking the News: Story from 1934.

Letter of 20 March 1941

WELLESLEY COLLEGE . . . : Letterhead.

From that night on . . . : Written vertically along the left margin of the letter's first page.

translations from Pushkin: He had begun a translation of Pushkin's mini-tragedy *Mozart and Salieri* in late December 1940 (published *New Republic*, 21 April 1941, pp. 559–60) and would publish other translations of Pushkin in *Three Russian Poets: Selections from Pushkin, Lermontov and Tyutchev* (Norfolk, Conn.: New Directions, 1944).

Soviet Short: The Soviet Short Story.

[tempest nighing] . . . : The opening of *Eugene Onegin*, Ch. I, stanza 33, was one of VN's favourite passages in Pushkin: 'Ya pomnyu more pred grozoyu: / Kak ya zavidoval volnam, / Begushchim burnoy cheredoyu / S lyubov'yu lech' k eyo nogam!' His 1945 translation ('From Pushkin's "Eugene Onegin", *The Russian Review*, 4:2 [Spring 1945], pp. 38–9) read: 'I see the surf, the storm-rack flying . . . / Oh, how I wanted to compete / with the tumultuous breakers dying / in adoration at her feet!' His literal 1976 translation renders the lines: 'I recollect the sea before a tempest: / how I envied the waves / running in turbulent succession / with love to lie down at her feet!' (*EO* [1976], I, l. 110).

Ich hab gedacht . . . : Ger.: 'I thought that I would get a letter from you today'. Ungrammatical: should be 'Ich hab(e) gedacht, dass ich heute einen Brief von Dir bekomme'. VN's German translator and editor Dieter E. Zimmer comments: 'His slips go to disprove the theory that he only pretended not to speak German fluently.'

Letter of 24 March 1941

WELLESLEY COLLEGE . . . : Letterhead

H.: Probably Hilda Ward.

L.: Lisbet Thompson.

Musinka Nabokov: DN.

Tatyana: Tatyana Nikolaevna Karpovich (née Potapov, 1897–1973), wife of Mikhail Karpovich.

Evgeny Rabinovich: Evgeny Isaakovich Rabinovich, pen-name Evgeny Raich (1901–73), biochemist, poet.

Pertsov's brother: Konstantin Aleksandrovich Pertzov (1899–1960) worked at various architectural firms in Boston before opening his own in 1945.

Lednitsky: Vatslav Aleksandrovich Lednitsky (1891–1967), literary historian, professor at Harvard and Berkeley, contributor to *Novyi Zhurnal*.

THE BIKE . . . : The bike VN was shipping to New York for DN.

Letter postmarked 25 March 1941

WELLESLEY COLLEGE . . . : Letterhead.

Mr Dimwitsvetov: Mansvetov, the 'fool and scoundrel' of the 18 March 1941 letter.

Chairman Sedykh: Andrey Sedykh, pen-name of Yakov Moiseevich Tsvibakh, whom VN first met in 1932 in Paris, came to the US in 1941. He soon became editor-in-chief of *Novoe russkoe slovo* and President of the Literary Fund in Aid of Russian Writers and Scholars in Exile.

Sergey Volkonsky: Sergey Mikhaylovich Volkonsky (1860–1937), theatre and dance theoretician and director of the Imperial Theatres, travelled to the US in 1893 to give a talk at the World's Fair in Chicago. 'What a charming sight it is to see these young girls surrounded by nature and science. And everywhere – in the woods, on the lake, in the lofty corridors, you hear the Wellesley cheer in young ringing voices': Prince Serge Wolkonsky, *My Reminiscences*, trans. A. E. Chamot (London: Hutchinson, 1924), vol. 1, p. 242.

the President: Mildred Helen McAfee (1900–1994; from 1945, Mildred Horton), President of Wellesley College 1936–49, with a three-year leave of absence 1942–5.

a professor of English literature: Presumably Charles Kerby-Miller (1903–71), assistant professor of English literature. He and his wife Wilma (1897–1990) would become friends of VN and VéN in their Wellesley and Cambridge years.

I kiss you on the clavicle, my bird: In Russian, a part-rhyme: 'Tseluyu tebya v klyuchitsu, moya ptitsa'.

Letter postmarked 26 March 1941

WELLESLEY COLLEGE . . . : Letterhead.

Vosstorg and Vdakhnovenia: Russ. 'Rapture' and 'Inspiration'. VN pointedly mistransliterates the Russian words to imitate his exaggerated pronunciation for an English-speaking audience. In his *Lectures on Literature*, he explains the terms (the pairing and the distinction derives from Pushkin): '*vostorg* and *vdokhnovenie*, which can be paraphrased as "rapture" and "recapture". . . the first being hot and brief, the second cool and sustained . . . the pure flame of *vostorg*, initial rapture . . . has no conscious purpose in view but . . . is all-important in linking the breaking-up of the old world with the building up of a new one. When the time is ripe and the writer settles down to the actual composing of his book, he will rely on the second serene and steady kind of inspiration, *vdokhnovenie*, the trusted mate who helps to recapture and reconstruct the world' (pp. 378–9).

Brown: Harper Glover Brown (1907–85), a lecturer in English.

Tatyana Nik.: Tatyana Nikolaevna Karpovich.

the Anyuta situation: Anna Feigin remained in occupied France and did not manage to escape until September 1941.

Karpovich . . . will do everything: Karpovich had already helped the Nabokovs move to the US, and VN solicited his support again in bringing Anna Feigin to join them.

Ridgefield: Ridgefield, Connecticut, where he was seeing Mikhail Chekhov.

Sov. short: 'The Soviet Short Story'.

refanglicize: From *perelitsevat'*, to take a piece of clothing apart, turn every piece of cloth inside out and stitch everything back together again (this way the unworn side of cloth will make the garment look like new).

'Spring' pretty soon: The VN–Peter Pertzov translation 'Spring in Fialta' was not published until May 1947, in *Harper's Bazaar*, pp. 138ff.

THINK IT WILL ARRIVE TOMORROW: VN's letter to DN occupies a separate page.

Letter of 28 March 1941

WELLESLEY COLLEGE . . . : Letterhead.

Dennis: Nigel Dennis (1912–89), assistant editor at the *New Republic*; in early 1941 he was in charge of the literary department.

'Art of Translating': 'The Art of Translation', *New Republic*, 4 August 1941, pp. 160–62.

March 28th: The anniversary of his father's death.

Bertrand: Thompson.

Schwartz: Delmore Schwartz (1913–66), American poet and short-story writer.

Wilson: VN's relationship with Edmund Wilson was about to become an intense friendship. For its full course, see *DBDV*.

Sedykh: Andrey Sedykh (Tsvibakh).

Edgar Fisher: Edgar Fisher (c. 1884–1968), of the Institute of International Education, which organized VN's lecture tours.

Lorrimer: Burford Lorrimer (1908–1952), editor at Bobbs-Merrill Publishing Company.

Aldanov: Mark Aldanov emigrated to the US in 1940, where in 1942 he would co-found *Novyi Zhurnal*.

the proofs: Of his translation of Pushkin's *Mozart and Salieri* (see note to letter of 20 March 1941).

Lilly Pons: Lily Pons (1898–1976), famous French-American operatic soprano.

elderly males and females of the New Yorker: In its cartooning style, presumably. Founded in 1925, the *New Yorker* had already become the leading outlet for American writers and readers.

Koussevitzky: Sergey Aleksandrovich Kusevitsky (Serge Koussevitzky, 1874–1951), Russian-born conductor and composer; music director of the Boston Symphony Orchestra (1924–49), he had performed in the Nabokov family home in St Petersburg. In 1940, Aleksandra Lvovna Tolstoy (1884–1979) of the Tolstoy Foundation had obtained from Koussevitzky a letter of support for VN, which may have eased his entry into the US.

Mansfield: Katherine Mansfield (1888–1923), New Zealand-born short-story writer.

Russian Tea-room: In New York City.

Wellesley-rein?: From the German for 'pure': will Véra be a presentable Wellesley wife?

Bobbs-Merr.: In 1938, the Indianapolis publisher Bobbs-Merrill published VN's *Laughter in the Dark*. Was the publisher wanting to sell film rights to the novel? In 1945, VN would sell the rights for $2,500, but no film of the novel was made until 1969.

M. M.: Karpovich. VN was seeking an affidavit for Anna Feigin, who was trying to leave occupied France for the US.

old man H.: Probably Iosif Hessen, who remained in occupied France. He would move to the US in 1942.

written to the Russian club for 50: Presumably to Andrey Sedykh (Tsvibakh), about the lecture discussed in the letter of 25 March 1941.

Norwork: Norwalk, Connecticut.

Chekh.: Mikhail Chekhov, with whom VN wanted to discuss the production of his play *Don Quixote*; he was based in Ridgefield, Connecticut.

MY DARLING: VN's letter to DN begins on a separate page. The word 'darling' (*dushen'ka*) features a prominently enlarged soft sign (Ь).

MY DEAR: This letter to DN is written on a separate page; it may have been enclosed in another letter to Véra and mailed either earlier or later than 28 March. Some Russian letters are replaced with English letters that look similar: Я (R) and И (U).

Letter of 31 March 1941

the collector Denton: A collection of approximately 1,500 specimens hosted at the Wellesley Historical Society. William Dixon Denton (1865–1923) and Robert Winsford Denton (1868–1941) collected butterflies and mounted them according to a method invented by their brother Sherman (1856–1937).

Tatyana: Mrs Karpovich.

M. M.: Mikhail Mikhaylovich Karpovich.

Zhukovsky's paintings: Stanislav Yulianovich Zhukovsky (1873–1944), Polish-born Russian landscape painter.

Zhdanov: VN had met with Georgy Zhdanov, actor and director, associated with Mikhail Chekhov, in Paris in 1936.

Undated note (1941–2?)

Date: Dated in pencil at the bottom of the note, possibly in VéN's later hand: '1941–2'.

1942

Note of May 1942 or later

May 1942 or later: This list requested from *Dead Souls* (1842) by Gogol was perhaps early on in VN's preparation for *Nikolai Gogol* (Norfolk, Conn.: New Directions, 1944), which he was commissioned to write in May 1942.

breakfast (two): In Russian at this time, *zavtrak* could refer to 'breakfast' (to be explicit, *pervyi zavtrak*, 'first breakfast') and to 'lunch' (to be explicit, *vtoroy zavtrak*, 'second breakfast'). 'Lunch' is now *obed*.

one day of 75 pages ( ): VN drew an arrow from the space between the empty brackets to the calculations at the top of the page. 115–38 = 76 is an error: the answer should be 77.

Letter of 3 August 1942

c/o Mrs Bertrand Thompson . . . : No stamp; possibly delivered by hand. At the top of the envelope, in VéN's hand: 'From Brattleboro, Karpovichs' summer home'. On the other side, in unknown hand, across the flap: 'Vladimirych asked you not to forget about rum and to buy him shoes (sneakers) probably size 10 and probably dark blue.' Vladimirych is a colloquial variant of VN's patronymic, Vladimirovich. The rum was for a sticky lure to catch moths.

West Wardsboro, Vermont: In 1942, the Nabokovs spent several weeks at the Karpoviches' spacious summer home in West Wardsboro. At the beginning of August, VéN travelled to Cambridge, Massachusetts, to find an apartment for the coming year in the vicinity of Harvard University, where VN was to start a job at the Museum of Comparative Zoology.

Newell: Unidentified.

Derricks: Unidentified.

Natasha: Nathalie Nabokov.

Mrs Levin: Elena Ivanovna Levin (née Zarudny, 1913–2006), wife of Harry Levin (1912–94), a professor of English literature at Harvard and from 1960 Irving Babbitt Professor of Comparative Literature.

'I. Feigin': Ilya Feigin.

Brombergs: Anna Feigin's relatives.

Marisha: The Karpoviches' daughter Marina (later Mrs Lee Hydeman).

Superman: Comic book series begun in 1939. VN had written a poem about Superman's and Lois Lane's honeymoon night, 'The Man of Tomorrow's Lament', which he sent to the *New Yorker* in June 1942, but which was not accepted for publication.

'The Nose': Gogol's short story 'The Nose' (1836).

Banks: Nathan Banks (1868–1953), head curator of insects at Harvard's Museum of Comparative Zoology. In October 1941 VN began to work gratis at the MCZ, reordering their butterfly collections; from 1942 to 1948 he was a paid research associate there and de facto curator of Lepidoptera.

Arctia virgo: Actually *Grammia virgo*, the Virgin Tiger Moth. *Virgo* had not been in the genus *Arctia* since 1866. The genera *Arctia* and *Grammia* look quite similar; perhaps VN remembered early nineteenth-century images where this moth still featured as *Arctia virgo*.

Goldenweiser: Aleksey Aleksandrovich Goldenweiser (1890–1979), Russian-born lawyer; in the 1940s he helped many of his compatriots emigrate from Europe to the United States, including the Nabokovs, the Feigins and the Hessens. (See Galina Glushanok, 'Vera Nabokova's Correspondence with A. Goldenveizer', *Nabokov Online Journal*, 1, 2007, http://etc.dal.ca/noj/articles/volume1/GLUSHANOK_Vera_Nabokova_A.A.Golqdenv.pdf)

Letter postmarked 2 October 1942

I arrived happily: The beginning of VN's lecture tour through the American South. His first stop was at Coker College in Hartsville, South Carolina.

Letter of 2–3 October 1942

Potter: Paulus Potter (1625–54), Dutch artist famous for his animal paintings in landscape settings.

Corot: Jean-Baptiste-Camille Corot (1796–1875), French landscape painter.
'enchantment of the eyes': VN echoes Pushkin's poem 'Osen'' ('Autumn', 1833), stanza 7, l. 1:
'Unylaya pora! Ochey ocharovan'e! / Priyatna mne tvoya proshchalnaya krasa . . .'
('Doleful time! Enchantment of the eyes! / Your farewell beauty pleases me . . .').
Coker: Coker College, Hartsville, South Carolina, where VN was to lecture.
Ingram: Dr Benjamin Clayton Ingram, professor of religion, head of the Christian Education Department at Coker College.
Mrs Coker: Vivian Coker (née Gay), widow of James Lide Coker (1863–1931), son of Major Coker.
belle-fille: Fr. 'daughter-in-law'.
the college founder, Major Coker: Major James Lide Coker (1837–1918) founded Welsh Neck High School in 1894; in 1908 it became Coker College.
President Greene: Dr Charles Sylvester Green (1900–1980), president of Coker College (1936–44).
'common sense': 'The Art of Literature and Commonsense', a revised version of 'The Creative Writer', *Bulletin of the New England Modern Languages Association*, January 1942, pp. 21–9, in LL, pp. 371–80.
tragedy of tragedy: Essay entitled 'The Tragedy of Tragedy', published in MUSSR, pp. 323–42.
tea olive: *Osmanthus americanus*, an evergreen native to south-eastern North America.
McCosh: Dr Gladys Kathryn McCosh, professor of zoology at Wellesley College.
Hesperids: Skippers.
Pierids: A large family of mostly white, yellow or orange butterflies.
Papilio: A genus of the Swallowtail butterflies, usually large and brightly coloured. The Tiger Swallowtail, *Papilio glaucus*, would be one of the largest in this region.
'eubule': *Phoebis sennae eubule*, the bright-yellow Cloudless Sulphur.
'Yid': *Zhid*, *zhidok*, a derogatory name for a Jew in Russia.
father of my hostess was a famous artist: Irish-American landscape painter Edward Gay (1837–1928).
beau-père: Fr. 'father-in-law'.
minister, Smythe: Ellison Adger Smyth (1903–98), Presbyterian minister.
the famous lepidopterologist Smythe: Ellison Adger Smyth (1863–1941), lepidopterologist, founding chair of the biology department at Virginia Polytechnic Institute.
Sphingids: Hawk Moths.

Charles Morgan: Charles Langbridge Morgan (1894–1958), British playwright and novelist, who had won the James Tait Black Prize in 1940 for *The Voyage*.
Valdosta: VN was to lecture at Georgia State Women's College in Valdosta.
museum: The Harvard Museum of Comparative Zoology.
Thecla: A genus of lycaenid butterflies.
'Geh zu deine Kabine: ich bin müde!': Ger. 'Go to your cabin: I'm tired!' *Geh zu deine Kabine: ich bin müde!* is ungrammatical. It should be *geh zu deiner Kabine* or *geh in deine Kabine*.
Acidalia: An abandoned name for a genus of Noctuid (owlet) moths.

Letter of 5 October 1942

Richmond: VN does not know yet that his lecture in Richmond has been cancelled.
not quite Tertiary: i.e. Cenozoic. In Russian, 'ne to tropicheskoe, ne to treteyskoe'.
Morrison: Samuel Eliot Morison (1887–1976), prominent historian, from 1941 Jonathan Trumbull Professor of American History at Harvard.

Letter postmarked 7 October 1942

the woman president: Florence Matilda Read (1886–1973), president of Spelman College (1927–53). She remained a friend and supporter of VN's for years.

Letter of 11 October 1942

Pushkin (Negro blood!): Pushkin's great-grandfather, Abram Petrovich Gannibal (1696–1781), was African, a fact of which Pushkin was proud. VN would explore Gannibal's uncertain origins in 'Abram Gannibal', an appendix to his 1964 *Eugene Onegin* commentary.
'Mozart and Salieri': Pushkin's verse drama *Mozart and Salieri* (1826–30) from the *Little Tragedies* cycle. On Edmund Wilson's suggestion, VN translated it for the *New Republic*, 21 April 1941, pp. 559–60; in book form in *Three Russian Poets* and *V&V*.
Lvov's music: The Russian composer Aleksey Fyodorovich Lvov (1798–1870). VN quotes from 'The Hymn of the Russian Empire' (1833–1917).

working on Gogol: On his book *Nikolai Gogol* (Norfolk, Conn.: New Directions, 1944).
Stuff the boxes: In VN's absence, VéN repinned butterflies in their trays at the Harvard MCZ under his instructions.

Letter of 12 October 1942

done with Gogol: With writing his book, *Nikolai Gogol*.
a short story: He would not write one until 'The Assistant Producer', his first in English, in January 1943 (*Atlantic Monthly*, May 1943, pp. 68–74).
the play: Possibly *The Event*, staged in Russian in New York on 4 April 1941. Molly Carpenter-Lee seems to have translated this or *The Waltz Invention* into English in 1939: see letters of 5 and 8 April 1939.
Bunny: The nickname of Edmund Wilson.

Letter postmarked 14 October 1942

Comstock's: William Phillips Comstock (1880–1956), a leading lepidopterologist, at the American Museum of Natural History.
'commonsense': 'The Art of Literature and Commonsense'.
president: Frank Robertson Reade (1895–1957), President of Georgia State Women's College in Valdosta.
Bunny's: Wilson's.

Letter of 17–18 October 1942

Enclosed is a letter from Charles A. Pearce (1906–70), poetry editor at the *New Yorker*.
the forms . . . laborious procedure: An application to the Guggenheim Foundation for a fellowship to allow VN to complete his current novel, which would ultimately become *Bend Sinister* (New York: Henry Holt, 1947).
Mikh. Mikh.: Mikhail Mikhaylovich Karpovich.
Browning: Robert Browning (1812–89), English poet, and one of VN's favourites.
Kadish: Journalist Mikhail Kadish, whom VN knew from Berlin.
Calocarpa americana: *Callicarpa americana*, American Beautyberry.

Myrica bushes: Myrica, a genus of small trees, the bayberries.

Neonympha: On 9 June 1941, on the south rim of the Grand Canyon, VN and VéN, at different altitudes, caught a specimen each of what VN would name as *Neonympha dorothea*, in 'Some New or Little Known Nearctic Neonympha (Lepidoptera: Satyridae)', *Psyche*, 49, pp. 3–4, 61–80 (see also *N'sB's*). The genus would be renamed, and the butterfly recognized as not a new species but as a new sub-species, *Cyllopsis pertepida dorothea*, of a butterfly hitherto not known north of Mexico. The *Neonympha* he has seen near Valdosta is of a different species within the same genus.

One picture shows . . . : See previous letter, where VN has asked VéN to imagine the paintings on his wall, as a telepathy experiment.

Letter of 20 October 1942

an Egyptian fresco with butterflies: According to Dieter E. Zimmer, the Egyptian fresco with several butterflies is in the Tomb of Nakht in West Thebes; there is a figure in his *Guide to Nabokov's Butterflies and Moths* (www.dezimmer.net/eGuide/Lep2.1-D-E.htm, under *Danaus plexippus*). VN began a book on *Butterflies in Art* in the mid-1960s, but did not complete the project; an Egyptian fresco features in *Ada* (1969, pt. 2 ch. 3).

Moe: Henry Allen Moe (1894–1975), secretary, administrator and then president of the John Simon Guggenheim Memorial Foundation (c. 1925–63).

the old man: Iosif Hessen, who had recently arrived in the US after escaping from occupied France.

Letter of 5 November 1942

an ideal trip to Chicago: On the second part of VN's 1942 American lecture tour, to Springfield, Illinois, St Paul, Minnesota, and Galesburg, Illinois.

Field Museum: Field Museum of Natural History, Chicago, one of the world's largest natural history museums.

RAILROAD STATION: Chicago's Union Station, built in 1925 and designed by Daniel Burnham (1846–1912).

Letter of 7 November 1942

Lincoln's house and grave: The only home that Abraham Lincoln (1809–1865) owned, and where he lived from 1844 to 1861, before becoming President. His tomb is also in Springfield.

the Club: The Mid-Day Luncheon Club, founded in 1915, hosting politicians, businessmen and celebrities as invited speakers.

a creepily silent melancholic: Elmer Kneale (1885–1944), bill collector for the Illinois State Register, a founding member of the Mid-Day Luncheon Club and its secretary for twenty-nine years (1915–44).

Shponka: A character in Gogol's story 'Ivan Fyodorovich Shponka and His Aunt' from *Evenings on a Farm Near Dikanka*, vol. 2 (1831).

McGregor: John C. McGregor, anthropologist, Acting Chief of the Illinois State Museum in Springfield (1942–5).

Carpenter: Frank M. Carpenter (1902–94), paleoentomologist, curator of fossil insects at the Harvard MCZ.

Paul Angle: Paul Angle (1900–1975), librarian of the Illinois Historical Library and state historian (1932–45).

Letter postmarked 9 November 1942

Turck: Dr Charles Joseph Turck (1890–1989), President of Macalester College in St Paul (1939–1958).

Annecy: Lake Annecy in France.

news is getting rosier: The Allies broke the Axis lines at El Alamein on 1 November, and the US invasion of North Africa began on 8 November.

Dasha: Dorothy Leuthold.

Vogelii Obthr: *Lycaena* (now *Maurus*) *vogelii* Oberthür, the Maurus Blue.

a bible and a telephone book . . . communication with the heavens and the office: VN would later refine this observation in the poem 'The Room' (1950) ('The room a dying poet took / at nightfall in a dead hotel / had both directories – the Book / of Heaven and the Book of Bell', *PP*, p. 164).

Letter of 11 November 1942

arrived here: Knox College in Galesburg, Illinois.

Commonsense: 'The Art of Literature and Commonsense'.

When he was small . . . : First published in *Atlantic Monthly*, January 1943, p. 116.

the third newspaper today: Perhaps also now to follow the Battle of Stalingrad, where the German advance was stalled by fierce resistance and worsening weather. On 19 November, the Soviet Army launched its eventually victorious counter-attack, a turning point of the Second World War.

Letter postmarked 7 December 1942

Honours College: Then part of the State Teachers College, now Longwood University, in Farmville, Virginia.

Barbour: Thomas Barbour (1884–1946), herpetologist, director of the Harvard MCZ (1927–46).

Pierce: Charles Pearce, poetry editor of the *New Yorker*.

Natasha: Nathalie Nabokov.

Zenzinov: Vladimir Zenzinov had left Europe for the US in 1939.

Frumkin: Yakov Frumkin, chair of the Union of Russian Jews, the Jewish rescue organization that helped the Nabokovs to cross to the US.

Kovarskys: Ilya Kovarsky, whom VN met in Paris in 1932 and 1936, and his wife.

Dasha: Dorothy Leuthold.

Hilda: Hilda Ward, who had helped VN translate 'Mademoiselle O' from French to English (*Atlantic Monthly*, January 1943, pp. 66–73).

Sanford: Dr Leonard Cutler Sanford (1868–1950), surgeon, amateur ornithologist, trustee of the American Museum of Natural History (1921–50).

Michener: Charles Duncan Michener (b. 1918), from 1942 assistant curator of Lepidoptera at the AMNH.

needed to prepare and draw the genitalia of my Lysandra cormion: Unclear why he needed to do this, since he had already published on *Lysandra cormion* in 1941 and would not do so again.

'types': See note to letter of 7 June 1939.

worked on her to my heart's content: This would give rise to the poem 'On Discovering a Butterfly', *New Yorker*, 15 May 1943, p. 26, republished as 'A Discovery' in *Poems* (1959) and *PP*.

Grainger's: Dr James Moses Grainger (1879–1968), professor from 1910, and chair from 1912 to 1950, of the Department of English at the State Teachers College, renamed Longwood College in 1949 and later Longwood University.

1943

Postcard postmarked 15 April 1943

18 years today: The Nabokovs' wedding anniversary.

Zyoka: Georgy Hessen and his father Iosif arrived in the US in December 1942.

museum: American Museum of Natural History, New York, where VN had carried out research in 1940–1.

A.: Presumably, Anna Feigin, who was now living in New York City.

1944

Letter 1 of 5 June 1944

To: 250 *W* 104 . . . : VéN and DN were staying in New York, with Anna Feigin, while DN had his appendix removed.

my novel: The novel that would end up being called *Bend Sinister*.

finish it before you get back: In fact he would not complete the first draft until late May 1946.

Gogol: His *Nikolai Gogol* (Norfolk, CT: New Direction, 1944).

Letter 2 of 5 June 1944

Wurst. H.: *Wursthaus*, a restaurant in Cambridge, Massachusetts, at 4 Boylston (now John F. Kennedy) Street from 1917 to 1996.

Loveridge: Arthur Loveridge (1891–1980), British biologist, curator of herpetology at the Harvard MCZ (1924–57).

I'VE THOUGHT UP A NEW AEROPLANE: VN marked the sketch with two labels, 'motor' and 'spare wheel'.

Letter of 6 June 1944

Clark: Unidentified.

T. N.: Tatyana Nikolaevna Karpovich.

M. Mikh.: Mikhail Mikhaylovich Karpovich.

Dobuzhinskys: The painter Mstislav Dobuzhinsky and his wife Elizaveta Osipovna Dobuzhinsky (née Wolkenstein, 1876–1965) had lived in the US since 1939.

truly horrendous hospital: In the margin, in VéN's hand: 'Massachusetts General'.

to the hospital where you'd been: In the margin, in VéN's hand: 'Harkness Pavilion Cambridge Hospital'. VN identified the hospital in a letter to Edmund Wilson as 'Mt. Aubrey Hospital' (9 June 1944, *DBDV* 148), in fact Mount Auburn Hospital, Cambridge.

this morning: 'This morning' is added above the line.

Dr Cooney: Unidentified. There is a horizontal line below this sentence.

Enfin: Fr. 'So'.

hasn't received the story: 'A Forgotten Poet'. *The New Yorker* would reject the story, which was published instead in the *Atlantic Monthly*, October 1944, pp. 60–65, and in *Nabokov's Dozen* (Garden City, NY: Doubleday, 1957), pp. 39–54.

invasion beach: VN was admitted to the hospital on 6 June, the day of the Allied invasion of Normandy (D-Day).

Postcard postmarked 8 June 1944

haemoraginal colitis: Haemorrhagic colitis.

Postcard of 9 June 1944

Dynnik: Unidentified, unless a nickname, or a mistake, for Dynkin, the Feigins' family doctor.

White: Katharine Sergeant Angell White (1892–1977), writer and (1925–60) fiction editor for The New Yorker.

I replied to her: VN accepted the offer.

Letter of 11 June 1944

Date: Since 'Sunday' is evidently correct, the actual date must be 11 June 1944.

Sergey's: Sergey Mikhaylovich Karpovich, son of Mikhail and Tatyana Karpovich.

Craigie: The Nabokovs' apartment at 8 Craigie Circle in Cambridge.

Letter postmarked 13 June 1944

The Russian departments we wrote to: Presumably in search of a position for VN, teaching Russian literature. At Wellesley, his position was renewed only a year at a time and until 1946 comprised only basic Russian-language teaching, not literature.

Grosya: Unidentified.

1945

Postcard postmarked 10 February 1945

A charming school: St Timothy's College, Stevenson, Baltimore County, Maryland.

Mrs Bush: Unidentified.

her namesake in 'The Gift': In The Gift, the Riga-born writer Bush becomes a laughing stock when he reads his play in broken Russian to a gathering of émigré Russian writers and readers in Berlin.

leave for New York: Where he would stay with Georgy Hessen.

1954

Letter of 18 April 1954

HUTSON HOTELS: Letterhead.

just arrived: VN had been brought to the University of Kansas at Lawrence for the annual Humanities Lecture and supporting talks and discussions.

Has Mityushok phoned: DN was then in his junior (third) year of a BA at Harvard University.

Letter of 20 April 1954

his typewritten memoirs: From 1948 to 1951, VN's own memoirs had been published serially, mostly in *The New Yorker*, but also in *Harper's Magazine* and *Partisan Review*, thus making him a celebrity in the world of American memoirs.

Elmer: Elmer F. Beth (1901–70), chair of the Department of Journalism and chairman of the Humanities Series Committee at the University of Kansas.

Ithacan: VN taught at Cornell University, Ithaca, New York, from 1948 to 1958.

the Winters: Unidentified.

Gatchina: A small town, former imperial residence, south-west of St Petersburg. Winter's having reached Gatchina, Dieter E. Zimmer notes, 'probably implies that he had been a translator in the German army during the siege of Leningrad; the ring around the city had been between the city of Gatchina and the Pulkovo Hills (now the St Petersburg airport). The German headquarters in that section of the front had been in Siversky, the estate of VN's relatives, the Falz-Feins.'

Andersen: Unidentified.

Cross: Samuel Hazzard Cross (1891–1946), diplomat, from 1930 professor of Slavic languages at Harvard. VN had a low opinion of Cross's knowledge of Russian grammar.

how he pulled out the wrong card: VN explained the intricacies of the card games in which Hermann, the protagonist, engages at the end of Pushkin's novella *The Queen of Spades* (1834).

1964

Note of 3 May 1964

A note to accompany a bouquet of flowers. It is written on one side of a small white card and addressed on the other. VéN had entered the clinic after abdominal pains over the previous month, and was operated on for appendicitis.

1965

Note of 15 April 1965

Date: The Nabokovs' fortieth wedding anniversary.

1966

Letter of 2 October 1966

in the local, Tulsa, newspaper: DN had a singing engagement for Tulsa Opera in Tulsa, Oklahoma.

Minton: Walter J. Minton (1923–), president of G. P. Putnam's Sons, which was about to publish *Speak, Memory: An Autobiography Revisited* (dated 1966, published January 1967), with these endpapers.

ask him for it, if you have a chance: VéN was visiting New York to discuss VN's publishing future. The Nabokovs had been dissatisfied with the size of the advances they had received from Putnam, their main American publisher since *Lolita* in 1958; as a result of the discussion with Minton, they asked the William Morris Agency to find another publisher, and in 1967 signed with McGraw-Hill.

the Grove edition of Miller's 'Tropic of Cancer': *Tropic of Cancer*, the erotic novel of Henry Miller (1891–1980), first published in 1934 in Paris, faced an obscenity trial after its 1961 American publication by Grove Press. In 1964, the US Supreme Court declared the novel was not obscene. That year, Grove Press published *Tropik raka*, a small-scale translation (200 copies) of the novel into Russian by émigré Georgy Egorov, made at the request of Miller, who wanted to honour the Russian characters in his book.

Elena: Elena Sikorski, VN's sister who, from 1949, had lived in Geneva and had come to Montreux to look after her brother during VéN's absence.

Vladimír: Vladimir Vsevolodovich Sikorski (b. 1939), Elena's son.

how to fold this thing: The letter is written on an aerogram sheet that folds into an envelope.

1968

Note of 8 June 1968

A note on an index card, in two coloured pencils, red and blue. The italicized lines are written in red, the rest of the note is in blue. In the lower-left corner, a later inscription, possibly in VéN's hand: '8–VI–68, to Verbier'. Verbier is a village in the Valais, south-western Switzerland.

1969

Note of 15 April 1969

Date: A 44th wedding anniversary note, in English, on an index card; only one side is inscribed. Dated at the bottom of the card, in a different pen, but probably also by VN. May have been inserted in a copy of *Ada*, which had arrived on 10 April.

Cymbidium lowianum: A species of Lady's Slipper Orchid.

Ada & *Lucette*: Characters in *Ada*, about to be published in May 1969, and strongly associated with orchids. VN drew a Cattleya orchid for the cover of the Penguin edition of *Ada* (1970), an image that Penguin adapted.

Note of 4 July 1969

Written on an index card. The Nabokovs were holidaying with Anna Feigin in Cureglia.

Note of 22 July 1969

Written on an index card. The cross indicates that at the end of 1976 VN selected this for inclusion in *Stikhi*, his selected Russian poems.

How I loved the poems of Gumilyov!: 'Kak lyubil ya stikhi Gumilyova!' first published in *Stikhi*, p. 297; translated by DN, *Atlantic*, April 2000, 75, and in *N's Bs*, p. 694.

1970

Letter of 6 April 1970

SAN DOMENICO PALACE HOTEL: Letterhead.

room 220: Added to the letterhead by VN.

Monza: A city near Milan where DN lived for many years, because of its Grand Prix racetrack (he raced cars) and proximity to La Scala (he was an opera singer).

the Montrome one: From Montreux to Rome.

Euchloe ausonia: The pierid butterfly, the Eastern Dappled White.

the Cyprian's silvery star: The Morning Star (Venus, who was reputed to come from Cyprus).

Letter of 7 April 1970

(Otherwise you will get what happened to Humbert): Echoes not only Humbert's fate, but also the mock-injunctions facing Humbert and Lolita: 'Some motels had instructions pasted above the toilet . . . asking guests not to throw into its bowl garbage, beer cans, cartons, stillborn babies'; 'Would sex crimes be reduced if children obeyed a few don'ts? Don't play around public toilets. Don't take candy or rides from strangers'; 'Do not throw waste material of any kind in the toilet bowl. Thank you. Call again. The Management. P. S. We consider our guests the Finest People of the World' (*Lolita*, pp. 146, 165, 210).

. . . Humbert) ¶: VN indicates the paragraph end here and elsewhere so that VéN does not have to struggle to decipher what could seem like the remainder of the line showing through from the other side of the sheet on the hotel's very transparent stationery.

and not ten years ago: VN and VéN had spent some of November 1959 in Taormina, at the Hotel Excelsior.

Letter of 8 April 1970

S. in Fialta: 'Spring in Fialta'.

red corvo: Corvo rosso, a Sicilian wine.

je m'excuse de ces mots un peu forts: Fr. 'Sorry for these rather strong words'.

Thais Zerynthia hypsipyle cassandra: A sub-species of the papilionid butterfly *Zerynthia polyxena*, the Southern Festoon. *Thais* is a superseded generic name, *hypsipyle* a junior (later, and therefore invalid, according to the law of taxonomic priority) species name.

'Où je peux laver le petit garçon?': Fr. 'where I can wash the little boy?'

phanodorm: A sleeping pill.

Janits: Or Yanits. Unidentified.

Galina Kuznetsova's diary: *Grasskiy dnevnik* (*The Grasse Diary*) by Bunin's mistress Galina Kuznetsova (Washington, DC: Viktor Kamkin, 1967).

Letter of 8–9 April 1970

Je tiens: Fr. 'I care'.

the 15th: Their 45th wedding anniversary.

Nebrodi Mountains . . . shame for us not to wander: 'Nebrodiyskie' is a pun on the name of the mountains (Nebrodi). The Russian *ne brodi* means 'do not wander'.

Anyuta: The Nabokovs had brought her from New York to Montreux in 1967 as her mental health began to decline.

Lifar's new memoirs: *My Life* (New York: World Publishing, 1970) by Serge Lifar.

Diaguiliev: Sergey Pavlovich Diaghilev (1872–1929), ballet impresario in Russia and Paris, founder of the Ballets Russes.

Markevitch: Igor Borisovich Markevitch (1912–83), Ukrainian-born composer and conductor, friend of VN's through his cousin Nicolas.

Topazia: Donna Topazia Caetani (1921–90), the second wife of Igor Markevitch.

allenburies: Allenbury's Pastilles.

Letter of 10 April 1970

Alfred Friendly: Journalist (1912–83), managing editor of the *Washington Post*; would visit VN in Sicily and write a short report, 'Nabokov the Collector', for the *New York Times*, 10 May 1970, vii, pp. 32–3.

tedesko: Ital. 'German'.

Puccinian: Sounding out music from operas by Giacomo Puccini (1858–1924).

correspondence: In Russian, *(pere)piska*.

Note of 15 April 1970

Date: The Nabokovs' wedding anniversary. The date and place '15-IV-70 Taormina' appears to have been added later by VéN. The card presumably accompanied flowers.

Forty-five springs: 'Sorok pyat' vyosen'. VN's 'springs' (*vyosen*) is a reference to Russian 'years' (*let*), which could also mean 'summers' (*let*) in the genitive plural: 'forty-five spring-like years' in effect.

1971

Note of 15 April 1971

A note on a white unlined card. Addressed on one side, inscribed on the other. Presumably the card accompanied flowers. VN's sketchy drawing of a small butterfly below his initial.

1973

Note postmarked 22 January 1973

Twelve tens: Presumably Swiss francs.

1974

Note of 5 January 1974

A note, on an index card, with a pen-and-ink drawing of a small butterfly.

thumb hurts: Inserted above the 'Happy Birthday' as an explanation for the rough lettering.

L'année d'Ada und 'Ada: The year when *Ada* was to be published in French and German. The German did appear (*Ada oder Das Verlangen*, trans. Uwe Friesel and Marianne Therstappen, Reinbek bei Hamburg: Rowohlt, 1974); the French translation, however, needed intensive reworking by VN and was not published until 1975 (*Ada ou l'ardeur*, trans. Gilles Chahine and Jean-Bernard Blandenier with VN, Paris: Fayard, 1975).

Note of 14 June 1974

Date: Dated by VéN 'To me from V. 14–VI–74'. Written on both sides of an index card. VN had traveled to Zermatt a week ahead of VéN in order to hunt butterflies.

1975

Note of 14 July 1975

On a checkered index card.

1976

Note of 7 April 1976

On a lined index card; a rhymed poem in Russian.

APPENDIX TWO: AFTERLIFE BY BRIAN BOYD

540: *an article on Nabokov that he understandably disliked*: For more detail, see *VNAY* 394–97. 'Under the pen name Jacques Croisé, Shakhovskoy declared that the emotional desert of Nabokov's years of Continental exile had been so complete that in his memoirs "he would even forget the friends of his darkest days." Shakhovskoy seems to have resented the fact that *Conclusive Evidence* did not name her, although the émigré pages of Nabokov's memoirs quite deliberately avoided his private life, limiting themselves to a few comments on those who contributed to Russian literature, in tones far from cold (Fondaminsky, "a saintly and heroic soul who did more for émigré literature than any other man'; Khodasevich, "wrought of irony and metallic-like genius, whose poetry was as complex a marvel as that of Tyutchev or Blok"; "wise, prim, charming Aldanov"). Citing the opinions of Hermann in *Despair* as if they were Nabokov's own and not those of a madman and murderer he despised, Shakhovskoy declared that in Nabokov's world "goodness does not exist, all is nightmare and deceit. Those seeking intellectual comfort would be better swallowing poison than reading Nabokov"' (*VNAY* 396).

Bibliography

ARCHIVES

Biblioteka-Fond 'Russkoe Zarubezhie', Moscow.

Irina Guadanini Papers. Private collection (Tatyana Morozov).

Vladimir Nabokov Archive, Henry W. and Albert A. Berg Collection, New York Public Library, New York, NY.

Vladimir Nabokov Papers, Library of Congress, Washington, D.C.

Vladimir and Véra Nabokov Papers (transcripts and photocopies) and Audiotapes. Private collection (Brian Boyd).

Zinaida Shakhovskoy Papers, Amherst Center for Russian Culture, Amherst College, Amherst, MA.

Zinaida Shakhovskoy Papers, Library of Congress, Washington DC.

WORKS BY VLADIMIR NABOKOV

Ada oder Das Verlangen, trans. Uwe Friesel and Marianne Therstappen. Reinbek bei Hamburg: Rowohlt, 1974.

Ada or Ardor: A Family Chronicle. New York: McGraw-Hill, 1969.

Ada ou l'ardeur, trans. Gilles Chahine with Jean-Bernard Blandenier. Paris: Fayard, 1975.

L'aguet: nouvelle inédite [*Soglyadatay*; *The Eye: Unpublished Novella*], trans. Denis Roche. *Œuvres libres*, 164, February 1935.

Anya v Strane chudes [trans. of Lewis Carroll, *Alice's Adventures in Wonderland*] Berlin: Gamayun 1923.

Bend Sinister (1947), reprinted with introduction by VN. New York: Time, 1964.

Camera Obscura [*Kamera obskura*], trans. Winifred Roy. London: John Long, 1936.

Chambre Obscure [*Kamera obskura*], trans. Doussia Ergaz. Paris: Grasset, 1934.

Conclusive Evidence: A Memoir. New York: Harper and Brothers, 1951.

La Course du fou [*Zashchita Luzhina*; *The Defence*], trans. Denis Roche. Paris: Fayard, 1934.

Dar [*The Gift*]. New York: Chekhov Publishing House, 1952.

Dear Bunny, Dear Volodya: The Nabokov–Wilson Letters, 1940–1971, ed. Simon Karlinsky (1979); rev. edn, Berkeley and Los Angeles: University of California Press, 2001.

The Defense (*Zashchita Luzhina*, *La Course du fou*, *The Luzhin Defence*). Trans. Michael Scammell with VN. New York: Putnam, 1964.

Despair [*Otchayanie*], trans. Vladimir Nabokov. London: John Long, 1937; rev. edn, New York: Putnam, 1966.

Drugie berega [*Conclusive Evidence*]. New York: Chekhov Publishing House, 1954.

'Entretien avec Vladimir Nabokov' by Pierre Dommergues, *Les Langues modernes*, 62 (January–February 1968), pp. 92–102.

Eugene Onegin, by Alexander Pushkin, trans. with commentary by Vladimir Nabokov, 4 vols; rev. edn,. Princeton, NJ: Princeton University Press, 1975.

The Eye [*Soglyadatay*], trans. Dmitri Nabokov with Vladimir Nabokov. New York: Phaedra, 1965.

Frühling in Fialta: Dreiundzwanzig Erzählungen [*Spring in Fialta: Thirty-one Stories*], ed. Dieter E. Zimmer, trans. Wassili Berger, Dieter E. Zimmer, Renate Gerhardt and René Drommert. Reinbek bei Hamburg: Rowohlt, 1966.

The Gift [*Dar*], trans. Michael Scammell [and Dmitri Nabokov] with Vladimir Nabokov. New York: Putnam, 1963; New York: Vintage, 1991.

Glory [*Podvig*], trans. Dmitri Nabokov with Vladimir Nabokov. New York: McGraw-Hill, 1971.

Gorniy put' [*The Empyrean Path*]. Berlin: Grani, 1923.

Grozd' [*The Cluster*]. Berlin: Gamayun, 1923.

Han som spelade schack med livet [*Zashchita Luzhina*; *The Defence*], trans. Ellen Rydelius. Stockholm: Bonnier, 1936.

Invitation to a Beheading [*Priglashenie na kazn'*], trans. Dmitri Nabokov with Vladimir Nabokov. New York: Putnam, 1959.

Kamera obskura [*Laughter in the Dark*]. Berlin and Paris: Parabola, 1933.

King, Queen, Knave [*Korol', dama, valet*], trans. Dmitri Nabokov with Vladimir Nabokov. New York: McGraw-Hill, 1968.

König, Dame, Bube [*Korol', dama, valet*; *King, Queen, Knave*], trans. Siegfried von Vegesack. Berlin: Ullstein, 1930.

Korol', dama, valet [*King, Queen, Knave*]. Berlin: Ullstein, 1928.

Laughter in the Dark [*Kamera obskura*]. Indianapolis: Bobbs-Merrill, 1938.

Lectures on Literature, ed. Fredson Bowers. New York: Harcourt Brace Jovanovich, 1980.

Lectures on Russian Literature, ed. Fredson Bowers. New York: Harcourt Brace Jovanovich, 1981.

Lolita. New York: Putnam, 1958.

Look at the Harlequins! New York: McGraw-Hill, 1974.

The Man from the USSR and Other Plays, ed. and trans. Dmitri Nabokov. New York: Harcourt Brace Jovanovich/Bruccoli Clark, 1984.

Mashen'ka [*Mary*]. Berlin: Slovo, 1926.

La Méprise [*Otchayanie; Despair*], trans. Marcel Stora. Paris: Gallimard, 1939.

The Nabokov–Wilson Letters: Correspondence between Vladimir Nabokov and Edward Wilson, 1940–1971, ed. Simon Karlinsky. New York: Harper & Row, 1979.

Nabokov's Butterflies: Unpublished and Uncollected Writings, ed. Brian Boyd and Robert Michael Pyle. Boston: Beacon Press, 2000.

Nabokov's Dozen. Garden City, NY: Doubleday, 1957.

'Neskol'ko slov ob ubozhestve sovetskoy belletriski i popytka ustanovit' prichinu onogo', ed. Alexander A. Dolinin, *Diaspora*, 2 (2001), pp. 7–23.

Nikolai Gogol. Norfolk, CT: New Directions, 1944.

'Notes on the Lepidoptera of the Pyrénées Orientales and the Ariège', *Entomologist*, 64 (November 1931), 255–57.

Otchayanie [*Despair*]. Berlin: Petropolis, 1936

Pale Fire. New York: Putnam, 1962.

'Pis'ma k Glebu Struve' ['Letters to Gleb Struve']. Ed. Evgeny Belodubrovsky, *Zvezda*, 4 (1999), 23–39.

'Pis'ma V. V. Nabokova k Gessenam' ['Letters of V. V. Nabokov to the Hessens']. Ed. V. Yu. Gessen, *Zvezda*, 4 (1999) pp. 42–45.

Pnin. Garden City, NY: Doubleday, 1957.

Podvig [*Glory*]. Paris: Sovremennye Zapiski, 1932.

Poems. Garden City, NY: Doubleday, 1959.

Poems and Problems. New York: McGraw-Hill, 1971.

Priglashenie na kazn' [*Invitation to a Beheading*]. Paris: Dom Knigi, 1938.

The Real Life of Sebastian Knight. Norfolk, CT: New Directions, 1941.

A Russian Beauty and Other Stories. New York: McGraw-Hill, 1973.

Selected Letters, 1940–1977, ed. Dmitri Nabokov and Matthew J. Bruccoli. New York: Harcourt Brace Jovanovich/Bruccoli Clark Layman, 1989.
Selected Poems, ed. Thomas Karshan, with translations by Vladimir and Dmitri Nabokov. New York: Knopf, 2012.
Sie kommt–kommt sie? [*Mashen'ka*; *Mary*], trans. Jakob Margot Schubert and G. Jarcho. Berlin: Ullstein, 1928.
Skital'tsy [*The Wanderers*], *Grani*, 2 (1923), pp. 69–99.
Soglyadatay [*The Eye*]. Paris: Russkie Zapiski, 1938.
Speak, Memory: An Autobiography Revisited. New York: Putnam, 1967.
Stikhi. Ann Arbor, MI.: Ardis, 1979.
Stikhotvoreniya, ed. Maria Malikova. St Petersburg: Akademicheskiy Proekt, 2002.
The Stories of Vladimir Nabokov, ed. Dmitri Nabokov. New York: Knopf, 1995.
Strong Opinions. New York: McGraw-Hill, 1973.
Three Russian Poets: Selections from Pushkin, Lermontov and Tyutchev (Norfolk, CT: New Directions, 1944).
Tragediya gospodina Morna, P'esy, Lektsii o drame [*The Tragedy of Mister Morn, Plays, Lectures on Drama*], ed. Andrey Babikov, St Petersburg: Azbuka-klassika, 2008.
The Tragedy of Mister Morn, trans. Anastasia Tolstoy and Thomas Karshan. London: Penguin, 2012.
Transparent Things. New York: McGraw-Hill, 1972.
Tyrants Destroyed and Other Stories, trans. Dmitri Nabokov with Vladimir Nabokov. New York: McGraw-Hill, 1975.
'V. V. Nabokov i I. A. Bunin. Perepiska' ['V. V. Nabokov and I. A. Bunin: Correspondence'], ed. R. Davis and M. D. Shrayer, *S dvukh beregov: Russkaya literatura XX veka v Rossii i za rubezhom*. Moscow: IMLI RAN, 2002, pp. 167–219.
Verses and Versions: Three Centuries of Russian Poetry, ed. Brian Boyd and Stanislav Shvabrin. New York: Harcourt, 2008.
Vesna v Fial'te i drugie rasskazy [*Spring in Fialta and Other Stories*]. New York: Chekhov Publishing House, 1956.
Vozvrashchenie Chorba: Rasskazy i Stikhi [*The Return of Chorb: Stories and Poems*]. Berlin: Slovo, 1930.
'Vtoroe dobavlenie k *Daru*' ['Second Addition to *Dar*'; 'Father's Butterflies']. Ed. Alexander A. Dolinin. *Zvezda*, 2001: 1, pp. 85–109.

BIOGRAPHICAL AND CRITICAL WORKS

Barabtarlo, Gennady, *Aerial Views: Essays on Nabokov's Art and Metaphysics*. New York: Peter Lang, 1993.

Boyd, Brian, *Vladimir Nabokov: The American Years*. Princeton, NJ: Princeton University Press, 1991.

—, *Vladimir Nabokov: The Russian Years*. Princeton, NJ: Princeton University Press, 1990.

Dolinin, Alexander A., 'Kubovyi tsvet. Iz kommentariya k slovaryu Nabokova'. In Lazar Fleishman, Christine Gölz and Aage A. Hansen-Löve, eds., *Analysieren als Deuten. Wolf Schmid zum 60. Geburtstag* (Hamburg: Hamburg University Press, 2004), 563–73.

Field, Andrew, *VN: The Life and Art of Vladimir Nabokov*. New York: Crown, 1986.

—, *Nabokov: His Life in Art*. Boston: Little, Brown, 1967.

—, *Nabokov: His Life in Part*. New York: Viking, 1977.

Glushanok, Galina, ed., 'Vera Nabokova's Correspondence with A. Goldenveizer', *Nabokov Online Journal*, 1, 2007.

Gul', Roman, *Ya unyos Rossiyu: Apologiya emigratsii*, Vol. 1, *Rossiya v Germanii*. Moscow: BSG Press, 2001.

—, *Ya unyos Rossiyu: Apologiya emigratsii*, Vol. 2, *Rossiya vo Frantsii*. Moscow: BSG Press, 2001.

—, *Ya unyos Rossiyu: Apologiya emigratsii*, Vol. 3, *Rossiya v Amerike*. Moscow: BSG Press, 2001.

Hessen, Iosif, *Gody izgnaniya: zhiznenniy otchot*. Paris: YMCA, 1981.

Khodasevich, Vladislav, *Kamer-fur'erskiy zhurnal*. Moscow: Ellis Lak, 2000, 2002.

Korostelyov, Oleg, and Manfred Shruba, eds., *'Sovremennye zapiski' (Parizh, 1920–1940), Iz arkhiva redaktsii [Sovremennye zapiski (Paris, 1920–1940), from the Editorial Archive]*, Vols 1 and 2. Moscow: Novoe Literaturnoe Obozrenie, 2012.

Mnukhin, L., M. Avril' and V. Losskaya, *Rossiyskoe zarubezh'e vo Frantsii. 1919–2000: biogr[aficheskiy] slovar': v 3 t [The Russian emigration in France, 1919–2000: Biographical dictionary in 3 Vols]*. Moscow: Nauka–Dom-muzey Mariny Tsvetaevoy, 2008–10.

Mukhachev, Yu. V., E. P. Chelyshev and A. Ya. Degtaryov, eds, *Literaturnoe zarubezh'e Rossii*. Moscow: Parad, 2006.

Parry, Albert, 'Belles Lettres among the Russian Émigrés', *American Mercury*, 29 (July 1933), pp. 316–19.

Schiff, Stacy, *Véra (Mrs. Vladimir Nabokov)*. New York: Random House, 1999.

Schlögel, Karl, Katharina Kucher, Bernhard Suchy and Gregor Thum, eds, *Chronik russischen Lebens in Deutschland 1918–41*. Berlin: Akademie Verlag, 1999.

Shakhovskoy, Zinaida. "Le Cas Nabokov, ou la blessure de l'exil" [as Jacques Croisé]. *La Revue de deux mondes*, August 15, 1959.

— *V poiskakh Nabokova* [*In Search of Nabokov*]. Paris: La Presse libre, 1979.

Zimmer, Dieter E., *A Guide to Nabokov's Butterflies and Moths*. Web version, 2012. www.d-e-zimmer.de/eGuide/PageOne.htm.

—, *Nabokovs Berlin*. Berlin: Nicolaische Verlagsbuchhandlung, 2001.

—, *Nabokov reist im Traum in das Innere Asiens*. Reinbek bei Hamburg: Rowohlt, 2006.

Acknowledgements

This project would have been impossible without the late Dmitri Nabokov's generously making available to us not only the letters to Véra, still in his possession in Montreux in 2002, but also the services of his staff, especially Antonio Epicoco, who located and photocopied the material, Aleksey Konovalov and Cris Galliker. Nikki Smith, Dmitri's then agent, enthusiastically endorsed the project. The staff of the Henry W. and Albert A. Berg Collection at the New York Public Library, especially its director, Isaac Gewirtz, and the cataloguer of the Vladimir Nabokov Archive, Stephen Crook, were always prompt in providing access to the originals once they arrived there later in 2002. Gennady Barabtarlo was enormously generous, meticulous, sensitive and insightful in his close reading of the Russian original manuscript, tapes and transcription and the English translation and notes, and in his solutions to the riddles embedded in Nabokov's letters of 1926. Andrey Babikov also contributed to the deciphering of the Russian. The late Omri Ronen's encyclopaedic knowledge of the Russian emigration helped solve some recalcitrant puzzles. Dieter E. Zimmer supplied invaluably precise information on topics he has made his own, Nabokov's Berlin, his butterflies, and his genealogy, and he and especially Ludger Tolksdorf continued to offer meticulous corrections through the book's multiple proof stages. Monica Manolescu combed through French periodicals in Strasbourg and Paris to confirm that the stories Nabokov had expected to be published in French journals in 1937 were not in fact published, and she and Maurice Couturier helped resolve a French crux. Maxim Shrayer provided information about Ivan Bunin and helped locate rare Bunin photographs. Bronwen Nicholson made valuable editorial suggestions and helped compile the bibliography. Stanislav Shvabrin offered astute suggestions about fine points of the translation. Galya Diment also checked the transcription of the Russian text. Michael Hurst digitized and enhanced the cassette tapes of Véra Nabokov reading out her husband's letters to her; Tim Page helped digitize the photographs. And, of course, a special thanks to Véra Nabokov herself, for not only occasioning and preserving these letters, but for reading out so much of them–despite her passion for privacy, her age and her ill-health–into BB's tape recorder in 1984–5.

Index

All literary works are by VN unless otherwise indicated. VN is also the default referent: 'aunt', if otherwise unspecified, will be *his* aunt; 'attitude to' (Berlin, say) will be *his* attitude to the term in question.

First names, first-name-and-patronymic combinations, nicknames, and initials referred to in the letters are listed and cross-referred to the surname, if known. Initials like 'B. G.' (for 'Berta Gavrilovna', surname unknown, or 'Berta Grigorievna Zeldovich') are listed under the first letter, since the second initial will be a patronymic, not a surname, whereas names like 'Misha L.' are listed under the initial for the surname before being cross-referred ('*see* Lubrzynsky, Mikhail Efimovich').

Place names are generally identified by the region relevant to the historical context (Russia *or* Soviet Union, for instance).

Page numbers in bold indicate core identifying or explanatory information or especially rich details in a long list of entries.

À la recherche du temps perdu (Proust), 51, 563
'A pomnish' grozy nashego detstva?' ('And do you recall the thunderstorms of our childhood?'), 520
Abbazia (Austria-Hungary; now Opatija, Croatia), 322, 323
'Abt Vogler' (Browning), 585
acacia, 71, 73, 106, 135, 137
Acharya, *see* Nakhman-Acharya, Magda Maksimilianovna
Acropolis, Athens, 177, 602
Ada, xix, xliv, xlvii, liii, 504, 518, **715**, **723**, **724**, **727**
Adamov, Nadezhda Konstantinovna, 191, 196, 198, 215, 292, **609**, **655**
Adamovich, Georgy Victorovich, 103, 153, 164, 167, 175, 194, 198, 223, 226, 244, 254, 257, 272–3, 288, 422, **577**, 593, 594, 598, 601, 613, 627; feud with Khodasevich and Nabokov, 240, 596, 609, **632–3**, 635; venality, 422, **695**
Adler Inn, Todtmoos, Germany, 73

'Admiralteyskaya igla' ('The Admiralty Spire'), 302, **623**, **627**
'Admiralty Spire, The', *see* 'Admiralteyskaya igla'
'Aerial Island', *see* 'Vozdushnyi ostrov'
'Aeroplan' ('Aeroplane'), 118, 137, **581**, 585
Africa, 4, 161, 313
African Americans, 465, 467, 469, 470–1, 472, 495
Agasfer (Ahasuerus), 21, **554**, **555**, review, 555
Aguet, L' (The Eye), *see* *Soglyadatay*
Ahasuerus, *see* *Agasfer*
Akhmatova, Anna (Anna Andreevna Gorenko), lx, 113, **579**, 695
Aksyonov, 272
Albertine disparue (Proust), 51, **563**
Albin Michel, publisher, Paris, 332, 350, 372, **669**
Aldanov, Mark Aleksandrovich, xxxii, xxxv, xliii, 18, 148, 190, 191, 193, 195, 200, 241, 243, 250, 254, 256, 257, 264, 269, 272–3, 281, 283, 285, 286, 291, 294, 338, 355, 380–1, 451, 452, 484, **554**, 616, **708**; as historical novelist, **676**; on VN, 254, 285, **639**, 650; VN on, 193–4, 195, 202, 206–7, 212, 216, 219, 225, 226, 273, 285, 321, 324, 329, 338, 587
Aldanov (Landau-Aldanov), Tatyana Markovna, 241, 250, 269, 304, 324, 338, **661**
Aleks. Fyod. *or* Aleksandr Fyodorovich, *see* Kerensky, Aleksandr Fyodorovich
Aleksandra Fyodorovna, Tsarina, 189, 607
Aleksandra Lazarevna, 278, **647**, *see* (?) Feigin, Anna Lazarevna
Aleksandr Yakovlevich, 235
Alexander I of Yugoslavia, 252, 638
Alfyorov, Anatoly Vladimirovich, 247, **636**
Algiers, 249
Alice's Adventures in Wonderland (Carroll), VN's translation of, see *Anya v strane chudes*
Alkonost, 37, 551, 559
Alsace, France, 187
Alta Gracia *or* Altagracia, *see* Jannelli, Altragracia de
Altai, Central Asia, 397, 567, 689
Altschuller, Grigory Isaakovich, 180, **604**
Altschuller, Isaak Naumovich, 179, 180, **603**
Amalia *or* Amalia Osipovna, *see* Fondaminsky, Amalia Osipovna
America, xxxvi, xxxvii, 14, 21, 27, 200, 265–6, 307, 314, 329, 334, 336, 387, 433
American Mercury, 299, 357, **658**, **677**
American Club, Paris, 197, 204
American Museum of Natural History, New York, 485, **718**
Amsterdam, 55, 126
Anchor, The, *see* *Yakor'*

'And do you recall the thunderstorms of our childhood?', *see* 'A pomnish' grozy nashego detstva?'
Andersen, 499
Andreev, Vadim Leonidovich, 215, **621**
Angle, Paul, 480, **716**
Anhalter Station, Berlin, 28, 161, 166, 186
Anna, 255
Anna, *see* Nabokov, Anna Pavlovna
Anna Maksimovna, 362
Anna Natanovna, 268, 269, 356, 361
anti-Semitism and philosemitism, xxiii, 25, 139, 165, 217, 230–31, 465, 557, 712
Anna Karenin (Tolstoy), lx, 123, 320, 582
Annecy, Lake, France, 481
Antibes, France, 441
Antonini, Giacomo, 288, 298, 324, **653**
Antwerp, xxxiii, 188, 210, 214, 232, 238, 239, 632
Antwerp Russian Circle, 188, 632
Anya v strane chudes (translation of Carroll, *Alice's Adventures in Wonderland*), xxiii, 184, 551, **605**
Anyuta or Anyutochka, *see* Feigin, Anna Lazarevna
Appel, Alfred, Jr., xliii
Arago, boulevard, Paris, 199
Arbatov, Zinovy Yurievich, 121, 127, 142, **581**
Arc de Triomphe, Paris, 338
Aristarkhov, 266
Ark: Anthology of Russian Émigré Literature, The (various authors), *see Kovcheg: Sbornik russkoy zarubezhnoy literatury*
arme Dichter, Der, 262
Army and Navy Club, London, 429
'Art of Translation, The', 452, **708**
Aschberg, Olga Nikolaevna, 224–5, 228, **625**
Aschberg, Olof, 228, **625**, **627**
Asia, 4, 651, 656, 681, 689
Asquith, Herbert Henry, Earl of Oxford and Asquith, 306, **661**
'Assistant Producer, The', **714**
Astrov, Nikolay Ivanovich, 166, 167, **595**
Atholl, Katharine Marjory Stewart-Murray, Duchess of, 387, **685**
Atlanta, Georgia, as VN address, 468–72, 477 (1942)
Atlantic, xxxvi, 440, 443, 444, 449, 451, 466, **702**, 704
Au Papillon bleu, restaurant, Paris, xlix, 198
Auerbach, 237
Augsburger Strasse, Berlin, 73
'Aurelian, The', *see* 'Pil'gram'
Australia, 427
Austria, xxxiv, 380
autobiography, VN's, early, xxxiv, 244, 260, 297, 301, 303, 304, 305, 306, 307–8, 309, 318, 330, 334, 336, 346, **634**, **658**, **660**, **673**. *See also* 'English Associations'; It is Me; Me; *Conclusive Evidence*; *Speak, Memory*

'Autumn', *see* 'Osen'' (Pushkin)
Average Man (Obyvatel'), pen-name of Mikhail Andreevich Osorgin, *q.v.*
Avg. Is. *or* Avgust *or* Avgust Isaakovich, *see* Kaminka, Avgust Isaakovich
Avinov, Andrey Nikolaevich, 336, **671**
Avksentiev, Aleksandra Nikolaevna, *see* Pregel, Aleksandra Nikolaevna
Avksentiev, Nikolay Dmitrievich, 167, 343–4, **596**
Aykhenvald, Yuly Isaevich, 59, 64, 65, 72, 81, 85, 87, 100, 105–06, 115, 117, 127, 135, 136–7, 142, 143, 155, 230, 248, **566**, 577, 584, 590, epigram on, 119, VN on, 248
Azef, Evno Fishelevich, 172, 203, **599**
Azef (Gul'), 378, 379, **683**

B. G., *see* Berta Gavrilovna *or* Zeldovich, Berta Grigorievna
Baby, Aunt, *see* Wonlyar-Lyarsky, Nadezhda Dmitrievna
Bad-Boll, Germany, 43, **561**
Badgers, *see Barsuki* (Leonov)
Bagrova (Filaretova-Bagrova), Maria Vasilievna Znosko-Borovsky, 312, **663**
Bakhareva (Princess Maria Aleksandrovna Tsitsianov), 319, 334, **665**
Bakhmeteff, Boris Aleksandrovich, 387, **685**
Balmont, Konstantin Dmitrievich, 262, 642
Baltimore, Maryland, xix, 459, 495
Banks, Leslie, 400, **690**
Banks, Nathan, 459, 466, 467, 472, 475, 711
Barabtarlo, Gennady Aleksandrovich, 525, 563, 617
Baratynsky, Evgeny Abramovich, 151, **588**
Barbey, Bernard, 383, **684**
Barbour, Thomas, 484, 493, **717**
Bardeleben, Albrecht von, 158, 162
Bardeleben, Frau von, 157, 351, 591, **675**
Baring, Maurice, 313, 319, 387, 392, 397, 402, 406, 411, **663**
Barnacle (Joyce), Nora, liii
Barsuki (*Badgers*, Leonov), 59, 566
Baryatinsky, Prince Vladimir Vladimirovich, 240, **632**
Bataud, Mme, 253
Baudelaire, Charles, 161, **592–3**
Baum, Vicki, 178, **603**
Bavaria, Germany, 42, 341
Bayerischer Platz, Berlin, 88
Baykalov, Anatoly Vaslievich, 304, **661**
Bazilevsky, Mme, 237, **631**
Bazilevsky, Pyotr Georgievich, 631
Beach, Sylvia, 350, 357, 362, **674**
Beaulieu, France, 173, 179. *See also* Domaine Beaulieu
Beaulieu-sur-Mer, France, 283
Beausobre, Julia, 415, 416, **693**
Bebesha, Aunt, *see* Wonlyar-Lyarsky, Nadezhda Dmitrievna
Bednye lyudi (*Poor Folk*, Dostoevsky), **627**
Belgium, xvi, xxxiii, xxxiv, 192, 207, 229, 230, 239, 253, 258, 260, 263, 290, 335, 344, 345, 399

Belgrade, Yugoslavia, 228, 290
Bell, Alexander Graham, 551
'Bells of Heaven, The' (Hodgson), 176, 601
Bellevuestrasse, Berlin, 64
Bely, Andrey, 301, **659**
Bem, Alfred Lyudvigovich, 177, 203, **602**
Benckendorff, *see* Ridley, Natalia Aleksandrovna
Bend Sinister, xix, xlvii, 476, 486, 490, 493, **695–6**, **714**, **718**
'Beneficence', *see* 'Blagost''
Benenson, Grigory Iosifovich, 393, **688**
Benois, Aleksandr Nikolaevich, 200, 208, 209, 345, **614**
Bennett, Arnold, xlix, 422, **695**
Béraud, Henri, xlix, 135, **584**
Berberova, Nina Nikolaevna, xxxi, xxxii, lx, 191, 193, 201, 202, 219, 223, 229, 243, 249, 254, 256, 281, 288, 298, 347, 355, **608**, 637, VN on, 193, 204, 206
Berdyaev, Nikolay Aleksandrovich, 247, 385, 387, **636**, **685**
'Berezhno nyos' ('I carefully carried'), xxiv, **544**
Berg Collection, New York Public Library, *see* Henry W. and Albert A. Berg Collection, New York Public Library
Berlin, Katherine, *see* Berling, Ekaterina Leopoldovna
Berlin, Germany, **xiv**, xvi, **xxii**, xxiii, xxiv, xxv, xxviii, xxix, **xxx**, xxxi, xxxiii, xxxiv, xlii, xlviii, 4, 23, 25, 28, 30, 33, 97, 167, 191, 209, 210, 213, 227, 228, 229, 244, 254, 256, 270, 285, 293, 305, 309, 317, 323, 328, 342, 354, 355, 356, 359, 375, 376, 395; as VéN address, 3–36 (1923–24), 39–41 (1925), 153–5 (1926), 157–68 (1930), 170–230 (1932), 232–268 (1936), 277–368 (1937); as VN address, 6 (1923), 48, 50–152 (1926), 156, 157 (1930), 270–5 (1936); attitude to, 27, 38, 117; eager to leave, 210, 214, 221; museums in, 162
Berlin Illustrirte Zeitung, newspaper, 123, 582
Berling, Ekaterina Leopoldovna, 264, 266, 297, **642**, **643**
Bernatsky, Mikhail Vladimirovich, 329, **668**
Bernstein, Henri, 197, **613**
Bernstein, Osip Samoylovich, 286, 292, **651**
Bers, 155
Bersky, 224
Berta Gavrilovna, 52, 71, 88, 133,
Berta Grigor., *see* Zeldovich, Berta Grigorievna
Bertman, 110
Bertran, Mme, as VéN alias, 18, **555**
Bertrand, *see* Thompson, C. Bertrand
Beth, Elmer F., 498, **721**
Biarritz, France, 94–95, 97, 98, 135, 228
Bible, 37

Bibliothèque Rose, 189, **607**
Bigland, Eileen, 301, 308, **659**
Bilig, Yuzya, 220
Billig, (Billik, I. M.?), 388, **686**
Birch, Francis (Frank), 435, 437–8, **701**
Birkett, George Arthur, 400, 407, **690**
Birmingham, England, 407
Blackborough, 213
Blagonamerenny (*The Loyalist*), journal, Brussels, 100, **576**
'Blagost'' ('Beneficence'), 69, 155, 569
Bliss, Mrs, 159
Blok, Aleksandr, 310
Blok, Aleksandr Aleksandrovich, 189, 607, **663**, quoted, 343, 544, **672**
'Blue Star, The', *see* 'Sinyaya zvezda' (Gumilyov)
Bluebird, The, *see* Sinyaya ptitsa
Bobbs-Merrill, publisher, Indianapolis, xxxv, 453, **643**, 709
Bobby, *see* De Calry, Count Robert Louis Magawly-Cerati
Bobrovsky, Pyotr Semyonovich, 155, 162, 167, 172, 173, **590**
'Bog' ('God', Derzhavin), 137, 585
Bogoslovsky, Boris Vasilievich, 440–1, 452, 453, **702**
Boileau, rue, Paris, 418, as VéN address, 417–39 (1939)
Bois de Boulogne, Paris, 281, 649
Boll, Germany, 42, 43, **561**
Bonaparte, rue, Paris, 283
'Bonfire', see 'Kostyor' (Bunin)
Bonham Carter, Lady Violet, 306, **661**
Bonnier, publisher, Stockholm, 289, **653**
Bordeaux, France, 126
Boris, Tsar, *see* Romanov, Grand Prince Boris Vladimirovich
Borman, 201
Bormes, France, 323, 325, 328, 341, 345, 354
Born, Bertran de, 192, **610**
Borodin, 440
Boronkin, xlv, 235
Boston, Massachusetts, 441, 443, 445, 451
Botticelli, Sandro, 397
du Bouche, Elena Karlovna, 362, **678**
Boulogne, *see* Bois de Boulogne
Bourne, H. J., 302, 307, 319, 347, 353, 366, **660**
Box, xxxi, 153, 155, 158, 159, 160, 163–4, 165, 169, 171, 174, 181, 598
Boyd, Brian, xxv, xxxii, xxxviii, xl, 170, as archivist and biographer, 539
Bradley, 210
Braykevich, Mikhail Vasilievich, 385, 387, 388, **684**, **686**
Brazil, 59
'Breaking the News', *see* 'Opoveshchenie'
Brechin Place, London (Sablins), 419, as VN address, 384–408 (1939)
Bremen (steamer), 467
Brisson, Jacques (Jean) Pierre, 233, **629**
British Museum, Great Russell Street, London, 405
British Museum (Natural History), now Natural History Museum,

Kensington, London, lv, 389, 391, 392, 397, 420, 423, 425, 430, **687**
Brodsky, Boris Yakovlevich, 283, **649**
Brodyachaya sobaka (Stray Dog), cabaret, St Petersburg, 270, **645**
Bromberg, Elena L'vovna, 271, 275, 290, 356, **645**
Bromberg, (Herman?), 340, 342, 346, **558**, **672**
Bromberg, Iosif (Osya), 387, 389, 391, 400, 413, 421, 685
Bromberg family, 459
'Bronze Horseman, The', see 'Mednyi vsadnik' (Pushkin)
Brooke, Rupert, 555
Brown, Harper Glover, 450, 707
Browning, Robert, 137, 476, 585, **714**
Brunst, Irina, *see* Kyandzhuntsev, Irina
Brussels, Belgium, xvi, xxxiii, xlv, xlviii, liv, 188, 202, 209, 210, 214, 239, 240, 244, 249, 252, 253, 254, 256, 259, 316, 395, as VN address, 232–6, 258 (1936), 277 (1937)
Bryanchaninov, (Aleksandr Nikolaevich?), 196, **613**
Bubka, *see* Nabokov, Dmitri Vladimirovich
Buchanan, 436
Budberg, Baroness Maria Ignatievna (Moura), 302, 304, 306, 307, 308, 313, 318, 335, 336, 347, 350, 354, 387, 388, 389, 392, 393, 397, 400, 403, 405, 406, 413, 415, 418, 420, 421, 429, 436, **659**, VN on, 307
'Budushchemu chitatelyu' ('To a Future Reader'), 223, **625**
Buffon, George-Louis Leclerc, Comte de, 14, 553
Bulgaria, 174
Bunin, Ivan Alekseevich, xxxii, xxxiii, xlviii, 71, 98, 99, 152, 162, 205, 207, 241, 250, 254, 256, 261, 264, 267, 269, 279, 281, 283, 286, 292, 294, 297, 317, 320, 338, 348, 365, 372, 394, **570**, **577**, 588, 618, 620, **633**, **638**; attitude to VN, xxxi, 254–5, 338, 348, 365, 370, 372, **681**; VN on, 148, 178, 241, 250, 256, 335, 365, 372
Bunny, *see* Wilson, Edmund, 473
Burd-Voskhodov, Aleksandr Pavlovich (Burov), 598
Burns, Robert, 115, **580**
Burov (Aleksandr Pavlovich Burd-Voskhodov), 598
Burr, Malcolm, 250, **638**
Bush, Mrs, 496
Butler, Richard ('Rab') Austin, 294, **656**
butterflies and moths, list of taxa (for role in VN's life, *see under* Nabokov, Vladimir Vladimirovich: butterflies and moths), *Acidalia*, 467–8, 713, *alveus*, 423, 697, *Antiopa*, 193, 610, *aphirape*, 97, Apollo (*see also Parnassius apollo*), 133, 151, 193, *Aporia crataegi-augusta*, 51 *arcilani* (*arcilacis*), 423, 696, *Arctia hebe*, 51, 563, *Arctia virgo*, 459, 711, *armoricanus*, 423, 697, *Brenthis*, 89, *Brenthis borealis*, 97,

butterflies – cont.
carpetiella, 117, 581, *carswelli*, 423, 696, *celerio*, 51, *Colias*, 475, Coridon, see *Lysandra coridon*, *Crestos lovitza* Sirin (drawing, crossword), 124–5, 582, *Daphnis nerii*, 51, *eubule*, 465, **712**, *Euchloe*, 475, *Euchloe ausonia*, 508, 725, *foulquieri*, 423, 697, *hebe*, 97, *Io*, 188, 193, 606, Hesperidae, hesperids, 397, 423, 425, 426, 430, 465, 466, 472, **697**, 712, *Jaspidea celsia* (drawing), 118, 581, *Larentia*, 594, *livornica*, 51, *Libythea celtis*, 177, 602, Lycaenids, 389–90, 472, 482, *Lysandra coridon/cormion*, xvii, 389–90, **484**, **687**, **717**, *meladon*, 423, 696, Melitaea/*Melithea*, 89, 249, 637, *Micropteryx*, 249, 637, *Neonympha*, 476, 479, **715**, *niceae*, 51, *Ornithoptera*, 249, 637, *pales*, 97, *Papilio*, 159, 465, 591, **712**, *Papilio alexanor*, 163, 594, Parnassians, 249, 637, *Parnassius apollo*, 133, 610, *pellonela*, 117, 581, *Pieridae*, Pierids, 465, 475, **712**, *Pieris*, 475, *Pieris brassicae*, 117, *podalirius*, 159, 323, 591, 666, *rumina*, 249, 637, Sphingids, 466, 712, *Thais*, 510, 725, *Thais rumina*, 156, 590, *Thecla*, 467, 713, *Vogelii* Obthr., 482, 716, Whites, 421, **694**, *Zerynthia hypsipyle cassandra*, 510, 725, *Zerynthia rumina*, 156, 590
Butterflies in Art (unfinished), 286, **652**, **715**
Byron, George Gordon, Lord, 289, **654**
Café de la Paix, Paris, 225
Café Murat, Paris, 241, 243
California, 206, 514
Calmbrood, as VN alias, *see under* Nabokov, Vladimir Vladimirovich: aliases
Cambridge, England (city), 42, 304, 310, described, 310–1, memories of, 310–1, 312, 407, 441, 444
Cambridge, Massachusetts, xxxvi, 459, 493
Cambridge, University of, xiv, 4, 17, 21, 98, 297, 308, 318, 403, 405, 409, 412, 420, 438
Camera Obscura, *see Kamera obskura*
Campaux, Suzanne, 257, **640**
Candide, newspaper, Paris, 209, 215, 219, 220, 315, 318, 319, 321, 324, 332, 342, 346, 352, 357, 367, **619**, 667
Cannes, France, xvii, xxxiv–xxxv
Cap d'Antibes, France, xvii, xxxv, 395, **688**
Carlton Hotel, London, 309
Carpenter, Frank M., 480, 487, 490, 492, 494, **716**
Carpenter-Lee, Molly (Mollie, Lee), 285, 301, 303, 307, 384, 387, 388, 397, 400, 425, 431, 433, 435, **651**, **662**
Carrefour, Le (dir. Bernhardt), 429, **699**
Carroll, Lewis (Charles Lutwidge Dodgson), xxiii, **605**
Castelmola, Sicily, 513
Castle, The (Kafka), 404, **691**
Catholic Church, 52, 77–78

Catoire, Ekaterina Andreevna, *see* Struve, Ekaterina Andreevna
Caucasus, 461
Cave, The (Aldanov), see *Peshchera*
'Cave, The' (Zamyatin), see 'Peshchera'
Caves du Vatican, Les (Gide), 165, **595**
Cement (*Tsement*, Gladkov), 67–8, 568
Chaikovsky, Pyotr Ilyich, 249, **637**
Champs-Elysées, avenue de, Paris, 336, 355, **670**
Chanel, fashion house, Paris, 409
Chapman, Thomas, 249, **637**
Charing Cross Station, London, 301, 387
Charleroi, Belgium, 259
Chardonne, Mme, 288, 290–1, **653**
Charlottenburg Station, Berlin, 53, 61, 96, 109, 130, 269
Charova, Vera Sergeevna, 403–4, 405, **691**
Chatto and Windus, publisher, London, 436
Chayka (*The Seagull*, Chekhov), 155, **590**
Chekhov, Anton Pavlovich, 65, 86, 155, 442, 464
Chekhov, Mikhail Aleksandrovich, 335, 443, 456–7, **670**, **704**, **709**
Chelovek iz SSSR (*The Man from the USSR*), 154, **589**
Chern., *see* Chernyshevsky, Nikolay Gavrilovich
Chernavin, Tatyana Vasilievna, 288, 292, 298, 302, 304, 306, 308, 394, 396–7, 424, 425, 427, 429, 433, 434, 439, **653**
Chernavin, Vladimir Vyacheslavovich, 397, **689**
Chernoviz, rue, Paris, 219
Chernysh, *see* Chernyshevsky, Nikolay Gavrilovich
Chernyshevsky, Nikolay Gavrilovich, xxxix, xl, 270, 323, 442, **644–5**, **666**, **704**. *See also Dar*, *and* 'Life of Chernyshevsky'
Chertok, Lev, 225, **626**
Chervinsky, Lidiya Davydovna, 248, **636**
Chez Angelo, restaurant, Taormina, 510
Chicago, Illinois, 477, 479, 481, 482, 715
Chichikov (*Myortvye dushi*), 248, 458
'Childhood', see 'Detstvo'
China, 367, 427
Chirikov, Evgeny Nikolaevich, 33, 35, 36–37, 160, **558**
Chisla (*Numbers*), journal, Paris, 339
Chlamydophorus (correctly *Chlamyphorus*) *truncatus*, 175
Chokhaev, Mustafa, 286, 294, **651**, **656**
Chorny (Glikberg-Chorny), Maria Ivanovna, 316, 322–3, 328, 331, 335, 341, 343, 344, 345, 350, 354, 357–9, 363, **664**
Chorny, Sasha (Aleksandr Mikhaylovich Glikberg), xxii, 316, 322, **556**, **664**
Christian Science, 159, 165
Chrysoptera, 466
Chukovsky, Korney Ivanovich, 207, **618**
Church, Barbara, 349–50, 432, 434, 435, **674**

Church, Henry, 349–50, 353, 432, 434, 435, **674**
Cingria, Charles-Albert, 350, **675**
Clark, 488
'Cloud, Castle, Lake', *see* 'Oblako, ozero, bashnya'
Club of Russian Jews, Brussels, 188, 259, **630**, 632, **641**
Cluster, The, *see Grozd'*
Cocteau, Jean, 190, 191, **608**
Coker College, Hartsville, South Carolina, 461–4, 712
Coker, James Lide, Major, 464, 466, 712
Coker, Vivian, 464–5, 712
Coker family, 464–7, 468, 469
Colas Breugnon (Rolland), xxiii, **565**
Collins, publisher, London, 419, 423, 427, 428, 429, 432, 433, 436, 439
Comstock, William Phillips, 474, 484, **714**
Comte de Monte Cristo, Le (Dumas), 14, 553
Conciergerie, Paris, 330, **668**
Conclusive Evidence, xix, xxi–xxii, xxxvii, 498, 543, **634**, 658, 721. *See also* autobiography; *Speak, Memory*
Concorde, Place de la, Paris, 355
Congo, 261
Constantinople, 21, 443
'Conversation between a Bookseller and a Poet', see 'Razgovor knigoprodavtsa s poetom' (Pushkin)
Cooney, Dr, 489, 491, 493
Corn is Green, The (Williams), 409, **691**
Cornell University, Ithaca, New York, xix, xxxvi, xxxvii, 499, 703, 721
Corsica, France, 245
Corot, Jean-Baptiste-Camille, 146, 461, 712
Correspondence with his Sister, *see Perepiska s sestroy*
Course du fou, La, *see Zashchita Luzhina*
Cowan, Tennessee, 477
Craigie Circle, Cambridge, Massachusetts, 493, as VéN address, 460–86 (1942), 495 (1945); as VN address, 486–93 (1944)
Crawford, Major, 391
Crimea, xiv, xxv, 180, 465, 554, 602, 622
Cross, Samuel Hazzard, 499, **721**
'Crosses, crosses', *see* 'Kresty, kresty'
crossword, 108–9, 110, 111–2, 124–25, 553, **579**, **582**
Cureglia, Ticino, Switzerland, 505, 506
Curran, Minnie Beryl, 407, 416, **691**
Curtis Brown, Albert, 301, **659**
Curtis Brown, literary agency, London, 301, **659**
Cymbidium lowianum, orchid, 504, **723**
Czechoslovakia, xiv, xvii, xxxiv, 148, 294, 326, 327, 328, 332, 339, 341, 343, 345, 346, 347, 363, 364, 367, 369, 375, 376

D-Day, xxxvi, 489, **719**
Dahl, Vladimir Ivanovich, 243, **634**
Dahlem, district, Berlin, 249, 638
Daily Times (?), 212, **620**

Dallwitz, von, 155
Damansky, Avgusta Filippovna, 207, 209, 282, **618**
'Dancing Snake, The', *see* 'Serpent qui danse, La' (Baudelaire)
Danechka or Danya, 85, 115, 143, 198, 199, 223, **573**
Danzig, Germany (now Gdańsk, Poland), 182
Dar (*The Gift*), xvii, xix, xxxix, liii, 260, 280, 281, 286, 291, 295, 302, 304, 314, 339, 349, 352–3, 353, 362–3, 366, 373, 496, 571, 594, 638, **641**, **644–5**, 648, **651**, **652**, **656**, **665**, 666, 669, 672, **674**, **681**, **689**, 720; excerpts in *Poslednie novosti*, 317, 331, 332, 334, 337, 345, 347, 352, 361, 367–8, 369, 671, 678, **680**, reception of, 367–8, 369, 370, 378, 397, **675–6**, **680**; second volume of, 441, **703**
Darien, Connecticut, 453, 702
Darling, Mr ('Mileyshiy'), xxx, lvi, 113, 126, 135–6, 140, 145–7, 148, 150
Darwin, Charles, xliii
Dasha, *see* Leuthold, Dorothy
'Dashing Fellow, A', *see* 'Khvat'
Dastakiyan, 226, 242, 243, 250, 257, 262, 264, 269, **627**
David, Father Armand, 427, **698**
Davos, Switzerland, as VN address, 520 (1975)
Davydov, Konstantin Nikolaevich, 325, **667**
'Day is Done, The' (Longfellow), 583
Dead Souls, *see* *Myortvye dushi* (Gogol)
'Decembrist, The' (steamboat), 343
De Calry, Count Robert Louis Magawly-Cerati (Bobby), 77, 78, 152, 245, **571**
Dedushka (*The Grandfather*), 6, **545**, **550**
Defence, The, *see* *Zashchita Luzhina*
'Delvigu' ('To Delvig', Pushkin), 366, **679**
Demidov, Ekaterina Yurievna, 224, **626**
Demidov, Igor Platonovich, 190, 191, 200, 224, 243, 370, **608**
de Monzie, Anatole, 288, **653**
'Demon' ('The Demon', Lermontov), 557
Denison Ross, Sir Edward, 302, 414, 416, **660**, **693**
Denis, *see* Roche, Denis
Dennis, Nigel, 452, 708
Denton, Robert Winsford, 456, 709
Denton, William Dixon, 456, 709
de Reul, Paul, 233, 278, **629**, **647**
de Rieux, *see* de Reul
Dernburgstrasse, Berlin, 103
Derricks, 459
Derzhavin, Gavriil Romanovich, 137, **585**, **639–40**
Despair, *see* *Otchayanie*
'Detstvo' ('Childhood'), 555
Diaghilev, Sergey Pavlovich, 512, **726**
Diary (Bennett), 422, **695**
Dickson, *see* Lovat Dickson, Horatio Henry
'Discovery, A', 718
Disraeli, Benjamin, 314

Dita, 187
'Ditty, A' ('Folk float up the town hall tower'), 125
'Ditty, A' ('Kit's so fit, Kitty, Kitty'), 125
Dobřichovice, Czechoslovakia, xiv, xxix, 558, as VN address, 32, 34 (1924)
Dobuzhinsky, Elizaveta Osipovna, 488, 492, **719**
Dobuzhinsky, Mstislav Valerianovich, 342, 345, 347, 357, 361, 488, 492, **672**, **719**
Dobycha (*The Plunder*, Tyrkov), 184, **604**
Docteur Blanche, rue du (Paris), 218–9
Döggingen, Germany, 42
Dolgov, General, 161, 592
Dolinin, Aleksandr Alekseevich, 570, 594, 659, 703
Domaine Beaulieu, France, xxv, 173, 179, 599, as VN address, 3 (1923)
Don Aminado (Aminodav Peysakhovich Shpolyansky), 191, 195, 205, 219, 220, **609**
Don Quixote (Cervantes, proposed adaptation by VN and Mikhail Chekhov), 456–7, **704**, **709**
Donici, Rostislav, 415, **692**
'Doorbell, The', *see* 'Zvonok'
Dostoevsky, Fyodor Mikhaylovich, xliii, 185, 220, 226, 464, **604**, **627**
Douglas, Norman, 247, 405, **636**
Doussia, *see* Ergaz, Ida Mikhaylovna
'Dragon, The', *see* 'Drakon' (Zamyatin)
'Draka' ('The Fight'), 69, 569
'Drakon' ('The Dragon', Zamyatin), 365, 679
Dresden, Germany, 179, 186
Drozdov, Aleksandr Mikhaylovich, 24, **556**
du Bos, Charles, 240, 252, 254, 256, **632**
Dubnyak (= Aykhenvald, Yuly Isaevich, *q.v.*), 106, **577**
Duckworth (Gerald Duckworth and Company), publisher, England, 307, 330, 393, **662**
Duggan, Stephen, 314, **664**
Dumas, Alexandre, 553
Dunkirk, France, 300
Dynkin, 287, 289, 491, **652**
Dynnik, 491, 720

E. I., 72, 81, 82
E. K., *see* Hofeld, Evgenia Konstantinovna
E. L., *see* Slonim, Evsey Lazarevich
Eastman, Elena Vasilievna, 212, **620**
Eastman, Max, 212, **620**
Edison, Thomas Alva, 8
Editeurs Réunis, bookstore and publisher, Paris, 247, **636**
Egerländer, Hotel, Marienbad, 381
Egorov, Georgy, 502, **723**
Ehrenburg, Ilya Grigorievich, 209, **619**
Eidel, 315, 324, 333, 338
Eiffel Tower, Paris, 261, 365–6
Eindhoven, Netherlands, 237
Eisner, Aleksey Vladimirovich, 160, **592**
Eitingon, Max (Mark Efimovich), 292, **655**

Eitingon, Mira Yakovlevna, 292, **655**
Eldridge Hotel, Lawrence, Kansas, 498–9
Elena or Elenochka, *see* Sikorski, Elena Vladimirovna
Eleonora, *see* Peltenburg, Leonora
Eliot, T. S., xliii
Elkin, Anna Aleksandrovna, 216, **622**
Elkin, Boris Isaakovich, 87, 153, 216, **574**, **622**
Elli, 233, 265, **629**
emigration, Russian, xiv, xvi, xxii, xxx, xxxi, xxxv, 154
Empyrean Path, The, *see Gorniy put'*
'Encounter, The', *see* 'Vstrecha'
England, xxii, xxxiii, xxxv, 273, 283, 297, 304, 314, 316, 326, 331, 332, 341, 350, 353, 360, 364, 366, 396, 402, 418, 421–2, 428
'English associations', 346, 673. *See also* autobiography
English-Russian Club, London, 394
Entomologist, The, journal, 158, 159, 389, 423, **591**, **687**
Epatiev, 154
'Epistle to James Tennant of Glenconner' (Burns), 580
Ergaz, Ida Mikhaylovna (Doussia), xxxii, 196, 210, 211, 212, 214, 225, 228, 229, 230, 240, 245, 256, 258–9, 281, 291, 318, 319, 321, 324, 357, 361, 372, 380, 382, 383, **612**, **667**, VN on, 212, 324,
Esther, 204
Etingon, *see* Eitingon
Etna, Mount, Sicily, 508
Eton, England, 308
Euclid, 442
Eugene Onegin (Pushkin), 194, **611**, early VN translation of, 445, 705, VN translation of and commentary to, xxxvii
Ev. K. or Ev. Konst., *see* Hofeld, Evgenia Konstantinovna
Eva, *see* Lutyens, Eva Efimovna
Evans, Brigadier William Harry, 397, 423, 430, **689**
'Evening', *see* 'Vecher'
Event, The, *see Sobytie*
Evg. Vasil., *see* Sablin, Evgeny Vasilievich
Evgenia Konstantinovna, *see* Hofeld, Evgenia Konstantinovna
Evreinov, Nikolay, xxxii, 202, 210, 213, 219, 220, **615**, VN on, 220
Evsey Laz., or Evsey Lazarevich, *see* Slonim, Evsey Lazarevich
Excelsior, Hotel, Taormina, Italy, 510, 725
Eye, The, *see Soglyadatay*

F., *see* Franzensbad
Falkovsky, Evgeny Adamovich, 142, 257, **570**, **641**
Falkovsky, Mme, 73, 85, 110, 127, 157, **570**
Falz-Fein, Lydia Eduardovna, 273, **646**
Fargue, Léon-Paul, 382, **684**
Farmville, Virginia, xviii, 484

Farrère, Claude, 245, **635**

Faulkner, William, xliii

Faust (Pushkin), *see* 'Stsena iz Fausta'

Favière, La, France, 323, 327, 354, 356, 357–9, 360, 363, 367, 369, **677**

Fayard, publisher, Paris, xxxii, 163, 187, 195, 196, 204, 234, 252, 337, 360–1, **594**

Fayard, Jean, 195, 361, **612**, **677**

Fedin, Konstantin Aleksandrovich, 69, **569**

Fedotov, Georgy Petrovich, 243, 248, 283, **634**

'Feet of the Young Men, The' (Kipling), 166, 595

Fehrbelliner Platz, Berlin, 123

Feigin, Anna Lazarevna (Anyuta, Anyutochka), xvi, xxxiii, 33, 54, 61, 62, 64, 74, 81, 95, 98, 100, 105, 107, 108, 120, 124, 126, 127, 131, 134, 141, 148, 151, 157, 160, 163, 165, 169, 174, 175, 185, 186, 187, 189, 194, 199, 204, 227, 228, 232, 234, 235, 238, 243, 251, 253, 258, 265, 267, 271, 272, 273, 274, 275, 277, 278, 280, 282, 283, 284, 289, 290, 292, 298, 301, 303, 304, 309, 314, 316, 320, 321, 324, 331, 334, 340, 345, 346, 351, 359, 361, 362, 371, 382, 390, 460, 467, 475, 477, 478, 485, 486, 494, 512, **558**, **563**, 576, 724, **726**, escape to America, 451, 453, 456, 459, 707, **718**

Feigin, Ilya (L., Lyusya), 81, 107–08, 131, 251, 255, 256, 258, 261, 264, 266, 280, 281, 284, 285, 286, 288, 289, 292, 294, 296, 298, 299, 302, 305, 312, 315, 316, 317, 320, 322, 325, 326, 329, 334, 340, 361, 362, 365, 375, 378, 380, VN on, 298, 315, 369, 383, 421, 459, 486, 496

Feldberg, Germany, 43, 44, 45

Felix, 245

Felsen, Yury (Nikolay Berngardovich Freydenstein), 194, 204, 206, 245, **611**

Fernandez, Ramon, 296, 320, **657**

Fet, Afanasy Afanasievich, **555**

Feux croisés, 230, 316, 318, **628**, 655

'Few Words on the Wretchedness of Soviet Literature and An Attempt to Establish the Cause Thereof, A', *see* 'Neskol'ko slov ob ubozhestve . . . '

'Fialta', *see* 'Vesna v Fialte'

Fiduciary Committee, 271, **645**

Field, Andrew, xxxix, xl, l– li, 539, 540, 636, 642

Fierens, Odetta, 233, 239–40, 248, 252–3, 256, 259, VN on, 252

Fierens, Paul, 233, 239–40, 248, 252–3, 256, 259, 265, 266, 267, 272, 279, **629**, VN on, 252, 266

'Fight, The', *see* 'Draka'

Field Museum of Natural History, Chicago, 479

Filippov, 333

'First Love', *see* 'Pervaya lyubov''

Fisher, Edgar, 452, 466, 467, 469, 474, 481, 482, **708**
Fisné, 317
Flaubert, Gustave, xxxi, xlix, 28, 174, 180, 452, **557**
Fletcher, Lady, 295, 296, 313, **657**
Flora *or* Flora Grig., *see* Solomon, Flora Grigorievna
Florence, Italy, 405
Florence, South Carolina, 461, 462, 468, 470
Florida, 473, 474, 476
Florovsky, Georgy Vasilievich, 203, **616**
Földes, Jolán, 291, 296, **655**, **657**
Folkestone, England, 384
Fomin, 284
Fond *or* Fondamin *or* Fondik, *see* Fondaminsky, Ilya Isidorovich
Fondaminsky, Amalia Osipovna, 190, 192, 193, 194, 219, 222, 223, 224, 225, 227, 228, 231, 240, 241, 246, 253, 262, 348, **607**, **610**, **633**, VN on, 225, 227
Fondaminsky, Ilya Isidorovich (Fond, Fondamin, Fondik, I. I., Il. Is., Ilya, Ilyusha), xxxii, xxxiii, lx, 3n, 163, 186, 190, 192, 193, 194, 195, 196, 202–4, 205, 206, 207, 211, 214, 217, 218, 219, 220, 221, 222, 223, 224, 225, 227, 235, 240, 241, 245, 246, 248, 255, 264, 265, 281, 283, 286, 290, 291, 294, 298, 305, 324, 326, 327, 329, 333, 338–9, 342, 343, 347, 348, 350, 352, 368, 372, 378, 382, 385, 391, 409, 434, **594**, **679**; on VN, 372; Russian Theatre and, 281, **649**; *Russkie zapiski* and, 352, **676**, **684**; VN on, 200, 207, 221, 223, 235, 240, 257, 267, 293, 315, 317, 319, 321, 351, 366, 378
Fontaines, Les, café, Paris, 254
'Fontan' ('The Fountain', Tyutchev), 585
'Forgotten Poet, A', 489, **719**
'Fountain, The', *see* 'Fontan' (Tyutchev)
Fox Film Co., 433, 434
France, xiv, xvi, xvii, xviii, xxii, xxv, xxvii, xxxiii, xxxiv, xxxv, xxxvi, 227, 303, 333, 350, 362, 363, 367, 369, 371, 374, 402
Franco, General Francisco, 316, **664**
François-Poncet, André, 270, **645**
Frank, Semyon Lyudvigovich, xlviii, lv, 234, **629**, **631**
Frank, Victor Semyonovich, 308, 436, **662**
Franzensbad (Františkovy Lázně), Czechoslovakia, xvii, 331, 334, 341, 345, 374, 376, 383
freemasons, 25, 226, **626–7**
Freiburg, Germany, xv, 113, as VN address, 42, 43 (1926), described, 42
Freud, Sigmund, 58, 220, 480, **566**
Freund, Gisèle, 350, **675**
Friendly, Alfred, 514, **726**
Frumkin, Yakov Grigorievich, 192, 196, 484, **609**, 717

Fulda, (Ludwig Anton Solomon?), 438, **701**
Fulda, (Oscar?), 438, **701**
Fyodorov, Mme, 163
Fyodorov, Vasily Georgievich, 161, 162, 185, **593**

G., Irina, *see* Guadanini, Irina
'Gadanie' ('Fortune-Telling'), 559
Galesburg, Illinois, 482, 483
Galina, *see* Petrov, Galina Nikolaevna
Gallimard, Gaston, 283–4, 285, 289, 291, 296, 315, 320, 321, **650**
Gallimard, publisher, Paris, xxxii, 200, 209, 210, 226, 228, 296, 332, 350, 352, 372, 540
Gamayun, almanac, 6
Gamayun, publisher, Berlin, 551
Gamayun, Russian mythology, 551
Gams, 416, 418
Gapon, Georgy Apollonovich, 193, **610**
Garbo, Greta, 234, **630**
Gare du Nord, Paris, 240
Garnett, Constance Clara, 307, **662**
Garnett, David, 319, **666**
Garsia, Lieutenant-Colonel Willoughby Clive, 420, 425, 427, 429, **694**
Gatchina, Russia, 499, 721
Gavronsky, Lyubov' Sergeevna, 288, 297, 298, 302, **653**
Gay, Edward, 466, 712
Gazdanov, Gayto Ivanovich, 175, **601**
Ge, Nikolay Nikolaevich, 199, **614**
Gedächtniskirche, Berlin, 59
Geisbergstrasse, Berlin, 133
Geneva, Switzerland, xxxvii, 500, 517
George V, hotel, Paris, 335
Georgia, 468–77
Georgia State Women's College, Valdosta, Georgia, 473–4
Germany, xv, xvi, xvii, xxx, xxxiii, xxxiv, 165, 290, 341, **631**; dislike of, xxii, 117, 372, **681**; reasons for remaining in, xxxi, xxxiv
Gertruda, 274
Gide, André, 165, **595**
Gift, The, *see Dar*
Gippius, Vladimir Vasilievich, 180, **604**
Gippius, Zinaida Nikolaevna, 169, 190, 194, 222, **597**, on VN, 608, VN on, 203
Giraudoux, Jean, 216, **622**
Girshfeld, 243
Girshman, Henrietta (Evgenia) Leopoldovna, 266, **643**
Gladkov, Fyodor Vasilievich, 67, 568
Gladstone, William Ewart, 314
Gleb *or* Glebushka, *see* Struve, Gleb Petrovich
Glory, *see Podvig*
Gobert, André, 394, **688**
God, 14, 20, 26, 35, 105
'God', *see* 'Bog' (Derzhavin)
Godunov-Cherdyntsev, Konstantin Kirillovich, *see Dar*
Goethe, Johann Wolfgang von, 177, 179, 602
Gogel, Aleksandra Ivanovna, 284, **650**

Gogel, Sergey Konstantinovich, 105, 127, 142, 284, **577**
Gogol, Nikolay Vasilievich, lv–lvi, lx, 174, 458, 459, 471, 473, 480, 549
Golde, Elena Ivanovna, 358
Goldenweiser, Aleksey Aleksandrovich, 460, 711
Golding, Louis, 426, **697**
Gollancz, Victor, 301, **659**. *See also* Victor Gollancz
Golovin, Aleksandr Sergeevich, 177, 291, **602**
Golovin, General Nikolay Nikolaevich, 286, 291, **651**
Golovina, Alla Sergeevna, 178, **602**
Golubev-Bagryanorodny, Leonid Nikolaevich, 71, 150, **570**
Gore ot uma (*Woe from Wit*, Griboedov), 179, 603
Gorguloff, Pavel Timofeevich, 330, **668**
Gorky, Maksim (Aleksey Maksimovich Peshkov), 211, 354, 442, **620**, **659**
Gorlin, Mikhail Genrikhovich, 162, **593**
Gorn, Mme, 166
Gorn, Vasily Leopoldovich, 166, **595**
Gorniy put' (*The Empyrean Path*), xxiii
Gorny, Sergey (Aleksandr Avdeevich Otsup), 64, **567**, 599
Goudy, Alexander Porter, 407, **691**
Goya, Francisco, 220
Grabbe, Countess Elizaveta Nikolaevna, 245, **635**
Gräger, 55, 105, 120
Grainger, James Moses, 484, **718**
Grande Armée, avenue de la, Paris, 283
Grandfather, The, *see Dedushka*
Grani (*Facets*), almanac, 21, **555–6**
Grasse, France, 225, 227, **626**
Grasset, publisher, Paris, xxxii, 187, 195, 196, 209, 228, 234, 317, 606
Grasskiy dnevnik (*The Grasse Diary*, Kuznetsova), 511, 725
Graun, Carl Heinrich, 238, **631**, 645
Gray, Elisha, 551
Greece, xiv
Greek, the, *see under* Nabokov, Vladimir Vladimirovich: psoriasis
Greene, Charles Sylvester, 464, 467, **712**
Greyhound, 470
Griboedov, Aleksandr Sergeevich, 179, 603
Grif, 59, 85
Grigory Abramovich, as VN alias, *see under* Nabokov, Vladimir Vladimirovich: aliases
Grinberg, Mikhail Lvovich, 338, **671**
Grinberg, Savely Isaakovich, 288, 302, 303, 304, 305, 308, 309, 310, 312, 391, 392, 403, 405, 407, 416, 417, 422, 426, 427–8, 432, 433, 616, **653**
Grinberg, (Sofia Maksimovna?), 338, 391, 392, 405, 426, **671**
Gringoire, newspaper, Paris, 220, 233, **624**
Grishen'ka, as VN alias, *see under* Nabokov, Vladimir Vladimirovich: aliases
Grosvenor House, London, 309
Grosya, 493

Grove End Gardens, London (Tsetlins), as VN address, 410–7 (1939)
Grove Press, 502, **723**
Grozd' (*The Cluster*, verse collection), xxiii, xxiv, 551
Grudinsky, 358
Grunelius, Alexandre, 250, 638
Grunelius, Antoinette (Mme Maurice), 188, 189, 194, 607
Grunewald, Berlin, xxx, 76, 90, 94, 97, 105, 109, 112, 114, 122, 126, 130, 139, 141, 145, 147, 151, 273, 274, **571**
Gruppa (the Group), 65, **568**
Gruzenberg, Oskar Osipovich, 194, 203, **611**
Guadanini, Irina Yurievna, 266, 269, 281, 286, 297, 313, 319, 321, 329, 339, 355, 368, **643**, affair with VN, xvi, xvii, xxii, xxxiv–xxxv, xxxviii, **643**, affair revealed, 540, **668**, denials of affair with, 354, 355, 676, VN on, 266, 324
Gubsky, Nikolay Mikhaylovich, 250, 294, 299, 302, 309, 319, 397, 400, 401, 402, 406, 412, 415, 416, 420, 421, 435, 437, 438, **638**, **656**, **694**, VN on, 309, 319–20, 403, 416, 421
Guggenheim Foundation application, 476, **714**
Guitry, Sacha, 391, **687**
Gul', Roman Borisovich, 378, **683**
Gumilyov, Nikolay Stepanovich, 160, 362, 506, **592**, **678**
Gurdjieff, Georgy Ivanovich, 220, **624**
Gurevich, Aleksandr Vissarionovich, 143, 149, 150, **586**
Gutmann Saal, Berlin, 141, 586

Hachette, publisher, Paris, 206
Halpern, Aleksandr Yakovlevich, xliii, 416, 417, **693**
Halsman, Philippe, xxi
Hamburg, Germany, 21
'Hamburg', steamer, 382
Hanna, 115
Harkness Pavilion Cambridge Hospital, Cambridge, Massachusetts, 719
Harper, Samuel Northrup, 415, 417, 424, 431, **693**
Harris, Angelica Vasilievna Allen, 307, 314, 384, 389, 405–6, 407, 411, 416, 418, 424, 438
Harris, Mr Allen, 384, 388, 389, 392, 393, 405–6, 407, 411, 416, 418, 424, 438
Harrison, Ernest, 308, 311–2, 353, **662**
Hartley, L. P. (Leslie Poles), 306, 307, 319, **661**
Hartsville, South Carolina, 462–5, as VN address, 460–1 (1942)
Harvard University, Cambridge, Massachusetts, xviii, xxxvi, 175
Haskell, Arnold, 250, 308, 314, 322, 361, 419, 420, 424, 425, 426, **638**, VN on, 419, 426–7, 427, 429, 431, 433, 436, 437, 438
Haskell, Vera Markovna, 304, 309, 392, 393, 418, 421, 423, 427, 429, 431, 435, 436, 437, 438, **661**

Heath, A. M. and Co., agents, London, 255, 261, 264, 290, 302, 317, **640**
Heaven, 14, 19, 27, 137
Heidelberg, Germany, 81
Heinemann, publisher, England, 309, 318, 330, 393, 394, **663**
Hellens, Franz, xxxiii, 208, 233, 234, 236, 239–40, 244, **619**, **629**, **632**, VN on, 234, 239, 252, 259, 260, 261–2, 279
Hellens, Maria Markovna, 239, **632**, VN on, 261
Heller, Vera, 409, 412, 413, 414, 421, 422, 423, 426, 427, **692**
Henie, Sonja, 226, **627**
Henry IV, 152, 588
Henry W. and Albert A. Berg Collection, New York Public Library, as repository for VN papers, including letters to Véra, 541
Hepner, Benno Pavlovich, 248, **636**
Herkulesbrücke (Hercules Bridge), Berlin, 101, 576
Herring, Erich Martin, 389, **687**
Hertz, Paul, 187, 188, **606**
Herzen, Aleksandr Ivanovich, 181, 291
Hessen, Evgeny Sergeevich (Zhenya), 178, **603**
Hessen, Georgy Iosifovich (Zyoka), 169, 192, 198–9, 216, 218, 243, 246, 247, 252, 271, 306, 335, 337, 349, 362, 370, 454, 485, 564, **609**, **638**, **718**, 720
Hessen, Iosif (Joseph) Vladimorovich ('old Joseph', 'the old man'), 66, 88, 96, 100, 110, 128, 130, 155, 157, 179, 186, 243, 246, 250, 254, 255, 273, 281, 282, 287, 290, 310, 324, 325, 349, 350, 355, 415, 453, 478, 552–3, 565, **568**, **709**, 715, **718**, memoirs, 253, 257, 265, 270, 275, 353, 367, **639**
Hessen, Sarah Yakovlevna, 243, 250, **634**
Hessen, Sergey Iosifovich, 157, 169, 173, 175, 180, **591**
Hessen, Sofia Grigorievna, 192
Hessen, Vladimir Iosifovich (Vava), 246, 257, **636**
Hessen, Zhenya, *see* Hessen, Evgeny Sergeevich
Hicks, (John Richard?), 400, **690**
Hill, Elizabeth Mary, 403, 405, 406, 407, 412, 424, 425, 432, 435, **690**
'Histoire morale d'un serin de Canarie' (Karr), 362, **678**
Historical Society, *see* Royal Historical Society
Hitler, Adolf, xvi, xii, xxxiii, xxxvi, xlviii, 391, 397
Hodgson, Ralph, xlix, 176, **601**
Hofeld, Evgenia Konstantinovna, 93, 158, 159, 170–1, 173, 174, 175, 181, 185, 186, 379, 387, 394, 400, 417, 431, 434, **575**
Hoffmann, E. T. A., 102, **577**
Hohenzollerndamm, Berlin, 122–3
Holland, 244, 279, 334, 394
Holstein, Christina Staël von, 440, **702**
Honours College, Farmville, Virginia, 484, **717**

'Hope', *see* 'Nadezhda' (Bunin)
Horace, 155, 265, 587
Hornton Street, London, 419, as VN address, 419–39 (1939)
Hôtel Magique (film idea), 243, 245, **634**
Houghton, Claude, 307, **662**
'How I loved the poems of Gumilyov!', *see* 'Kak lyubil ya stikhi Gumilyova!'
Human Countenance, The, *see* *Lik chelovecheskiy* (Vladimir Gippius)
Humbert, Humbert, xliv, xlvii, 509, 725
Hundred Russian Short Stories, 318, 336, **665**
Huntington, Constant, 306, **661**
Huxley, T. H., xliii
Hyde Park, London, 427
Hyde Park Hotel, London, 313

I. I. or Il. Is., *see* Fondaminsky, Ilya Isidorovich
I. V., *see* Hessen, Iosif Vladimirovich
'I carefully carried', *see* 'Berezhno nyos'
'I know, coldly and wisely', *see* 'Ya znayu, kholodno i mudro'
Ida Mikhaylovna, *see* Ergaz, Ida Mikhaylovna
Igor, *see* Demidov, Igor Platonovich
Ilf, Ilya (Iehil-Leib Arnoldovich Faynz), 351, **675**
Illinois Historical Library, Springfield, Illinois, 480
Illinois State Museum, Springfield, Illinois, 480
Ilya, *see* Fondaminsky, Ilya Isidorovich
Ilyashenko, (Vladimir Stepanovich?), 237, 631
Ilyin, Ivan Aleksandrovich, 65, **568**
Ilyusha, *see* Fondaminsky, Ilya Isidorovich
'In the desert a telephone rang', *see* 'Zvonil v pustyne telefon'
'In what heaven', *see* 'V kakom rayu'
'Inconnue de la Seine', 339, **672**
India, 397
'India invisible I rule, An', *see* 'Ya Indiey nevidimoy vladeyu'
Indochina, 4
Ingram, Benjamin Clayton, 463, 712
'Inspiration, pink sky . . . ', *see* 'Vecher na pustyre'
International Herald Tribune, 509
Invitation to a Beheading, *see* *Priglashenie na kazn'*
Ioann, Father, later Archbishop, *see* Shakhovskoy, Dmitri Alekseevich
Ioffe, Mlle, 58, 85, 89, 143
'Ionych' (Chekhov), 86
Ira or Irina, *see* Kyandzhuntsev, Irina
Irving Place, Ithaca, as VéN address, 497–8 (1954)
'Istreblenie tiranov' ('Tyrants Destroyed'), 401, 403, 444, **690**
'It is me,' 244, 260, **634**. *See also* autobiography
italics, indicating non-Cyrillic characters, 3n
Italy, xxxiv, 95, 322, 323, 335
It's Not Always Shrovetide for the Cat (*Ne vsyo kotu maslenitsa*, Ostrovsky), 66, 568

Ithaca, New York, 498, 721, as VéN address, 497–8 (1954)
Ivan Alekseevich, *see* Bunin, Ivan Alekseevich
'Ivan Fyodorovich Shpon'ka i ego tyotushka', ('Ivan Fyodorovich Shpon'ka and His Aunt', Gogol), 480, **716**
Ivan the Terrible, 204
'Ivan Vernykh', 49, **563**
Ivanov, Georgy Vladimirovich, 161, 167, 169, 191, 194, 283, **592**, **595**, 598, attack on VN, 592, 594–5, VN on, 283, 608–9
Izgoev, Aleksandr Samoylovich (Aron Solomonovich Lande), 169, **596**
Izobretenie Val'sa (*The Waltz Invention*), lx, 388, 390, 395, 399, 400, 430, 432, 433, **686**, **714**

Jacob, Dr, 187
Jacobson, see Yakobson
Jaloux, Edmond, 239, 253, 256–7, **632**
James, Henry, 72, 74, **570**
Janits, 511
Jannelli, Altagracia de, xxxv, 247, 289, 307, 317, 329, 343, 347, 348, 382, **636**, **674**
Jannings, Emil, 159, 592
Japan, 25
'*Je veux lire en trois jours*' (Ronsard), 216, **621**
Je veux qu'on se voit (Kashin-Evreinov), 220, **624**
Jeanne, 282, 288, 334, **649**
'Jeeves' (Sablins' butler), 385, 387, 412, **684**
Jesus Christ, 20, 144, 152, 586
Joan of Arc, 67, 79, 107, 571
'John Bottom' (Khodasevich), 148, 587
John Long, publisher, London, 239, 241, 242, 246, 247, 256, 261, 264, 270, 272, 281, 283, 285, 288, 304, 306, 307, 328, 350, 393, 394, 397, 406, 413, **632**, **646**
Joseph, old, *see* Hessen, Iosif Vladimirovich
Journalists' Union, Berlin, *see* Union of Russian Writers and Journalists
Joyce, James, xliii, xlix, liii, 181, 185, 266–7, 269, 295, 306, 350, **604**, VN on, 295, 604, VN critiques and parodies *Work in Progress*, 267, **643–4**
Jubilee, The (*Yubiley*, Chekhov), 65, 568

K., *see* Kortner, Fritz
K., Otto, *see* Klement, Otto
K., Achilles, 403
'K Muze' ('To the Muse'), 223, **625**
Kadashev-Amfiteatrov, Vladimir Aleksandrovich, 21, 160, 169, 556
Kadish, Mikhail Pavlovich, 59, 72, 85, 115, 127, 142, 476, **566**, 714
Kafka, Franz, 404, 445, **691**
Kaiserdamm, Berlin, 102, 121
'Kak lyubil ya stikhi Gumilyova!' ('How I loved the poems of Gumilyov!'), 506, **724**
Kalashnikov, Mikhail, 242–3, 245, 255, 375, **633**

'Kalina' (Larionov), 121, **581**
'Kamennyi gost'' ('The Stone Guest', Pushkin), 294, **656**
Kamera obskura (*Camera Obscura*, *Laughter in the Dark*, *Chambre obscure*), xv, xxxv, 172, 173, 181, 185, 190, 196, 205, 211, 212, 214, 229, 266, **599**, 605, **620**, **626**; film versions of, 297, 309, 317, 453, **709**; reception of, 181, 190, 201, 257, 615: reviews of, 601, 613–4, **635**, VN on, 173, 599; translations of, into English (as *Camera obscura*), 307, 309, 599, **632**, **662**, (as *Laughter in the Dark*), **643**, into French (*Chambre obscure*), 196, 212, 234, 291, **630**
Kaminka, Avgust Isaakovich, 67, 157, 202, 211, 223, 269, 310, 333, 552–3, 565, **568**
Kaminka, Elizaveta, 169, 597
Kaminka, Mikhail Avgustovich, 163, 165, 169, **594**, **597**
Kannegisser, Elizaveta Ioakimovna, 286, 310, **652**
Kannegisser, Leonid Ioakimovich, 286, 297, **651**, **652**
Kansas, University of, xxxvi–vii, 498–9, **721**
Kaplan (father), 203
Kaplan, Mme, 51, 55, 61, 62, 66, 67, 70, 72, 75, 79, 88, 90, 94, 98, 102, 107, 133
Kaplan, Sergey, 58, 64, 66, 70, 72, 76, 78, 82, 85, 90, 94, 98, 100, 102, 105, 112, 133, 135, 237, 244, **563**, 635
Kardakov, Nikolay Ivanovich, 64–65, 249, 393, **567**, **638**
Karlsruhe, Germany, 172
Karpovich, Marina Mikhaylovna (Marisha), 459, 711
Karpovich, Mikhail Mikhaylovich, 175, 275, 442, 443, 447, 451, 453, 456, 459, 476, 488, 489, 490, 491, 493, 494, **601**, **703**, 707, 709
Karpovich, Sergey Mikhaylovich, 492
Karpovich, Tatyana Nikolaevna, 447, 451, 453, 456, 459, 488–9, 490, 491, 492, 493, 494, **706**
Karr, Alphonse, 362, **678**
Karsavin, Lev Platonovich (?), 58–59, **566**
Kartashev, Anton Vladimirovich, 203, 204, **616**
Kashin-Evreinov, Anna Aleksandrovna, 220, **624**
Kasim-Bek, Aleksandr Lvovich, 388, **686**
Katkov, Georgy Mikhaylovich, 155, **589**
Kaun, Alexander, 200, 206–7, 210, 211–2, 228, **614**
Kedrova, Elizaveta Nikolaevna, 338, **671**
Kelly, Amy Ruth, 441, 443, 445, 453, 456, 457, 473, 478, **703**
Kensington Gardens, London, 391
Kensington Park, London, 434
Kensington Park Road, London (apartment of Valentin Tsetlin), as VN address, 297, 300–13 (1937)
Kensington Regiment monument, 428, **698**
Kent, England, 301

Kerby-Miller, Charles, 449, **707**
Kerensky, Aleksandr Fyodorovich, 190, 193, 221, 222, 243, 256, 269, 304, 329, 342, 343–4, 347, **608**, VN on, 193, 203, 342
Kernahan, Coulson, 319, 328, **666**
Key, The (*Klyuch*, Aldanov), 203, **616**
Khmara, Grigory Mikhalyovich, 320, 338, **666**
Khodasevich, Vladislav, xxxii, xxxiii, xliii, 148, 191, 193, 194, 195, 201, 223, 243, 244, 245, 250, 255, 265, 280, 281, 288, 298, 378, 381, **587**, **608**, 618, **635**; death, 434, **700**, **701**; double bill with VN, 240, 245, 254, 635, 639; feud with Adamovich, 240, **632–3**, 635; on VN, 280, 378, **648**, **683**; Pushkin and, 266, **643**; VN on, 193, 195, 201, 206–7, 217, 240, 241, 245, 250, 255, 266, 280
Khokhlov, German Dmitrievich, 178, **602**
'Khvat' ('A Dashing Fellow'), 218, 324, **623**
Kiesewetter, Aleksandr Aleksandrovich, 163, **593**
Kiev, Soviet Union, 105, 238
King, Queen, Knave, *see* *Korol', dama, valet*
Kipling, Rudyard, 166, 382, **595**
Kirkhner (Kirshner?), 317, 318, 320, **665**
Kislovodsk, Russia, 206
Kleiststrasse, Berlin, 105
Klement, Otto, 309, **662**
Klyachkin, Roma (Romochka, Kliatchkine), 197, 198, 199, 204, 223, **613**
Klyachkin, 198, 613
Klyuch (Aldanov), 203, **616**
Kneale, Elmer, 480, **716**
Knox College, Galesburg, Illinois, 483
Knut, Dovid (Duvid Meerovich Fiksman), 201, 247, **615**
Kodryansky, Natalia Vladimirovna, xl, 546
Kogan, Israel, 292, 334
Kogan-Bernstein, Elena Yakovlevna, 318, 324–5, 337, 341, 347, 349, 378, **665**
Koka, *see* Rausch von Traubenberg, Nikolay Nikolaevich
Kokoshkin, Vera Evgenievna, 265, 266, 281, 286, 297, 321, 339, 355, 368, **642–3**
Kolbsheim, xvi, xxxii, 199, 213, 605, 638, as VN address, 186–8 (1932)
Kolomeytsev, Nikolay Nikolaevich, 205, 250, 257, **617**
Kolomeytsev, Nina Dmitrievna (aunt), 205, 218, 223, 250, 257, 266, 283, 291, 334, 339, 365, **617**
Komissarzhevskaya, Vera Fyodorovna, 338, **671**
'Komnata' ('Vot komnata. Eshcho poluzhivaya'; 'The Room': 'Here is the room. Still half alive'), xlix, 110, **571**, **575**; composition of, 73–74, 90, 91, 575; publication, 132; reception, 100; text, 91–93
Konoplin, Ivan Stepanovich, 89, **574**
Konovalov, Aleksandr Ivanovich, 402, **690**

Konovalov, Sergey Aleksandrovich, 384, 386–7, 389, 399, 401–2, 404, 407, 415, **684**
Konstanz, xv, xxix, 45, 47, 99, **562**, as VéN address, 42–7 (1926)
Konyus, Tatyana Sergeevna (née Rachmaninov) (?), 208, 217, **619**
Korniloff's, restaurant (Chez Korniloff), Paris, 241, **633**
Korol', dama, valet (*King, Queen, Knave*), xv, xxx, 157, 208, 211, 212, 216, 228, 229, 286; translation, into English, 229, into German (*König, Dame, Bube*), 591, **699**
'*Korolyok*' ('*The Leonardo*'), 302, 382, **660**
Korostovets, Vladimir Konstantinovich, 36, 86, 110, **559**
Kortner, Fritz, 287, 297, 309–10, 313, 315, 317, **652**
Korvin-Piotrovsky, Nina Alekseevna, 272, 274, **645**
Korvin-Piotrovsky, Vladimir Lvovich, 422, **645**, **695**
Kostya, Uncle, *see* Nabokov, Konstantin Dmitrievich
'Kostyor' ('Bonfire', Bunin), 178, **603**
Koussevitzky, Sergey Aleksandrovich, 452, **708**
Kovalevsky, Evgraf Petrovich, 166, 175, 180, **595**
Kovalyov, Elena Aleksandrovna, *see* Peltser, Elena Aleksandrovna
Kovarsky, Ilya Nikolaevich, 196, 202, 213, 229, 261, 484, **612**, **717**
Kovcheg: Sbornik russkoy zarubezhnoy literatury (*The Ark: Anthology of Russian Émigré Literature*; various), 546
Kovno (Kaunas), Soviet Union, 107, 232
Kozhevnikov, Vladimir, 182, **604**
Kramář, Karel, 11, 14, 17, 31, 163, **552**
'Krasavitsa' ('A Russian Beauty'), 245, 254, 259, **635**
Krasnaya nov' (*Red Virgin Soil*), Soviet journal, 155, **589**
Krasnov, Pyotr Nikolaevich, 25, **557**
Kremenetsky, see *Klyuch*
Kresty, prison, St. Petersburg, 37, 560
'Kresty, kresty' ('Crosses, crosses'), 173, 179, **603**
Kreul, 187, 196
Kreutzer Sonata (Beethoven), 141
'Kreytserova sonata' ('The Kreutzer Sonata', Tolstoy), xxx, 122, 125. *See also* Pozdnyshev trial
Krumme Strasse, Berlin, 54
Krug (*The Circle*), journal, Paris, 271
Krummhübel, Germany (now Karpacz, Poland), 546
Krymov, Berta Vladimirovna, 214–5, **621**
Krymov, Vladimir Pimenovich, 214, **621**
Ksyunin, Aleksey Ivanovich, 290, 294, 299, **654**
Küfferle, Rinaldo, 264, **642**
Kulisher, Aleksandr Mikhaylovich, 207, 238, **618**
Kuprin, Aleksandr Ivanovich, xxxii, 195, 218, 229, 230, **611**, VN on, 230–1
Kuprin, Elizaveta Moritsovna, 229, **627**

Kuprin, Ksenia Aleksandrovna ('Kissa Kuprine'), xliii, 231, **628**
Kuzmin-Karavaev, Dmitry Vladimirovich, 203, **615**
Kuznetsova, Galina, *see* Petrov, Galina Nikolaevna
Kyandzhuntsev, Elizaveta Samoylovna (mother), 205, 221, 223, 242, 245, 263, 270
Kyandzhuntsev, Irina (married names Brunst, then Komarov), 205, 221, 223, 242, 243, 262, 263, 270, 281, 283, 287, 324, 329, 339, 340, 350, 353, 355, 373, **642**, VN on, 242, 324
Kyandzhuntsev, Savely (Saba, Sava), 202, 205–6, 211, 215, 217, 221, 222, 223, 225, 228, 242, 243, 245, 261, 262, 263–4, 265, 266, 270, 283, 287, 324, 339, 340, 350, 353, 355, **615**, 625, VN on, 205, 213, 242

L., *see* Feigin, Ilya
L., Misha, *see* Lubrzynsky, Mikhail Efimovich
La Coupole, restaurant, Paris, 269, 313
La Skaz, *see* Las Cases
Ladinsky, Antonin Petrovich, 191, 269, 357, **608**
Ladyzhnikov, 57, 58, 64, 70, **565**
Lalodya ('littlie'), 68
Landhausstrasse, Berlin, as VéN address, 6–36 (1923–4)
Landau, Grigory Adolfovich, 149, 155, **588**, 590
Landau, Mme, 21, 149–50
Lannes, boulevard, Paris, 192, 194, 610
Larionov, Ivan Petrovich, 121, 581
Las Cases, rue, Paris, 222, 255, 339, 615, 640, 648
Last Advent, The (film, Murnau: *Der letzte Mann*), 159
Laughter in the Dark, *see* *Kamera obskura*
Lausanne, Stéphane, 332, 335, **669**
Lausanne, Switzerland, xx, 502
Lavandou, Le, France, 294, 316, 323, 359
Lawrence, David Herbert (D. H.), 175, 196–7, 278, **601**, **647**
Lawrence, Kansas, xix, as VN address, 497–8 (1954)
Lawrence, Lieutenant-Colonel Thomas Edward, 278, 420, **647**, 694
Lazarus, 114, 131
Le Boulou, France, 156, 227, **627**
Le Cerf, Ferdinand, 249, 430, **637**
lectures, *see* Nabokov, Vladimir Vladimirovich: lectures
Lednitsky, Vatslav Aleksandrovich, 447, **706**
Lee, Asher, 313, 388, 391, 392, 397, 400, 425, 435, **686**
Leeds, University of, xxxv, xlii, 386, 389, 392, 396, 399, 402, 404, 407, 410, 411–2, 413, 414, 415, 416, 418, 424, 428, 436
Lefèvre, Frédéric, 337, 346, **671**
Leipzig, Germany, xvi, 33, 273, 283, as VéN address, 270–5 (1936)
Lena, *see* Massalsky, Elena Evseevna

Lenin, Vladimir Ilyich, 30, **558**
'Lenin' (steamboat), 343
Léon, Lucie (Elizaveta Matveevna) Léon Noel, 297, **638**
Léon, Pavel (Paul) Leopoldovich Léon, 250, 264, 266–7, 294, 297, 357, **638**, 643
Leonov, Leonid Maksimovich, 59, **566**
Leopold III of Belgium, 259, 265, **641**
Le plaa, 240
Lermontov, Mikhail Yuryevich, 18, 28, 169, 555, 557, 600
Leskov, Nikolay Semyonovich, 171, 185, 344, **598**, **673**
letters to Véra, post-1970, 539–41
'Lettres de femmes et femmes de lettres', 322, **666**. *See also* Nabokov, Vladimir Vladimirovich: unrealized literary projects
Leuthold, Dorothy (Dasha), 443, 482, 484
Levin, Elena Ivanovna, 459, 711
Levin, Isaak Osipovich, 204, **616**
Levinson, Andrey (André) Yakovlevich, xxxii, xliii, 196, 201, 202, 210, 214, 606, **612**, VN on, 214–5
Levinson, Lyubov' Shlemovna, 214–5, **621**
Levinson, Maria Andreevna, 215
Levitsky, (Aglaida Sergeevna Shimansky, née Levitsky?), 425, **697**
Lexington, Massachusetts, 492, 493
Liberal Club, London, 308, 314, 360
Library of Congress, Washington, DC, lx, 540
Lifar, Sergey Mikhaylovich, 339, 512, **667**, **672**, **726**
Life of Arsen'ev, The (*Zhizn' Arsen'eva*, Bunin), 620
'Life of Chernyshevsky' (ch. 4 of *The Gift*), xxxix–xl, 270, 291, 293, 294, 347, 349, 352, 370, **644–5**, **655**, **666**
'Life of Vasily Travnikov, The' ('Zhizn' Vasiliya Travnikova', Khodasevich), 254, **639**
'Lik', 388, **686**
Lik chelovecheskiy (*The Human Countenance*, Vladimir Gippius), 180–1, **604**
Likhosherstov, Aleksandr Aleksandrovich, 324, **667**
Limousin poets, 192, **610**
Lincoln, Abraham, 480, **716**
Linia Brungil'dy (Aldanov), 321, 324, **666**
Linnaeus, Carl, 117
Linz, Austria, 381
'Lips to Lips', *see* 'Usta k ustam'
Lisa or Lisbethsa, *see* Thompson, Lisbet
Lit. Dig., *see Literary Digest*
Literary and Artistic Circle, Berlin, 117, 121
Literary Digest, weekly, New York, 357
Liteyny Prospect, St Petersburg, 206
'Little Angel, The', *see* 'Sam treugol'nyi, dvukrylyi, beznogiy'
littlies, 68, 142, 153, *and see under* individual names, Lalodya, Show, Tuftikins

'Living Water, The' (Nabokov-Lukash), *see* 'Voda zhivaya'

Lizaveta, *see* Thompson, Lisbet

Lockhart, Sir Robert Hamilton Bruce, 354

Logos, 196, **613**

Lolita, xix, xxii, xxxvii, xliv, xlvii, liii, lvii, lviii, 509, 540, 725

Lolly, *see* Lvov, Lolly

London, England, xiv, xvi, xvii, xviii, xxxiv, xxxv, xlii, xlix, liv, 122, 216, 254, 256, 281, 282, 287, 288, 289, 290, 291, 292, 293, 294, 295, 297, 298, 299, 302, 307, 312, 315, 316, 318, 320, 322, 323, 328, 331, 332, 335, 337, 338, 342, 343, 345, 347, 348–9, 353, 354, 356, 357, 360, 361, 364, 379, 384, 386, 389, 396, 399, 404, 406, 411, 412, 415, 432, 434; as VN address, 300–13 (1937), 384–439 (1939); described, 302, 304, 305, 308, 387, 391, 393, 408, 416, 425–6, 427

London Zoo, 426, 427

Long, *see* John Long

Longfellow, Henry Wadsworth, 126–7, **583**

Look at the Harlequins!, xx

Lord Baltimore Hotel, Baltimore, Maryland, 495

Lorrimer, Burford, 452, **708**

Lourie, 391, 393, 395, 396, 408–9, 414, 416, 418, 431, 438

Louvre, Paris, 266, 286

Lovat Dickson, Horatio Henry, 429, 431, 433, 435, 437, **699**

Loveridge, Arthur, 487, **719**

Lubrzynsky, Mikhail Efimovich, 413, 414, 419, 422, 423, 429, 430, 432, **692**

Lucy, as alias for Feigin, Ilya, *q.v.*, 320

Ludovic (Louis Gosselin, 'Georges Lenôtre'), 312, **663**

Ludwiga, 99, 130, 576

Lugano, Switzerland, 506

Luitpoldstrasse, Berlin, as VéN address, 39 (number 13, Rilcke, 1925), 158–67 (number 27, Bardeleben, 1930)

Lukash, Ivan Sozontovich, 17, 27, 101, 195, 197, 201, 204, 456, **554**, 555, **614**

Lutherstrasse, Berlin, 105

Lutyens, Eva Efimovna (née Lubrzynsky), 257–8, 389, 400, 408, 409–10, 411, 414, 415, 420, 426, 427, 435, 436, **641**

Lutyens, Robert, 409, 420, 436, **692**, VN on, 436

Luxembourg, Jardin de, Paris, 208

Luzhin or *Luzhin's Defense*, *see* *Zashchita Luzhina*

Lvov, Aleksey Fyodorovich, 471, 713

Lvov, Lolly Ivanovich, 204, 208, 217, 255, 281, 302, **616**

Lvovsky, Mme, 210

Lyaskovsky, Aleksandr Ivanovich, 65–6, 162, **568**

Lyussya, *see* Shul'gina, Valentina Evgenievna

Lyusya, *see* Feigin, Ilya

M., *see* Milyukov, Pavel Nikolaevich
M. Mikh., *see* Karpovich, Mikhail Mikhaylovich
McAfee, Mildred Helen, 449, 453, **706**
Macalester College, St Paul, Minnesota, 481–2
McBride, 266
McCosh, Gladys Kathryn, 465, 469, 476, **712**
McDougall, Lady, 395, 397, 406
McGregor, John C., 480, **716**
McLoughlin, Maurice Evans, 394, **688**
Macmillan, publisher, London, 429, 433, 436
Macomba, Café, Taormina, Italy, 514
Madame Bovary (Flaubert), 28, 173, 178, **557**
'Mademoiselle O', xxxiii, xliv, 234, 235, 236, 240, 242, 243, 244, 245, 247, 249, 252, 254, 259, 261, 262, 268, 295, 465, 476, **629**, 642
'Magda's Childhood', excerpt from *Kamera obskura*, 172, **599**
'Magda's Visit', intended excerpt from *Kamera obskura*, 172
Magentanz, 491
Magnolia Street (Golding), 426, **697**
Makeev, Nikolay Vasilievich, 249, 254, **637**
Maklakov, Vasily Alekseevich, 210, 257, 281, 282, 285, 292, 315, 325, 329, 331, 344, 346, 363, 365, 375, 376, 377, **619**, **648**
Makovsky, Sergey Konstantinovich, 17, **554**
Malevsky-Malevich, Svyatoslav Andreevich, 279, **648**
Malevsky-Malevich, Svyatoslav Svyatoslavovich (Svetik), xlv, 235, 238, 279, 280, **630**, **648**, VN on, 238
Malevsky-Malevich, Zinaida Alekseevna (née, and pen-name, Shakhovskoy), *see* Shakhovskoy, Zinaida Alekseevna
Mallarmé, Stéphane, 318, **665**
Mamchenko, Victor Andreevich, 283, **650**
Man from the USSR, The, *see* *Chelovek iz SSSR*
Manchester, University of, 418
Mandelstam, Yury Vladimirovich, 201, 226, **615**, 627
Mann, Thomas, xliii
Mansfield, Katherine, 452, 708
Mansvetov, Vladimir Fyodorovich, xxxix, xl, 178, 440, 449, 484, **602**
Marcel, Gabriel, xxxii, xliv, 196, 201, 208, 212, 228, 229, 230, 240, 245, 247, 248, 250, 253, 256, 259, 261, 267, 268, 269, 288, 294, 315, **612**, **628**, 636, **655**
Margarita, *see* Masui, Margarita
Margolin, Olga Borisovna, 245, **635**
Maria, Mother (Elizaveta Yurievna Skobtsov), 203, 246, 248, **615**, **636**
Maria Antoinette, Queen of France, 330
Maria Pavlovna, Grand Duchess of Russia, 335, 336, 368, **670**

Maria Vasilievna, *see* Rausch von Traubenberg, Maria Vasilievna
Marianne, journal, Paris, 385, **685**
Marienbad (Mariánské Lázně), Czechoslovakia, xvii, 153, 382, 383, as VéN address, 381–3 (1937)
Markevitch, Igor Borisovich, 512, **726**
Markevitch, Topazia, 512, **726**
Markovich, *see* Morkovin, Vadim Vladimirovich
Marois, rue Le, Paris, 402, as VéN address, 384–416 (1939)
Marseilles, France, 4, 252, 638
Marshall, Mrs, 390
Martin du Gard, Roger, 97, **576**
Martini, Freddie, 508
Martyre de l'Obèse, Le (*The Martyrdom of the Obese Man*, Béraud), 135, **584**
Mary, *see Mashen'ka*
Mashen'ka (*Mary*), xv, xxix–xxx, 54, 55, 57, 66, 68, 96, 98, **564**, reviews of, 70, 87, 115, 121, 132, 153, translations of, 95, 163, 564, 699
Massachusetts General Hospital, Boston, 488, **719**
Massalsky, Elena Evseevna (née Slonim, VéN's sister), 78 (?), 95, 212, 369, 567
Massalsky, Prince Nikolay, 162–3, 593
Massary, Friederike (Fritzi), 301, **659**
Masui, Jacques, 238, 259, 278, 289, 631
Masui, Margarita, 238, 279
Match, magazine, Paris, 389, **686**
Matin, Le, newspaper, Paris, 325, 332, 335, **667**
Matusevich, Iosif Aleksandrovich, 243, 266, **634**
Matveev, Arina Rodionovna, 266, 267, **636**
Maurois, André, 236, 289, **630**, **654**
Mayakovsky, Vladimir Vladimirovich, 565
Maysky, Yan Lyakhovetsky (Ivan Mikhaylovich Maysky), 307, **662**
Me, 297, **658**. *See also* autobiography
'Mednyi vsadnik' ('The Bronze Horseman', Pushkin), 113, **579**
Melnikov-Papoushek, Nadezhda Fyodorovna, 70, 103, **567**
Mélot du Dy, Robert, 253, 286, 295, **639**, **657**
Menton, France, xvii, xxxv, 322, 323, 389, 443, 704
Méprise, La, *see Otchayanie*
Merana, Italy, 438
Mercure de France, journal, Paris, 289, 654
Mercury, *see American Mercury*
Merezhkovsky, Dmitry Sergeevich, 194, 203, 222, **597**
Mesures, journal, Paris, 187, 279, 286, 289, 346, 347, 349, 350, 382, 606, **674**
Meudon, France, 201
Meurant, René, 233, 234, **629**
Meurice, hotel, Paris, 379
Mexico, Gulf of, 476
Michaux, Henri, 350, **674**
Michel, *see* Albin Michel

Michener, Charles Duncan, 484, **717**
Mickey Mouse, 427
Micropteryx, 249
Mid-Day Luncheon Club, Springield, Illinois, 480, **716**
Mikh. Mikh., *see* Karpovich, Mikhail Mikhaylovich
Mil., *see* Milyukov, Pavel Nikolaevich
Milan, Italy, xxxvii, 511
Miller, Henry, 502, **723**
Milyukov, Pavel Nikolaevich (Mil., 'old man Pol', Pavel, P.N.), 194, 196, 243, 282, 283, 285, 290, 292, 294, 295, 299, 317, 318, 324, 329–30, 332, 335, 352, 425, 563, **611**, **616**, VN on, 204, 334, 370, **670**
mimicry, 471, 476
Minton, Walter J., 502, **722**
Minneapolis, Minnesota, 481
Misha, *see* Kaminka, Mikhail Avgustovich, *or* Lubrzynsky, Mikhail Efimovich
Miskhor, Crimea, 177, **602**
Mississippi, 481
Miten'ka, *see* Nabokov, Dmitri Vladimirovich
Mitina lyubov' (*Mitya's Love*, Bunin), 241, **633**
Mityushen'ka, Mityushonok, *see* Nabokov, Dmitri Vladimirovich
Mochulsky, Konstantin Vasilievich, 87, 248, **574**
Moe, Henry Allen, 478, 484, **715**
Mokropsy, Czechoslovakia, 35
Moldau (Vltava, river), Czechoslovakia, 16, 28, 554
'Molitva' ('Prayer'), 34, **559**
Molly, *see* Carpenter-Lee, Molly
Moment sud'by (Teffi), 334, 335, **670**
Mond, Sir Alfred, 415, **693**
Monnier, Adrienne, 349, **674**
Montanard, Angèle, 358
Montherlant, Henry de, 299, **658**
Montparnasse, quarter, Paris, 214, 243, 350
Montreux, Switzerland, xix, l, li, 507, 513, as VéN address, 507–13 (1970), 516 (1971), as VN address, 500 (1964), 502 (1966), 504 (1969), 516 (1971), 517 (1973), 518 (1974), 521 (1976)
Montreux Palace Hotel, Montreux, xix, 539, 540, 541
Monza, Italy, 507, **724**
Morevsky, Mme, 281, 284, 285, 298, 332
Morgan, Charles Langridge, 466, 468, 713
Morgan, Louise, 421, **695**
Morkovin, Vadim Vladimirovich, 177–8, 602
Morocco, 482
Morison, Samuel Eliot, 468, 713
Morrison, 399, 407, 412
Morskaya Street, St Petersburg, Russia, 113, **579**
Moscow, Soviet Union, 107, 124, 151, 292, 444
Moskva, bookstore, Berlin, 64, 70, 567

'Motsart i Salieri' ('Mozart and Salieri', Pushkin, translated by VN), 470–1, 476, **708**, 713
Moulinet, France, xvii
Mount Auburn Hospital, Cambridge, Massachusetts, 489–92, **719**
Moura, *see* Budberg, Baroness Maria Ignatievna
'Mozart and Salieri', *see* 'Motsart i Salieri' (Pushkin, translated by VN)
Much Ado about Nothing (Shakespeare), 425
Muller, Henry, 195, 196,
Mulman *or* Mulmanovich, 180, 185–6
Muma, *see* Zapolsky, Maria Sergeevna
Murat, boulevard, Paris, 221, 269
Muravyov, *see* (?) Ugrimov, Irina Nikolaevna
Muromtsev-Bunin, Vera Nikolaevna, 269, 297, 338, 366, 372, **633**, VN on, 372
Mus disneyi, 427
Mus flavicollis, 434, 435, 436
Musée national d'Historie naturelle, Paris, France, 430
Museum of Comparative Zoology (MCZ), Harvard, Cambridge, Massachusetts, xviii, xxxvi, 459, 486, 487, 488, 492–3, 494, VéN helps sort butterflies at, 467, 472, 475, 478, **714**
'Music', *see* 'Muzyka'
Mussolini, Benito, 193, 222, 387
'Muzyka' ('Music'), lv, 198, 204, 210, 211, 212, 218, 219, 223, 314, 315, 318, 319, 321, 346, 382, **548**, **614**, 665, **666**
My Double and I (Gubsky), 421, **694**
My Life (Lifar), 512, **726**
Myortvye dushi (*Dead Souls*, Gogol), 458, **636**, **710**
Myrica, 476

N. I., *see* Sablin, Nadezhda Ivanovna
N. R. F., see *Nouvelle Revue Française*
Nabokov, Anna Pavlovna, 279, **631**
Nabokov, Dmitri Vladimirovich (son; Bubka, Miten'ka, Mityushen'ka, Mityushonok, Musin'ka), xxxvii; allows access to letters to Véra, 541; appendix operation, xviii, xxxvi, xxxix, 487, 489, 490, 491, 493, 494, 502; birth, xvi, xxxiii, **628**; butterflies, attempt to interest him in, 424, 437, 459, 465, 469, 472, 476; death, xx, lxi, **628**; edits *Selected Letters*, 540–1; in hospital with VéN, 488; leaves Germany, xvii, xxxiv; Montreux years, 541; Nabokov's tenderness toward, xlv–xlvi, 250, 262, 264, 265, 270, 276, 309, 340, 352, 369–70, 382; opera singer, xxxvii, 242, 502, 722, 724; others send wishes or gifts, 254, 257, 305, 312, 335, 412, 478; racing car driver, xlii, 724; role in *Letters to Véra*, lxi, 541; translator, lxi; VN asks

Nabokov Dmitri Vladimirovich – *cont.* after, 241, 284, 333, 334, 337, 371, 490, 491, 496; VN buys gifts for, 327, 403, 451; VN draws for, 238, 255, 264, 271, 273, 274, 284, 291, 299, 302, 312, 367, 385, 398, 445, 446, 448, 449, 451, 454, 455, 475, 487, 490, 494; VN dreams of, 235, 260, 304, 334, 377, 422; VN imagines, xlv, 232, 236, 237, 253, 264, 265, 350; VN misses or wants to rejoin, 267, 272, 282, 292, 293, 314, 315, 328, 331, 332, 337, 343, 344, 352, 353, 359, 365, 368, 369–70, 375, 380, 406, 408, 492; VN promises to look after, 247, 346, 374, 431, 439, 459; VN sends kisses or wishes, 244, 251, 258, 268, 280, 285, 287, 296, 303, 308, 318, 345, 348, 361, 364, 373, 379, 383, 390, 460, 481, 484, 499; VN shows photographs of, 234, 238, 250, 298; VN thanks for message, 440, 447, 500, 507; VN thinks tenderly of, 242, 252, 262, 270–1, 272, 275, 276, 278, 283, 288, 291, 294, 309, 317, 321, 325, 327, 329, 336, 354, 437; VN writes messages for, 385, 387, 388, 392, 394, 395, 398, 401, 408, 410, 412, 413, 416, 418, 420, 422, 424, 426, 428, 429, 431, 433, 435, 437, 438, 439, 448, 450, 451–2, 454, 455, 457, 468, 471, 474–5, 478, 479, 483, 486, 487, 494

Nabokov, Elena Ivanovna (mother), 21, 153, 157, 161, 162, 165, 324, 377, **550**; birth, xiii; conditions in Czechoslovakia/Prague, 11, 21–22, 28–29, 32, 54, 61, 93–94, 158, 163, 169; death, xviii, **693**; depicted in *Glory*, 172–3, 599; financial support from VN, lv–lvi, 74, 78, 107, 133, 134, 221, 296, 313, 316, 354, 383, 385, 387, 400–1, 406, 411, 415, 417; forwards letter from Sergey, 77; health, xxii, 155, 158, 159, 165, 182–3, 184, 186, 294, 394, 415, 417, 481; letters quoted, 93–94, 158; 'mama' to VN, lix; marriage, xiii; mood, 33, 54, 159, 165, 170, 175, 182, 187; move to Prague, xxviii, 10–11, 551; spiritualism, 175; touched by VéN's letter about Sergey, 109; understanding of VN's work, 12; unsupported by Milyukovs, 204, 616; visited by VN, xvii, xxxi, 10–11, 32, 34, 37, 177, 179, 181; VN asks after, 253, 371; VN awaits letter from, 189, 288, 369; VN's concern for, 4; VN eager to show Dmitri to, xxxiv, 298, 330–1, 334, 339, 341, 343, 346, 348; VN entices her to read Joyce, 181; VN expects visit from, 227; VN forwards letter from, 91; VN hopes to visit, 310, 317, 327–8, 330–1, 362, 363, 364, 365, 376, 380; VN letter to, 539; VN reads work to, 171; VN receives letter from, 109, 131, 236, 273, 290; VN reports on, 154, 160, 382; VN sends kisses to, 375, 378; VN writes to, 56, 67, 74, 87, 95, 107, 149, 235, 243, 284, 299, 333, 379

Nabokov, Elena Vladimirovna (sister), *see* Sikorski, Elena Vladimirovna

Nabokov, Ivan Nikolaevich (Ivan, Vanya), 202, 205, 214, 216, **605**

Nabokov, Kirill Vladimirovich (brother), 22, 93, 154, 171, 173, 177, 178, 181, 183, 184, 185, 186, 234, 261, 262, 289, 354, **551**, **630**; birth, xiii; literary aims, xxxi, 169, 203; move to Prague, xxviii, 11; VN on, 154, 159, 161, 162, 169, 170, 175, 234, 237, 238, 259, 278–9, 279–80

Nabokov, Konstantin Dmitrievich (Uncle Kostya, Uncle K), 71, 98, 99, 100, 152, 386, 397, **570**, 577

Nabokov, Maria Ferdinandovna (grandmother), 313, **663**

Nabokov, Musin'ka, *see* Nabokov, Dmitri Vladimirovich

Nabokov, Nathalie (Natasha), xvi, xxxii, 188, 190, 199, 202, 205, 211, 213, 214, 215, 216, 217, 219, 223, 228, 336–7, 443, 459, 484, 576, **605**

Nabokov, Nicolas (cousin, Nika), xvi, xxxii, xxxvi, 169, 187, 188, 190, 192, 194, 196, 197, 199, 205, 210, 216, 217, 223, 225, 230, 250, 273, **597**, **605**, snob, 238, 336–7

Nabokov, Nikolay Sergeevich (Niki), xlvi, 279, **631**

Nabokov, Olga Vladimirovna (sister), *see* Petkevich, Olga Vladimirovna

Nabokov, Sergey Sergeevich (cousin), xlvi, 237, 238, 279, **631**

Nabokov, Sergey Vladimirovich (brother, Seryozha), 87, 109, 131, 154, 159, 171, 185, 187, 194, 202, 208, 213, 215, 223, 228, 230, **571–2**; birth, xiii; letter to mother quoted, 77–78; VN on, 78, 196, 229

Nabokov, Véra Evseevna (née Slonim), *passim*; alias (Mme Bertran), 18, 56; birth, xiii; book dedications to, xxi, xxii; character, xli–xliii; death, xx; depression and anxiety, xv, xxix, xlii, 52, 75, 76, 80, 83, 140, 382, 482; determination, xl, xli–xlii, 3; driver, xlii; early awareness of VN, xxiii, xxv, 543; editing *Selected Letters*, 540–1; endearments and salutations for, xxx, lvi–lvii, 50, and *passim*; English, knowledge of, 559; final years, 539–41; first exchanges with VN, xxiv–xxviii, 545; gun, xlii, **580**; health and weight, xv, xxii, xxix, 100, 106, 110, 115, 117–8, 120, 121, 131, 137, 140, 154, 168–9, 174, 326, 328, 329, 333, 334, 341, 346, 349, 351, 354, 362, 368, 374, 378, 435, 441, 449, 451, 472, **563**, **704**, **722**; letter to Elena Ivanovna Nabokov, with VN, 546;

Nabokov, Véra Evseevna – *cont.*
letters from VN, preserves, 539, tape-records, xxxii, 170, 539–40, 541, 1932 letters lost, 541; letters to VN, xxvii–xxviii, **xxxviii–xxxix**, **xl–xli**, l, 16, 24, 135, 146, 152, 164, 173, 185, 199; marriage, xxi, xxix; meets VN, xiv, xxiv–xxv, 3, 544, 550; muse, 29; poems for, xxi, **xxv–xxvii**, 4, 6, 520, 521; privacy, 539, 541, 555; public image, xxiii; reproaches in letters of, xlii, 3, 8, 228, 297, 342, 376, 377, 397–8, 398, 406, 432; roles in VN's life, xxiii, xli, 543; secretary, xxxi; support of VN, 195, 543; tutoring, xxix; understanding of VN's work, 12; voice, 491, 505, 513

Nabokov, Vladimir Dmitrievich (father), 166, 391, **552**, 565; birth, xiii; death, xiv, xvi, xxv, xxxiii, 335, **575**, **656**, **670**; founds and edits *Rul'*, xiv, xxii; imprisonment for Vyborg Appeal, 37, 560; marriage, xiii; understanding of VN's work, 12–13; VN letters to, 539; writings, 37

Nabokov, Vladimir Vladimirovich, *passim*;
acclaim, attitude to, xliii–xliv; aliases in letters, xlviii, liv–lv, 549, Calmbrood, xlviii, 282, **554**, **649**, Grigory Abramovich, xlviii, liv–lv, 256, 261, 268, 287 ('Ger.Abr.'), **640**, 644, Grishen'ka, 260, Victor, xlviii, lv, 278, 279, 283, 285, 286, 287, 288, 289, 290, 296, 308, 310, 319, 324, 329–30, 331, 333, 337, 345, 349, 359, 360, **549**, **647**, **648**, **665**; animals, drawings of, 166, 168, 168, interest in, xliv–xlv, 53, 71, 80, 96, 112, 117, 174, 176, 177, 180, 182, 185, 188, 189, 192, 199, 220, 230, 232, 234, 246, 260, 276, 277, 334, 427, 623, toy, 109, 142, 153, *see also* Box, Zen-Zin;
anniversaries commemorated, 11, 180, 319, 331, 335, 351, 354, 365, 373, 401, 452, 485, 501, 504, 512, 515, 516, 518, 552, **666**, **668**, **670**, **674**, **675**, **676**, **679**, **682**, **690**, **718**, **722**, **723**, **726**, 727;
birth, xiii; butterflies and moths (*see also* list of taxa in main sequence under *butterflies and moths*), xvii, xxxii, xxxvi, xliv, li, lv, 34, 89, 97, 110, 146, 154, 163, 166, 171, 173, 177, 182, 185, 193, 198, 227, 259, 286, 308, 316, 328, 334, 336, 367, 384, 393, 397, 424, **425**, 431, 432, 437, 450, 454, 456, 459, **465**, 466, 467, 468, 469, 470, 471, **474**, 475, **476**, 477, 478, 480, 482, 502, 506, 508, 509, 510, 512, 513, **700**, **710**, as code for money, 290, 308, 654, 657, 662, at British Museum (Natural History), 389–90, 396, 420, 423, 425, drawings of, 118,

124, 166, 518, hopes for job working with, 295, 430;
character, xliii–xlvii; chess, liv, 35, 69, 117, 153, 154, 155, 159, 167, 169, 175, 178, 440, 513, **569**; children, attitude to, xlv–xlvii, 373; codes for finances, xlviii, liv–lv, 365, 631, 632, 640, 641, 644, 647, 648, 649, 650, 653, 654, 656, 657, 658, 661, 662, 664, 665, 666, 668, 669, 673, 676, 679; composition, xlix–l, 12–13, 14, 17, 20, **23**–24, **29–30**, 54, **55–56**, 57, 58, **60–61**, 70–71, 78, 80, 81, 90, 91, 120, 134, 272, 319, 332, 340, 347, 366, 368, 422, 486; copyright, concerns about, 302, 307, 343, 347, 366;
death, xx, 539; dislike of deference, xliii; drawings, for Dmitri, 238, 255, 264, 271, 273, 274, 284, 291, 299, 302, 312, 367, 385, 398, 445, 446, 448, 449, 451, 454, 455, 475, 487, 490, 494, for Véra, 116, 118, 124, 147, 166, 168, 168, 442, 518; dreams, 23, 29, 41, 79, 102, 113, 140, 253, 260, 293, 304, 334, 345, 375, 377, 422, 434;
enthusiasm for VéN's letters, 16, 24, 28, 41, 90–91, 96, 115, 246, 255, 312, 343, 347, 354, 373, 390, 392, 410, 435, 453, 473;
farm labourer, xxv; food poisoning, 488–94, **719**;
German, knowledge of, 705; gymnastics, 87, 101;
homosexuality, attitudes to, 78, 159, 208, 249, 254, 283, 405, 512;
illnesses, 156, 441, 445, 469–70; inspiration explained, 707;
job-seeking in England, 306, 307, 308, 386, 389, 399, 402–3, 404, 407, 414–5, 418, 430, 433, 434, 439; job-seeking in US, 493, **720**;
lectures, American tours, xviii, xxxvi, 449, 460–84, **703**, 711, composition of, 445, 447, 450, **703**, delivery of, 449, on Art of Literature and Common Sense, 464, 474, 483, 498, **712**, on Gogol, 499, on Gorky-Chekhov, 442, 447, on mimicry, 471, 476, on Nineteenth Century, 442, on Proletarian Novel, 443, on Pushkin, 470, on Russian Novel, 442, on Short Story, 442, on Soviet Drama, 443, on Soviet Short Story, 445, 451, 456, on Technique of Novel, 447, 450, 481, on Tolstoy, 498, on Tragedy of Tragedy, 465, 466, 472, **712**, on War Novel, 474, reception of, 443, 449, 450, 453, 456, 460, 464, 470, 474, 495; letter to mother, with VéN, 546; letters of 1932 lost, xxxii; letters to parents, l, 539; love for Véra, xxi–xxii, and *passim*;
marriage, xxi, xxix; meets Véra Slonim, xiv, xxiv–xxv, 3; memory, VN on, 304, 312, 391; modesty, xliii–xliv, 18; music and, xlix, 471;

Nabokov, Vladimir – *cont.*
on reading process, 433;
passports, permits, visas, and identity cards, xxxiv, xxxvi, xxxviii, xlviii, lv, 31, 95, 162, 177, 179, 180, 183, 184, 210, 213, 224, 229, 258, 259, 262, 265, 282, 287, 288, 293, 301, 304, 308, 309, 314, 315, 316–7, 320, 323, 326, 327, 331, 333, 337–8, 340, 341, 343, 344, 345, 346, 350, 353, 363, 364, 365, 367, 368–9, **370–1**, 371–2, 373, **373–4**, 375, **376–7**, 377, **378**, **379**, 380, 381–2, 383, 414, 415, 416, 418, 427, 428, 429, **643**, **682**; post offices, aversion to, 7, 30; psoriasis, xxxiv, xxxviii, 127, 279, 284, 285, 286–7, 288–9, 292, 293, 296, 298, 308–9, 316, 318–9, 324–5, 330, 332, 339, 347–8, 349, **378**, 583, **648**;
questionnaire (with Raisa Tatarinov), 137, 138–9, 148, 149;
reading, xlix, 28, 57, 59, 67–8, 69, 72, 74, 135, 312, 420, 421, 422, 513; readings, xvi, xvii, xxxii, xxxiii, xxxiv, xlviii, lx, Antwerp, 188, 210, 214, 232, 239, **632**, Belgrade, 228, Berlin, 64–6, Brussels, 188, 202, 209, 210, 214, 232, 236, 240, 244, 249, 252, 253, 256, 258, 278, 395, 399, **630**, **641**, **647**, Cambridge, 318, 403, Dresden, 179, 186, 605, Eindhoven, 237, **635**, London, 302, 303–4, 307, 313, 314, 316, 347, 350, 353, 360, 384, 388, 390, 391–2, 397, 399, 401, 403, 405–6, 407, 410, 411, 416, 420, 423, 425, Oxford, 318, Paris, 194–5, 203, 214, 218, 219, 220–1, 221–4, 238, 244, 245–6, 251, 253, 254–5, 256, 258–9, 261, 263, 268, 269, 280, 291, 294, 295, 298, 306, 331, **615**, **635**, **644**, **648**, **652**, **655**, **657**, Prague, 382, Strasbourg, 188, 192, 209, 210; religion, 78, 366, 471; relocation suggestions, Brussels, 242, 259, 260, London (or England), 314, 332, 341, 410, 414–5, 416, 418, 421–2, 428, 438, 439, Paris (or France), 210, 214, 216, 221, 227, 260, 262, 267, 281, 289, 290, 292, Riviera/South of France, 283, 286, 288, 293, 295, 298, 308, 313, 314, 316, 320, 321, 322–3, 326, 327, 328, 331, 332, 341, 343, 344–5, 348, 363, 367, 369, 371; reproaches, laments, or exhortations about VéN's infrequent letters, xl–xli, xlviii, 18, 20, 21, 23, 34, 67–68, 72, 74, 80, 83, 88, 105, 106, 113, 133, 143, 148, 151, 152, 154, 160, 163, 165, 168, 174, 213, 242, 250, 272, 387, 430, 471, 483, 493, 511; reputation, xxii, xxxi, xxxii, xxxv, xxxix, xl, xliii–xliv, l, 18, 64–66; riddles in letters, xxx, liv, lviii, 103, 108–9, 110, 111–2, 114, 116, 117, 128–9,

132, 133, 136, 145, 146, 147, 150, discussion of, original Russian text of, and solutions to, 525–37; Russian, desire to write in, 481–2;
search for escape from Germany, xxxiii, 117; shaving, 83, 133, 188, 461, 463, 509; Sirin pen-name, xiv, xxii, 27, 52, 197, 310, 355, 444, 553, **554**, 559; skiing, 546; smoking, 62, 81, 87, 91, 105, 106, 114, 116, 133, 137, 279, 404, 489; soccer, 174, 185, 311, 333, 340, 391, 392; suntanning, 126, 127, 130, 143, 144, 145, 149, 151, 191, 350, 362, 378; style in letters, xlvii–xlviii; swimming, 41, 43, 53, 54–55, 90, 94, 97, 105, 109, 111, 143;
teeth, 292, 371, 372, 373, 374, 375, 377, 382; tennis, xxx, 52, 55, 60, 69, 79, 83, 95, 96, 98, 105, 107, 110, 112, 114, 121, 123, 127, 129, 130, 132, 133, 134, 139, 141, 144, 145, 149, 152–3, 394, 395, 396, 431, 438, 466, 471, 476, 488, 564, 588, 688; testimonials for, 387, 390, 396, 399, 402, 407, 420; theatre, 324, 335, 408–9, 425–6, 438, 456–7 (*see also*, in main sequence, Russian Theatre); time, thoughts on, 151; translations for money, 14, 25, 36, 157, 286, 287, 332, 406, 425, 434, 435, 436, 437, 438; travel suggestions, 94–5, 97, 98, 135 (Biarritz, France), 148 (Czechoslovakia), 162, 163, 165, 174 (Varna, Bulgaria), 224–5, 227 (Pau, France), 225 (Grasse and Saurat, France), 412, 426 (mountains); tutoring, xxix, xxxi, xxxvi, xxxvii, 33, and see main pupils, Aleksandr Sack and Sergey Kaplan;
unrealized film projects, *Hôtel Magique*, 243, king's son, 252; unrealized literary projects: 73–74, story about room (see 'Komnata'); 105, poem about letters to God; 112–3, 134, story in form of 'review' of non-existent literary almanac, with Akhmatova parody; 155, story not about Horace; 171, 177, 181, 182, novel about examination; two lectures in French, 295, 316 (about women writers, or exhibitions), 322, 332, 348; play, 315, 318, 319, 325, 332, 335, 340, 343, 346; poem about Paris, 366; poem about Clem Sohn, 366; story, 366, 369; Russian grammar for English speakers, 386; lecture, Cambridge, England, 403, 412; book project in English, 422, 424, 437; story in English, 444

Nabokov family home, 163

Nabokov: His Life in Art (Field), 540

Nabokov: His Life in Part (Field), 539, 540, 636, 642

Nadezhda or Nad. Iv. or Nadya, *see* Sablin, Nadezhda Ivanovna

'Nadezhda' ('Hope', Bunin), 178, **603**
'Nad ozerom' ('Over the Lake', Blok), 343, **672**
'Nagrada' ('The Reward'), 347, **674**, excerpt from *Dar*, q.v.
Naif, Le (Hellens), 261, **642**
Nakhman-Acharya, Magda Maksimilianovna, 193, 233, **610**
Nalyanch, Sergey Ivanovich, 164, **594–5**
names, treatment of, 3n
Napoleon III, 466
Nash vek (*Our Age*), weekly, Berlin, 173, **599**
Natasha, *see* Nabokov, Nathalie
National Museum, Prague, xxxii, 162, 173
Navashin, Dmitry Sergeevich, 288, **653**
Ne vsyo kotu maslenitsa (*It's Not Always Shrovetide for the Cat*, Ostrovsky), 66, 568
Nebrodi Mountains, Sicily, 512, 726
Nebuchadnezzar, 146
Nedelya (*The Week*), newspaper, Prague, 167, **596**
Nef, 395
Nekrasov, Nikolay Alekseevich, 145
Nemirovich-Danchenko, Vasily Ivanovich, 22, 160, 162, **556**, 593
Nemirovsky, Irina Lvovna (Irène), 196, **613**
Neskin, 243
'Neskol'ko slov ob ubozhestve sovetskoy belletristiki i popytka ustanovit' prichinu onogo' ('A Few Words on the Wretchedness of Soviet Literature and an Attempt to Establish the Reasons Thereof'), xxx, **570**, composition of, 70–71, delivery of, 72–73, preparation for, 51, 52, 57, 59, 67, 566, reception of, 72–73
Nestorstrasse, Berlin, 293, as VéN address, 236–68 (1936), 277–336 (1937), as VN address, 270–4 (1936)
Neue Winterfeldtstrasse, as VéN address, 41 (1925)
Neva, river, Russia, 79
New Mexico, 468
New Republic, weekly, Washington, DC, xxxvi, 440, 452, **702**
New Statesman, weekly, London, 513
New York, New York, xviii, xxxvi, xxxix, 444, 447, 451, 459, 461, 484, 485, 496; 35 West 87 Street, as VéN address, 440–56 (1941); 250 West 104 Street (Anna Feigin), as VéN address, 486–93 (1944), 502 (1966)
New York Times, 245, 292, **635**, **656**
New Yorker, xix, xxxvi, 452, 466, 489, 491, 708, 719
Newell, 459
News Chronicle, newspaper, London, 421, **695**
'Neznakomka' ('Incognita', Blok), 544
Nice, France, 4, 194, 345, 348, 381
Nicholas I, Tsar, 189
Nicholson, *see* Nicolson, Harold George
nicknames, lx, 3n

Nicolson, Harold George, 307, 313, 319, 388
Nielsen, Asta, 29, **557**
Nika, *see* Nabokov, Nicolas
Nikolai Gogol (*Nikolay Gogol*), 471, 473, 486, 493, **710**, **714**, **718**
Nikolay (cat), 253, 262, 320–1, **639**
Nikolay Pereslegin (Stepun), 193, **610**
Nikolka Persik (translation of Rolland, *Colas Breugnon*), xxiii
Nilus, Sergey Aleksandrovich, 25, **557**
Nina, Aunt, *see* Kolomeytsev, Nina
Nollendorfplatz, Berlin, 89
Nord-Express, 305
Norfolk, Connecticut, 454
Norwalk ('Norwork'), Connecticut, 454
'Nos' ('The Nose', Gogol), 459, 711
'Notes on the Lepidoptera of the Pyrénées Orientales and the Ariège,' 171, **590**
Nouvelles littéraires, newspaper, Paris, 187, 209, 219, 332, 337, 342, 346, 354, 367
Nouvelle Revue Française, journal, Paris, 192, 195, 196, 202, 204, 209, 236, 252, 284, 286, 289, 293, 315, 320, 352, 382, **610**, 612
Nov' (*Virgin Soil*), journal, Russia, 576
Novotvortsev, Mlle, lx, 223, 228, 255, **623**
Novyi grad (*New City*), journal, Paris, 204, 299, **610**, 649
Nuki, 75
Nürnberger Strasse, Berlin, as VN address, **563** (1926)
'O Khodaseviche' ('On Khodasevich'), 437, **701**
Obenberger, Jan, 165, **595**
Oberthür, Charles, 249, **638**
'Obida' ('A Bad Day'), 212, **620**, **626**, translation into French ('L'Outrage'), 279, 282, 284, 286, 316, 346, 349, **648**, 649, **650**, 664, **673**
'Oblako, ozero, bashnya' ('Cloud, Castle, Lake'), 382, **679**, **683**, 705, translation into English, 443, 447, 450, 452, **704**
Obolensky, Maria Nikolaevna, 205, 218, **617**
Obolensky, Prince Vladimir Andreevich, 226, **627**
Observer, newspaper, London, 54, 61, 89, 103, 121, 144, 153, 306, 512, **564**
Obstein, *see* Stein
Obyvatel' (Average Man), pen-name of Mikhail Andreevich Osorgin, *q.v.*
'Odd', *see* 'Skazka'
'Odelia dear' (Vyazemsky), 174–5, **600**
Odéon, Place de l', Paris, 349
Odessa, Russia, 241
'Odinochestvo' ('Solitude'), 361, 367, **671**, **678**, excerpt from *Dar*, q.v.
Odoevtseva, Irina Vladimirovna (Iraida Gustavovna Heineke), 194, **611**
Œil-de-Dieu (Hellens), 208, 619
Œuvres libres, book series, Fayard, 249
Ofrosimov, Yuri Victorovich, 65, 72, **568**
'Okno' ('The Window'), 223, **625**

'Old Grace', *see* Jannelli, Altagracia de
'old Joseph', 'old man, the', *see* Hessen, Iosif
'On Discovering a Butterfly', 718
'On Khodasevich', *see* 'O Khodaseviche'
'Opoveshchenie', 245, 254, 304, 325, 332, 444, **635**, **669**
orchid, 500, 504, **724**
Original of Laura, The, 541
Orlov, 110
Ornithoptera, 249
Orthodox Church, 76–8
'Osen'' ('Autumn', Pushkin), 461, 712
Osnabrücker Strasse, Berlin, as VéN address, 337–68 (1937)
Osorgin, Mikhail Andreevich (Mikhail Andreevich Ilyin), 121, 194, 198, 203, 212, 217, 415, **581**, **603**, VN on, 217
Ostrovsky, Aleksandr Nikolaevich, 66
Osya, *see* Bromberg, Iosif
Otchayanie (*Despair*), xvi, 194, 210, 219, 223, 227, 228, 238, 241, 242, 243, 244, 245, 260, 261, 298, 312, 365, 598, **611**, 623, **626**, **627**, **631**, **635**; translation, into English (*Despair*), xxxiii, 246–7, 248, 249, 253, 256, 261, 263, 266, 272, 281, 283, 288, 296, 306, 308, 314, 319, 320, 321, 328–9, 348, 349, 350, 352, 353, 357, 360, 365, 372, 391, 634, 639, 645, 648, **662**, **665**, **674**, reviews of, 366–7, **679**; translation, into French (*Désespoir*, *La Méprise*), 247, 248, 249, 256, 259, 268, 295, 296, 315, 320, 321, 352, 361, 372, 385, 640, **644**, 681
Otsup, Nikolay Avdeevich, 217, **622**
Outcry, The (James), 72, **570**
'Outrage, L'', *see* 'Obida'
Oxford, England, xiv, 318, 407
Oxford Book of Poetry, 338

P. N., *see* Milyukov, Pavel Nikolaevich, *or Poslednie novosti*
Pale Fire, xix, xliv
Pamyati Amalii Osipovny Fondaminskoy (*In Memory of Amalia Osipovna Fondaminsky*), 348, **674**
Panchenko, 66, 71, 78
Panin, Countess Sofia Vladimirovna, 166, **595**
Paramount, film studio, 394
Parchevsky, Konstantin Konstantinovich, 247, **636**
Pares, Sir Bernard, 308, 314, 389, 392, 394, 396, 398, 399, 402, 406, 407, 412, 415, 417, 423, 424, 427, 436, **662**, VN on, 424
Paris, France, **xvi**, xvii, xix, xxxi, xxxii, xxxiii, xxxiv, xxxv, xxxvi, xlii, xliv, xlix, liv, lx, 4, 37, 87, 95, 126, 167, 171, 186, 187, 188, 189, 210, 225, 227, 234, 235, 236, 238, 239, 240, 258, 259, 260, 278, 280, 283, 293, 294, 295, 303, 304, 307, 310, 312, 313, 314, 323, 324, 328, 331, 338, 354, 355, 356, 359, 361, 382, 386,

388, 389, 390, 399, 402, 404, 409, 411, 415, 416, 417, 419, 423, 429, 430, 431, 432, 434, 461, 479; as VéN address, 417–39 (1939); as VN address, 190–231 (1932), 239–58, 260–8 (1936), 278–300, 315–80 (1937); described, 218–9, 244, 261, 284, 294, 338, 340, 349, 350, 360, 365–6, 368, 399; eagerness to move to, 210, 214, 216, 221, 227, 260, 262, 267, 281, 289, 290; international exhibition (1937), 338, 365–6, **671**; VN's reputation in, 198, 221–4, 226–7, 288, 294, 321, 355

Pariser Strasse, Berlin, 273

Parry, Albert, 418, **677**, **693–4**

Pascal, Germaine, 210, 619

Passauer Strasse, Berlin, 85, as VéN address, 155 (1926)

'Passazhir' ('The Passenger'), 292, 334, 433, **656**, **700**

'Passenger, The', see 'Passazhir'

Passy, quarter, Paris, 193, 207

Pasternak, Boris Leonidovich, 178, **602**

patronymics, Russian, lx

Pau, France, 224, 227, 229

Paulhan, Jean, xxxii, 192, 195, 202, 204–5, 209, 210, 236, 240, 252, 262, 270, 272, 279, 281, 282, 283, 284–5, 285, 286, 289, 293, 296, 299, 316, 332, 349, 350, 352, 354, 382, **610**, VN on, 204, 282, 293, 351

Paulhan, Sala, 210

Pavel, *see* Milyukov, Pavel Nikolaevich

Pavlova, Anna Pavlovna, 236, **630**

Pearce, Charles, 484, **714**

'Pearl, The', *see* 'Zhemchug'

'Pegas' ('Pegasus'), 206, **617**

Peltenburg, Leo, 107, **578**, **630**

Peltenburg, Leonora, 235, 238, 261, 278, 279, **630**

Peltenburg, Vera, 235, **630**

Peltser, Elena Aleksandrovna (née Kovalyov), 253, 347, **639**

Pen Club, Brussels, 232, 235, 236, 629

Pen Club, London, 307

Pen Club, Paris, 405

Perekryostok (Crossroads), literary circle, Paris, 191, **609**

Perepiska s sestroy (Correspondence with his Sister), xl

Pereslegin, see Nikolay Pereslegin

Pereverzev, Pavel Nikolaevich, 292, 655

'Perfection', *see* 'Sovershenstvo'

Perkins, Agnes Francis, 442, 443, 444, 450, 453, 457, 467, 473, 476, **703**, VN on, 453

Perpignan, France, 228

Persky, Dominique Desanti (Dominika Sergeevna Persky), 338–9, **672**

Perts, I., 103, **577**

Pertzov, Konstantin Aleksandrovich, 447, **706**

Pertzov, Pyotr Aleksandrovich, 443, 444, 447, 451, **704**, 705

'Pervaya lyubov'' ('First Love'), 223, **625**

Peshchera (*The Cave*, Aldanov), 207, 272–3, 275, **618**, **646**, **647**
'Peshchera' ('The Cave', Zamyatin), 362, 365, **678**
Peter the Great, 113, 579
Petersburg (Bely), 301, **659**
Petit, Eugène, 329, **668**
Petit, Sofia Grigorievna, 332
Petkevich, Boris Vladimirovich, 159, 167, 169, 170, 172, 174, 185, **592**, chess, 155, 159, 167, 175, 181, 558
Petkevich, Olga Vladimirovna (sister), xlvi, 27–28, 56, 93, 131, 154, 159, 161, 165, 167, 169, 170, 172, **558**; birth, xiii; marriages assessed by VN, xxxi, 170, 185; move to Prague, xxviii; parenting, xxxi; singer, 33; VN on, 174, 175, 181, 382
Petkevich, Rostislav Borisovich (Rostik, nephew), xxxi, xlvi, 170, 172, 174, 181, 185, 379, 434, 439, 575, **597**, **683**, **700**
Petrov, Evgeny (Evgeny Petrovich Kataev), 351, **675**
Petrov, Galina Nikolaevna (née Kuznetsova), 250, 511, **638**, 725
Petya, *see* Skulyari, Pyotr Mikhaylovich
Petrograd, xxiii. *See also* St Peterbsurg
Petropolis, publisher, Berlin, 162, 225, 244, 298, 312, **593**, **626**
Pevzner, 499
Pfalzburger Strasse, Berlin, 309
Phalero, Greece, 223
Piccadilly, London, 416, 417
Pierce, *see* Pearce, Charles
'Pikovaya dama' ('Queen of Spades, The', Pushkin), 499, **721**
'Pilgram' ('The Aurelian'), 161, 163, 167, 226, 239, 252, 257, 259, 265, 268, 336, 346, **593**, 594, **673**
Pilsky, Pyotr Moiseevich, 367, **680**
Pio, *see* Korvin-Piotrovsky, Vladimir Lvovich
Piotrovsky, Mme, *see* Korvin-Piotrovsky, Nina Alekseevna
Piquet, 210
Pirandello, Luigi, 100, 576
Plaksin, Boris Nikolaevich, 220, **624**
Pletnyov, Rostislav Vladimirovich, 175, 185, **601**
Plevitskaya, Nadezhda Vasilievna, 291, **655**
Plisnier, Charles, 233, 234, **629**
Plon, publisher, Paris, 208, 228, 268, 619, **628**
Plunder, The, *see* *Dobycha* (Tyrkov)
Pnin, xix, xxxvi, xxxvii, liii, lv, 579
'Podarok' ('The Present'), excerpt from *Dar*, q.v.; 332, 335, 337, 345, **669**, **671**
Podolsk, Russia, 159
Podvig (*Glory*), xv, 173, 198, 200, 204, 205, 210, 211, 213, 216, 217, 229, 261, 312, **599**, 612, 622, **626**, **628**, translation of, 204, 209, 226, 228
Poems (1979), see *Stikhi*
'Poet' ('The Poet,' Pushkin), 120, 581
Poets' Hermitage, *see* Skit Poetov, 159

Pohl, Anna Mikhaylovna (Yan-Ruban), 217–8, **622**, VN on, 217
Pohl, Vladimir Ivanovich, 217, 602, **622**
Pol, old man, *see* Milyukov, Pavel Nikolaevich
Pole, The, *see Polyus*
Poletika, Vladimir Ivanovich, 86, **573**
Politzer, Ronald, 419, 423, 429, 435, 436, **694**
Polonsky, Yakov Borisovich, 206, **618**
Poltava, Soviet Union, 220
Polyakov, Aleksandr Abramovich, 191, 286, 294, **608**, **651**
Polyakov, Anna (Alma) Eduardovna, 337, 342, **671**
Polyakov, Solomon Lvovich (pen-name Litovtsev), 294, 387(?), 390(?), 408(?), **656**
Polyakova, Anastasia Alekseevna, 198, **613**
Polyus (*The Pole*), play, 6, **545**, **550**, 551
Pomerania, Germany, xxix
Poncet, *see* François-Poncet
Pons, Lily, 452, **708**
Poor Folk, *see Bednye lyudi* (Dostoevsky)
Poplavsky, Boris Yulianovich, 243, **634**
'Port' ('The Seaport'), 69, 569
Portnov, 217
'Poseshchenie muzeya' ('The Visit to the Museum'), lix, 388, 426, **686**, **698**
poshlost', 584
Poslednie novosti (*The Latest News*), newspaper, Paris, 162, 163, 164, 167, 172, 175, 178, 185, 189, 190, 192, 194, 195, 198, 200, 201, 203, 207–8, 226, 227, 228, 231, 235, 240, 243, 244, 257, 265, 281, 286, 331, 333, 335, 345, 347, 348, 354, 361, 402, 422, **593**, 627, **632**; VN's hopes of regular column in, 281, 285, 292, 299, 324, 330, **649**
Post, newspaper, London, 389, **686**
Potresov, Sergey Victorovich (Yablonovsky), 346, 347, **673**
Potsdamer Platz, Berlin, 107
Potsdamer Strasse, Berlin, 66
Potter, Paulus, 461, 711
Pourtalès, Guy de, 297, **658**
'Pouchkine, ou le vrai et le vraisemblable' ('Pushkin, or the Real and the Plausible'), 279, 282, 284–5, 285–6, 288, 293, 295, 296, 315, 350, 352, 400, **648**, 651, **654**, **657**, **666**
Pozdnyshev trial, and VN's speech for, xxx, 105, 106, 115, 117, 121, 127, 135, 137, 139–40, 141–2, 149, 577. *See also* 'Kreytserova sonata'
Pozner, Vladimir Solomonovich, 209, **619**
Prague, xiv, xv, xvii, xxviii–xxix, **xxxi**, xxxiv, xli, xlviii, l, liii–liv, 11, 17, 32, 33, 35, 37, 56, 94, 143, 164–5, 179, 219, 290, 292–93, 299, 310, 316, 319, 324, 326, 327, 331, 333, 340, 348, 350, 371, 374, 375, 376, 377, 378, 380, 381, 417; as VéN address, 370–80 (1937); as VN address, 10–31, 36 (1923–24), 153–5 (1926), 158–69 (1930), 170–86 (1932), 381–3 (1937); described, 13, 16, 19–20, 27, 162, 175–6, 186

'Prayer', *see* 'Molitva'
Pregel, Aleksandra Nikolaevna, 301, **659**
Pregel, Sofia Yulievna, 220, **624**
Priel, Jarl, 385, 391, 392–3, 401, 403, 404, 406, 412, **685**, **687**
Priglashenie na kazn' (*Invitation to a Beheading*), xvi, 236, 237, 239, 243, 245, 248, 250, 268, 302, 333, 418, **630**, **687**
'Printemps à Fialta', *see* 'Vesna v Fialte'
Problemist, The, 513
Procope, Le, restaurant, Paris, 195, **612**
Proffer, Ellendea, xliii
Protocols of the Elders of Zion (Nilus), 25, **557**
Proust, Marcel, xlix, 51, 70, 96, 191, 267, 304, 336, 452, **563**
'Provans' ('Provence'), 550
'Provence', *see* 'Provans'
Prozrachnost' (*Transparency*, unpublished collection), 409
Prusak, Sala, 210, 619
Prutkov, Koz'ma, 585
Pteridophora alberti, 174
Puccini, Giacomo, 514, **726**
puddle, 68, 83, 132, 134, 135, 137, 584
Pumpyansky, Leonid Semyonovich, 239, **632**
Püngeler, Rudolf, 159, **592**
Purishkevich, Vladimir Mitrofanovich, 59, **566**
Pushkin, Aleksandr Sergeevich, xxxiii, xxxvii, xliii, 63, 86, 107, 120, 145, 174, 186, 217, 248, 265, 266, 278, 288, 294, 311, 325, 354, 366, 367–8, 461, 470, 472, 499, **555**, **574**, 578, 579, 581, 600, 636, **639–40**, 643, **663**, **679**, **707**, **713**,
Pushkin exhibition, 325, **667**,
translations from, 445, 470–1, **705**
'Pushkin, or the Real and the Plausible', *see* 'Pouchkine, ou le vrai et le vraisemblable'
'Pustyak,—nazvan'e machty, plan—i sledom' ('A trifle—a mast's denomination, plans—trailed'), **573**, **581**; composition, 82; text, 83–84; publication, 87; reception, 85, 89
Put' (*The Way*), journal, Paris, 155, **590**
Putnam, G. P. Putnam's Sons, publisher, New York, 306, 308, 318, 330, 333, 336, 343, 346, **722**
puzzles, *see* Nabokov, Vladimir Vladimirovich: riddles
Pyrenees, 66, 227

'Queen of Spades, The', *see* 'Pikovaya dama' (Pushkin)

Rabinovich, 263
Rabinovich, Evgeny Isaakovich, 447, **706**
Rachmaninov, Natalia Aleksandrovna (?), 208, 217, **619**
Rachmaninov, Sergey Vasilievich, lx, **618**
Radio Belge, 302
Raevsky, Georgy Avdeevich, 609
Raevsky, Nikolay Alekseevich, 173, 174, 185, **600**
Raisa, *see* Tatarinov, Raisa Abramovna

Rami, 397
Rashel, 286, 372
Rasputin, Grigory Efimovich, 220, **624**
Rathaus, Daniil Maksimovich, 160, 161, 178, 592
Rathaus (Klimenko-Rathaus), Tatyana Danilovna, 178, **602**
Ratner, 264, 269
Rausch von Traubenberg, Aleksandr Nikolaevich, 213, 218, **621**
Rausch von Traubenberg, Baron Evgeny Aleksandrovich (Zhenya), 218, **623**
Rausch von Traubenberg, Baron Georgy Evgenievich (Yury, Yurik), 218, 284, **623**
Rausch von Traubenberg, Maria Vasilievna, 205, 210, 211, 218, 220, **617**
Rausch von Traubenberg, Baron Nikolay Nikolaevich (Koka), 191, 199, 202, 205, 206, 210, 211, 218, 220, 221–2, 223, 224, 225, 226, 228, **609**, **617**, VN on, 204, 211, 218
'Razgovor knigoprodavtsa s poetom' ('Conversation between a Bookseller and a Poet', Pushkin), 555
Read, Florence Matilda, 469, 470, 471, 472–3, 478, **713**
Reade, Frank Robertson, 474, 476, 477, **714**
Real Life of Sebastian Knight, The, xviii, xxxv, xxxvi, 389, 393, 399, 400, 403, 405, 413, 416, 417, 419, 421, 423, 428–9, 429–30, 433, 436, **686**, **695**, **699**
'Recompense, The', *see* 'Voznagrazhdenie'
Regensburger Strasse, Berlin (address of Anna Feigin, Evsey Slonim, Sofia Slonim), 51, 58, 72, 76, 80, 81, 82, 83, 89, 98, 107, 124, 131, 149, **563**
Regent's Park, London, 425
Regina, 238, 395
Reiselfingen, Germany, 43
'Remarkable Case of Davidson's Eyes, The' (Wells), 122
Rembrandt van Rijn, 106
Remizov, Aleksey Mikhaylovich, 217, 252, 330, **622**
'Return of Pushkin, The', see 'Vnov' ya posetil' (Pushkin)
Revue de France, journal, Paris, 382
Revue de Paris, journal, Paris, 216, 337, 342, 346, 355, 367, 382, **622**
Revue hebdomadaire, La, journal, Paris, 383, **684**
'Reward, The', *see* 'Nagrada'
Richmond, Virginia, 468, 469, 713
riddles, *see* puzzles
Ridel, S., 259, 269, 270, 286, 287, 288, 289, 291, 361, 365
Ridelius, *see* Rydelius, Ellen
Ridgefield, Connecticut, 451, 453, **707**, as VN address, 456 (1941)
Ridley, Lady Natalia Aleksandrovna, 306, 308, **661**
Riga, Latvia, 37, 194, 324, 496
Riley, Norman Denbigh, 423, **696–7**
Rilke, Rainer Maria, 236, **630**

Rimsky-Korsakov, Nikolay Andreevich, 557
Riviera, France, 282–3, 461, 467
Roche, Denis, xxxii, 188–9, 196, 198, 199, 201–2, 209, 210, 223, 225, 228, 243, 245, 248, 249, 255, 256, 257, 288, 290, 298, 334, 336, 352, 353, 361, 369, 372, 382, 393, **607**, VN on, 259
Rochebrune, *see* Roquebrune
Rockefeller Institute, New York, 478
Rodzyanko, Lidiya Erastovna, 342, **672**
Rodzyanko, Nikolay Mikhaylovich, 285, 342, 346, 365, 368–9, 428, **650**, **672**, **698**, VN on, 368
Rodzyanko, Sergey Nikolaevich, 195, **612**
Rodzyanko, (Sergey Pavlovich?), 388, 390–1, 395, 400, 406, 413, 422, 431, **686**
Roerich, Nikolay Konstantinovich, 175, **601**
Le Roi Louis XVII et l'enigme du Temple (Lenôtre), 312, **663**
Roland, Manon (Marie-Jeanne Philippon), 233, **629**
Rolland, Romain, xxiii, 565
Romains, Jules, 405, **691**
Romania, 290
Romanov, Grand Prince Boris Vladimirovich, 211, **620**
Romanov, Grand Prince Vladimir Kirillovich, 408, 409, 425, **691**
Romanov, Grand Prince Vsevolod Ioannovich, 422, **695**
Rome, Italy, 174, 481, 507, 508, 509
Romochka, *see* Klyachkin, Roma
Ronsard, Pierre de, 4, 216, 550, 621
'Room, The', 'A Room for Rent', 'Rooms,' *see* 'Komnata'
'Room, The' ('The room a dying poet took'), 482, **716**
Roquebrune-Cap-Martin, France, 288, 320, 321, 322, 323, 325
Roshchin (Nikolay Yakovlevich Fyodorov), 286, 373, **651**
Roshchin, Mme, 373
Roseneck, Berlin, 90
Rosny jeune, J.-H., 110, **579**
Ross, Alan Strode Campbell, 416, **693**
Rossiya i slavyanstvo (Russia and Slavdom), newspaper, Paris, 167, 172, 173, 208
Rostik, *see* Petkevich, Rostislav Borisovich
Rostov-on-Don, Russia, 239
Rostovtsev, Mikhail Ivanovich, 333, **669**
Rotenshtern (Zvezdich), Pyotr Isaevich, 85
Rousseau, Jean-Jacques, 82
Royal Historical Society, London, 416, 417
Rozhdestveno, Russia, 30, **558**
Rubchik, 383
Rubinstein, Dmitry Lvovich (Mit'ka), 223, **625**
Rudnev, Vadim Victorovich, lv, 190, 223, 255, 256, 267, 270, 275, 279, 281, 291, 305, 319, 352, 353, 368, 369, 437, 549, **608**, **644**, 665, **680**

Rukavishnikov, Elena Ivanovna, *see* Nabokov, Elena Ivanovna
Rukavishnikov, Vasily Ivanovich (Uncle Vasya, 'Ruka'), 228, **558**, 627
Rul' (*The Rudder*), newspaper, Berlin, **xiv**, **xxii**, xxiv, xxv, xxvii, xxxi, lx, 13, 21, 27, 34, 45, 52, 55, 66, 67, 69, 71, 86, 88, 89, 91, 95, 96, 98, 99, 102, 107, 113, 120, 127, 130,132, 133, 134, 141, 149, 152, 155, 168, **552–3**, 576
'Ruler, The', *see* 'Ya Indiey nevidimoy vladeyu'
'Rupert Bruk' ('Rupert Brooke'), 555
Rusina, 85, 573
Russia, xvi, xxii, xxiii, xxx, xxxi, lix, 26, 55, 70, 100, 150, 157, 312, 343, 386, 403, 416, 418
'Russian Beauty, A', *see* 'Krasavitsa',
Russian Club, New York, 454
Russian Culture Day, xxx, xxxi, l, 55, 58, 64–66, 121, 565, **566**, 568
Russian orthography, lviii–lx, 3n, 549, 551, 584, 624
'Russian River, A', *see* 'Russkaya reka'
Russian Tea Room, New York City, 453
Russian Theatre, 281, 286, 309, 315, 378, **649**
Russkaya mysl' (*Russian Thought*), journal, Sofia-Prague-Paris, 6, 173, 183, 551
'Russkaya reka' ('A Russian River'), 34, **559**
Russkie zapiski (*Russian Annals*), journal, Paris, 352, **676**, **684**
Russkie zapiski, publisher, Paris, **626**
Russkoe bogatstvo (*Russia's Riches*), journal, St Petersburg, 183
Russkoe slovo (*The Russian Word*), newspaper, Harbin, 115, **580**
Rutenberg, Pyotr Moiseevich, 193, **610**
Rydelius, Ellen, 302, **660**
Ryss, Pyotr Yakovlevich, 204, **616**

S., Sofia, 81
S. A., *see* Sack, Sofia Adamovna
S. F. Protection, *see* Society for the Protection of Science and Learning
S. G., *see* Sofia Grigorievna Hessen
S. Z., *see* *Sovremennye zapiski*
Saba, *see* Kyandzhuntsev, Savely
Sablin, Evgeny Vasilievich, 281, 285, 288, 297, 302, 304, 305, 312, 313, 314, 322, 347, 352, 360, 361, 364, 384, 386, 388, 390, 391, 393, 395, 397, 398, 400, 403, 405, 406, 412, 414, 415, 417, 418, 419, 425, **649**, VN on, 404
Sablin, Nadezhda Ivanovna, 284, 297, 305, 322, 337, 350, 352, 360, 364, 384, 386, 388, 390, 391, 393, 395, 398, 403, 405, 406, 408, 412, 414, 415, 417, 418, 419, 425, **650**, VN on, 404, 422
Sack, Aleksandr Iosifovich (Shura), xv, xxix, 42, 44, 51, 52, 53, 54, 61, 64, 66, 68, 76–77, 82, 87, 88, 89, 90, 94, 95, 96, 97, 98, 102, 103, 104, 109, 110, 112, 120, 121, 122, 123, 129, 132, 133, 134, 141, 145, 147, 152, **561**

Sack, Sofia Adamovna, 42, 52, 74, 133, 153, **561**
Säckingen (Bad Säckingen am Rhein), Germany, 46, 47, **562**
Sacks, Oliver, xlix
Sadko, 27, **557**
Sadko (Rimsky-Korsakov), 27, **557**
Saïgon, rue de, Paris, 402, **690**
St Blasien, Germany, 44, 45, 50, 57, 69, 89, 95, 98, 100, 102, 103, 106, 146, 167, **561**, as VéN address, 50–152 (1926), as VN address, 44–6 (1925)
St-Cloud, Paris, 350
St Paul, Minnesota, 481, 482, 483
St Peter's, Rome, 481
St Petersburg, Russia, xiii, 162, 175, 205, 403
St Timothy's College, Baltimore County, Maryland, 495–6, 720
Sainte-Hélène, petit île (Aldanov), 216–7, **622**
Salmon Hotel, Florence, South Carolina, 462
'Sam treugol'nyi, dvukrylyi, beznogiy' ('The Little Angel'), 223, **625**
San Domenico Palace Hotel, Taormina, Italy, as VN address, 507–15 (1970)
Sanford, Leonard Cutler, 484, **717**
Sapozhnikov, Vasily Vasilievich, 397, **689**
Saurat, France, 217, 225, 227, **623**, **626**, 627
Sav. Is. or Savely or Savely Isaak., *see* Grinberg, Savely Isaakovich
Savoy, France, 428, 429
Sayn-Wittgenstein, Elizaveta Dmitrievna, 135, **584**
Schiff, Stacy, xxxiv, 541, 543, 545
Schillstrasse, Berlin, 59, 101, 109
Schlesinger, Fanni Samoylovna, 290, 316, **654**
School of Slavonic Languages, University of London, 423, 431
Schubert-Saal, Berlin, 586
Schwartz, Delmore, 452, 708
Schwarzsee, Germany, 519
Schwarzwald, Germany, xv, xxix, 44, 45, 75, 83
Schwarzwaldhaus Hotel-Pension, as VéN address, 68–86 (1926)
Seagull, The, *see* *Chayka* (Chekhov)
'Seaport, The', *see* 'Port'
Seb. Knight, or *Sebastian*, *see* *The Real Life of Sebastian Knight*
Sedykh, Andrey, *see* Yakov Moiseevich Tsvibakh
Segodnya (*Today*), newspaper, Riga, 34, 37, 201, **559**
Seine, river, Paris, 244, 245, 284, 366, 479
Selected Letters, **1940–1977**, xlvii, reasons for including letters to Véra, 540–1, 668
Sergey, or Seryozha, *see* Nabokov, Sergey Vladimirovich or Nabokov, Sergey Sergeevich
'Serpent qui danse, La' ('The Dancing Snake', Baudelaire), 592–3

Seven Pillars of Wisdom (T. E. Lawrence), 420, **694**
Seyfullina, Lidia Nikolaevna, 59, **566**
Seythenex ('Pneumothorax', 'St Thorax'), France, 420, 431, **694**, **700**
Sh. (Shura), *see* Sack, Aleksandr Iosifovich
Shabelsky-Bork, Pyotr Nikolaevich, 89, **575**
Shakespeare, William, xliii, 265, 424, 425, 588–9
Shakh, Evgeny Vladimirovich, 212, **620**
Shakhovskoy, Princess Anna Leonidovna, 272, **646**
Shakhovskoy, Dmitri Alekseevich (Father Ioann), 99, 152, 238, 241, **576**, **633**
Shakhovskoy, Olga Vladimirovna, *see* Petkevich, Olga Vladimirovna
Shakhovskoy, Prince Sergey Sergeevich, 154, 155, 165, 185, 558, **589**
Shakhovskoy, Princess Zinaida Alekseevna (Zina, Zinochka; married name Malevsky-Malevich), xlv, 188, 232, 234, 235, 240, 253, 259, 260–1, 262, 277, 279, 280, 285, 289, 290, 344, 354, 392, 399, **606**; later antagonism toward VéN and VN, 540, 606; reveals VN affair with Irina Guadanini, 540; VN on, 234, 235, 236, 237, 238, 239, 242, 244, 249, 259
Shalyapin, Fyodor Ivanovich, 159, 592
Sharshun, Sergey Ivanovich, 248, **636**
Shaykevich, Anatoly Efimovich, 220, **624**
Shcherbatov, Anna Vladimirovna, 237, 238, 240, **631**
Shcherbatov, Prince Pavel Borisovich, 237, 238, 240, **631**
Sheffield, University of, xxxv, 386, 389, 400, 407
Sheremetev, Count Dmitry Aleksandrovich, 226, **626**
Sherman, Savely Grigorievich, 161, 162, 166, 167, 190, 243, 245, 246, 247, 248, 250, 255, 257, 270, 281, 290, 324, **593**
Shifrin, Semyon Savelievich, 243, 245, 250, 251–2, 257, **634**
Shik, Aleksandr Adolfovich, 261, **642**
Shklovsky, Zinaida Davydovna, 397, 401, 405, 407, 424, 425, **689**
Shklyaver, Georgy Gavrilovich, 197, 198, 226, 227, 249, 251, 257, 296, **613**
Shmelyov, Ivan Sergeevich, 209, **619**
'Shopot, robkoe dykhan'e . . .' ('Whisper, timid breathing . . .', Fet), 555
Shpolyansky, *see* Don Aminado
Shpon'ka, *see* 'Ivan Fyodorovich Shpon'ka i ego tyotushka'
Shpunt, 405
Shor, (Nadezhda Rafailovna?), 141, **586**
Show ('littlie'), 83, 100, 140
Showen'ka, *see* Show
Shul'gina, Valentina Evgenievna ('Lyussya'), 220, **624**
Shura, *see* Sack, Aleksandr Iosifovich

Shuvalov, Aleksandr Pavlovich, 394, **688**
Shuvalov, Count Pavel Aleksandrovich, 388, 394–5, **686**
Shvarts, 289, 654
Sicily, Italy, xix, xxxvii, 51, as VN address, 507–15
Siewert, Svetlana Romanovna (Svetik), xiv, xxiii–xxiv, xxv–xxvi, 18, 540, 544, 545, **554**, **630**, **633**
Siewert, Tatyana Romanovna, 109, 245, 578
Sikorski, Elena Vladimirovna (sister), xxxvii, 27–28, 56, 93, 154, 158, 159, 161, 170, 185, 502, **555**, **723**; birth, xiii; favourite sibling of VN, xxv, 555; first marriage (Skulyari), 169, 170; interest in VN's love-life, 544; letters to VN, xl; move to Prague, xxviii; VN on, 169, 170, 175. *See also Perepiska s sestroy*
Sikorski, Vladimir Vsevolodovich, 502, **723**
Sikorski, Vsevolod Vyacheslavovich, 176, 179, 180, 601
Silbermann, *see The Real Life of Sebastian Knight*
'Silentium' (Tyutchev), 248, **637**
Singapore, 21
Sinyaya ptitsa (The Bluebird), cabaret, Berlin, 29, **558**
'Sinyaya zvezda' ('The Blue Star', Gumilyov), 362, **678**
Sirin, Vladimir, **xiv**, **xxii**, xxiii, xxiv, xxv, xxvii, xxxi, xxxii, xxxix, xl, xli, xlvii, lix, 18, 27, 52, 66, 69, 124, 125, 197, 215, 226, 310, 355, 444, 529, 543, 553, **554**. *See also* Nabokov, Vladimir Vladimirovich
Sirin, in Russian mythology, 551, 559
Siverskaya, Russia, 220, **624**
Sizif (pen name of Adamovich, Georgy Victorovich, *q.v.*), 103, **577**
'Skazka' ('A Fairy Tale,' 'A Nursery Tale', 'Odd'), 99, **572**; composition, 78, 80, 81, 85; publication, 86, 88, 95, 96, 102; reception, 85, 108, 110
Skit Poetov (The Poets' Hermitage), literary group, Prague, 159, 160–1, 173, 177, **592**
'Skital'tsy' ('The Wanderers'), 18, **554**
Skulyari, Elena Vladimirovna, *see* Sikorski, Elena Vladimirovna
Skulyari, Pyotr Mikhaylovich, 154, 155, 169, 170, 178, 589
'Slice of Life, A', *see* 'Sluchay iz zhizni'
Slonim, Elena (Lena; VéN's sister), *see* Massalsky, Elena
Slonim, Evsey Lazarevich (VéN's father), xxiii, 34, 55, 58, 61, 72, 95, 98, 107, 126, 368, **563**, attitude to VN, 108, VN's attitude to, 89–90, 565
Slonim, Mark Lvovich, 143, 253, 270, **586**, translation office, 229, 252, 257, **628**, **639**
Slonim, Slava Borisovna (VéN's mother), xxiii, 50, 57, 61, 94, 98, 99, 107, 130, **563**, **567**

Slonim, Sofia Evseevna (VéN's sister, Sofa, Sonya), xxiii, 51, 72, 80, 131, 198, 229, 249, 251, 255, 263–4, 267, 269, 280–1, 284, 286, 294, 296, 356, **563**, VN's attitude to, xliii, 251, 263–4, 269, 296,

Slonim, Véra Evseevna, *see* Nabokov, Véra Evseevna

Slovo (*The Word*), newspaper, Berlin, xliii, 88, 97, 103

Slovo, publisher, Berlin, 54, 121, 162, 212, 565, 574, **613**

'Sluchay iz zhizni' ('A Slice of Life'), 245, **635**

Smichov, district, Prague, as VN address, 10, 12, 18 (1923–34)

Smolensky, Vladimir Alekseevich, 193, 201, 609, **610**

Smyth, Ellison Adger, 466, 712

'Snare, The' (Stephens), 185, **605**

Sobytie (*The Event*), 272, 281, 388, 390, 395, 399, 400, 430, 432, 433, 473, **645**, **649**, **665**, **686**, **714**

Société Protectrice des Animaux, 188, 217–8

Society for the Protection of Science and Learning, 396, 433, 436, **689**

Society of Northerners, 256, 302, 305, **640**

Sofa, *see* Slonim, Sofia Evseevna

Sofia Ad., *see* Sack, Sofia Adamovna

Sofiev, Yury Borisovich, 247, **636**

'Soft Sound', *see* 'Tikhiy shum'

Soglyadatay (*The Eye*), novella, xv, 159, 161, 167, 225, 228, **592**, in translation, French (*L'Aguet*), 249, 252, 257, 259, 298, **637**

Soglyadatay, proposed collection, 225–6, **626**

Sohn, Clements Joseph, 362, 366, **678**

Solliès-Pont, France, xiv, xxv, 3

'Solnechnyi udar' ('Sunstroke', Bunin), 148, **587**

Solntse myortvykh (*Sun of the Dead, The*, Shmelyov), 209, **619**

Solomon, King, 38

Solomon, Flora Grigorievna, 304, 305, 308, 312, 341–2, 353, 379, 380, 387, 393, 404, 411, 417, 419–20, 421, 422, 423, 425, 429, 431, **661**, VN on, 411,

Somov, Kontantin Andreevich, 345, 388, **673**

Sonya, *see* Slonim, Sofia

Sorbonne, Paris, 288

'Sovershenstvo' ('Perfection'), 212, **621**

Soviet literature, xxx, xlix, 51, 52, 57, 59, 67, 69, 70, 71, 566. *See also* 'Neskol'ko slov . . . '

Sovremennye zapiski (*Contemporary Annals*), journal, Paris, **xxxi**, xxxii, xxxiii, xxxix, lv, 121, 132, 141, 148, 153, 163, 190, 194, 205, 211, 225, 235, 257, 265, 270, 273, 294, 302, 317, 319, 332, 339, 345, 348, 349, 352, **581**, **665**

Sovremennye zapiski, publisher, Paris, 225, **626**, 628

spaced lettering, indicating non-Russian words spelled in Cyrillic, 3n

Speak, Memory, xix, liii, 502, **634**, **722**. *See also* autobiography; *Conclusive Evidence*
Spectator, The, magazine, London, 513
Spelman College, Atlanta, Georgia, 469–73, 475, 476, 477
Spiresco, Kosta, 206, **617**
Spolokhi (*Northern Lights*), journal, Berlin, 22, **556**
Spree, river, Germany, 27
'Spring in Fialta', *see* 'Vesna v Fialte'
'Spring Thunderstorm', *see* 'Vesennyaya groza' (Tyutchev)
Springfield, Illinois, 479, 480–1
Spurrier, 413
Squire, John Collings, 72, **570**
Stakhanovites, 343, **673**
Stalin, Iosif Vissarionovich (Dzhugashvili), xxxvi, 464
Stanford University, California, xxv
Stein, Semyon Ilyich, 54, 55, 69, 71, 1 69, **564**
Stempffer, Henri, 423, **696–7**
Stendhal (Marie-Henri Beyle), xliii, 257, **640**
Stephens, James, 185, **605**
Steps to Parnassus (Squire), 72, **570**
Stepun, Fyodor Avgustovich, 192–3, **610**
Stettin, Germany, 81
Steuart, Douglas Sturt Spens, 427, **698**
Stewart, Dr, 308, 312, **662**
Stikhi (*Poems*, 1979), **724**
Stock, publisher, Paris, 259, 268, **641**
'Stone Guest, The', *see* 'Kamennyi gost'' (Pushkin)
Strasbourg, France, xvi, xxxii, 188, 190, 192, 209, 210, 293, 316, 321, 323, 354, 356
Straus, Ralph, 319, **666**
Strawson, Frank, 305, 308, **661**
Stray Dog, *see* Brodyachaya sobaka
Struve, Aleksey Petrovich, 230, 332, **628**
Struve, Andrey Glebovich, 397
Struve, Antonina (Nina) Aleksandrovna, 228, 229, 230, **627**
Struve, Danila Glebovich, 397
Struve, Ekaterina Andreevna (née Catoire), 230
Struve, Gleb Petrovich (Gleb, Glebushka), xlvi, 15, 167, 216, 230, 254, 256, 273, 285, 288, 292, 297, 301, 302, 303, 304, 306, 312, 314, 318, 336, 347, 349, 350, 360, 361, 364, 369, 386, 387, 388, 389, 390, 392, 394, 396, 397, 399, 401, 402, 403, 407, 412, 415, 420, 422, 423–4, 435, 436, **553**, 606, **685**, on VN, 273, **646**, VN on, 288, 297, 304, 312, 347, 360, 364, 369, 403, 404
Struve, Marina Glebovna, 397
Struve, Nikita Alekseevich, 332, **669**
Struve, Nina Glebovna, 397
Struve, Pyotr Berngardovich, 203, 204, 228, 229, 230, **553**, **616**
Struve, Yulia Yulievna, xlvi, 15, 197, 217, 218, 230, 303, 397, **553**, VN on, 312
'Stsena iz Fausta' ('Scene from *Faust*', Pushkin), 186, 605
suffering, aphorisms on, 81, 85, 100

Sumarokov-Elston, Count Mikhail Nikolaevich, 394, 395, **688**
'Summit, The', *see* 'Vershina'
Sun of the Dead, The (Shmelyov), *see* *Solntse myortvykh*
'Sunstroke', *see* 'Solnechnyi udar' (Bunin)
Superman, 459, 711
Supervielle, Jules, xxxii, 190, 191, 194, 195, 209, 245, 249, 256, 350, 360, **608**, VN on, 192, 195, 197, 210, 243, 247, 252, 256, 259, 352
Svetik, *see* Malevsky-Malevich, Svyatoslav Svyatoslavovich *or* Siewert, Svetlana
Svyat. Andr., *see* Malevsky-Malevich, Svyatoslav Andreevich
Sweden, 337
'Swelter', *see* 'Znoy'
Swinburne, Algernon Charles, 233, 629
Switzerland, xix, xx, xxxiv, 47, 380

T. N., *see* Karpovich, Tatyana Nikolaevna
Taboritsky, Sergey Vladimirovich, xvi, xxxiii, 89, **575**, **656**
Tair, publisher, Paris, 208, 281, 289, 302, **618**, **648**
Taormina, Italy, xix, xxxvii, xli, li, liv, 510, 512, 513, 725, as VN address, 507–15 (1970)
Tatarinov literary circle, Berlin, xxx, 135, 136–7, 139, 148, 149–50
Tatarinov, Raisa Abramovna, 15, 34, 54, 58, 70, 71, 72, 81, 85, 95, 100, 115, 124, 127, 135, 137, 143, 149, 151, 161, 197, 198, 217, 223, 238, 240, 244, 247, 250, 253, 256, 259, 269, 281, 286, 289, 292, 296, 297, 318, 319, 324, 329, 331, 334, 342, 357, 368, 369, 370, 381, **553**, questionnaire (with VN), 137, 138–9, 148, 149, 150
Tatarinov, Vladimir Evgenievich, 13, 15, 24, 54, 58, 65, 70, 71, 72, 81, 85, 95, 100, 115, 127, 135, 142, 143, 148, 149, 150, 297, 324, 329, 342, 357, 368, 381, **552**
Tatischev, Count Boris Alekseevich, 428, **698**
Tatyana Vasilievna, *see* Chernavin, Tatyana Vasilievna
Teffi (Nadezhda Aleksandrovna Buchinsky), xxii, 269, 270, 281, 291, 297, 334, 338, **644**, **670**, **671**
Tegel, district (and cemetery), Berlin, 32, 33, 74, 120, 124, 133, 333, **559**, 571, 669
Teisch, Mme, 219
telepathy, 475, 477, 715
Tenishev School, St Petersburg, 143, 223, 235, 243, 255, **586**
Tennessee, 473, 477
Terapiano, Yury Konstantinovich, 193, 248, 257, 339, **610**, **672**
Terijoki, Finland, 83, **573**
'Terra Incognita', 204, 210, 254, **616**
'Terror', *see* 'Uzhas'
Teryuz, 204
Teslenko, Nikolay Vasilievich, 316, **664**

Thames, river, London, 421
Theis, Otto, 420, 421, 427, 429, 433, 436, **694**
'There was never a Queen like Balkis' (Kipling), 166, 595
Thiébaut, Marcel, 337, 345, 382, **671**
Thieme, Hermann, 77–78, 131, 185, 208, 215
Thien, Otto, *see* Theis, Otto
Third Rome, The, *see* *Tretiy Rim* (Ivanov)
Thomas Cook, travel agency, 268, 381
Thompson, C. Bertrand, 171, 173–4, 196, 197, 200, 211, 213, 217, 218, 220, 225, 230, 286, 299, 301, 302, 305, 308, 313, 343, 347, 353, 452, **598**, VN on, 197, 220, 301, 476
Thompson, Lisbet (Lisa, Lisbetsha, Lizaveta), 186, 189, 192, 196, 197, 200, 211, 213, 217, 218, 219, 220, 225, 230, 286, 290, 292, 296, 301, 302, 313, 440, 443, 447, 459, 460, 493, **598**, VN on, 220, 301
Thomson, David Cleghorn, 433, 436, 438, **700**
Thorndike, Sybil, 409, **692**
1001 Nights, 197
Thyrse, journal, Brussels, 240, **632**
Thyssen (?), 196
Tiergarten, Berlin, 101, 160
Tiessen (?), 196
'Tikhiy shum' ('Soft Sound'), xlix–l, **567**, **568**, composition of, 55–56, 57, 58, 60–61, reception of, 64–66, reviews of, 69, 121, 569, text of, 62–63,
Tissen (?), 196
Titisee, Germany, 57, 75, as VN address, 43 (1925)
'To a Future Reader', *see* 'Budushchemu chitatelyu'
'To Delvig', *see* 'Delvigu' (Pushkin)
'To the Muse', *see* 'K Muze'
Todtmoos, Germany, 46–47, 50, 57, 59, 69, 72, 73, 76, 78, as VéN address, 72–86 (1926)
Tolstoy, Aleksey Konstantinovich, 585
Tolstoy, Count Aleksey Nikolaevich, 336, **671**
Tolstoy, Count Lev Nikolaevich, xxx, xliii, 140, 142, 204, 215, 256, 386, 464, 498, **577**, 586
Tomsk, Russia, 397
Toulon, France, xxv, 60, 323, 328, 331, 333, 342, 345, 348, 354, 356, 359
Tragediya gospodina Morna (*The Tragedy of Mister Morn*), xxix, xlix, 11, 12–13, 14, 17, 18, 20, 22–23, 23–24, 24–25, 27, 28, 29, **545**, **552**
Tragedy of Mister Morn, The, *see* *Tragediya gospodina Morna*
transliteration, lx. *See also* Russian orthography
Transparency, *see* *Prozrachnost'*
Transparent Things, xx
Trautenaustrasse, Berlin, 74
Treptow, district, Berlin, 102
Tretiy Rim (*The Third Rome*, Ivanov), 167, **596**
Trida Svornosty, Prague, as VN address, 10–18 (1923–4)

'Trifle—a mast's denomination, plans—trailed, A', *see* 'Pustyak,—nazvan'e machty, plan—i sledom'
Trinity College, Cambridge, 312, 414, 442, 447
Trinity Street, Cambridge, 312
Trocadero, Paris, 267
Trofimov, Mikhail Vasilievich, 418, **694**
Tropic of Cancer (Miller), 502, **723**
Trotsky, Ilya Markovich, 85, 167, **573**
Truda, *see* Gertruda
Tsetlin, Maria Samoylovna, 292, 297, 305, 331, 347, 384, 386, 387, 398–9, 406, 419, 421, 423, 431, 432–3, 438, 439, **656**, 700
Tsetlin, Mikhail Osipovich, 283, 292, 293, 297, 331, 347, 384, 398, 406, 419, 421, **650**, **656**
Tsetlin, Valentin Mikhaylovich (Valya), 304, 386, 418, **685**, **694**
Tsement (*Cement*, Gladkov), 67–8, 568
Tsitsianov, Princess Maria Aleksandrovna, *see* Bakhareva
Tsvetaeva, Marina Ivanovna, 31, 33, 318, **558**
Tsvibakh, Yakov Moiseevich (Andrey Sedykh), 194, 200, 210, 226, 449, 452, **611**, 615, **706**
tub, 35, 87, 146, 198, 321, 329, 331, 333, 344, 345, 352, 357, 368, 369, 385, 420, 613
Tuftikins ('littlie'), 68, 69, 83, 594
Tuileries, Jardin des, Paris, 266
Tulsa, Oklahoma, 502, 722
Turck, Charles Joseph, 481, 482, **716**
Turovets, 280
type, taxonomic, 699
typographic conventions, 3n
'Tyrants Destroyed', *see* 'Istreblenie tiranov'
Tyrkov-Williams, Ariadna Vladimirovna, 184, 392, 395, 401, 403, 406, 423, 431, 432, 433, 434, **604**
Tyrrell, William George, 1st Baron, 388, **685**
Tyutchev, Fyodor Ivanovich, 78, 136–7, 248, **572**, 637

Ugrimov, Irina Nikolaevna, née Muravyov (?), 329, **668**
Ullstein, publisher, Berlin, 157, 187, 429, 565, 591, **699**
Ulysses (Joyce), 306, **604**
Uncle Sam, 466
Union of Russian Writers and Journalists, Berlin, 105–6, 117, 186, 566
United States, xxii, xxxv, xxxvi, xxxix, lvii, 14
'Universitetskaya poema' ('A University Poem'), 154, 155, 166, **589**
University of Chicago, 415, 417
University of London, 230, 386, 389, 399, 412, 424
'University Poem, A', *see* 'Universitetskaya poema'
Updike, John, xlvii
Usoltsev, 124
Usoltsev, Mme, 124

Ussuri, Russia, 64
'Usta k ustam' ('Lips to Lips'), 171, 178, 184, 236, 237, 255, 256, **598**
'Uzhas' ('Terror'), story, 154, 155, **589**

'V kakom rayu' ('In what heaven'), xxiv, **544**
V. M-ch, *see* Zenzinov, Vladimir Mikhaylovich
Vacek, 181
Valdosta, Georgia, 466, 467, 469, 470, 472, 473, 713, as VN address, 473–5 (1942)
Valéry, Paul, 316, 318, **664**
Vanya, *see* Nabokov, Ivan Nikolayevich
Var, France, 323, 328, 344
Varna, Bulgaria, 162, 163, 165
Varshavsky, Sergey Ivanovich, 169, **597**
Varshavsky, Vladimir Sergeevich, 169, 257, **597**
Vasya, Uncle, *see* Rukavishnikov, Vasily Ivanovich
Vava, *see* Hessen, Vladimir Iosifovich
'Vecher' ('Evening'), 4–5, **550**
'Vecher na pustyre' ('Inspiration, pink sky . . . '), 223, **625**
Venice, Italy, 381
Vera (Mrs Vladimir Nabokov) (Schiff), 541
Vera Markovna, *see* Haskell, Vera Markovna
Vera Nikolaevna, *see* Muromtsev-Bunin, Vera Nikolaevna
Verbier, Switzerland, 503, 723
Vergun, Irina Dmitrievna, 181, **604**
Vermont, 456, 458, 459, 488, 494
Versailles, avenue de, Paris (Fondaminskys), 240, **632**, as VN address, 239–63 (1936), 278–300, 315–80 (1937), diagram, 370
'Vershina' ('I Like That Mountain,' 'The Summit'), 45, 46, **561**
Veryovkin, 76, 127, 571
Veryovkin, Mme, 222–3, **625**
'Vesennyaya groza' ('Spring Thunderstorm', Tyutchev), 78, 125, **572**, **582**
'Vesna v Fialte' ('Spring in Fialta'), 281, 304, 324, 510, **649**; translation into English, 318, 447, 451, **707**, into French ('Printemps à Fialta'), 298, 334, 336, 346, 352, 353, 361, 369, 372, 378, 382, **677**, into German, 324
Vestnik Evropy (*The Messenger of Europe*), journal, St Petersburg, 183
Vevey, Switzerland, xx
Victor, *see* Nabokov, Vladimir Vladimirovich: aliases
Victor Gollancz, publisher, London, 301, **659**
Victoria Station, London, 301, 431, 433
'Videnie' ('A Vision'), 25–26, **557**
Vienna, Austria, 324, 381, 383
Viktoria-Luise-Platz, Berlin, 146
Vilenkin, Mark Vladimirovich, 308, 335, 337, 390, 391, **662**
Vinaver, Evgeny Maksimovich, 324, 399, 400, 404, 415, 418, 424, 425, **667**
Virginia (state), xviii, xxxvi, 474, 484

Vireneya (Seyfullina), 59, **566**
Vishnyak, Mark Veniaminovich, 167, 190, 193, 206–7, 211, 243, 256, 291, 294, 368, **596**, VN on, 203, 214
'Vision, A', *see* 'Videnie'
'Visit to the Museum, The', *see* 'Poseshchenie muzeya'
Vlad. Mikh., *see* Zenzinov
Vladimir Nabokov Archive, Henry W. and Albert A. Berg Collection, New York Public Library, xxxix, 541
VN: The Life and Art of Vladimir Nabokov (Field), 540, **668**
'Vnov' ya posetil' ('The Return of Pushkin', Pushkin), 311, **663**
'Voda zhivaya' ('The Living Water', Nabokov-Lukash), 29, **558**
Volkonsky, 176
Volkonsky, Irina Sergeevna (née Rachmaninov) (?), 208, 217, 229, **619**, 628
Volkonsky, (Prince Pyotr Petrovich?), 342, **672**
Volkonsky, Sergey Mikhaylovich, 449, **706**
Volkov, Nikolay Konstantinovich, 191, **608**
Volkovyssky, Nikolay Moiseevich, 72, 73, 100, 115, 127, 142, 155, 166, **570**
Voloshin, Maksimilian Aleksandrovich, 18, **554**
Volya Rossii (*Russia's Will*), journal, Prague, 61, 64, 70, **567**
Voronina, Olga Yurievna, 541
Vorontsov-Dashkov, Countess Lyudmila Nikolaevna, 405, **691**
Voyna i mir (*War and Peace*, Tolstoy), 238, 386, **631**, **685**
'Vozdushnyi ostrov' ('Aerial Island'), 223, **625**
'Voznagrazhdenie' ('The Recompense'), 337, 347, **671**, excerpt from *Dar*, q.v.
Vozrozhdenie (*Renaissance*), newspaper, Paris, 166, 207, 221, 226, 244, **596**, **632**
'Vozvrashchenie Chorba' ('The Return of Chorb'), 292, 324, 334, 336, **656**
Vozvrashchenie Chorba (*The Return of Chorb*), collection, 211
'Vrai, Le', *see* 'Pouchkine, ou le vrai et le vraisemblable'
Vrubel, Mikhail Aleksandrovich, 37, **559**
'Vstrecha' ('The Encounter'), xxv–xxvii, **544**, 545
Vyazemsky, Pavel Petrovich, 175, **600**
Vyborg Appeal, 37, **560**
Vyra, 37, 409
Vysotsky, 408–9

Wagner, Richard, 357, **677**
Waldman, Milton, 428–9, 430, 436, **699**
Waldshut, Germany, 47
Wallace, 253, 324
Walpole, Sir Hugh Seymour, 400, 405, 406, **690**
Walrus, 75
Walrus, Mrs, 157, 591
'Wanderers, The', *see* 'Skital'tsy'
'Wanderings' (Volkonsky), 449

Wannsee, Berlin, 55, 142, 143
War and Peace, see Voyna i mir (Tolstoy)
Ward, Hilda, 440, 443, 447, 484, **702**, **717**
Warsaw, Poland, 121
Ways to Strength and Beauty, see Wege zu Kraft und Schönheit
Weeks, Edward, 440, 443, 447, 449, 450, 451, 452, 468, **704**
Wege zu Kraft und Schönheit (*Ways to Strength and Beauty*, Kaufmann and Prager), 76, **571**
Wehr, Germany, 45, 46, 47, **562**
Weidle, Lyudmila Victorovna, 201, **615**
Weidle, Vladimir Vasilievich, 195, 248, 254, 268, 271, 286, **611**, on VN, **645**, VN on, 257, 286, 289
Wellesley, Massachusetts, 441, 473
Wellesley College, xviii, xxxvi, xxxix–xl, lix, 441, 444, 449, 453–4, 456, 465, 466–7, 469, **708**; as VN address, 440–55 (1941); described, 441, 443, 445, 450; reception at, **704**
Wells, Herbert George, 61, 122, 304, 305–6, 307, 354, 397, 399, 406, **567**, **659**
West Wardsboro, Vermont, 710, as VN address, 458 (1942)
Westend, Berlin, 96
Whale, Winifred Stephens, 386, 393, 395, 400, **685**
'When he was small, when he would fall', 483, **717**
'Whisper, timid breathing . . .', *see* 'Shopot, robkoe dykhan'e . . .' (Fet)
White, Katharine Sergeant Angell, 491, **720**
Wilding, Anthony Frederick, 394, **688**
Wilhelm, 210
Williams, George Evelyn, 409, **691**
Wilmersdorfer Strasse, Berlin, 54
Wilson, 298, 320
Wilson, Edmund (Bunny), xxxvi, xliii, l, 452, 473, 474, 476, 485, **708**, **714**, VN on, 476
Windsor Hotel, Paris, 335
'Window, The', *see* 'Okno'
Winter, 499
'Winter Morning, A', *see* 'Zimnee utro' (Pushkin)
'Winter Night', *see* 'Zimnyaya noch''
Winter Palace, St Petersburg, 79, 572
Winterfeldtstrasse, Berlin, 67, 133
Witte, Count Sergey Yulievich, 115, 580
Wittgenstein, Aunt, *see* Sayn-Wittgenstein
Wittenbergplatz, Berlin, 79
Wodehouse, P. G., 385, **684**
Woe from Wit, see *Gore ot uma* (Griboedov)
Wolf, 304
Wonlyar-Lyarsky, Nadezhda Dmitrievna (Aunt Baby), 302, 308, 422, 438, **660**
Woolf, Leonard, liii
Woolf, Virginia, liii
World War II, xxx, 464, 482, 483, 489, **716**, **717**, **719**

Wursthaus, Cambridge, Massachusetts, 487, 488, 491, 493, 494, **719**

'Ya Indiey nevidimoy vladeyu' ('The Ruler', 'India invisible I rule, An'), xxiv, 179, **544**
'Ya znayu, kholodno i mudro' ('I know, coldly and wisely'), 103–04, 115, **580**
Yakobson (?), 27
Yakobson (Jakobson), Roman Osipovich, **697**
Yakobson (Jakobson), Sergey Iosifovich, 424, 431, 433, **697**
Yakor' (*The Anchor*), 235, **630**
Yalta, Crimea, 171, 177, 598
Yan-Ruban, *see* Pohl, Anna Mikhaylovna
Yanovsky, Vasily Semyonovich, 248, 283, **636**
Yasinsky, Ieronim Ieronimovich, 65, **568**
'You call – and in a little pomegranate tree an owlet', *see* 'Zovyosh'– a v derevtse granatovom sovyonok'
Yu. Yu. *or* Yulia *or* Yulen'ka, *see* Struve, Yulia Yulievna
Yubiley (*The Jubilee*, Chekhov), 65, 568
Yurik, *see* Rausch von Traubenberg, Baron Georgy Evgenievich
Yuzhny, Yakov Davidovich, 24, **556**

Za svobodu (*For Freedom*), newspaper, Warsaw, 121, 164, **581**
Zack, Léon (Lev Vasilievich), 233, 234, **629**
'Zagovor' ('Conspiracy', Aldanov), 148, **587**
Zamyatin, Evgeny Ivanovich, 171, 227, 322, 324, 362, 365, **598**, **666**
Zapolsky, Maria Sergeevna (Muma, cousin), 205, 214, 219, 220, **617**
Zapolsky, Vladimir Evgenievich, 205, 219, 220, 617
Zashchita Luzhina (*The Defence*, *The Luzhin Defence*), xv, xxxi, 192, 195, **610**; reviews of, 164, 167, 211, 212, 215, 312, 593, 594, 596, **635**; translation into English, 302, 413, 428–9, 430, 436, into French (*La Course du fou*) 198, 199, 201–2, 225, 228, 234, 291, 361, 365, 428–9, 430, 436, 612, 613, 615, 627, **630**, **699**, into Swedish (*Han som spelade schack med livet*), 312, 337, **653**, **660**, **663**
Zaytsev, Boris Konstantinovich, xxxii, 206–7, 217, 245, 250, 264, 339, 348, **617**, VN on, 250, 335
Zaytsev, Kirill Iosifovich, 65, 203, 204, **568**
Zaytsev, Vera Alekseevna, 217, 245, 339, 348, **622**
Zeldovich, Berta Grigorievna, 243, 247, 255, 257, 269, 271, **634**
Zen-Zin (cat), 220, 227, 240, 253, 298, 320, **639**
Zenzinov, Vladimir Mikhaylovich (V. M-ch, Vlad. Mikh., Zinzin), xxxii, xxxiii, xli, 190, 220, 222, 241, 242,

Zenzinov – *cont.*
248, 255, 281, 286, 291, 298, 315, 319, 324, 329, 333, 338, 343, 347, 348, 349, 350, 366, 378, 484, **607**, **717**, VN on, 203, 240, 262, 270, 293, 321, 378
Zermatt, Switzerland, as VN address, 519, 728 (1974)
Zetlin, *see* Tsetlin
Zhdanov, Georgy Semyonovich, 272, 286, 287, 297, 302, 313, 317, 457, **645**, **709**
'Zhemchug' ('The Pearl'), xxiv, **543–4**
Zhemchuzhnikov, Aleksandr Mikhaylovich, 585
Zhemchuzhnikov, Aleksey Mikhaylovich, 585
Zhemchuzhnikov, Vladimir Mikhaylovich, 585
Zhenya, Uncle, *see* Rausch von Traubenberg, Baron Evgeny Aleksandrovich
Zhizn' Arsen'eva (*The Life of Arsen'ev*, Bunin), 620
'Zhizn' Vasiliya Travnikova' ('The Life of Vasily Travnikov', Khodasevich), 254, **639**
Zhukovsky, Stanislav Yulianovich, 456, 709
Zimmer, Dieter E., 681, 705, 715, 721
'Zimnee utro' ('A Winter Morning', Pushkin), 557
'Zimnyaya noch'' ('Winter Night'), 183, 599
Zina or Zinaida, *see* Gippius, Zinaida Nikolaevna
Zina or Zinochka, *see* Shakhovskoy, Princess Zinaida Alekseevna
Zin. Dav., *see* Shklovsky, Zinaida Davydovna
Zinzin, *see* Zenzinov, Vladimir
Znosko-Borovsky, Evgeny Aleksandrovich, 199, 202, **614**
'Znoy' ('Swelter'), xxvii, 4, 5, 6, 544–5, **550**
Zoo (station), Berlin, 103, 143
Zoological Garden, Berlin, 53, 140
Zoologisches Museum, Berlin, 389
Zoppot, Germany (now Sopot, Poland), xv, xxix, **560**, as VN address, 41 (1925)
Zoshchenko, Mikhail Mikhaylovich, 57, 58, 565, 566
'Zovyosh'– a v derevtse granatovom sovyonok' ('You call – and in a little pomegranate tree an owlet'), xxviii, 545
Zurich, Switzerland, 253, 324
Zurov, Leonid Fyodorovich, 372, **681**
Zyoka, *see* Hessen, Georgy Iosifovich
Zvezdich (Pyotr Isaevich Rotenshtern), 85, **573**
Zveno (*The Link*), weekly, Paris, 50, 61, 82, 87, 103, 121, 153, **563**
'Zvonil v pustyne telefon' ('In the desert a telephone rang'), 521
'Zvonok' ('The Doorbell'), 334, **606**, **667**, translation into German, 187, 324, 606

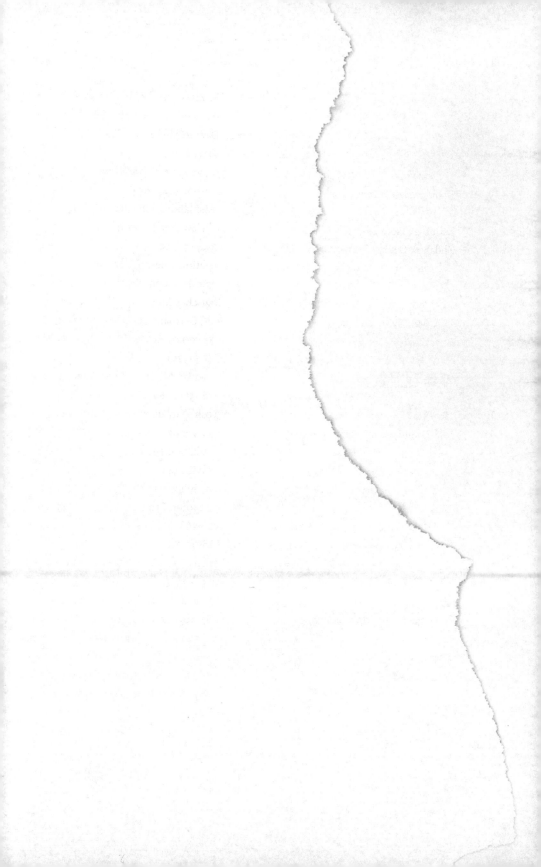

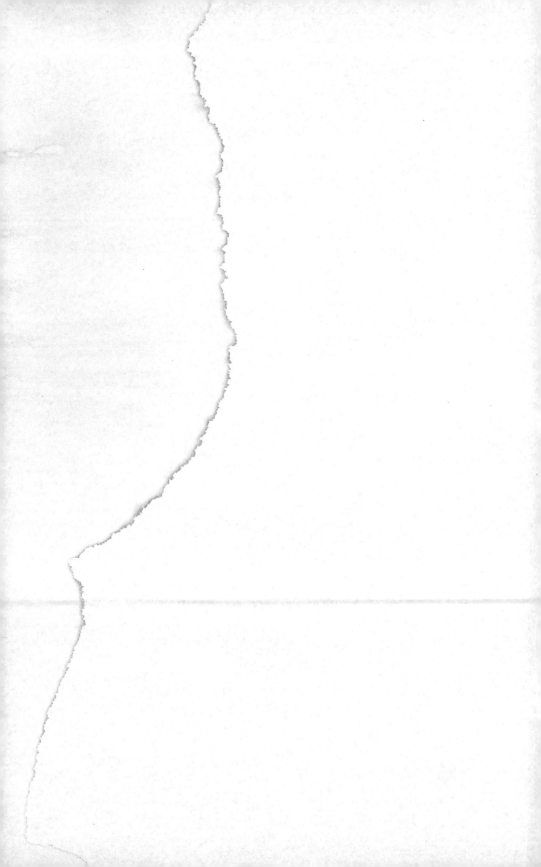